Birkhäuser Architectural Guide
Spain

Birkhäuser Architectural Guides

Previously published
Germany
Japan
Switzerland

Forthcoming
Netherlands, Belgium, Luxembourg
Scandinavia
USA

Birkhäuser Architectural Guide
Spain 1920-1999

Selection Committee	Ignasi de Solà-Morales
	Antón Capitel
	Gabriel Ruiz Cabrero
	Víctor Pérez Escolano
	Pedro de Llano
	Javier Cenicacelaya
	Peter Buchanan
Introductory Essay	Ignasi de Solà-Morales
Guide Entries	Antón Capitel
	Susana Landrove
	Massimo Preziosi
	Aurora Fernández
	Javier Mozas
	Ramón Pico Valimaña
	Garlos García Vázquez
	Plácido Lizancos
	Carmen Jordá
	José María Fernández Isla
	Federico García Barba
	Francisco J. Noriega
	Eduardo Fernández Abascal
	Víctor Pérez Escolano
Final Essay	Luis Moreno Mansilla and Emilio Tuñón
Scientific Direction	Gerardo Mingo Pinacho
	Guillermo Vázquez Consuegra
Edited by	Raúl Rispa

Birkhäuser Verlag
Basel · Berlin · Boston

Originally published in 1998 under the title
Guía de arquitectura. España. 1920-2000
a book-format version of the
Register of Spanish Architecture, a
🏛 **Ministerio de Fomento** and Tanais Ediciones, s.a. joint project

Publishers: *María José Aguaza and Raúl Rispa*

Guide entry texts written by
Antón Capitel Asturias, Castile and León, Madrid. *Susana Landrove* Aragón, Balearic Islands, Catalonia.
Massimo Preziosi Aragón, Balearic Islands, Catalonia. *Aurora Fernández* Navarre, Basque Country, La
Rioja. *Javier Mozas* Navarre, Basque Country, La Rioja. *Ramón Pico Valimaña* Andalusia. *Carlos García
Vázquez* Andalusia. *Plácido Lizancos* Galicia. *Carmen Jordá* Valencia. *José María Fernández Isla* Castile-La
Mancha, Extremadura. *Federico García Barba* Canary Islands. *Juan Francisco Noguera* Murcia. *Eduardo
Fernández Abascal* Cantabria. *Víctor Pérez Escolano* Andalusia. *Tanais editorial team* Ceuta and Melilla,
introductory sections to the Autonomous Communities, provinces and cities, engineering works.

English editor: *Erica Witschey*
Translation into English: *Victoria Hughes, Bryony Persson, Erica Witschey* and *Clare Godfrey*

Design and content structure *Tanais editorial team, Carlos Navas (Subdirectorate General for Architecture).*
Documentation *Carmen Ortín, María Benítez, V. León (CA, s.a.), Salomé Fajardo, Marta Rubio* and *Marta
Rodríguez (Subdirectorate General for Architecture).* Coordination of inventories *Miguel A. Baldellou.* Data
base and electronic processing *J.L. Medina (CA, s.a), Isabel Fernández Hiraldo, A. Prieto.* Layout *J.L. Medina
(CA, s.a), María Benítez, María José Chacartegui, Manuel G. Cordero, Ricardo Martín.*

Library of Congress Cataloging-in-Publication Data
A CIP catalogue record for this book is available from the Library of Congress, Washington D.C., USA

Deutsche Bibliothek Cataloging-in-Publication Data

Birkhäuser architectural guide Spain 1920-1999 / Solà-Morales...
[transl. into Engl.: Victoria Hughes...]. - Basel ; Berlin ; Boston :
Birkhäuser, 1998
(Birkhäuser architectural guides)
Einheitssacht.: Guía de arquitectura. España. 1920-2000 <engl.>
ISBN 3-7643-5748-7 (Basel ...)
ISBN 0-8176-5748-7 (Boston)

Cover design: Ott + Stein, Berlin
Colour reproduction, filmsetting and printing: Monterreina s.a., Madrid
D.L. M -44941-1997
Printed on acid-free paper produced of chlorine-free pulp. TCF ∞
Printed in Spain
ISBN 3-7643-5748-7
ISBN 0-8176-5748-7

9 8 7 6 5 4 3 2 1

Contents

Drawing up an inventory of Spain's architectural heritage and fostering excellence in contemporary architecture are just two of the missions of the Spanish Directorate General of Housing, Architecture and Urban Planning, which are carried out by the Subdirectorate General for Architecture. This governmental office has recently developed a new approach to adapt to the new scenario resulting from the unification of Europe and the globalisation of the economy. Within this new framework, and given that Spain lacked a catalogue of its architecture, in 1994 the Ministry of Development and Tanais Arquitectura set up a multimedia project to develop a *Register of Spanish Architecture*. This guide is the first fruit of stage one of this project.

The set of works collected herein, selected by a qualified committee of independent experts, shows the high level of architecture in our country – which not so long ago was struggling in isolation to achieve modernity and has now become one of the world's focal points for its architectural relevance – and the international competitiveness of Spanish architects. The fact that the guide is published in five languages by prestigious European and American publishers means readers from all corners of the world will have access to contemporary Spanish architecture. The publication unveils the great masters of the sixties – until now hidden by the cloak of isolation imposed by a non-democratic regime –, which for many will be a revelation, and marks a milestone without any comparable precedents.

This guide is a multipurpose tool, but as a source book that provides a canon of works and architects, its central aim is to provide a greater understanding of the rich diversity of our built-up environment and to invite readers to experience Spain's real architecture for themselves.

Gerardo Mingo Pinacho
Subdirector General for Architecture, Ministry of Development

GUIDE TO THE GUIDE

This introduction provides the reader with what we like to call the genesis of the guide, how it came about, why and for whom, followed by an explanation of its contents and how they were selected. It also describes how it is organised, with a detailed breakdown of its different entries, and gives clues as to how best to use it.

"Architecture is the frame of life". This quote from Frank Lloyd Wright is simply a statement of fact. In our Western civilisation, nine out of every ten people live in cities, in a built-up, man-made environment. Buildings, other constructions and, indeed, all changes wrought on our surroundings to facilitate human life are, above all, creations of the spirit. Architecture is the art generated by the creativity of men and women, architects; the professional discipline that covers the basic human need for a home and a living space to shelter us from nature. Everything that helps us better to understand these works will mean greater appreciation of their creators. Everything that makes their authors more widely known will lead to a deeper critical awareness of cities and built-up environments, a wiser demand for good architecture.

Culture is the root and the identity of people. No other component of the collective heritage of human groups is as lasting and significant as its architecture. In fact, when an entire town, community or nation wants to make itself known, it nearly always displays itself through its architectural icons. This legacy from the past is a collective good that we should preserve, a heritage that we should all try to add to with new contributions, the best expressions of creativity that the architects and engineers of each age can offer. Getting to know this heritage, with points of reference and keys to help us assess new architectural styles and ideas, will help individuals to enjoy their beauty and will enhance the cultural level of the community as a whole.

This guide is the most exhaustive single, portable source of information on Spanish architecture of the 20th century. It was conceived for a wide range of readers and users, from those wanting to satisfy occasional curiosity to those teaching at academic level. It is really directed at anyone interested in architecture: historians, critics, professionals, students, politicians, civil servants, whoever; and at the growing sector of the general public that, as "culture consumers", are open to enjoying the aesthetic pleasure aroused by the beauty of form and the efficiency of function. It is both for Spaniards and non-Spaniards, for all those whom it may help to discover or study from their desktop the wealth of Spain's architectural heritage of this century. We hope it will encourage you to visit the works it describes, as part of a new wave of architectural tourism. And we should also remember the "person-on-the-street" and the builders themselves, who will realise how important it is to demand excellence in the architecture of their next house, building, industrial premises or offices. This book is for everyone, for those who are already fans of good architecture and those who simply feel attracted by this world of professionals who create, design and build up spaces.

Genesis

In the beginning was the project to *Register and Disseminate Spanish Architecture*. This publication forms part of that project, which has been a joint effort between Spanish state authorities for architecture and an independent professional publishing house committed to disseminating the country's best works and architects. An agreement was signed in November 1995, between the Spanish Ministry of Development, through the Subdirectorate General for Architecture of the Directorate General for Housing, Architecture and Town Planning, and Tanais Arquitectura, the architectural imprint of Tanais Ediciones, S.A., to draw up this Register of Spanish Architecture. It was to provide a basic instrument for detecting contemporary works of value; to document them as soon as possible and make them more widely recognised as epitomes of excellence in architecture and in the creativity of architects.

The register has been programmed over three different stages. The first (this one) covers the years from 1920 until the end of the century, perhaps the era most in need of critical appreciation and explanation, given society's widespread tendency to misunderstand prophets of their own time. The second and third stages will go back in time to the very beginnings. The register has been planned to be a living, open entity, that will be periodically updated to incorporate new works of special value as they come into existence, whilst including and excluding other previous works in the light of different factors. It has not been created as a closed repository, but as an open instrument intended to disseminate architecture and architects. It has thus been published in multimedia, based on data, text, plans and photographs, with drill-down possibilities. The guide is one of the instruments in this register, a printed version, alongside a version prepared for CD ROM and another on-line version for InfoVia and Internet. Thus, the *Architectural Guide. Spain, 1920-1999* is not a mere reshuffling of old documents. It is a new, specific concept in its own right, its design obeying the state-of-the-art criteria reached only after its authors had researched more than a hundred similar guides from other countries in other languages.

Contents

The guide features 767 top-quality works produced during the years from 1920 to 1999. It includes not only architectural objects in the strictest sense of the term – rehabilitations of existing buildings and new ones – but also engineering works, as seen from the "architectural" viewpoint, i.e. in terms of their composition, formal beauty and harmony, and landscaping and garden works, town planning projects, etc. The central focus of the register and the guide are the works as such, rather than the towns or locations in which they stand, whilst the architects (or engineers) take their due place as authors of these works. The period covered reflects the widely accepted idea that the 19th century did not really end in 1900, but rather continued until the end of the First World War. It was in the twenties that a radical paradigm shift took place in architecture, with the emergence of the Modern movement, which, as always occurs, had been preceded by pioneers and works that anticipated the new "rationalism" in the layout and new kinds of formal expression.

Cutting up reality into time periods is always somewhat arbitrary, cutting off the flow of real life. But in this case, the team of consultants heading the project thought that, as in other similar works in Western countries, this periodification contributed most accurately to establishing a coherent body of information. Its scope in space covers the entire sovereign territory of Spain, with works located in the Peninsula, the Balearic Islands, the Canary Islands, and Ceuta and Melilla in Africa, whatever the nationality of their architects. Finally, moving beyond the conventional idea of an architectural guide, this publication does not just present the works on Spanish soil, but also ensures that readers will not get a blinkered view of the subject, by giving some coverage to the work of Spanish architects abroad, something that has been a deep-rooted tradition since the 16th century. In the 20th century, there have been two specific circumstances that have made it even more important: the 1939 exile after the Civil War, and the increasing globalisation of architectural competition since the eighties.

The first level of content is the selection of the works: the list, catalogue, guide. The detailed contents of each work is limited to bare essentials, namely its identification (names, dates and location) and its iconography (photograph, plan or sketch), along with a description and evaluation in words. This is all combined in an entry for each building (see explanation on p. 12). The entries form the core of the guide as such, as a descriptive catalogue of the works. But apart from the 767 works representing the best of 20th century Spanish architecture, another 333 works are referred to, offering supplementary information about an architect, a specific work, an urban area, a city or a tendency. Finally, in order to identify historical and architectural reference points in different towns and regions, mention is made of 286 buildings from prior to the 1920-1999 period, ranging from prehistory to the beginning of the 20th century. However, a mere succession of disjointed entries on individual buildings would not be enough to meet the demands of readers for useful information. Much of the context would be lost, in terms of its space, time, economic and cultural conditions from which the works spring, against which they react and which they finally transform. Moreover, this is a comprehensive guide. So additional sections contain introductory articles, as well as documentary information and other useful appendices.

Selection of the Works

There was no single, systematic, exhaustive work presenting a selection of the best contemporary Spanish architecture, although, as the reader knows only too well, there is a veritable mass of guides, compendia, rankings, catalogues and selections of restaurants, hotels, discotheques, bars, wines, nature treks... So, starting from scratch, we established a basic inventory of approximately 8,000 entries. The sources used by the expert committee listed on page 3 were not, however, limited to this inventory. The committee also consulted Schools of Architecture and Architects' Chambers. But it was their exclusive duty to make the choices required. The process was similar to giving architects a site and asking them to build freely within it. After that, the different attributes of value for classifying the works were established in national terms, for Spain as a whole, bearing in mind the country's general posi-tion in the history and culture of the world. This scheme of reference means that, as we have explained above, the guide contains works that, whilst important at Spanish level, may not be so relevant at European level, although some of them are in fact renowned as part of the universal architectural heritage. And then, at a lower order of things, what is selected for Spain is not just the sum of works that would be chosen for Spain's individual regions (the Autonomous Communities). The main criterion used to select a work was its cultural excellence, the quality of the architecture constructed. In sum, this is not just a catalogue of a predetermined style or tendency, but rather contains a wide range of types, architects, periods, etc. Along with the essential criteria of top-quality design, other lesser factors have come into play in the committee's choice, such as the degree to which a work exemplifies a certain style or fashion, or is unusual, or is highly visible and therefore forms a point of reference in the landscape.

Organisation

This Guide is structured in three main parts:
• a general introduction or presentation (pages 16-43);
• the guide as such (pages 45-341), the entries on the works;
• the apparatus to facilitate use (pages 342-408): directories, indexes and maps.

In the first part, the architect, professor and critic, Ignasi de Solà-Morales (Barcelona School of Architecture) provides the keys to interpreting Spanish architecture from 1920-1999. His article is not only highly enlightening for non-experts, but also gives food for thought to professionals. Many foreign analysts have said that the weak point of Spaniards in the 20th century is their constant desire to criticise their own output negatively. Professor Solà-Morales, however, turns criticism into a *virtuoso* act that stimulates architects to greater things. After this introduction, the reader will find a comparative chronology, a double-spread for each decade, showing a number of architectural works and events set in their time, in Spain and worldwide, alongside other historical, political, cultural, technological and social milestones. Obviously such a table cannot be exhaustive, but it is a useful map for those wishing to situate the works in terms of *Zeitgeist* (the "vibes" that each age gives off), although in no way intended to be read as an historical narrative.

The second part is the central, major body of this volume. The guide, in the strictest sense of the word, i.e. the entries, broken down by Autonomous Communities, which are covered in alphabetical order of their Spanish name. Note that the order is established by the substantial word in the official name, e.g. Rioja in La Rioja. Within each region, an initial text gives a succinct introduction to its geography, history, economic, social and architectural structures. Data is also provided on the population (1991 census) and the per capita GDP (Gross Domestic Product) taken from the BBV Foundation's publication, *Renta Nacional de España y su Distribución Provincial, Avance de 1995*. Each Community is further broken down into provinces, in alphabetical order. Again, concise information is given on the context of the town or province being covered, with data on altitude, climate and inhabitants (1991 census). Under each town, the works appear in chronological order. After the guide to works in Spain, under the title Casting Shadows, the architects and professors (Madrid School of Architecture), Luis Moreno Mansilla and Emilio Tuñón Alvarez provide readers with an incisive overview of works of Spanish architects abroad.

The third main block of the guide is like a toolkit, which readers can use in order to get the most out of its wealth of contents: a directory of practising architects and engineers with biographical dates (of birth, graduation and death in the case of deceased professionals), addresses and contact numbers; an alphabetical list of works; an alphabetical list of architects and engineers; a typological list of works; a glossary of the terms used; a selected bibliography for readers wishing to find further information; a list of photograph and illustration credits; and general maps of Spain.

Entries
Each of the 767 works selected are presented as a separate entry, consisting of three parts: a header with key data, a text and an illustration. In the header, the name given of the work is usually the current one, although in cases where despite the change in use, the original name has been widely retained in published sources or in common parlance, then this has been showed first, with the new use or name between square brackets. Two years are usually given for the dates (e.g. 1964-71), indicating the date of design and the year when the work was finished; in other cases, however, there is a single date when the design was executed the same year as the building, or when due to the time in which it was made and if its architect has already died, there is no reliable source. In the case of current interventions on existing buildings, we give the date of the original building, followed by that of the intervention, e.g. 1911 • 1990-94. To the right of the name and date of the work is an identification tab, consisting of a letter (for the name of the province) plus a number which serves several purposes, as references on indexes, etc. The address of the work comes next. This appears in Spanish to facilitate its location. The names and abbreviations used stand for the following:

Autovía is Dual Carriage Motorway	Parque is Park
Av. is *Avenida* or Avenue	Pasaje is Alley or Passage Way
Barrio or Barriada is Quarter	Paseo is Boulevard
Ciudad Universitaria is University Campus	Pol. is *Polígono* or Industrial Estate
Colonia is Estate	Pza. is *Plaza/Plaça* or Square
Ctra. is *Carretera* or Road	s/n is *sin número* or without a number
c/v is *con vuelta* or on the corner with	Urb. is *Urbanización* or Development
Muelle is Dock	Vía/Via is an Urban Thoroughfare

When the street is followed by a comma and a second name (e.g. Rosales 4, Tafira), the second name refers to the neighbourhood. Outside cities, the address is followed by a full stop and the name of the town (in bold) where the work is located. Finally, the surname(s) of the author(s) appears (the full name appears in the directory on page 342), followed by the initial or the full first name only in cases where two or more architects share the same surname, together with an indication if it is an engineer [eng.]. Alongside the block of data and text is one or more photographs, or a photograph and plan, elevation or section of the work. Finally, there are works that have been finished too recently or were still in progress when this guide went to press in December 1997, which have been provisionally selected and classified, and the jury has reserved its right to ratify or remove them in the future. In such cases the safety helmet symbol has been used in the margin to indicate provisionality.

As the perspicacious reader will notice immediately, not all the entries are the same length. The quality ranking of a work can be judged by the amount of space devoted to it, an entire page being given over to those that consistently received top marks in all the committee's evaluation sessions and from all the members. There are other entries that occupy a full page spread (either vertically or horizontally across two half pages), but are placed on a light grey background, in order to show that they were not accorded top ranking but nonetheless are special cases which, because of their size, extension or scale, require extra space in the guide.

Authorship and Language

This has been a collective endeavour, but not an anonymous one. The selection of the works covered has been the exclusive responsibility of the expert committee of specialised consultants (see list on page 3). The essays are signed by their authors, who are named in the table of contents on page 5. The entries for the 767 works have been written by specialists – architects, professors, critics and historians – whose names are shown on page 4. The remaining unsigned texts were drawn up by the editorial team of the publishing house.

The data of the works were provided by the architects, except in the case of those who have died, where it has been their heirs, relations or foundations that provided them, duly checked against all available sources. The plans and drawings or sketches have been submitted by the architects, heirs or documentary archives and, except for the odd exception (see credits on page 399), have not been redrawn, in order to keep them as true to the original as possible. As regards the photographs included, wherever possible they came directly from the architects or administrators of their documentary archives, for we believe that the pictorial representation of works should respond to the idea that its creators have of it. When these photographs were not made available, we used the archives of the Subdirectorate General for Architecture of the Spanish Ministry of Development and of Tanais Arquitectura. Pictorial contributions from important institutions in architecture have also been employed. Finally, a number of new photographs have been taken in accordance with the indications of the scientific and editorial board when required.

The language tries to maintain a balance between the rigour of strict architectural and engineering terminology and jargon, and the kind of communication needed to ensure that the average reader can understand what is being said. Nonetheless, the glossary on page 386 will provide readers with a succinct explanation of more than one hundred and fifty terms, along with the acronyms and abbreviations used in the guide. Some expressions have been condensed, such as temperatures in towns, which always appear in degrees Celsius, where the first figures are the maximum temperatures, the average highest temperature in summer and the average highest temperature in winter (e.g. 34°-18°), and the second are the minimum temperatures, the average lowest temperature in winter and the average lowest temperature in summer (e.g. 1°-18°), so that they typically read as follows: 34°-18° and 1°-18° C. Likewise, several standard abbreviations have been used. Thus, the term century is abbreviated as c., metres as m, kilometres as km, gross domestic product as GDP, national as nat., average as av., approximately as approx., collaborator as coll., and before Christ as BC. Finally, in those instances when Spanish terms have been used, these appear in italics to denote the foreign provenience of the word.

How to Use the Guide

The guide is an extraordinarily versatile, user-friendly publication. It provides nearly all the forms of use that a reader can imagine. Amongst the most typical uses, apart from reading it from cover to cover, following the text, we could mention browsing, to obtain an overall view of its contents. It can also be used as a work of reference. The guide provides a comprehensive set of ways to "navigate" through the information stored in it. In other words, there is a set of routes established so that readers will not get lost and can search and find whatever they are after.

Readers may wish to use the guide as an aid to lead them through Spanish 20th century architecture, or they may wish to research or know more about a certain period, region, town, architect or type of building. Several indexes or directories facilitate access to or complement the guide's information:
- an alphabetical list of addresses of architectural and engineering firms, including further information on the architect or engineer, such as year of birth, graduation and death, where applicable (page 342).
- an alphabetical list of works (page 353).
- an alphabetical list of place names (page 364).
- an alphabetical list of authors (page 366).
- a typological list of works, listing hospitals, residential buildings, airports, etc. (page 375).

Final Words

This guide is the outcome of a decision reached by a few and made reality by the efforts of hundreds. We have aimed at maximum reliability in the data. However, the editor must proffer his apologies for any error or omission that may have involuntarily slipped into it. We would encourage readers to send in any corrections, suggestions or futher information that they would like to see included as part of the ongoing enhancement of the register and the desire to update the guide in future editions.

My final comment may seem obvious, but we sometimes get carried away by the fascination of new media and fall into a kind of architectural consumerism: nothing can replace the experience of the real thing. Photography and the printed word cannot be a substitute for visiting the work and seeing it in its own context. So we must beg you to abandon your armchairs and get out onto the street where you can enjoy real architecture in its element.

The Editor

Acknowledgements

This guide has been made possible by a confluence of efforts and resources, public and private, corporative and professional, institutional and individual. To mention everyone involved would make a very long list. Although all collaborators have been thanked by the people in charge of the project, we would like to reiterate our appreciation to the architects and engineers whose works appear in the Register, most of whom have made a special effort to supply us with the necessary information and illustrative material, as shown in the list of credits on page 399.

We would also like to give special credit to Rafael Fernández del Amo (Madrid); the Alejandro de la Sota Foundation and its chairman, José de la Sota (Madrid); the César Manrique Foundation (Lanzarote); the Office of Architecture and Housing of the Andalusian Department of Public Works (Seville); the Eduardo Torroja Institute of Building Sciences and its Deputy Director, Antonio Ruiz Duerto (Madrid); the Architects' Chamber of Asturias and the person in charge of its Cultural Counsel Centre, Miguel García Pola (Oviedo); the Civil Engineers' Chamber (Madrid) and its Documentation Service, for which Marisa Marco is responsible; the Architects' Chamber of Madrid; the Architects' Chamber of Catalonia and its cultural councillor, Gerardo García-Ventosa (Barcelona); the Mies van der Rohe Foundation and the DOCOMOMO Register (Barcelona); the Juan March Foundation (Madrid) and its Museum of Abstract Art (Cuenca); the CAAM, Atlantic Centre of Modern Art, and its director, Martín Chirino (Las Palmas de Gran Canaria); Miguel Martín Fernández de la Torre's heirs (Las Palmas de Gran Canaria); the Architects' Chamber of the Canary Islands/Tenerife District and its chairman, Ramiro Cuende Tascón (Santa Cruz de Tenerife); the Architects' Chamber of the Balearic Islands (Palma de Mallorca), and the chairman of the Architects' Chamber of Castile and León/Segovia District, Luis Llorente Alvarez, for their collaboration in helping us secure the materials needed for this guide. Special mention must also be made of the civil engineers, Jesús Jiménez Cañas, for his counselling, and Fernando Sanz Ridruejo, for the data supplied.

The Spanish Council of Architects' Chambers was helpful in contacting the professional associations. The Architects' Chambers of Western Andalusia, Eastern Andalusia, Aragón, Asturias, the Balearic Islands, the Canary Islands (Gran Canaria District), Cantabria, Eastern Castile and León, Castile-La Mancha, Catalonia, Extremadura, Galicia, Madrid, Murcia and La Rioja furnished us with useful suggestions, data and references for the selection of the works. We also thank the Schools of Architecture that have contributed to this work.

We want to express our gratitude to those persons whose collaboration has exceeded their duties: architect, writer and critic Susana Landrove (Barcelona), journalist Aurora Fernández, and architects Javier Mozas (Vitoria), Plácido Lizancos (Santiago de Compostela) and Carmen Jordá (Valencia).

Last but not least, credit must be given to Cristina Narbona, Borja Carreras and Fernando Nasarre, the high officials directly responsible for architecture and town planning in the Ministry of Development during the course of these works.

The Publishers

SPANISH 20TH CENTURY ARCHITECTURE
THREE IDEAS TO INTERPRET IT

I do not intend to examine the complexities of the Spanish architectural culture over the last 75 years in just a few pages. The wide range of buildings selected for this guide is as many-sided as the values they represent. Their very variety highlights the difficulty of isolating either any common or any differentiating features for Spanish architecture over such a long period. So, with a rather more modest aim in mind, in the following lines I will simply propose some conceptual knots that seem to me to be especially significant in tying up the strands of Spanish architecture through this century.

When Fernando Chueca Goitia published his book, *Invariantes Castizos de la Arquitectura Española* (1947), he was working within the regenerationist tradition of the *Revista de Occidente* journal towards a formalist-empathetic definition of all Spanish architecture from the Middle Ages down to his time. It was an attempt at a new approach, more like a manifesto than a description. In fact, the book provided the theoretical foundations for the *Manifiesto de la Alhambra* (1953), which Chueca himself prepared and which was disseminated as presenting a specifically Spanish position contrary to the internationalism of modern architecture between the wars.

Whether an aesthetic manifesto or a tendency programme, the kind of self-questioning it produced dealt, above all, with how we perceive space and how we define form. Until then, these issues had been considered as invariables in Spanish architecture over the centuries; the new approach intended to change the face of Spain following the disasters of the Civil War and the Second World War. But analysing what has been the most intentionally significant architecture of this century does not bring us to any common pattern that might help us unravel what, to paraphrase Pevsner writing of England in the fifties, we could call the Spanishness of Spanish architecture.

The method proposed here is almost the opposite. Rather than seeking the essence of the *castizo*, the typically Spanish, as the common content over the length and breadth of space and time, what I want to examine in this essay are the changing conditions encountered by Spanish architecture in its deployment.

I shall do this not so much in terms of a permanent creative drive, as in terms of factual coordinates or events that have contributed to defining certain features that occur repeatedly in Spanish architectural works throughout the century. By using three ideas of a very different nature, I suggest that we can understand what Spanish architecture this century has been like both in the realm of ideas and at the more down-to-earth level of specific objects constructed in equally specific places.

All this must be done dynamically, that is to say, by changing this reference framework over time. If there is any general statement that I would like to make, it is precisely that Spanish architecture has undergone enormous transformations. Rather than invariables, we should speak of variables. Rather than searching for the *castizo* or purely Spanish, with all its racial and geopolitical overtones, what

Palace of Charles V, Granada, Pedro Machuca, 1527. El Escorial, Madrid, Juan de Herrera, 1563-84. El Prado Museum, Madrid, Juan de Villanueva, 1785. Crypt, Güell Estate, Barcelona, Antoni Gaudí, 1908-15.

we shall try to find is the *mestizo* or crossbreed, the eclectic, the interactive character that Spanish architects have increasingly displayed both in their internal professional relations and in their relationships with urban places and with the architectural cultures of the world. To what degree we can still detect common features, similar sensibilities or dominant stereotypes from these processes of dispersion and globalisation will be the corollary of the three starting points for interpretation that I lay out herein.

1. From Peripherality to Globality
In order to situate Spanish architecture within a broader framework, we have habitually resorted to using the centre-periphery model. Ever since the Renaissance, at least, Spanish architecture has been on the periphery of things: it received currents drifting in from abroad and shaped them into very *sui generis* versions of their originals.

It is true that some works of great quality have been produced in this task of appropriation and elaboration. We have only to think of the architecture of Machuca (16th c.), Villanueva (18th c.) or Coderch (20th c.). However, we cannot deny the evidence that the routes along which architectural ideas and tastes travelled were one-way roads. Spanish architects were creative receivers, without a doubt. Receivers with their own initiative that could bring characteristic tints and hues to the models and styles emanating from Italy, France, Germany or whatever source the breezes of innovation were blowing in from. Nonetheless, when all is said and done, they were peripheral receivers in that the force of the incoming flow was incomparably stronger than that of any possible novelties that they themselves might have produced and sent outwards to the changing focal nodes of culture.

Of course, this does not mean there was any dearth of quality, nor lack of creative ingenuity, figurative drive or sensibility. But it is equally true that, in the history of Western architecture, the best of Spanish works from Modern and

Ugalde House,
Caldes d'Estrac,
Barcelona,
by José A. Coderch,
1949

contemporary times show a significant degree of conformity in their ideas and tastes, occupying the space left for dependent peripheries. Even when architectural culture has thrown up exceptional talents, such as Juan de Herrera (16th c.) or Antoni Gaudí (19th-20th c.), they have shown little sign of making much impact – if any at all – on the centres of European and Western culture. When quoting Gaudí's case, Eugenio d'Ors referred to it as one of our great anomalies.

Only in very recent times, since the seventies, has this asymmetric position been reversed. We repeatedly discuss the fact (not without certain traces of *parvenu* pride) that over the last twenty or twenty-five years, Spanish architecture has managed to excite international interest as it perhaps had never done before. Several monographic works in the most prestigious journals, travelling exhibitions, international prizes, a high profile in the most renowned universities and cosmo-politan fora are just a few of the many symptoms of this changing position.

The explanation behind this phenomenon would on its own merit a detailed analysis. In this introduction, however, let us just remark that although the political change from dictatorship to democracy has played its part, it cannot be the sole cause of this transformation. It actually has more to do with the fact that the recent architectural output of some Spanish architects has been taken up on the world-wide web of *conoscenti* as a genuinely new contribution, with its own personality.

But I should immediately point out that what we are experiencing now cannot be interpreted within the traditional centre-periphery model that I referred to above. Because what has changed has not been Spanish architecture itself as such, but the model with which architectures blossoming around the world establish their inter-connections and exchange-nodes. For what has occurred in the world, and not just in Spanish architecture, is that over the last thirty years we have shifted from a hierarchical system towards a globalised system, from a dualist model to a pluralist one. Spanish architects nowadays are surprised that the work of Sáenz de Oíza, de la Sota, Coderch and Sostres has not yet received world-wide public recognition. But let us not deceive ourselves. It was not just the cycles of classical architecture of the Modern Age or of the Eclectical architecture of the first Industrial Revolution that failed to enter into the cultural framework of world architecture. Actually, the same thing happened with our avant-garde and Rationalist works, and with the Organic and Expressionist architectures that followed later. The cycle of what we can call the Spanish Modern move-ment continued to lie outside the world map.

> It is surprising that
> "... the work of
> Sáenz de Oíza,
> de la Sota,
> Coderch and Sostres
> has not yet received
> worldwide public
> recognition."

Despite our devotion and enthusiasm for the generation of our teachers, we should realise that the qualitative change in our world position has only come about when the deep cultural mutation that we usually call the Post-Modern crisis took place. This has something to do with the crisis of the dominant cultural model, but also with the rampant intensification in consumption and the mass interchange of information in all directions, both of which form part of globalisation.

It is true that the Post-Modern crisis meant, amongst other things, the end of the centre-periphery dualism. In the search for other alternatives to the central development of the Modern movement, attention became focussed on episodes removed from these centres (Spain, Ticino, Portugal, Holland, California, Japan...). The powerful apparatus for producing dominant culture, the most prestigious critics and the most renowned central display cases in the United States and Europe, which had not previously shown much interest or enthusiasm for these architectural products, now opened their arms to them. But the Post-Modern phenomenon of looking out and about very soon linked in with another, no less decisive phenomenon: multiple networking and the growing simultaneity of all information sources, both accompanied by a dramatic increase in people's mobility.

Spanish architecture is now on the world map because its output contains aspects of interest and singularity not to be scorned. But Spanish architecture is also on the multipolar networks that now form the fabric of global architectural culture because the consumption of architecture through journals, exhibitions, lectures, conferences and presentations has expanded exponentially in comparison with such information flows only thirty years back.

A few Spanish architects, indeed a notable number of them, are on the network because the global market for talent to participate in competitions, present ideas or teach in universities anywhere in the world is now infinitely more complex and plural than it was just a few years ago. Being on the network is not exactly the same as being at the centre used to be, as opposed to being on the periphery. It clearly means being present on the international, global market. A merciless, difficult market. A plural, mobile market. A kind of jungle in which nearly everything goes, as long as it can stand being permanently subjected to the unstoppable dynamism of total consumption.

2. Economics, The Primacy of Practice
Being an architect in Spain has, for the last century and a half, meant being in a well-defined profession that enjoys high social prestige. Since the mid-19th century, architects have no longer been formed within the Academies of Fine Arts, their training being structured according to the new French model of polytechnical education. In both Europe and America, this dichotomy has been far from insignificant. Under the classical tradition, architects were trained in the context of the arts. Painters, sculptors and architects were the experts, educated at institutions whose core values consisted in the art of drawing, the development of aesthetic sensibility and the interaction between all the artistic genres.
Beaux Arts architects were (and in some cases still are) predominantly artists, not just in France, but also in countries as diverse as Germany, Austria, Russia, the United States and Argentina, to mention but a few. Their main attributes were and are, consequently, those that derive most immediately from their privileged condition, linked to creativity and taste, and their competence is considered to be of special importance in areas related to meaning, monumentality and singularity.

Contrary to this, technical architects (in the original sense of the word, coming from the Greek *teknos*), educated in polytechnical institutions, along with the other technical specialists trained with them, give priority to the specific knowledge of a building's static behaviour and the know-how required to understand the needs and organisation of spatial systems intended for the most varied functions that the complex industrial city may demand. Of course, their artistic training forms a vital part of this, and knowledge of architecture past and present is also necessary. But representational techniques will simply be a vehicle for training taste, in a process whose final aim is the detailed analysis of structure and the production of objects, their factuality and their durability. Ever since the School of Architecture was founded in Madrid in 1844 and then in Barcelona in 1875, architectural training in Spain has shown a decisive orientation towards technical specialisation and the development of the abilities required to cope with any kind of building need, from a flexible, broad technical base.

The breadth of skills related to building at the same time entailed an equally broad-ranging burden of responsibility. In Spain, unlike in many other Western countries, architects have been, almost exclusively, the only professionals with legally recognised powers to assume the responsibility for any building work. To this date, civil engineers still do not exist as such in Spain, and although there are obviously people with similar specialisations and affinities in different branches of engineering, their involvement in the legal responsibility for building works is extremely limited. Something along these lines has also occurred with the figure of the chartered surveyors (*aparejadores*), more recently renamed technical architects (*arquitectos técnicos*). Although their training overlaps in part with that of architects, from the legal viewpoint, their involvement and responsibility for most building processes does not cover anything like the scope established under prevailing Spanish law for professional architects. This situation, which is indeed rapidly changing at present, with evident consequences for the medium-term future, has meant that over the last 150 years architectural professionals have been the key experts through whose hands all the output of the building industry had to pass.

Apart from this highly important quantitative and qualitative aspect of architects' competences and powers in Spain, we should also add that Spanish legislation is also exceptional in comparison to other Western countries' in that architects hold ultimate liability for all the problems that may come up in a building, not just whilst it is being built but also throughout the terms laid down to guarantee the quality of any edifice. In other words, this means that technical responsibilities are laid on the shoulders of architects that could not be given to them had they not first been endowed with the know-how to cope with them and had they not first been involved with the decisions about the project from the outset.

My opinion regarding these aspects is that, although they may not appear to have much to do with criteria of cultural excellence, in fact it is impossible to understand many of the characteristic features of Spanish architecture if we ignore or underestimate the factors that define the architectural profession in Spain. In other words, Spanish architecture has contained and still contains a requirement of realism in building terms, a highly practical sense of how to deal with functional specifications and how to understand the specific feasibility of projects, which is not at all comparable with the *modus operandi* of architects elsewhere.

> "Spanish architecture is now on the world map because its output contains aspects of interest and singularity not to be scorned."

This is something that could still change in Spain, precisely due to the globalisation and standardisation already mentioned above. But until it does, the Spanish architect continues to be someone called in to find a high-quality, efficient and economically feasible way of solving the enormously wide range of technical problems involved in building. Technical competence, multi-skill abilities and an orientation towards practical rather than theoretical, teaching or experimental activities are all features that very specifically define the majority, as well as the significant minority of Spanish architects.

"...it is impossible to understand many characteristic features of Spanish architecture if we ignore or underestimate the factors that define the architectural profession in Spain."

When international critics repeatedly call attention to the sense of tectonicity in Spanish buildings, often lacking in buildings outside Spain, they are recognising values that are almost inevitable for architects who have been trained in and are constantly exercising practical responsibilities both in the design and the material execution of plans. Nor are international specialist critics mistaken in appreciating the tangible, sensual, non-abstract, tactile and colouristic condition, linked to the building trades and the details of the physical execution of architectural objects. But these attributes which, regardless of fashions and tendencies, are habitual in the works of Spanish architects, are merely the evidence of the necessary attention that results from the liability that they assume and from a social practice that is closely bound to the definition of their professional practice.

An immediate corollary of the situation described is that the architectural profession in Spain, in general terms (because architects are necessarily involved in the construction industry), moves a lot of money. This is especially important if we bear in mind the corporative links binding architects together and the control that they exercise, both corporately and individually, over a sizeable flow of economic resources. On the threshold of a new century, there are processes about that will alter all this. One inevitable consequence will be the reorganisation of the profession, the change in the volume and sources of resources and the sharing out and dissipation of more superstructural activities which we are used to calling cultural activities.

The panorama of Spanish architecture, the excellence of certain names and works, not just those that have emerged in more recent times but also, really, from any time during this century, may change suddenly and quickly if we do not apply intelligent alternatives vis-à-vis the future. The past situation is unlikely to survive in similar form, but it would be equally false to think that the attention that the world is currently paying Spanish architecture can act as any kind of guarantee for that future. On the global web, everything is broken down and built

Alejandro de la Sota
at the Gymnasium
of the Colegio
Maravillas, Madrid,
1962

up again with glibly changing performances and optimisations, which will make it difficult for Spanish architects to maintain the coherence of their professional organisation and profile.

3. The End of the Century, The Beginning of a New Millennium

If we compare the importance of avant-garde output with the professional production of architecture throughout the century, the balance is tipped in favour of the latter category. What we could call the "classical" avant-garde, or the works pertaining to the period between the wars, had a late, minority impact in Spain and, for political reasons but also for considerations of social acceptance, it was never widely accepted by the general public. The talent drain following the Civil War – with Sert and Lacasa leaving the country, for example, and many others going into a "domestic exile" – broke down a movement that, although strong, did not achieve collective success in an environment that could not offer more than very limited possibilities of continuity. The Spanish avant-garde, moreover, lagging almost a decade or so behind the German and Parisian ones, arose when the central protagonists had already initiated processes of revision that were developed before and after the Second World War, with only a sporadic Spanish presence that was largely unrepresentative of the architectural culture of Spain in those years.

The later brilliant and powerful Expressionisms of the seventies were, above all, individual shouts, critical gestures that were never sufficiently articulated in any programme. The innovative venture of Sáenz de Oíza, Coderch, de la Sota and Bohigas, amongst others of their generation, showed great internal efficacy, in that the climate these architects created around them was one which brought about the deepest change in Spanish architecture as a whole. This was the generation of a decisive cultural watershed, the generation that changed the linguistic and figurative methodology they inherited to the one that to a large extent still lives on in today's architecture. Frenetically aware of what was happening around them, in Italy, Great Britain, the United States and the countries of Northern Europe, these architects, who were not even especially

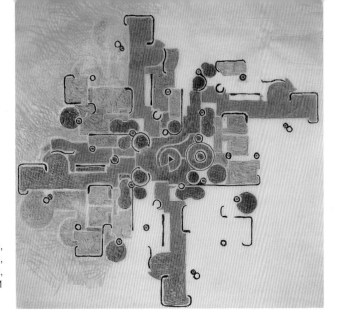

Ground plan,
Torres Blancas Building,
Madrid, by Sáenz de Oíza,
1961

progressive or revolutionary in their leanings, liquidated the remains of the decrepit 19th century Eclectic-Academic culture and opened up architecture to a wide range of possibilities for experimentation, innovation and personal expression.

But this generation did not receive foreign recognition, only domestic attention. It was the generation that recomposed the professional profile, the productive realism, the balance between individual expression and public service. We should explain, in rather less innocent terms than is common, how the foundations of today's Spanish architecture were laid down, and by whom, not in terms of anyone's specific choices of style or their greater or lesser attention to technical, typological or urbanistic experimentation, but in terms of their overall feel for architecture as part of a broader whole, linked to social integration, the priority of public over private, and the moderation with which architects act as interpreters of the demand for public and private spaces.

When we look at more recent architecture, we can see that the way that most architects work is not that different from the way those who are now seen as the masters of the sixties did. Nowadays, the renowned, widely praised work of Rafael Moneo and of his large group of faithful followers is characterised by an intelligent approach, highly sensitive to the needs of town planning, widely cultured in its definition of types and elegant in the way it finishes off the individual buildings. In Madrid, Seville, Galicia, Barcelona and Navarre, the work of many of today's most highly accredited architects are based on this highly developed professional definition. The discourse has been internalised, becoming an integral part of the discipline's arsenal. The gestures have been restrained, always within the limits of the politically correct. A certain exchangeability of names and works is the characteristic note struck by the dozens of talented and flexible architects, between the ages of forty and sixty, who elegantly and carefully define a way of doing architecture that has now become the paradigm of civil language.

"... dozens of talented and flexible architects, between the ages of forty and sixty... elegantly and carefully define a way of doing architecture that has now become the paradigm of civil language."

National Museum of Roman Art, Mérida (Extremadura), by Rafael Moneo, 1982

However, in my opinion, in the cult that praises beauty over expression, where well-mannered form is only offset by the odd flash of wit or some clever allusion for those in the know, there is a tendency for energy to turn into entropy and the elaborate processes of definition into Mannerism. I must admit that, at present, I view the works of my generation with a certain amount of disenchantment, seeing only tiny glimmers of hope for a forthcoming renewal, if it is not going to continue churning out more of the same. Part of the best Spanish architecture appears to have turned in upon itself, become narcissistic and increasingly risk averse. Even the climate of public recognition and institutional respect merely seems to be allowing us to relax further into complacency.

For me, there are now very few positions and careers that have escaped this general tonic of things. Perhaps only works such as those by Miralles, Navarro Baldeweg, Elías Torres, Antonio Sanmartín, Abalos and Herreros, Yago Conde[1], and presumably other younger and less highly publicised names as well as those that I have simply forgotten or do not know, are heading along different lines, taking risks in different directions. These other lines are extremely diverse. Sometimes I think that they are more an illusory desire than a consolidated reality. But I am convinced that, in the beautiful calm waters of this end-of-the-century Spanish architecture, we are in greater need than ever of echos and awareness of the challenges that lie before us. The societies and towns in which we live are neither integrated nor respectful to the message and manners that much of our

1. The premature victim of a fatal disease, he was the author of suggestive designs, such as the school and fire station for the Olympic Village, Barcelona, never built. [Editor's Note].

"... works [that are] heading along different lines, taking risks in different directions."

Convention Centre and Exhibition Hall, Salamanca, by Juan Navarro Baldeweg, 1988-92

architecture continues to give out. The current threats and opportunities in terms of technology, land distribution and production could easily just wipe out the system of mutual bolstering that we have established, if we are not able to enhance the tension, open up new fronts and increase the riskiness of our ventures.

The guide that follows these lines tells a long story. The story of how the first, impossible wave of modernisation was squashed; how an abortive avant-garde came into being and how we have collectively and elaborately constructed a tightly rationed architectural culture with which to make and unmake our towns and cities, and respond (sometimes directly and others evasively) to the greatest transformation of the Spanish territory ever to take place in our history.

I hope that in ten years time, when I flick through the pages of this guide, some new chronological chapter will have been added, in which I shall see that we have been able to respond to the magnitude of these new challenges with the rigour and vigour that the times require of us.

Ignasi de Solà-Morales
July 1997

1920

Jujol builds the Bofarull House in El Pallaresos

Social revolts take place in Barcelona. José Solana paints *La tertulia del café de Pombo*. The writer, Pérez Galdós dies. Total population: 21.2 million. Average life expectancy: 41 years

1921

Arturo Soria i Mata, town planner responsible for the design of the Ciudad Lineal Development in Madrid in the 19th c., dies

The Spanish are defeated at Annual (Morocco). The Communist party appears in Spain. The head of government, Eduardo Dato, is murdered. Ortega y Gasset publishes *Invertebrate Spain*

1922

The Law of Low-priced Housing goes into effect

Jacinto Benavente receives the Nobel Prize for Literature

1923

Zuazo draws up the proposal for the Inner Bilbao Reform; Bastida, the proposal for the Bilbao General Plan

Primo de Rivera's coup in Barcelona marks the beginning of his dictatorship. Salvador Dalí paints *Cubist self portrait*. Ortega y Gasset launches the magazine, *Revista de Occidente*

1924

The Decree-Law of 8 March, a council statute which requires all cities with 10,000 or more inhabitants to draw up an expansion plan, is approved

Rafael Alberti writes *Sailor on Land*. Joan Miró paints *The hunter*. Valle Inclán writes *Lights of Bohemia*. Radio Barcelona, the first commercial radio station, starts broadcasting

1925

The 11th National Congress of Architecture and the 1st Congress of Town Planning are held in Madrid

Salvador Dalí paints *Muchacha de espaldas*. New car sales registered: 21,934

1926

The Alfonso XIII canal and bridge are inaugurated in Seville. The Bilbao Expansion Plan is put out to tender. Antoni Gaudí dies

Juan Gris paints *Guitar with sheet of music*; Joan Miró, *Dog barking at the moon;* Salvador Dalí, *Harlequin*. Worker strikes erupt all over Spain

1927

The design of the Ciudad Universitaria campus in Madrid is drawn up under López Otero, Head of the Technical Office in charge of the works

Homage to Góngora in Seville's Atheneum and birth of the *Generation of '27* (García Lorca, Alberti, Guillén, Alonso, Diego...). A. Ferrant sculpts *Woman's head*. Juan Gris, one of the founding fathers of Cubism, dies. Worker strikes continue

1928

Aníbal González builds the Plaza de España in Seville; García Mercadal, the Rincón de Goya in Zaragoza

García Lorca writes *The Gypsy Ballads*. Three women become town councillors in Seville

1929

Mies van der Rohe builds the German Pavilion in Barcelona. In the international competition for the Madrid Expansion Plan, Zuazo and Jansen's proposal stands out. Rubió i Tuduri draws up the Greater Barcelona Plan. The Telefónica Building in Madrid becomes the first European skyscraper

On 9 May, Alfonso XIII inaugurates the Ibero-American Exhibition in Seville, and on 19 May, the International Exhibition in Barcelona. García Lorca publishes *Poet in New York*. Buñuel and Dalí direct *Le Chien Andalou*

The magazine *L'Esprit Nouveau* is founded. The unprecedented urban development of Chicago in the twenties turns it into a "social laboratory"

Mies van der Rohe designs the Glass Skyscraper project for Berlin. Max Weber publishes *The City* (an independent territorial unit based on loyalty links among its inhabitants)

R. Schindler builds the Schindler/Chase House, Hollywood. Competition for the Chicago Tribune

Le Corbusier publishes *Vers une architecture*. Gropius establishes the Bauhaus in Weimar. Gustave Eiffel dies

E. Mendelsohn builds the Einstein Tower, Potsdam; G.T. Rietveld, the Schröder House, Utrecht; J.J.P. Oud, the Workers' Housing, Hook; Wright, the Freeman House, Los Angeles, CA

The Exhibition of Decorative Arts is held in Paris. The Bauhaus moves to Dessau. Le Corbusier builds the La Roche/Jeanneret House in Paris

Gropius builds the Bauhaus, Dessau. M. Breuer designs the Wassily armchair. Pierre Lavedan publishes *What is Town Planning?*

Melnikov builds the Rusakov Workers' Club, Moscow; Le Corbusier, the Villa Stein, Garches, Paris. The Weissenhofsiedlung, Stuttgart, is designed. 1925-30 E. May publishes *Das Neue Frankfurt*, Römerstadt. W. Ruttmann directs *Berlin, Symphony of a Great City*

The 1st CIAM is held in La Sarraz, Switzerland, with S. Giedion as secretary. Radburn is the first garden city with pedestrian walkways. E.G. Asplund builds the Stockholm Public Library. E. Freyssinet invents prestressed concrete

The 2nd CIAM is held in Frankfurt. R. Neutra builds the Lovell House, Los Angeles, CA; Eileen Gray, the Cap Martin House, Roquebrune; E. Mendelsohn, the Schocken Department Store, Chemnitz. B. Taut publishes *Die neue Baukunst in Europa und Amerika*

1920
Mondrian paints his *Composition in red, black, blue, yellow and grey*. R. Wiene directs *The Cabinet of Dr Caligari*. Gandhi starts his campaign of civil disobedience in India. Modigliani dies

1921
Pirandello writes *Six Characters in Search of an Author*. The Italian Communist Party is founded by Gramsci. Einstein receives the Nobel Prize for Physics. The tuberculosis vaccine is developed

1922
Mussolini rises to power in Italy. Joyce publishes *Ulysses*. The USSR is created

1923
Stalin succeeds Lenin in the USSR. Mustafa Kemal becomes the first president of the Republic of Turkey. Catastrophic inflation hits Germany. E. von Stroheim directs *Greed*

1924
The Labour party tops the polls in England. Mussolini's Fascist party wins the elections in Italy. T. Mann writes *The Magic Mountain*. Malevich launches his suprematist manifiesto. Lenin, Kafka, Conrad and Puccini die

1925
With 10,000 travellers a year, Tempelhof airport in Berlin is the busiest in the world. Hitler writes *Mein Kampf*. 1st Ku-Klux-Klan congress is held

1926
The Nazi Youths are established in Germany. J. Logie's television system is demonstrated. Fritz Lang directs *Metropolis*

1927
Allied military control in Germany comes to an end. Civil War breaks out in China. Stalin expels Trotsky from the Communist party. Heidegger publishes *Being and Time*. Lindbergh flies across the Atlantic. *The Jazz Singer* is the first talkie. Picasso paints *The painter and his model* series

1928
Fleming discovers the first antibiotic: penicillin. D.H. Lawrence publishes *Lady Chatterley's Lover*; B. Brecht, *Three-penny Opera*. Ravel composes *Bolero*; G. Gershwin, *An American in Paris* Magritte paints *Trying the impossible*

1929
The US stock market crash leads to a worldwide economic crisis: the Great Depression. Mussolini and Pius XI's treaty gives rise to the independence of the Vatican City. D. Vertov directs the first documentary film, *The Camera Man*. The MoMA opens in New York

1930
Aizpurúa and Labayen build the Sailing Club, San Sebastián; Zuazo, the Casa de las Flores, Madrid. The GATEPAC group is founded in Zaragoza

1931
Sert builds the Apartment Building on Muntaner street, Barcelona

1932
Martín designs the Town Hall in Las Palmas de Gran Canaria. Indalecio Prieto creates the Technical Office for Madrid's Accesses and Suburbs. Rubió i Tuduri draws up the Catalonian Territorial Distribution Plan
1933
Sert, Torres Clavé and Subirana design the Tuberculosis Clinic in Barcelona; Bergamín and Blanco, the Colonia El Viso Residential Estate in Madrid
1934

1935
Arniches, Domínguez and Torroja (engineer) build the Zarzuela Racetrack, Madrid
1936
S. Esteban de la Mora translates P. Abercrombie's Town and Country Planning, introducing the term "planning" in Spain. The Falangist architect, Aizpurúa is murdered in San Sebastián

1937
The Comitee for the Reconstruction and Rehabilitation of Madrid is established. Sert and Lacasa design the Spanish Pavilion for the Paris Exhibition
1938
Franco creates the National Committee for Devastated Regions

1939
Over 250,000 buildings are destroyed during the Civil War. Many architects go into exile, including Sert, Lacasa, Candela, Bonet

Primo de Rivera's dictatorship comes to an end. Ortega y Gasset publishes The Revolt of the Masses. L. Buñuel and S. Dalí direct L'Age d'Or. Julio González sculpts Head with large eyes. Total population: 23.4 million

King Alfonso XIII abdicates and goes into exile. The Second Republic is established. On 15 April, the proclamation of a state of war is followed by a violent general strike: 16 men die as convents are burned down during Spain's Tragic Week

On 30 August, General Sanjurjo's uprising against the Republic fails. Buñuel directs Land without Bread. Catalonia obtains the status of an autonomous region. Anarchist revolts take place. The Gaceta del Arte magazine is first published

Women are allowed to vote. J.A. Primo de Rivera establishes the Spanish Falangist Movement. García Lorca writes Blood Wedding. The right-wing party tops the polls in the general elections

Revolutionary strikes take place in Asturias. García Lorca's Yerma goes on stage

Unemployment (667,898 persons) grows and strikes intesify. New car sales fall to 21,369

In February, the Popular Front wins the elections. On 18 July, the Civil War (1936-39) breaks out in Spain as generals Mola and Franco lead the army in a revolt against the Republican government. Writers Unamuno and Valle Inclán die. Playwright García Lorca is shot

Guernica is bombarded. Picasso paints Guernica. Radio Nacional de España starts broadcasting nationwide. Thomas Mann backs the Republicans

The Ebro Battle is fought. Franco establishes his first government

On 1 April, the Civil War ends and Franco's dictatorship begins. The country is shattered. There is strong repression: 30,000 are shot, 270,000 are imprisoned, 700,000 are processed for political reasons. There is a massive exile. The poet, Antonio Machado dies

The third CIAM is held in Brussels. W. van Alen builds the Chrysler Building, New York; Mies van der Rohe, the Tugendhat House, Brno; R. Maillart, the Salginatobel Bridge, Schiers; Hood and Howells, the Daily News Building, New York

Le Corbusier builds the Savoye Villa, Poissy; R. Schreve, T. Lamb and A. Harmon, the Empire State Building, New York; P. Chareau and B. Bijvoet, the Maison de Verre, Paris; W. Dudok, the Town Hall, Hilversum. R. Hood designs the Rockefeller Center, New York

The Bauhaus moves to Berlin. Sir O. Williams designs the Daily Express Building, London. H.R. Hitchcock publishes *The International Style, Architecture Since 1922*; A. Sartoris, *Gli elementi dell'architettura funzionale*

Led by Le Corbusier, the CIAM held in Athens applies the tenets of the Modern movement in town planning. A. Aalto builds the Paimio Sanatorium. Hitler closes the Bauhaus

B. Lubetkin and Tecton build the Penguin Pool, London Zoo

E. Mendelsohn and S. Chermayeff build the de la Warr Seaside Pavilion, Bexhill

G. Terragni builds the Fascio House, Como; P.L. Nervi, the Aircraft Hangar, Orvieto; E. Mendelsohn, the Schocken Library, Jerusalem; J. Duiker, the Gooiland Hotel, Hilversum. The Hoover Dam (Nevada and Arizona) is built. Pevsner publishes *Pioneers of Modern Movement*

The 5th CIAM and the International Art Exhibition are held in Paris. Wright builds Fallingwater, Bear Run, PA. The Golden Gate is built in San Francisco

Wright builds Taliesin West, Scottsdale, AZ; Gropius, the Gropius House, Lincoln, MA. L. Mumford publishes *The Culture of Cities*

Wright builds the S.C. Johnson Wax Offices, Racine, WI; E. Mendelsohn, the Hadassah Hospital, Monte Scopus, Jerusalem

1930
The Nazis come second in Germany's general elections. The planet Pluto is discovered. W. Carrothers, of Du Pont, invents nylon. A. Bialetti invents the Moka coffee maker. Moholy-Nagy is in Paris

1931
Austrian and German banks close, giving rise to a financial crisis in central Europe. Al Capone is arrested and imprisoned in the US. The Japanese occupy Manchuria and begin to assert their military dominance of the Far East. Thomas A. Edison dies

1932
Franklin D. Roosevelt becomes president of the US. Elections in Germany lead to major gains for the Nazi party in the Reichstag. A. Huxley publishes *Brave New World*

1933
Roosevelt launches the New Deal. Hitler is named chancellor of Germany and consolidates his power eliminating opposition parties. He also bans Modern art: several artists go into exile

1934
Hitler becomes Führer of the Third Reich. A. Calder designs his mobile sculptures

1935
Mao Zedong starts the Long March. Penguin launches the pocket book. Gardel dies

1936
Roosevelt is reelected president of the US. Hitler and Mussolini form the Berlin-Rome alliance. Stalin initiates a purge of the Communist party. Cárdenas institutionalises the Mexican revolution. J.M. Keynes propounds a new economic theory. England and Germany broadcast television

1937
Japan invades China. The Stalinist processes take place. F. Porsche designs the Volkswagen *beetle*, a popular car commissioned by Hitler

1938
L. Biro invents the ballpoint pen; Baird, colour TV. H. Moore sculpts his *Recumbent figure*. D'Annunzio dies

1939
Hitler occupies Poland and Czechoslovakia. England and France declare war on Germany. World War II begins. DDT is used for the first time. The World Fair, "World of Tomorrow", is held in New York. Chagall paints *The cellist*

1940

The Institute of Local Administration Studies is founded. The 2nd National Assembly of Architects is held

1941

The OSHA, Union's Housing and Architecture Organisation is established. Gutiérrez Soto ends work on the Apartment Building on Miguel Angel street, Madrid, designed in 1936

1942

Torroja finishes work on the Martín Gil Viaduct

Total population: 25.7 million. The Communism Repression Law is enacted. Spain declares its neutrality in World War II

The INI, National Industry Institute is created. 50% of the active population is employed in agriculture, whereas only 22% works in the industry sector

The poet, Miguel Hernández dies in prison. The writer, Camilo José Cela publishes *The Family of Pascual Duarte*. The sculptor, Julio González dies

1943

Palacios Ramilo builds the Veracruz Sanctuary, O Carballino

Benjamín Palencia paints *Cesta en el campo*. The shortage of food and resources increases

1944

The engineer, Carlos Fernández Casado, designs the Aqueduct over the River Najerilla

The poet, Alfonso R. Castelao publishes *Sempre en Galiza*. The US enforces an oil embargo on Spain

1945

Luis Moya designs the Technical College of Gijón. The Spanish-Portuguese Town Planning Congress is held

The writer, Carmen Laforet publishes *Nada*. The country starves. Per capita income is 35% lower than in 1935. New car sales descend to 4,101 units

1946

The Madrid General Plan, by Pedro Bidagor, and several other city plans (Valencia, Seville...) are drawn up. The Madrid Town Planning Committee is set up

1947

An arm of the River Guadalquivir is blocked at Chapina, Seville

Foreign ambassadors abandon Madrid as the Spanish borders are closed down. Dalí paints *Saint Anthony's temptation*

Spain is excluded from the Marshall Plan to help rebuild Western Europe. The Basque Country is plagued with strikes

1948

Sota designs the Esquivel Settlement in Seville

The *Dau al Set* magazine is launched by the group of Barcelona painters (Tàpies...) and writers of the same name. The "maquis" guerrilla fighting Franco is defeated

1949

Cabrero and Aburto design the Trade Union Building, Madrid; Bonet Castellana, the La Ricarda Villa, El Prat de Llobregat. The National Town Planning Headquarters are established. Construction work begins on the new docks and banks of the River Guadalquivir after blocking its course at Chapina, Seville

The composer, Joaquín Turina (*Sevillian Symphony*) dies. The playwright, Buero Vallejo receives the Lope de Vega Prize for *The History of a Stairway*. The GDP grows 0.5%

1940

E.G. Asplund builds the Woodland Cemetery at Enskede, Stockholm

Germany, Italy and Japan are allied. Pétain establishes his pro-Nazi government in Vichy. Orson Welles directs *Citizen Kane*. Paul Klee dies

1941

A. Aalto builds the Villa Mairea, Noormarkku. The *Charter of Athens* is inspired by Le Corbusier. S. Giedion publishes *Space, Time and Architecture*

Germany invades the USSR and begins the siege of Leningrad. Japan attacks Pearl Harbour. The US declares war on Japan and Germany. Joyce, Tagore and Virginia Woolf die

1942

G. Guerrini, E. la Padula and M. Romano build the Palazzo della Civiltà Italiana, Rome; A. Libera and C. Malaparte, the Malaparte House, Capri; Hassan Fathy, the House for an Artist, El Cairo

Fermi builds the first nuclear reactor in Chicago, leading to the development of the atomic bomb. Peggy Guggenheim opens the Art of this Century Gallery, New York, designed by Kiesler

1943

Sir Patrick Abercrombie draws up the London Plan that served as a model for the great town planning works of the forties and fifties worldwide. O. Niemeyer builds the Restaurant in Pampulha

Mussolini is removed from office and the Italian Facist party is dissolved. Jackson Pollock exhibits in New York. Sartre publishes *Being and Nothingness*. M. Curtiz directs *Casablanca*

1944

J. LL. Sert publishes *Can our Cities Survive?* Sir Edward Lutyens dies

The Bretton Woods agreement establishes a new international economic order. The allied troops land in Normandy. Rossellini directs *Rome, Open City*. Mondrian and Kandinsky die

1945

L. Barragán starts work on the El Pedregal Estate, Mexico City. Mies van der Rohe designs the Farnsworth House, Plano, IL

US drops the first atomic bombs on Hiroshima and Nagasaki. Japan surrenders, ending World War II (40 million victims). Mussolini is shot. Hitler commits suicide. The world is divided into spheres of influence in Yalta and Potsdam

1946

R. Neutra builds the Kaufman Desert House, Palm Springs, CA

Victor Manuel III abdicates; the Italian Republic is voted in by referendum under prime minister De Gasperi. C. d'Ascanio designs the Vespa motorcycle for Piaggio; L. Réard, the bikini

1947

L. Barragán builds the Barragán House, Mexico City; M. Breuer, the Breuer House I in New Canaan, CT

US launches the Marshall Plan. India gains its independence. A. Camus publishes *The Plague;* Tennessee Williams, *A Streetcar Named Desire*. D. Hume makes the first kidney transplant

1948

Mies van der Rohe designs the Lake Shore Drive Apartments, Chicago, IL. H. Seidler builds the Seidler House, Sydney

The first transistor is invented by Schockley, Bardeen and Brattain (Bell labs.). The OECD and FAO are set up. Israel is declared a Jewish state. Gandhi is murdered. The Cold War begins

1949

The Copenhagen Plan (with roots in A. Soria's Ciudad Lineal Development) acts as a model for the plans of Warsaw (1957), Hamburg (1960), Washington (1961). C. Eames builds the Eames House, Santa Monica, CA. K. Tange designs the Peace Memorial and Museum, Hiroshima

Mao Zedong proclaims the People's Republic of China. Germany is divided into two states: the Federal Republic and the Democratic Republic. S. de Beauvoir publishes *The Second Sex*. NATO is formed as a defensive alliance by western nations. W. Faulkner receives the Nobel Prize for Literature

1950
Fisac designs the Church of the Dominican Fathers in Alcobendas (Madrid)

Total population: 27.9 million (37% live in cities). The US Congress grants Spain a loan. Laín Entralgo publishes *Spain as a Problem*

1951
Coderch and Valls design the Ugalde House (Caldes d'Estrac) and the Apartment Building in Barceloneta (Barcelona)

Camilo J. Cela publishes *The Hive*. Eduardo Chillida forges the iron stele, *Ilarik*. One million tourists visit Spain

1952
Santos et al. design the Technical College of Córdoba

Twelve years of rationing cards come to an end. The 35th International Eucharistic Congress is held in Barcelona, breaking Spain's isolation

1953
Vaquero Palacios designs the Grandas de Salime Dam

US signs an agreement with Spain to establish American military bases in Spain. Oteiza designs the sculptures for the Arantzazu Monastery, designed by Saénz de Oíza. The first SEAT car is manufactured in Barcelona

1954
Fernández del Amo designs the Vegaviana Settlement (Cáceres). The Managed Settlements Programme builds social housing blocks for Madrid's immigrants

The 5th Congress of the Spanish Communist party triggers a national reconciliation policy. Antoni Tàpies paints *Painting with a red cross*. Together with Arp and Ernst, Miró receives the Grand Prix in Venice

1955
Sostres builds the Agustí House, Sitges. Sert designs the Joan Miró Studio, Palma de Mallorca. Yordi designs the Dam over the River Eume

Spain joins the UN. The 1st National Housing Plan goes into effect. Sánchez Ferlosio publishes *The Jarama*. New car sales increase to 67,628

1956
The new land and town planning law, the "Ley de Suelo" (a valuable regulation which, nonetheless, is complex and difficult to apply) goes into effect. The Aldeadávila Dam is designed

Televisión Española starts broadcasting on a regular basis. Spain grants Morocco its independence. Juan Ramón Jiménez receives the Nobel Prize for Literature

1957
Alejandro de la Sota builds the Civilian Government Building, Tarragona

The new government, formed by Opus Dei ministers who abandon the Falange's state intervention policy and lean towards economic liberalism, gives rise to modern reforms. The *El Paso* group of artists (Saura, etc.) is formed

1958
Corrales and Molezún build the High School Institute, Herrera de Pisuerga, and the Spanish Pavilion for Expo'58, Brussels

The post-war period comes to an end. Spain joins the OECD. Alberto Sánchez sculpts *Iberian bull*. Antoni Tàpies receives the UNESCO Award at the Venice Biennial. The SEAT 600 sets the car boom in motion in Spain

1959
Fisac builds the Hydraulics Laboratory, Madrid; Fernández del Amo, the Villalba de Calatrava Settlement, Ciudad Real. The National Congress of Town Planning is held in Barcelona

The stabilisation plan puts an end to Spain's autarchy. J. García Hortelano publishes *Nuevas amistades* (social realism). Severo Ochoa receives the Nobel Prize for Medicine

J. O'Gorman et al. build the National Library of the University of Mexico City. C.R. Villanueva designs the University City, Caracas. B. Zevi publishes *Storia dell'architettura moderna*

The 8th CIAM is held in Hoddesdon. Le Corbusier starts the Chandigarh Parliament. P.L. Nervi builds the Gatti Factory, Rome. Sert publishes *The Heart of the City*; A. Hauser, *A Social History of Art*

A. Aalto builds the Säynätsalo Town Hall; SOM, the Lever House Building, New York. A. Jacobsen designs the Ant chair

The CIAM meets in Aix-en-Provence. Le Corbusier builds the Unité d'Habitation, Marseille. Eero Saarinen designs the MIT Chapel, Cambridge, MA. Sert is Dean of the Harvard Graduate School of Design

Mies van der Rohe designs the Seagram Building, New York; Le Corbusier builds the Ronchamp Chapel.

Le Corbusier finishes the Chandigarh Supreme Court

E. Saarinen designs the TWA Terminal, Kennedy Airport, New York; A. Aalto, the Vuoksenniska Church, Imatra

The UIA Congress on "The Modern City" is held in Moscow. L.I. Kahn designs the Richards Medical Laboratories, Philadelphia, PA. A. Jacobsen builds the Christensen Factory, Aalborg. Lucio Costa draws up the layout of Brasilia

L. Barragán builds the Fuente y Plaza del Bebedero, Mexico City; O. Niemeyer, the Plaza de los Tres Poderes and Alborada Palace; E. Dieste, the Church of Atlántida, Uruguay; E. Rogers and E. Peressutti, the Velasca Tower, Milan

The Guggenheim Museum opens in New York; its designer, Frank LL. Wright, dies. O. Niemeyer builds the Cathedral of Brasilia. H. Rosenberg publishes *The Tradition of the New*

1950
The Korean War begins. Vietnam is divided. Diner's Club card appears. P. Neruda publishes *Canto General*. Matisse receives the Grand Prix of the Venice Biennial

1951
The Coal and Steel European Community is established. US tests the H bomb. Jackson Pollock leads abstract Expressionism. The colour TV is manufactured. Wittgenstein dies

1952
Hemingway writes *The Old Man and the Sea*. S. Donen and G. Kelly direct *Singing in the Rain*. Picasso paints *War and peace*

1953
Stalin dies. The Korean War ends. An agreement is signed to set up the first transatlantic telephone cable. M. Bich designs the first disposable Bic ballpoint pen. F. Crick and J. Watson discover the double helix structure of DNA

1954
The US Supreme Court rules that segregation in schools is unconstitutional. Salk develops a vaccine for polio. Bill Haley gives birth to rock' n' roll. War in Indochina ends. Nasser leads the Arab nationalist movement. Matisse dies

1955
The Bandung conference condemns colonialism. Nabokov publishes *Lolita*. The Warsaw Pact unites the eastern bloc nations in a defense treaty. Perón goes into exile. James Dean dies

1956
Egypt nationalizes the Suez canal. Morocco gains its independence. In Hungary, Soviet tanks crush the revolt against the communist regime. A. Resnais directs *Night and Fog*, on Nazi concentration camps. Kruschev denounces Stalinism

1957
France, Germany, Italy and Benelux create the European Community (Rome Treaty). The first artificial satellite, *Sputnik*, is launched. I. Bergman directs *Wild Strawberries*. Brancusi dies

1958
De Gaulle is elected president of France. John XXIII becomes Pope. Pacifism spreads. The American Express card is issued. Elvis Presley reaches the zenith of his career. The Brussels Expo' 58 is held. The NASA is created

1959
Castro overthrows Batista's regime in Cuba. J. Kilby and R. Noyce invent the semiconductor. A. Resnais directs *Hiroshima, Mon Amour*. The Boeing 707 flies New York - Paris in 8 hours

1960
Alejandro de la Sota designs the Gymnasium for the Colegio Maravillas, Madrid

There is strong immigration from the country to the city and to Europe. Total population: 30.3 million (42.5% live in cities). The 2nd National Housing Plan is launched. There is fast economic growth and social change. The GDP grows 0.9%

1961
Sáenz de Oíza designs the Torres Blancas Building, Madrid. The master engineer, Eduardo Torroja dies

Joan Miró paints *Blue III*. Buñuel's *Viridiana*, winner of the Venice Award, is banned in Spain. The GDP grows 11.3%

1962
Antonio Fernández Alba builds the El Rollo Abbey, Salamanca

Franco establishes a new government. The royal wedding of Prince Juan Carlos with Princess Sophia of Greece takes place in Athens. The GDP grows 9.6%

1963
Construction work on the Aldeadávila Dam comes to an end

Communist leader, Julián Grimau is executed. Picasso paints *The painter and his model*. Immigration to Europe reaches its zenith. The GDP grows 9.5%

1964
Bohigas, Martorell and Mackay build the Casa del Patí Building on Ronda del Guinardó, Barcelona. P. Bidagor publishes *Situación general del urbanismo en España*

The *Equipo Crónica* group (pop-style critical art) is established. 48.4% of the total population lives in cities. The unemployment rate is 2%. The GDP grows 6.6%

1965
A plan to rehabilitate palaces and castles for tourism accommodation goes into effect

Student demonstrations begin. New car sales grow to 341,039. The GDP grows 7.5%

1966
The architectural journal, *El Inmueble* (later *Nueva Forma*) is first published

C. Saura paints *The hunt*. Zóbel, Rueda and Torner open the Abstract Art Museum in Cuenca. The GDP grows 7.6%

1967
Vázquez Molezún designs the Summer House in A Roiba

Over one million Spaniards have emigrated since 1960. The GDP grows 4.6%.

1968
Coderch designs the Las Cocheras Apartment Building Complex, Barcelona

Miró donates many of his works to Barcelona, thus creating the basis for the Miró Foundation. The Basque terrorist organisation, ETA starts its terrorism campaign

1969
Fullaondo finishes building the High School in Txurdinaga, Bilbao

Franco establishes a new government and appoints Prince Juan Carlos, future King of Spain, his successor

The last CIAM congress is in Otterlo. C. Testa designs the Banco de Londres y Sudamérica, Buenos Aires. R. Banham publishes *Theory and Design in the First Machine Age;* K. Lynch, *The Image of the City* (the city as a cultural problem)

Gio Ponti and P.L. Nervi build the Pirelli Building, Milan; Lasdun, the Royal College of Physicians, London. L. Mumford publishes *The City in History*

Mies van der Rohe designs the New National Gallery, Berlin; Eero Saarinen, the Gateway Arch, Saint Louis, MI. R. Venturi builds the Vanna Venturi House, Philadelphia, PA

H. Scharoun builds the Philharmonic Concert Hall, Berlin; J. Stirling and J. Gowan, the Engineering Department, Leicester University. P. Ramírez Vázquez designs the National Museum of Anthropology, Mexico

J. L. Sert builds the F.G. Peabody Terrace residence hall for married students, Harvard University; A. and P. Smithson, the *Economist* Building, London. L.I. Kahn designs the Salk Institute, La Jolla, CA

Le Corbusier dies. P. Collins publishes *Changing Ideals in Modern Architecture*

J. Stirling builds the History Department, Cambridge University; Breuer and Smith, the Whitney Museum, New York

Fuller's Geodesic cupola is built for the Montreal Universal Exhibition

L. Barragán and A. Casillas build the Egerstrom House and San Cristóbal Stables, Los Clubes, Mexico City; D. Lasdun, the University of East Anglia, Norwich; R. Legorreta, the Camino Real Hotel, Mexico City

A. Rossi designs the Gallaterese Apartment Building, Milan; L. I. Kahn, the Kimbell Museum of Art, Fort Worth, TX. Roche and Dinkeloo build the College Life Insurance Building, Indianapolis, IN

1960

John F. Kennedy becomes president of the US. Congo and Nigeria gain their independence. The laser is developed. The pill is put on the market. The US *Triton* does the first underwater circumnavigation of the world

1961

The Berlin Wall is erected. Soviet cosmonaut, Yuri Gagarin becomes the first person in space. R. Wise directs *West Side Story*

1962

De Gaulle resigns. Algeria gains its independence. The US *Telstar* telecommunications satellite is launched. Amnesty International is founded. Marilyn Monroe and W. Faulkner die

1963

President Kennedy is assassinated. M. Luther King Jr. leads a major civil rights march in Washington. J. Cortázar publishes *Rayuela;* H. Böll, *The Clown.* The Kodak Instamatic camara is designed. Pope John XXIII dies

1964

Kruschev falls. M. Luther King receives the Nobel Prize for Peace. Nelson Mandela is imprisoned for life. J.P. Sartre rejects the Nobel Prize for Literature. U.S. Pop Art success at the Venice Biennial: Rauschenberg receives the Grand Prix. The Beatles become famous. Nehru is murdered

1965

The Vatican's Index of Banned Books is abolished. A. Leonov is the first person to move in space

1966

Philips develops the cassette. Mao Zedong initiates the Cultural Revolution. Minimal Art is exhibited for the first time in museums. Giacometti dies

1967

The Six Day War takes place. García Márquez publishes *One Hundred Years of Solitude.* Barnard does the first heart transplant

1968

There are student movements in Paris and demonstrations against the Vietnam War in the US. Martin Luther King is assassinated. Soviet tanks crush the reform movement of the Czech leader, Dubček. Kubrick directs *2001: A Space Odyssey.* M. Duchamp dies

1969

Neil Armstrong (*Apollo XI*) is the first man to walk on the moon. Y. Arafat becomes the leader of the PLO. Gaddafi rises to power in Lybia. The *Concorde* makes its first journey. 250,000 people demonstrate against the Vietnam War. Nabokov publishes *Ada.* Beckett receives the Nobel Prize for Literature

1970
ACTUR, the Urgent Urban Works Law-Decree, is passed

1971
Sáenz de Oíza designs the Banco de Bilbao, Madrid. Sota's Exact Sciences Department Building, University of Seville, receives the National Architecture Award

1972
The architectural journal *2C. Construcción de la ciudad* is first published

Population: 33.6 million. 26 million tourists visit Spain. 2.1% of all Spanish women take the pill (US 16%).

The Spanish authorities close the liberal newspaper, *Madrid*. The left-wing magazine, *Triunfo* suffers a temporary closure

The unemployment rate is 2.2%

1973
Moneo and Bescós design the Bankinter Building, Madrid

The new government's president, Carrero Blanco is assassinated by the ETA terrorist group. Buñuel directs *The Discreet Charm of the Bourgeoisie*

1974
Sert builds the Miró Foundation, Barcelona. Lack of planning leads to the contamination of the Greater Bilbao area

Franco's last government is established. Albert Ràfols Casamada paints *Fruit bowl*. The Dalí museum opens in Figueras. The PSOE socialist party is renovated at the Suresnes congress

1975
The architectural journal, *Nueva Forma*, ceases to be published

New car sales rise to 693,590. Franco dies. H.M. Juan Carlos becomes king

1976
García de Paredes designs the Granada Auditorium; Manterola and Fernández Troyano, the Sancho III el Mayor Bridge. Peña Ganchegui builds the Plaza del Ténis, San Sebastián

The first democratic municipal elections are held. H.M. the King designates Adolfo Suárez president of the new government. The Spanish fertility rate (2.8) is twice that of Germany

1977
The journal, *Arquitectura* publishes a special issue on a new generation of Sevillian architects

On 9 April the PCE communist party is legalised. On 15 June, the first democratic general elections are held, in which the UCD centre party wins

1978
The journal, *Arquitectura bis* publishes a monograph on 28 Madrilenian architects

On 6 December the new liberal and democratic Spanish Constitution that decentralises the state into regional autonomies, with their own parliament and government, is approved through a popular referendum

1979
Martínez Lapeña and Torres Tur build the Boenders House, Ibiza. Construction work starts on Yamasaki's Torre Picasso in Madrid, at 165 m the highest building in Spain

The UCD centre party obtains a relative majority in the general elections. The Statutes of Autonomy for Catalonia and the Basque Country are approved through referenda. At the municipal elections, the left-wing parties win (PSOE and PCE); their involvement at town hall-level opens up a key period for architecture and town planning.

SOM builds the John Hancock Center (designed by B. Graham), Chicago; TVA engineers, the Paradise Power Station, KT

H. Lefèbvre publishes *La révolution urbaine*. The Regional Plan for South-East England is drawn up

J. Utzon builds the National Assembly Building, Kuwait. The Moscow Plan is drawn up. H. Lefèbvre publishes *Marxist Thought and the City*

I.M. Pei & Partners build the Hancock Tower (designed by Henry N. Cobb), Boston, MA. Ch. Jencks publishes *Modern Movements in Architecture*

A. Isozaki builds the Prefectural Museum of Modern Art, Takasaki City

L.I. Kahn builds the National Assembly Building, Dacca

D. Lasdun builds the National Theatre, London; G. De Carlo, the Free University of Urbino

A. Siza designs the Quinta da Malagueira Housing, Evora. R. Rogers and R. Piano build the Georges Pompidou Centre, Paris

I.M. Pei & Partners build the National Gallery of Art East Wing, Washington, D.C. P. Johnson and J. Burgee design the AT&T Building, New York

Gehry builds the Spiller House, Venice, CA. R. Rogers designs the Lloyd's Building, London. M. Tafuri and F. Dal Co publish *Architettura contemporanea*. Philip Johnson receives the Pritzker Prize

1970
S. Allende is elected president of Chile. Greenpeace is born. In US, 50% of the female population works outside the home. Jimi Hendrix dies
1971
IRA terrorism increases in Northern Ireland. Communist China is admitted in the UN. Luchino Visconti directs *Death in Venice*. Bacon is the painter of the year. Louis Armstrong dies
1972
Kassel's *Documenta* brings Hyper-Realism to the fore. The Watergate scandal is exposed. H. Böll receives the Nobel Prize for Literature. Ireland, UK and Denmark join the EEC. Ezra Pound dies
1973
A military coup overthrows S. Allende in Chile. US launches its first spatial laboratory: *Skylab*. OPEC's oil embargo causes worldwide energy crisis. Pablo Picasso and John Ford die
1974
President Nixon resigns as a result of the Watergate scandal. A coup in Portugal ends president Caetano's repressive right-wing dictatorship, the oldest in Europe
1975
The Vietnam War ends. Philips and Sony develop the videocassette. Bic designs the disposable safety razor. M. Thatcher leads UK Conservatives
1976
Vietnam is reunited as a Socialist Republic. Jimmy Carter becomes president of the US. Jasper Johns's works are exhibited at the Whitney Museum, New York. Mao Zedong dies
1977
The US *Space Shuttle* does its first flight. The *Apple II* personal computer is developed. Lucas releases *Star Wars*. Steven Biko is murdered
1978
Louise Brown, the first test tube baby, is born. Karol Wojtyla becomes Pope John Paul II. Egypt and Israel normalise relations after meeting at Camp David. Woody Allen directs *Annie Hall*. Aldo Moro is assassinated by the Red Brigade
1979
Margaret Thatcher becomes the first female prime minister of Great Britain. Muslim fundamentalists overthrow the shah of Iran and establish an Islamic theocracy under Ayatollah Khomeini. Egypt and Israel sign a peacy treaty backed by president Carter. The Sandinistas overthrow the Somoza dictatorship in Nicaragua. Vietnam invades Cambodia and deposes Pol Pot. Soviet troops enter Afghanistan. Sony develops the Walkman cassette. H. Marcuse dies

1980
Moneo designs the National Museum of Roman Art, Mérida; Cruz and Ortiz, the House with Patio on Doña María Coronel street, Seville

Total population: 37.5 million. The Statute of Autonomy for Galicia is approved in a referendum (74% abstention rate)

1981
Viaplana, Piñón and Miralles design the Plaza de los Países Catalanes, Barcelona. Félix Candela and J.L. Sert receive the CSCAE Gold Medals

On 23 February, the 23-F coup takes place. The New York MoMA returns Picasso's *Guernica* to Spain. The writer, Josep Pla dies

1982
Martínez Lapeña and Torres Tur design the Hospital in Mora de Ebro. The architectural journal, *El Croquis* publishes its first issue

Unemployment rate: 17.1%. The PSOE socialist party wins the elections with an absolute majority. Felipe González becomes president of the government

1983
Bonell and Rius design the Horta Cycle Track, Barcelona. The architectural journal, *Arquitectura bis*, established in 1971 by Bohigas and Correa, ceases publication

Unemployment rate: 17.3% (Germany, 7.1%; Italy, 9.6%; The Netherlands, 12.9%; US, 10.1%). The painter, Joan Miró dies

1984
Vázquez Consuegra designs the Social Housing Block on Ramón y Cajal street, Seville

The first test tube baby girl is born in Spain

1985
Navarro Baldeweg designs the Salamanca Convention Centre and Exhibition Hall

J.M. Sicilia's paintings are exhibited at the Paris Biennial. Cristina Hoyos and Antonio Gades star in *Carmen*

1986
H.M. King Juan Carlos I proclaims Seville the venue for the Universal Exposition of 1992

On 1 January, Spain joins the EEC. Spain's permanence in NATO is approved by referendum. For the second time, the PSOE socialist party gets an absolute majority in the general elections

1987
Bonell and Gil design the Municipal Sports Pavilion of Badalona (Barcelona). The Seville General Plan gives rise to the construction of a whole gamut of works throughout the city

The PSOE wins the municipal elections with a simple majority. Barcelona is chosen as the venue for the 1992 Olympic games

1988
Alejandro de la Sota and Alvaro Siza receive the CSCAE Gold Medals

Chillida sculpts *Gure Aitaren Etxea*, Guernica. Almodóvar directs *Women on the Verge of a Nervous Breakdown*

1989
The MONARK group designs the Finnish pavilion for Expo'92, Seville. F.J. Sáenz de Oíza receives the CSCAE Gold Medal

For the third time, the PSOE tops the general election polls with an absolute majority. Camilo J. Cela receives the Nobel Prize for Literature. Salvador Dalí dies

M. Yamasaki builds the World Trade Center, New York; Johnson and Burgee, the Crystal Cathedral, Garden Grove, CA. K. Frampton publishes *Modern Architecture, a Critical History*

T. Ando builds the Koshino House, Tokyo; M. Botta, the Rotonda House, Stabio, Switzerland. R. Meier designs the Arts and Crafts Museum, Frankfurt. J. Stirling receives the Pritzker Prize

Stirling and Wilford design the extension for the Tate Gallery, London. C. Correa builds the Bharat Bhavan, Bhopal. Kevin Roche receives the Pritzker Prize

R. Bofill builds the Palais d'Abraxas Housing, Marne-la-Vallée; M. Graves, the Portland Building, Portland, OR; A. Galfetti, the Tennis Club, Bellinzona, Switzerland. I.M. Pei receives the Pritzker Prize

J. Stirling and M. Wilford build the Neue Staatsgalerie, Stuttgart. N. Foster designs the Library and Gallery of Art, Nîmes

N. Foster builds the Hong Kong and Shanghai Bank, Hong Kong. Work starts on the construction of La Défense, Paris (1985-88)

F. Venezia builds the Small Open Air Theatre, Salemi, Sicily; R. Piano, the Menil Collection, Houston, TX; A. Isozaki, the Contemporary Art Museum, Los Angeles, CA

R. Salmona designs the Casa de Huéspedes, Cartagena, Colombia. J. Nouvel builds the Institut du Monde Arabe, Paris; Herzog & de Meuron, the Ricola Storage Building, Laufen, Switzerland

T. Ando builds the Church-on-the-Water, Tomamu. Oscar Niemeyer receives the Pritzker Prize

P. Eisenman builds the Wexner Center for the Visual Arts, University of Ohio, Columbus; Makovecz, the Paks Catholic Church, Hungary; I.M. Pei, the Bank of China, Hong Kong (369 m high). Frank Gehry receives the Pritzker Prize

1980
Reagan becomes president of the US. The Polish labour union, Solidarity is led by L. Walesa. Border disputes lead to war between Iran and Iraq. John Lennon is murdered in New York

1981
Mitterrand becomes president of France. The US *Columbia* space shuttle initiates a new era of space exploration. The AIDS virus is detected in New York. Anwar Sadat is assassinated

1982
Argentina invades Britain's Falkland Islands. Israel invades Lebanon. US marines invade Grenada. D. Hockney paints *My mother*. G. García Márquez receives the Nobel Prize for Literature

1983
President Reagan escalates the arms race ("Star Wars"). For the second time, M. Thatcher wins the elections. Democracy is reinstated in Argentina, with R. Alfonsín as president. The CD is developed. L. Buñuel and J. Miró die

1984
Indian prime minister, Indira Gandhi is assassinated. The AIDS virus is pinned down. M. Duras publishes *The Lover*. Truman Capote dies

1985
Gorbachev, the new Soviet leader, initiates a series of reforms to increase personal freedom and liberalize the economy. Orson Welles dies

1986
Chernobyl has a nuclear accident. The Iran-Contra scandal shakes the Reagan administration. Swedish prime minister, Olof Palme is murdered. L. Borges, Henry Moore and J. Beuys die

1987
Margaret Thatcher is re-elected for the third time running. Reagan and Gorbachev agree on major arms reductions. Andy Warhol and Rita Hayworth die

1988
A ceasefire is reached between Iran and Iraq. Moscow begins to withdraw its troops from Afghanistan

1989
Communist control begins to collapse in Eastern Europe. The Berlin Wall is torn down. Hungary declares itself a democratic republic. Ceausescu is deposed in Romania. Soviet republics demand independence. Havel is elected president in Czechoslovakia. Chinese students occupy Tiananmen square. Khomeini condemns Rushdie for blasphemy. The *Voyager II* reaches Neptune

1990
Moneo designs the Kursaal in San Sebastián. O. Bohigas and F. de A. Cabrero receive the CSCAE Gold Medals

Juan Navarro Baldeweg receives the National Plastic Arts Award. Chillida sculpts the *Elogio del horizonte*, Gijón. The Madrid-Barajas airport caters to 15 million travellers

1991
Cruz and Ortiz build the Santa Justa Train Station, Seville. Seville is completely transformed: new avenues and ringroads, railway lines and parks are laid out as old buildings are refurbished. J. Cano Lasso receives the CSCAE Gold Medal

Spain occupies the eighth place in the GDP world ranking. Total population: 39.4 million. Total number of foreigners visiting Spain annually: 50 million

1992
Vázquez Consuegra builds the Navigation Pavilion, Seville. J.A. Corrales and R. Vázquez Molezún receive the CSCAE Gold Medals. Investments in Barcelona for the Olympics reach 926,438 million pesetas

The AVE high-speed train between Madrid and Seville (540 Km) is inaugurated. Seville's 1992 Universal Exposition, Expo'92, receives over 41 million visitors in 6 months. The Olympic games are held in Barcelona

1993
Siza builds the Galician Centre of Contemporary Art, Santiago de Compostela. Sáenz de Oíza receives the Príncipe de Asturias Prize for the Arts

For the fourth time running, the PSOE wins the general elections, this time with simple majority. Felipe González forms a new government

1994
Miguel Fisac receives the CSCAE Gold Medal

Only 8% of the population lives of agriculture. The PP right-wing party wins the elections for the European Parliament

1995
Gallego builds the Museum of Fine Arts, A Coruña. The 3rd Biennial of Spanish Architecture is held: Moneo and Solà-Morales' Illa Diagonal Building receives the Biennial Award

According to the UN, Spain occupies the 9th place in the life standard world ranking. It has the lowest (1.2) birth rate in the world. The old city quarters are abandoned: Toledo loses 55% of its inhabitants since 1950, and Barcelona 135,000 dwellers in 5 years

1996
Foster & Partners build the Bilbao Underground. The Museo del Prado competition is unawarded. J. Vaquero Palacios receives the CSCAE Gold Medal. Alejandro de la Sota dies

The PP right-wing party wins the general elections. José M. Aznar becomes the new president of the government with the backing of the CiU and PNV parties. The painter, Gerardo Rueda dies

1997
Gehry builds the Guggenheim Museum, Bilbao. A new "Ley del Suelo" land law is approved. The 4th Biennial of Spanish Architecture takes place

Digital TV is broadcasted by satellite. The NATO Summit held in Madrid gives a green light to the incorporation of formerly Communist Eastern European countries into the organisation

1998
The Ist Biennial of Ibero-American Architecture and Engineering is held. The architectural journal, *Arquitectura*, celebrates its 80th anniversary

The centenary of the *Generation of '98* and of the loss of Cuba, the last Spanish colony in America (that marked the end of a historic era) is celebrated

Gehry builds the Schnabel House, Brentwood, CA; Murphy and Jahn, the Fair Tower, Frankfurt; Murcutt, the Maguey House, Kempsey, Australia. Aldo Rossi receives the Pritzker Prize

East and West Germany reunite. US and USSR agree to weapon reductions in Europe. Violeta Chamorro wins the elections in Nicaragua. War ends in Lebanon and El Salvador. Iraq invades Kuwait; the invasion is condemned by the UN

1991

Venturi, Scott Brown & Associates build the Seattle Arts Museum. Robert Venturi receives the Pritzker Prize

Iraq is defeated in the Gulf War. Apartheid laws are abolished in South Africa. Fighting breaks out between Serbs and Croats in Yugoslavia. A coup against Gorbachev ends under popular pressure led by the president, Boris Yeltsin. The environmental crisis increases worldwide

1992

A. Predock builds the American Heritage Center and University Art Museum, University of Wyoming. Alvaro Siza receives the Pritzker Prize

Yugoslavia disintegrates; the EC recognises Croatia and Slovenia's independence. Warfare increases in Bosnia. The US and USSR sign the STAR II treaty calling for the elimination of nuclear warheads by the year 2003

1993

Gehry builds the Frederick R. Weisman Art Museum, Minneapolis. J.M. Montaner publishes *Después del movimiento moderno: arquitectura de la segunda mitad del siglo XX*

Bill Clinton is inaugurated president of the US. Huntington predicts the clash of civilisations in lieu of state conflicts. Internet experiences an explosive growth

1994

T. Ando builds the Chikatsu-Asuka Historical Museum, Minami-Kowachi; M. Botta, the San Francisco Museum of Modern Art, CA

Deng, the father of China's economic aperture to the world, makes his last public appearance

1995

R. Koolhaas builds the Congress and Exhibition Hall, Lille; D. Perrault, the Grande Bibliothèque, Paris; F. Gehry, the Disney Concert Hall, Los Angeles, CA

In the US, 76% of all women work outside the home, and 43% of all executive positions are held by females. In Central Asia, the Aral Sea has lost 60% of its water since 1960

1996

W.J.R. Curtis publishes *Modern Architecture Since 1900*, third edition. R. Moneo receives the Pritzker Prize and the commission to build the Cathedral of Los Angeles, CA

Clinton is re-elected president of the US, the only superpower in the world. US space probes find traces of water on the Moon and of primitive life on Mars

1997

César Pelli's Petronas Towers (450 m), Kuala Lumpur, are the highest in the world. Norman Foster's Commerzbank (259 m), Frankfurt, is the highest building in Europe. Navarro Baldeweg builds the Music Center, Princeton, NJ; Peter Eisenman, the Aronoff Centre, Cincinnati, OH. Aldo Rossi dies

1 out of 5 Americans is connected to Internet. Muslim fundamentalists kill hundreds of citizens in Algeria. Digital Television via satellite makes its appearance in Great Britain. China recovers Hong Kong. The *Mars Pathfinder* arrives in Mars and transmits images direct via TV. Scotland's Dolly is the first cloned animal

1998

In Shanghai, work is scheduled to end on SOM's Jin Mao Tower (421 m) and to continue on Kohn, Pedersen and Fox's WFC Building which, at 460 m, will be the highest building in the world when construction work finishes in 2001

The 12 cm DVD (Digital Video Disk) appears on the market. The Expo 98 Exposition is held in Lisbon (Portuguese Pavilion designed by Alvaro Siza)

ANDALUSIA

Andalusia has the largest population and the second largest area of all Spanish regions. Its impressive size, diverse landscape (snowy mountains towering to heights of 3,300 m contrast with deserts and wetlands) and rich past (brimming with milestone events, assimilating a potpourri of cultures and spreading local values far and wide), all lie behind the region's highly complex and yet instantly recognisable personality. Andalusia is many regions in one: inland Andalusia, coastal Andalusia, Guadalquivir valley Andalusia, with an Atlantic vocation, and Mediterranean Andalusia. It is a region blending eastern base notes with European input and American trends. The landscape is essentially rural but articulated through well-structured cities and towns alongside the settlements built through past and present colonisation attempts. All of Andalusia's cities overflow with history, although the passing of time has marked them in different ways. The road stretches right back to 4,000-year old Cádiz, with the ancient town of Tartessus shrouded in the mists of mythical times, and *Baetica*, the area in the grip of the Romans and birthplace of emperors before the region took the path of Islam, which turned *Al-Andalus* into the southern hemisphere's destiny. Andalusian architecture picks up all these threads and knits them with the European soul of the Carolingian Renaissance, with the major link of American colonisation and the equally influential African connection. Reference has always been made to the lack of any bourgeois or industrial revolution in a region excessively bound by its agricultural backcloth and hedonistic soul. Hence the reason why the 20th c. has only been taken on board and integrated into the dynamic values of modern-day Spain at a very late stage. This oversimplification makes better sense in view of what Andalusia has to offer to those who seek to discover it through its architecture. Although no guide can cover all the varied facets of the forms it takes, mention must be made of the mining works scattered from Huelva to Almería, the incipient industrial manifestations in Málaga, the hydroelectric works and territorial alterations which intensified in the mid-20th c. to further the programme of rural settlement and which act as a counterpoint to the infinite wealth of Andalusian vernacular architecture that does not stop at the traditional country estates – the *haciendas* and *cortijos* – but is expressed in a thousand different ways. As to be expected, the face of present-day architecture is ambiguous: the Regionalist thrust best exemplified in the works designed for Seville's Ibero-American Exhibition and by Aníbal González in Seville and Rodríguez Acosta in Granada is tempered by innovative works: González Edo (Málaga), Sánchez Esteve (Cádiz), Lupiáñez (Seville) or Langle (Almería) can put together as good a panel of modern architects as any that Andalusia can offer for a greater understanding of the overall Spanish scene. Local Andalusian architects (Medina Benjumea, García de Paredes, La Hoz) together with architects from outside the region (Sota, Moneo) have made their own particular mark. On the threshold of the new millennium, it is impossible to evoke the architecture of the region without the names of such renowned exponents as Cruz and Ortiz or Vázquez Consuegra coming to mind, or the public sector architecture found in the towns and villages scattered over the length and breadth of Andalusia.

Geography: 87,268 km², very varied, with the Guadalquivir river valley acting as a backbone separating the mountain ranges to the N and the SE and with a coastline bathed by the waters of two different seas. **Climate:** equally varied, with long, hot summers and mild winters. **Population:** 7,040,627. **GDP:** 74% of nat. av.

ALMERIA. The golden age of Muslim *Al-Maryya* (mirror of the sea) lasted up to the Christian reconquest in 1484, as seen in the Arab citadel, the Alcazaba (8th c.), and its gardens. In the 20th c., Langle emerged as one of the most outstanding Andalusian Rationalist architects. After the arrival of new architectural blood from outside Almería in the seventies, the latter years of the century have taken on a more plural tinge, with local architects working alongside those who have settled in the province, such as Ramón de Torres, Lasaosa and Jaramillo (see AL 5), Martínez Durban (20 social housing units in La Chanca, 1979-80), Fernández y Pastor (Cervantes housing estate, Roquetas, Aguadulce, 1982-85), Pérez Rollano (40 houses in Fiñana, 1985-87) or Centellas (Vícar secondary school, 1986-89). Rainfall: approx. 200 mm and 50 days. Sunshine: 3,075 hrs. Temperatures: 31°-17° and 8°-23° C. Population: 159,687.

Garden City 1940-47   AL 1
Barriada Ciudad Jardín
Langle Rubio
The road layout of this neighbourhood was treated with special care. As a result, the roads establish a basic skeleton, articulated with varied morphological elements, that allow the free spaces and public buildings (the school complex deserves attention) to structure the core of the "city".

Bus Station 1952-53   AL 2
Pza. de Barcelona s/n
Langle Rubio
The design is an interesting mixture of an orthodox Rationalist language with the Late Modernism of the fifties, which places the finishing touches to the work. Two built-up volumes close off the corner of the station, linked by a convex central corpus, whose horizontality is systematically enhanced.

Technical College 1967-75   AL 3
Ctra. Almería-Níjar, km 7
Cano Lasso/Campo Baeza/Martín/Más-Guindal
On the outside, white volumes contrast with the naked earth. Inside, the architecture looks towards several inner courtyards, sheltered from the sun, wind and dust. A masterpiece of order and flexibility, it cleverly introduces a sense of high culture into the vernacular language of the old Mediterranean culture.

Music Conservatory 1985-88   AL 4
Av. Padre Méndez s/n
Ruiz-Larrea
Located between two new neighbourhoods whose buildings showed no particular order, the conservatory's linear floorplan is drawn together by two focal points and is encased in a shell of quality brickwork. Inside there is an interplay of spaces with controlled lighting along an ordered structural passage.

Refurbishment of the Church of AL 5
San Pedro el Viejo 1985-88
San Pedro c/v Guzmán
de Torres/Lasaosa/Jaramillo
This unobtrusive reform project tried to recover the spaces, materials and textures of the original building, incorporating new elements into the resulting container. It is exemplary of an architecture based on mutual contemplation and respect.

CADIZ. Few cities can rival Cádiz's ancestral character forged over four millennia. Its foundation dates back to mythological times – Hercules placed one of his columns here – before it was chosen in 1100 BC as a strategic enclave in the Atlantic by the Phoenicians, who named it *Gadir*. Later it would make its mark as a trading, sea-faring city whose destiny and sights were set on American shores. The historic city, which was truly consolidated in the 18th c. and at the forefront of Liberalism in the 19th c., stands on a rocky platform joined to the mainland by a narrow, sandy isthmus. Its layout is Neo-classical and its buildings white and fairly uniform, with no great palaces or monuments, but with Romantic gardens and good examples of buildings of the thirties by Sánchez Esteve. Outside the boundaries of the former walled city, on the other side of the Puerta de Tierra gateway, lies modern Cádiz. Built in the sixties, it has little town planning value but does hold some notable examples of modern-day

architecture. An industrial city and working port, the visual symbol of its progress are the Light Towers (see CA 2) in the Bay of Cádiz, a protected natural area of wetlands and salt marshes which, in the space of few kilometres, embraces San Fernando (78,845 inhabitants), Rota (25,291 inhabitants and a large naval base) and Puerto de Santa María (61,032 inhabitants, wineries, and a popular resident-ial and holiday area). Further inland, some 35 km N of Cádiz, lies Jerez de la Frontera (176,238 inhabit-ants), home of the world famous sherry wines and

wineries (see CA 14 and page 55). Turning SE, some 40 km down the coast is Conil (13,289 inhabitants) and its beaches; 45 km away is Sanlúcar de Barrameda (48,390 inhabitants), with attractive churches and wineries; 54 km away is Chipiona (12,398 inhabitants) and its beach; 99 km away is Tarifa (15,220 inhabitants), the southern tip of Europe, with its 10th c. Arab castle and the strong winds that provide the other technological face of Cádiz (see CA 21); 124 km away is Algeciras (86,042 inhabitants), the port with the greatest volume of traffic and gate-way to Africa; and 136 km away, on the Mediterranean edge of the province, is the residential estate of Sotogrande (Vázquez Molezún, 1978). All in all, Cádiz is an extremely varied province with excellent public sector architecture. Rainfall: approx. 450 mm and 75 days. Sunshine: 3,035 hrs. Temperatures: 28°-16° and 8°-22° C. Population: 157,355.

Transmediterránea Company CA 1
Building 1938-40
Av. Ramón de Carranza 26
Sánchez Esteve
The architect established a dynamic discourse of volumes with particular interpretations based on Rationalist orthodoxy in this new and radical proposal for an urban frontage that looked both back to the past and for-ward to the future: the commercial port.

Light Towers 1955

Puntales-Trocadero, Bahía de Cádiz

Toscano [eng.], ENI

Alongside the gantry cranes of Astilleros Españoles, especially the one in Puerto Real (1950s), these two twin electricity towers have become the point of reference for this ancient city, founded four millennia ago. Besides acting as a landmark, their verticality also emphasises the horizontality of the ineffable bay. Designed by the Italian engineer, Toscano, each tower consists of a mast (150 m high) crowned by a crosstree. Their elegant and functional metal structure was impeccably executed to support the overhead electricity distribution through 1,600 m-long cables over the estuary in the inner sac of the Cádiz Bay, from Trocadero to Puntales. The Spanish National Institute of Industry (INI) bought them from the Italian ENI, which manufactured them at the same time as some others that were placed in the Messina Straits (220 m tall). They immediately became the highest and second-highest electricity towers in the world. Their outer shape is the result of developing a circular form upwards, creating a cone-shaped upright with a slight curvature. The metal trunk has a diameter of 20.7 m at the base and tapers off to 6 m at its highest point, where the horizontal crosstree is placed, to hold the overhead cabling. Inside, a spiral staircase leads up to the top, running around the inside of the exterior metal-work walls. This creates a dynamic space, set off by this graceful formal solution that makes the spiral appear to continue on travelling forever upwards. The towers are lit up at night, which further contributes to display their nature; for apart from being a masterly display of industrial engineering at its best, they are also an aesthetically pleasing landmark.

Refurbishment and Extension to the Cádiz Museum 1980-90

Pza. de Mina s/n

Feduchi

The project refurbished a stark Neo-Classical building (1852), focussing on the creation of a space – a courtyard covered by glass, into which the parts of the museum flow – to articulate the museum visit. The stairway was treated as if it were a work of sculpture.

Adaptation of the Candelaria Bastion for a Maritime Museum 1986-89

Paseo de Carlos III

Cruz/Ortiz

The sea defences have long served as the bastions of this city. In an effort to endow them with new use, Cruz and Ortiz were commissioned to convert the 1673 bulwark built along the sea wall into a sea museum. Showing enormous discretion in their work, they created an institution that now forms an indispensable part of Cádiz's legacy. It is an exercise in juxtaposition and twinning, in which architecture uses unifying elements to link up porches, roofs and pre-existing volumes, each with its own individuality, to create a continuous route for museum visitors through the inner garden and out on to the seafront itself.

Other works. The Drago State School (1989-92) on Marianista Cubillo 15, by Campo Baeza, is an exercise in essentialist architecture, whose abstraction sits well against the sea. The Ciudad del Mar development and the new Dockland (1990-94) in Punta de San Felipe, by Carbajal and Otero, is another example of formal abstraction and subtle use of materials.

Social Housing 1986-91

Barbate 58-62, Barriada de La Paz

Vázquez Consuegra

The blocks, set in an area much spoilt by the uncontrolled spread outside the old city walls, were intended to break away from the autonomous nature of the rest of the buildings and make a cohesive urban statement. This was achieved by setting up two linear blocks to form a continuous façade along the main street, marking out a free space inside which linked the third block. The formal treatment of the blocks containing a double gallery housing programme provides unity along the continuous façades, using a single type of window opening, no terraces and a continuous brick plinth. The buildings curve at the corners, formalising the statement made on both streets and establishing a rich dialogue at their point of inflection. This is completed with a reference to the Cádiz lookout tower. This dialogue is tightened up and enriched with the creation of an interior street across which the blocks face each other. All in all, the housing complex shows a successful amalgamation of carefully thought-out techniques in both composition and expression.

Reform of the Gran Teatro Falla 1987-90

Pza. Manuel de Falla s/n CA 6

Carbajal/Otero

A brilliant Neo-Mudejar building from the end of the 19th c. and a cultural and urban symbol since, the theatre was reformed with great discretion and respect, maintaining the spatial layout of the original building whilst consolidating its structure and restoring its brick shell.

Telecommunications Tower and CA 7
Telefónica Building 1989-93

Av. Fernández Ladreda 4

Vázquez Consuegra

Along with the Light Towers (see CA 2), this tower has become an integral part of the urban skyline. Its robust white concrete upright is placed upon a discreet plinth that resolves the urban contact, and is set off by a platform of matching white concrete.

Social Housing 1992-96 CA 8

Concepción Arenal s/n, Campo del Sur

Siza/Otero

The 36 dwellings built under the Official Protection Plan face the ocean and the strong prevailing westerly winds of Cádiz, closing the perimeter of the old city centre. To cope with this placement, the design laid out the 3-storey building in the shape of a "U" with a continuous enclosure, opening up an open courtyard on its main façade. The composition of this continuous shell takes up the composition that informs the traditional middle-class Neo-Classical housing in Cádiz: a two-level local stone-clad plinth and a rigorous development of the upper floors in a neutral, stark surface of white mortar, interrupted only by the impeccably cut window openings set within carefully constructed frames. [First stage constructed; second stage starting in 1997.]

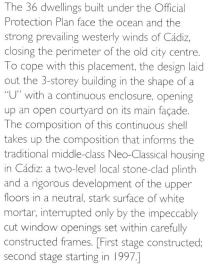

Wholesalers Market 1934-35 CA 9

Pza. de Ntra. Sra. de la Palma. **Algeciras**

Sánchez Arcas/Torroja Miret [eng.]

A thin concrete membrane with a skylight window reinterprets the centrality of the Roman Pantheon, covering a unique space where the stalls act as singular elements. This display of technical virtuosity is success-fully supported by a clear formal expression and an outstanding dominion of detail.

Port Facilities 1994-95   CA 10
Chipiona
Cruz/Ortiz
A set of buildings serving different purposes
– workshops, stores, shops and a control
post – was scattered around on the site,
without significance, until the architects
unified them with a Minimalist expression
based on serialisation and reiteration of
concrete latticework panels.

Sáenz House 1976-77   CA 11
La Fontanilla. **Conil de la Frontera**
Barrionuevo, A./Torres Martínez
In a continuous line of summer villas, this
house-studio is laid out in the vernacular
style. The inner courtyard, reached by an
alley onto the street, provides the central
focus to the design. From an inset plinth, it
opens upwards in search of sea views and is
topped by the studio with its terrace.

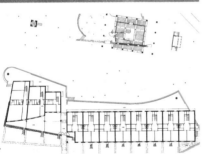

Row Housing and Villa 1982-85   CA 12
Urb. El Manantial. **El Puerto de Santa María**
González Cordón
This complex of 11 homes nestles amongst
dunes and pinetrees on a high point overlooking the Bay of Cádiz. They are distributed
into two main cores by aligning eight of
them in a row and grouping the remaining
three in an independent set. Laid out on a
common brickwork plinth, they are brought
together to create a single urban image
through the serialisation of S-facing open
terraces, with vaulted roofing that is extended
into the houses themselves, configuring the
particular shape of the sitting rooms. Access
is from a rear street, at intermediate level,
leading into a house layout that establishes
the upper floor as a living area and the
ground floor as a sleeping area. The N
façade overlooks this rear street, closed off
with wood slatwork.

Barriada de La Plata 1940-56   CA 13
Pizarro c/v Asta. **Jerez de la Frontera**
Cuadra e Irízar
This social housing complex on the outskirts
of Jerez dates back to the period following
the Civil War, when the 4-storey blocks were
built on a parallel layout. Between them lies
a large communal area, enhanced by the use
of spatial resources such as open alley ways
and lower-rise building volumes.

Tío Pepe Wineries 1960-63 CA 14
Manuel María González, 16. **Jerez de la Frontera**
Cuadra e Irízar/Torroja Cavanillas [eng.]
Torroja favoured new building techniques
and systems little known in the region, such
as vaulting with thin sheets of reinforced
concrete, which established spaces that
differ from the traditional cellar architecture
of the Sherry area and whose originality was
emphasised by their horizontal plinth.

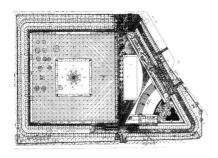

Trade Fair and Exhibition Hall 1985-92 CA 15
Parque González Hontoria. **Jerez de la Frontera**
Vellés/Casariego, M./Posada/Soto
The architect set this independent exhibition
hall in an urban park with views to creating
a pavilion that also provided a monumental
touch to its surroundings. It is compact,
enclosed in a decisive yet subtle treatment
of its geometric volume, exploiting all the
expressive qualities of red brick, which is so
intelligently laid as to emphasise the quality
of the building's formalisation. Thus, against
a continuous, vibrant background, the points
of conflict that sometimes cause problems
in this kind of building have been given an
exquisite treatment in the brickwork: lintels,
crests and corners. This carefully worked
shell contains a large, generous, versatile
space that can easily accommodate the
open-ended requirements of any trade fair
programme.

Social Housing Apartments 1984-88 CA 16
Av. de la Marina 75. **Rota**
González Cordón
The overlap of a diverse programme for
maisonette-style apartments, alternated on
the last three storeys, configures a large-scale
urban façade that links up the historical city
centre with the more anonymous spread of
buildings towards the suburbs, a connection
that is reinforced by the original curved roof.

Hermanos Laulhé Day-Care Centre 1954
Ctra. de la Carraca s/n. **San Fernando** CA 17
Cavestany
This successful, Modernist design in a site on
the periphery of the city is set in a double
L-shaped gallery joining two party walls and
achieving interesting interplays of volume. It
adopts the Cádiz-style façade composition,
both in terms of the materials used and the
hierarchy of the different floors.

Palace of the Dukes of Lerma 1945   CA 18
Finca La Viña. **San Roque**
Talavera
A singular interpretation in the Neo-Baroque style of the Andalusian country residence, it represents a rejection of Rationalist values and a return to more traditional language during the post-Civil-War period in Spain, bringing elements of urban Baroque into the typical vernacular architecture of rural Andalusia.

Sotogrande Hotel 1963-65   CA 19
Urb. Sotogrande. **San Roque**
Corrales
The topography of this site in the foothills was complicated, leading the architect to fragment the hotel complex into two wings of room modules that are set in staggered fashion around the common and service areas, with a sloping roof and private garden that softens the sometimes harsh sunlight.

Municipal Hall 1989-92   CA 20
Pza. de la Victoria s/n. **Sanlúcar de Barrameda**
García Márquez/Rubiño/Rubiño
The original complex had been put together piecemeal over the ages, but the architects managed to endow it with formal and spatial unity by a coherent use of materials, especially in the new roof and, although to a lesser extent, in the stairs and the skylight windows.

Wind-Energy Park 1992   CA 21
Dehesa de los Zorrillos, Sierra Enmedio. **Tarifa**
Sociedad Eólica de Andalucía/KWT/PEESA
An enormous park for generating electricity from high-tech windmills, it is located on the seaward side of a mountain. In this setting the design becomes almost sculptural, the technological artefacts creating a metaphor for the wind that brings to mind the landscaping exercises of American Minimalism.

Gaspar House 1990-92   CA 22
Pinar de San José. **Zahora**
Campo Baeza
In this hermetic square building, covered and open-air spaces are mixed in an atmosphere that is intimately welcoming. The sparseness of the vocabulary and the precision of the building techniques turn the containing wall, whiteness and water into the keys to an exercise in personal lyricism.

More on the Province of Cádiz. Amongst the works of relative value scattered throughout the province, take note of Anasagasti's Expressionist Vilamarta Theatre (1916) in Jerez de la Frontera, on Pza. Romero Martínez s/n, which has undergone recent restoration; and Fisac's Bodegas San Patricio cellars (1969), on Av. de Circunvalación, which show the brilliant application of structural prefabs to a traditional winery building.

CORDOBA. Once the Roman capital of *Hispania Ulterior* in the 2nd c. BC, then the Moorish capital of the independent caliphate of *Al Andalus*, Córdoba has been Christian since the 13th c. Its Mosque (8th-10th c.) is a jewel of universal architecture and the Jewish quarter, with its narrow lanes and whitewashed houses and courtyards, a true benchmark for vernacular architecture. Its contemporary side can be discerned through the Modernist works of Castiñeyra. The Civil War ravaged the Pedroches area to the N of the province and required action to be taken by the Committee for Devastated Regions (see CO 6). Colonisation with the development of new settlements also affected the local countryside, an olive oil producing area, in places such as La Vereda (see page 63). The driving force in the fifties was provided by de la Hoz. One particular field in which he and other architects (Cuenca, Serrano, leading members of the Equipo 57 normative art initiative of the post-war avant-garde movement in Spain) worked was public sector housing, such as the Las Palmeras estate (1985) designed by Asensio et al. Rebollo Puig, Benítez and Asensio laid out the new train station (1991-94) designed for the high-speed AVE train. Altitude: 124 m. Rainfall: approx. 500 mm and 80 days. Sunshine: 2,930 hrs. Temperatures: 39°-15° and 2°-20° C. Population: 310,468.

Chamber of Commerce 1951-52   CO 1
Pérez de Castro 1
García de Paredes/Hoz, R. de la
A series of concatenated scenarios generate a spectacular compositional discourse that begins at the reception desk, leads up the staircase to the upper floors and culminates in the conference hall. This understated, free formalism, however, finds no expression in the total symmetry of the façade.

Technical College 1952-56   CO 2
Ctra. N-IV, 2.5 km from Córdoba
Santos/Sánchez Puch/Robles/Cavestany
This complex housing the Universidad Laboral consists of a set of parts that are ordered along a central axis configured as a large, landscaped public space. This is bordered to the sides by two pergolas that link up the different student residence halls, located in buildings built on a cross plan, which in turn join up with the seminar and teaching rooms. At one end of the axis is the communal building, and at the other, a peculiar church with tower, which is the ideological and visual focal point of the complex. Pilasters, cornices and porticoes establish an intelligent architecture that uses abstract Classicism to deal with the demands for monumentality that the Franco regime always imposed on its most important commissions.

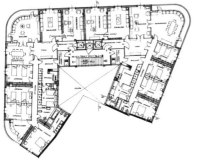

Apartment Building 1954-55   CO 3
Cruz Conde c/v Pastores c/v Eduardo Lucena
Hoz, R. de la
The design was carried out in two stages to fill in an entire block in the expansion plans for Córdoba. Rafael de la Hoz tried to apply his own Expressionism to round off the corners on the street of Cruz Conde and to emphasise the ground floor and the cornice, resolving it with a thin cantilevered slab of concrete. This desire to change the shape of the corner was not gratuitous, consolidating the opening up of a double gallery parallel to the façade by swivelling it out from the corners. The double gallery contains the apartments. In the corpus of the building, a clearly vertical layout of spaces exploits the relationship with the slabs in the building frame and the use of hard materials like stone and gressite. The second stage plays with alternating window openings.

Canals House 1956   CO 4
Ctra. de las Ermitas 22
Hoz, R. de la
A strict volumetric and functional intention breaks the house down into two clearly differentiated parts, set at an angle from each other: one for daytime areas and the other for bedrooms. The texture of the stone, the wood-slatted *brise-soleil* and the garden all help to underline the house's character.

Urban Block of Housing 1988-91   CO 5
Barriada Las Palmeras
Daroca/Díaz/Muñoz/Valverde
The U-shaped block with a large central plaza is defined by grouping the housing into two 4-storey volumes on a double gallery layout, linked up along the perimeter, with entrances set at their points of union. The unity of the design is reinforced by a continuous running portico that acts as plinth to the complex.

Town Hall, Main Square, Church 1941-46
Los Blázquez   CO 6
Rebollo Dicenta/Sánchez Puch et al.
This public space articulates a set of edifices with which the Committee for Devastated Regions endowed the village with a central focus. The layout of the main square and its representative buildings is regular, and the design has clearcut roots in traditional Andalusian architecture.

GRANADA. The city stands in an impressive setting, with the peaks of the Sierra Nevada mountains as a backdrop and the fertile plains of the River Genil spread out below it. Under Muslim rule for almost 800 years, it was capital of the Kingdom of Granada which did not fall until 1492, the same year Columbus set foot in America, witnessing its golden age under the Nasrid dynasty (12th-15th c.). Its great legacy bequeathed to Andalusia is the Alhambra, a true palatial city (12th-14th c.) and paradigm of universal architecture, and the Generalife gardens. Granada's claim to fame is also Renaissance – Charles V palace, cathedral and Royal chapel – and Baroque, with the 17th c. Carthusian monastery or Cartuja. Washington Irving spread its fame in the 19th c. By the 20th c. a host of works abounded in the sphere of the "red mount": the Rodríguez Acosta house (see GR 1); the open-air Generalife theatre (see GR 2), the best of the period; the Manuel de Falla Auditorium (see GR 3), García de Paredes's masterwork; the Alhambra accessways (see GR 4), the rehabilitation of the Charles V palace (see GR 5), seeking the true nature of the work under the Francoist make-up, and the new Rey Chico (1992-97), by Soler Márquez. Over all these works hangs the inevitable shadow of rejection for any intervention that strikes at the heart of Spain's cultural heritage. The very strength of the place has become an ongoing challenge in the 20th c., whose ins and outs give plenty of food for thought regarding contemporary architecture in Spain. The establishment of the Granada School of Architecture (1994) raises hopes that it will provide a much needed boost to young architecture in the eastern part of Andalusia. Altitude: 682 m. Rainfall: approx. 360 mm and 85 days. Sunshine: 2,980 hrs. Temperatures: 36°-14° and 2°-17° C. Population: 287,864.

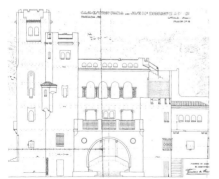

José María Rodríguez-Acosta GR 1
Garden House 1914-28
[now the **Rodríguez-Acosta Foundation**]
Callejón del Niño del Rollo, La Alhambra
**Rodríguez-Acosta/Santa Cruz/Cendoya/
Anasagasti/Jiménez Lacal**
Under the technical guidance of all these architects, especially Anasagasti, the painter Rodríguez-Acosta articulated a set of prismatic volumes in the upper part of a lush terraced garden, exploiting the traditional concept of the Grenadine *carmen* (house with garden). The architecture is an exercise in avant-garde Formalism using more classical compositional mechanisms to resolve the issue of historical references, which were inevitable in this time, and to adapt to the open-plan programme the painter needed for his studio. This has a clever concatenation of spaces, in which the exhibition room, the sitting room-library and the studio are set at different levels. The landscaping and architecture are complementary in creating a unitary interpretation of the whole, so that there is a continuum between the inner rooms and the outer gardens, by virtue of a precise spatial articulation of open space, based again on historical references to the Nasrids. The composition of the white, stylised prisms on the slopes is reinforced by the lines of cypress trees that act as a discontinuous plinth for the architecture.

Open-Air Theatre and Gardens 1954 GR 2
Generalife
Prieto-Moreno
Chief architect of the Alhambra for forty years, Prieto-Moreno's sure hand made a clean, clearcut design, which prolongs the exceptional Generalife gardens with geometrical terracing, following a spatial succession reminiscent of Islam, that leads up to the open-air theatre.

Manuel de Falla Auditorium 1975-78 GR 3
Paseo de los Mártires s/n
García de Paredes
The Auditorium tries to project a neutral image, discreetly articulated in the out-standing landscape along the Paseo de los Martires. García de Paredes's design is based on a philosophy of integration and responsibility, albeit within the context of the way that this was understood in the seventies, so that it responds to all the possible conditioning factors on different scales: it must fit into the delicate surroundings of the Alhambra and reflect the urban nature of the city of Granada, as well as fulfil the meticulous requirements for high-quality acoustics that any music auditorium must satisfy. Thus, with functionality as its guiding principle, the Auditorium has been made as a compact building, whose grandeur is on a human scale, with pure volumes based on the use of materials in keeping with Brutalist tenets: bricks and concrete. The octagonal shape is cleverly integrated into a single space, stretched lengthways. Using imaginative mobile furnishings and fittings, the architect has made an interior that is flexible to the possibilities of changing programme requirements, so that it can fit into different combinations: the hall seating 1,311 spectators can be turned into three different halls with varying capacities.

New Accessways and Parking Area GR 4
for the Alhambra 1989-97
La Alhambra
Hubman/Vass
The new car parks and accessways to the palatial ensemble were the winning designs in an international competition. The Viennese architects recovered the natural surroundings through a terraced system with exposed concrete water drains.

Refurbishment of the Charles V Palace GR 5
for the La Alhambra Museum 1993-95
La Alhambra
Rodríguez Frade
The architect recovered a room in the Palace
for exhibitions. Originally designed by Pedro
Machuca in the 16th c., the introduction of
modern shapes and materials, stairs, mezzanine and entrance all articulate a new compositional discourse around the central wall.

Bus Station 1994-95 GR 6
Ctra. de Jaén s/n
Torres Martínez
A large wall divides the building into two
functional areas located at different levels:
the bus stop platforms on one level and the
shopping and passenger area on another.
Outside, there is a markedly horizontal feel
created by the skylights, laid out like folds
over the plane of the roof.

Sierra Nevada High Performance GR 7
Sports Centre 1990-95
Monachil
Junquera/Pérez Pita
Ski slopes and indoor training areas were
laid out as high performance sports facilities
for top class sportsmen and sportswomen.
The work slots neatly into the natural park
surroundings through the emphatic interplay
of staggered volumes.

Social Housing 1991-93 GR 8
Barriada de las Angustias. **Motril**
Martín/Martín/Ruiz
This project was built on three different
sites. The typological solutions vary from the
block patio (block A) to the linear block
giving directly onto the street, sealed by a
long party wall (block B). The expressive
force of the buildings is mainly focussed on
the roofs and corners.

More on Granada. In chronological order, the works of interest in the capital and the province
of Granada are: the Belén district garden houses (1932-36), by Castillo Moreno and the
painter, Lanz, in Granada, two family houses with Rationalist gardens that stand out in the
Historicist milieu; the University Hostel in Sierra Nevada (1933), by Prieto-Moreno and
Robles, a pioneer mountaineering resort in Spain which later became world-famous as a ski
resort, in Monachil, 8 km from Granada; the 158 dwellings in the social housing project
(1985-90), by Soler, Mateos and Herrera, in the Polígono Almanjayar industrial estate, in
Granada; the Palacio de Deportes sports centre (1988-92), by Clotet and Paricio, on Ctra.
de la Zubia s/n, Granada; and the 15 dwellings in Domingo Santos and Jiménez Torrecillas's
social housing project (1992-94), in Cijuela, 20 km from Granada.

HUELVA. Phoenician *Onuba* and Arab *Ghelbah*, Huelva blends sea coast with countryside and is home to the most emblematic of Spain's National Parks: Doñana. Mining has been carried out in Huelva since ancient times: the Río Tinto mineworks date back over 2,000 years. In the 19th c., when the mines were run by an English company, colonial-style houses were built on the nearby beaches and grew into Punta Umbría (8,490 inhabitants, a popular resort). Its architectural highlight is Villa Pepita (1938), on Cerrito s/n, by Pérez Carasa. In the capital, Huelva, the service station (1955) on Av. Federico Molina, by Herrero, and the social housing, such as the 50 units built in Tharsis (1988-92), by Cruz and Ortiz, and the 49 units in Huelva (1990-93), by Pozo Soro and Torres Galán, are interesting. Rainfall: approx. 520 mm and 75 days. Sunshine: 3,020 hrs. Temperatures: 36°-17° and 4°-19° C. Population: 144,579.

Bus Station 1990-94   HU I
Doctor Rubio s/n
Cruz/Ortiz
The architects solved the difficult conditions imposed by the triangular site and the peculiar manoeuvring space needed by buses to turn around full circle with a single flourish. One flat roof covers the station concourse and the bus stop bays, thus avoiding dispersion and generating a landscaped area inside.

Federico Mayo Group   HU 2
of 50 Fisherman Houses 1950-55
In front of Severo Ochoa. **Ayamonte**
Herrero Ayllón
Based on the typical vernacular architecture of fishing villages, the houses are marked by the simple, highly economic use of building materials, techniques and language, and are laid out in serial order along the perimeters of the site to create a pleasant interior space.

López Bueno House 1993-95   HU 3
Finca La Estacada Nueva. **Hinojos**
González Cordón
Located in a generous natural environment, the house is set in its own small territory, marked by its own walls and volumes. The work and service areas give onto the access patio, whilst the leisure and living areas are concentrated in a prism that stands above the rest.

JAEN. After its Carthaginian, Roman and Muslim past and the splendour of its Renaissance age – take Ubeda, Baeza and the cathedral in Jaén as living proof – the province now slumbers in the midst of a sweeping landscape dominated by olive groves, source of the locally-produced olive oil. The River Guadalquivir rises in this province and has prompted some of the most outstanding examples of Spanish hydroelectric works, such as the Salto del Jándula dam (see J 2). The efforts channelled into housing developments at two particularly active moments in time are well known: during Franco's dictatorship, with the active involvement of the Committee for Devastated Regions, and over the last two decades of the 20th c., under the auspices of the Regional Government of Andalusia. Altitude: 574 m. Rainfall: approx. 370 mm and 75 days. Temperatures: 35°-13° and 5°-22° C. Population: 107,413.

Banco de España 1982-88   J 1
Paseo de la Estación 57
Moneo
The requirements in terms of expression and scale in this kind of public building – textures, portico, graphics – are met by a series of geometric exercises that regulate how the different elements of the building are positioned in plan and elevation. It is a minor masterpiece by Moneo.

Salto del Jándula Dam 1924-32   J 2
La Lancha. **Andújar**
Aguila [eng.]/Fernández-Shaw
The architect collaborated with engineers on several dams. Open to the progressivist ideas coming from Europe at the beginning of the century, Fernández-Shaw built this gravity dam, 90 m high and 240 m long around its crown, as a symbiosis between Expressionism and Rationalism, already tried out in his Madrid petrol station (see M 13).

The expressive side of the work is dominant here, defined by powerful use of massive material that begs for a direct, dramatic reading of the function of this dam, due to its monumentality and the connotations of Man's dominion of Nature. This forcefulness is slightly attenuated with the wave-shaped forms that break its plinth, which are clearly an eloquent simile of the thrust of the waters contained inside to regain their freedom.

MALAGA. No other Andalusian city has kept up with modern times in the same way as Málaga. Since *Malaka* was founded by the Phoenicians 3,000 years ago, the city has made its way through the centuries as a port and trading centre, with a venture into the industrial age in the 19th and early 20th c., opening to tourism in the second half of the 20th c. The Rationalist city revolves around the architect González Edo, who designed Málaga's general plan in 1950 and the housing block (1935) on Paseo de Reding c/v Cervantes. The city's planning and architecture has been in the hands of the younger generation of local architects over recent decades, with the Trinidad-Perchel plan by Moreno Peralta and the bus station (1989) by Seguí. However, the milestone of Málaga's contemporary years has definitely been the transformation of its coastline into an extended urban tourist resort. Countless architects have played their part in this 50-year long process during which Málaga's tiny fishing villages have been built up into towns and cities, turning the coast into one continuous development. Some of the best works have been produced by Gutiérrez Soto in Marbella (67,882 inhabitants), 56 km from Málaga city, with his house in Guadalmina Baja (1950); by Higueras, with the Fierro house (1970) on the El Batatal estate and the 172 apartments (1980) constructed in Guadalmina Baja; and by Junquera and Pérez Pita, with the apartments (1982-85) built in Nerja, on Hernández Carabeo, 78.

Lange House 1959   MA
Monte Miramar 6, Urb. Santa Paula
Mosher/Relaño
The organic architecture of this house is very much in keeping with the criteria of Frank Lloyd Wright. The use of traditional materials, the incorporation of Nature into the house and the spatial articulation on the basis of crossed axes that mobilises the entire design all refer back to the master architect.

Church of Belén,   MA
Carmelitas Descalzos Convent 1961-64
Paseo de la Alameda c/v Tomás Heredia
García de Paredes
This vertical development of a programme for a convent uses a container box that superimposes the different functions on different planes. The church, which has a single nave where light is guided to fall on the austere shapes and materials with which it is built, is located on the ground floor and, over it, the office spaces. Further up, the box opens to house the cloister, designed as a continuity of the surrounding plant life in an internal space, which also serves as the plinth for the cells incorporated within the truss that covers the cube-shaped volume. Outside, the design draws one into the 19th c. Paseo de la Alameda, a tree-lined path, through the neutral use of materials and colours to fit the surroundings.

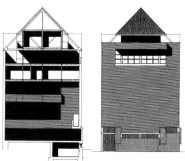

Torcal Cinema Theatre 1933-34   MA 3
Ramón y Cajal 4. **Antequera**
Sánchez Esteve/Rubio
The vitality of the cinema in the thirties made it possible to set this unconformist building amidst a neighbourhood of more historical architecture. After the reception area, which respects traditional urban values, the cinema presents a dynamic play of volumes with a careful *Art Déco* decor in horizontal bands.

Trade Union Holiday Resort 1956-63   MA 4
Ctra. N-340, km 197. **Marbella**
Aymerich/Cadarso
The organic variety of the urban planning of this holiday resort, where free spaces and public buildings form an attractive focal point, has provided enormous morphological and typological variety in the design and layout of the 199 houses, some of which are free standing, others back-to-back.

Settlements of
La Vereda 1963, **Peñaflor** (Córdoba)
Miraelrío 1964, **Vilches** (Jaén)
Cerralba 1964, **Pizarra** (Málaga)

Following illustrious precedents, such as the colonisation of the Sierra Morena in the 18th c. by Charles III, the 20th c. witnessed the unsuccessful settlement attempts of the Second Republic, followed by the reservoir and irrigation land settlement policy of the Franco years. In Andalusia, it encompassed both the Atlantic and Mediterranean parts of the province, with regional works affecting the Guadiana, Guadalquivir and the SE areas, with the construction of 54, 85 and 45 developments in each case. By the time Franco died, over 9,000 houses had been built under such programmes in Andalusia, accounting for 30% of the national total. The Land Settlement Institute was in overall

Although traditional techniques were used, more Rationalist forms were often sought. Important architects were involved in a few developments of this kind, but apart from the example in Esquivel (Sota, SE 55), the most outstanding work in Spain was carried out by José Luis Fernández del Amo. In Andalusia he designed the settlements of La Vereda[1] (Peñaflor, Córdoba) and Miraelrío[2]

charge, but each regional authority laid out different areas with settlements designed for between 20 and 200 housing units. These developments were interlinked through the road network and had a regular layout drawn up around the main square where the administrative services and church were sited, although in some cases architects did try out rather more innovative designs.

(Vilches, Jaén), together with Cerralba (Pizarra, Málaga), which was a joint project carried out with Antonio Fernández Alba. La Vereda was a small-scale design for 21 houses. Miraelrío was laid out for 68. The initial project for 100 units in Cerralba was cut to 88 houses, together with a church, social club, crafts centre, school, hospital, bakers shop and administrative building.

SEVILLE. Founded in the mists of time – "Hercules built me" are the words from the legend – Seville was home to the kingdom of Tartessus over 2,500 years ago. Later the Romans renamed it *Hispalis*, Julius Caesar surrounded it with walls and saw the rival city of *Italica*, cradle of future emperors (Hadrian, Trajan), spring up across the river. Remains of Seville's past can still be found in the city. Heading the list are those dating back to *Isbiliya*, when Andalusia was under Arab rule. The Giralda tower and the Alcázar palace (12th c.) from the Almohade period take pride of place alongside the fruits of the Gothic period – the cathedral (15th-16th c.), Santa Ana de Triana – and the syncretic Mudejar style – Peter the Cruel's Alcázar fortress (14th c.) and a host of churches. This mish-mash of architectural styles forged a culture which the impetus of a city that was the economic node between the Old and the New World (16th-17th c.) transformed into Renaissance, Mannerist and Baroque jewels

ranging from work in the cathedral, the city hall and the Lonja market, with outstanding architects such as Hernán Ruiz the Younger, up to the work of Figueroa (El Salvador and San Luis churches). The city walls were knocked down in the 19th c., but no urban expansion plan was developed to mirror those of Madrid and Barcelona. The early years of the 20th c. were marked by the impact of the 1929 Ibero-American Exhibition, which brought Regionalist architecture to the fore. A. González, J. Talavera and J. Espiau Muñoz were the leading exponents of this movement, which reached its peak just as Rationalism began to make its first gentle waves felt through the work of local architects such as Lupiáñez, Arévalo and Galanares or Sert's very first work, the Duclós House (see SE 9). The outbreak of the Civil War in Spain did not stand in the way of continued innovation in Seville (the bus station, the technical college complex) whose guiding hands, the Medina Benjumea brothers, set up the OTAISA group, whose guiding principles were those of the American professional corporations and fitted in with the moves towards industrialisation in Seville. Architecture in the fifties and sixties, with local designs by Abaurre and Recaséns interspersed with the work of professionals from outside Seville such as de la Sota (see SE 16 and SE 55), came to a head with the first generation of architects graduating in 1966 from the Seville School of Architecture, the third school to be founded (1960) after Madrid (1844) and Barcelona (1875). In the early seventies, young architects led the way in the debate on a new Spanish architecture which was then floundering in the crisis-ridden waters of the Modernist movement. Rossi and Venturi's influence was answered with analysis and proposals, while the Architects' Chamber flung itself into opposition to the dictatorship with studies on town planning published through its Studies and Services Centre (CEyS). The first works by Cruz and Ortiz, Vázquez Consuegra and Sierra proved to be a modest and yet significant indication of the sign of the times, as was the involvement of the younger generation (Trillo, Barrionuevo, Villanueva, Díaz Recaséns) in important studies incorporating this shift in direction. The new democracy, the 1979 municipal elections and the appearance of a regional government were to provide a fillip to public sector architecture. Seville, the political-administrative capital of Andalusia, was then a city bereft of any kind of structure and suffering from town planning ailments. When Expo'92 came around it was to be an expression of the city's cosmopolitan side, bringing together the best works from all around the world, and the perfect excuse to tackle the most far-reaching urban change in Seville's long history: namely, the advanced modernisation suiting its position as a Southern European metropolis. Today, this city, with a dominant services sector treads a delicate tightrope between tradition and modernity, between the attraction of the historic city which has left such a deep imprint on life and culture in Seville and the new city with its close-lying suburbs in a metropolitan area with no real formal shape whose architecture is badly in need of an overhaul and a new impetus to take it forward into the 21st century. Altitude: 12 m. Rainfall: approx. 450 mm and 75 days. Sunshine: 2,950 hours. Temperatures: 38°-17° and 5°-21° C. Population: 704,857 (city) and 1,638,218 (province).

Southern Expansion Plan and the 1929 Ibero-American Exhibition 1929
González, Aníbal et al.

Seville has always pulled southwards, down-river[2], as shown by the Paseo de las Delicias (1827-64), laid out on the orders of Arjona, the city's Mayor at the time, or the gardens of the San Telmo Palace (18th c.). In 1911, Forestier, keeper of the parks in Paris, was commissioned to turn the gardens granted as a gift to the people of Seville in 1893 by the Infanta María Luisa into a public park. This important work, with its ingenious layout pooling a basic French design with English picturesque and Spanish-Muslim elements, brought Seville to the forefront of the world landscape gardening scene. The María Luisa Park (1914) was to be the focal point around which the Ibero-American Exhibition (planned for 1910 and eventually opened in 1929) was laid out. The event was to be the crucial driving force behind the urban transformations of the time, together with the great hydraulic works that diverted the course of the River Guadalquivir and opened up the Alfonso XIII Canal (1910-26), by Moliní (eng.), and Bridge, by Delgado Brackenbury. Two huge ensembles eventually saw the light of day from Aníbal González's original plan: the Plaza de América (1911-1919) on the S edge of the park, whose Historicist-style (Mudejar, Gothic and Renaissance) pavilions[3] are the ultimate expression of the Regionalist vision of the time, and the Plaza de España (1914-28) on the E edge (see SE 2) of the park.

This same extensive area still holds buildings designed by other architects after 1925: the Lope de Vega Theatre and the Exhibition Casino (see SE 5), and many pavilions including that of Peru (by Piqueras, 1927-29), Chile (see SE 6), Cuba (see SE 8), Argentina (by Noel, 1925-29) and Mexico (by Amábilis, 1926-28). Their degree of conservation

is not always to the same standard and the prevailing style is Neo-Colonial. At the same time that the El Porvenir district[1] was being developed to the E, there was little worthy of note further south, on the W side of the long Paseo de la Palmera, laid out in the early years of the 20th c. and now a port area and university campus. There is not even anything but the site left of the stadium, now belonging to the Betis Football Club. The only reminder of the milestone year of 1929 left on this southern city boundary is the Heliópolis[2] district (1926-29) designed by Mondrilla.

Plaza de España 1914-28

González, Aníbal

The largest of the buildings (186 × 93 m) constructed for the 1929 Exhibition (see SE 1) slots into the tradition of great properties that Seville once built around its walls, such as the neighbouring San Telmo Palace and the old Tobacco Factory (18th c.). Aníbal González's first outlines for the Exhibition had a distinctive monumental slant that took on full-blown shape in this Plaza de España. If the 1893 Columbus Exposition in Chicago laid down a precedent for such monumental bias, this work actually came about in response to the hegemony of Spanish architectural nationalism. The first design was prepared in 1914 when the María Luisa Park, relandscaped by Forestier, was opened and the work on the Plaza de Armas was progressing, although the development of the project had reached a stage of frustrating delay. The plan originally revolved around the future headquarters of the Worker's College complex, which was to house the School of Crafts and Trades in its central section. That particular section, with other pairs in the middle and with 70 m high towers at either end, form a huge arc shape that is taken even further by arcades,

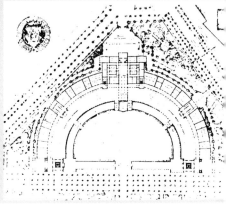

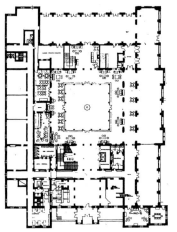

Alfonso XIII Hotel 1915-28

San Fernando 2

Espiau/Urcola

In 1916, the council held a competition for architects to design a luxury hotel. Amongst fierce competition from other professionals, all working in the Historicist style, the pure "Sevillian Style" of this project won through, a version of traditional high-class architecture, adorned with a profusion of glazed tiles and using laboriously crafted techniques in the bricklaying for the central volumes. This interpretation of the style prevailed over another that aimed to develop the rural language of whitewashed walls and pure volumes. Eaves with iron strut tenons, wooden lintels, delicately curved metalwork, and round arches are just a few of the many decorative elements that enhance the structure. The floor plan is square, set around a central courtyard, with two main façades looking outwards, whose composition is united by a turret reinforcing the corner between them.

platforms and a tidal inlet with its bridges (the fountain was added on to González's proposals). This left a central space to be used for sports events, processions and other mass gatherings such as the opening of the exhibition itself. The outright geometrical emphasis of the design continues a long tradition of this type of Classical matrix shape. In this case, the Eclectic style of Aníbal González, by then a mature architect, opened up the way for a powerful free hand to incorporate different Historicist references, particularly to the Spanish Baroque, at the same time as it backed the revival of traditional trades, the use of pressed brick and the application of ceramic tilework and ironwork in a whole host of different ways. This lively use of materials consistent with the principle that it should be "colour that enhances the construction's values" conceals the early structural use of reinforced concrete. Spaciousness, typological forcefulness and the vibrant use of figurative elements, together with its utility for festive purposes are all attributes of this singular example of Sevillian contemporary architecture.

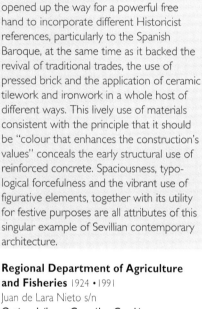

Regional Department of Agriculture and Fisheries 1924 • 1991

SE 4

Juan de Lara Nieto s/n
Ortiz e Iríbar • González Cordón
González Cordón fit a complex administrative programme into the old cotton mill, respecting the urban layout and the Neo-Mudejar façades of the old industrial complex. In another part of the site, he put up two singular buildings, far from the old manufacturing tradition, using contemporary urban materials and techniques.

Exhibition Casino and Lope de Vega Theatre 1925-28
SE 5

Av. de María Luisa s/n
Traver
This Classical-style composition resolves two independent programmes by articulating volumes formally clad in the Historicist language of the twenties. The unity of language and treatment given to the access-ways links the central space in the casino and the symmetry in the theatre layout.

Chile Pavilion at the Ibero-American Exhibition 1927-29 SE 6
Paseo de las Delicias s/n
Martínez Gutiérrez
An outstanding reconciliation between the traditional language of the Spanish colonies and the avant-garde lines of European Expressionism, the complex is articulated with volumes of monumental impact and enhanced by the tower that centres it.

Headquarters of the Real Maestranza de Caballería 1927-30 SE 7
Paseo de Colón s/n
González, Aníbal
The façade is designed in a Regionalist style that is highly fitting for the building joining up the Paseo de Colón on one side and the Real Maestranza Bull Ring (18th c.) on the other, housing the institution that owns the bull ring and gives it its name.

Cuba Pavilion at the Ibero-American Exhibition 1927 • 1983 SE 8
Av. de la Palmera s/n
Govantes/Cavarrocas • Torres
The Colonial Revivalist style articulates a Classical composition of volumes subject to an extension within a very specific context. The extension provides a formal, tectonic analogy in the new space built up and subtly linked to the existing Pavilion.

Duclós House 1929-30 SE 9
Ceán Bermúdez 5
Sert
José Luis Sert's first building is unashamedly guided by Corbusian principles. The Modernism of the design also stands out when it is considered that it was built at a time when the Ibero-American Exhibition was making Regionalist architecture all the rage throughout Seville and Southern Spain. The building programme established the need to design both a home and an office. These were housed in two wings, with Sert's out-and-out Modernism shining through in all of the building's details: the organisation of space, the open portico on the façade, the modular treatment and the surface work on its concrete structure, the texture and the whiteness unifying its volumes and the large open roof terrace wall that acts as a fifth façade.

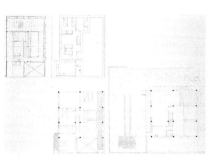

Anatomical Institute 1935

SE 10

Av. Sánchez Pizjuán s/n

Lupiáñez/Arévalo

The architects consider this work to be a "Rationalist design, but in terms of American Rationalism, from inside out, and not like European Rationalism, from outside in". The interplay of volumes is articulated by the unit system of strict modulation and highly expressive structural framework.

Bus Station and Housing 1938-40

SE 11

Prado de San Sebastián s/n

Medina Benjumea, R.

This twofold unit shows clear influence of the Viennese *Hof* model. A continuous brickwork plinth serves as base for the volumes closing the urban block, twinning two different uses and allowing access into the central space through very cleverly placed parabolic gaps.

HYATSA Factory, Stage 1 1938-41

SE 12

Héroes de Toledo 71

Talavera/Galnares

Strictly ordered along lines of economy and functionality, this building displays a stark architecture developed in pointed brick-work, which acts as the backdrop for the entire industrial estate. The overall unity of the complex allows for certain outbreaks of Expressionism in some of the key buildings.

Technical College 1942-53

SE 13

Ctra. Sevilla-Utrera, km 4

Medina Benjumea/Gómez Estern/Toro Buiza

The complex programme for an integrated, across-the-board training of students leads to a rich and varied architecture in the different container buildings. These are closely related to each other and to the natural surroundings in which they are located by a plan that recognises the routing and the hierarchies inherent to the university function. The definition of the architecture is based on the conscious use of Rationalist shapes as an alternative to the stereotypical image of Regionalist designs so common under Franco's regime. The volumetric layout of the teaching buildings and the ancillary buildings (church, theatre, sports facilities) is stark and practical, whilst the inherent plainness of the materials stands in contrast to the use of bright colours.

Los Diez Mandamientos Neighbourhood 1958-64
SE 14

Av. del General Merry c/v Malvaloca

Recaséns

An interesting application of the H-shaped block layout that is open to two readings: outside, it presents the stark image of a contention wall, reinforced by the use of brick and a standard distribution of the openings; inside, the space is welcoming.

Head Offices of the Sevillian Electricity Company 1969-71
SE 15

Av. de la Borbolla 5

Medina Benjumea, F. et al.

Glass and steel in a horizontal modulation constitute the image of a sculpture-building that, as such, generates its own space in its surroundings. The building programme is met with open-plan floors around a central core of services.

Department of Science 1971-73
SE 16

Av. Reina Mercedes s/n

Sota, A. de la

The layout of an independent building enclosed around a landscaped central courtyard – covered with awnings from spring to autumn – enabled the architect to shut out the surrounding wasteland before it was developed. The programme is symmetrical. The conference room and cafeteria, an isolated element in the general programme, are placed close to the block of seminar and lecture rooms. The lecture rooms that are most intensively used are located on the ground floor, while the rest are poled up in curious tower blocks at either end of the main corpus of the building. The seminar rooms, as far away as possible from the hustle and bustle created by the students flocking to the lecture rooms on the ground floor, are reached via lightweight galleries through the courtyard. The building is closed off from the outside with walls and blinds, but opens onto the garden inside with an expressive metal structure. Recipient of the National Architecture Award 1973.

Other works. The evolution of the incipient Sevillian Rationalism of the thirties can be seen in two other buildings: the office building between party walls on Rodríguez Jurado 6 (1935-36), by Galnares, and the independent building of apartments with shops on the ground floor known as "Cabo Persianas" (1938-40), on San Pablo 2, by Arévalo and Lupiáñez, both showing unequivocal support for the new Rationalist principles.

Courtyard House 1974-76 SE 17
Doña María Coronel 26
Cruz/Ortiz

A pioneer work of the style created by a
new generation of Andalusian architects
interested in overcoming some of the short-
comings of the Modernist movement that
were, in the seventies, the focus of much
international criticism, this building is an
exponent of the new sensitivity to the old
town centres that Aldo Rossi's writings
had awoken and which met with heartfelt
response in the hard-done-by city centres of
Andalusia. In its day, this work by Cruz and
Ortiz provided a magnificent example of
how to deal with the cultural, typological
and scaling requirements of historical town
centres, without abandoning the legacy of
the Modernist tradition in terms of sparsity
and economy of line. The formal innovation
of the kidney-shaped courtyard was fully
justified by the need to rationalise the
complex geometry of the site, guaranteeing
decent visual and light conditions to the
inward-facing apartments, without access
to the very short façade giving on to the
street. The contained expressivity and the
reconciliation of traditional codes with
contemporary materials and shapes has
made it possible for the building to blend
in with its urban landscape without being
self-effacing.

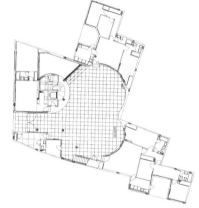

El Porvenir Housing Block 1976-81 SE 18
Juan Pablo c/v Valparaíso c/v Colombia c/v
Progreso
Barrionuevo, F.

The building stands in a district developed
during the 1929 Ibero-American Exhibition.
It is an area of low-density residential housing,
where detached and semi-detached houses
stand alongside low-rise apartment buildings.
Here, several sites were grouped together
to launch a single operation. Six terraced
apartment buildings form a city block, closed
around a large landscaped courtyard, whose
different levels make it possible for the
underground carpark to come partially out
to the surface, thus providing it with natural
ventilation and lighting. On the brick façade,
the large window openings are alternated
with slatted board surfaces and a series of
glass cylinders that articulate an urban
discourse charged with expressive force.

Architects' Chamber
of Western Andalusia 1977-83

Pza. de Cristo de Burgos 35
Ruiz Cabrero/Perea Caveda
Located in the historical centre, the building reconciles the different forces that have shaped the delicate urban environment around it. It acts as a hinge between the six storeys and colonnade over the noisy Imagen street, and the four storeys and gardens of the peaceful Pza. de Cristo de Burgos, a space that was well configured except to its N side, where the Architects' Chamber and the nearby church of San Pedro (14th c., Gothic-Mudejar) are located. Whilst the street façade establishes a clearcut urban alignment facing the traffic, the Cristo de Burgos façade successfully absorbs the scale of the urban square, which is reflected in its large window and door openings. The diagonal that the plan articulates from the vertex of the corner establishes the frontier between street and square and forms a courtyard opening onto the façade which, with its benches, fountains and tiles becomes a kind of extension of the square itself.

Social Housing 1978-84   SE 20
Antonio Maura 3
Trillo, M./Trillo, J.L./ Martínez, A.
The monolithic character of this linear block is emphasised by the use of brickwork panels growing up from the ground. To the N side, it presents a strict modulation of openings which is fragmented by cores of vertical communications; to the S, a series of balconies open up the façade.

Chamber of Commerce 1979-82   SE 21
Pza. de la Contratación 8
Cabrera/González Cordón/Lerdo de Tejada
This small palace from the beginning of the century was rehabilitated for administrative offices and official acts. Setting the leftovers of the past within a new spatial configuration, the design purposefully leaves the conflicts inherent in any intervention on an historic building unsolved and open to contemplation.

More on Seville. Luis Marín de Terán (see SE 24 and SE 31) was instrumental in training the young Sevillian architects of the seventies. He worked with Del Pozo and Haro on the housing block (1974-75) on Av. de Pío XII c/v Av. de Pino Montano. The Sierra brothers, apart from their large-scale designs (see SE 23 and SE 33), established their very own style in refurbishing old houses from the historic city centre, as in the Sierra Studio (1980-84) on Monsalves 13.

Kindergarten 1980-81 SE 22

Barriada de Pino Montano

Trillo, M./Trillo, J.L./Martínez, A.

Responding to the typological chaos reigning in the area, this building shows a clear formal identity capable of ordering its own spaces without reference outside itself. Following a grid layout, the school rooms are organised in a series of modules that enclose the courtyard and establish an interior street.

Housing on Urban Block B-2 and SE 23
Housing on Urban Block A-2-1 1981-83

Barriada de Pino Montano

Sierra, J.R./Sierra, R. • Torres/Durán

The Partial Plan for the Pino Montano district (to the NE of the city), designed by Cruz and Ortiz in 1980, provided a new alternative for urban growth inspired in the 19th c. expansion plans. The orthogonal grid pattern of closed blocks and inner garden court-yards reinstated the concept of "street corridors" as a response to the alienation and deterioration of the suburbs. Different architects were commissioned to construct the urban blocks to avoid the monotonous repetition of shapes so common in modern cities. The Sierra brothers (urban block B-2) responded with an ambitious project to contain a circular courtyard[1] within the square perimeter of their two blocks[2], thereby circling the square in a manner without precedent in traditional layouts. The Neo-Realist stamp clarifies the symbolic intentions behind this fortress-building that establishes a different image of this kind of mass housing. Torres and Durán's design (urban block A-2-1)[3], two linear blocks run-ning along an interior road, follows patterns more common to the area, proposing an appearance that rather than compacting inwards, looks out, jeopardising the very concept of the closed block.

Apartment Buildings 1982-86 SE 24

Barriada de La Corza

Marín de Terán/Pozo, A. del

Located in the suburbs, this housing complex uses models deeply rooted in vernacular Andalusian architecture to reinterpret the typology of quality Andalusian housing. The design goes beyond the limits of the house and impregnates the urban surroundings, which become a space for social relations.

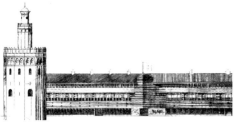

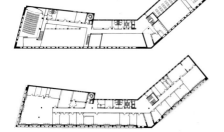

La Prevision Española Building 1982-88   SE 25
Paseo de Cristóbal Colón 26
Moneo
Located on the W edge of the city centre, where the disjointed layout of narrow streets opens up along the Guadalquivir river with more emblematic architecture, this insurance company building responds to the delicate urban environment in two ways. Firstly, it closes the inner city, entering into a relationship with the monumental landmarks close to it, especially the Torre del Oro tower (to which it acts as a kind of back-drop) and the San Telmo Palace. Secondly, it establishes itself as a clearly contemporary proposal of much greater cultural scope, related to the architectural tradition of the entire city. This duality is resolved with a twofold scaling, playing off the large brush-strokes responding to the far-sighted vision (deep horizontal shadows, the massive gablet on the corner and the opaque mezzanine) with a series of traditional elements that bring the building into line with the more sentimental image of Seville (latticework, turrets, glazed tiles).

Housing on A-2-2 Block 1982-83   SE 26
Barriada de Pino Montano
Barrionuevo, A.
Another part of the Partial Plan for Pino Montano (mentioned in SE 23), this is a closed urban block, opening to the outside through its corners. The Neo-Regionalist (or perhaps Neo-Vernacular) ornaments, symbolism and language express a search for identity in one of the harshest suburbs of the city.

Housing Block 1983-85   SE 27
Hombre de Piedra 9-11
Cruz/Ortiz
This is one of the last housing blocks Cruz and Ortiz built in the historical city centre. In this case, their characteristic way of closing off the outside of their buildings hides an exciting inner space, generated by successive porches, galleries and staircases, articulated around two linked courtyards.

Other works. Other works by Cruz and Ortiz, architects of wide renown who have also established Sevillian landmarks, include the housing complex (1978-80) on Lumbreras 24, which continues to use the courtyard house concept; and a complex of detached and terraced houses (1977-80), creating two façades that form a new street in Villanueva del Ariscal, 15 km from Seville.

Social Housing 1984-87
Av. Ramón y Cajal 10
Vázquez Consuegra

This building is located in the oldest suburb of the city's first expansion, in a confused, complex environment where buildings of all styles and heights converge. The project moved within the strict limits imposed by the town-planning ordinances and the rules for eligibility to social housing funding. Despite these constraints, the architecture manages to articulate a valuable proposal for social housing that reconciles the tendency towards low-density housing so clear in the early Modernist designs with the need to establish a powerful urban nucleus capable of making its voice heard over the cacophony of building languages. The four storeys in the block are made of two maisonette apartments, superimposed and inverted, so that the lower maisonettes enjoy a rear courtyard and the upper ones have access to a private terrace on the roof. This profusion of open spaces in no way undermines the overall image of a single, surprisingly long block with access galleries. Quite the opposite, the modular repetition of the openings in the façade cut back into the outer wall actually adds to the emphasis on unity achieved by continuity and repetition in the functional elements, like the plinth, the upper gallery, the canopy over the gallery and the curved corner. The resulting building speaks in clear, decisive tones, generating its own references in an urban setting very much in need of landmarks. However, the small scale is also important in defining the building: the stair-cases, banisters, window bars and other such smaller architectural details manage to consolidate and add tone to the overall design, meeting a demanding level of resolution in the architectural fittings.

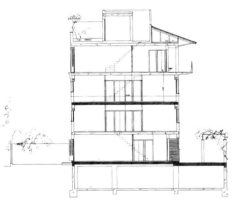

Other works. Vázquez Consuegra's open-minded sensitivity is present in all his designs, including his refurbishment works, as in his adaptation (1985-88) of an 18th c. house on Patio Banderas 14, in the old city, for the Andalusian Architectural Institute, and, on a larger scale, the first stage of the careful rehabilitation of the 18th-19th c. San Telmo Palace (1991-92) as the Presidential Offices of the Regional Government of Andalusia. As the city was endowed with state-of-the-art telecommunications equipment for Expo'92, he was commissioned to build the International Centre and Telephone Teleport (1990-91) for Telefónica, on Ctra. de Pineda s/n. During these years, Bravo and Martínez designed four housing blocks (1990-93) articulated in two rings around a courtyard, inspired in the traditional Sevillian housing style, on Estrasburgo 2-8, in Los Bermejales, a new suburb to the south of the city.

**La Cartuja Island and
Expo'92 Exhibition Grounds** 1984-92

The 1992 Universal Exposition was the great-est event ever to have taken place in Seville's contemporary urban history. The decision to award the holding of the Expo to Seville had been taken a decade earlier, and once the site for the event was chosen, the process of defining the layout of the La Cartuja Island began. The area covered 415 ha. of land close to the historic centre and around the ancient charterhouse of Santa María de las Cuevas (1400), which had been turned into building land after the river course was diverted (1975-82). Between the two river channels, the boundaries of the layout were

Calle Torneo 1986-92

The great legacy bequeathed to Seville by the Universal Exposition held in the city in 1992, whose impact has been even greater than the transformation of the exhibition grounds on La Cartuja island, was the striking urban facelift given to the city as a result of the huge investments made to re-equip the smallest, southernmost, and least developed of all the cities that had been host to such an event. The almost simul-taneous green light given to the plans for the Expo'92 grounds and the new Town Planning General Plan (1985), with their fair share of differences and cross-over areas of responsibility, did, however, enable the right support to be given to the operations required for the road and railway systems, transport facilities, the seven new bridges spanning the Guadalquivir (see SE 32, SE 43 and SE 44) and other infrastructure and public buildings which had to live up to Seville's position as the capital of Spain's Autonomous Community of Andalusia. The most significant work done on the urban street layout was the City Council's striking redesign of Torneo street. The opening up of the old historic quarter to the stretch of the river that had previously been closed off by blank walling and railway lines and the joining up of the city with the Expo'92 exhibition grounds, almost equal in area to that of the historic quarter, which is

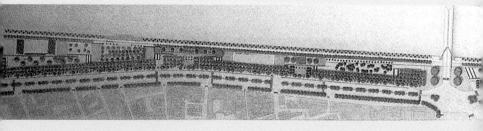

the Alamillo park to the N and an urban edge to the S formed by roads such as the Ronda de la Exposición ringroad. Years later, the layout's unconvincing intensive appearance is evident. One of its elements, the lake of Spain, has been drastically altered to make way for the Isla Mágica theme park now occupying this area, close to a planned new university campus. The rehabilitation of the old charterhouse, however, is an architectural oasis. Several architects worked on the different areas: gardens; orchards; outer chapel; monumental area (see SE 33), which will be housing the Contemporary Art Centre of Andalusia; 19th c. factory buildings (see SE 35 and photograph above); as well as the new Fifteenth Century pavilion (Torres).

The most extensive part of the area is now given over to a technological park which has never really taken off, although it still keeps some of the notable buildings put up for Expo'92. The Japan (Ando) and Great Britain (Grimshaw) pavilions have been taken down, but a number of other pavilions can still be seen: Spain (Cano Lasso), Finland (see SE 46), France (see SE 45), Hungary (Makovecz), Czechoslovakia (Nemec/Stempel), Castile-La Mancha (see SE 41), the Central Theatre (see SE 50) on the N side and the Navigation Pavilion (see SE 42) on the S edge of the grounds, as well as the World Trade Centre (Vázquez de Castro) and the REDESA Red Eléctrica regional centre by Bayón (1989-92), in the photograph above.

possibly the biggest in Europe, entailed a whole host of layout problems and required a new river front, several kilometres long, to be set up. The architects Díaz Recaséns and Fernández de Castro were not in charge of the overall work, but they did design a clever section whose upper level functions as a thoroughfare which, although it is the leading ringroad and has considerable traffic running through it, succeeds in maintaining the street's urban character with the help of a series of sizeable street lights. The wide side platform opens up to the lower level, the Paseo Juan Carlos I, a spacious avenue that widens out in places and pleasantly meets up with the river at times. All in all,

the design created a new landscape in the very heart of Seville both for the river and for the outline of La Cartuja island with the Guadalquivir garden, the old industrial chimneys of the 19th c. Cartuja factory and the silhouettes of MBM's Plaza del Futuro building (1989-92).

La Maestranza Theatre 1986-91 SE 31
Paseo Cristobal Colón 22
Marín de Terán/Del Pozo
The cylindrical drum shape of the concert hall rises up behind the façade of the 18th c. military building, acting as an integral part of the monumental skyline between the historic city centre and the river. On the opposite side of the site the building is fragmented to fit the surrounding urban landscape.

Centenary Bridge 1987-92 SE 32
Autovía de Circunvalación SE-30
Martínez Calzón/Fernández Ordóñez
The biggest of the suspension bridges built for Expo'92 with 2,018 m between piers, 110-m high pilasters and a central anchored span 564 m long. The high-tech engineering is based on careful structural, constructional and economic logistics and facilitates access to the S of the city and the Guadalquivir.

Refurbishment of the Abbey Area SE 33
on La Cartuja Island 1987-92
Camino de La Cartuja, Isla de La Cartuja
Sierra, J.R./Sierra, R.
This project converted the abandoned 15th c. Charterhouse into an administrative and exhibition centre for Expo'92. Reconstruction of the missing part of the old cloister made restoration an integral part of the overall rehabilitation process.

Santa Justa Train Station 1988-91 SE 34
Av. de Kansas City
Cruz/Ortiz
The site chosen for the new train station had hardly been developed at all, although it was expected that the new building would turn the surrounding neighbourhood into a busy urban nucleus. Consequently, the architects planned to build a modern, functional station that would also act as an urban monument. From the outside, the building gives the impression of austerity, dominated by strong horizontality and extensive use of brickwork.

Refurbishment of the Ceramics Factory SE 35
of La Cartuja for the IAPH 1987-95
Isla de la Cartuja
Vázquez Consuegra

The La Cartuja factory (15th-19th c.) on the island needed to be refurbished to house the offices in charge of the Historic Heritage of Andalusia. Former transformations had turned the factory into a labyrinthian group of buildings from all ages. The project only kept those that met certain quality standards and demolished the superfluous ones. The sections constructed defined the edges of the new complex, respecting its cumulative, fragmented structure. In the new spaces opened up, the architecture is very carefully controlled in terms of scale, proportions and fittings, in order to establish a dialogue between its new, contemporary style and the rich voice of the past, established over so many centuries.

Airport Terminal 1987-91   SE 36
Autovía Madrid-Cádiz, km 532
Moneo

The new terminal turns the isotropic, rather anonymous space of most airports halls into a building of architectural value, without in any way interfering with its functionality, by incorporating traditional references into the design: glazed tile vaults, inner courtyards and Islamic mosque architecture.

The main entrance, 14.65 m above ground level, is defined by a curved, somewhat asymmetrical canopy leading into the main concourse, where the ticket offices, waiting areas and shops are located. These inner areas are surprisingly spacious, their generous dimensions further enhanced by the careful choice of materials and intelligent use of light. The gently coloured concourse is mainly lit through enormous vertical picture windows. Although this space is clearly defined, the glass divisions make visible the transitional spaces behind. The large open-ings in the side walls also reveal the functional aspects of the station, whilst emphasising its monumental quality. The raked roof indicates the unity of the internal route through the concourse and down the escalators to the platforms. Once over the platforms, how-ever, the roof folds over the different tracks, vaulted in such a way as to enable the penetration of natural light through panels. The materials used, in this case exposed concrete, once again help to manifest the functional change. Recipient of the National Architecture Award 1992.

Catalana Occidente Building 1987-91 SE 37
Av. San Francisco Javier s/n
Sierra, J.R./Sierra, R.
Located on one of the main arterial roads
of the new city, as it spreads to the E, this
building purposely combines and twists a
series of Classical elements, such as a plinth,
porticoes and cornices, to generate a very
powerful metropolitan image that evokes a
multiplicity of references.

Capitular and Colombina SE 38
Libraries 1989-91
Alemanes (Cathedral complex)
Sierra J.R./Sierra, R.
The project required the conversion of two
naves enclosing the 12th c. Patio de Naranjos
courtyard to house the Cathedral Archives
and the Archbishopric Library. The Almohade
character of the building was recovered and
a new functional organisation established.

Torretriana Building 1989-97 SE 39
Camino del Guadalquivir, Isla de La Cartuja
Sáenz de Oíza
This unique building, intended to act as the
main offices of several Regional Government
Departments for Andalusia, was designed to
act as a W gateway to the city. A square
inserted into the circle composes the well-lit
plan of a building whose façade makes clear
reference to the vocabulary of Louis Kahn.

Plaza de Armas Hotel 1989-92 SE 40
Marqués de Paradas s/n
**González Cordón/Pérez Escolano/García
Vázquez**
The plan takes up the curve marking the edge
of the historic centre where it meets with
the open spaces of La Cartuja Island. This
duality is expressed in the radical counter-
positioning between the urban, traditional E
façade and the abstract, high-tech W façade.

Castile-La Mancha Pavilion 1990-92 SE 41
Paseo del Lago, Isla de La Cartuja
Casas, M. de las
The pavilion is a closed prism, the interior of
which is split in two by an open corridor
from which the stairs rise up towards the
exhibition areas and the administration
offices. The inner gallery is walled in glass,
whilst the outer volume is enclosed in
laminated wood.

Navigation Pavilion and Tower 1989-92   SE 42
Isla de La Cartuja
Vázquez Consuegra

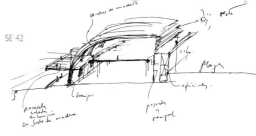

Located next to the river, to the S of La Cartuja Island, the pavilion and its tower team up with the Alamillo Bridge (to the far N) to form the main urban landmarks defining the edge of the Expo'92 grounds as seen from the city itself. This, along with the representation role played by the building during the Expo'92 and afterwards, meant that the pavilion could not be seen as a mere container for exhibits, but rather had to commit itself to a definitive image of its own individuality. A single, continuous roof that starts on the vertical plane, then curves and slopes, ending up like an eye-shade, gives the building just such character. It is the unifying element, broken only on the riverside where it is perforated with glass openings and a glazed volume (the temporary exhibition hall) that breaks up the great expanse of metal to its NW corner. A set of platforms, stairs, ramps and terraces link up the exterior with the interior, which is of necessity open-plan to allow for optimal flexibility in housing exhibitions. The white tower rises up from the waters of the river, as a complement to the pavilion, twinning two vertical communication corpuses: an open, structural shaft of lifts and a stairwell, which is much more closed and opaque.

La Cartuja Bridge 1990-91   SE 43
Torneo and Isla de La Cartuja
Leonhardt/Viñuela

This slim, streamlined bridge is 238 m long. Made up of 22 sections, it crosses the old riverway, linking up the historical city centre with La Cartuja Island at the site of the Santa María de las Cuevas Monastery. It was conceived as a continuous, asymmetrical steel box-girder bridge crossing the River Guadalquivir in a single 170-m span, without any intermediate support. It thus met the requirements of the administration, that planned to use this unbroken stretch of water for international rowing races. The bridge melds discreetly with its environment, its elegant, functional beauty distinguishing it from the rightly named exhibitionist aesthetics of much of the nearby architecture.

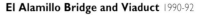

El Alamillo Bridge and Viaduct 1990-92 SE 44
Autovía de Circunvalación SE-30
Calatrava
The design established two symmetrical
bridges united by the 526.5-m long viaduct,
supported on sloping columns, crossing
La Cartuja Island. The idea was to create a
metaphor of the gateway to the Guadalquivir
valley. In the end, however, only the bridge
over the old riverway was built, at the level where the N part of the ringroad crosses the
river. The bridge consists of a large reinforced concrete pile, in a metal sleeve, sloped at 58°,
and compensated by the counter-stress of 13 pairs of cables from which the deck seems to
be hung. The metal deck covers a span of 200 m. The result is an immense lyre, 142 m high,
which has completely reshaped the traditional skyline of the city and become one of its most
important visual landmarks.

France Pavilion 1990-92 SE 45
Isla de La Cartuja
Viguier/Jodry/Seigneur
On the ground, the pavilion seems no more
than an enormous square canopy supported
on four piles to its corners, under which a
sophisticated glass prism allows for access.
The glass platform that serves as the floor
announces the authentic exhibition space of
the building, that extends below the ground.

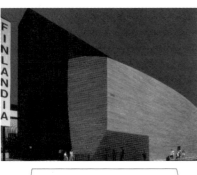

Finland Pavilion 1990-92 SE 46
Av. de las Palmeras, Isla de La Cartuja
MONARK Group
The Finnish pavilion for Expo'92 is made
up of two parallel but clearly differentiated
parts, between which a tense dialogue is
established. One, named "The Keel", is
made of Finnish pinewood and follows the
principles of wooden boat-building, thereby
taking on the role of representing traditional
craftsmanship. The other, known as "The
Machine", is a totally modular, prefabricated
steel parallelepiped, a clear metaphor for
industrial culture. A narrow passageway, 15 m
high and 2 m wide, the abstract translation
of a landscape known in Finnish mythology
as the "Throat of Hell", runs between the
two sections. Access to the pavilion is
through a ramp that goes up through this
symbol-laden gap between wood and steel,
Nature and Technology.

Spanish Television Centre in Andalusia 1990-93

SE 47

Parque del Alamillo, Isla de La Cartuja
Ayala
Seen from the N of La Cartuja Island, this building looks fragmented, combining stone walls with other lighter cladding. The tower is clearly what gives the whole its most outstanding characteristic: a skin of metal sheeting filters the light and hides a lift and stairs.

Social Housing 1990-93

SE 48

Manzana 120, Pol. Los Bermejales
Frechilla/López Peláez/Sánchez
The two linear housing blocks with 120 units were built in parallel and have access galleries; the lower maisonette apartment has access to a private garden and the upper one to an open terrace. The little indigo dents and the pronounced balconies over the street add character to the building.

Police Station 1991-92

SE 49

Cortijo de Cuarto, Bellavista
Carrascal/Fernández de la Puente
The complexity of the programme is solved with an outer wall closing the perimeter, turned into the axis that vertebrates the entire operation. The many, very different parts making up the whole are all set back onto this wall, leaving three large free spaces between them, at different levels.

Central Theatre 1991-92

SE 50

Ronda de la Exposición, Isla de La Cartuja
Ayala
This multi-purpose theatre built for Expo'92, based on a simple geometrical composition, consists of a square-base prism in whose diagonal another higher, rectangular-base prism housing the stalls of the theatre is set. Stone, glass and electronic parasols give the volume a very clean, high-tech definition.

New Headquarters of the Provincial Government 1991-95

SE 51

Av. Menéndez Pelayo 32
Cruz/Ortiz
The design included the rehabilitation of an 18th c. barracks and their extension in a new building, linked to the old by a green space. The new building is clad in green stone and responds to its irregular surroundings with different heights and degrees of opening.

Priest Seminary 1992-97   SE 52
Av. de Bonanza c/v Av. de la Palmera
Carbajal
The comb-like volumes are set on a single
plinth to make the most of the site. The
building is enhanced by a diaphanous, roofed,
ventilated storey between the base and the
bedroom sections, which combines with the
roof to give the ensemble areas for ritual
ceremonies, leisure activities and views.

Town Hall, Library and   SE 53
Constitution Square 1984-91
Pza. de la Constitución. Camas
Noguerol/Díez
This sophisticated proposal fitted well into
the context of an empty lot between party
walls, where a series of architectural pieces
intended to serve as town hall, library and
shopping centre were all linked up to form a
large public area.

Housing Complex (136 Units) 1989-96   SE 54
Ronda Sur de Circunvalación. Los Palacios
García Márquez/Rubiño/Rubiño
Taking rural Andalusian architecture as their
reference, the architects designed a series of
terrace houses based on the austere repetition
of modules and volumes. The visual unity of
the complex regenerates the fragmented
outskirts of this village, 28 km from Seville.

SE 55 **Esquivel Settlement** 1948-52
Alcalá del Río, Viar
Sota, A. de la. coll.: Herrero Urgel

Esquivel was one of the first settlements
built as part of the colonisation programme
and highlights the underlying principles of the
project which sought "to take as teachers
the people who have always made villages ...
the village builders". Those were Sota's own
words to explain the "architectural orientation" of the plan, since the *ex novo* design
here went down a different path. The layout
is symmetrical albeit eccentric, regular albeit
with curved lines, and the way the streets
and spaces are divided and organised in
hierarchy is certainly modern. The church
and the town hall are placed at the entrance
"to show off their best side to anyone who
passes by" and the arts and crafts square is
set at the far end of the axis. The villagers
"are to live in houses that form narrow,

intimate streets and even more intimate
squares", in the quest for "human scale".
Six different types of houses were designed:
with one or two storeys, between two and
five bedrooms, with a yard leading into a
storeroom, an animal stable, a shed and an
outside WC. The way in which the formal
components are cut down and used
randomly endorses the principle that under-
pins the whole project: "simplicity [was] ...
our preoccupation when doing things,
despite the wealth of theory that explains

Rolando House and Studio 1980-83
Ctra. Almensilla, km 7.6. **Mairena del Aljarafe**
Vázquez Consuegra
Home and office are coordinated along an
L-shaped plan, which segregates a portion
of space from the agricultural land, marked
out by a pergola. The building techniques
used and the strong rural component in the
architecture are evidence of the influence
of the olive-growing estates that surround it.

Uhtna Hus House 1983-85
Urb. Simón Verde. **Mairena del Aljarafe**
Vázquez Consuegra
The house is articulated in three blocks.
The central block contains the living room,
and the two side ones the smaller rooms.
A series of recesses and shifts alter the
initial symmetry of the building, thereby
generating several porches, terraces and
galleries opening onto the garden.

SE 57

Canal Sur Television Centre 1985-88
Ctra. San Juan de Aznalfarache-Tomares, km 1.3
San Juan de Aznalfarache
Díaz Recaséns
As an alternative to the high-tech world of
telecommunications, this broadcasting centre
is based on the Andalusian architectural
tradition, closing the building off from the
outside and articulating it with inner courtyards that lead to a panoramic tower.

SE 58

them, with total simplicity ... with the minimum science ..." Sota's approach was applied
at all levels, from the layout down to each
of the elements, including the most relevant
ones, such as the church, the town hall
building or the primary school, as well as the
secondary elements such as the benches,
walkways and fountains, "the salt and pepper
seasoning it". In an overall catchment area
of 2,152 ha., Esquivel was built on 14 ha.,
with 160 houses, 110 for the settlers and a
further 50 added subsequently (1953-56).

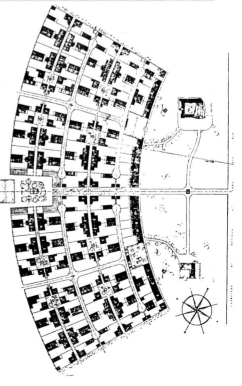

ARAGON

Land of great contrasts (high mountains, deep valleys and desert plains), Aragón achieved the status of a kingdom in 1035. Following unification with the County of Barcelona in the 12th c., it became a Mediterranean power, with territories in Roussillon, Valencia, the Balearic Islands, Corsica, Sardinia, Sicily... Ferdinand II of Aragón married Isabella I of Castile and created the first modern state (15th-16th c.). Its three provinces boast of beautiful Romanesque buildings and magnificent examples of the Mudejar style (13th-16th c.). Industry and wealth are concentrated in Zaragoza, the most strategically located city, set at a crossroads for domestic and international trading routes. Huesca and Teruel are more rural. Although the region was the official birthplace of the Modernist movement in Spain, with the foundation of the GATEPAC group in 1930, the "revivals" of the beginning of the century – looking back to Renaissance and Mudejar art forms – coloured the Aragonese Rationalist designs. Characterised by their austere language and widespread use of brick, these buildings showed a markedly different tone, more related to central European radical orthodoxy than to Spanish Modernism, placing the emphasis on adaptation to local climate and materials. These traditional roots were reaffirmed in the post-war era, with a strong ideological content: Teruel, almost totally destroyed during one of the bloodiest battles in the Civil War, became one of the symbols of Franco's victory and emblematic of the kind of urban planning to which General Franco's regime aspired in reconstructing Spain.

Geography: 47,669 km², varied landscape set between the Pyrenees and the Sistema Ibérico range, on the Ebro river valley, the most important river in Spain. Climate: continental, dry in the capital. Rainfall: approx. 320 mm and 90 days. Sunshine: 2,800 hrs. Population: 1,221,646. GDP: 106% of nat. av.

HUESCA. This rural province can be enjoyed driving 53 km along the road from the capital to Sabiñánigo (see the Technical College, 1958, by Basso, Bohigas et al.), and then crossing a series of valleys to the ski resort of Cerler, 154 km from the capital. Huesca, a city state under Sertorius in 83 AC, conserves stretches of Roman road (Coso Alto, Coso Bajo). Its historical city centre, full of narrow Mediaeval streets, houses outstanding monuments: the 13th c. Gothic cathedral and the 12th c. Romanesque cloisters of San Pedro el Viejo. Many authors (including Rábanos) consider Huesca's Rationalist architecture to be of great purity: see the Polo house (1931) on Pza. de la Justicia 1, by J. L. León, and the Casa de Las Lástimas (1933) on Las Cortes 17, by Beltrán Navarro. Origin: village of *Illerda* and then Roman city of *Osca*. Altitude: 466 m. Temperatures: 34°-10° and 2°-19° C. Population: 50,085.

Sports Centre 1988-94   H 1
Camino de San Jorge s/n, Cerro de San Jorge
Miralles/Pinòs
The surrounding landscape and topography established the defining constraints for this sports building, along with its daring, much cited roof, which stands suspended over different depths of excavated space. Its collapse during construction lead to a new design.

Lavert Apartments 1976-79   H 2
Cerler ski station, Benasque Valley
Bach/Mora
This residential complex of split-level apartments, specifically designed for a mountain resort, was organised along three staggered, partly overlapping lines. The purity of the traditional construction in local stone is eclectically undermined by a series of conventionally Modernist references.

TERUEL. Teruel is the capital of the rural province of the same name, featuring towns of splendid mediaeval vernacular architecture, such as Albarracín (1,170 m altitude), 36 km from Teruel, with an extreme climate (harsh winters and hot summers), an ancient city under Muslim rule until 1171, remains of which time can still be seen in the Mudejar towers of several 12th and 13th c. churches. In the new ski resort of Javalambre (municipality of Camarena de la Sierra), San Martín, Ortiz and Elena Cánovas have built an interesting Ski Services Centre (1994-96). Altitude: 952 m. Population: 27,226.

ZARAGOZA (also Saragossa). City on the banks of the River Ebro, home to Iberians, Romans, Visigoths, Muslims and Christians as of 1118, it has an important cathedral, La Seo, which is a conglomeration of historical styles, from Romanesque to Churrigueresque; a 16th c. corn exchange, La Lonja, and an 18th c. basilica, La Virgen del Pilar, by Ventura Rodríguez. During the 20th century, it has exemplified the encounter between tradition and new ideas within a provincial socio-political framework. Although featuring designs inspired by the avant-garde (the Matías Bergua house, on Paseo de Ruiseñores 55, designed by Bergamín and Blanco-Soler, 1930-33), until well into the fifties, the traditionalism of the Regionalist movement reigned supreme. Emblematic in this sense is the career of the Borobio brothers who, except for some clearly contemporary residential buildings (in appearance rather than layout), continued to use traditional elements, albeit often transformed by a timeless composition: see the Caja de Previsión Social building (1931), on Costa 1, and the old trade fair grounds, Feria de Muestras (1940-58, together with Beltrán Navarro), on Paseo de Isabel la Católica s/n. Under Franco's regime, after the war, monumental buildings found favour, such as the Capuchinos Abbey (1940), in Eusa, on Paseo de Cuéllar 22. Later, the rapid growth of the city until 1975-77 followed urban development models linked to fast industrialisation. In the eighties, with the return of democracy, there has been an increase in public works, with special focus on re-habilitating old buildings and areas. In the province, at approximately 80 km, the walled town of Daroca and the Mudejar town of Tarazona also show this mixture of old and new. Origin: Iberian city state of *Salduie* (2nd c. BC), and Roman city of *Caesaraugusta* (19-14 BC). Altitude: 200 m. Temperatures: 35°-12° and 3°-19° C. Population: 622,371.

Rincón de Goya 1926-28   Z 1
Parque Primo de Rivera
García Mercadal
A manifesto of the Rationalist movement in Spain, this building was commissioned to celebrate the Goya centenary. The architect, the sole Spanish participant in the CIAM congress celebrated at La Sarraz, designed this municipal hall with a very compact composition of pure volumes.

Housing Block 1930
Ram de Riu c/v Supervía
Zuazo
During the first half of the thirties, the urban expansion of Zaragoza began to overflow the city limits defined in earlier times. In this context, Zuazo applied Rationalist principles to this low-budget open housing area, laying it out in linear blocks that became locally famous after the war.

Ebro Water Authority Building 1933-38 Z 3
Paseo de Sagasta 24
Borobio R./Borobio J.
Located on an important 19th c. avenue, this unfussy building combines the use of traditional brick facing in the local style with new Functionalist ideas. Its design achieves both enormous structural clarity and compositional simplicity with a straight-forward layout.

Law School 1935-39 Z 4
Pza. de San Francisco, Ciudad Universitaria
Borobio, R./Borobio, J./Beltrán Navarro
This building was part of the University campus that the Borobio brothers planned with Beltrán Navarro (1935), along similar lines to the Madrid campus. The Law School is of classical composition, closer to the earlier works of Regino than the more avant-garde ideas of his brother.

Diestre Factory 1964-67 Z 5
Ctra. N-II, km 314
Moneo
Moneo's first solo commission, this building clearly reveals the influence of his recent working experience in the Jørn Utzon studio: the different ceiling levels required for the operations in the industrial assembly line became the leitmotif for the composition of an authentic artificial topography in the Ara-gonese landscape, which is predominantly flat. The usual industrial corrugated iron roofing was turned into a succession of gentle volumetrics at varying heights, which are structured along a retiform set of girders, one stacked atop the other. The colour of the building's cladding, its horizontal develop-ment and its position in the environment contribute to its successful contextualisation.

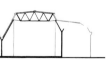

Los Enlaces Service Station 1960-63   Z 6
Av. de la Hispanidad and Ctra. N-II
Yarza García
The parts of the programme – service station, petrol pumps and restaurant – are united by a roof consisting of a metal structure supported on concrete pillars. This elegant architectural solution has turned the building into an eloquent image of urban modernisation in the sixties.

Aragón Public Library 1984-89   Z 7
Doctor Cerrada 22
López Cotelo/Puente/García
The Urban Development Plan established that the library facilities should be housed in two high blocks, constructed against existing buildings, and a lower block in the centre, set slightly apart so as to allow access to the public space inside. The architects, however, proposed that the two volumes should be condensed into one to establish a more compact, singular solution. There is one high block, on a line and at a height with the façade of the neighbouring buildings, and respecting similar proportions in windows and doors. From it springs a lower floor, set back from the street line, containing the reading room with natural overhead lighting. Artistic expression is circumscribed to the façade of the six-storey building, clad in wood with outside maintenance galleries.

Municipal Auditorium 1990-94   Z 8
Eduardo Ibarra 1
Pérez Latorre
The architect's tendency to use different materials and architectural references is reflected in this building. The programme consists of several concert rooms, set in a single container, established by an imposing volume with porticos along its perimeter. Inside, the separate rooms are like water-tight boxes, where different atmospheres are created for the music. The Mozart Room makes explicit reference to the typical terraced concert halls that Scharoun used in Berlin. In the space between the music rooms and the main volumes is the foyer, where the high reinforced concrete pillasters mark a spatial rhythm that is taken up by the coffered ceiling. The alabaster enclosure adds the final touch to the welcoming atmosphere inside.

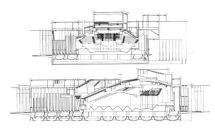

Sports Centre 1991-92   Z 9
Ciudad Universitaria
Tobías Pintre
Turning to an image of great formal
simplicity, with evident allusions to typical
industrial building techniques and materials
– metal cladding, corrugated iron roofing,
etc. –, the building successfully introduces
new order into the confused urban design
of the campus.

Extension to the Law Courts 1985-94   Z 10
Prudencio c/v Pza. de Nuestra Señora del Pilar
Sota, A. de la/Capella
Over 30 years after the Civilian Government
Building (TA 1), Sota was commissioned to
design a great Administration building. And
with the same idea of avoiding any imposing
frippery, he distributed pure volumetric
shapes around a tree-filled courtyard,
separating the different circulation routes.

More on Zaragoza. Amongst the numerous rehabilitation projects carried out during the
eighties, of special interest is the remodelling of the Aljafería Palace, an originally Islamic
complex (9th-11th c.), which has been expanded in successive stages: in Mediaeval Christian
times (12th-14th c.), the Renaissance (15th-16th c.) and in the modern era, declared National
Monument in 1931. Franco and Pemán, with a set of subtle, one-off operations (1986-87)
have removed the parts of little interest added whilst it served as barracks, and reformed the
whole to house the Autonomous Regional Parliament, the Archaeological Museum and a
library. The Pablo Serrano Museum (1986-93), on Paseo de María Agustín 18, is another
excellent example, where Pérez Latorre turned the fragmented parts of an industrial building
designed in 1916 into a single, open exhibition space.

Church of San Juan 1980-82   Z 11
Pza. de San Juan s/n. **Daroca**
Burillo/Lorenzo
These architects have become renowned
for their work in restructuring and
recovering historical buildings. Here, they
completely overhauled the existing building
(a 13th c. Romanesque church) with a
careful game of analogies and details that
are reminiscent of Scarpa's sensitivity.

City Museum 1982-83   Z 12
Pza. del Palacio Episcopal. **Tarazona**
Burillo/Lorenzo
The remodelling plan focussed on ridding
the building of additions to the lower
levels of the Episcopal Palace (13th-18th c.
complex), to enhance the rhythm
established by the double order of
segmental brick arches, consolidated and
integrated by an airy exhibition walkway.

ASTURIAS

Asturias is known for its emerald-green valleys, prehistoric cave dwellings, Celtic settlements and Roman roads and ruins. Its architectural fame stretches far back to the pre-Romanesque buildings erected under the Visigothic dynasty of the kings of Oviedo. Their magnificence reached its zenith under King Ramiro I, in the 9th c., with the *aula regia* or Royal Hall of Santa María del Naranco and the Church of San Miguel de Lillo, both in Oviedo, and the Church of Santa Cristina de Lena in Pola de Lena, 34 km from Oviedo. In the Middle Ages, numerous abbeys and churches were built, especially during the Romanesque period, many of which were reconstructed in later centuries. The architectural highpoint of the mediaeval period, however, was the Gothic cathedral of Oviedo (begun in the 14th c.). Following the unification of Spain, Renaissance, Baroque and Neo-Classical architecture developed consecutively in the region, and important ecclesiastical and civilian buildings were designed. But perhaps it is its vernacular or rural architecture that most catches the eye: not only the picturesque farmhouses and out-buildings, but also the elegant houses of the local nobility, the rural churches and chapels and the beauty of the small coastal towns – such as Cudillero and Ribadesella – and picturesque villages set in impressive mountain landscapes. In this rural architecture one unique construction stands out, the *hórreos* or granaries. Although as big as a small house, farming families nevertheless still consider them moveable. Perched on stone or wooden piles, to keep grain dry, their design manages to be both functionally and aesthetically pleasing. In the boom following the local industrial revolution – focussed around the massive coal and steel industry in Avilés and the steelworks, seaport and shipyards in Gijón – and the nation-wide economic growth during the second half of the 19th c., the region's towns began to expand and were rebuilt, first along academic classical *Beaux Arts* guidelines, then in Eclecticist and Historicist architectural styles. This Historicism was common throughout the first third of the 20th c., although it overlapped in the twenties and thirties with the new Modernist architecture that partly substituted it. Architects such as the Bustos, Marín de la Viña (Casa Vallina building, Av. de la Costa 100, Gijón, 1933-35), Sáinz Heres or Somolinos (Aramo building, Uria 21, Oviedo, 1935-42), and engineers such as Sánchez del Río spearheaded the movement in the region. After the Civil War, the architect, Luis Moya and his studio built Gijón's Technical College, the Universidad Laboral, the biggest, most important and most beautiful example of 20th-c. Classicism in Spain. Under Franco, Asturias suffered from the cultural depression that affected all of Spain, but as new ideas started moving again, the Modernist architect, Alvarez Castelao made his name for consistent excellence in the region, with a few Modernist contributions by Vaquero Palacios. Over the last two decades, a new architectural culture has flourished, taking advantage of the policies to combat industrial decline (renovation of the old La Curtidora factory as a business park in Avilés, Gutiérrez Herrero s/n, by Nanclares, Ruiz and González Moriyón, 1989-94) and the new interest in civic buildings (Gijón's Sports Centre, Paseo Dr. Fleming s/n, Barrio de La Guía, by Pérez Arroyo, 1989-92). The nineties style is both universal and local, a combination that provides exciting new scope for further development.

Geography: 10,565 km², a narrow strip about 50 km wide between peaks of up to 2,500 m and the Cantabrian Sea. Climate: humid, with fine drizzle (the *orbayu*). Rainfall: approx. 1,100 mm and 200 days. Sunshine: 1,800 hrs. Population: 1,098,725. GDP: 84% of nat. av.

OVIEDO. Once capital of the Asturian Kingdom created by the successors of Don Pelayo in the 8th c., it is now the capital of the Principality of Asturias and, along with Gijón (29 km away), one of its main metropolitan areas. Oviedo is known for its magnificent pre-Romanesque monuments, the mainly Gothic cathedral and its late Gothic tower. With a university that dates back to 1534 (38,688 students in 1995-96), it also has the most significant historic town centre in the region, whose narrow streets, 16th-18th c. palaces and quaint squares are described by Clarín in *La Regenta*. Gijón and Aviles boast similar heritages. All three towns have excellent examples of the eclectic Historicist architecture of the burgeoning 19th c. middle classes, as well as of the development of Modernist architecture. Origin: end of the 8th c. Altitude: 265 m. Temperatures: 23°-12° and 4°-16° C. Population: 204,276.

Casa Blanca Building 1929-31   O 1
Uría 13
Busto, M. del/Busto, J.M. del
This is the first building by Manuel del Busto with his son José Manuel, after his Historicist period, conceived midway between the end of Secessionism and the beginning of *Art Déco*. One of the first Modernist buildings in Oviedo, it is considered an important city monument.

Apartment Building 1932   O 2
Independencia 7
Busto, M. del/Busto, J.M. del
An attractive example of the *Art Déco* period of the Bustos, the architects who constructed several town, residential and civic buildings in this style in Oviedo and Gijón. Their residential buildings are still standing in Gijón, but the architecturally interesting cinemas have disappeared.

INP Building 1934-42   O 3
Argüelles c/v Pza. Carbayón
Vaquero Palacios/Casariego Terreros
Along with the El Termómetro Building (see O 4), this is one of the best conceived Modernist residential buildings in the region. It was built during the thirties by the architects Vaquero (also a well-known painter) and Casariego (famed for his earlier Historicist designs). Using a busy city corner, they constructed a personal but attractive interpretation of Rationalism, searching for a domestic interpretation of the new Modernism that would be as valid as the earlier Historicist vocabulary. The building adds character to its location, turning it into one of the most attractive spots of modern Oviedo. The interior stained-glass windows are by Vaquero, while the reliefs decorating the lower façade of the building are by Goyco Aguirre of Gijón.

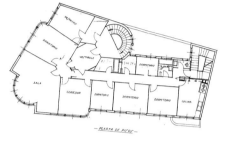

El Termómetro Building 1936-43 ○ 4
Fruela 18 c/v San Francisco
(Pza. de la Escandalera)
Sáiz Heres
Constructed some years after the INP Building (see ○ 3) by Vaquero and Casariego, the El Termómetro Building, which occupies the most important corner in modern central Oviedo, on Pza. de la Escandalera, has become one of the most emblematic buildings in the city. It is much identified with Mendelsohn's ideas, incorporating Expressionism into Rationalist architecture, especially in its daringly radical curved glass corner. Sadly, its lower levels have been ill-treated and abandoned, although a well-deserved face-lift could return the building to its attractive original state. The El Termómetro Building is worth restoring as an important part of the city's architectural heritage.

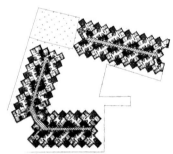

ALSA Bus Station and Housing 1957-64 ○ 5
Pza. Primo de Rivera 1
Alvarez Castelao
Independent and cut off from the mainstream, Ignacio Alvarez Castelao is a typical example of the many regional architects working during the Franco dictatorship. This is his most original and attractive work, conceived in a style both austere and expressive, which cunningly combines the twofold functionality of housing and bus station. The work is characterised by its overwhelming massiveness.
Castelao was also responsible for the adaptation of the ancient San Pelayo Convent for government use (1958-66, on Diecinueve de Julio). The reform was based on a radical design, with modern architecture efficiently and coherently superimposed on the old. It has recently been re-restored, but not faithfully.

Sports Centre 1960-65 ○ 6
Río Caudal s/n
Sánchez del Río [eng.]
Many years after his most important work, the Pola de Siero market (see ○ 19), the engineer, Sánchez del Río designed this sports centre, with interesting multiple-layer reinforced concrete vaulting, showing the consistency in his personal architectural style.

Cantabrian Hydroelectric ○ 7
Building 1964-68
Pza. de la Gesta 2
Vaquero Palacios
The architect and painter, Vaquero Palacios designed this building in the style of Mies van der Rohe, but with many personal touches that enhance its volumetric complexity. It is typical of the architecture of the sixties in Oviedo.

Department of Biology 1965-69 ○ 8
[now **Geology Dept.**], Jesús Arias de Velasco s/n
Alvarez Castelao
This building shows the more international side of Alvarez Castelao, incorporating references to Le Corbusier and also the Smithsons. It is more successful than his Medical School Building (Av. Julián Clavería s/n), even if the latter is more original and experimental.

Refurbishment of the Banco de España ○ 9
for the Regional Government 1983-86
Suárez de la Riva 11
Nanclares/Ruiz Fernández
Representative of the architecture of the generation exercising the profession after the death of Franco, the sensitivity with which the Bank of Spain building was renovated shows its architects' successful touch and personal commitment.

Administration Building for ○ 10
the Regional Government 1989-92
Coronel Aranda 2
Hernández Sande, M. and E./Perea Caveda
This office building was constructed in such a way as to recover the Rationalist tradition in a high-tech, internationally oriented version, representative of the economic optimism at the end of the eighties and the excitement over regional autonomy.

Bridge over the River Sella 1989-90 ○ 11
Arriondas
Manterola/Fernández Troyano [engs.]
In this arched steel construction with an 80 m span, for the first time, the loads from the arch are transmitted via triangular bays onto the supports, in a solution that works well for ground with different sheers. The shape is simple, clear and minimalistic, impeccably set and related to the surrounding landscape.

Refurbishment of the Covadonga Sanctuary 1958-64

O 12

Real Sitio de Covadonga. **Cangas de Onís**
García-Lomas
An interesting refurbishment of the historic sanctuary, consisting of the bishop's house, chapter house, the areas of the Basilica and the Cave. The attractive Historicist style can be considered a very personal interpretation of the ambiances that were there before.

GIJON. The second biggest city in Asturias by population and the biggest in size, this industrial capital and main port of the Principality constitutes a unique, sprawling metropolitan con-urbation with Oviedo. Gijón conserves interesting Roman remains, recently rediscovered. Its old city centre and fishing port deserve a visit, as do its 17th and 18th c. palaces. Its rapid development during the last third of the 19th c. and the beginning of this century, with the enormous industrial port of El Musel, is reflected in its *Beaux Arts* and Historicist-style buildings, interspersed with fine examples of Modernism. In the fifties and sixties, it suffered from overcrowding and land speculation. However, more recently it has undergone many improvements and rehabilitations. Origin: Roman city of *Gegio*, on prehistoric settlement on the Santa Catalina Peninsula. Temperatures: 23°-13° and 4°-18° C. Population: 260,267.

Apartment Building 1934

O 13

Pza. del Instituto 3
Busto, M. del/Busto, J.M. del
Although Manuel was famed for his Eclectic buildings, and both had been outstanding architects in the *Art Déco* style, this housing block was a superb foray into Rationalism. Their other, earlier residential building on Pza. de San Miguel 10 (1931) is also worthy of note.

ALSA Bus Station 1939-42

O 14

Magnus Blisktad 2
Busto, M. del/Busto, J.M. del
As original and personal as it is international, the Gijón bus station is designed in a Realist Expressionist style, searching for a new language apt to establish a building characteristic of modern life as an integral part of the urban surroundings. It is these architects' most progressive, radical design.

Reform of the Inner Port 1986-92

O 15

Puerto de Gijón
Nanclares/Ruiz/González Moriyón
The project brought about the successful, sensitive reform of the old city port, turning it into a Marina and managing to transform the nearby urban landscape and inject new life into the area by designing and inserting very varied elements. It is located next to a rehabilitated urban zone.

Technical College 1945-56
Ctra. de Villaviciosa km 68. **Cabueñes**
Moya, L./Rodríguez Alonso de la Puente/
Moya, R.

A highpoint of Spanish post-war Historicism, this building represents the culmination of the ambitions that spurred a unique and cultivated architect, Luis Moya Blanco (1904-1990, professor at the Madrid School of Architecture), in his personal crusade to prove the superiority of traditional over modern architecture. Conceived as an "ideal city", it consists of a main square, surrounded and formed by an enormous tower and the key institutional buildings of a university: the Church, the Theatre, the Rectory and the Administration Building. The church is of special interest. Spread out on an original, elongated elliptical layout, with a daring groin vault, it shows excellent dominion of brickwork and masonry. Its domes are supported by ridge and vault ribbing, without using either concrete or iron reinforcement, thereby making it materially true to the principles of Classical Historicism.

Understood as a polemic against Modernist architecture, the layout of the large, complex set of buildings rejected the academic composition criteria of the *Beaux Arts* method and took up what the author interpreted as the tools and techniques of traditional Spanish architecture: scattering elements in a landscape, without symmetries or compositional axes, ordering them around squares and courtyards. The different parts of the whole are not standardised, but display their own character, with a close, but not closed relationship between construction and expression. The intensity of the polemic led the architect to use all the resources of traditional architecture in this vocational training centre. However, some modern techniques managed to slip in, especially those related to Expressionism. It is the masterpiece of Spanish 20th-c. Classicism and one of the best and most original examples of this style worldwide.

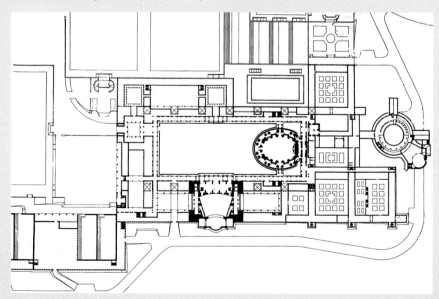

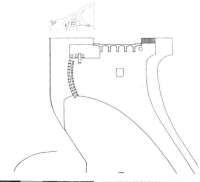

Electrical Power Plant 1953-54   O 17
Grandas de Salime
Vaquero Palacios

This power plant, with a reservoir dam and generator plant designed by Vaquero Palacios, is a masterpiece of engineering. The artist's talent for working in three dimensions was given freer rein here than in other projects. Endowed with the great formal intensity of Expressionism, built in reinforced concrete, and including a mural by Vaquero Turcios, Vaquero Palacios's son, the plasticity of the Grandas dam is illustrative of the close relationship between engineers and artists often observed in well-designed public works. The same architect also designed the power plants in Miranda (1958), Proaza (1964), Aboño (1969) and Tanes (Ríoseco, 1980, also with the help of his son), which are all important for their use of sculpture and painting.

Municipal Hall 1991-92   O 18
La Quintana. Nueva de Llanes
Diego Llaca

Exemplary of the new respect for regional architecture and included here as an example of Asturian Regionalism, this public building in Llanes is a small, sensitively designed work that fits into a traditional environment without having to compromise its modern identity to do so.

Market Building 1928-30   O 19
Alcalde Parrondo 5. Pola de Siero
Sánchez del Río [eng.]

Pola de Siero's market is the masterpiece of the great engineer, Sánchez del Río, who brought the use of reinforced concrete to the region. Although not a prolific designer, his intentions and quality put him on an equal footing with better known figures, such as Nervi, on an international level, or Torroja and Candela in Spain. The structure – great arches with delicate vaults of reinforced concrete – is spectacular. Expressionist and organic in style, the Pola de Siero market is not only attractive, but also shows the truly welcoming character that all public-service buildings should have. Sánchez del Río built it at the same time as he undertook other lesser works, like the urban canopy in Oviedo, popularly known as *El Paraguas* (the Umbrella).

BALEARIC ISLANDS

This archipelago is made up of five main islands – Majorca, Minorca, Ibiza, and the smaller Formentera and Cabrera – as well as several tiny isles. Each island has a different climate, vegetation, topography and history. Minorca is furthest N, relatively low-lying (max. alt.: 358 m), rainy (635 mm) and cooled by prevailing northerly winds. Majorca is more varied, with two ranges of hills (Puig Mayor is 1,445 m), a coastline broken up into bays, beaches and gulleys, low precipitation (450 mm) and long hours of sunshine. Ibiza is the furthest S, closest to the mainland, hilly but low-lying (Atalaiassa, 475 m), warm and dry, basking in almost constant sunshine. Typical vegetation grows abundantly in all of them. Their strategic position in the Middle Sea of the Ancient World has made them a crossroads, a refuge and a strategic objective over the last four thousand years, ever since a human culture began to produce the megalithic architecture of the *talayots* (watch towers), *navetas* (ancient burial chambers) and *taulas* (central altars). The islands have seen Phoenicians, Greeks, Carthaginians (a Golden Age for Ibiza), Romans (who founded the city of Palma and called the large island *Majorica*), Vandals, Byzantines, Muslims (whose engineering skills provided water technology and techniques for farming the rugged slopes)... James I of Aragón conquered them in 1229, initiating another era of prosperity which culminated in the 14th c., when the islands were a great trading centre, with 900 vessels, 30,000 sailors and cartographers of world-wide prestige. Later, in the 16th c., Berber and Turkish pirates forced the inhabitants to build walls and fortifications around their towns and to settle further inland, away from the coast. In the 18th c., Charles III granted special protection to the *xuetes* (Majorcan Jews) and generated new wealth in trade and farming. The architectural legacy of this era includes monumental buildings – La Lonja (15th c. merchants hall), the Gothic cathedral in Palma (14-16th c.), and the Castle (16th c.) in Ibiza – and noble Gothic and Renaissance houses (Palma), as well as vernacular buildings (villages, such as Deyá in Majorca and Ciudadela in Minorca) and cube-shaped, white and dry-stone houses in the countryside and in clusters (Sa Penya and Dalt Vila in the city of Ibiza and Puig de Missa in Santa Eularia d'en Riu). The islands constitute a political unit, an Autonomous Community with devolved government powers in many areas, but what really binds them together is tourism, their most lucrative trade. Back in the 19th c., the islands attracted intellectuals and artists (George Sand and Chopin in La Cartuja de Valldemosa, Archduke Ludwig Salvator of Austria who studied the islands and then settled in Majorca). In the 20th c., Churchill and other intrepid tourists discovered Formentor on Majorca. In the thirties, Ibiza served as refuge to Germans fleeing the Nazis, and its vernacular architecture attracted the Rationalist GATCPAC architects. But by the sixties, mass tourism began to transform the economy and the image of the islands. Tourist income made them richer (the richest province in the national ranking), but also plagued the coasts (especially of Majorca and Ibiza) with tourist facilities. Although parts of the coastline and the interior still conserve their old charm, some of the most beautiful seaviews were ruined. Architects such as Sert raised the alarm over this environmental disaster, but no policy was implemented to conserve the magnificent island scenery until the nineties, when building restrictions were imposed, existing eyesores given a facelift and infrastructure improved.

Extension: 5,014 km², archipelago in Western Mediterranean, 299 km av. distance from Iberian Peninsula. Climate: Mediterranean, varying between islands and zones. Population: 745,944. GDP: 148% of nat. av.

MAJORCA. This island offers a wide scope of possibilities in terms of natural landscape and different tourist attractions for its millions of visitors each year. Royalty, millionaires, and package tourists all flood in, some for a week of sea and sun and others to visit their second homes. Approximately 150,000 Germans have houses here – increasingly preferring typical island homes suitably fitted with mod cons –, as do Spanish and foreign film-, rock- and pop-stars in search of a place to get out of the public eye – looking for secluded luxury homes and quality decor. However, in general, the island's 20th c. architecture reflects its calling as a leading tourist resort worldwide (77% of its GDP). But although mass tourism, sixties-style led to the indiscriminate mass building of unaesthetic hotels and housing with the sole aim of packing in more people during the summer season, Domènech i Muntaner's design for the Gran Hotel Mallorca in 1903 also initiated a taste for attractive, tasteful hotels, which lived on in later projects, with the classical rehabilitation of old palaces (as in Son Vida), ancient towns (as in Puerto de Andraitx), noble houses (as in Deyá) and country houses (as in the road from Orient to Alaró), and with contemporary new designs that respect their privileged setting, as in the Punta Negra hotel, by Sánchez Cuenca (1965, on the road from Palma to Palma Nova, km 25) and produced some of the architectural successes covered in this section. In the nineties, architects of all nationalities have built homes for discerning clients (Hassan Fathy, the Alpha Bianca House, 1990; John Pawson, the Neuendorf House, 1996). Several decades before, at the turn of the century, the city of Palma de Mallorca, set around an open bay, was influenced by Catalan Modernism. In 1981, it started rehabilitating the historical

city centre, which had remained within the city walls from the time of James' I Christian Reconquest (1229) down to the 19th c., when some of the fortified walls were knocked down. Neither the Rationalism of the thirties (Juncosa and his contemporaries) nor the plans for urban reform and expansion (Alomar, 1943; Ribas i Piera, 1969-73) succeeded in substantially altering its mediaeval charm. Origin: Roman settlement, 123 BC. Rainfall: 90 days. Sunshine: 2,950 hrs. Population: 308,616.

Miró Studio 1954-55 PM 1
Joan Saridakis 29. **Palma de Mallorca**
Sert/Juncosa/Ochoa [eng.]
The painter employed great architects and engineers to build his studio. The outcome is a refined building, running down staggered stone terraces and set in a skin of ceramic elements and overhead windows. The space provides the light and fresh air necessary for painting.

Fénix Hotel 1957 PM 2
Paseo Marítimo. **Palma de Mallorca**
Gutiérrez Soto
This building was originally designed as an extension of the Victoria Hotel, requiring the rearrangement of the exterior spaces and the construction of an entirely new building to prolong the seafront parade along from an existing block. In 1980, it was turned into an apartment building.

Camilo Cela House 1961-62 PM 3
Francisco Vidal, Bonanova. **Palma de Mallorca**
Corrales/Molezún
The house was designed as a home for the
writer, Camilo Cela (1989 Nobel Prize for
Literature) and the editorial office of his
magazine, *Papeles de Son Armadans*. The
volumetrics were scaled into three clearcut
cuboids, cantilevered horizontally, in order
to afford sea views from all the rooms.

Reform of the Ronda PM 4
and Baluartes Promenades 1983-92
La Portella. **Palma de Mallorca**
Martínez Lapeña/Torres Tur
Rehabilitating different spaces is another
facet of the mastery shown by the architects
who designed the access stairway to Ibiza's
Castle. Their awareness of the setting and
the original buildings, which they modify but
do not alter, is exemplary.

Escarrer House 1985-88 PM 5
Son Vida. **Palma de Mallorca**
Martorell/Bohigas/MacKay
This 3,000 m^2 luxury residence is big enough
to contain references to Palladio, Lutyens,
the 19th c. Catalan Revival and MBM's own
architecture. A fascination for detail and the
expressive force of the materials reach their
apotheosis in a personal reinterpretation of
historical tradition.

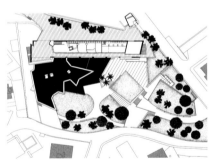

Joan and Pilar Miró Foundation 1987-92 PM 6
Joan de Saridakis 29, Son Abrines.
Palma de Mallorca
Moneo
Thirty years after Sert's refined design for
Miro's studio (see PM 1), the painter decided
to complete the "Miro Estate" in Palma with
his own foundation, which contains a study
centre and exhibition rooms. Here, Moneo
establishes a virtual relationship with the
surrounding landscape: a long parallelpiped,
which defines access ways and contains the
study centre, shuts off the view of the
immediate environment, now highly urban.
In the exhibition area, with its stark play of
volumes and shapes, the strong Mediterranean
light that filters through alabaster surfaces
creates a welcoming atmosphere. The
garden and the furrowed surfaces of the
brise-soleils contribute to further emphasise
the building's isolation from its context.

Ciudad Blanca Residential Estate 1961-63
Alcudia
Sáenz de Oíza. col.: Fullaondo

The last CIAM meetings saw the Team X win through with its efforts to "give a more human face" to Rationalist orthodoxy. Sáenz de Oíza was in close contact with this group, and its new principles served as one of the leitmotifs running through the design for this large 100-apartment tourist complex. The architect carefully studied the through-fare routes, the taxonomy of the public spaces, the sense of "community" and the visual interaction with the coastal landscape and used his findings as the foundation for a composition in which he also successfully avoided the risk of monotony by using a progressive shift in plan and section for the modular repetition of the cells. With this system, he managed to create a very special, authentic artificial landscape.

Hotel del Mar 1961-64
Paseo de Illetas 7, Illetas. **Calvià**
Coderch

With elements already tested in earlier designs (aggregation of parts, volumes set back and forward to produce a serrated profile in plan, wooden slats, ceramic cladding and blind surfaces), Coderch managed to build a hotel that was quite different from the other coastal hotels without substantially altering its capacity or scheme. The 8-storey building for rooms presents a virtually blind façade to the road running along the edge of the property. However, it is opened up to the coast in a zig-zag plan, the bedrooms being set back diagonally and protected from the sun by wooden lattice boards. The services use up two floors, which are adapted to the sloping terrain by terracing the storeys. The interiors were designed by Correa and Milà.

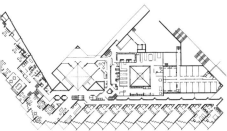

Manacor Hospital 1991-96
Ctra. Manacor-Alcudia s/n. **Manacor**
Fernández Alba, Angel

The architect articulated the complex and dense hospital programme in a compact composition, adding and concentrating the building's sections in a single unit. The small volumes placed around the large block of hospital units diminish the impact of the building on its surroundings.

Utzon House 1971-72 PM 10
Acantilado (by the cliff). **Porto Petro**
Utzon
The pure, elementary volumetrics typical of
Mediterranean architecture are interpreted
in a radically "archaic" manner in this house.
It is made up of four main bodies, set into
the rugged coastal landscape, right on the edge of a cliff, and linked up by a series of totally
inward-looking courtyards at the back. Halfway between the ancient megaron of the
Mycenaean palaces and the vernacular farmsteads of Majorca, Utzon's buildings are made of
local stone, including some of the furniture, which uses stone slabs. The living area is in
continuous relationship with the sea, which can always be glimpsed through the courtyards
and the porticos of the rectangular pilasters

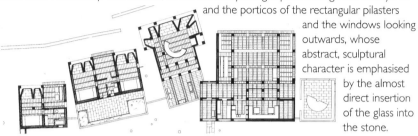

and the windows looking
outwards, whose
abstract, sculptural
character is emphasised
by the almost
direct insertion
of the glass into
the stone.

IBIZA. Ibiza's architectural wealth bears witness to the island's strong agricultural economy
(cereals, fruits and vegetables) and its strategic position in the Mediterranean. Colonised by
the Carthaginians in 7th c. BC, it remained under Roman rule for five centuries before
passing to Spanish Muslim hands from 901 to 1235. The capital's fortifications, the look-out
towers and the rural architecture fascinated the GATCPAC architects in the thirties, who saw
it as confirmation of their own Rationalist ideas in vernacular architecture: a spontaneous
balance between the clearcut lines that they espoused and the adaptation of design to the
climate and landscape, without any superimposed historical traditions. The island architecture
was made famous by Erwin Broner, a German architect fleeing from the Nazi regime, who
arrived there in 1933. Since then, successive generations of architects have been fascinated
by its buildings. Sert, deeply tied to the
island despite his time in the US, wished to
be buried in Ibiza. The sixties saw many
attempts at imitating the Ibizan style and
much of the more recent architecture maintains a strong relationship to the local vernacular. Origin: founded by Carthaginians as
Ebysos or *Ibosim*, 654 BC. Altitude: 9 m.
Rainfall: 300 mm and 65 days. Sunshine:
2,850 hrs. Temperatures: 32°-16° and 9°-
23° C. Population: 30,378.

Broner House 1960 IB 1
Travessía de Sa Penya 15. **Ibiza**
Broner
In the harbour area of Sa Penya, beneath
the fortress of Santa Lucía overlooking the
sea, this German architect built his home,
establishing a seemingly natural balance
between the simplicity of local Ibizan
architecture and the Modernist techniques
and vocabulary.

Reform of L'Hospitalet Church 1981 IB 2
Santa Faz, Dalt Vila. **Ibiza**
Martínez Lapeña/Torres Tur
The design created mechanisms to allow the
original building to be used both as a church
and as a forum for exhibitions and music:
the religious insignia are movable, the slate
floor is inset with small pieces of marble
where panel supports can be placed. The
shell modulates the intense sunlight.

Can Pep Simó Residential Estate 1965 IB 3
Cap Martinet. **Santa Eularia d'en Riu**
Sert
In the early sixties, Sert developed this truly
Ibizan estate, together with Rodríguez Arias
and Font Gorina. Six detached houses were
planned (one for Sert himself), an apartment
building and a common garden area and
swimming pool. The community bylaws
established the materials, colours, style and
landscaping to be used and authorised the
governing board to "access the site and
carry out such works as may be required to
restitute its aspect" should anything occur to
affect the overall appearance of the estate.
The design was generated by an iterative
methodology, articulating volumes on a
common scale throughout the length of a
path. The use of local materials and building
techniques refers to a long-standing Ibizan
tradition: dry-stone terracing to cling to the
slopes; flat roofs; whitewashed porches and
surfaces. Local plants and the absence of
fences or walls further integrate the estate
into the landscape. The appearance of
the whole is not so much the outcome of
holistic design specifications as of the formal
composition of a series of pieces. Gradually,
new houses were added to the estate,
including designs by Broner, Rodríguez Arias,
Illescas and, more recently, Martínez Lapeña
and Torres Tur (see IB 4).

Gili House 1985-87 IB 4
Can Pep Simó. **Santa Eularia d'en Riu**
Martínez Lapeña/Torres Tur
Located on the edge of the Can Pep Simó
Estate, the house's outer walls shape the
development of the building plan. They mark
the boundaries, protect and model the views,
and elevate and organise the distribution of
the house, which has much in common with
Coderch's Ugalde house (see B 108).

More on Ibiza. Amongst the public works in Ibiza, of special interest is the Island Health Centre, built in 1991 by Basterra, Canalis and Llinás on Vía Romana 81, to house the Department of Health and Social Security, whose simple volumetrics are well suited to the urban environment around it.

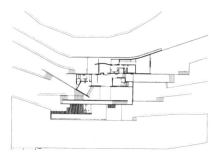

Boenders House 1979-83   IB 5
Camí de Benimussa, Can Portes. **San Antonio**
Martínez Lapeña/Torres Tur
With a deep understanding of vernacular Ibizan architecture, the architects planned this holiday house, surrounded by pine-woods, on the basis of successive terraces, which the house itself then incorporates. Modelled on the traditional stone terracing found in rural settlements throughout the island, the terraces are turned into load-bearing walls, articulating the zig-zag layout inside the house, which in turn opens it to the landscape outside: the gentle slope of a mountain with splendid views over the sea and the San Antonio Bay. The multiplicity of accessways and the lack of definite boundary markings further emphasise the house's relationship to its rural surroundings. The swimming pool, reminiscent of a spark-ling channel for running water, is located at the lowest point in the site. The house is built simply, with a taste for perfectionism that serves as the theme tune for all its architects' works, adding value and meaning to all its different spaces.

MINORCA. Conquered by Rome in 122 BC, it was taken by the Vandals (427), then Byzantium (554). Under Spanish Muslim rule, its capital was in Ciudadela. When Alfonso III of Aragón reconquered it for Christianity, he settled it with Catalans and Aragonese. The Treaty of Utrecht passed the island to the British, who held it as their main Mediterranean sea base throughout most of the 18th c. until 1802. For strategic reasons, the British established the capital in Mahón, on a natural bay, and left a legacy of architecture with clear references to Palladio. During the Civil War, it held out as a Republican stronghold until February 1939, which explains the lack of investment in public works under the subsequent rule of General Franco. However, light industries have provided it with a sound economic base, allowing it to remain closed to mass tourism, becoming a focal point and holiday home for Spanish architects and publishers, rather than foreign masses. Interesting contemporary architecture includes the Francés house, in El Fanduco, Mahón Port (1976), by Circi and Bonet. Rainfall: 120 days. Sunshine: 2,700 hrs. Temperatures: 31°-15° and 7°-23° C. Population: 23,097.

Law Courts 1992-96   ME 1
Santa Eulalia s/n. **Mahón**
Navarro Baldeweg
The architect solved the public character of this parallelepiped volume through the use of vernacular building techniques – rubble wall-ing, dubbing out walls and small openings – which also integrate it into its surroundings.

CANARY ISLANDS

The six islands and seven bigger isles of the Canaries, Spain's tropical paradise, are located in the Atlantic Ocean, close to the Tropic of Cancer, 1,100 km SW of the Iberian Peninsula and 115 km from the African coast. They are divided into two provinces, Las Palmas (including Gran Canaria, Lanzarote and Fuerteventura) and Santa Cruz de Tenerife (including Tenerife, Gomera, La Palma and Hierro), which together form the Autonomous Community. Volcanic in origin, the archipelago is so extreme that it is easiest to refer to it as a miniature continent in which the landscape ranges from desert to thick woods of conifers and sabine trees typical of the Tertiary Era, and from the highest peak in Spain, the Teide (3,718 m) to long sandy beaches. The *Guanche* natives lived in a Neolithic Age culture when they were taken over under the reign of Isabella I of Castile, as her kingdom stretched out westwards between 1483 and 1496. Canary architecture has been influenced by the landscape, which has given a special touch to the different stylistic movements. The 20th c. architecture has also been affected by the economic development in the archipelago: in the twenties, the banana became the staple cash crop, traded from the large ports of Las Palmas de Gran Canaria and Santa Cruz de Tenerife, obligatory stopping places for the main sea-routes of the time. Later, in the sixties, the influx of money from the tourist boom, as holidays became a form of leisure for Europeans, meant building up much of the empty land on Gran Canaria, Tenerife and Lanzarote. The archipelago architecture has also been affected by the cosmopolitan character of the islands. The European avant-garde made its presence felt in the island through the charismatic journal *Gaceta de Arte*, published in Tenerife until the Civil War, with contributions from such influential figures as Breton, Picasso and Le Corbusier, and with articles discussing the ideas of movements such as Surrealism, Purism and De Stijl, the Bauhaus and Soviet Constructivism. The Rationalism of the Canaries in the thirties and forties was perceived as relevant throughout Spain, for it stood alongside Madrid and Barcelona as a focal point for a large group of architects, including Martín Fernández de la Torre in Gran Canaria and Marrero, Blasco, Pisaca and Hardisson in Santa Cruz de Tenerife. In the sixties, the hotels and housing developed to accommodate the influx of tourism was deeply influenced by Brutalist and Organicist experiments. In 1962, the international competition of ideas for the Maspalomas Costa Canaria development was held to plan the future tourist resort on the sandy beaches of S Gran Canaria and served to set up the guidelines for the zoning throughout the island. Meanwhile, individual housing estates were defined by local architects, such as Manuel de la Peña, who created several tourist complexes and works such as the Albergue Arinaga (1963-66) in Agüimes, Gran Canaria, and Díaz Llanos and Saavedra in Tenerife. Although the profession was enhanced by the new School of Architecture in Las Palmas (1968-69), the last two decades of the 20th c. have seen both good and poor architecture and no clear tendency to speak of. Young architects are emerging, however, whose high-quality designs show their concern for expressing and understanding the local context – see TF 8 and TF 10 by Artengo, Ménis and Pastrana, or their San Agustín Hall of Residence (1989-93) in La Laguna, and the San Clemente Apartment Building (1990-92) in Santa Cruz de Tenerife.

Geography: 7,479 km², very varied. Climate: predominantly dry, 20° C average annual temperature, with 6° yearly variation and 8° daily variation. Population: 1,637,641. GDP: 101% of nat. av.

LAS PALMAS DE GRAN CANARIA. The city of Las Palmas (N of the island of Gran Canaria), conquered by Juan Rejón in 1478, is set on a small sandy isthmus and a tiny peninsula, La Isleta (literally the little island). The old town was located to the S, on an estuary, but has shifted N towards the isthmus where, at the end of the 19th c., Puerto de La Luz was located, the biggest port in this part of the Atlantic, which has injected much dynamism into the local economy. Town planning (see GC 4) and architecture from the twenties to the fifties was dominated by Rationalism, through the work of the local architect, Miguel Martín-Fernández de la Torre, who designed the Ciudad Jardín gardened city as well as several public and private buildings. In the last years of the 20th c., there has been a highly speculative environment, with heterodox contributions from architects linked with the School of Architecture, such as F.J. Bordes and M.L. González. Population: 384,877.

Provincial Psychiatric Hospital 1930-32   GC 1
Hoya del Parrado 2, Ctra. Marzagán
Martín Fernández de la Torre
The pavilions are symmetrically articulated along a main axis along which the different architectural parts are placed. Two of the pavilions in the main access way have overtones of certain Dutch Rationalist designs. The main buildings are simple prisms with horizontal bands of sliding windows.

Parque Hotel 1931-36   GC 2
Muelle de Las Palmas 2 and 4
Martín Fernández de la Torre
This complex occupies an entire city block, making a significant contribution to defining the surrounding urban landscape in a key part of the city: San Telmo Park. The 8-storey rectangular volume is distributed with two groups of 4 apartments in the head-walls and the actual hotel in the centreline.

Speth House 1932-34   GC 3
Rosales 4, Tafira
Martín Fernández de la Torre/Oppel
The house is constructed on large horizontal planes linked up by wooden enclosure structures that form large shaded areas. The programme is laid out with the main rooms looking towards the W, below the eaves, and the access and service areas looking towards the E.

Urban Planning of Las Palmas de Gran Canaria and the Garden City 1922-38

Martín Fernández de la Torre

In 1922, Mesa y López, then Mayor of the city, commissioned the architect to draw up an urban plan. At that time the city had two main focal points: the historical city centre (districts of Vegueta and Triana, on either side of the Guiniguada Gully) and the La planned a new kind of urban development consisting of low-density detached houses with gardens and roadways designed with picturesque criteria to include cul-de-sacs and trident-shaped road layouts that make the place much more of an upper-middle

Luz Harbour (districts of La Isleta and Las Canteras), on the extremes of a long coastal strip between the ocean and the mountains. For eight years, Martín designed the roads and infrastructures needed for urban growth: seaside boulevards, avenues running N-S and perpendicular streets. The flexible design respected the old layout but also established and consolidated the different neighbourhoods that were springing up in the urban environment. One of the most important of these in the history of Canarian urbanism is the Ciudad Jardín (1937), placed between the historical city centre and the La Luz Harbour. English influence meant the inhabitants of Gran Canaria were attuned to the ideas of Unwin and Howard's garden city. Working along similar lines to those laid down in Letchworth or Hampstead, Martín

class residential estate than a solution for low-income bracket housing. The development contains many Rationalist buildings (see GC 6), making it comparable to the Colonia El Viso in Madrid (see M 41), with more than a hundred designs by Martín himself, including the Santa Catalina Clinic [2] (now much changed). The architect also acted as the developer of a complex of 35 medium-sized houses in a specific sector, known as the Colonia Icot [3] (1937). This estate contains many references to the German *Siedlungen:* low-rise housing set in generous gardens with ample open spaces whose architecture follows the principles of the Central-European Rationalism as known through the journals of the time. There are two kinds of housing: terraced houses and semi-detached houses on the corners. All of them are determinedly simple, with clearcut volumes and no concessions to decorative principles, reflecting the formal and ethical repertoire of Ernst May's proposals for the suburbs of the Nidda Valley in Frankfurt.

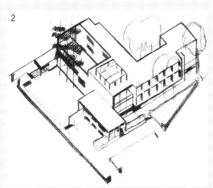

2

3

Cabildo Insular Building 1932-38   GC 5
Bravo Murillo 23 c/v Pérez Galdós
Martín Fernández de la Torre/Laforet
The Island Government Building is perhaps the most important Rationalist work on the Canary Islands, recognised throughout Spain as a masterpiece of the movement. Its dramatic volumetric composition in a focal area establishes a clear distinction between the historical centre and the expansions already beginning in the thirties (see GC 4). The building's impact is enhanced by its location in a busy corner, from which three avenues fork out, trident-form. The design exploits the visual potential of the corner setting and establishes a radical break with the traditional forms of urban aggregation. The clearcut volumes, without concessions to unnecessary decorative details, are in no way related to the alignment of the surrounding buildings. The government building consists of a lower corpus, whose recessed building joinery emphasises its horizontal lines. A more massive prismatic volume is set symmetrically above, topped by a tower set back from the building line, which acts as an urban reference point. The tower also establishes a dialogue with the spires of the cathedral, in an attempt to clearly articulate the new city layout. The entrance is to the side, through a small square that serves as a base to the building, set back from the building line on the road, in a solution that allows visitors to enjoy a sense of directionality in their entrance and to fully appreciate the architecture and the idea of progress it is intended to represent.

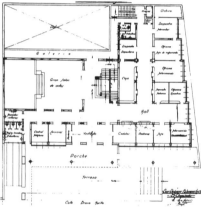

Ley-Lenton House 1932-33   GC 6
León y Castillo 295, Ciudad Jardín
Martín Fernández de la Torre
This detached 2-storey house is located at one end of the garden city (see GC 4) and opposite the sea. The use of sweeping horizontal planes in its composition allows for the creation of generous terraces that take advantage of the magnificent views over the Las Alcaravaneras beach.

Other Works. Miguel Martín Fernández de la Torre's enormous productivity — hundreds of projects of different scales, from town planning to furniture design — has left its mark in Las Palmas and the surrounding areas. The city bears clear signs of his presence in many architectural gems, including cinemas, public buildings and houses, such as the Juan Domínguez house in Lope de Vega 10, in Tafira, or the Quevedo house on Tomás Quevedo.

Vega House 1932-33   GC 7
Rosales 2, Monte Lentiscal, Tafira Alta
Martín Fernández de la Torre/Oppel
The shape of this house results from the symmetrical placing of several prisms that intersect and perforate each other with horizontal strips of sliding windows and breaks in the edge lines. The studied joinery in the pergolas, balconies and exterior doors makes it a work of purist aesthetics.

Shell STAIBS Building 1933-36   GC 8
Eduardo Benot 11
Martín Fernández de la Torre
The dynamic composition of this small office building between party walls, with a façade overlooking the harbour, is defined by the horizontality and open plan of the interior spaces, which are all focussed on the views. The building is set off with a canopy that acts as support to an advertising display.

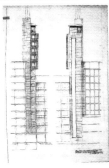

Casa del Marino Building 1958-63   GC 9
León y Castillo 322
Martín Fernández de la Torre
A unique architectural solution successfully tackles the difficult location and complex use patterns of this building that combines housing, offices, cultural and service areas. The different spatial elements are combined in a single reconstituted unity articulated around the main tower containing lifts and stairs, which manages to fit cleverly into the triangular shape of the site. The principal access space, under a canopy that borders the entire building to the W, deserves special attention. In an original flourish, the volumetric unity thus defined is once again fragmented by the application of different vocabularies to the different façades. This creates surprising formal variety and has overtones of certain Latin-American architects working at the end of the fifties.

Petrol Station 1956   GC 10
Tomás Morales c/v Senador Castillo Olivares
Suárez Valido
This small office building with a petrol station on the ground floor takes advantage of a unique location, on the angle between two streets, to make a statement of Expressionist style that was the first sign of Modernism making its comeback in the Canary Island archipelago following the Civil War.

Atlantic Centre of Modern Art 1988-89   GC
Balcones 8, Vegueta
Sáenz de Oíza
Behind a conserved Neo-classical façade, the reform has opened up a rich interior exhibition space, focussed around traditional Canary Island courtyards. Using a clearly contemporary language, the courtyard design establishes a central volume that organises the routing and the views.

Tafira University Campus 1990-   GC I
Tafira
Standing under a grove of palm trees, this campus is a successful attempt to conjugate conservation of the agricultural environment with the needs of the university, favouring high-quality planning and individual buildings of special merit. Behind the Brutalist School of Architecture, by Bordes and Juárez (1979-83) and the Computing and Mathematics Department (1988-91) by the well-known member of the Tendenza, Gianugo Polesello, and Palem, Martínez Santa María built the University Library (1990-95), which won the National Architecture Award. Navarro Baldeweg planned the Legal and Economic Sciences area, which consists of several buildings with lecture rooms (1992-96, photograph), departmental buildings, etc., where he tried to articulate the common spaces, especially the library and the main hall.

Alfredo Kraus Auditorium 1985-97   GC I
Av de Las Canteras s/n, Las Arenas
Tusquets/Díaz
The use of massive stone walls in this imposing building next to the sea is clearly reminiscent of the old defensive ramparts of past ages. In the auditorium's main concert hall, an enormous picture window opens up directly on to the sea behind the main podium.

Regional Government Building 1990-97   GC I
Av. Marítima
González García
This three-block complex integrates offices, facilities and a hotel. The large covered atrium that organises the different circulation flows acts as an ambiguous transition area between the outside and the inside, where the textures, colours, and technological solutions have all received special attention.

LANZAROTE. This is an island of spectacular volcanic scenery (the last big eruptions took place in 1730 and 1824), with craters, fields of lava known as *malpaís* and ashes, on which agriculture sprung up, making economic use of the scarce water available and protecting the plants and crops from the dry NE wind with stone walls that made their imprint on the landscape, especially in the La Geria area of the island. The volcanic scenery is at its most dramatic in the National Timanfaya Park, with the Fire Mountains, *montañas de fuego*, located 28 km from Arrecife. The onslaught of mass tourism at the beginning of the seventies radically transformed the island's life style, but its effects have been kept in check under the ecology-

conscious leadership of the renowned artist and landscape architect, César Manrique, working with other architects determined to save the land-scape (see LZ 3). 8 km NE of the capital is Costa Teguise, a new international resort named after the old capital of the island, with the Guanapay Castle (16th c.) standing right on the edge of an extinct vol-cano. Population: 88,475.

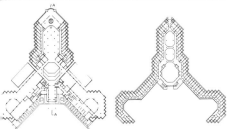

Las Salinas Hotel 1973-77 LZ 1
Av. Islas Canarias s/n. **Costa Teguise**
Higueras/Manrique
A hotel of this size and on such a privileged location – the coastal plane right next to the sea – required a singular architecture. The design revolves around a main line of symmetry, like a rhythmic variation on an octagonal honeycomb, that uses the room as the basic unit. The varied repetition establishes multiple combinations of open spaces that create a very direct relationship between the inside and outside of the hotel. The vertical tapering of the building facilitates its integration with the surround-ing landscape, whilst the virtuoso work with reinforced concrete defines generous spaces in which the tropical plants so typical of the Canary Islands can bloom. The landscaping is the work of the multi-skilled artist, César Manrique.

National Timanfaya Park LZ 2
Visitors Centre 1989-93
Abarca/Cano/Cano/Corella/Cosín/Fariña
The building is subtly shaped out of white planes and pure volumes, creating an elegant filigree that stands out against the black craggy rockscape of lava. The main space is the exhibition hall, around which other lesser volumes are set for the different service areas.

**Landscaping Treatment
of Lanzarote** 1968-1989
Manrique et al.

The Canarian artist, César Manrique, who had always wanted to conserve the beauty of the island's landscape, exerted great influence over the changes that this unique volcanic area underwent from the sixties to the nineties. Both his aesthetic training and his personal relationship with the volcanic island have contributed to imbue the local

people with an unusual sense of environment, the island architecture being characterised by maximum respect towards nature, with new buildings being modelled on vernacular works. The set of projects in which César Manrique received unstinted support from the local government and cooperation from other architects and engineers, such as E. Cáceres and F. Higueras, has turned the island into a living collective work of art. Apart from the "low-profile" architecture dotted all over the island, the most significant works that Lanzarote spearheaded in the sixties and seventies began with Manrique's own residence in Tahíche (6 km N of Arrecife, now the César Manrique Foundation[2]), in which the set of spaces that made up his home and studio (1968) are half-buried in the lava scenery, while the tropical plants and volcanic nooks and crannies are used to enhance the volumes that pay homage to the popular architecture of the area. These criteria anticipate the aesthetic ideas behind his later interventions on the island. The Timanfaya Restaurant[1], the reconditioning of the Jameos del Agua, a volcanic grotto with a seawater lagoon (30 km NE of Arrecife), the Mirador de la Batería del Río (20 km N of Arrecife) look-out point and the refurbishment of the San José castle in Arrecife for use as the Museum of Contemporary Art[3] were all undertaken between 1970 and 1974, establishing a paradigm of Lanzarote as a tourist area that conserves existing environmental conditions. This initial stage was marked by concern for integration, altering natural spaces as little as possible and searching to make new buildings fit in with their surroundings. This stage was characterised by the abundant presence of lush vegetation and contrasting colours, as well as the use of local materials (volcanic stone or aged wood). The projects of the second stage, as the El Almacén cultural centre, the recovery of the Charco de San Ginés (both 1984) and the Guatiza cactus garden (1989), however, do not show such a powerful sense of design, and are perhaps contaminated by a certain amount of triteness that, unfortunately, belies the driving intensity of the earlier decade.

TENERIFE. The island is characterised by the orography around the high Teide Peak, now a protected area (the Cañadas del Teide National Park), lush and wet on the N side and drier on the S. To the NE is the conurbation of La Laguna (117,718 inhabitants) and Santa Cruz de Tenerife (202,674 inhabitants), with their old city centre and port, respectively, which has developed fast in the 20th c. The Rationalist architecture, although in evidence, is less important than in Gran Canaria, the outcome of a more conservative view of society, where a certain Eclectical character was imprinted upon the purist principles of the avant-garde. Nonetheless, there are several residential buildings of interest, such as the Schwartz house (1936), on Severo Ochoa 13, by Marrero. In the seventies, there was strong architectural renovation, when architects such as Henríquez, Díaz Llanos and Saavedra went back to reassess the assumptions of Brutalism in their works. At the end of the century, young local architects, such as Artengo, Menis and Pastrana have been working with geological characteristics – see their natural pool on the El Guincho Coast (1988), 62 km S – and outsiders have begun to design important buildings, such as the Trade Fair Grounds of Tenerife, by Calatrava (1992-96).

Círculo Mercantil Trade Hall 1932 TF 1
Pza. de Candelaria 6
Marrero

This prize-winning design used a steel frame structure and different prefab elements of artificial stone to give the hall what can be classified as a stark Classical look from the outside. Its tower, however, was specifically designed to establish a significant dialogue with the other surrounding buildings.

Cabildo Insular Building 1933-50 TF 2
Pza. de España s/n
Marrero

The building tried to impose order in the sea front, establishing guidelines that could be used in the city's expansion. The layout is based on a double bay design in which the offices are placed next to the façade and an interior courtyard is articulated within three surrounding monumental volumes.

Lecuona Building 1933-36 TF 3
Robayna c/v Méndez Núñez
Marrero

This building is organised on 4 storeys with 11 apartments. The design takes advantage of the corner site to make a stylistic exercise whose composition follows the Expression-ist models of Mendelsohn, emphasising the horizontal elements and setting them against the clearly defined edges.

Marrero House and Studio 1933   TF 4
San Francisco 5 (Glorieta Arquitecto Marrero)
Marrero
The ground floor is used as the architect's office, while the other two floors are taken up by two independent apartments. In the centre of the façade are some terraces oriented towards the harbour; adjacent to them the service rooms. The architect also designed his furniture in the *Art Déco* style.

Architects' Chamber   TF 5
of the Canary Islands 1968-71
Rambla del General Franco 123
Díaz Llanos/Saavedra
Conceived as a multiple service complex, the building formed part of a town planning exercise, opening up the most important road from the city to the mountains. The use of reinforced concrete enabled the architects to create a container for extremely generous spaces and achieve a high degree of complexity in the construction, which is translated into a sophisticated version of Brutalist aesthetics. The building is organised around the tower for the lifts and stairs, which is hooked onto the different spaces and volumes. The main office block is on the ground level; the auditorium and access to the exhibition hall under the square at mezzanine basement level; and the material testing laboratory in the basement.

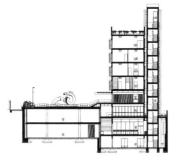

Multi-Tiered Housing 1969   TF 6
Urb. Ifara
Henríquez
Set on a difficult topographical site, the lay-out uses a 4 x 4 m construction module which is open to multiple combinations, creating homes of up to 120 m². The volumes are set to guarantee privacy, whilst at the same time providing impressive views, optimally oriented with relation to the sun.

Head Offices of Caja Canarias 1979-83   TF 7
Pza. del Patriotismo
Artengo/Domínguez Anadón/Schwartz
The complex is organised in two volumes: the high one houses the administration areas of the bank, whilst the low-rise is divided into two sectors, with the trading floor and the meeting and exhibition rooms separated by a small square. A certain monumentality in the architecture adds to the bank's image.

Petrol Station 1981 TF 8
Acceso Mercatenerife, Pol. Costa Sur
Artengo/Martín Menis/Rodríguez Pastrana
This small industrial building was constructed according to a clearcut programme. The Minimalist canopy, the clear reference to oil derricks in the towers and the integration of the corporate image into the overall design all add to the masterly simplicity with which the station defines its space.

Hovercraft Station 1986-91 TF 9
Muelle Norte
Martínez/Pérez Amaral/Corona
The renovation of the old fish market is now the new gateway to the city. The building is linearly organised following a strict grid construction to establish a clear exchange between the urban access ways and the embarkation jetties. A unique bow roof marks the sea front.

Ana Bautista Sports Centre 1988-93 TF 10
Alvarez de Lugo s/n
Artengo/Martín Menis/Rodríguez Pastrana
This pavilion for rhythmic gymnastics stands in a key part of the city. The composition is based on an S-shaped section in the laminated wood structure, which attenuates the necessary building volume. The delicacy of the building solutions is, perhaps, the centre's most outstanding feature.

Industrial Premises 1988-91 TF 11
Cruce del Porís de Abona. **Arico**
García Barba
A small industrial building in a semi-desert landscape close to the coast, its austerity and its delicate sensitivity to the climate and the landscape are of great impact. A rectangular volume houses the technical facilities at ground level, whilst the management and services are at mezzanine level.

Ramón y Cajal / Vintersol Centre 1962-66 TF 12
Av. de Suecia 11, Los Cristianos. **Arona**
Díaz Llanos/Saavedra
This small clinic stands in an isolated spot on the coast, next to an old fishing village. The residential and service areas are ordered around a generous solarium with two pools. The architecture is deeply rooted in Le Corbusier's ideas, as evidenced in the way it links up the interior and exterior spaces.

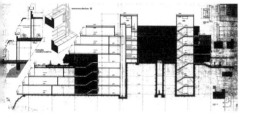

Ten-Bel Hotel and Apartments 1970-72 TF 13
Costa del Silencio. **Arona**
Díaz Llanos/Saavedra

The creation of the first tourist resort on the S of the island enabled the architects to apply theoretical principles elaborated for the Maspalomas international competition of ideas (Gran Canaria). With clear deference to the latest CIAM and the contributions of Team X, the Ten-Bel estate is structured on a main ring road for motor traffic, to which independent, low-density residential units and pedestrian throughways are gradually connected. These, along with careful respect towards existing landscape and plant life have provided an exemplary model of how ecotourism can make for attractive holiday towns. The architects also experimented in different typologies coming from roots as disparate as the suburban complexes of Utzon and the North African *casbahs*.

Housing Estate 1984 TF 14
Av. de Los Majuelos, Taco. **La Laguna**
Cabrera Domínguez/Febles

In response to the widespread phenomenon of self-built houses in this area, the local administration set up this estate with a set of designer houses that provide alternatives to the uncontrolled spread. The estate is established around a wealth of open spaces according to Rationalist principles.

Social Housing 1988 TF 15
El Gramal, Pol. del Rosario. **La Laguna**
Sosa/Gutiérrez

This complex consists of 33 terraced houses in two rows on a single urban block. The intelligent solution of the plan was based on a close study of the general layout, to establish housing along Rationalist principles which, nevertheless, continue incorporating the Mediterranean courtyard.

Science and Cosmos Museum 1989-93 TF 16
Vía Láctea c/v Av. de los Menceyes. **La Laguna**
Garcés/Sòria

This small interactive museum belongs to the Canary Islands Astrophysics Institute. Access to the 2-storey building is through the upper floor, from a plaza that acts as the roof. The main areas are located in the mezzanine basement floor, around a large ovaloid hall reminiscent of an exploding star.

CANTABRIA

This Autonomous Community comprising a single province, Santander, formed part of Castile until the eighties. Its ports – Santander and San Vicente de la Barquera – exported Castile's wool to the Netherlands from the 13th c. and handled most of the kingdom's commerce up to the 17th c. The early Cantabrians were mountain people who put up famous resistence against the Romans until Augustus' victory ended the war of 29-19 BC. Millennia before, its inhabitants painted the world-famous Paleolithic cave paintings of Altamira (near the Mediaeval town of Santillana del Mar), which will be exhibited in the museum Navarro Baldeweg is building. Cantabria's lush, verdant valleys provide grazing land for livestock, while Santander and Torrelavega are active urban centres, working in several industries: dairy, chemicals, iron and steel, and shipbuilding. A popular retreat for the 18th c. nobility and a prosperous area throughout the 19th c. (which brought Catalan artists such as Gaudí to the small town of Comillas, full of vernacular architecture), the province generated a tradition of grandiose stone houses. Eminently conservative, the architectural panorama was dominated by Eclecticism. Rucabado's dreams of a national architecture based on mountain tradition, which also found followers in the Basque country, left its mark. In the thirties, this conservative tendency hampered the creative freedom of architects attuned to the Modernist movement, among them Lastra, and after the Civil War, it dominated reconstruction, with strong influences emanating from Madrid.
Geography: 5,299 km², in a strip of land between the Cantabrian Mountains and the Bay of Biscay. Climate: humid and moderate. Rainfall: 1,100 mm and 217 days. Sunshine: 1,775 hrs. Population: 530,281. GDP: 91% of nat. av.

SANTANDER. Splendidly located on a south-facing slope with views over the bay as well as the mountains, this city is the lieu of the Architecture Biennial, a meeting place for music-lovers and a centre for university summer courses. The original fishing village, set around the old abbey and the port, spread upwards over the top of the hills around the bay and wrestled land from the sea. Expansion in the 19th c. created its now famous promenade, the Paseo Pereda. Royal summer visits during the first quarter of the century brought big architectural commissions, such as the Banco de España building, by Martínez del Valle and Yámoz (1924-25) and the development of the El Sardinero area, consolidated into the city limits in the seventies. Much of the old quarter has been rebuilt after the fire in 1941. Origin: Port of San Emeterio, 11th c. Temperatures: 26°-13° and 7°-18° C. Population: 196,218.

Apartment Building 1930   S 1
Fernández de Isla 27 c/v Pza. Juan Carlos I
Lastra
Lastra used the graded city building, in the style of Sauvage in Paris, to resolve the street front and the corner onto the square. The dynamic volumetrics, with projecting vertical elements, are enriched with a purified Rationalist language and the treatment of the joineries and metal mouldings.

Siboney Building 1931-32   S 2
Av. Castelar c/v Paseo Pereda c/v J. de la Cosa
Marrero
Along with Miguel Martín-Fernández de la
Torre and Richard Oppel, Marrero formed
part of the remarkable group of pre-Civil
War architects from the Canary Islands. In
this design, an exception outside the islands
where he normally worked, the building
takes up an entire city block and is placed
facing the bay, its shape suggesting a ship,
with references to Expressionist vocabulary.
The emphatic horizontalness of the
openings is moulded with sculpted curving
elements, set into the two planes of the
façade. Two intermediate semi-cylinders
bring order to the elevation. The curving
corners mark the front limit of the work and
introduce a dimension of continuous
volume suggested by the dynamic rotating
image, accentuated in the upper cylinders.

Sailing Club 1934   S 3
Malecón de Puertochico s/n
Bringas
Following the modern metaphor of the ship
building with a nearby precedent in the San
Sebastián Club (see SS 1), Bringas anchors
the building in the bay and creates two
façades: one, opaque and volumetric, faces
the city; the other, light, transparent with
horizontal terraces, looks towards the bay.

Office Building 1987   S 4
Pasaje de Peña, Pza. de San José Ruano and
Jesús del Monasterio
Bayón
This block is formed by an older building, to
which additional storeys have been added,
and a layered block with a concave wall
facing, articulated by a glazed passageway.
The other façades, of heavy stone, are
broken by regular openings.

Olano House 1957   S 5
La Rabia, 5.5 km from **Comillas**
Coderch/Valls
Successfully transferring their Mediterranean
model to the Cantabrian landscape, the
architects juxtapose two pentagonal pieces,
accompanied by a line of walls that enclose
the courtyard. The main part opens onto the
landscape through a beautiful perimetral
terrace built of wood and metal.

Casa de la Lluvia (Rain House) 1978-82   S 6
Navarro House, Alto de La Hermosa,
Ctra. de La Hermosa. **Lierganes**
Navarro Baldeweg

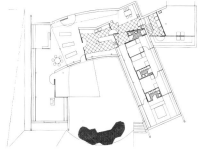

The architect's first work, widely written
up in architectural literature, the Rain house
is located in the small country village of
Lierganes (28 km from Santander), which
still conserves its noble houses. Navarro
constructed a summer house with a
U-shaped plan opening to the valley. The
building is organised on formal, functional
lines that can be best seen in the volumetric
solution of the roof. Stone, glass and zinc
are horizontally stratified in the façades,
with slight alterations that emphasise the
entrance ways and open up the view.
The imaginative design and clever use of
materials, reminiscent of de la Sota, anticipate
a new sensitivity which Navarro exploits in
later works.

Parish Church 1957   S 7
Pza. de Baldomero Iglesias. **Torrelavega**
Moya

The spatial and structural model inspired in
late-Romanesque and Baroque architecture
used by Moya in his previous churches
(see O 16 and M 52) acquires new meaning
in the Torrelavega parish church both in
regard to its construction and the way it is
fitted into the surrounding landscape. Moya
designed the crypt eliptically. The cupola
soars above it, with its central dome eye
and very elaborate vault ribbed with brick
segmental arches, which rest on a wall
articulated with pilasters. Spatial uniformity
is manipulated by the tension introduced in
the axes, accesses, chapel and main altar.

The architect used complex volumetrics
to resolve the presence of the church in
the square and on the alley. The main
elevation was resolved by superimposing
an independent façade. All in all, this is "a
church that is unique in modern European
religious architecture" (Antón Capitel),
surprisingly little known by the general
public.

Other Works. Also of interest in Torrelavega is the Ceferino Calderón building block, by
Lorenzo and Calatayud (1956). It is a worthy example of a project done in the years when
Spain was still cut off from the international scene. In Santander, the Cantabria Festival Hall by
Sáenz de Oíza (1988-91), well-situated on Gamazo street with a view to the bay, continues to
elicit contradictory interpretations amongst experts.

CASTILE AND LEON

Castile and León, on the Castilian meseta through which the River Duero runs, is the largest Autonomous Community in Spain, and probably the richest and most varied in terms of its historical architecture. It is also the heart of Spain, historically, aesthetically and culturally. It was created by joining together the province of León with the eight provinces of Old Castile – Avila, Burgos, Palencia, Salamanca, Segovia, Soria, Valladollid and Zamora – and covers approximately the same area as the old kingdoms of Castile and León. As early as the 8th c. there was a royal court in the city of León, so when Count Fernán González won his independence from the Leonese king and started building castles (castillos) all over the meseta in the 10th c., he little dreamed that he was providing the foundations and the name (Castilla) of what would become the largest kingdom in the peninsula, a European power and the nucleus for one of the first ever nation states, formed out of the union of Castile under Queen Isabella I and Aragón under her husband, Ferdinand I. Indeed, in the 16th and 17th c., several towns, such as Valladolid under Philip III, were royal courts, and the region was a world superpower, one of the largest empires in history. Castile and León contains important remnants and monuments from Roman culture (León, Astorga, Segovia....), a comprehensive range of Mozarabic architecture, as well as a varied collection of Romanesque (with magnificent churches, abbeys and cathedrals, as in Zamora and the old Salamanca cathedral), Gothic (splendid cathedrals in León and Burgos), Late Gothic and Early Renaissance (Segovia cathedral and the new Salamanca cathedral), High Renaissance (including Juan de Herrera's Valladolid cathedral), Baroque, Neo-Classical and Academic architecture, although the importance of the former categories rather outshines that of the later ones. Academic architecture gave way to the Eclecticism and Historicism, which prevailed in the intensive renovation of the housing stock and of civil and institutional buildings, triggered off by the economic boom throughout Spain in the last third of the 19th c. This was another period of (albeit relative) splendour, with buildings such as Gaudí's famous Episcopal Palace in Astorga and his savings bank building, the Caja de Ahorros, in León. Until the thirties, Eclecticism lived alongside the incipient Modern architecture of the architects, Torbado and Cañas in León, Gil González in Salamanca (as in the building located on Zamora 83 c/v Plaza San Marcos, 1935), Carrasco Muñoz in Valladolid (the Trade Union Housing Project on Málaga street, 1937) and in Zamora (the block on Núñez de Balboa, 1939), among others. However, the best 20th c. buildings were constructed after the Civil War, when Modern architecture definitively established its supremacy over the Late Historicism of the forties. The buildings were nearly always designed by architects practicing in Madrid, some born in Castile and León and some not. In the final decades of the 20th c., with the creation of the Valladolid School of Architecture (1974), and more professional architects than ever, the region has developed its own architectural style, in close connection to national and international trends, which is very promising and full of potential.

Geography: 94,147 km², with a very varied mosaic of fields, high moors and riverbanks. Climate: long, harsh winters alternate with short, dry summers. Rainfall: between 500 mm (Salamanca) and 1,000 mm (León), and between 130 days (Zamora) and 150 days (Segovia). Sunshine: between 2,500 hrs (Segovia) and 2,700 hrs (Valladolid). Population: 2,562,979. GDP: 92% of nat. av.

BURGOS. An historically important mediaeval town situated on the banks of the River Duero and with a magnificent 13th-c. Gothic cathedral, Burgos has expanded enormously in recent times. Origin: Christian fortress 884. Altitude: 856 m. Temperatures: 32°-7° and -1°-13° C. Population: 169,111.

Business School 1981-83   BU 1
Av. Francisco de Vitoria s/n
Rodríguez Partearroyo/Capitel/Ortega
Detached from the surrounding buildings, this small college conveys order by its absence of mass and its frontal façade, that blends perfectly with its location. It has an interesting layout and an attractive interior. The design is reminiscent of university buildings from the thirties.

LEON. Roman, Gothic and Muslim, it was resettled by Ordoño I in the 9th c. and became the seat of the Kingdom of León from the 10th c. to 1230. Today it is a provincial capital with an historically important town centre, including the 13th c. Gothic cathedral, and a modern quarter with 19th c. and newer housing. Origin: 7th *Gemina* Roman Legion settlement in 1st c. Altitude: 822 m. Temperatures: 26°-7° and -1°-13° C. Population: 147,825.

Apartment Building 1935   LE 1
Av. de Roma c/v Cardenal Lorenzana
Torbado/Cañas
An interesting example of early Modernist architecture in the region, its sophisticated use of resources associated with Expressionism and the Amsterdam School is especially attractive. Its three façades are articulated by cylindrical bay windows on the two corners from which the balconies stem.

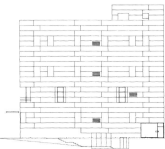

Post Office and Telecommunications   LE 2
Building 1980-84
Pza. de San Francisco
Sota, A. de la
A mature example of Alejandro de la Sota's work, this functional building exemplifies the purist and compositional aspects of this architect's work, as well as the muted Brutalism of his singular technique. Despite this, the building manages to emphasise the value of its urban nature through the use of very modern materials and geometries which are dexterously combined with other, more native elements, such as the bay window and the false stone-coloured ashlars, which stand somewhere halfway between reality and concept. The compact, enclosed volume, broken up by its various window and door openings, establishes an appealing simplicity and an effective sobriety, both trademarks of de la Sota's architectural elegance.

Barrios de Luna Bridge 1979   LE 3
Autovía León-Campomanes, km 47.5
Manterola/Fernández Troyano [engs.]
Its 440 m span (plus two additional 66 m arch spans) established the world record in suspension bridges in 1979 and held it for ten years. Since the vessel of the 50 m deep reservoir constructed on potholed karstic ground could not hold the foundations for a traditional bridge, the engineers arrived at the solution of an elegant suspension bridge, 22 m wide and with a 2.2-m deep lintel, suspended by 54 pairs of tied beams, set 8.08 m apart, hanging from two towers, 101 m and 122 m tall.

PALENCIA. Vaccei *Pallantia* was an important city in Roman times. Later it bcame an episcopal seat in the 4th c. Today, the city has a beautiful 14th-15th c. Gothic cathedral. The province, in turn, is one of the largest European concentrations of Romanesque architecture, including the Church of Fromista (1066), 30 km from Palencia. On a different plane, but nonetheless equally interesting, is the Municipal Hall (1992-94) in Villamuriel de Cerrato, by Gallegos and Sanz. Altitude: 781 m. Population: 81,988.

Department of Agriculture 1983   PA 1
Av. Viñalta s/n
Fernández Alba, Angel
Together with Burgos' Business School (see BU 1), this university building is an excellent example of the Eclectic Rationalism of the Madrid School during the eighties. It is famous for its orderly urban composition and its allusion to Stirling in its overhead window lighting.

PA 2 **Secondary School** 1955
Av. María Auxiliadora s/n. **Herrera de Pisuerga**
Corrales/Molezún
The Palencia Secondary School designed by Corrales and Vázquez Molezún, is a masterpiece of the Spanish architecture of the fifties. Although these architects were generally considered to be amongst the most important representatives of the Modernist movement after the Spanish Civil

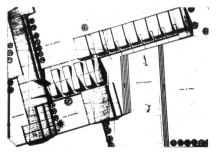

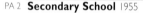

War, here they were already working along more revisionist and also more sophisticated lines. The detached building's stark, diagonal composition in the site, a typically Modernist feature, contrasts with the use of traditional materials (brick and tiles) and the typically Castilian large raked roofs. By searching for a design set within its environment, the architects moved from pure Rationalism towards a more appropriate combination of

SALAMANCA. While all Castilian provincial capitals are characterised by their attractive town centres and architectural monuments, Salamanca possesses the most striking ambience and personality. Situated on a rise overlooking the River Tormes, it has a large Roman bridge from the 1st c. and one of the most attractive skylines on the Iberian peninsula. As a frontier fortress for Muslim *Al-Andalus*, it was repeatedly destroyed during the Middle Ages. After it was rebuilt during the 12th c., Alfonso IX set up a university in 1215, one of the three oldest learning centres in the world and the most important in Spain during the Renaissance, with 7,000 students in the 16th c. Even today, Salamanca owes its flourishing culture to the university (31,776 students in 1996). The city was constructed largely with the special "Salamanca stone", a golden-hued sandstone that gives it its characteristic look. Other architectural gems include a 12th c. Romanesque cathedral; a 16th c. Gothic Renaissance cathedral; several exceptional Plateresque works such as the old 15th c. university; the splendid Baroque Plaza Mayor square built in 1729, and a lively intellectual ambience, a focal point for academics working in the Spanish language. Origin: *Helmatike* or the *Salmantica* of the Vaccei, who fought against Hannibal in the 3rd c. Altitude: 800 m. Temperatures: 32°-8° and -1°-14° C. Population: 186,322.

Apartment Building 1962
Prior c/v Prado
Sota, A. de la
This is an interesting example of the way in which the Modernist architect, Alejandro de la Sota took into account the surrounding environment, in this case the city of Salamanca, without losing sight of his very own purist Rationalist principles.

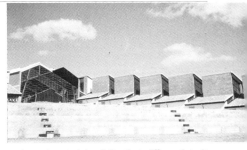

modernity and tradition. The conceptual model behind this design can be traced to the Amsterdam School and Nordic architectural movements, and more specifically to Alvar Aalto's emblematic works, particularly the Town Hall he built in Säynätsalo. The school is very sophisticated in its volumetric layout, conceived as a series of large blocks covered by long roof-lines raked at counterposing angles. In this way, it achieves a use,

scale and material solidity that differentiate it from its formal inspiration in the USSR Pavilion designed by Melnikov for the 1925 Decorative Arts Exhibition in Paris. Nonetheless, it is the most important Melnikovian interpretation in Spanish architecture, although it also contains a few references to Jacobsen's works. The building deserves to be restored and much better maintained with due respect to its high quality.

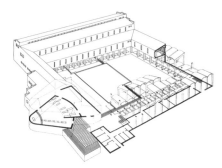

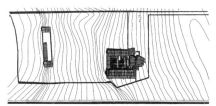

El Rollo Abbey 1958-62 SA 2
Paseo del Rollo 44
Fernández Alba, Antonio
The cloistral Carmelite convent of El Rollo received the National Prize for Architecture. It is the most significant work demonstrating the changing ideals in Spanish architecture (and, more specifically, in the Madrid School) on the cusp between the Modernist Rationalism of the fifties and the Organicism that was to find full expression in the following decade. Antonio Fernández Alba was the architect who spearheaded this change, acting as a bridge between the generation of the early pioneers and the generation of Higueras and Moneo. In this Abbey, he established an Organicism that was both Spanish and traditionalist, with intentional references to Aalto's revisionist designs. He made a cloistral layout, that is compatible with a clever orientation of the nuns' cells towards the sunlight, by staggering the cells along two sides of the cloister. As such, it is a representative work of an alternative Modernism that seeks to incorporate functionality and hygiene, so important to a cloistered order. The use of partitioned brick vaults, pioneered by the Classicist Luis Moya, and the golden Salamanca sandstone add the finishing touches to this great work, splendidly situated in the Castilian landscape.

Carmelo Abbey 1969-70 SA 3
Arenal del Angel, Cabrerizos
Fernández Alba, Antonio
Influenced by Kahn and by the later works of Le Corbusier, Fernández Alba created an intriguing design for this other Carmelite Abbey using reinforced concrete and substituting the enclosed cloister layout with a linear one. As in the Abbey at La Tourette, the cloister walk extends to the roof.

Reconstruction of the Casa de las SA 4
Conchas Building 1984-93
Rua Mayor c/v Compañía
López Cotelo/Puente
This reconstruction demonstrates sensitivity towards the present-day needs of a historical 15th c. building, reconstructed as a library. The delicate touch of its contemporary architects melds the modern reconstruction with the original building.

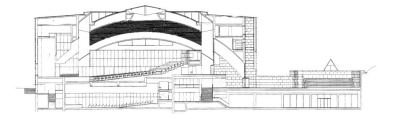

**Convention Centre
and Exhibition Hall** 1985-92
Cuesta de Oviedo s/n
Navarro Baldeweg

Salamanca's convention centre, the Palacio de Congresos y Exposiciones, is without a doubt the most important work of Navarro Baldeweg, the Madrid School architect that is considered only second to Rafael Moneo. As in the majority of the buildings reviewed in Salamanca, it holds special interest for the manner in which the new architecture is adapted to the context of an historical city of the first magnitude. Navarro resolved the convention centre's siting on a steep slope just below the cathedral by envisioning it as a kind of stone plinth for the cathedral. He took advantage of this situation to place the bulk of the installations that this type of building requires below ground level, and thus allowed the large stone prism housing the auditorium – conceived as an enormous vaulted interior space – and the small, glazed

exhibition hall – designed rather like a modern temple – to rise above the ground uncluttered by functional requirements. Thus, the basic ideas inspiring the building are the interior dome (the "pantheon") and a temple (Greek-style, but adapted to the teachings of Mies van der Rohe). Of these, the dome assumes special importance: it is spherical, executed in layered concrete supported by the lightest of ribs, an example of Soane's ideas but on a much larger scale. Navarro Baldeweg, a disciple of Alejandro de la Sota and a renowned painter in his own right (1990 National Plastic Arts Award), is a conceptual architect known for expressing his ideas through reduced (even minimalistic), subtle architectural forms and layouts. This important work in Salamanca qualifies him as one of the main protagonists of the Spanish style of the eighties known as Eclectic Rationalism.

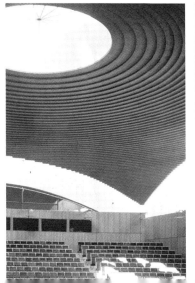

Aldeadávila Dam 1956-63

Aldeadávila de la Ribera
Iberdrola, Technical Department
Dir. Martínez Artola [eng.]

Across the River Duero, right on the border with Portugal, the Aldeadávila dam holds back the waters of the Aldeadávila falls in a reservoir massed behind a thick concrete cupola-vault dam, 139.5 m high (the 5th highest in Spain), with 8 sluice gates, 250 m long at the crest of the dam. The reservoir has a water holding capacity of up to 115 hm³ (the 90th biggest in Spain) and is exclusively used to produce hydro-electricity. Although all the above data conjures up an image of a rather non-descript dam, Aldeadávila has several features that make it quite unique. In the first place, it is located in an extraordinarily sheer granite gorge, whose vertical walls and difficult access were a serious obstacle to the engineering works. Moreover, the work had to resist the sudden surges in the Duero's flow rate, caused by flash floods, of more than 12,500 m³/sec. To stop these waters from scouring the bed, such influxes had to be guided back to the river. The solution entailed the marked curvature and ridging of the dam at the crest (with a 120 m radius) to create, using the words of the engineer, Martínez Artola, "a thick vault profile in which the downstream face acts as support and guide for the overflow".

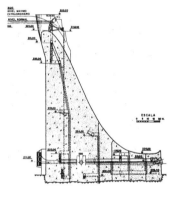

Almendra Dam 1965-70

Almendra and Villar del Buey
Iberdrola, Technical Department
Galíndez/Guinea [engs.]

Near Aldeadávila, on the River Tormes, the Almendra complex consists of a main dam and two side weirs. The main structure is a double-curved vault dam supported on strong concrete abutments with ribs, also made of concrete, and an overflow spillway with sluice gates. 202 m high (the highest in Spain). It has a 1,047.7 m long dam crest and a water holding capacity of 2,643 hm³ (third biggest in Spain) in its reservoir. The Almendra complex is used to produce hydroelectricity.

SEGOVIA. One of the most important monumental Castilian cities, it includes the great Roman aqueduct from the 1st c.; the Gothic Renaissance cathedral from the 16th c.; a picturesque castle; and numerous civic buildings from its Golden Age in the 15th-16th centuries, all set in stunning landscape. Its old quarter has been preserved in isolation from the modern urban sprawl. Origin: Roman settlement, 1st c. BC. Altitude: 1,005 m. Population: 57,617.

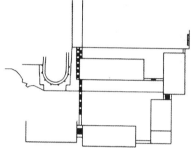

Pío XII Neighbourhood Cooperative Apartments 1962-66

SG 1

Taray 9

Aracil/Viloria/Miquel

This design clearly dates from the time when Rationalist architecture was giving way to more complex tendencies, tied both to Italian Neo-Realism and to the English experiments of the sixties, as well as those of Team X. Located in the middle of the historical quarter, on a very steep incline, these five staggered apartment blocks, three to eight levels tall, are linked together by airy walkways and steps, housing 114 split-level apartments. The group of blocks is integrated into the Segovian urban landscape with few Figurative concessions but with intense spatial relations. The language is a Spanish version of Roman Neo-Realism as well as the so-called *Arte Povera*.

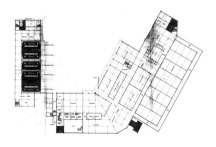

Sausage Factory 1963-66

SG 2

Ctra. de San Rafael 42

Inza/Dols

This 16,000 m² industrial complex, the masterwork of Francisco de Inza, represents one of the most conspicuous positions within Revisionist Modernism in Spain during the sixties, and more specifically within the Madrid School. In this sense, it can be set alongside other works which, like the El Rollo Abbey in Salamanca (see SA 2) by Fernández Alba, are geared to this Revisionism without making any concessions to the International Style. The factory shows the influence of German Expressionism, perhaps more markedly that of Poelzig, although it stands alone as an excellent design. From afar, it looks rather like a fortress, with its red-brick blocks, laid out functionally for its intended use in sausage production, as well as to fit in with the topography of the site. This castle-like profile is well suited to the granite Castilian plateau, although certain unfortunate modifications and somewhat negligent maintenance of the surroundings diminish the effect.

SORIA. Frontier stronghold of Christians and Muslims for centuries, it was rebuilt in 1120. The city contains an historic Mediaeval quarter. The province, a wide barren plain lashed by the wind and furrowed by the River Duero, has inspired many poets. Origin: Arevaco township. Altitude: 1,050 m. Temperatures: 32°-7° and -2°-13° C. Population: 35,840.

Religious and Cultural Centre 1983-87   SO

Parque de San Francisco. **Almazán**

Bellosillo

The church, chapel which doubles as a meeting hall, nursery, apartments and offices form an interesting example of the Formalism of Bellosillo, an outstanding figure in the Madrid architectural scene, whose style is often compared to Scarpa and the school that followed after him.

VALLADOLID. Founded in 1078, it was the seat of the imperial court until Philip II transferred it to Madrid in the 16th c. Today the regional capital, it has grown from 124,212 inhabitants in 1950 to 345,891 in 1991, keeping pace with its industrialisation. Its old quarter, not very well conserved, lies on the left bank of the River Pisuerga; the newer part on the right bank. It has a university with 37,413 students. Altitude: 694 m. Temperatures: 32°-8° and 0°-15° C.

Apostolic School of the   VA
Dominican Fathers 1952-54

Ctra. de las Arcas Reales s/n

Fisac

This is one of Fisac's masterpieces, both for its church design (to which he brought special intensity and skill) and for its early Revisionism. The work represents the completion of the architect's passage from Modernist Classicism, which he practiced in the forties, to his own personal Organicism, without having exercised the International Style. The group of buildings is articulated in an orthogonal manner. Of special interest is the church, which includes a bronze statue of Saint Dominic by Oteiza. It is an attractive configuration of spaces with bare wall-coverings, in which the sunlight takes on a special relevance, and which is influenced by the freedom ensuing from the use of re-inforced concrete and facing brick. Together with the Theological School and Church in Alcobendas (see M 157) and the chapels and Technical College for Vocational Training Teachers in Madrid (see M 61), it forms a definite group in Fisac's work. This one in Valladolid, with its sophisticated details in the treatment of the exterior has been considered his most successful design. The architect is one of the main influences in the Modernist revival of Spanish architecture after the Spanish Civil War.

La Rondilla Health Centre 1990-93 VA 2
Cardenal Torquemada 54
Frechilla/López-Peláez/Sánchez
The initial requirements for a health centre
and a separate administrative management
area were resolved by the architects through
the creation of two different volumes with
elegant façades, which, despite their sparseness, seek to elevate the overall quality of
the location, a suburb of Valladolid.

More on Valladolid. Within the capital city, known for its 16th c. cathedral by Herrera and
15th c. Colegio de San Gregorio, interesting reform works include the transformation of the
Palace of the Counts of Benavente (1985-90) on Pza. de la Trinidad into a public library, by
Casas; and the transformation of the 15th c. Fuensaldaña Castle (1984-86), 5 km N of the
city centre, for use by the Parliament of Castile and León, by E. de Teresa and P. González.
The eighties saw a proliferation of new buildings for social uses, such as the Health Centre in
the Arturo Eyries industrial estate (1986) by Casares and Ruiz Yébenes. In the province
there are interesting towns such as Simancas (11 km distant), with its Royal Public Records
Office, Medina de Rioseco (42 km distant), and Medina del Campo (43 km distant), with its
15th c. Military-Gothic Castle of La Mota.

Reconstruction of VA 3
the Church of Santa Cruz 1985-88
Calle Mayor. **Medina de Rioseco**
Linazasoro
This interesting analogic reconstruction of an
important Renaissance church and its ruined
vault is representative of the Spanish Critical
Restoration of the eighties and of the architectural solidity and historical knowledge of
its restorer-architect.

School of the Carmelite Fathers 1968-70 VA 4
Calle del Rey s/n. **Medina del Campo**
Casas, M. de las
This radically modern, technological, specialist intervention, exemplary of the reaction
of a new generation of architects against the
excesses of the Organic Revisionism carried
out by the Madrid School, heralds the type
of works that the architect, Manuel de las
Casas, would build later in his career.

Los Zumacales Sports Complex 1990-91 VA 5
Camino Hondo s/n. **Simancas**
Abalos/Herreros
A translucent box, very austere in structure
as well as in cost, it is purely technological
and figurative, and very representative of its
architects' work which, twenty years after
passing through the era of "disciplinary
recovery", connects with Casas' school in
Medina del Campo (see VA 4).

ZAMORA. Founded on a rocky bank of the River Duero, this city was the Vaccei *Ocelodurum,* the Roman *Ocellum,* and the Moorish *Samurah,* destroyed during the Muslim invasion but reconstructed by Alfonso I in 747. It then became a Christian Medieval city known for its textiles and numerous churches. Along with an interesting old quarter, it has one of the most original Romanesque cathedrals (1151-74). The quality of its architecture continued in the 16th and 17th c. Today, with an attractive skyline along the riverfront and with modern extensions, it continues to safeguard its past, as evidenced by the restoration of the Principal Theatre (1984-88) by Vellés, Casariego, Somoza and Posada, that adds to its new architectural patrimony. Altitude: 650 m. Temperatures: 30°-8° and 1°-17° C. Population: 68,202.

Apartment Buildings 1939　　　　ZA
Núñez de Balboa c/v Reyes Católicos c/v
Alcalá Galiano
Carrasco Muñoz
Representative of Modernist architecture in the region during the thirties, albeit rather late Modernism, this open block of apartment buildings laid out linearly was one of the most radical but successful examples of Rationalist Expressionism.

Technical College 1947-53　　　　ZA
Av. Príncipe de Asturias 53
Moya, L./Moya, R./Ramírez, P.
A younger sister to the Technical College of Gijón (see O 16), it facilitates an understanding of Luis Moya's passionate yet cultured opposition to Modernist architecture. Conceived in the manner of a large convent, the building successfully mixes the Spanish Classical tradition with a more personal interpretation of enlightenment. The group of buildings is developed around a large open patio of partitioned arches resting on Greek Doric columns. The use of partitioned brickwork arches is authentically late Classicism, one of the most original, skilled works of this European and American style of the 20th c. Its greater moderation and lesser institutional emphasis than the Gijón college makes it more representative of Moya's Traditionalism, which is more constructive and functional than compositional.

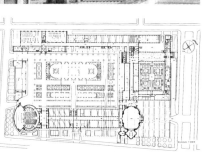

Zamora Museum 1989-95　　　　ZA
Pza. de Santa Lucía I
Moreno Mansilla/Tuñón Alvarez
This small, interesting archaeological museum resolves its difficult location by use of a cubic geometry and formal techniques that are as economical as they are subtle and efficient. It provides clear proof that the architects are destined to stand out amongst the emerging generation of the nineties.

Spanish-Portuguese Institute 1993-97   ZA 4
Av. Nazareno de San Frontis s/n
Casas/Lleó
This interesting intervention on an ancient
ruin, originally the Gothic Abbey of San
Francisco, uses a language true to Rationalist
tradition. Without recourse to the old
method of contrast between styles, the
architects have preferred to seek intense
conceptual analogies between them.

Trade Fair Grounds 1993-96   ZA 5
La Aldehuela
Fraile/Revillo
On farmland near the River Duero, this
square-plan pavilion conceived in a radical
high-tech Modernist style demonstrates a
subtle syntactic concern that integrates it in
the successful tradition of Mies van der
Rohe but at the same time overcomes the
formal constraints of the German master.

Martín Gil Railway Viaduct   ZA 6
over the River Esla 1942
Palacios del Pan
Martín Gil/Torroja/Villalba [engs.]
The viaduct takes the Zamora-La Coruña
railway over the Ricobayo reservoir. Initial
studies for its design were carried out in
1929, and the first plan, by Martín Gil and
Villalba, dates back to 1930. After Gil's early
death, Villalba altered the original design in
1934-35, but then, in 1936 the Civil War
put a stop to such public works. After the
war, Torroja took over the project and
added an arched metal structure for building
the viaduct, which was then filled with
concrete. This mixed structure required
new structural calculations. The final viaduct
has a total span of 209 m (for a long time
the world record for concrete arch stayed
bridges) with a rise of 64.75 m and a height
to the central close of 110 m over the
depth of the reservoir. On either side of the
central arch, there are five and three
rounded-arch tranches, each arch with a
22-m span.

CASTILE-LA MANCHA

This Autonomous region of sprawling cereal fields, vineyards and olive groves spanned by two large rivers, the Tagus and the Guadiana, boasts Toledo (Heritage of Mankind), the city that formed the cornerstone of Spanish history and accommodated a remarkable combination of races, religions and communities, as its capital. Bordering the Mediaeval kingdoms of Islam, these lands were fortified with castles and strewn with public squares. Today, Castile-La Mancha is made up of five provinces – Albacete, Ciudad Real, Cuenca, Guadalajara and Toledo – whose continuing socio-political relationship with the capital has converted their cultural policies into an extension of those formed in Madrid. Throughout the 20th c., the spontaneous display of a pride in local tradition has co-existed with the cosmopolitan aura imported from Madrid. If anything, time will resolve this formal division and grant a legitimate form to the architecture developed in this region.

Geography: 79,226 km², S of the Meseta. Climate: continental. Population: 1,651,833. GDP: 92% of nat. av.

ALBACETE. This province half way between the Mediterranean coastline of the Spanish Levante and Madrid has flat lands, extreme temperatures and an economy heavily dependent on agriculture. Its capital, Albacete (135,889 inhabitants), has suffered the typical chaotic, nebulous growth which has characterised the recent urban development in Spain, an issue which is currently being remedied. Cañada del Agra is located 65 km SE of Albacete.

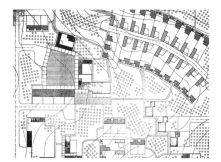

Cañada del Agra Settlement 1962-63   AB 1
Fernández del Amo

The architect followed up his work for the Land Settlement Institute (see Andalusia, Extremadura and Valencia) with this new scheme, where the houses were introduced at the same time as the green areas. The village's design was based on the creation of large blocks containing units which were projected onto the interior of the block. The differences in level between the blocks were adapted to the sloping lie of the land, while the houses opened out onto wooded areas created between the blocks. The village is surrounded by a ringroad with access to the civic centre located on the most even-surfaced plot of land: the porticoed square has a town hall, a doctor's surgery and house and a social centre with bar. In the words of the architect, "the plastic expression of this architecture coloured by the local soil may be identified with the image of a transformed geographical setting".

CIUDAD REAL. The southern-most province of Castile-La Mancha has based its economy on agriculture, with Valdepeñas (on the A-4 dual-carriageway to Andalusia, 25,067 inhabitants and porticoed main square) as one of the main producers of table wine in Europe. Ciudad Real (60,138 inhabitants), the capital of the province, was founded in 1225 by Alfonso X the Wise. Villalba de Calatrava is located 57 km SE of the town.

Motel 1959-60 CR 1
Ctra. N-IV, Km 193. **Valdepeñas**
Lamela
Undoubtedly the first attempt at adapting the American concept of the motel to the Spanish mentality, Lamela's design combines regionalist references with a pragmatic scheme, clearly ahead of its time, in a building which has been remarkably and efficiently blended into the surrounding area.

Villalba de Calatrava Settlement 1955-57
Fernández del Amo CR 2
Sáenz de Oíza best defined this scheme when he described Villalba de Calatrava and Vegaviana (see CC 5) as no more, yet no less, than an experimental new village. And this is surely where the greatness of the architect, Fernández del Amo lies: in his ability to use new typologies to solve old problems with a boldness that is only inherent to true creators. Like Vegaviana, Villalba de Calatrava classifies as a new settlement precisely because it rejects the mediocrity of popular building. This explains its ongoing conceptual modernity. Villalba de Calatrava is situated 57 km SE of Ciudad Real in the Encomienda de Mudela estate, a large hilly area ploughed up by the INC (Land Settlement Institute) and dedicated partly to dry farming and partly to irrigated farming with water extracted from the River Fresnedas reservoir. Located on a high plateau, the village is arranged into equal, elliptical-shaped blocks with truncated edges. It accommodates 100 houses for tenant farmers, with agricultural outbuildings and six workers' houses, a church, two schools with housing for teachers and a local government building including a doctor's surgery. There are three different types of houses for tenant farmers: two of which are two-storey units and the third is a single-storey model. All are provided with stock-yards, stables, porches for storing carts and machinery, henhouses and pigsties. The houses contain a covered passage which is used as an open-air living area.

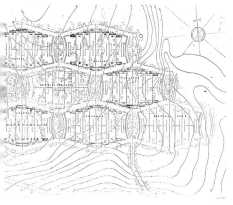

CUENCA. This picturesque, almost dream-like town springs from the heart of a landscape contoured by the gorges of the Júcar and Huécar rivers. Its hanging houses (see CU 1) offer a surprising spectacle effected by its bold construction and symbolic dynamism. The individualist old town gradually emerged hewn out of swirling hillsides and rocky headlands. Its Roman origins, four centuries of Moorish occupation, Gothic-Norman style cathedral (12th-13th c.), streets lined with vernacular architecture, distinctive spaces such as the Pza. de los Descalzos, rocky headlands and wooded areas all combine to produce an area of physical beauty. Altitude: 923 m. Temperatures: 32°-6° and 0°-11° C. Sunshine: 2,725 hrs. Population: 46,047.

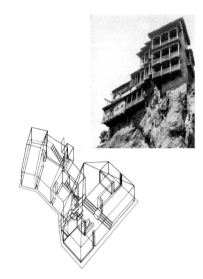

Hanging Houses 1928-29   CU 1
Canónigos s/n
Alcántara
Museum of Abstract Art 1963-66   CU 2
Rueda/Torner/Zóbel/Barja
In 1926, Alcántara's programme to restore a series of dilapidated houses (a compact floor plan with spacious wooden galleries hanging over the rocky walls of the Huécar gorge) created an image which has become the symbol of the city. Later, the museum was perhaps the first decentralising project to take place in the cultural scene under the Franco dictatorship. The scheme was carried out as a private project developed by many distinguished artists: Rueda, Torner and, in particular, Fernando Zóbel, all of which, for professional or sentimental reasons, had some connection with the town of Cuenca and who, with the collaboration of the architect Fernando Barja, renovated one of the Hanging Houses to accommodate a permanent collection of Spanish abstract art. Its great simplicity and the elegance of its forms combined to produce a memorable end result. In 1971, it was given a special award from among the first of the COAM architectural awards to be issued.

GUADALAJARA. Its proximity to Madrid, only 55 km away by dual-carriageway, inevitably tends to categorise it as a satellite town, while its historical heritage, including the Infantado palace of 1480, a beautiful example of Isabelline style architecture with a subtle mixture of Mudejar details and flamboyant Gothic motifs, turn Guadalajara (67,847 inhabitants) into a complex phenomenon which can only be described as the periphery interpreted as abstract reality.

Regional Government Building 1983-88   GU 1
Av. de España s/n, Pol. El Balconcillo
Mingo
The building's multifunctional design (shared by different departments: Traffic, the Geographical Institute, Statistics) was resolved through the insertion of a clearly hierarchical floor plan that manages to efficiently reflect its intention in an elevation of sincere and effective volumes.

TOLEDO. Toledo rises up from the centre of a plain like an island encircled by the meandering course of the River Tagus. The *Toletum* described by Titus Livy as the capital of the Roman *Carpetania* later became capital of the Visigothic kingdom (6th-8th c.). Occupied by the Moors until 1085, it was reconquered by Alfonso VI and two years later became the Imperial City. Brimming with architectural jewels in a unique urban setting, with the cathedral (12th-15th c.) as its main attraction, it now suffers from the problems usually encountered in

historical towns and the alarming depopulation of its centre. Although in the 12th c. it was the paragon of tolerance with Christians, Muslims and Jews living side by side, it now maintains an awkward relationship with the 20th c., when three Toledos have emerged: the historical city, an unimpressive residential estate on the road to Aranjuez, and the so-called suburbs at the lowest part of the town, where the middle classes have now made their residence. Toledo also suffers from an excess of regulations designed to preserve the historical-cultural character of the town but which, in fact, are often overly conservative and undermined by the diversity of institutions responsible for their application: the National Trust, the Council and the Autonomous Government of Castile-La Mancha. Other than the production of cloned replications, there seems to be little room for the development of modern architecture in Toledo's historical centre. Altitude: 923 m. Temperatures: 36°-11° and 1°-20° C. Sunshine: 2,900 hrs. Population: 63,561.

Reform of the Rojas Theatre 1984-89   TO 1
Pza. Mayor s/n
Tuñón/Rodríguez Noriega/Iglesias
One of the best examples produced under the decentralising and renovation policies applied by the Ministries of Culture and Public Works during the eighties, it has a magnificent Italian-style auditorium with a daring, well-proportioned and imposing entrance hall.

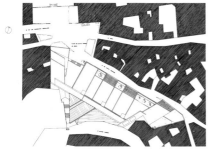

Regional Department   TO 2
of Agriculture 1989-93
Pintor Matías Moreno 4
Casas, M. de las/Casas, I. de las
The only attempt at integrating modern architecture into the historical centre, its success lies in its ability to come to terms with the awkward unevenness of the site. Manuel de las Casas studied the site and subsequently established a modular fraction-ation concept to ensure the work's total compatibility with the typological character of the surrounding area. Despite its expres-siveness, and without compromising the building's institutional image, the complex is perfectly blended into the urban context, with the aid of a light, elegant chipped stone cladding in total coherence with the local colouring. However, its greatest achieve-ment lies in its long-distance unobtrusive-ness and its close-up objective neutrality.

Health Centre 1989-93   TO 3
Barcelona c/v Av. Barbeiri, Barrio Palomarejos
Frechilla/López-Peláez/Sánchez
The centre's extension was built on pilotis forming a single complex with the previous health centre. The new building is a 2-storey L-shape which occupies two sides of the site. Five pavilions are placed in parallel to the lower side, creating a sequence of suggestive covered patios.

Technological Timber Centre 1993-96   TO 4
Pol. Industrial de Toledo
Corrales
A bold industrial building with clearly-defined volumes, under the ventilated plane of its double roof it houses laboratories, lecture rooms and other highly specialised facilities. The special format and colour of the Facosa blocks applied to the façade help to blend the building into the surrounding landscape.

Enlargement and Renovation   TO 5
of the Maqueda Castle 1984-87
Burillo/Lorenzo
Initially destined to be used as premises for the Civil Guard, the enlargement and renovation of the castle may be seen as an exercise in precision, achieving the sharp definition of the old structure and the new spaces through the introduction of distinctly modern elements.

Talavera de la Reina. 70 km from Toledo and 116 km from Madrid, this industrious town in the province of Toledo boasts the second largest population in Castile-La Mancha and the fastest growth in the last three decades of the 20th c. due to its strategic location and varied industries: agriculture, cattle raising, trade and services. Its world-famous ceramics can be seen in the new Ceramics Museum (1996) designed by Manuel Barbero. The town centre combines examples of Gothic architecture, such as the Santa María collegiate church, and magnificent Talaveran tiles, as in the Virgen del Prado hermitage, with geometrical yellow tiles (14th-15th c.) in the vestry and Renaissance blue tiles (16th-18th c.) in the porch and on the inner walls, with various examples of contemporary architecture scattered over the uninspiring urban setting typical of a rapidly developing town. Population: 69,136.

Lucas Prieto House 1960   TO 6
Av. de Extremadura 17
Sáenz de Oíza
Constructed after what may be termed as an experimental phase (1955-58) in the works of Oíza, this piece clearly illustrates Moneo's comment following a study of Oíza's works: "obsession with measurements as the basis of the project, together with an impressive accuracy in the preparation of floor plans".

Moro House 1964-67 • 77 TO 7
Av. Extremadura 16
Casas, M. de las
Situated beside the Prieto house (see TO 6) designed by Sáenz de Oíza and opposite Paseo del Prado, its architecture presents a very successful structural modulation based on load-bearing walls in an attempt to give maximum priority to the entrance of light by the repetition of a number of small patios.

Girls' Boarding School 1975-77 TO 8
Santo Domingo 21
Casas, M. de las/Casas, I. de las
This work, which won the National Architecture Award, develops a free, open-plan scheme connected to the main building. Of special interest are the treatment of its brick walls to obtain a uniform skin (which is in some ways reminiscent of Stirling's works) and the skylights.

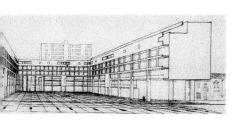

Cabeza del Moro TO 9
Housing Complex 1977-84
Cabeza del Moro c/v Ronda del Cañillo
Casas, M. de las/Casas, I. de las
A new urban space was developed in the interior of a large block in the form of a porticoed square, designed to link the town with the river. The project placed particular emphasis on form, reinforced by the rows of balconies which act as a double façade.

Family House 1986-88 TO 10
Finca El Mecachón
Vicéns/Ramos
The central space consists of a large, almost floating ridged roof which links the different functions of the house along its length. On the outside, the building springs out of the ground in the form of an irregular brick wall whose protruding volumes stand out in search of light and views.

CATALONIA

This triangular area to the NE of the peninsula, between the Pyrenees and the Ebro, the river that gave its name to the peninsula and its inhabitants, was occupied first by the Greeks, who established their colonies in the 6th c. BC, and then by the Carthaginians, who founded *Barcino* (Barcelona) in the 3rd c. BC. Under the Romans, *Tarraco* (Tarragona) became the capital of *Hispania Citerior*. Later, at the end of the 5th c., Teudis the Visigoth made Barcelona his capital. In the 8th c., Charlemagne, resisting the Moorish invasion, occupied the strip of land stretching from Navarre to the coast, creating the Spanish March or frontier between the two civilisations. In the 9th c., Wilfred the Hairy combined various estates to form the dynasty of the house of Barcelona. Ramón Berenguer IV then united the earldom with the crown of Aragón, which in the 13th-14th c., under James I, became a Mediterranean force to be reckoned with, supported by a flourishing middle class of traders and bankers. The marriage of Ferdinand I of Aragón to Isabella I of Castile united the two crowns and marked the beginning of the modern age, although the leading Catalonian political institutions founded in the 13th c. remained unaffected. In 1716, with the formation of the new centralised state under the first Bourbon monarch, Philip V, Catalonia eventually lost its independence. The enlightened policies of Charles III led to the industrial revolution and the subsequent cultural *Renaixenca* of the 19th c. (the School of Architecture opened in Barcelona in 1875), which culminated in the Modern movement and the cultural dominance of the universally acclaimed Gaudí. Thus ended a chain of events which endowed Catalonia with the Romanesque churches of the Pyrenees, the Cistercian monasteries of Santes Creus and Ripoll, the Gothic church of Santa María del Mar and palace of the Generalitat, the Neo-Classical buildings and the Eclectic works. At the close of the 20th c., its historical-cultural heritage and its enterprising middle class singled Catalonia out from other Spanish regions for its combination of nationalist sentiment and strong leanings towards Europe. Catalonian architecture of the twenties should be interpreted within this context and that of the Primo de Rivera dictatorship, former Captain General of Catalonia. The pronounciation of political independence in Catalonia led to a style of architecture which, although conservative and non avant-garde in design, was clearly searching for new forms of urban expression. Under the *Noucentisme* heading different expressive styles came to light, from an initial recovery of the Classical tradition which involved a return to architectural origins, to the recovery of the Baroque rural architecture that characterised the construction of school buildings. The Second Republic and the creation of the autonomous government of Catalonia, the Generalitat, provided a positive setting for the introduction of the Modern movement. Thus, a new official style was born embodying the progressive Republican ideas in construction works promoted by the Generalitat, which were a key element in the founding of the GATCPAC, a group whose dissolution was accelerated by the Civil War. The years between 1939 and the seventies involved a period of reflection and academic reevaluation for Catalonian architecture. In the dark years of the reconstruction, Coderch together with other Catholic

Geography: 31,930 km² of highly complex and varied land, from the peaks of the Pyrenees (3,400 m) to the lowlands at the mouth of the River Ebro, with a central depression and coastal mountain ranges. Climate: Mediterranean (see information on each town entry). Population: 6,115,579. GDP: 123% of nat. av.

architects in Madrid introduced Mediterranean ingredients in an appreciation for vernacular forms which counteracted the new regime's preference for imperial forms. In the fifties, Barcelona renewed its contacts with Europe through the activities of Aalto, Sartoris, Gio Ponti and Zevi, who reintroduced Modern themes based on a systematic revision of the Functionalist style. These developments were spearheaded by the R Group amid fierce debate at a time of cultural isolation. In his writings, Bohigas envisaged a collective scheme for Catalonian architecture: by recovering the Modernist tradition (the conscious use of the popular tradition in a socially oriented architecture) and the more recent Rationalist style (concerned with resolving sociological problems) he created the concept of Realism which characterised the Barcelona School in the sixties. All this took place in Barcelona, the in-official capital of Catalonia during the 40 years of the Franco regime, now the indisputably official capital under the democratic government. The other provinces and their capitals, Girona, Lleida and Tarragona, also offer fields of activity to Barcelona architects.

BARCELONA. At the end of the 20th c. Barcelona is internationally considered to be one of the most thriving architectural cities in view of its ability to apply an urban reorganisation scheme through the introduction of a series of rational alterations to the existing framework. The city underwent a first period of dramatic growth with the development of capitalism in the 19th c. This involved demolishing the old city walls and introducing in 1854 the *eixample* scheme completed in the thirties and based on Cerdà's plan for a permanent urban layout which was approved by the central Government, despite opposition from the City Council and local institut-ions. The construction of a modern middle class Barcelona was founded on the concept of the city as the product of the community's labours and its harmonious insertion into the surrounding region. With the Modern movement, the idea of the city as communal property led to utopian schemes such as those described in the Macià Plan, drawn up in collaboration with Le Corbusier. As in other areas of
Europe, this model would not be applied to housing estates until the sixties. The relatively few urban constructions relating to the field of social housing were mainly built from the fifties onwards, when the land bordering the city limits was occupied by a series of residential areas in response to the high influx of working-class immigrants. In the sixties, Barcelona acquired metropolitan status amidst scenes of chaos and decay, unresolved even by the new network of motorways regulated by the 1962 plan. Then during the transition to democracy, the General Metropolitan Plan was introduced in 1976. The arrival of the Socialists and Bohigas' involvement as town planning councillor became key factors in the transformation which took place in the eighties. With a policy based on the reconstruction of the existing city and a confidence in its capacity to regenerate the surrounding area, a series of specific city plan-ning interventions were proposed. Special attention was given to neglected areas, equipping them with facilities and public spaces in an attempt to monumentalise the suburbs. The 1992 Olympic Games gave special impetus to an urban renovation project which affected the whole of Barcelona. The Games provided the pretext for a series of works which completed the previous policy and established the new bases for growth: the construction of the ring-road, the Olympic Village and the remodelling of the Hebrón valley and Montjuïc park, as well as a whole host of schemes related to these projects. In the years following the olympic euphoria, an urban renovation policy was implemented focussing on the reevaluation of the old town through a series of evacuation and refurbishing schemes and the creation of cultural enclaves. Meanwhile there was a surprising drop in the population over 1991-1996, a phenomenon which may be explained by the redistribution of the population. Rainfall: approx. 600 mm and 105 days. Sunshine: approx. 2,450 hrs. Temperatures: 29°-12° and 5°-23° C. Population: 1,643,542.

Pere Vila School 1921   B 1
Paseo Lluis Companys 18-22
Goday i Casals
In his search for a language that would best
express the Novecentist ideas of the Catalan
upper middle class, Goday imitated the rural
Baroque style of architecture in his school
buildings, incorporating the transposed forms
of popular buildings and using serigraphed
surfaces and terracottas.

Casa Cambó Building 1921-25   B 2
Via Laietana 30
Florensa
This office block reflects the architectural
backdrop at the opening of the Via Laietana.
The Modemist, reinforced concrete structure
is cloaked in a Renaissance style façade, save
for the tripartite openings, which make clear
reference to the office blocks produced by
the Chicago School.

Coliseum Cinema Theatre 1923   B 3
Gran Via de les Corts Catalanes 595-599
Nebot
The grandiloquence of this direct application
of the *Beaux Arts* style of composition, which
in this case alludes to the Paris Opera house
model, reflects the cultural preferences and
climate of the Primo de Rivera dictatorship
years, both fully shared by Barcelona's upper
middle class.

Myrurgia Factory 1928-30   B 4
Mallorca 351
Puig i Gairalt
A building representative of a generation of
local architects belonging to a progressive,
cultured and cosmopolitan middle class, the
composition of its façades is clearly rooted
in a certain Classicism, while a more modem
approach is evident in its organisation and
technology.

Other works of the twenties. Jujol's Casa Planells building (1923) is located on Av. Diagonal
c/v Sicilia. Examples of architecture outside the avant-garde style which dominated the city's
design aesthetics during this period are the Fénix Español building (1927), on Paseo de Gracia
c/v Diputación, in which Bona took advantage of the spatial potential of the corner using a
wide range of ingeniously combined and repeated Classical elements (balusters, cornices and
sculptures). Mestres i Fosses, using a similar style to the GATCPAC, also applied traditional
concepts to the composition of his only partially constructed project (1930-33) for the
Blanquerna school on Via Augusta 140 (now the Menéndez Pelayo Institute), although he
also adopted Functionalist concepts in its distribution and used modern building systems,
reconciling avant-garde ideas with a more traditional approach.

Montjuïc and the 1929 International Exhibition in Barcelona 1914-29

The 1929 Exhibition ended the restructuring of the city that had begun in the early 20th c. and was seen by many as a catalyst in the creation of a Great Barcelona due to its capacity to stimulate investment. The selection of Montjüic to house the fair was based on the structure of the property, which was mainly rural, and therefore easy to acquire, and was also suitable for the construction of an urban park. Furthermore, if the 1888 exhibition had "reconquered" the Citadel area, the 1929 exhibition, taking over yet another bastion that had dominated the city for centuries, would conclude the process towards urban reappropriation. In preparation for the event, the roads were restructured by Amargós (1914), the

gardens landscaped by Forestier (1915) and the project defining the basic structure of the exhibition drawn up by Puig i Cadafalch (1915). Despite Puig i Cadafalch's exclusion from the project in 1923, at the time of the Primo de Rivera dictatorship, the groundwork had already been completed when the government took it over in a display of political rhetoric. The exhibition was laid out along an axis which stemmed from Pza. de España (a new urban focal point aligned to the Gran Via), rose up the hill on either side of what is now Av. María Cristina and culminated in a series of terraces at the monumental Palau Nacional (1925-29), designed by Catà, Cendoya and Domènech Roura, on Pza. del Mirador s/n. It explored the full compositional spectrum of the *Beaux Arts,* from the *pompier* grandiloquence of the Palau Nacional to the folklorist populism of the Spanish Village[2] (1926-28), designed by Folguera and Raventós, a reconstruction of the different styles of regional architecture with special attention given to the spatial composition and with clear references to Sitte. Eclectic accents were also apparent in the exhibition pavilions, of which the following stand out: the Alfonso XIII Palace[1] (1923-29), by Puig i Cadafalch, on Pza. del Marqués de Foronda, and the Palace of Graphic Arts[3] (1928), by Durán Reynals and Martínez Paricio, on Paseo de Santa Madrona 39, recently refurbished (1984-89) by Josep Llinás for use as an Archaeological Museum[4].

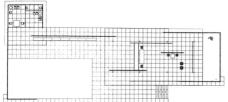

German Pavilion at the
1929 International Exhibition 1928-29
Av. Marqués de Comillas s/n, Montjüic
Mies van der Rohe
Reconstruction: **Solà-Morales/Ramos/Cirici**

The construction of this small travertine, glass and marble building, designed by Mies van der Rohe for the German authorities' reception of King Alfonso XIII during the inauguration of the 1929 International Exhibition, is universally recognised as one of the events that helped launch the language of contemporary architecture, or the International Style. This was due to its capacity to fuse spatial and plastic qualities alluding both to 20th c. avant-garde art as well as to the history of architecture in general. Interpreted both as a classical temple and the greatest known example of spatial fluidity in modern architecture, it stimulated constant study and interest from the moment it disappeared when the exhibition was closed down. Despite repeated proposals for its reconstruction at the beginning of the fifties, it was not until 1980, with Oriol Bohigas as town planning councillor, that the project was assigned to architects Ignasi de Solà-

Morales, Fernando Ramos and Cristian Cirici. Convinced that the pavilion could not be considered as a temporary construction in view of the quality of the materials used and the care invested in the details, they decided to carry out a philological reconstruction of the building, based on the few remaining original documents and on the sketches which still existed of the original foundations indicating its exact dimensions. The only modifications introduced in the new building concerned aspects problematic for its permanent duration, such as the collection and drainage of rain water, which had not been taken into account in the original design, or the quality of the roof; these aspects were resolved with contemporary technology. In addition, it was decided to complete other areas which, due to the urgency with which the original building was constructed and the lack of funds available at the time, were incorrectly performed for the 1929 exhibition, such as the green marble lining on a section of the pond wall dominated by the Kolbe statue or the travertine in the office area, which was replaced by stucco in 1929.

Gardens for the Pedralbes Palace B 7
Av. Diagonal 686
Plaza Francesc Macià and Plaza Eduard Marquina (Turò Park) 1928-34
Rubió i Tudurí

These are three examples of the garden projects designed by this versatile architect and critic. The Pedralbes gardens were re-designed, incorporating the existing trees into a project based on parterres and a picturesque geometrical arrangement. The alterations to Pza. Frances Macià resolved the intersection of the city's main arteries with a tranquil, almost melancholic garden, which unfortunately has now become over-ridden with traffic. In contrast, the same author defined the Turò Park as a square. This urban park, located in a built-up area of the city, pays homage to Cerdà's original idea which was disregarded amidst vying plans for the city's growth in the 20th c.

Sant Jordi Building 1929-31 B 8
[now Catalonian Ministry of Justice]
Pau Claris 81
Folguera

The Sant Jordi edifice inverted the traditional horizontal division of the buildings found in the *eixample* area, with the owner's quarters situated on the first floor and rented flats on the upper floors, to adapt it to more modern requirements. Thus, the offices were located on the first few storeys, rented flats above, and the owners' apartments on the two top floors, opening onto a terrace with a garden area. This arrangement was reflected on the outer façade as well as in the inner court-yard area, with references to the Viennese architecture in vogue at the beginning of the 20th c. The internal spatial arrangement was reorganised and the flats were converted to offices during a remodelling designed to accommodate the regional Ministry of Justice.

Apartment Building 1931 B 9
Via Augusta 61
Rodríguez Arias

Despite being a member of the GATCPAC, Rodríguez Arias designed this building using his own criteria. An interesting asymmetrical effect was created in the façade by subtle variations in the fenestrations and balconies, an effect which he accentuated during a re-furbishment of the top two storeys (1960).

Sert

This building, Josep Lluis Sert's first important urban project and one of the best examples of Spanish Rationalism, swells up between 19th c. façades with all the violence of a manifesto. Made possible by family funding, the housing block makes an emphatic and controversial statement on modernity, both through its formal expression and through its distributional arrangement. By creating maisonette apartments, each with its own entrance hallway directly accessed from outside and with a sitting room open onto both storeys at the corner of the volume, where the staircase internally links the two levels, Sert provided a solution to the traditional arrangement between typical middle class homes, with their sequence of rooms and narrow corridors. This meant that the kitchen and the dining room were on different storeys, a problem that was solved through the inclusion of a food lift. The façade directly reflects the internal organisation, with alternating rhythms of strongly contrasting spaces (sliding windows for communal areas and balconies for the bedrooms), smooth surfaces, piped railing, standard metal carpentry and

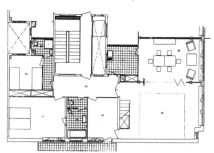

pronounced edges. The problem of its positioning between party walls and the style chosen by the architect were reconciled by providing the two flats on each storey with a very irregular distribution of natural light and ventilation, while the overhanging balconies suspended from each corner offered a solution to the joining of the two planes of the façade, which are separated by a flight of steps justified by their function (the cleaning of adjacent windows). The block was renovated in 1975, the first time a building produced by the Modern movement in Barcelona was to undergo restoration, amid debate on the re-evaluation of this type of architecture and its maintenance. Despite the renovation, its current state is one of serious deterioration.

Collasso i Gil State School 1931-35 B 11
San Pau 109 bis
Goday i Casals
Goday applied a purer language to this new
state school made up of three blocks placed
in a U-arrangement around a central courtyard (consequence of the Educational Reform during the Second Republic), breaking
away from his previous educational buildings
and aspiring to Dutch proto-Rationalism.

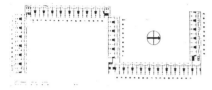

Bloc House B 12
Workers' Housing Development 1931-36
Paseo Torres i Bages 91-105
Sert/Subirana/Torres/GATCPAC
On the cover page of issue number 11 of
A.C., the magazine published by GATEPAC, a
text is printed over a picture of the Bloc
House model asserting the worker's right to
decent housing. This complex of 207 units,
based on the single model of a split-level
apartment accessed from open corridors,
was the first to be built in Spain following
the concepts of the new Rationalist theory
and language. Communal facilities, baths, co-
operatives, clubs and day-care centres were
included in the general scheme, which was
never actually completed. The subsequent
construction of an additional block, together
with the poor state of conservation of the
former have spoilt the overall image of the
complex.

Astoria Building 1933-34 B 13
París 193-199
Rodríguez Arias
This building includes a cinema and bar on
the ground floor and basement, and housing
units tightly distributed over eight storeys as
reflected in the façade. Rodríguez Arias (see
B 9) projected a symmetrical composition
with cantilevered balconies reminiscent of
Walter Gropius' works.

Roca Jewellers 1933-34 B 14
Paseo de Gràcia 18
Sert/Bonet
An example of Modern interior design of
the thirties, it stands in the *eixample*. The
front bearing wall was replaced by a series
of metal pillars and girders, giving the front
section of the building an effect of continuity.
All elements, both internal and external,
were designed by the architects.

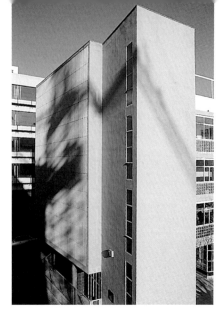

Tuberculosis Clinic 1934-38
Torres Amat c/v Pasaje de Sant Bernat 10
Sert/Torres Clavé/Subirana

The authorities of the autonomous government of Catalonia commissioned this clinic in the thirties, during a campaign against tuberculosis aimed at eradicating the illness from the most densely populated and unsanitary part of the old city, which was claiming the highest number of victims. The commission was taken on applying the most militant form of Rationalism; besides the clinic, the programme also included a tuberculosis study centre and the headquarters of the association fighting against tuberculosis in Catalonia, standing out as an example to the neighbouring area. The building was arranged in an L-shape, making no attempt to align itself to the surrounding site. It opens onto a south-facing patio through which air, sun and light were allowed to enter, providing an environment in which locals were able to get back into contact with nature. The multi-storey scheme was divided into two blocks, one linear and modulated and the other more complex in form. Each of the three sections of the programme ran throughout the complex. The clinic was situated on the ground level, adapting itself to social needs, while the research and assembly units were

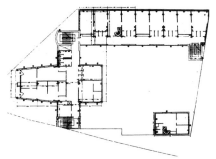

distributed between the two upper floors. The project brief justified the structure and choice of materials from the point of view of the clinic's functionality and optimisation of available space. The structure consisted of pillars instead of bearing walls, obtaining spacious halls, whilst the structural material selected was rolled steel in view of its fineness, constructability and flexibility for future enlargements. The external features were reduced to the sole function of enclosure. Facilities were practical, the reduced height of the storeys implying material and energetic economising. The finishing adhered to autochthonous tradition, using ceramics and various textures and colours. Thus emerged a genuine GATCPAC building and the most distinguished work produced for the Modern movement throughout the peninsula. In 1982, a sympathetic renovation was completed.

Apartment Building 1934-35   B 16
Aribau 243 c/v Campo Vidal 16
Durán Reynals
This building between party walls is the most significant work produced by Durán Reynals during his allegiance with the GATCPAC. Opening out onto two streets, it offers an alternative to the traditional distribution of houses between party walls. Its façades are solemn and its composition Rationalist.

Other works. The Civil War (1936-39) affected all areas of society. There was a radical paralysation of building and a clamping down on modern design projects. Some architects went into exile, while others even lost their lives. Nonetheless, a certain continuity was maintained with the design of such constructions as the Fábregas building, by Gutiérrez Soto, on Pza. Urquinaona, commissioned in 1934, interrupted in 1936 and completed in 1942-44.

Barraquer Clinic 1934-40   B 17
Laforja 88
Lloret Homs
Commenced in 1936 and concluded after the Civil War in 1940, this private clinic, which aspired to scientific Rationalism and an openness to the most advanced techniques in the field of ophthalmologic surgery, has come to gain world-wide recognition. For its construction, Ignacio Barraquer, who was the first of a dynasty of distinguished ophthalmologists, contacted a series of specialists, including the architect, Lloret Homs and numerous interior designers, marble-setters, painters and plasterers who introduced new techniques in the use of materials and the construction of installations. The result was a building with an *Art Déco* feel to it achieved through the technical refining of a preestablished style, rather than through a rationalisation of the construction process and the use of materials which characterised the Rationalist movement. The original building was increased in height during the seventies, altering its volume considerably.

Apartment Building 1935-40   B 18
Av. Diagonal 419-421 c/v Enrique Granados
Churruca Dotres
This large-scale complex, sited in an irregular block of the *eixample* area, is made up of five buildings sharing a common ground floor, yet have a certain autonomy of height. The views from Enrique Granados are impressive, showing the central courtyard and the rear façades.

Housing Block for Officials 1939-40   B 19
Av. Diagonal 667
Solà-Morales de Roselló
This was one of the few projects in Barcelona commissioned by the state in the early post-war years. The author, one of the most important figures during the transition years leading into the fifties, minimised the usual monumental overtones in favour of a well-defined floor plan and stark façade.

Frare Negre Residential Complex 1940   B 20
Paseo J.F. Kennedy c/v Paseo San Gervasi c/v Paseo Maluquer
Bona
The main façade resolved the building's urban character by applying the composition-al laws of a purified Classical language re-duced to a means of projection, while the rear façade emphasised its domesticity with a purer style.

Other works of the forties. While the most acclaimed works of the Second Republic were those that adhered to the most orthodox avant-garde movements, other more Historicist works coexisting with them became the protagonists, backed by the new regime during the earlier years of the dictatorship and by a continuity in academic education. The works of Francesc

Mitjans may be situated in this context, alternating between constructions of clear Academicism, as in the residential buildings (1945-48) on Balmes 182, and designs more closely related to Rationalism, as the housing block (1940-43) on Amigó 76, with a highly functional floor plan and an open façade, some-thing unheard of in Spain at that time. Both were born out of a stance which refused to be converted into a manifesto of a particular style, preferring to introduce more spontaneity in the rationalisation of the functionality of the building in terms of the overall programme as well as the techniques used, while adapting itself to the conditions of the surrounding area.

Park Hotel 1950-54   B 21
Av. Marqués d'Argentera 11
Moragas i Gallissà
The architect resolved the long, drawn-out proportions imposed by the site through the presentation of the lateral façades as abstract two-dimensional surfaces, in con-trast to the main façade, which conserved a calibrated equilibrium between the visible structure, the enclosure walls and the over-hanging balconies.

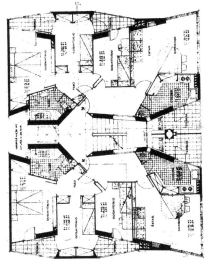

Apartament Building in La Barceloneta B 22
(Marina House) 1951-54
Paseo de Joan de Borbó 43
Coderch/Valls

One of the first clear examples of how the architecture of the fifties suceeded in breaking away from the Eclectic style which characterised the first decade of the Franco dictatorship, this apartment building is also an illustration of how younger generations of architects rediscovered and reinterpreted contemporary language and poetry in the light of the architectural events taking place in Europe at that time. According to Antón Capitel, in this particular case reference was made to the house in Alessandria designed by Ignazio Gardella. The project involved a low-budget housing block constructed in a popular area of the city and commissioned by the Social Institute of the Marina. The pronounced objective and abstract character of the block stands out against the fragmented urban context, despite the Classical language involved in its volumetric composition, including the base, vertical development and crowning. Coderch and Valls justified the fragmented geometry of the floor plan, reflected in the broken line of its perimeter, by the meagreness of the site in relation to the programme required: two flats for six people on each floor. The use of poor materials, such as ceramic cladding, and of traditional techniques, such as the adjustable horizontal slats of the blinds are transformed in a composition that is made up of vertical strips corresponding to the broken geometric layout of the floor plan. This results in introverted volumes of pronounced plasticity. Here, Coderch was engaged for the first time with the issue of urban housing and established a relationship with the context which he was to maintain throughout his career: the skin of the building was converted into a surface undergoing constant development, gaining a sense of weight and rhythm which is merely sensed from the outside, as if contact with the atmosphere of the modern city could only be sustained by avoiding direct openings and by using filtering devices. The project is thus illustrative of Coderch's controversial anti-urban crusade, which he maintained throughout his works within the restructured city.

Apartment Building 1954   B 23
Tavern 34 c/v Rector Ubach
Barba Corsini
In an attempt to domesticate the spaces of modern housing, Barba Corsini worked from a structure of bearing walls clearly marking and classifying the different atmospheres and functions of the apartments, going to the extreme of even providing a floor plan defining the position of the furniture.

F.C. Barcelona Stadium 1954-57   B 24
Travessera de les Corts c/v Av. Joan XXIII
García-Barbón/Mitjans Miró/Soteras Mauri
The huge investment in the construction of the first important architectural work in Barcelona at a time when Spain was on the verge of opening up to the outside world responded to the increased popularity of football in Europe (see Real Madrid stadium, page 239), and provided an opportunity to affirm the Catalonian identity. Involving highly innovative systems which allowed for the 40 m-overhang of the grandstand roof and the installation of a cinema and swimming pool beneath the tiers of seating, the football pitch was sunk below the entrance level. This calculated altimetric difference reduced the vertical circulations of the public. The extension to the stadium (1982) by Mitjans, Soteras, Mitjans Perelló, Cavaller and Bergnes spoilt the appearance of the façades.

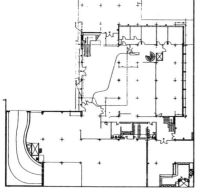

Gustavo Gili Publishing House 1954-61   B 25
Roselló 89
Bassó/Gili
Sensitive to the plans to do away with the gardens designed by Cerdà in his *eixample* plan, the Gustavo Gili publishing house, which accommodates offices and ware-houses (the latter located in the basement), lies back on the limits of the site to define a new façade and liberate a central space.
In line with the tradition of the Modern movement, the three volumes forming the complex incorporate the use of pilotis, large and varied surfaces and sliding windows. Great care was taken in the design and extraordinary conservation of each of the elements within the interior. Unfortunately, the construction of a high-rise apartment building in front of the publishing house has diminished the external permeability of the block.

Social Housing 1955-59
Pallars 299-317
Bohigas/Martorell
The architects turned to the expressive quality of brick to resolve the appearance of this low-cost building estate organised in six independent volumes, which form a zigzag emphasised by the vertical accesses and openings and the glazed ceramic sections of the drainpipes.

School of Advanced Business Studies 1955-61
Av. Diagonal 696
Carvajal/García de Castro
Developed from a winning competition design, this building, which was originally to be sited elsewhere, takes its main reference from the ambitious programme, capitalising on the topography and adhering to the Rationalist tendency of the campus.

Law School 1957-58
Av. Diagonal 684
Giráldez/López Iñigo/Subías
The rush to transfer the faculties from the Central University to the upper part of the city was the catalyst for this project, which was designed and built in just ten months. The architects undertook their first project with enthusiasm and confidence in the new technologies at their disposal. They made clever use of materials and procedures which up until then had been rarely used (asphaltic shingles, light prefabs, rubber paving), designing other elements which were not available at a time when the country was on the verge of opening up to the free market (metal structures, replaceable panels, electrowelded meshing structures). The outcome was a project resolved by a variable structural grid which, when applied to the floor plan and projected onto the façade, produced a spatial clarity that had a considerable impact on the design aesthetic of that period. In 1993-96, Llinás built a bar and lecture room annex in an awkward strip of sloping land, resolved by a clever adaptation to the topography, embedding the 85 m building into the ground.

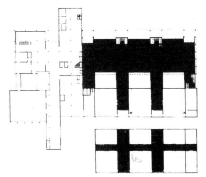

More works of the fifties. Confirming the diversity of results characterising the R Group, the building (1953) on Av. de L'Hospital Miltar 125, by Moragas and Riba, may be contrasted with the Escorial housing estate (1952-62), constructed by the Alemany, Bohigas, Martorell, Mitjans,

Ribas Casas and Ribas Piera group on Escorial 50. Moragas tackled the issue of popular housing with two brick buildings, incorporating prismatic volumetrics and a gable roof "free of both pediments and gilding, *brise-soleils* and bright colours". In the Escorial project, however, an attempt was made to provide an alternative to the traditional urban block, focusing on semi-public open spaces and using a blatantly contemporary language.

Apartment Building 1957-61   B 29
Johan Sebastián Bach 7
Coderch/Valls

If the geometrical arrangement of the Barceloneta building (see B 22) can be compared with the expressive vitality of the Ugalde house (see B 108), a comparison which does not appear excessive given the coherence of the architect's style, then the carefully planned layout of these apartments, which were designed for upper class residents, make direct reference to the Catasús house in Sitges (see B 140). The service areas look onto an inner patio. The entrance hall, accessed by a private lift for each of the apartments, minimises the circulation flows by serving the different areas of the house. The daytime area is positioned towards the main façade, resolved with a layer of lattice-work and a modern version of the bow window, while the bedrooms are conceived as a rigid sequence of spaces positioned along the lateral brick façade.

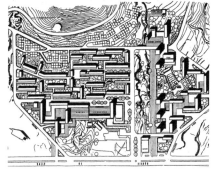

Housing Estate in Montbau   B 30
[Partial Plan and Sector 1] 1957-65
Paseo del Vall d'Hebron c/v Angel Marques c/v Arquitectura c/v Poesía
Giráldez/López Iñigo/Subias

The programme for this estate set out five main objectives: 1. to establish a nucleus of flats of a specific size and character that would stand out in contrast to the rest of the city, 2. to organise and differentiate the estate's functions, 3. to mark out the large green areas, 4. to use public buildings as focal points in the composition of the estate, 5. to distinguish the circulation flows. At a time when social housing was under speculation, Montbau was distinguished as an exemplary housing complex, allied to the concepts advocated by the CIAM and reflecting the style of the Berlin Interbau. If, in practice, the estate is less generous and rather more built up than initially planned, the overall arrangement may still be considered as a reference point for low-cost housing in Barcelona.

Architects' Chamber of Catalonia 1958-62

B 31

Pza. Nova 5

Busquets

Despite its location in one of the most monumental and representative areas of the city, this design, which won the second round of the competition organised by the Architects' Chamber, avoids any attempt at adapting itself to the surrounding historical context. Instead, through its volumes and forms Busquets made an urgent statement on the Modernist typology of the curtain wall block (which, in the original version, was composed purely of glass). This design base was conditioned by a strong tendency towards the "internationalism" of foreign contemporary architecture, fiercely defended by Catalonian architects during that time in clear reaction to the cultural isolation brought about by the Franco regime. Of the original interior design, entrusted to the most distinguished designers of the time, only the meeting and conference room has been preserved, which may be identified from the outside by its blind volume and trapezoidal floor plan, decorated following a design by Pablo Picasso.

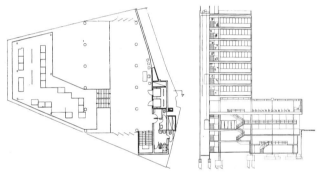

Apartment Building 1959-65

B 32

Av. Meridiana 312 bis-318

Bohigas/Martorell/Mackay

The project was intended to invest a nondescript peripheral area with an urban character and to stress the importance of the façade. The windows which clamber upwards in search of the sun reflect the adaptation of a single housing module to minor variations.

Manzana Seida Apartments 1959-67

B 33

Av. de Sarriá 130-152

Mitjans i Miró

This complex is composed of six different units linked by their vibrant façade and a careful juggling of the shadows and transparencies produced by the shuttered windows and false balconies. The result is a visually compact urban structure scaled to urban dimensions.

Other works. Spain's reticent entry into the cultural scene of the fifties led to the rediscovery of the masters of Rationalism and a familiarisation with the latest international activities. The office and housing block for the Caixa d'Estalvis savings bank (1956) on Rosselló 36, by Terradas, whose composition involved the repetition of a small number of elements and a two-dimensional façade, is a good example of this. Also, heralding the rapid industrialisation and development that would take place in the following decade are the works of Ortiz Echagüe and Echaide, who constructed a series of buildings (1954-60) based on meticulously defined design projects for the car company SEAT. Of special mention are the warehouse and offices on Pza. Cerdà and the laboratory in the Zona Franca, clearly inspired by the American Mies van der Rohe, and one of the most significant reference points of the era.

Apartment Building 1960-62   B 34
Johan Sebastián Bach 28
Bofill
The awkward urban location of the project, on a rather narrow chamfered site situated between two buildings, whose rear façade only partially coincided with the inner courtyard of the block, was tackled through the establishment of a deep cut into the volume of the building, considerably reducing the volume of the apartments, forming a series of setbacks and directing the façade towards the sources of natural light. The night area of the apartments, two on each floor, whose internal distribution was subject to detailed study, looks out onto this patio. The main façade on Johan Sebastián Bach involves a system of abstract surfaces composed of slatted blinds and brickwork lattices protecting the glass surfaces of the daytime area.

Antoni Tàpies Studio-House 1960-63   B 35
Saragossa 57
Coderch/Valls
The separation between the house and city is emphasised as if out of a desire to protect the artist's work. Beyond the abstract façade, the interior accommodates a 2-storey high studio at the rear of a narrow site in contrast to the 4-storey residence that is crowned by the blind volume of the library.

Hispano Olivetti Building 1960-64   B 36
Ronda de la Universitat 18
Belgioioso/Peressutti/Rogers
Since the thirties, the Olivetti group applied a conscious policy to the design of its products and buildings, entrusting its works to famous architects. In this instance, the Milanese BBPR Group was given the commission. The design is inspired by the façades of the *eixample* area of Barcelona.

Casa del Pati Housing Block 1961-64 B 37
Ronda del Guinardó 42-44
Bohigas/Martorell/Mackay
Following a revision of the conventional architecture produced during the Modern movement and, in particular, the type that led to the multiplication of uniform blocks surrounded by neutral spaces on the outskirts of the city, Bohigas reasserted values concerned with human issues and personal exchanges. Translated into architectonics, these values led to a constructional flexibility, a variety of styles and a hierarchy of public and private spaces, recreation and circulation areas, while underlining the importance of the housing block in the development of the city. This perspective gave rise to an interest for communal spaces shared by multi-unit housing blocks: in the case of the Casa del Pati, these spaces became the determining factor in the overall layout. Within the limited space available, identical blocks were arranged perimetrically in such a way that the whole site was taken up. From this configuration, the form of the patio emerged and, treated in such a way that its limits were left undefined, it recreated the atmosphere of a town square. In answer to a desire to accentuate communal space, the blocks are grouped around the patio, which takes on this function and screens the flats from the outside road.

Meridiana Dogtrack 1962-63 B 38
Concepción Arenal 165
Bonet Castellana/Puig Torné
The project was brilliantly resolved by means of a roof formed by two concentric parabolas which were adapted to the oval shape of the dogtrack, enhancing the scale of the building and introducing a spatial quality into the service areas (betting area, bar and other zones) of the design.

Apartment Building 1962-65 B 39
Nicaragua 97-99
Bofill
The building's awkward orientation to the N provided the architect with the opportunity to inject the façade with an intense dynamism. This was developed on practically blind surfaces. The incorporation of a series of setbacks into the floor plan allows the daytime area to be opened to the E and W.

El Noticiero Universal Building 1963-65 B 40
Roger de Llúria 35
Sostres

Situated between party walls in an *eixample* block, the office and workshop building for the newspaper *El Noticiero Universal* tackles the issue of integrating modern buildings into historical centres. Sostres, the founder of the R Group, decided to introduce an abstract quality into the traditional façade and, by basing his design on a single element, the vertical window, he imitated the proportions of the adjacent façades, thus alluding to the strictest form of Rationalism. Inside the building, the free floor plans allow the façade to be interpreted in a new light. The windows are perceived as a series of strips establishing a new, this time narrative relationship with the traditional façade of the opposite building, converting the view into a sequential vision.

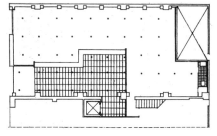

Mare Güell B 41
Hall of Residence 1963-67
Esperança 5-7
Cantallops/Rodrigo

By applying a linguistic repertoire based on a knowledge of both traditional and contemporary Rationalist materials, the building is structured in a rigid H-shaped layout which creates two separate courtyards, one for the nuns and one for the students.

Apartment Building 1964-67 B 42
Muntaner 271-273 c/v Avenir 35-37
Solà-Morales Rubió de Roselló

The desire to separate the bedrooms off from the sitting room area and to provide the building with an equal proportion of sunlight led to an original design. The bedrooms occupy two bays parallel to the façade, while the dining-living room area forms part of an additional body separated by a patio.

Banca Catalana Building 1965-68 B 43
Paseo de Gràcia 84
Fargas/Tous

Based on a winning design, this building was resolved with technological spirit, applying the formal capacities of a warped panel to the façade and using a structure that makes it possible to free the ground floor and basement of pillars by converting the first floor into an enormous truss.

Trade Building 1966-69 B 44
Gran Via Carles III 86-94
Coderch/Valls

Based on volumes previously established by the Council, the design for these towers chiefly concerned their facing which the architects, opposed to the use of the sharp angle, resolved with an undulating perimeter to which the moulded curtain wall adapted in a serrated edge.

Fullà Housing Block 1967-71 B 45
Génova 27
Clotet/Tusquets

The works produced by these two prolific architects in Spain during the sixties marked the introduction of design themes which up until then had been barely touched upon. They were almost always characterised by a great linguistic freedom, employing elements extracted from the Vernacularism of Venturi and the Classical or Rationalist Minimalism of the avant-garde. In this case, Clotet and Tusquets experimented with the field of multi-unit housing. Inside a block whose volumes had been established by council regulations, they offered a broad scope of distributional solutions and annexations which range from the simple study to the split-level apartment with five rooms, maintaining the service areas as the "centre of gravity" of the entire block.

Apartment Building on the Old Bus B 46
Depot in Sarriá 1968-73
Paseo Manuel Girona 71-75
Coderch

The system used in the composition, based on the annexation of modules that were tested out in the Banco Urquijo buildings (see B 48) and taken up again by Coderch in other projects, is applied here on a totally different scale and with different proportions.

La Caixa Building 1968-73 B 47
Av. Diagonal 530
Busquets

Built at a time when the Diagonal was being transformed into the main artery of the city, the materials and contemporary technology used give the savings bank an air of affluence, while the continuous transparent glass façade is protected from the sun by an abstract sequence of bronze glass *brise-soleils*.

Six Housing Blocks
for the Banco Urquijo 1968-73
Raset c/v Modolell c/v Vico c/v Freixa
Coderch

Despite the City Council's orders to build a single block in this extensive area, Coderch proposed a careful composition, sensitive to the proportions and scale of the surrounding area, made up of small palatial residences and gardened houses dating back to the beginning of the 20th c. The volumetric composition of the six blocks, each containing two apartments per storey, was based on the annexation of a series of staggered housing modules. This type of solution, reminiscent of the single-unit houses that were designed by Coderch in the fifties, made it possible to do away with the typical inner courtyards found in most urban blocks. The complex is delicately linked to the outside context both by the floor plan arrangement, which thrusts the daytime area out onto the carefully landscaped common space that exists between the six units, and by the timber louvres forming the surface of the façade.

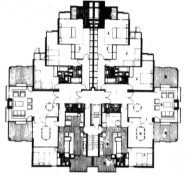

Other works of the sixties. The block of apartments (1964-67) on Muntaner 271 c/v Avenir 35-37, designed by Solà-Morales Rosselló and Manuel Solà-Morales Rubió, with its sober yet expressive façades, is noteworthy. During the boom years there was a considerable increase in high-rise buildings in Barcelona. Of the few works of interest is the Atalaya building (1966-70) on Av. Sarrià 71 c/v Av. Diagonal, designed by Correa and Milá.

Diagonal-Carles III Underpass 1971-73
Carlos Fernández Casado, S.L.,
Manterola/Fernández Troyano [engs.]

In the early seventies a series of road infra-structures were constructed in Barcelona, including the opening of what is now known as Ronda del Mitg. Its intersection with Av. Diagonal was resolved with a careful engineering design which took into account the surrounding urban conditions.

Apartment Building 1971-76
Av. Coll del Portell 52
Rius Camps

This building is a testimony to the confidence in technological experimentation during this period: all structural and external enclosure elements were prefabricated, from the network of pillars to the pyramidal mesh welding making it possible to create a single bay without resorting to intermediary supports.

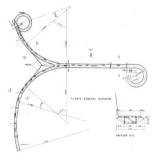

Suspended Footbridge 1972-74   B 51
Ronda del Litoral near Rambla de Prim
Carlos Fernández Casado, S.L.
Manterola/Fernández Troyano [engs.]
This suspended footbridge, winner of the
European Metal Construction award in
1975, highlights the formal capacities of
quality engineering constructions. Towards
the end of the sixties, the Pza. de las Glorias
had been converted into an intersection of
motorways cutting it off from the surrounding area. The engineers resolved the connection by linking the Mataró motorway
with Av. Meridiana by means of a footbridge
divided into two curved branches and
suspended by a series of cables to a free-
standing pile secured at three points at
97 m-intervals, forming an isosceles triangle.
The footbridge was transferred to its
current location during Arriola's remodelling
of the square in the early nineties (see B 97).

Frégoli I Building 1972-74   B 52
Madrazo 54-56
Bonell
This building sums up recurrent themes in
Catalonian architecture of the seventies: the
typological restructuration of housing blocks
of the Modernist movement, translated in
an excessive complexity of spatial solutions,
was accompanied by a desire to control the
project through an emphasis on detail.

Thau School 1972-75   B 53
Ctra. d'Esplugues 49-53
Bohigas/Martorell/Mackay
With the aim of introducing innovations into
the field of education, a large complex was
designed to accommodate the different stages
of schooling (kindergarten, primary and
secondary), divided into two independent
buildings positioned around an amphitheatre.
Whereas their earlier buildings incorporated
a linear arrangement running along an access
corridor, this school marks a turning point in
their design, turning to models based on a
central arrangement, introducing an open-
plan design in which a multi-use arrangement
calls for an educational system based on
teamwork. The building solution continues
to give special importance to detail and the
expressivity of materials, which in this case
do not only allude to artisan tradition but
also to more industrialised production.

Miró Foundation and Contemporary Art Studies Centre 1972-75

Pza. Neptú s/n, Parc de Montjuïc
Sert/Jackson & Associates
The Miró Foundation is based on an idea proposed by Miró together with a group of friends, including Joan Prats, an active promoter of Barcelona culture: that of creating a building which, apart from accommodating the works donated by Miró to his home town, was to include a centre dedicated to the study, dissemination and promotion of contemporary art, equipped with exhibition halls, a library and an auditorium. Developed in Sert's study in Cambridge, the design was based on ideas already tested out by the architects in the Maeght Foundation in Saint-Paul-de-Vence: a clear circulation plan, use of roof-lighting and the incorporation of external spaces (gardens, patios or terraces) adapted to the scheme and to the site chosen by Miró from several sites offered by the Council due to its location in a park on the mountain. The overall arrangement, made up of small defined units around a patio, employs simple materials combining concrete with traditional techniques, such as Catalonian jack arches and ceramic paving. In 1988, Jaume Freixa, who was assigned the execution of the initial project, built an enlargement which intensified the complex and closed off the N patio.

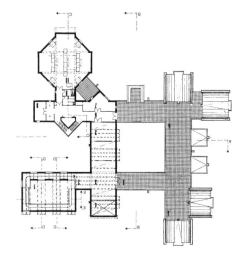

Apartment Buildings in Sarrià 1975-79

Ossio 43-44 c/v Eduard Conde 50
Martorell/Bohigas/Mackay
In contrast to the narrow streets of the Sarrià district and in response to its lack of well-defined public spaces, this MBM project offered a variety of internal open spaces providing access to the three independent buildings housing 95 apartments grouped around the courtyard area.

Les Cotxeres de Sants Civic Centre 1977-84

Ctra. de Sants c/v Olzinelles
Pérdigo/Pujol/Rodríguez
The closure of the city's bus depot served to stimulate this design, produced in the euphoria of the post-Franco era. The addition of new buildings affected the overall arrangement of the block, which gravitates around a pedestrian area.

La Balsa Restaurant 1978-/9   B 57
Infanta Isabel 4
Tusquets/Clotet
While preserving the structure of the old
laundrette, the owner's living quarters were
concealed within the building, taking the
form of an introverted house-cum-patio
and acting as a base to the restaurant,
whose traditional timber structure conjures
up the image of a rural pavilion.

Río de Janeiro Housing Estate 1978-81   B 58
Río de Janeiro c/v Paseo Valldaura
Nadal
This complex made up of two 10-storey
tower blocks and two 5-storey blocks, sited
on premises once belonging to a railway
station, present a sequence of volumes
which define the public space in an attempt
to restructure and revitalise the area in
which they stand.

Extension to the Advanced Technical   B 59
School of Architecture 1978-82
Av. Diagonal 649
Coderch
Coderch offsets the International style that
characterises the university area with the
horizontality of this severely introverted
building, which is cleverly defined by the
modular repetition of abstract, curved brick
walls.

Eduard Fontseré State School   B 60
(La Teixonera) 1978-82
Farnés 60
Donato/Geest
Taking advantage of the marked unevenness
of the site, the architects pushed through
their design for this school in an attempt to
open up the neighbourhood – characterised
by the chaotic configuration of its public
spaces – and reconstruct its urban scenery.

Rehabilitation and Enlargement   B 61
of the Science Museum 1979-80
Teodoro Roviralta 55
Garcés/Sòria
By totally remodelling a series of extensions
to the Domènech i Estepà building (1904),
the architects obtained a considerable
transparency in the central area, providing
direct access to the garden as well as a
significant layout clarity.

Other works of the seventies. The decade of the seventies began and ended with two works by Bohigas, Martorell and Mackay: the 33-unit housing complex (1970-73) on Paseo de la Bonanova 92, consisting of two L-shaped buildings that generate a series of open spaces for inhabitants of this pricey area, and the Serras house, the single-unit residential building on Bellmunt s/n, in Canovelles, a farming village (13,056 inhabitants) 29 km from Barcelona. Built in the lapse of time between these two projects were the housing block (1972-74) on Tokio 2, by Bonet Bertán and Cirici; the La Farigola del Clot school (1977-80) on Hernán Cortés s/n, by Bosch, Tarrús and Vives; and the l'Alzina state school (1977-82) on Pasaje Salvador Riera 2, by Bach and Mora.

Apartment Building 1981-82   B 62
Bertrán 67
Ferrater
The scheme for this small, residential building of multi-storeyed split-level apartments, designed for the upper middle class, is enhanced by a series of spatial episodes dating back in time, from the arcade of ground floor shops to the "Romantic" back garden.

Creueta del Coll Park 1981-87   B 63
Av de la Mare de Déu del Coll 89
Martorell/Bohigas/Mackay
The development of the old stone quarry located in this densely populated district was divided into two sectors: on the one hand, the reafforestation of sloping areas; on the other, the introduction of a clearly defined geometry in the interior of the crater marking out the recreational and bathing areas.

Extension to the   B 64
Picasso Museum 1981-86
Montcada 19
Garcés/Sòria
The programme focussed on the creation of a throughway connecting the three buildings in the Gothic quarter of the city chosen to house the Picasso museum. The throughway imitated the geometry and planimetric proportions of Montcada street and internally linked the three courtyards with traditional stairways and loggias. The architects introduced the connecting areas naturally, almost imperceptibly, imitating the surrounding area while succeeding in defining the circulation flows of visitors and identifying the museum spaces as distinct units. The integration of the new with the old was achieved by an epidermic treatment of the surfaces which fused the different textures of stone, brick and marble, paying special attention to the details.

Plaza dels Països Catalans
B 65
or Plaza de la Estación de Sants 1981-83
Viaplana/Piñón. coll.: Miralles

This public space had to be designed for an area offering minimal possibilities for the development of its topography and with no surrounding buildings of value from which to take reference. The project accepted the immediacy of the site, its emptiness, size, horizontality and other determining factors, such as the railway lines that cross it below the ground. Avoiding any real attempt to protect the space with parapets or split levels, the scheme proposed a flat area that extends over the railway lines all the way up to the station. It is with this sense of stark immediacy that the project came into being, based on a very natural reaction: that of striving for immobilisation in response to an over-charged environment. The constructed elements help to reinforce this attitude: from the outside, the square blends into the city, but on entering the square, it takes on larger dimensions and the pergolas lend a new dynamism to an area, which is little more than the space resulting from an urban configuration. Since its controversial construction, this "hard square" (as it is popularly referred to) has been converted into the paradigm of a type of architecture which has come to be known as Minimalist in abstract formal terms.

Remodelling and Extension
B 66
of the Palau de la Música 1981-89
Sant Francesc de Paula s/n
Tusquets/Díaz

The restructuration of this building, the florid culmination of Catalonian Art Nouveau, brilliantly resolved by Doménech i Muntaner in 1905 in a narrow site of the Gothic district of the city, was achieved by creating new relationships with the urban context. By partially demolishing a neighbouring church, an Academic construction built in 1940, the Palau gained a new façade facing towards the Via Laietana artery which was opened in the 18th c. The façade was reinforced by the addition of a cylindrical brick structure in clear reference to the angular solutions of the surrounding Eclectic architecture. The duplication of entrances that this entailed was resolved by the construction of a stairway offering direct access to the gallery.

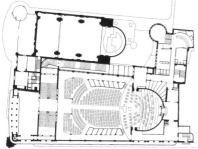

Moll de la Fusta and Paseo Colón 1981-87
Solà-Morales Rubió, M. de   B 67
This was the first project constructed on the
sea front. After a meticulous study of the
section, a cutting was introduced for the
passage of fast traffic beneath the wide
coastal tree-lined promenade looking onto
the port. The addition of urban furniture
and fixtures gives the complex a domestic
character.

Via Júlia 1982-86   B 68
Via Júlia
Sola Susperregui/Julià i Capdevila
The Via Júlia stood on the space left over by
a series of indiscriminate building processes
and presented a series of difficult problems:
the buildings constructed on different levels
and the underground train, whose tunnel
rose to surface level, had caused a marked
difference in level between the two lanes.
The project, which was developed over a
length of 900 m, resolved the layout by means
of two differentiated sections: one involved
the widening of pavements, while the other
involved the creation of public space marked
by a pergola between the two lanes. A
careful design united the overall arrangement, giving it an urban image accentuated
by sculptural elements: a light tower inspired
by industrial chimneys and a sculpture by
Sergi Aguilar and Antonio Roselló.

Fossar de la Pedrera 1983-86   B 69
Mare de Déu del Port s/n
Galí
The design was based on the scenic value of
the cavity produced in the mountain by this
unused stone quarry. A path leads to an
area of emotive space which was once a
common ditch and has now been converted
into a monument to those who died defend-
ing Catalonia's freedom during the Civil War.

Arquitecte Jujol State School 1983-87   B 70
Riera Sant Miquel 41
Bach/Mora
Located on the site formerly occupied by
the Manyac offices designed by Jujol, of
which one of the staircases has been preserved, the school presents a compact and
regular typology, reflected in the calm
composition of the brick façade, adorned
with tripartite openings.

Horta Cycling Stadium 1983-84
Paseo del Vall d'Hebron c/v Paseo Castanyers
Bonell/Rius

The successful insertion of this sports arena, one of the first facilities to be built for the 1992 Olympics, into a peripheral area of the city characterised by a diversity of elements was achieved by establishing a harmonious relationship between the design and the surrounding context, thus imposing a new urban order. The oval-shaped cycle track was inscribed into a low, regular cylinder whose cross section was adapted to the slight gradient of the surrounding structure, while the radial pillars of reinforced concrete injected a sense of rhythm and helped to define the outer ring. The perimeter of the outer ring underwent various treatments: on one level, in the upper zone, strips of concrete framed the entrance. In the areas flanking the points at which the ellipse meets the circle, the services were accommodated forming a blind concrete wall broken only by the side entrances. In the area opposite the entrance, the structure pushed away the blind enclosure once again and opened it out to offer a view of the city. The use of a unit as defined as the circle did not stop the architects from following the direction established by the mountain-sea axis in the track, thus expressing the real meaning of this structure, which offers open views of the surrounding landscape along a route leading from the entrance to the belvedere.

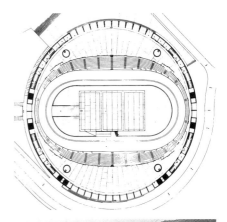

This is also the function of the areas between the track and the external perimeter, which confirm both the sporting character and the public nature of these spaces. This simple but far from elementary spatial and distributional design employed inexpensive materials which lended themselves well to the "poor" construction techniques that had to be adopted due to the low budget and little time available to develop the programme (the stadium was constructed in ten months): reinforced concrete pillars assembled on site, concrete block enclosures, ceramic and brick facing tiles. The tiers of seating and the four large angled lighting masts were the only prefabricated elements included in the design.

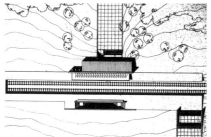

Universidad Autónoma Train Station 1984 B 72
Bellaterra
Bach/Mora

This simple yet effective project was based on the elementary and synthetic presence of a wall constructed in parallel to the line of the tracks and platforms. The wall is backed by a narrow structure containing the services and ticket office, and is highlighted by a large segmental arch which crowns the access stairway, vesting the station with an atmosphere of serenity and with very clear "civic" and urban references on its town-side façade. The platforms are dominated by a large metal canopy supported by braces in allusion to the history of railway architecture. Its presence is revealed from the opposite part of the wall by the projecture of three abstract prisms which act as a counter-weight.

Conversion of the CATEX Factory into a Pool and Sports Centre 1984-90 B 73
Pallars 275, Poble Nou
Mateo

Mateo tackled the conversion of this old factory in Poble Nou from a narrative stand-point. He accepted the value of the existing building and avoided Post-Modernist senti-mentalism, establishing tensions by the juxtaposition of new elements.

Bach de Roda-Felipe II Bridge 1985-87 B 74
Calatrava

This peripheral area was converted into a landmark by the construction of an infra-structure which imposed a clearly defined aesthetic on a characterless environment. The bridge is only one part of a general plan to restructure the area, which included the creation of a linear park on either side of the railway track and a triangular plaza.

Santa Mónica Art Centre 1985-90 B 75
La Rambla 7
Viaplana/Piñón

Without altering the existing building, a 17th c. convent later converted into a barracks, the project superimposed the different elements required for its new use as an exhibition centre and small library, inverting the functions of the unit and accentuating the quality of its spaces.

Other works of the eighties. The reconstruction of the less structured areas of the city put forth by Bohigas with backing from the Council had a particularly strong impact on certain areas of the urban landscape, such as the Baró de Viver housing development (1985-88) on Paseo de Santa Coloma c/v Cinturón del Litoral, designed by Donato Folch, or the Parque de España Industrial park (1981-86) constructed by Peña Ganchegui and Rius Camps.

Illa Diagonal Building 1986-94   B 76
Av. Diagonal, Numància, Déu i Mata, Entença
Moneo/Solà-Morales Rubió, M. de
The decision to reestablish the continuity of the urban façade in the context of the isolated buildings characterising this section of Av. Diagonal led to a successful combination of project designs scaled to the proportions of the surrounding area. The unitary image of the 300-m long volume was developed through the coherent and uniform repetition of openings which may be interpreted as an "anonymous standard" or as an "urban architectural element *par exellence*". The building was scaled down to human proportions by a series of successive setbacks in the surface of the façade and variations in the upper profile of the building which helped to soften the visual impact of the complex without falling into mediocrity. The rear façade opening onto a park housing a conference centre, schools and a hotel, rejected the immediacy of the initial gesture, providing a rhythm of strong horizontal openings and a rather more defined set of volumes.

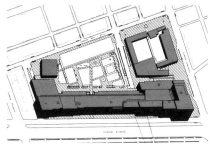

School of Civil Engineering   B 77
Library and Lecture Rooms 1987-90
Campus Nord, Gran Capità 1
Llinás
This project involved the construction of two brick volumes, defined by clean contours and careful details, which could easily form part of the regular grid of the new campus. The library stands out as a completely blind volume resolved by roof-lighting.

Antoni Tàpies Foundation 1987-90   B 78
Aragó 255
Amadó/Domenech
The restructuration of one of the buildings that pioneered Catalonian Art Nouveau displayed sensitivity and restraint towards the spatiality of the original structure, which is interrupted by the use of cast iron pillars. Tàpies's aerial sculpture places the building in virtual alignment to the urban façade.

Other works of the nineties. Also by Llinás is the single-unit house, Can Caralleu (1991-93), on Capella de San Caralleu 12, in an area of self-built houses on a S-facing site with magnificent views of the city. The building stands on a steep hillside which, rather than being a problem, is capitalised on by further embedding the structure into the ground, creating a house which is at once secluded and linked by retaining walls to the neighbouring houses.

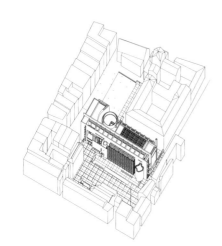

Museum of Contemporary Art 1987-96   B 79
Pza. dels Angels 1
Meier & Partners
This building forms part of a series of urban upgrading projects in the historical quarter of El Raval, discussed in the study entitled *Del Liceo al Seminario* (From the Lyceum to the Seminary), by Clotet, Tusquets and Bassó (1980), which focused on the renewal of religious buildings in this area for cultural purposes and the creation of wide open spaces. Turning to compositional methods previously tested out by Meier in the construction of buildings housing works of art, and clearly inspired by the Modern tradition, the building was inserted into its historical context, establishing the boldness of its own design as its point of reference. The *promenade architecturale* formed by an imposing ramp constructed across the main façade provides an entrance to the museum's different exhibition areas: on the ground floor, large halls dedicated to temporary exhibitions and, on successive storeys, natural intimate spaces housing the permanent collections.

Auditorium and Music Centre 1987-   B 80
Padilla c/v Alí Bei c/v Lepant
Moneo
In an area on the edge of the *eixample,* where the geometrical grid of streets and avenues seems to lose its rigid definition, Moneo proposed a compact, restrained building adapted to the alignment proposed by Cerdà in the 19th c. This complex and extensive programme, which incorporated different scales and included two concert halls designed to seat 2,500 and 700 people, was resolved by the use of a reinforced concrete grid, clad with dark stainless steel panels and lined with oak panelling. The floor plan was dictated by variations in density establishing relationships between the different rooms, from the external crown of the lecture room, which protects the two halls, to the patio, which acts as a covered urban space dominated by a lantern.

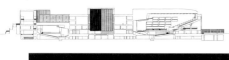

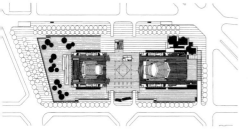

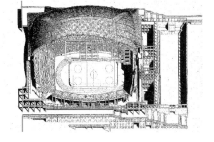

Sant Jordi Palace 1988-91 B 81
Anillo Olimpico, Montjuïc
Isozaki

Isozaki's project for this olympic pavilion established the enormous domed shell of its roof as the compositional vertex of the work and as a scaled-up symbol of reference in an attempt to blend the building in with the topography of the Montjuïc mountain. In actual fact, it is the simplified and some-what disappointing version of the original competition proposal, which propounded a single undulated surface covering both the main hall and the multi-purpose centre of which the wavy perimeter that now forms the base is a mere token in comparison. The system used to elevate the large framework structure is the Pantodome, consisting of the on-site assembly of a series of highly resistant elements which were progressively elevated during the construction phase.

New Building for the B 82
Crown of Aragón Archives 1988-93
Marina c/v Almogàvers
Amadó/Domenech

This complex project provided a two-fold solution to the programme's desire to re-affirm the centrality of the Las Glorias area and convert the archive building into a modern place of study, resulting in a build-ing of complex urban arrangement.

Poble Nou Park 1988-92 B 83
Paseo Calvell, Carmen Amaya, Paseo M. del Bogatell
Ruisánchez/Vendrell

This park was designed as a continuation of the interventions planned and built along the sea front and as an extension of the Olympic Port park, recovering areas of industrial wasteland to provide the Poble Nou district with a new image. The project proposed the construction of a landscape by incorporating characteristic elements from N Spain's beach areas (such as pine clusters and sand dunes) and confining the constructed elements to an essential mini-mum, concentrating them around the old railway tracks passing through the area. By using a language that links it to its surround-ings, the park takes on the character of an area in the process of evolution, in contrast to the Olympic Village constructions.

Montjuïc: 1992 Olympic Facilities

Taking advantage of the Olympic Games to "complete" the city, the Council's policy was not limited to the installation of strict sporting facilities, including such projects as the Montjuïc mountain (see B 5), which underwent a series of interventions[4] to reinforce its status as the largest urban park in Barcelona and the setting for a host of facilities geared to leisure activities, entertainment and mass demonstrations. Construction activity was centred around the Olympic Ring designed to hold prize-giving ceremonies and athletic events, which was based on the winning design project by Buxadé, Correa, Margarit and Milà, whose proposal was selected for providing the best means of assigning a specific building project to each of the teams invited to participate. The winning team, in collaboration with Gregotti, was assigned the restructuration of the Montjuïc Olympic Stadium[1] (1929, by P. Domènech) of which only the Eclectic outer casing was conserved, whilst Isozaki was commissioned the Sant Jordi Palace (see B 81), the most effective of the group. The Calatrava Telecommunications tower with its somewhat excessive fifties style dominates the olympic area in the form

of an urban-scaled sculpture rising to a height of 120 m. The pedestrian entrance to the area was resolved by a series of escalators which scale up the terraces of the monumental shaft of the Palau Nacional of the 1929 Exhibition (see B 5). Beth Galí was assigned the Sot del Migdia park[2], improving the connection between the Montjuïc cemetery and the Olympic Stadium by means of a series of promenades. As far as cultural facilities are concerned, the Miró Foundation (see B 54) was extended and the Palau Nacional restored by Gae Aulenti for use as the headquarters of the National Art Museum of Catalonia[3]. A series of pavilions for the 1929 exhibition were also restored as conference centres and exhibition areas situated around the urban centre of Pza. de España, in which Garcés and Sòria reconstructed the Plaza Hotel (1990-93) inspired by its original volumetrics.

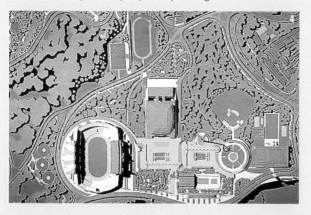

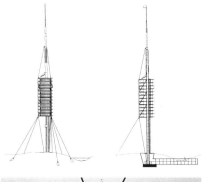

Telecommunications Tower B 85
in Collserola 1989-92
Vallvidrera-Tibidabo, Collserola
Foster

The competition for this project defined the programme as a "monumental element of technology", and was thus resolved by Foster, with his winning design involving a 288-m high tower which dominates all of Barcelona's landscape over the Tibidabo mountain range. Furthermore, taking into account the surrounding conditions and in order to minimise the impact on the natural park in which it was sited, Foster reduced the hollow reinforced concrete shaft to a diameter of 4.5 m, supported by braces of high-resistance prestressed steel. The technological body was resolved in thirteen triangular planes which incorporate the services, antennae and vantage lookout points open to the public.

Archery Pavilion 1989-91 B 86
Granja Vella, Vall d'Hebron
Miralles/Pinòs

This design scraped up the ground in a *frottage*-like motion in order to give rise to two configurations, several retaining walls and roofs which encompass a rather austere programme, endorsing the poetical approach proposed by Bru in his plans to develop the area (see B 87).

Restructuration B 87
of the Vall d'Hebron Area 1989-92
Paseo del Vall d'Hebron
Bru

The task of equipping this peripheral area with sports facilities for the Olympic Games was converted here into an opportunity to explore the new concept of public space as an urban vacuum through the artistic application of recycling techniques and collage.

House in San Gervasi 1989-91
Infanta Isabel 12
Sunyer/Badía
As in the Herrero house (1986), the work involved an elegant application of Minimalism: the nucleus of communications was concentrated in an elongated area three storeys high, which distributes the different levels of the pure prism, superimposed by the cubic shape of the guest-room area.

Other works. Works produced by the generation of architects emerging in the first few years of the democracy include the Juan Carlos I Hotel (1988-92), by Ferrater, located at the entrance to the city, on Av. Diagonal 661-671, a bold construction project including two enormous reinforced concrete walls and a courtyard serving the entire height of the building, which stand in sharp contrast to the subtle underground volumes of the Fitness Center (1992-97) situated alongside; the Collserola town hall (1988-90), by Rahola, on km 47 of the Vallvidrera-Sant Cugat road, with its subtle definitions and sensitivity towards the natural surroundings; and the Municipal sports centre in the Vall d'Hebrón valley (1989-91), by Garcés and Sòria, in Granja Vella, involving clearly defined brick volumes that manage to create a tension with the curved geometries of the Olympic Park by Eduard Bru (see B 87).

Olympic Village or Nova Icària 1985-92
(General Park and Town Planning)
Marina, Moscou, Doctor Trueta, Av. Bogatell, Bisbe Climent, Cinturón del Litoral
Martorell/Bohigas/Mackay/Puig Domènech
The Olympic Village embraces 150 ha of coastal land formerly occupied by obsolete industries and railway lines which formed a barrier between the city and the Mediterranean. The development of the area was not only promoted to host the 1992 Olympic Games, but to culminate an urban reconstruction project funded by the Council and leading to a series of specific regenerating works within a larger context. The construction of ringroads and the deviation of the railway line helped to upgrade an area which had been until then a peripheral part of the town and which due to its location as an extension of a series of buildings along the urban coastline could be converted into a new recreational epicentre, as well as a quality residential area. The architects in charge of the development project defined a coastal park, a marina – known as the Olympic Port, also designed by MBM – that culminates in two 44-storey towers, a residential area containing 2,000 apartments and a series of installations (see B 90 and B 94). Based on the 19th c. grid of the Cerdà area, they proposed the extension of this

old industrial area, converting it into a single zone while incorporating variations on the model as alternatives designed to enrich the monotony of the expansion area. It has the form of a detailed project which not only dictates the volumes and the shape of public spaces but also, in accordance with works already performed by the architects in the field of multi-storey housing from the seventies onwards, concentrates its attention on small details and on fragmentation, co-ordinating and controlling the contributions made by the different architects participating in the project. The Cerdà grid was modernised by grouping the blocks into three parcels, reducing built up space, interrupting the continuity of the perimeter and introducing a series of superblocks left partially open to allow for the public use of the interior courtyard. A series of entrance buildings, among which the one designed by

Hospital del Mar 1989-93
Paseo Maritim 25
Brullet/Pineda

The rehabilitation of this hospital centre completed the series of construction works carried out on the sea front at the end of the eighties for the 1992 Olympics. The design entailed the application of an apparently superficial treatment to the existing buildings, a high-rise block and a series of pavilions, which actually redefined the internal organisation and provided the complex with a uniform image. The emphasis of the project fell on the intermediate spaces and, although its urban character was resolved with the two redesigned parts of the complex, its most representative space was located inside the building and invested with an air of tranquillity, which resulted in an open but protected area that comes as a relief to the tensions usually found in a hospital.

Bach and Mora for the Telefónica company (1989-92) is of special mention, located on Joan Miró c/v Av. de Icària, provide access to these semi-open public spaces from Av. de Icària, filled with a series of pergolas designed by Miralles and Pinòs (1991-92). The most outstanding housing blocks were designed by Bonell, Rius and Gil (see B 91) and Martínez Lapeña and Torres Tur (see B 92). Also of special mention are the buildings (1990-92) by Viaplana and Piñón, on Av. de Icària 174-184, that attempt to abstract normative detail in a construction which, without competing with the buildings surrounding it, establishes the determining factors of the area.

Olympic Village Apartments 1990-92   B 91
Salvador Espriu 81, Villa Olímpica
Bonell/Rius/Gil
The design introduced variations on the standard façade proposed by the authorities, defined independent porches and played with the continuity of the façade, thus distinguishing the buildings from other designs on the Ronda del Litoral and offering an interesting solution to the three blocks.

Apartment Building 1990-92   B 92
Pza. Tirant lo Blanc, Villa Olímpica
Martínez Lapeña/Torres Tur
In an attempt to define the pedestrian axis of the Av. del Bogatell, the Olympic Village authorities proposed this circular building complex, which was broken up by the architects with the addition at one end of a tower using an architectural style that is reminiscent of Coderch.

Hilton Hotel 1990-92   B 93
Av. Diagonal 589
Viaplana/Piñón
The Hilton Hotel in Barcelona is defined by the distance it establishes with the buildings surrounding it, proposing a new public space, mirroring the existing area and, as is usual in the works produced by architects Piñón and Viaplana, placing emphasis on subtle variations.

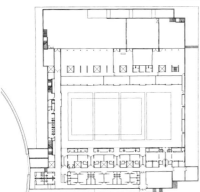

Mar Bella Pavilion 1990-92   B 94
Paseo Marítim de la Mar Bella c/v Ronda del Litoral
Ruisánchez/Vendrell
Once the reconstruction of the surrounding landscape had been completed with the Poble Nou Park (see B 83), Ruisánchez and Rius extended their design to the River Besós with a sports and leisure centre that contained various amenities for public use. While the landscaping recaptured the natural environment, the buildings were situated in such a way as to not affect the surrounding area. Both buildings accommodate their services under a large concrete platform, minimising the constructions to a mere surface area or skin containing the space and emphasising its transparency. The result is the formation of simple volumes, perhaps in reference to the industrial architecture designs previously occupying the area.

Meteorological Centre 1992   B 95
Arquitecte Sert 1, Villa Olímpica
Siza
From the apparent simplicity of this cylindrical tower located at the point where the wharf meets the coast, the architect from Porto developed a complex internal system of openings to the exterior defined by the relative positioning of concentric skins and radial partitions.

Trinidad Junction Park 1990-92   B 96
Ronda Litoral, Autopista A-17 and A-18
Batlle/Roig
Situated inside the cloverleaf resolving the connection between the new ringroad and the city's N exit, the park was developed taking the surrounding area into account, solving different fragments of the junction and transforming the park into a landmark at the entrance to the city.

Plaza de las Glorias Catalanas 1990-93   B 97
Arriola
The project resolved this complicated road junction by raising it above ground level and constructing a ring capable of accommodating a car park under the raised section as well as a park at its centre, precisely in the site where Cerdà, in his 19th c *eixample* arrangement, had planned to transfer the centre of Barcelona.

Caritat House   B 98
Contemporary Cultural Centre 1990-93
Montalegre 5
Viaplana/Piñón
In the context of an ambitious plan to revive the old Raval district, one of the most dilapidated of the historical part of Barcelona, and in an attempt to convert it into a cultural enclave, the rehabilitation of the Caritat House, an old hospice, was undertaken to house the headquarters of an urban studies centre. The existing building was organised around a courtyard, under which the new entrance hall was situated. Plans to conserve the character of the courtyard entailed substituting one of its sides with a large glass surface accommodating a nucleus of vertical communications. By inserting an inflection in the façade above the cornice line, the architects cleverly introduced the profile of the town itself into the patio.

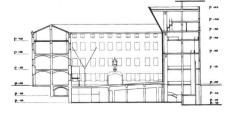

Apartment Building 1992-95 B 99
Carme 55-57 c/v Roig 28-36
Llinás

The insertion of this building into a compact urban section of the old town was achieved by a careful orchestration of its volumes in an attempt to create a space among the narrow streets of this neighbourhood. The housing programme was divided into three volumes stemming from the first floor which, through a dynamic effect created by a series of setbacks and vacuums, strike up a complex relationship with the geometrics of the surrounding buildings, with the exception of the façade facing Carme street, placed in parallel. In the same way, the ground floor, linking the isolated volumes of the apartments and a series of shops to a continuous passage way, makes no attempt to conserve the alignments, thus increasing the visual angle of Roig street.

Reorganisation B 100
of the Port Vell Buildings 1993-95
Muelle de España
Viaplana/Piñón

A leisure and shopping centre replaces the old port facilities of this marina which, linked by a mobile walkway to the Rambla avenues (the spine of the old town), completes the renewal of Port Vell, opening this area of the town out to the sea.

Conversion for the B 10
Pompeu Fabra University 1993-97
Ramón Trías Fargas 25-27
Bonell/Gil

The rehabilitation of a former barracks for student accommodation conserved the character and volume of the original building. The programme was developed around a central patio, which acts as a main square and incorporates a partially sunken library.

Reconstruction B 102
of the Gran Teatre del Liceu 1995-98
Rambla 63-65
Solà-Morales, I. de

The controversial alterations to the Gran Teatre del Liceu (1847) involved the reconstruction of the hall destroyed in a fire in 1994 and the enlargement of the theatre, equipping it with the technical elements and conditions of comfort it formerly lacked.

Metropolitan area and province of Barcelona. As is the case in other large European cities, the influence of the city of Barcelona extends beyond its central government to a territory including many other municipalities. Its urban realm therefore no longer refers merely to the inner city – the capital, with a surface area of 97.6 km^2 and a population of 1.5 million – but to a much larger urban agglomeration, contained within 33 municipalities making up what is today the metropolitan area – with an area of 585.3 km^2 and 2.9 million inhabitants. In view of the remarkable transformation that has taken place (see pages 138-139), stimulated by economic development and the transfer of industries to the first outer ring in the sixties, and to a second ring and other less central areas in subsequent phases, the surrounding villages, many of which were small, rural communities, now play a supporting role in production work and urban services. The main areas of growth have focussed on three fronts: along the axis of the River Besós, NE of the capital; along the axis of the River Llobregat, to the SW; and beyond the Collserola mountain range, to the W. Whereas the inner city is principally concerned with activities relating to the tertiary sector with middle and upper class residents employed in the service, business, leisure and culture industries, the working class area is located towards the NE and SW and the wealthy area towards Sant Just and Sant Cugat. (Note: the distances stated below refer to Barcelona proper). Situated on the Llobregat axis are two industrial centres: Hospitalet, practically converging with the S of Barcelona (255,050 inhabitants, 5000% growth since 1900), and Esplugues, only 5 km away (46,810 inhabitants, a 10-time increase in four decades), were the villages most affected by the high level of immigration in the sixties and early seventies, as reflected in the development of numerous mass housing estates. El Prat del Llobregat (64,987 inhabitants), 7 km away, is an extensive urban area in which the airport and several sizeable new industries are located. Sant Just Desvern (11,022 inhabitants), 7 km away, and Sant Joan Despí (22,867 inhabitants), 12 km away along the Collserola mountain ridge, also abandoned their agricultural activities to dedicate themselves to industry. Viladecáns (see page 189) followed suit, as did Molíns de Rei, located 17 km to the SW and of particular historical interest with its Carles III bridge. Along the second axis, the River Besós, 6 km away is Sant Adrià (36,397 inhabitants), and 9 km away is Badalona (217,983 inhabitants), the Iberian *Baitolo* and Roman *Baetulo*, a modern industrial town dating back to the 19th c. Both are densely populated urban con-glomerations characterised by light industries and large shopping centres. On the third front and on the other side of the mountain range is the district of Vallés, with its rolling hills and rich landscapes, whose economy is based partly on its industrial activities, but mainly on the service sector. It includes Ripollet (25,833 inhabitants), 13 km away, Cerdanyola (84,315 inhabitants), 15 km away, with its private university, and 18 km away, at the foot of the mountain range, San Cugat (31,184 inhabitants), a residential community with a

Sant Cugat del Vallés
Molíns de Rei
Cerdanyola
Sant Just Desvern
Sant Joan Despí
Esplugues
Viladecáns
Badalona
Hospitalet
Barcelona
Sant Adrià
El Prat del Llobregat

13th c. cloister. The authorities are currently planning a metropolitan region of Barcelona, which, in addition to the area mentioned above, would include approx. 163 municipalities, 3,236 km² and 4.2 million inhabitants, two thirds of the total population of Catalonia. Within the Vallés region, this area embraces the industrial town of Mollet (35,494 inhabitants), 17 km away, Sabadell (189,184 inhabitants), the second largest industrial centre in Catalonia, 20 km away; Canovelles (13,508 inhabitants), 29 km away; and L'Ametlla (4,467 inhabitants), 42 km away. Along the coast, towards the NE, is Vilassar de Mar (see page 188); Mataró (101,479 inhabitants), the Roman *Iluro*, now an industrial town, 28 km away; Caldes d'Estrac (1,652 inhabitants), 36 km away, and Palafolls (4,069 inhabitants), 60 km away. Towards the SW is Sitges (see page 188), a popular tourist resort. Further inland, 70 km away, is the industrial town of Igualda (32,460 inhabitants); 44 km W is Sant Sadurní d'Anoia (8,596 inha-

bitants), the *cava* bubbly wine capital; and 25 km N is Palau de Plegamàns (9,689 inhabitants). Besides these areas, with works featured in this guide, 55 km N is Els Hostalets de Balenyà (3,203 inhabitants) and 42 km NE is Canyamars (313 inhabitants).

Parish Church of Sant Jaume 1957   B 10

Marqués de Montroig 214. **Badalona**

Moragas i Gallisà

In this small chapel, the architect adopted a stance which Bohigas described afterwards as "Realist", typical of the Barcelona School: the poor materials used, both traditional and contemporary, were recomposed in a fusion of asymmetrics inspired by the Brutalist movement.

Piher Factory 1959-64   B 10

Riera Cañadó. **Badalona**

Bohigas/Martorell

The complex incorporates an electronic products factory and consists of two buildings, one designed for industrial production and the other, which is smaller in size, for the changing rooms, a dining room and the porter's office. By adopting the standard elements used in the construction of industrial bays – such as the aggregation of modules, use of metal ridge roofs and incorporation of roof-lighting – but intensifying its expressivity and optimising its assets, the project acquires a unitarian image. Following its first enlargement, the same team of architects demolished the factory in 1970 and replaced it with a more flexible building with a larger capacity, setting it up as an open space which could easily be adapted for enlargement or changes in function.

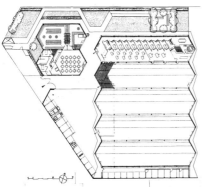

Remodelling of La Llauna Factory for School Use 1984-86   B 105
Industria c/v Sagunto. **Badalona**
Miralles/Pinòs
A desire to preserve the size and span of the building during the scaling implied by its new use as a school led the architects to keep an open-plan ground floor and to lean the constructed elements against the existing structure.

Law Courts 1986-90   B 106
Germà Juli c/v Prim. **Badalona**
Mateo/Moliner
The architects decided to let the urban structure surrounding the building define its tripartite distribution, which is reflected on the outside in the composition of the very solemn frontal façade and which, in contrast, is dramatised inside with a courtyard uniting the vertical circulation flows.

Municipal Sports Pavilion 1987-91   B 107
Ponent 143-161. **Badalona**
Bonell/Gil
The architects' determined efforts to transform this urban environment with the introduction of a "sports cathedral" resulted in the selection of a scheme that had already been employed in this type of building: the application of a design language, similar to that used in the Horta cycle track (see B 71). The perfect ellipse is inserted into the urban surroundings with the clear intention of striking up a two-way osmotic relationship: if the regularity of its shape is capable of creating a new order and a new hierarchy within the context, the site is also capable of conditioning the arrangement of the

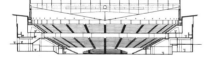

building, producing a slight incline and breaking the long plan view axis of the outer ring with its grand entrance. As in the Horta cycle

track, the architects made no attempt to impress their public with the selection of costly materials or advanced technology. The most representative element of this design economy is the structure of its roof, involving a one-way, non-radial scheme, superimposed onto the ellipse of the amphitheatre. It is made up of six long metal beams (86, 78 and 60 m) joined by a central nerve designed to reduce the stress and allow for the entry of natural light.

B 108 **Ugalde House** 1951-52
Caldes d'Estrac
Coderch/Valls

The house is one of the best examples and most important symbols of the rebirth of Modern architecture after the gloomy years of the *Beaux Arts* imposed by the post-war regime. The traditional Mediterranean motifs found in the houses designed by Coderch in the forties, such as the Garriga Nogués house in Sitges (see page 188), lose all their vernacular or anecdotic connotations when incorporated into a design language directly inspired by the Rationalist masters of the twenties and thirties, particularly in view of the artist's interest in the simple, basic forms of the "white architecture" associated with Mediterranean Europe. In the case of the Ugalde house, the design is based on the creation of an artificial platform, imitating the typical farming terraces, which clearly defines the scope of the house and provides the framework for the sculptured composition of its volumes. A clearly centrifugal dynamic is applied in an attempt to present the construction as an echo of its context, mindful of the trees populating the area, the magnificent views of the surrounding landscape and the gradient of the site. By isolating the guest-room, which was transformed into an abstract polyhedron linked to the house by a roof, and by raising the owner's room above ground level, with its privileged view of the natural surroundings, a series of intermediate zones were created which open onto the landscape emphasising the synthesis of the domestic and natural environments. This highly successful experiment goes down as an *unicum* in Coderch's works, who later tended towards the application of strict compositional and attributive laws which were converted into the standards and codes of his language, applied to both single-family houses and urban housing with the coherence and order that characterises the architect's profession. When referring to the dynamic and turbulent volumes used in the Ugalde house in later years, Coderch admitted that he should perhaps have imposed "a little more order".

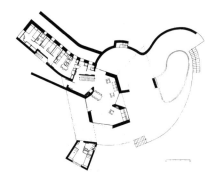

Simón Warehouse 1986-88 B 109
Isaac Peral, Pol. Industrial Congost. **Canovelles**
Clotet/Paricio
The large bay (35 m) required for storage
purposes was resolved with a series of
metal trusses resting on large reinforced
concrete columns, supported by concrete
block wall facing which acts as a counterpart
to the light metal skin of the cover and the
end walls.

Family House 1964 B 110
Mas Silvestre. **Canyamars** (Dosríus)
Martorell/Bohigas/Mackay
In order to establish a closer contact with
nature and, at the same time, allow a certain
flexibility of use, the building was divided
into three distinct units linked by a series of
porches. A simple construction system was
used, involving brick walls and sloping ridge
roofs.

Apartments 1976-79 B 111
Jaume Mimó c/v Les Vinyes. **Cerdanyola**
Clotet/Tusquets
This complex of 18 apartments is divided
into two rows, one straight and one curved,
separated by a common space. The different
zones of the house are distributed upwards,
following the development of the staircase,
while a complex system of galleries lead to
the individual studios on the top floor.

M.M.I. House 1955-58 B 112
Apel.les Mestres 8-10, Ciudad Diagonal. **Esplugas**
Sostres
This single-unit residence, initially conceived
as a plane of reinforced concrete positioned
over a grid of uniform metal pillars, was
eventually adapted to the relative positioning and neoplasticity of a series of walls,
creating an interesting effect of transparencies
and visual relationships.

Iranzo House 1957 B 113
Apel.les Mestres 19, Ciudad Diagonal. **Esplugas**
Sostres
This housing programme was distributed
with certain autonomy into compact units.
Similarly, the occupation of the site and the
external arrangement of each of the outer
skins complied with this volumetric grouping
in clear reference to the central European
Rationalist style of architecture.

Family House 1958   B 114
Av. Paissos Catalans 23. **Esplugas de Llobregat**
Correa/Milà
This was the first in a series of three houses
built in this family estate around the grand-
mother's house in response to the need of
a growing family. The house, dominated by
an arrangement of horizontal lines, is built of
brick, closed to the outside and open to a
central courtyard.

Extension to the   B 115
Godó y Trías Factory 1954
Pol. Torrent Gomal. **Hospitalet de Llobregat**
Correa/Milà
The new pavilion annexed to this industrial
complex containing a cafeteria, day-care
centre and two apartments, was introduced
as an exercise in the pre-existing language,
recovering the dexterity and expressivity of
facing brick.

Pau Sants State School 1981-83   B 116
Pasaje Miner. **Hospitalet de Llobregat**
Bosch/Tarrús/Vives
The peculiarity of the site occupied by this
primary and secondary school building, at
the end of a row of houses situated inside
an industrial block, was resolved by intensifying the volume of the structure in such a
way that the line was formally completed
and the inside of the block liberated.

Cemetery 1985-96   B 117
Av. de los Países Bajos s/n. **Igualada**
Miralles/Pinòs
The construction of the cemetery was based
on a previous examination of the shape of
the site, whose contours were moulded in
such a way that what was once just a landscape was converted into a formal site. The
elements constructed, partly underground,
partly above it, reinforce the modifications
introduced by the design. The churchyard
was developed on a split level, with the
concrete retaining walls accommodating
the vaults. The graves were located in an
elliptical space situated on the lower level.
Beyond the opaque service wall at the
entrance, the cemetery was drawn out in a
descending course towards the heart of the
valley and away from the noise. To leave
the site, one has to turn on one's tracks and
walk back along the same path.

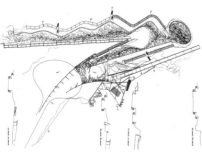

Uriach House 1962
B 118

Sant Pere s/n. **L'Ametlla del Vallés**
Coderch/Valls
Confirming the coherence of the architects'
objectives, this project, a true variation on
the theme of the single-family house, tones
down the geometrics of the Catasús house
(see B 140) with the insertion of modulated,
recessed volumes previously used in the
Rozes house (see GI 15).

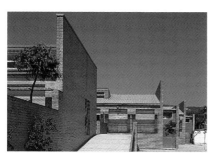

Puig i Cadafalch Block 1971-75
B 119

Av. Puig i Cadafalch c/v Salesianos. **Mataró**
Clotet/Tusquets
The recessed surfaces of two of the building
façades are clearly defined by a taut line. In
contrast to the traditional typology of the
housing block with patio, the ground floor
design follows the course of the urban
artery which closes off the surrounding
area, opening onto a semi-public space.

Camí del Cros State School 1984-86
B 120

Ronda del Cros 13. **Mataró**
Brullet
The basic structure of this enclosure-building
contains the communal services and screens
the school from the suburban surroundings.
From this point, the units housing the classrooms extend towards the farmland, providing the space needed for the installation of
vegetable gardens, walkways and squares.

Twin Bridges
B 121
over the River Llobregat 1972

Ctra. N-II. **Molins de Rei**
Villar/Torroja Cavanillas [engs.]
Built at the site formerly occupied by the
Carles III bridge, these bridges are illustrative
of Torroja's mastery. The structures of
prestressed, reinforced concrete are
supported by pillars with a 125 m central
span.

Gardened Housing Estate 1985-93
B 122

Residencial Sud Gallecs. **Mollet del Vallés**
Garcés/Sòria
This residential estate is formed by two
blocks built around interior courtyards set
in symmetrical relation to the square and
main avenue. The public spaces exercise
direct influence over the layout and
the composition of the accesses to the
common spaces.

Sports Centre 1987-96 B 12?
Ramón Turró c/v Ribera de la Burgada. **Palafolls**
Isozaki
Here, the architect developed his initial proposal for the Sant Jordi Palace in Barcelona (see B 81). Adapting the design to the new scale of the site, he introduced a semi-circular roof composed of a two-layer spatial triangular grid, whose undulations define the requirements of the programme.

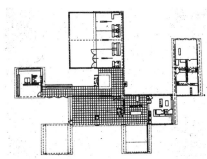

Correction Centre 1984-86 B 12
Garraf s/n. **Palau de Plegamans**
Bru
Subtly avoiding any reference to the image of the "specialised" building and paying thorough attention to the topographical conditions of the surrounding area, the architect placed a finely calibrated, tense architectural composition within the context of the natural landscape.

La Ricarda Villa 1949-61 B 12
Camí de l'Albufera. **El Prat de Llobregat**
Bonet Castellana
Having recently completed his Punta Ballena constructions in Maldonado, Uruguay (see page 335), Bonet Castellana received the commission for this residential building on his first trip to Spain after his exile in Argentina during the Civil War. The project took four years to complete; after rejecting an initial Le Corbusier type proposal, a design relating more closely to his experience in South America and showing greater sensitivity to the site – the delta of a river, in a pinewood near the beach – was adopted. A reinforced concrete roof, supported at each corner by four metal pillars, was the organisational element behind a design which, despite the large size of the programme, was arranged on a single level. Repeating this 8.8 x 8.8 m module, the same element was used to cover both external and internal spaces. The project extends over the site, breaking it up into sections and avoiding the organisation of the units around a central nucleus. In the same way, the trees and vegetation invade these intermediate spaces, drawing the external space into the interior of the building and extending the projections produced by these roofs into the garden area, which is ordered by the incorporation of small elements.

Remodelling and Extension of El Prat Airport Terminal 1989-92
B 126

El Prat de Llobregat
Bofill Levi

Inspired by the typology of the *rambla*, or dry river bed, Bofill created a 870 x 18 m raised rectangular passage way linking the different areas. Four triangular terminal buildings are positioned along its length catering for both departures and arrivals.

Medical Centre 1982-85
B 127

Tarragona c/v Ctra. Sabadell-Barcelona
Ripollet
Llinás

Situated at the junction between a series of fast lanes of traffic, the building is screened from the aggression of the surrounding area by the large platform which covers the parking area. Its staggered volumes have a predominantly horizontal arrangement.

Council Apartments and Shops 1989-94
B 128

Ctra. de Prats, Antoni Forellad, Barrio de Torreguitart. Sabadell
Bach/Mora

In order to invest these apartments with an urban character (as part of a suburban area project) the architects used the materials and structures of the surrounding buildings, introducing a slightly raised patio to screen the area from the surrounding traffic.

Besós Park 1982-87
B 129

Cristóbal de Moura. Sant Adrià del Besos
Viaplana/Piñón

Located on the very edge of the outskirts of Barcelona, the design, whose borders are protected by vegetation, created a public place with objects positioned on levelled ground. The area between these objects was left to grow freely, loosely defined by the general layout.

Can Bonet - El Pla House 1976-83
B 130

Camí del Vallserena. Sant Antoni de Vilamajor
Bonet/Cirici

Despite the modesty of the project design, which took the henhouses as its main source of inspiration, this small house was designed with highly refined spatial and morphological devices which range from the "pure architecture" of the porticoes to a meticulous attention to detail.

Fortuny Apartments and Swimming Pool 1972-74

Mozart 7. **Sant Cugat del Vallés**
Clotet/Tusquets

This was the first adaptation of the housing scheme previously implemented by these architects in Cerdanyola in 1976 (see B 111). The different areas, arranged along the length of the staircase, are directly inter-connected through the use of sliding walls.

Municipal Hall 1990-93

Paseo Torreblanca. **Sant Cugat del Vallés**
Artigues/Sanabria

The design, which also includes the sloping square, became the new civic point of refer-ence in the semi-urban area of Sant Cugat. The complex programme was divided into three regular horizontal volumes which are dominated by the blind box of the theatre, clad with louvres.

Medical Centre 1984-86

Carrer de la Vinya s/n. **Sant Hipolit de Voltregá**
Viaplana/Piñón

While the project by the same architects for the enlargement of the Sant Pere de Badalona cemetery (1984-90) in Camí del Xiprers, Ctra. Badalona-Mollet, was dictated by the topography, the building designed for this public health centre took no such consider-ations into account, existing in its own right.

Negre House 1915-30

Llobregat c/v Torrent del Negre. **Sant Joan Despí**
Jujol

This project involved the renovation of an old country house or *masia* built in 1680. Here, the architect injected the old zones with an entirely new character through a series of detailed, colourful restructuring and cladding operations which bring to life the typical symbolic elements used by Jujol. Without modifying any of the original open-ings of the façade, Jujol applied scratchwork coating to the façade and crowned it with an undulating cornice line, at the same time that he converted the central balcony into a bold overhanging gallery. The renovation of the interior focused on the stairway area, which was given the spatial treatment of a church dome, and on the creation of a small chapel, which was designed using a clearly Baroque style.

Jujol House 1931
B 135

Jacint Verdaguer 31. **Sant Joan Despí**
Jujol

The architect's holiday home in Sant Joan Despí, where he was municipal architect, incorporates an intentional economy of resources. A tall structure emerges from the centre of a symmetrical floor plan, with windows positioned at its angles (a recurrent technique in the solution of towers).

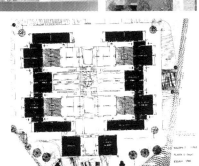

Walden Building [Phase I] 1970-75
B 136

Av. de la Industria s/n. **Sant Just Desvern**
Bofill

In *Walden, or Life in the Woods*, the 19th c. sociologist, Thoreau, proposed an alternative way of community life. This modern adaptation of Fourierism was intended as an attempt at illustrating Thoreau's theory, constructed on the terrain of a disused cement factory in the modern "woodlands" of the industrial suburbs. Amid controversy from upper middle class authorities, a standard multi-functional 30 m² cell was conceived and annexed to form the different apartments. The complex consists of 18 towers whose 16 storeys are recessed as they extend upwards and are joined and separated by different types of ringed or branched flows of circulation, following the scheme previously implemented by Bofill in his Gaudí quarter in Reus (1964-70).

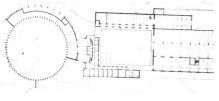

Raventós i Blanc Cava Wineries 1985-88
B 137

Pza. del Roura s/n. **Sant Sadurní d'Anoia**
Bach/Mora

The acknowledged tendency of these two architects towards a calculated, elegant style of architectural composition is illustrated in this wine-making centre, one of their most popular and successful statements, attached to the building constructed for the same company by Puig i Cadafalch in 1904. The design bases were conditioned by a decision to preserve an old oak tree, which was incorporated into the project, giving rise to a peaceful entrance patio defined by a circular porch of brick pillars. The entrance to the wine-making area itself is defined by a series of representative spaces linked to the porch, conserving a figurative balance between the image of industrial buildings at the beginning of the 20th c. and traditional farming constructions.

Department of Arts and Crafts 1987   B 1.
Pompeu Fabra. **Sant Sadurní d'Anoia**
Garcés/Sòria
The commission entitled the reorganisation
of a building constructed in 1884, which was
never formally completed, composed of
two back-to-back volumes, a block of three
open storeys containing classrooms and an
apsed chapel, topped with a new N-facing
roof, used as a mural painting workshop.

More on the coast. 25 km N of Barcelona capital is Vilassar de Mar (12,110 inhabitants), with an
interesting group of schools and secondary school (1990-94), on Av. Ferres Puig, by Brullet and
Luna. Within the metropolitan area, 12 km S is the industrial town of Viladecáns (53,235 inhabitants) and then, 43 km away, between the Garraf massif and the sea, Sitges, a small white-washed
village built up at the end of the 19th c. when it was discovered by painters such as Ruisiñol and
architects such as Puig i Cadafalch, Domènech and Sunyer, who built a considerable number of
Modernist houses in this area. Now an important holiday town within a country which is one of
the leading tourism centres in the world, this attractive village, that multiplies its population of
13,096 inhabitants in the summer, preserves Modern works produced by Sostres (see B 139) and
Coderch (see B 140), who also designed the Garriga-Nogués house (1947) in Zumalcárregui s/n.

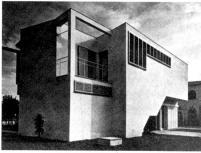

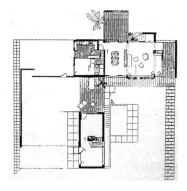

Agustí House 1955   B 1.
Terramar. **Sitges**
Sostres
When referring to the Agustí house, and as
a means of justifying the use of white, empty
volumes at a time when their combination
with a pure, uncluttered art lacking stylistic
contamination was losing ground to a more
spontaneous architecture, such as that produced by the Scandinavian Schools, Sostres
stressed the influence that these concepts
continued to exert in the formation of the
architects of his generation as well as in the
local tradition. This point of view reflected
an attitude present in all of Sostres works,
including a style of architecture reminiscent
of the great masters of the Modern movement. Unendowed with the temporality
factor that impregnates the rest of Sostres's
works, the Agustí house is one of his most
individual works. Located in a housing
development beside the sea, this single-
unit house is organised in two blocks: one
contains the living quarters and the other a
study or possible guest room. Between
them, two axes are drawn defining the
programme and giving form to the garden.
The circulation flows established give rise to
an interesting volumetric effect. Interesting,
too, are the spatial effects created around
the staircase, which inject the project as a
whole with a sense of dynamism.

Catasús House 1956-58 B 140

Onésimo Redondo-Torres Quevedo. **Sitges**
Coderch/Valls

One of the best examples of a programme based on the clearly defined separation between the service area, the daytime zones and the bedrooms distributed over a T-shaped arrangement, this design mirrors the architects' meticulous concern with the distributional nature of the house.

Social Centre 1986-94 B 141

Mayor s/n, Hostalets de Balenyá. **Vic**
Miralles/Pinós

Through the use of projections and recesses, the architects defined the central space of this social centre in the form of a large hall, whose presence is felt throughout the building and whose appearance is defined by a lack of concrete walls and metal trusses. The remaining spaces and the organisation of the programme stem from the hall and contain workshops, meeting rooms, lecture areas, a bar and terraces.

Apartment Building 1969-73 B 142

Sol 6. **Viladecáns**
Martorell/Bohigas/Mackay

This complex of 52 low-budget apartments was vested with an urban character in an attempt to revive the dilapidated area of Viladecáns, part of the industrial belt circling Barcelona. The design adopted the curved form of the street, which offsets the verticality of the brick façade and gives form to the ground floor porch.

GIRONA. Before the construction of the Roman *Gerunda*, an Iberian settlement occupied the hill surrounded by the rivers Ter and Onyar. The latter separates the modern from the old town, characterised by its mediaeval splendour, narrow, winding, occasionally staggered streets, and the *call* or Jewish quarter, one of the most important in Europe. The two areas are linked by bridges which offer good views of the traditional houses beside the river and the Gothic cathedral (14th-15th c.), with its Romanesque cloisters and Baroque façade (17th c.). Today, the importance of pre-Rationalist Noucentiste figures such as R. Masó confirm the Catalonian rather than purely Barcelonan identity of the movement and explain the limited influence of Rationalism during the Second Republic. After the war, fairly neutral urban growth was followed in the sixties by housing developments giving rise to the jumbled residential areas of the town and by the restoration of the old Jewish quarter, while the majority of the high quality works were concentrated along the coast. The stylish construction of La Miranda house (1974-77), by Manuel de Solà-Morales Rubió, on Ctra. Santa Coloma km 0.8, is an exception to this rule. It was not until the eighties that the public sector began to see the development of quality modern installations and works, while the Council's efforts to restore public spaces turned Girona into a pleasant and orderly town. Altitude: 70 m. Rainfall: approx. 700 mm and 105 days. Sunshine: approx. 2,450 hrs. Temperatures: 31°-13° and 0°-17° C. Population: 70,409.

Banco de España 1982-89   GI
Gran Via Jaume I
Clotet/Paricio
The desire to illustrate the representative character of the central bank of Spain was expressed through a cylindrical volumetric solution, whose segmental arches and false pilasters set the rhythm of the design. The building now acts as an important visual link with the 18th c. city.

Adaptation of the Les Aligues Complex   GI
for the University 1987-93
Pza. de Sant Domènech s/n
Fuses/Viader
All that remained of the religious complex of Les Aligues, dating back to the 16th c., were the ruins of an L-shaped building that backed onto the remains of a Roman wall. Further, the only part of the complex still intact was the façade and remains of the entrance to a small chapel. The restoration design completed the plan of the figure with an inner courtyard on whose limits the newly designed extended building accommodating the library and the cube-shaped building integrating the façade of the former chapel were placed. The original buildings, forming the Rector's offices, were completed with a combined use of materials and reinforced concrete structural supports which were deliberately and expressively exposed.

Law Courts 1988-92   GI
Av. Ramón Folch c/v Reial Fontclara
Bonell/Gil
The L-shaped design that resolved both the integration of the building into its urban context and its functional division blended into the surroundings by means of a curved façade, aligned with the Post Office building, and the staggering of a secondary structure which looks out onto the Devesa park.

Costa Brava. The landscape between Blanes in the SW and the French border in the NE sums up the spirit of the Mediterranean: crystal blue waters, coves, pine forests and small fishing villages. At the beginning of the 20th c., painters and writers like Picasso, García Lorca, Dalí, Thomas Mann, Chagall, Eluard all sang its praises. Although the area has been spoilt by the buildings designed to accommodate the waves of tourism that poured in from the sixties onwards, the area still has some beauty spots. From N to S, with distances from Barcelona: 69 km away is El Port de la Selva (760 inhabitants) and the neighbouring Romanesque monastery (10th c.) of Sant Pere de Rodas. Also 69 km away is Cadaqués (1,814 inhabitants), the sunny little fishing village with an atmosphere dominated by architects, artists and intellectuals. The Senillosa house (1956), by Coderch and Valls, on Santa María s/n, and the

Cruylles House 1967-68 GI 4
Aigua Blava. **Begur**
Bonet Castellana

The use of a domed modular element (see B 125) helped adapt this house to the rugged coastal topography. The zones are arranged around the alternation of trapezoidal shapes, which are emphasised by the grand structure of the inverted dome that rises up abstractly over the rocky cove.

Llinás House 1978-80 GI 5
Ctra. Begur - Sa Tuna km 0.8. **Begur**
Llinás

This work is based on the relationship between the regular, almost blind volume which forms the house and the gallery composed entirely of glass and screened by a light canopy. This relationship dictates the internal communication system and defines a balance between domesticity and nature.

Romeu House 1958-63 GI 6
Paratge de S'Olivera s/n. **Cadaqués**
Correa/Milà

Correa and Milà's Romeu house is one of the most typical examples of the single-family housing produced by these architects, who began working in cooperation with Coderch and who, despite the theoretical debates of the fifties, were acclaimed for their meticulous designs and constructive techniques, confirming Catalonian interest in paying special attention to details. The three hexagonal-shaped volumes clad in rough stone define the different functional areas of the house, angling the openings towards views of the surrounding land-scape. The calm image of a country villa is obtained through the use of traditional materials and techniques, such as wooden structures, slate cladding and ceramic-tiled roofs.

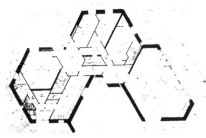

Correa house (1962), by Correa and Milà, on Guillermo Bruguera 4 (see also GI 6) are examples of the new architectural designs built in these predominantly vernacular towns. 56 km away is Roses (10,303 inhabitants), the former Greek *Rodhe*, now a large tourist area on the bay. 37 km inland, the industrial town of Figueres houses the famous Dalí Museum-Theatre with its geodesic dome (1970-72) by Pérez Piñero. L'Estartit, 35 km away, preserves the atmosphere of a small fishing village. Beyond this is Begur (2,734 inhabitants), 45 km away, with scenic places including the Aigua Blava cove, 3 km to the SE, and Palafrugell, 38 km away, with beaches such as Calella (5 km away), and rural communities such as Llofriu (3 km away). Sant Feliú de Guixols (16,088 inhabitants), 35 km away, has several Modernist houses and Amadò, Domènech and Puig's apartments (1970-71) on Ctra. Palamòs 126.

Castanera House 1963-64   GI 7
Es Golfet. **Calella** (Palafrugell)
Bonet Castellana
The architect was chiefly concerned with
the generous platform of the terrace, which
was interpreted as a large open space under
which the night area evolved, and which
was accentuated by a reinforced concrete
pergola, intentionally overdimensioned in an
attempt to turn it into a landmark.

Photographer's Studio-House 1992-93   GI 8
Llampaies. **Camallera**
Ferrater/Guilbernau
The old stone granary formerly situated in
this orchard was converted into the key
element of this design, which was based
on the juxtaposition of a series of cubic
volumes that closely imitated the original
building. Beside the original building, which
was partially restored for use as a sitting
room and provided with a new roof, Ferrater and Guilbernau constructed a "box" of
similar proportions to house the night area
of the studio-house. Linking the old area
with the new, the architects introduced a
low structure which functions as a kitchen
and dining room. The guest pavilion, lined
with wood and slightly set apart, helps
to inject dynamism into this volumetric
distribution. It is backed by the large blind
box containing the photographer's studio.

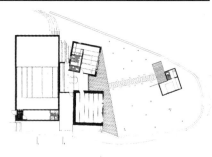

Ballvé House 1958   GI 9
Paseo de Maristany. **Camprodón**
Coderch/Valls
The strict distributional scheme previously
applied in the Catasús house (see B 140) was
taken up again in a nearly identical scheme.
However, this time the design was adapted
to the requirements of the geographical
context, a mountainous area, with the addition of a ridge roof and local stone cladding.

Arco de les Fosses Bridge 1994   GI 10
Eje Transversal Lleida-Girona. **Fosses**
Viñuela/Reventos [engs.]
Two metal-arched bridges, each formed by
two parallel arches with 83-m spans and
copper steel mixed floors, are supported by
circular pillars and suspension hangers placed
every 9.2 m. The construction is perfectly
blended into the landscape by the acute
slenderness of its form.

El Guix de la Meda House 1984 GI 11
El Guix de la Meda. **L'Estartit**
Ferrater

This detached house was resolved as a detailed "stratigraphic" sequence of materials which were progressively reduced in weight; from rough stone to the use of wood and from artificial block facing to the final application of reinforced concrete projecting canopies and copper roofs.

Sailing Club 1990-92 GI 12
Paseo Marítim. **L'Estartit**
Ferrater

Within a triangular layout scheme that responded directly to the geometries dictated by the harbour and marina, the architects created a series of transparencies leading towards the sea, which is evoked in the slight inclinations of the central bearing wall and roof.

Georgina Belvedere 1971-72 GI 13
Llofriu (Palafrugell)
Tusquets/Clotet

Following closely on Venturi's legacy, this ironic exercise adapted an over-scaled object inspired by Classical architecture to the minimal typology of the single-unit residence, resolved in an entirely contemporary floor plan, whose intention was to use the belvedere terrace as a garage.

María Victoria Hotel 1953-58 GI 14
Querol 7. **Puigcerdà**
Sostres

In this project, located at the centre of Puigcerdà, a mountain village with an altitude of 1200 m in the Pyrenees, near the French border, Sostres combined references to the International Style with allusions to mediaeval typologies. The façade, whose design was based on its perception from neighbouring streets, incorporated many different types of openings, similar to those found in mediaeval houses and, while avoiding the introduction of hierarchies, their organisational arrangement was successfully rationalised. The materials used, mainly perforated sheet steel and wood, acted in a similar way, characterising the façade in a material and repetitive rather than compositional manner. The space inside was fragmented into different zones by means of a series of slanting walls.

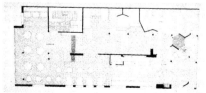

Rozes House - La Almadraba 1961-62 GI 15
Ctra. de l'Almadrava, Canyelles Grosses. **Roses**
Coderch/Valls

This exemplary illustration of a design used on various occasions by the architect involved the annexation of regular modules, set back from each other. The day area revolves around a patio, while the night area is defined by a series of cubic volumes that are adapted to the topography.

Salgot House 1988-89 GI 16
Urb. Vista Alegre. **Sant Feliú de Guixols**
Garcés/Sòria

Situated near the coast, the composition of this house is based on the juxtaposition of two pure prisms, whose geometries create a tension by impacting one volume against the other, creating an external area which opens out onto magnificent views of the sea.

Rehabilitation of the Monastery GI 17
of Sant Pere de Rodas 1988
Sant Pere de Rodas (El Port de la Selva)
Martínez Lapeña/Torres Tur

The restoration of this Romanesque monastery was concerned with the conservation of its ruins rather than their reconstruction. The minimal amount of alterations introduced prepared the site for visitors and equipped the monastery with the services required.

Ullastret Restoration 1982-85 GI 18
Ullastret
Mateo

Located between the capital city of Gerona and the sea, this originally Iberian town conserves the remains of its walls, a Romanesque church and several Gothic buildings. To prevent its deterioration and as part of a policy to revive historical centres, the regional government of Catalonia decided to redefine its infrastructure and public spaces. Mateo's design for Ullastret was concerned with detail and fragmentation, characteristics which are typical of the juxtaposition of buildings commonly found in mediaeval towns. The adaptation to each particular case of the elements used in constructing slopes to transport and channel water has led to a diversification of solutions and materials which all add to the interest of the surrounding area.

LLEIDA. Capital of a diverse land extending from the high Pyrenees to the fruit and vegetable farming plains and the arid lands of the S, Lleida reached the peak of its glory in the 14th c. with its *Estudio General* university. Later, the historical town centre fell into severe decline, subject to a town planning policy which has failed to provide effective solutions. The policies adopted in the democratic era proposed three plans for future development: a well-defined urban restructuring scheme for the attractive fortress hill where the 13th-14th c. cathedral is located, at the historical heart of the city; the regulation of urban growth in a radial direction; and the linking of the city to the surrounding area by means of a series of ringroads. Origin: Hispanic-Roman village of *Ilerda*. Altitude: 151 m. Rainfall: approx. 300 mm and 115 days. Sunshine: approx. 2700 hrs. Temperatures: 34°-9° and 0°-18° C. Population: 119,380.

Old People's Home 1966   LL 1
Ctra. de la Vall d'Aran, Partida de Gualda
Domènech/Puig/Sanmartí/Sabater
The programme for this old people's home, which belongs to a religious order, defined a strict partitioning and complex network of circulation flows which have led to an architecture based on the addition of components extending over the site in search of the most favourable light.

Restoration of   LL 2
the District of El Canyeret 1981-90
La Seu de Lleida
Amadó/Domenech/Puig
The imposing construction resolved the difficult relationship between the centre of the town and the historical nucleus, caused by an uneven topography, with a wall-building structure that emerges from a coil-shaped floor plan and is emphasised by a tower.

TARRAGONA. The hill on the left shore of the mouth of the River Francolí saw the construction of Megalithic temples and was the site for the battle between the Cossetans and the Escipions who, in 218 BC, turned the Iberian *Tarrakon* (6th c. BC) into *Tarraco,* capital of *Hispania Citerior* which, under Augustus Caesar became the imperial city and regional capital of *Tarraconensis.* Following its occupation by the Visigoths (5th c.), the city declined from the time of the Moorish invasion in 714 until the Christian reconquest in the 12th c., when the cathedral was built. The widening of the streets which demolished the mediaeval walls (1854) established a central axis in the Rambla Nova, while the ancient port was expanded in the 20th c. with the industrialisation of the city at the end of the fifties. At the end of the 20th c., this city-region, located on the coastal plain of El Camp de Tarragona, has experienced the migration and scattering of its inhabitants. Although it conserves its important historical centre, witness to the splendour under Augustus Caesar (see the Archaeological Museum), more than half of its population lives in isolated municipalities and communities. Besides others (see page 200), the ancient port of Salou (8,236 inhabitants), 10 km SE, and the old fishing port of Cambrils (14,903 inhabitants), 18 km SE, joined by an uninterrupted beach, are both ports originally involved in exporting industrial products from Reus (88,595 inhabitants), 14 km W, and have become important centres since the tourism boom that took place in the seventies. On the other hand, Els Pallaresos (670 inhabitants), 6 km away, is still a rural village. The area is due for a complete restructuring operation and the application of an impartial development policy. Rainfall: approx. 500 mm and 100 days. Sunshine: approx. 2,700 hrs. Temperatures: 33°-16° and 6°-22° C. Population: 111,869.

Civilian Government Building 1954-57
Pza. Imperial Tarraco s/n
Sota, A. de la

In 1956 the General Board of Architecture launched a preliminary design competition for the construction of the Civilian Government building in Tarragona, to be located on Plaza Imperial Tarraco, a central space in the *eixample* area of the city. The design principles stressed the importance of giving the main façade a unitary character and the cornice line a height of at least 21 m. In addition, they imposed the use of natural stone ashlar in a programme which, apart from its administrative functions, was to include a large number of apartments. De la Sota won the competition with a project that focussed on two themes: the volumetric organisation of the different functions to be served and the definition of an axis whose impact on the façade introduced a hierarchy into the design, resolving the representative character of the building, although not without some irony. The volumetric arrangement results from the juxtaposition of the uses: the administrative functions are arranged in a horizontal unit on which the living quarters are positioned, including the Governor's residence and the guest and staff quarters. By separating the shared network of pillars enclosing these two volumes, the architect emphasised their autonomy, pushing back the outer skin of the ground and second floors and allowing the structure to emerge. Even if there is a diversification of use, the distribution maintains the same principle in each storey: organisation around an axis incorporating the main entrance and Governor's balcony, which becomes the reference point for the other openings on the main façade. The clarity of the initial design is maintained from the spatial definition of the interior and the application of constructive solutions to the design of the woodwork and furniture. At a time when the official buildings produced by the Franco regime were marked by an academic Eclecticism, the Civilian Government building, a masterful piece of singular architecture, backed the values of the Modern movement, flying the flag for Spanish modernity. In 1985, Josep Llinás worked with de la Sota to complete the restoration of the building.

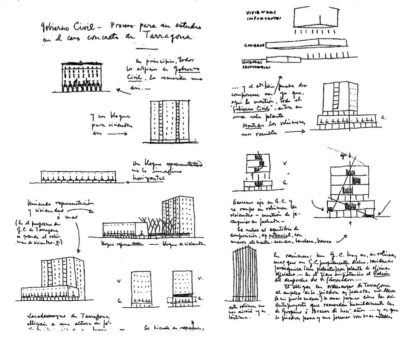

Holiday Resort 1955   TA 2
Ctra. de Barcelona s/n
Monravà/Pujol Sevil
Commissioned by the Union for Education
and Leisure Works, the resort was designed
to provide a place for workers to spend
their holidays. Staggered over three levels
due to the passing of the road and railway,
the 200-unit design is defined in small units
characteristic of the Mediterranean language.

Urban Solid Waste   TA 3
Incineration Plant 1988-90
Pol. Industrial Riu Clar
Bach/Mora
Catering to the needs of each of the different sections, the project was articulated in a
series of blind, cubic volumes. Contrasting
with these, the intentional exposure of the
machinery was turned into a symbol of the
plant's function.

More on Tarragona. The headquarters for the Architects' Chamber (1985-92), on Sant Llo-
renç 20-22, was designed by Moneo. During the eighties, there was an increase in outfitting
operations. These include the Medical Centre (1983-87), by Garcés and Sòria, on Francesc
Macià s/n, in Mòra la Nova (2,662 inhabitants), 62 km to the W. Its neighbouring town is
Mòra d'Ebre (4,487 inhabitants), whilst Montferri (153 inhabitants) is 25 km N of the capital.

Metropol Theatre 1908-10 • 1992-95   TA 4
Rambla Nova 46
Jujol • Llinás
This theatre, funded by the Workers Union
and designed by Jujol in an irregular section
of the centre of Tarragona, stood in a state
of disrepair following the bombs that fell on
its gallery during the Civil War and its subsequent conversion into a cinema, which
cut out all natural light. The adaptations
made by Llinás, based on the few remaining
structures and the documents available from
the time, was concerned with recapturing
the original spatial sequence. The idea of
the design is reflected in the marine symbol-
ogy of its decorations. Through the use of
bold chromatics, typical of Jujol's palette,
which enhance the penetration of natural
light, Llinás managed to (re)create a free-
flowing, watery atmosphere. The gallery
which led from the street to the first level of
the amphitheatre was extended to include
the foyer; a staircase parallel to the existing
one was added in the hall and the services
and dressing rooms were accommodated
behind the stage.

Catering and Tourism Training Centre 1988
TA 5

Estel c/v Paseo Marítimo. **Cambrils**
Rahola

The different uses to which each section was to be put are reflected in the volumetrics of this complex. The training centre occupies the ground floor, forming the base which supports the two storeys used as a student residence.

Bofarull House 1915-30
TA 6

Els Pallaresos
Jujol

As in the case of the Negre house in Sant Joan Despí (see B 134), in Els Pallaresos the architect was concerned with the transformation of a rural house into a suburban villa for a rich provincial family. Jujol spent 15 years working on this project, which gave him plenty of time to produce one of his greatest works as far as the richness of spatial and decorative solutions is concerned. The renovation was primarily concerned with the rehabilitation of the staircase structures which were elevated above the cornice, creating a rectangular tower crowned by a light iron structure and the statue of an angel, a symbol which is frequently found in Jujol's work. By varying the form of the staircase from square to hexagonal, the ascent to the tower belvedere was illuminated through a series of oculus openings letting in the light. The façade looking onto the owner's land was enhanced by a porch of Gothic-Arabic brick arches, supported by cast iron pillars. Jujol concluded the design with a pergola of parabolic arches which shade the laundry room patio and a garden fence in the form of a blind wall, whose strong plastic expressivity is only interrupted by an abstract triangular opening.

Montserrat Sanctuary 1926-31
TA 7

1 km outside Montferri. **Montferri**
Jujol

This work, which was abandoned on the outbreak of the Civil War, is one of the best examples of the architect's religious involvement, creating, with a sequence of parabolic arched structures, an itinerary which is clearly processional in character. It is now undergoing works for its "completion".

Hospital 1982-88 IA 8
Castell s/n. **Mora d'Ebre**
Martínez Lapeña/Torres Tur
Whereas Martínez Lapeña and Torres Tur's housing designs, park projects and restoration works bear the stamp of a personal exchange, their approach to this 25,000 m² hospital programme followed a very strict organisational perspective which, nonetheless, respected the surrounding area. The hospital is located on the edge of a high plateau, with its main axis lying low over a 200-m stretch, thus accentuating the building's horizontality and blending it into the surrounding landscape. From this central axis, the different hospital wings stem like vertebrae from a spine in a design which, apart from defining function through volumetrics, reduces the scale of the building, conferring on it an aura of domesticity. The hospital wards are situated on the N side of the plateau, which descends sharply into a valley. They are arranged along a corridor opening out to the E and W-facing patios and are thus protected from the harshest winds and the intensity of the summer sun. To the S, a long drawn out building marks the entrance to the hospital. The exterior is layed out as if it were a patrol route, which as it travels, defines the site and as it nears the construction, highlights the building itself.

Chipre Apartments 1960-62 TA 9
Salou
Bonet Castellana. coll.: Puig Torné
Based on the modular use of a gallery with 5-m spans and the standard employment of construction elements (weldings, carpentry), the design strategy of this complex focussed on its adaptation to the site, achieved by the pure volumes of the apartments, which are staggered over six levels.

Municipal Library 1989-92 TA 10
Carrer de Ponent 16. **Salou**
Pérez Jové
The design articulated the programme in relation to the pine wood occupying the site. It concentrated the services at one end and positioned the lecture rooms facing the trees, separating the structure from the enclosure, which was punched to incorporate the external space into the building.

The surrounding area. Torredembarra (6,218 inhabitants), 12 km to the NE of Tarragona, is a tourist town with beaches and a fishing port. 9 km inland towards the W, Vilaseca (11,432 inhabitants) boasts the municipal library (1985-86) intelligently designed by Llinás, on Rambla de Catalunya s/n. Finally, Vistabella is a small village bordering La Secuita, 13 km to the N.

Holiday Apartments 1954-57

Aragó 11. **Torredembarra**
Sostres

This staggered complex of four split-level apartments was constructed just before the tourist boom using a simple design (Catalan roofs, bearing walls and one-way spanning slabs) but paying special attention to the typology and the composition of the façades.

Secondary School 1993-96
TA 12

Av. de Sant Jordi 62. **Torredembarra**
Llinás

On a gentle hill on the outskirts of the town, Llinás created a regular square-plan volume organised around the well-ventilated and illuminated space of the covered, inner court-yard. The external surfaces of the parallele-piped were designed to generate a dialogue with the immense blue sky of Tarragona.

Parish Church
of San Bartolomé 1918-23
TA 13

Pza. Dr. Josep Gaspé i Blanc. **Vistabella**
Jujol

Jujol demonstrated his fully-developed skills in the structuring of this small church, one of his masterly constructions. An advocate of popular Catholicism, Jujol worked with the participation of the small village, which until that time had been denied a place of worship, in a design that converted it into one of his most personal projects, even from an ideological point of view. The building bears witness to a typological "defilement" between the central and longitudinal floor plan, created by the diagonal positioning of the typical Basilican entrance-altar axis across the square plan, whose sides house the chancels positioned at opposing angles. The large parabolic rib dome occupying the central space and the belfry structure are supported by four isolated pillars at the centre of the church. Adopting the typical procedure used in rural chapels, the almost bare exterior contrasts with a rich interior, which features a series of frescos produced by the architect himself.

CEUTA AND MELILLA

Ceuta and Melilla, two very different cities, very different territories, are both Spanish enclaves in the N African coast, enjoying lifestyles that are closely linked to S Europe.

CEUTA. On the E side of the Gibraltar Straits, the most northerly point in Africa, Ceuta is surrounded by sea, set on a small isthmus beneath the Hacho Mountain. An ancient port, the Roman *Septem Fratres,* under the rule of the Hispanic Muslims after the 10th c. it changed its name to *Sebta.* Portuguese from 1415, then Spanish since 1580, it has a 15th c.

cathedral (1421) and 16th c. royal walls and moat. The city was active in the twenties, embracing Rationalism from very early on, especially in the works of José and Gaspar Blein. Both were responsible for the 7-storey apartment building (1929) on Isabel Cabral I, a "skyscraper" by Ceutan standards. The macled volumes and the curved corners confer a highly expressive sculptural feel to it. José Blein also designed the façade of the Maritime Station (customs building) which was originally built by Gallego, Amar de la Torre [eng.] and Galmes Nadal (1930) on the Alfonso XIII Dock. The Town Hall was extended by Cruz and Ortiz in 1989-93. Climate: warm Mediterranean. Population: 70,864.

MELILLA. On the N coast of Africa opposite Almería, on a rocky promontory of the peninsula of Tres Forcas Cape, the Phoenician *Rusaddir* later became first Roman, then Visigothic, and then Christian. Muslim from the 8th c., it became part of the newly unified Spain in 1497, 15 years before Navarre did. With a beach and port, its attractive old city centre, with steep, narrow streets and Andalusian-style vernacular architecture is surrounded by three walled

precincts (15th-18th c.), with the Santiago Gate (15th c.) opening into the first of these. Its architecture, in the first half of the 20th c. was dominated by the Barcelona-trained Enrique Nieto, municipal architect whose abundant output was very Modernist in approach. Modern architecture did not arrive until the end of the twenties, in the Monumental Cinema (1929) designed by Lorenzo Ros. Nieto was not immune to its influence, but bent more in the direction of *Art Déco.* Among the most recent works carried out in Melilla's old quarter (Moreno Peralta special plan) is Vellés's restoration of the Conventico caves, in the bastions (1990-95), which features a spectacular parabolic arch. Climate: benign, approx. annual average 19° C. Population: 58,449.

EXTREMADURA

On the W border with Portugal, with the Sierra de Gata mountains to the N and the Sierra Morena mountain range to the S, Extremadura is divided into two administrative provinces: Cáceres and Badajoz (the largest province in Spain with 21,757 km²). This rural region of large estates has always suffered from its off-centre position on the sidelines of Spain's geography and from the endemic lack of a business fabric, which have perpetuated an insufficient, depressed economic model that the region is fighting to overturn. Extremadura's paradox-filled landscape is an architectural treasure trove. Land settlement programmes brought irrigation to substantial expanses of this dry region that also lays claim to the largest reservoir in Spain, La Serena, one of the largest in Europe. Populated since prehistoric times, its long years under Roman rule bequeathed structures that have survived to the present day: the exceptional, unrivalled engineering work of the 2nd c. Alcántara bridge (194 m long, 70 m high) and the masterly public architecture of Mérida, a city that was once capital of *Lusitania* and is now the capital city of the Autonomous Community. It also has a breathtaking urban legacy from the Middle Ages – Cáceres' old quarter (Heritage of Mankind), Coria –, the Renaissance period – Trujillo, the cathedral in Plasencia – and vernacular architecture – Guadalupe, with its 14th c. monastery, and the villages of La Vera. Since the eighties, some of the most influential names on the Spanish architectural scene have been commissioned to build works in Extremadura. Moneo, Navarro Baldeweg, Sáenz de Oíza, Calatrava and Vázquez Consuegra point the way ahead to continuity.
Geography: 41,602 km². Climate: continental with slight nuances. Population: 1,056,538. GDP: 69% of nat. av.

BADAJOZ. On the banks of the River Guadiana (spanned by Herrera's 16th c. Palmas bridge), it doubles as a border post with Portugal, 6 km away. It has a 10th c. Arab fortress and remains of the 16th c. city walls. The Archaeological Museum, restored by Capitel and Riviere in 1981-87, is interesting. Talavera la Real, an air force base, is 18 km away; Almendralejo (25,325 inhabitants) 60 km SE, and Don Benito (29,324 inhabitants) 120 km away. Altitude: 184 m. Rainfall: 440 mm and 95 days. Temperatures: 36°-14° and 2°-17° C. Population: 122,407.

Kindergarten 1986-89   BA 1
Barriada Antonio Domínguez
Prieto Fernández
Located in a district of sprawling housing on the outskirts of the city, the building enhances its surroundings. The brief was implemented through the use of an inner corridor which combines the functions of a multi-purpose playground in winter with monitoring and control activities. This organising element is the starting point from which the whole scale of the building stems. The modular ground plan allows for a good arrangement of the teaching areas and the sloping section helps regulate the light coming from the W.

Open Block of 64 Housing Units 1987-92
Cuestas de Orinaza BA 2
Carrasco López/López Alvarez/Prieto Fernández
Six different types of social housing units were distributed within four storeys in buildings that run together. The split-level apartments were located on the third floor. The buildings were arranged around a square in an attempt to raise the standard of a rather unimpressive outlying urban area.

Social Housing Units 1988-92 BA 3
Ortega Muñoz c/v García Lorca. **Almendralejo**
Vázquez Consuegra
These three blocks, built on two plots of land on the edge of the town in an as yet undeveloped sector, contain 73 units of subsidised housing apartments. Vázquez Consuegra tried to create a new urban fabric through the design of intimate spaces (take the tiny pedestrian-only square) and the reinstatement of the façade as a unitary element. Two of the blocks alternate split-level apartments with single-storey flats, while the third block contains double bay apartments.

Municipal Hall 1994-97 BA 4
Pza. de España s/n. **Don Benito**
Moneo
The centre was built on the site of the old town hall. Built with the idea of integrating the building into Pza. de España by placing its entrance on the corner of that same square, the result is an exercise in dense, compact architecture with an extensive programme for such a small building.

MERIDA. Founded in Roman times in 25 BC as a strategic point on the banks of the River Guadiana (the junction of the Silver Way, joining Salamanca and Seville, and the road linking Toledo and Lisbon), Mérida's golden age came in the 2nd c. Successive domination by the Alani, Suebi, Visigoths, Muslims and Christian Military Orders eventually ruined it. An extraordinary archaeological site, ruins not hidden under the city's modern-day buildings include the masterly 792 m-long Roman bridge (1st c. BC); Trajan's Arch (2nd c.); the House of Mithras (1st c.), a patrician residence with magnificent mosaics; the Amphitheatre (8th c. BC), with seating capacity for 14,000 spectators; and the famous Theatre donated by the Emperor Agrippa in 24 BC, large enough for 6,000 spectators and with excellent acoustics. Providing a sense of continuity and paying tribute to this heritage, Moneo took Mérida right to the fore of the international cultural scene and set a crucial benchmark in contemporary Spanish architecture with his museum (see BA 5). Navarro Baldeweg (see BA 6) and Sáenz de Oíza, with his School of Public Administration (1988-92), have also played a part in this contemporary architectural boom. Population: 51,135.

National Museum of Roman Art 1980-85
José R. Mélida s/n   BA 5
Moneo

Marking a milestone in contemporary Spanish architecture, the unquestionable high architectural standard of this masterpiece has already elevated Moneo's building to the same level as the most famous historic monuments in the city of Mérida. However, its design also raised the question of how to fit a new work harmoniously into a truly consolidated old quarter. The only answer possible was for the museum to accept this two-fold challenge, making a stand for purity in a building that delights in recreating the aura of the past, whilst reflecting on the key elements that helped to shape a particular cultural and social order in times gone-by. Thus, the first contribution of this irresistible architectural proposal was the way in which its modest urban surroundings accept a series of successive skewed buttresses – a constructive metaphor for the obvious solidity of Roman structures – as if it were the most natural thing in the world. Moneo managed to perfectly reconstruct this type of closed universe – an abstract framework for the historic remains it was designed to house – by stressing and repeating one constructive theme that runs through the museum and partly defines its very structure: the buttresses. The repetition does not end there, as breaks in continuity, proportions and openings are other key elements that Moneo handles as subtly and cleverly as if they were Chinese boxes, around the age-old theme of art within art. The result is an

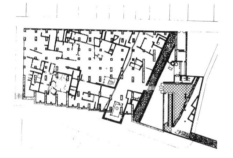

examination of the encounters between a system of parallel walls that are transformed as they meet up with the longitudinal system created by the void produced through the arches in them. The main museum space arises out of this dialectic relationship between the transversal order created by the walls and the longitudinal structure created by the nave of successive arches. The secondary naves help to accomplish the project's aim, that of shaping a huge library of stone remains.

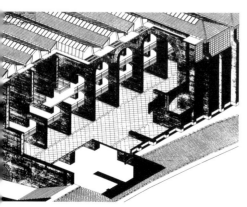

Regional Government Buildings 1991-95
Av. del Guadiana s/n   BA 6
Navarro Baldeweg
On the banks of the River Guadiana, next to the Alcazaba fortress and between the Roman bridge and Calatrava's bridge (1988), this building is clad in local stone and groups together the openings in a quest to balance out its different masses. The structural regularity of the construction stands in sharp contrast to its irregular-shaped site. To a certain extent, the building takes up the architectural heritage approach set by Moneo's Museum – the building stands on 60 concrete piers over an archaeological deposit – and on the façade facing the river there are three glazed inner courtyards that break up the regularity of the elevation.

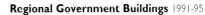

30 Social Housing Units 1989-92   BA 7
Aldea del Conde. **Talavera la Real**
López Alvarez
This public sector housing development consists of 30 interesting, low-cost, semi-detached 80 m^2 units with three bedrooms each. The structure is reinforced concrete with ceramic enclosure walling and polyure-thane injected sandwich panels. The doors and windows are lacquered aluminium.

CACERES. The Almohade wall of the *Hizn Qariz* conserves Roman remains (*Norba Cesarina*, 35 BC) and is supplemented by a Christian mediaeval structure. It encloses an old and well-preserved ensemble of Gothic and, most of all, Renaissance architecture: mansions, palaces, churches, convents and public spaces all form part of the heritage bequeathed to Cáceres by the prosperous nobility in the Middle Ages and the Spanish conquerors who made their fortune in America: the Pza. de Santa María, Golfines de Arriba palace, Cigüeñas house (15th c.), and Moctezuma palace are just a few examples. The old quarter now rubs shoulders with the modern city built outside the walls, with its interesting main square and avenues and buildings of scant architectural interest. Altitude: 439 m. Rainfall: approx. 500 mm and 105 days. Sunshine: approx. 2,950 hrs. Temperatures: 35°-9° and 3°-19° C. Population: 84,319.

Apartment Building 1931   CC 1
Av. de España 7-9
Pérez, Angel
The most significant example of the Modern movement in Extremadura, the design of the façade and the treatment given to the cornered openings turn this building into the prototype of the contemporary formal approach. The ensemble is reminiscent of some of the works by Fernández-Shaw.

Rehabilitation of the Camarena Palace CC 2
for the Architects' Chamber 1986-89
General Ezponda 9
Ayala
The decisive reform of a former house-cum-fortress dating back to the 15th c., whose magnificent inner cloister and restoration of its corner tower are two of its most notable features, brought out all the tension between the existing and the new elements.

Fine Arts Section CC 3
in the Museum of Cáceres 1991
Pza. de las Veletas 1
Aranguren, M./González
The ensemble includes three buildings: the main one (Casa de las Veletas, 15th c.), the extension (Casa de Caballos, 17th c.), and a new, small pavilion built as a restoration workshop in the extension's courtyard. A double metallic string staircase that can be taken apart allows for different circulation routes in an intervention whose use of traditional materials in contemporary designs is reminiscent of Scarpa.

The province. 62 km separate Cáceres from Alcántara (2,264 inhabitants), with the Roman bridge (see page 202) that gave its name to the town (*Al Qantara*, meaning the bridge) in Arab times and to the Military Order during the Middle Ages under Christian rule (13th c.). The village of Vegaviana (see CC 5) lies 88 km N of Cáceres and 20 km from Coria.

Restoration of the CC 4
San Benito Monastery 1962-65
Regimiento de Argel s/n. **Alcántara**
Hernández Gil/Oriol
Hernández Gil and Oriol first restored the monumental part of the monastery, a 16th c. Gothic-Renaissance building used as the headquarters of the Military Order of Alcántara, before incorporating a number of new elements into the original building. The solution chosen was perfectly in keeping with the prevailing ideas at the time of the design and successfully picked up pointers from the Italian school, mainly those usually associated with the work of Scarpa and Gardella. Essentially, great care was taken over the choice of building materials, which had to belong to the area. The approach taken, however, was contemporary through and through. During the eighties, Hernández Gil worked on further restoration of the same ensemble.

Vegaviana Settlement 1954-58   CC 5
Vegaviana
Fernández del Amo

Of all the town planning work carried out
by José Luis Fernández del Amo for the
Land Settlement Institute, Vegaviana is
definitely his most resoundingly successful
work, even more so than his excellent
input to the Villalba de Calatrava (see CR 2)
and Cañada del Agra settlements (see AB 1).
The village is located in the Borbollón area,
near the reservoir of the same name on
the River Arrago that made it possible to
irrigate the lands that had been covered by
huge expanses of holm oak and cork oak
forest. This is where Fernández del Amo's
sensitive handling of the project made its
presence felt. Taking the surrounding
landscape into account, he drew up an
urban layout which respected these mature
trees, keeping them both in and around
the village as a reminder of how the area
had once looked. The housing units built
– 340 for settlers and 60 for workers –
opened onto common areas and formed
large blocks around which a road network
for vehicles and animals was laid out.

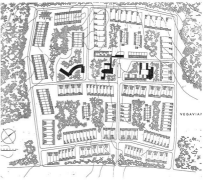

Together with the housing units, he also built a church, seven schools with housing for the
school teachers, six arts and crafts centres, seven shops, a clinic with accommodation for the
doctor, an administration building, a multi-purpose social centre and the local association
headquarters. Fernández del Amo also made a point of using local materials and techniques
whenever possible, so that only the structural elements are made of reinforced concrete.
This work methodology contributed to highlight the local atmosphere and the traditional
nature of the proposal. Nevertheless, the settlement's most salient feature results from the
architect's conscious decision not to exploit any "popular" clichés. As a result, the prevailing
aesthetic criteria in Vegaviana is the harmonious blending of the different elements of nature,
formalised in architectural terms by the serial grouping of identical houses that seek to make
the most of their volumes rather than create an idealised reproduction of a pretentious,
preconceived scenario. All in all, the outcome responds to Fernández del Amo's definition of
architecture: "the organisation of space for human life".

GALICIA

The NW of the peninsula, a land of green fields and oak-clad rolling hills on the shores of the Atlantic ocean and the Cantabrian sea, was settled by Celtic communities who lived in *castri* (6th c. BC). The Romans took over in 137 BC, bringing the region into the domains of *Hispania* and turning *Lucus Augusti* (Lugo) and ancient *Gallaecia* into provinces of the Empire. Lugo then became the capital of the Suebi kingdom (5th c.), annexed to Visigothic *Spania* in 585. Never conquered by the Arabs, it later formed part of the kingdom of Asturias (8th c.) and still later came under the crowns of Castile and León, only enjoying fleeting periods as an independent kingdom. In 1980 Galicia became an Autonomous Community made up of four provinces (A Coruña, Lugo, Ourense and Pontevedra) with its new regional government – the *Xunta* – and Parliament in Santiago de Compostela.

Galician architecture has come under the influence of consecutive architectural styles: Romanesque (11th-12th c. cathedral), Plateresque (Royal Hospital), Renaissance (Fonseca College), Baroque (17th-18th c. Obradoiro façade) and Neo-Classical (Raxoi Palace), to mention a few of the works in Santiago de Compostela. The city itself grew up after the discovery in 813 of the tomb of the Apostle St. James, patron saint of Spain. The Pilgrims' Way to Santiago has been a magnet for European spiritual and intellectual forces since then. Galicia also offers a treasure trove of vernacular architecture, with its *hórreos* (see page 91), small elevated granaries, and its *pazos*, 17th-19th c. homes built in stone by the rural nobility, porticoed streets and squares, trimmed glass and timber galleries...

The structure of Galicia's society and economy at the start of the 20th c. did not differ too much from that of the 18th c., when a steady stream of Galicians began a process of emigration that intensified in the 19th-20th c., when one million people left for America in half a century. The dominant feature of the region was the division of its rural property into small holdings, most of its population making a living out of subsistence farming, and the peculiar dispersion of dwellings into tiny villages, hamlets and parishes. In fact, Galicia has as many communities as the whole of Spain put together. The main economic activity and architecture of interest were concentrated in its port cities, Vigo and A Coruña. In A Coruña, González Villar, Caridad, Tenreiro and Rey Pedreira, alongside Jenaro de la Fuente (father and son) and the Gómez Román brothers in Vigo all tried to bring the avant-garde message home to Galicia. They moved from the prevailing Eclecticism to Modernism (with some good examples dating from 1910) and on to Rationalism. Little was built during the long post-war years. Official tastes followed their own dictates which here mimicked the Baroque style. In the sixties, Fernández-Abalat and Bar Boo tackled the revival of creative architecture as economic development prompted the success of architects such as López-Zañón, Laorga, Cano Lasso and Castañón from outside Galicia's cultural environment. The firm basis on which Galician architecture now stands is largely the result of Bar, Albalat and a group of young architects' efforts to establish the Galician Architects' Chamber; the foundation of the A Coruña School of Architecture in 1974 and the celebration of the International Seminary of Contemporary Architecture in Santiago in 1976. At the end of the 20th c., rural, sea-faring and industrial (ship-building, car manufacturing, oil refining...) Galicia is a hive of creative architectural activity within Spain.

Geography: 29,434 km², a uniform area conditioned by the Galician massif which descends in steps down to the coastline, indented by tidal inlets known as *rías*. Population: 2,720,445. GDP: 86% of nat. av.

A CORUÑA. Marked on the map by the geographers in Antiquity, it was used as a stopover point by the Phoenicians, who may have built the 58 m-high Hercules Tower (the oldest working lighthouse in the world), and rebuilt by the Roman inhabitants of *Cruinia* in the 2nd c. Repopulated in 1208 by the King of León, today it boasts chemical and canning industries as well as a flourishing services sector and an active port. The old city and the 19th c. urban expansion which created the city's Av. de la Marina was, during the early 20th c., the only middle class centre in Galicia. At that time, it underwent a complete overhaul when architects such as Rey Pedreira, Tenreiro and Estellés introduced the new European avant-garde influences and techniques in the city. This renewal was interrupted by

the Civil War and was not taken up again until the sixties, when the city launched a large-scale expansion plan with low-level town planning and housing and the demolition of many historic buildings. It took the arrival of democracy in the seventies for the authorities to bring this destruction to a halt and implement a quality control policy. This reencounter with architecture of a high standard is fuelled by a new generation of architects led by Manuel Gallego and linked to his young School of Architecture (1974). Rainfall: approx. 1,170 mm and 200 days. Sunshine: 2,150 hrs. Temperatures: 23°-13° and 8°-16° C. Population: 254,822.

Villa Molina 1928   C 1
Pza. de Portugal c/v Paseo de la Habana
González Villar
Under the disguise of a detached house, this building actually consists of two houses plus ground floor shop premises, all built on a raised plinth to offer good views of the bay. The façade decoration consists of two bands of colour that run along the four sides of the building.

San Agustín Market 1932   C 2
Pza. de San Agustín
Rey Pedreira/Tenreiro
A bold concrete sheet forms a paraboloidal section vault (linked with Freyssinet's tests in Reims) and heals the long-standing open rift between the old quarter of the city and its outskirts. The design of this light, airy building seems perfect for any kind of outdoor village market.

Coca Cola Factory 1960   C 3
Av. de Alfonso Molina s/n
Fernández-Albalat/Tempeiro Brochón
This glass and steel box was built to house the manufacturing facilities of a then new drink on an exceptional site at the entrance to the city. The hygienic and sophisticated industrial process was left on view to anyone from outside. Recent extensions spoil the design somewhat.

Social Housing in Elviña [Unit 5] 1964-65   C 4
Ronda de Camilo J. Cela, Pol. de Elviña
Corrales
This complex of social housing units, shops, a market, a church, a kindergarten, a parking area and open spaces makes up a residential estate that for thirty years marked one of the city's fronts, facing the main road leading into it. The housing units are grouped into four blocks: one is formed by housing units in row formation and the other three are longer, have more storeys and are arranged in parallel, S-facing and slightly set back to gain more sunlight. The blocks are linked by a network of walkways which give onto the different facilities on the estate. They also take pedestrians to the generous system of open spaces set aside for public use, the outcome of the partial plan for the estate which was also drawn up by Corrales, as well as the parish church (1971) close-by. After standing up to the vandalism inherent in two decades of neglect, the church itself, with a resemblance to certain Le Corbusier style constants, has just succumbed to an unfortunate rehabilitation scheme.

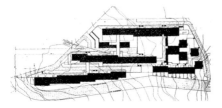

Collegiate Church   C 5
Sacred Art Museum 1982-87
Puerta de Aires 23
Gallego
Designed to house the artistic treasures of the Santa María Collegiate Church (13th-14th c.) as part of an overall plan to boost its image in the interesting but dilapidated old quarter (N of the port), the dimensions of the building justify the attention paid to details and its intimate scale. The problems of placing a staircase in the small enclosure and giving spatial unity to the whole were solved by building the museum around the staircase itself. As a result, the light, floorings, colour and the sculptural handrail are the prominent features of the museum's interior. The façade fulfils the two-fold function of protecting the treasure and detaching the building from its surroundings, notable for a diversity of constructive typologies.

Other works. A good example of the renewing trend of the early twenties can be found in the head offices of the Banco Pastor (1920-22) on Cantón Pequeño 1, by Tenreiro and Estellés, the tallest building in Spain at the time. Jumping forward in time and moving to the S of the new city, Noguerol and Díez designed the Elviña Health Centre (1996-97) in the second phase of the Elviña estate that was originally laid out by José A. Corrales (see C 4).

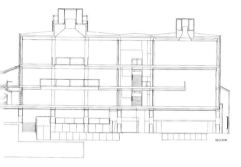

SECCION

Museum of Fine Arts 1988-95   C 6
Panaderas c/v Av. de Zalaeta
Gallego

The museum occupies a site between two urban areas: on one side, the old Pescadería quarter, whose buildings are of the standard befitting a historic centre, and on the other, the new area resulting from a recent demolition and expansion plan, with few works of interest. The brief entailed the rehabilitation of the main façade and one remaining bay of the old Capuchin order convent (1715) and the construction of a new building to house the collection. Thus, the restored main façade and its bay (6 m) were used as a basis for structuring the new building, whose complexity prompted the architect to use a reticulate pattern to order the layout and shape the building. The stone ground floor is a roofed extension of the city's spaces. The actual museum takes shape from this point onwards, created on the basis of a box formed by aluminium sandwich panels, light elements, and glass, all flexibly arranged. As a result, the light that filters in here and there actually defines the spaces instead of illuminating the objects on show. Two sections face up to the neighbouring buildings. One is transparent, in sharp contrast to the old convent, and the other one, blind this time, stands powerfully opposite its more garish fellow buildings.

Red Eléctrica, S.A.
Regional Operations Centre 1990-94   C 7
Av. de Zalaeta 48
Perea. coll.: González Mariscal/Hernández

This industrial building located in a residential setting was arranged around the computer centre that regulates the flow of electric power throughout Galicia. In a subtle metaphor, its transparency both captures and radiates the light it brings to Galicia.

Domus Museum Casa del Hombre 1993-95
Angel Rebollo c/v Ctra. de Circunvalación   C 8
Isozaki/Portela

The steep terrain of a quarry on a clifftop, the last urban space between the city and the Atlantic, is the site of this striking building. Constructed on a territorial scale, with a symbolic curved façade made of concrete pieces, it rather resembles a ship that has run aground on the seashore.

A Coruña province. The granite subsoil of the wettest province in mainland Spain gives way to a landscape of oak, pine and chestnut trees interspersed with natural green fields that provide a basis for beef and dairy farming, timber operations and crops (maize and potatoes). The land is divided into many small holdings and the population scattered in countless tiny villages. Opposite the provincial capital, across the tidal inlet, lies Perillo and, 3 km further, O Carballo, both towns in the municipality of Oleiros. 9 km S and 38 km SE is Culleredo. A Capela is 60 km NW. Nearer the coast, Valdoviño is 68 km N. Santa Comba is 58 km SW, with the school (1989-91) by Noguerol and Díez on Papamoscas street. Corrubedo, 135 km away, next to the cape of the same name, has several architects' summer houses, including Manuel Gallego's pioneering example (1972), that of Iago Seara (1991) in Pedra do Pino, and that of David Chipperfield (1997-).

Dam across the River Eume 1955-60   C 9
San Pedro de Eume. **A Capela**
Yordi de Carricarte [eng.]
The huge dimensions – 103 m high and 284 m long at the crest of the dam – of the first vault dam ever built in Spain set a record in constructions of this type. Designed in the mid-fifties, the dam across the River Eume was built in order to feed a hydro-electric power station located some 2 km downstream in Parrote, in the municipality of Monfero, through an underground conduit. Slotted into a deep, closed valley, the dike's slender outline reveals the ease with which Yordi de Carricarte moulded concrete and the self-assurance with which he was able to dam a river. He put these same skills into practice in other subsequent dams (such as the one in Belesar, 1959-60, see page 216) throughout the whole of Galicia, creating dams that were to keep breaking different engineering records. Nevertheless, this emphasis on huge scale did not prevent him from looking after the minor details of his projects. As a result, his dams always went hand in hand with magnificent auxiliary buildings (houses, equipment rooms, etc.) and careful land-scaping specifically designed to alleviate the impact of the engineering work on the environment.

Tuberculosis Sanatorium 1927 C 10
Parque do Sanatorio. **Cesuras**
González Villar

The Galician Centre in Havana commissioned Villar to build a sanatorium in the woods of Cesuras at a time when Galicia was being decimated by tuberculosis. The programme consisted of a complex made up of two sections, three storeys high, to be used as bedrooms and joined up by a third, one-storey section for the common services. The whole construction was raised off the ground slightly by a stone plinth to protect it from the negative effects of the wet ground. A number of problems cut its construction short when one of the bedroom pavilions had been built (never to be used). Today, the building has been divested of its worth-while elements and now stands on its last legs, almost swallowed up by the forest that was once its *raison d'être*.

Technical College 1961-63 C 11
Av. de Acea da Má. **Culleredo**
Laorga/López-Zanón

The extensive programme for these training facilities was divided up into a number of buildings scattered through a forest. Covered pathways gave the ensemble some sense of structure. Where required, the blank walls were built in slate-based rough stone, while the other walls opened to the surroundings.

Caramés House 1937 C 12
Av. das Mariñas 4, Perillo. **Oleiros**
Caridad Mateo

Built by an architect trained in Barcelona, this house is one of the very few examples of Rationalist architecture found in Galicia. Constructed in an environment dominated by Eclectic architecture, the compositional freedom of the work breaks up the volume and eliminates all ornamentation.

Gallego House in O Carballo 1977-79 C 13
Urb. El Pinar, O Carballo. **Oleiros**
Gallego

This detached house, built by and for the architect, adapts to its natural surroundings without compromising its categorical presence, opening up to its environment by gradually giving up the intimacy of its spaces. The materials used – stone, concrete, oak, steel – are both traditional and modern.

SANTIAGO DE COMPOSTELA. Born in the 9th c. when the tomb of the Apostle, James the Greater was located in an ancient cemetery, *Campus Stellae*, the city has attracted pilgrims from all over the Christian world ever since. The historic quarter of the city with its Mediaeval, Renaissance, Baroque, Neo-Classical and 19th c. architectural jewels is actually even more impressive than its individual works, all masterpieces in their own right: the cathedral, with its Doorway of Glory (12th c.), the Obradoiro façade (17th-18th c.), its striking streets and squares such as Pza. de la Quintana, Rúa Nova, Rúa del Villar or Rúa del Franco, with their traditional architecture. The city remained quite unchanged until the sixties, but subsequent growth, its new status as capital of the autonomous region and part of the heritage of mankind have all entailed an unprecedented phase of expansion. A strict municipal policy fosters constructions in new urban areas and rehabilitation work in the old quarter. The outcome is an architecture of very high standard, including projects by Siza, Kleihues, Foster and Grassi. One of the Cultural Capitals of Europe in the year 2000, this milestone will push Mediaeval Santiago still further into the modern world. Altitude: 260 m. Rainfall: approx. 2,050 mm and 200 days. Sunshine: 1,950 hrs. Temperatures: 25°-12° and 4°-13° C. Population: 105,851.

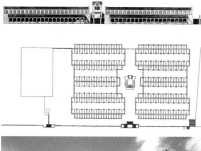

Market 1937-41   C 14
San Agustín
Vaquero Palacios
Standing in the heart of the historic quarter of Santiago, the market replaced an old Modernist building in ruins. The gap between two old churches on one of the cornices of the city was filled by this building where the architect managed to overcome a serious lack of resources through a feat of architectural integration. Romanesque and Baroque-style elements can be glimpsed in the work, as well as ideas borrowed from vernacular architecture. Thus, when the building fills up with the local people from the country who come to the city to sell their produce in the market, the ensemble takes on that eternal aura of a time-honoured building. The paving, inherited from preceding buildings, unifies the ensemble whose eight internal routes and central square are reminiscent of a Galician village.

Other works. The sixties saw work begin in the W part of the city, where Cano Lasso built the housing units on the Polígono de Vite estate (1959-60) and in San Caetano (1970-71) and then, the Galicia Auditorium (1986) on Av. Burgo das Nacións, all of these works whose architectural language and constructive materials aim to link up with the vernacular tradition.

Department of Philology 1988-91   C 15
Av. Burgo das Nacións s/n
Nogerol/Díez
The layout split the university building into two parallel wings linked up by a central section housing the most notable spaces. The triple-height lobby area is particularly impressive, opening onto a spectacular staircase which provides a foretaste of the spatial virtues of the rest of the building.

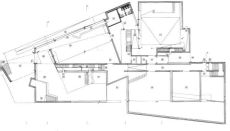

Galician Centre of Contemporary Art 1990-95

Valle Inclán s/n

Siza

This work is more than just the simple implementation of a brief requiring a building for the exhibit of contemporary art works. Its significance is far greater and results from its siting on the edge of the historic quarter, requiring it to change the face of an area of the city hard hit by the tensions produced by the encounter between its old and the new layouts. A further factor of influence was the imposing presence of the significant Bonaval convent (the Museo do Poblo Galego, the Pantheon of Illustrious Galicians) and the urban void that offered up many possibilities at the time the centre was planned. With the aid of Isabel Aguirre (landscaping) and Chillida (sculptures), Siza was able to turn these possibilities into something tangible and successful: the magnificent **Santo Domingo de Bonaval Park** (1990-95). The Art Centre's volume has a mediating effect on the different scales of the buildings and the urban spaces around it. The building is structured as an ensemble of different sized sections around the main section, laid out in a N-S orientation, in keeping with specific and apparently unfathomable geometric rules. In the centre of the composition, a triangular courtyard opens up the three storeys of the building, organising the areas for different purposes. The outer skin is made of local granite, applied in an industrialised format which it makes no attempt to disguise. White is the predominant colour of the interior: white paint or white marble are used on the wall faces and on some tiled floors. The different spaces within the building are layed out following a sequential route which ends on an open terrace with a view over the rooftops of the historic quarter of Santiago.

Conference and Exhibition Centre 1991-95

Barrio de San Lázaro

Noguerol/Díez

This austere and yet welcoming box-shaped building on the edge of the city looks onto the new fast access ringroads on the divide between the city and its suburbs. It was built with a versatile ground plan, volumetric simplicity and restrained construction materials.

University Research Institutes 1992-97   C 19
Av. López G. de Marzoa, Campus Sur
Gallego
The site lies on the edge of the city, forming a cornice looking onto one of its access roads. Although the buildings are independent, free-standing structures, they were actually designed as an ensemble where each piece was arranged to fulfil a specific sequence following concrete lines and an orientation springing from the manifest intention to restore some kind of structure to a dismembered area of the university campus. The buildings themselves stand as prismatic stone elements on their pedestals. The impact of their repetition is toned down by subtle differences in form, volume and colour. The internal organisation of each building results from its independence within the ensemble and fulfils a detailed programme based on scientific research.

Municipal Hall 1986-91   C 20
A. Gándara, Atios. **Valdoviño**
Gallego
The building manages to impose order on its surroundings in a municipality with no urban centre. It alternately folds in and opens out to create new covered or open spaces. Simple materials are used on the exterior, with warm materials suited to the cultural purpose of the building inside.

LUGO. Built over a Celtic *castrum*, Roman *Lucus Augusti* was an important crossroads and capital of the *conventus juridici*. It was also home to the court of the Suebi kingdom under Remismund (5th c.) and was reconquered from the Muslims by Alfonso I in 746. Its walls (3rd c.) stretch for 2 km and form an enclosure around which today's new city has grown up. Inside, notable buildings include the cathedral (12th-18th c.) and its colonnaded streets and squares (Pza. de Santa María and Pza. del Campo) lined by old noble houses. The province of Lugo is rural and farming-based. 55 km S of the capital is Chantada, just 1 km before the Belesar reservoir dam designed by Yordi de Carricarte (see C 9), with its offices and sluice gate outhouse (1958-62) by Castañón de Mena. Altitude: 485 m. Rainfall: 1,175 mm and 200 days. Sunshine: 1,800 hrs. Temperatures: 25°-12° and 2°-11° C. Population: 73,986.

Municipal Hall 1987-90   LU 1
Pza. do Mercado. **Chantada**
Gallego
This work took a mansion house and local landmark as its starting point. The old building was emptied out and then restructured. The interior was designed for visitors to work their way up following a route supported by pre-existing elements and giving a prominent role to the lighting from the roofing.

OURENSE. Its origins are unclear, but it has a Roman bridge. Today Ourense encompasses the old city, with its cathedral (12-13th c.), together with a more modern area built in the 19th c. and several contemporary districts including facilities designed by Alex Reinlein, a local architect. Carballino lies 27 km NW. Baños de Molgas, with its Pauline school (1963-69) by Laorga, is 36 km SW, close to the Os Milagres shrine. Altitude: 125 m. Rainfall: 870 mm and 170 days. Sunshine: 2,050 hrs. Temperatures: 31°-15° and 2°-13° C. Population: 108,584.

Technical College 1974-75   OR 1
Av. da Universidade s/n
Cano Lasso
The programme (a hall of residence, lecture rooms, workshops, other facilities) was split up into blocks that meander through the forest and slot neatly into the landscape. Hermetic walls of crude concrete with an attractive patina look N, glazed galleries S.

Veracruz Religious Shrine 1943-57   OR 2
Evaristo Vaamonde. **O Carballino**
Palacios Ramilo
This lighthouse of faith in a tiny spa town with metropolitan pretensions was built at a time when there was a shortage of every-thing but faith, hence the lack of ornament-ation. The shrine exudes symbolism in its forms, which have been copied from the history of architecture.

PONTEVEDRA. The bridges spanning the River Lérez gave the city its name: the *Pontis Veteris* of Roman and mediaeval times. A working port from the Middle Ages until the 18th c., when the delta silted up, it had its golden age in the 16th c., as evidenced by the Church of Santa María la Mayor, with an impressive façade by Cornelis of Holland and Juan Nobre. Today, it is a peaceful city with an interesting historic old quarter of arcaded streets, imposing houses and beautiful squares (Pza. de la Leña and Pza. de Teucro) and a new sector that has grown up outside the city walls demolished in the 19th c. and which spread to new districts after the sixties. Close to the provincial capital, to the NW is the municipality of Poio, with Vila-garcía de Arousa (32,000 inhabitants) 25 km away. To the SW is the Morrazo peninsula, with Bueu (12,371 inhabitants) 19 km away on the shores of the Pontevedra inlet. On the N side of the narrowest and deepest inlet in Vigo, 28 km away, is Cangas de Morrazo (22,737 inhabitants), a dormitory town. Vigo, 24 km to the S on the A-9 motorway, is Galicia's main industrial city. It is Spain's leading fishing port and one of the most important ones in Europe (see page 220). Rainfall: around 1,700 mm and 175 days. Sunshine: 2,220 hrs. Temperatures: 27°-16° and 7°-13° C. Population: 71,182.

Galician Biological Centre 1949-51   PO 1
Av. de Vigo s/n, Salcedo
Sota, A. de la
Sota closed the decade of the forties with a building in which the features of popular architecture are clearly present, albeit tinted by his personal way of doing things. "In times of great doubt, it is wise to recur to the truth underlying vernacular architecture," he said a short time after building the centre.

Municipal Sports Centre 1966 PO 2
Av. de Compostela s/n
Sota, A. de la
Designed for a competition with a limited budget, its vertical communications were solved through towers at the four corners while the rest was designed with concrete structures, minimum spatial mesh, translucent sheet roofing and good soundproofing. It was modified in 1987 without Sota's advice.

Apartment Building 1972 PO 3
Conde de Gondomar 12
Sota, A. de la
The site, located opposite some wonderful gardens, provided a good excuse for master architect Alejandro de la Sota to recreate urban Galician architecture. The façades made of stone gradually lose mass as they rise, turning into a glazed gallery at the very top of the building.

Auditorium, Conference and PO 4
Exhibition Centre 1992-98
Av. Alexandre Bóveda, A Xunqueira
Casas, M. de las
On the river bank, the ensemble consists of three buildings that can be used jointly or independently. Their complex volumetric features take the ensemble idea further by evoking the strength of this new landmark for the new city.

Summer House PO 5
in A Roiba 1967-69
Beluso beach. **Bueu**
Vázquez Molezún
The half-ruined walls of the A Roiba jetty (an old fish salting plant) that were sinking into the high tide were used as a basis for this summer home. The ground floor opens directly onto the sea, as does the upper floor, where the living quarters were located. The upper storey contains four bedrooms, a kitchen-dining room, a living room and a terrace, all of which are very small. The new walls were built in reinforced concrete painted white. Nevertheless, no effort was made to disguise their rough texture, so similar to the pitted geological texture of this coastline. As a result, far from disrupting the shoreline, the convulsed geometry of the building seems to form part of its geology.

PLANTA GENERAL Y CUBIERTAS

Domínguez House 1976 PO 6
Av. da Caeira. Poio
Sota, A. de la

The idea of the human dwelling as symbolic expression might well sum up this house, better known as the "house in A Caiera", designed by the master architect, Alejandro de la Sota. The rooms in contact with the ground were designed for rest and leisure, whilst those above ground level were better suited to the performance of a physical or intellectual activity. Thus, the bedrooms are arranged under the horizontal plane. Above them are the rooms and areas set aside for human activity. The whole building is topped by a terrace which acts as a launching pad, a space reserved for the imagination to run wild. The building materials were chosen to suit the objectives of the design: earth and stone materials were used for the rest areas, whereas lighter, more transparent materials were chosen for the activity areas. Colour underlines the messages transmitted: ochre for the base, white or transparent in the main section and nothing, just thin air, at the very top.

Other works. Palacios Ramilo (see OR 2 and page 220) designed the Town Hall building (1919-24) in Porriño, 34 km from Pontevedra and 15 km from Vigo. César Portela, who constructed very little in the city where he was born but who created notable works in other parts of the province and the region, worked with Pascuala Campos on another Town Hall building (1973-75), that of Pontecesures, 35 km N of Pontevedra.

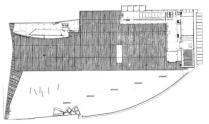

Town Hall 1984-95 PO 7
Av. de Castelao 2. Cangas de Morrazo
Noguerol/Díez

This rather complex brief was developed on a plot of land reclaimed from the sea and facing the town buildings. The municipal offices, local police headquarters and offices belonging to other authorities are all on the ground floor. Also on this floor is the public reception area, with a large counter, and the general hall area built to triple height. Here, the stairs and the glazed lift function both as sculptural elements and as the link with the first floor, with the plenary assembly room and administrative offices, and the second floor, with the mayor's office and the main premises of the political groups. This huge glass box standing on its black stone plinth and topped by a roof which seems to levitate imposes its serious institutional image on the chaotic surroundings.

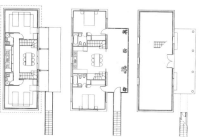

Arturo Estévez House 1980-83   PO

San Martiño de Salcedo. Pontevedra

Portela

The compact main body, glazed gallery and unitary roof of this house, built for a family of modest means, are all features typically found in local vernacular architecture. Load-bearing walls in granite ashlar, chestnut wood work and a roof made of clay tiles slotted over a wooden structure are just some of the elements expressing Portela's own interpretation of the vernacular architecture of the area, based on the use of traditional building materials and techniques implemented with modern technology and rationalisation processes. This blend is also found in the layout of the house around the fireplace. All in all, Portela managed to fulfil the programme requirements, keeping within the low budget and building a house to suit the geography of the location.

VIGO. The city known as *Vicus Spacorum* in Roman times stands at the foot of a hill on the S side of the Vigo tidal inlet. Although it was the most important port in N Spain during the 16th c., it was little more than a fishing village until the 19th c., when it underwent serious expansion thanks to the fishing and canning industries and its use as a port to emigrate to South America. In 1899, the middle classes prompted an expansion that filled the city with Eclectic houses first and Modernist works later. Palacios Ramilo, designer of the Town Hall building (1919-21) in Porriño, 15 km S, drew up an utopian project to turn Vigo into the "Barcelona of the Atlantic", at the same time as the Rationalist trends of the thirties made their mark. Three decades later, Bar Boo relit the pre-Civil War torch with his new vision of architecture (see PO 9 and the 1963 building on Pza. de Compostela 39). Thus began a phase of swift growth, intensive speculation and a development policy that brought wealth to the industrial city through car manu-facturing, shipyards and metallurgy at the same time that

it triggered its deterioration. In the nineties, Vigo faced a large-scale urban improvement operation to save the port installations and some rather dilapidated urban areas (see page 221). Rainfall: around 2,100 mm and 165 days. Sunshine: 2,180 hrs. Temperatures: 27°-12° and 5°-15° C. Population: 278,050.

Plastibar Building 1957-62   PO

Marqués de Valladares 27

Bar Boo

Bar's first work, accomplished when he was still a student, consists of several storeys of offices and three apartments whose staggered sections endow them with a spatial richness comparable to that of separate houses. The building was constructed using traditional materials and experimental solutions.

Department of Economic Sciences and Library 1989-95

As Lagoas Campus, Marcosende
Penela

This complex was adapted to suit the lie of the land. Its two wings (lecture rooms and teaching departments) practically venture into the forest. The wing housing the lecture rooms has a saw-tooth outline that allows space to be optimised without it losing any of its attributes.

Opening up Vigo to the sea. 1994 marked the start of a process to revamp a section of the coastline in Alcabre, a remote city district, together with the construction of the Museum of the Sea[1], by Rossi and Portela. Located on a small, rocky cape and taking advantage of the premises of an old abattoir, the design draws its strength from the use of emphatic new forms. In another section, traffic lanes are being taken underground between Pza. de la Estrella and the Berbés quarter; Vázquez Consuegra is reorganising the seafront[2] (1995-97) along a 2 km

stretch. His plans (1995-) include the construction of a number of new buildings[3], including restaurants, a pavilion and gardens, plus the conversion of the old Maritime Station into the City Museum and the creation of an Aquarium on a platform jutting out into the sea. The design also includes an administrative building by Esteve Bonell, a shopping centre by Sáenz de Oíza and a swimming pool by Andrés Perea. The overall intention is to set up a new focal point for the city that points the way to a future brimming with possibilities.

Seafront Promenade and Aquarium 1983-87

Vilagarcía de Arousa
Portela

The design of a new pedestrian walkway in this former spa town attempts to rebuild its façade, joining up the landmarks which have been conserved from the past to other new ones. The aquarium, with its striking iconography, is one of these new landmarks.

MADRID

In Madrid and its region, the oldest architecture still standing mainly dates back to the times of the Catholic Monarchs (15th c.), although the area did not really take off until 1561, when Philip II established his capital in the small town of *Magerit*, founded by the Arabs, for the essential reason that it stood right in the middle of his peninsular domains. The building of El Escorial (16th c., by Herrera) first, and then the main square, the Plaza Mayor (17th c., by Gómez de Mora) and the Royal Palaces of El Pardo (9 km W of Madrid) and Aranjuez (16th-18th c., 45 km S) gradually formed the large metropolitan structure that still dominates the Madrid region. The Hapsburg court expanded the city slightly beyond the low valley known as El Prado (where the royal Retiro Gardens and their enormously scaled-down palace now stand). When the old Arab palace, the Alcazar, burned down, the new Bourbon dynasty, which began with Philip V, commissioned the construction of the Royal Palace (18th c., by Juvara, Sabatini, Sachetti and Ventura Rodríguez) and oversaw the expansion of the metropolitan structure of the region, while Fernando VI founded the royal grounds of San Fernando de Henares. Under Charles III, the layout of the new capital was established, with the Prado boulevard (18th c., by Ventura Rodríguez) marking the beginning of what is now the Paseo de la Castellana, a 12 km thoroughfare running N-S through Madrid and comprising the trident-shaped junction at Atocha and Juan de Villanueva's masterpiece, the Prado Museum (1785). During the 19th c., the housing stock was systematically renewed, reaching a high average quality that can still be appreciated today. In the second half of the century, the city was expanded northwards, its streets laid out according to a gridwork pattern established by the engineer and architect, Castro (1859). At the turn of the century, the ambitious operation of opening up the Gran Vía, an avenue running W-E, entailed the demolition of old houses and the construction of new blocks.

Plans to extend the Castellana as the modern axis of Madrid were put out to tender in 1929, in a competition won by Zuazo and Jansen, but the extension was not open to the traffic until after the Civil War. Around the same time the city also expanded W with the Ciudad Universitaria, the campus area, in a project commissioned in 1927. By then the city had already expanded its 19th c. limits, having constantly pushed outwards, absorbing neighbouring villages and developing outlying districts. In 1920, Madrid Province had only 1.07 million inhabitants and was mainly a political and administrative capital, where incipient Modern architecture developed alongside the better established Historicist, Academic and Eclectic styles. The area thus features examples of Flórez's school and university complexes, with Rationalist features that make them virtually Modern, which stand alongside works by Palacios Ramilo, the most brilliant, highly respected Eclectic Classicist. In the first group, apart from Flórez, architects such as Fernández Shaw, Gutiérrez Soto, Bergamín and Feduchi were very much in touch with the new international trends. Besides these two major groups, there were others, equally qualified,

Geography: 7,995 km², on the Southern Meseta, between the Guadarrama mountains (peaks of up to 2,430 m) 40 km N, and the Tagus River to the S. Altitude (city): 646 m. Climate: continental, rather dry, with cold winters and hot summers. Rainfall (city): 440 mm and 95 days. Sunshine: 2,750 hrs. Temperatures: 34°-10° and 2°-18° C. Population: 5,030,958 (community), 3,010,492 (city). GDP: 127% of nat. av.

who occupied the middle ground between Palacios Ramilo and Flórez. The work of Zuazo, Arniches and Domínguez, the architects of the university campus, and Fernández Balbuena displayed an alternative modern style, which the city and the province made its own, reflecting the best and most genuine side of culture in the capital (and really, the rest of Spain too) in the twenties and thirties.

The Civil War wrought havoc on Madrid, severely punished for its resistence, but afterwards the city and the region were transformed at the hands of the pro-Franco architects (rather than by the regime itself) who worked in the Historicist revival. The Historicist flavour of the new times radically altered the development of the works designed by Gutiérrez Soto and Moya, the most authentic and talented Late Classicist, and even the younger generation (Fisac, Cabrero) was for a time held in its sway. But soon, Modern architecture arose anew, and the architects already mentioned embraced its precepts in the city's buildings, their works standing alongside those of the new masters, such as de la Sota, Corrales, Vázquez Molezún and Sáenz de Oíza, who were the leading lights in the fifties (characterised by the triumph of Rationalism) and the sixties, when Organicism came to the fore, and who were succeeded by the likes of Fernández Alba. Besides their highly committed avant-garde works, other strictly professional constructions of equally outstanding high quality also started to emerge. Immigration doubled the population in less than twenty years, reaching 3.8 million in 1970. The influx was housed in state-developed projects such as the *Poblados Dirigidos* (managed settlements) and the *UVA's* (neighbourhood absorption units) which perhaps represented the culmination of the Modern thesis of rationalist social housing, although the same set of ideas also gave birth to such unique works as Sáenz de Oíza's Torres Blancas (White Towers) building. The latter work, above all, shows how rapidly Spain ran through the entire gamut of Modern architecture, from out-and-out Rationalism to the most radical Organicism, both understood as "true modernity" in this condensed time frame.

Whilst all this was going on, the city grew way beyond its 19th c. limits, becoming the metropolis that the 18th c. monarchs had envisaged when they built their royal palaces. In the seventies and eighties, when architecture was overwhelmed by an ongoing identity crisis, a new way of thinking arose with the arrival of new generations, educated by the architects mentioned above and increasingly spearheaded by Rafael Moneo. The period began with his small, but brilliant Bankinter building, a true symbol of its time, and ended with his Atocha station. Yet it is best characterised by the state and municipal housing projects developed by democratic institutions. The remodelling of the old peripheral suburbs and the creation of new ones (Palomeras to the S, with housing for workers, is the key example) were exemplary exercises in this new kind of architecture. This stage was very closely linked to the great cultural and professional drive that the old School of Architecture, founded in 1844, took on at this time.

At the end of the 20th c., Madrid is Spain's leading financial and services market, and its second biggest industrial conglomeration. It is Spain's capital, the seat of its two-chamber parliament, its government and its central state administration. In the first half of the nineties, when public investment was not especially buoyant, it was in a paradoxical situation in which it had achieved international recognition as a focal point of architectural development, with a School that turned out well-qualified, well-rounded professionals, whilst at the same time the real output of large works of excellence, reflecting this culture, was tailing out, although there were many outstandingly good smaller works. Although Madrid has always been renowned for exporting good architecture, at the end of the 20th c. there was more ignorance than ever about how to use its new and old genius to transform the city itself, and this despite the fact that Madrid and its region, along with Barcelona and Catalonia, contain the greatest amount of architectural works designed this century. The systematic protection of Spain's architectural heritage, which began in the seventies, served to save some of its best old buildings, but also limited to a certain extent the possibilities of the new. However, the Madrid School's constant output of new professionals augurs a future where there will be no shortage of talent.

Fine Arts Circle 1919-26 M 1
Alcalá 42
Palacios Ramilo
This building marked a watershed in Palacios' career, as he moved from the Spanish Eclecticism of his Post Office Building (1904-17) on the Pza. Cibeles, toward an updated, more Classical style, better suited to fight against the Modernism that he wished to ignore. It is also contemporaneous with the Matesanz Building (1919-23) on Gran Vía 27, and the Commercial Building (1919-21) on Mayor 4. The Fine Arts Circle is special in the way it superimposes different building programmes and meeting rooms at different heights. The resulting complexity in section is surprisingly successful. The exterior expresses this complexity by setting different Classical episodes within a chaotic, exultant melange, thus stamping its character on an already architecturally important area of the city.

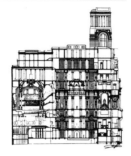

Madrid-Paris Building 1920-34 M 2
Gran Vía 32
Anasagasti/López Sallaberry
This building is typical of the second stage of the Gran Vía development. Initially it was built up to half level, only later being duplicated upwards by the same architects. In one of its street-level sites, Anasagasti made a sophisticated cinema theatre, which has now been transformed and spoiled.

Menéndez y Pelayo M 3
State School 1923-29
Méndez Alvaro 16
Flórez
Representative of the educational complexes that Antonio Flórez designed as part of the 1923 plan, this one is very much in keeping with the kind of public works that Primo de Rivera promoted to improve infrastructure during the first years of his dictatorship. As Head of the School Buildings Department of the Ministry of Public Instruction, Flórez changed the very concept of what a school should look like. This one shows a strict Academicism with some overtones of future Modernist architecture, as in its use of metal curtain walls. Other Madrid school buildings of interest are General Zumalacárregui, on Bravo Murillo 162, and Concepción Arenal, on Antonio López 1, both built at the same time with similar characteristics.

Monumental Cinema 1922-23   M 4
Atocha 65
Anasagasti
Although its exterior is more conventional, its interior shows a full-blown Modernism in its technical and aesthetic details. The refined structure is of reinforced concrete. Anasagasti also designed the Real Cinema (1921), now renovated out of recognition, and the Pavón Theatre (1924) on Embajadores 9.

Apartment Building 1924   M 5
Viriato 20
Palacios Ramilo
With this building, Palacios Ramilo moved away from the Eclecticism of his earlier works and constructed the housing around a courtyard opening onto the street, according to a more Modernist layout that, nonetheless, in no way undermined the forward-looking Classicism of his language.

Red Cross Central Clinic 1924-28   M 6
Av. Reina Victoria 26
Cárdenas, M. de
This U-shaped building with a landscaped courtyard modernised and gave continuity to the Madrid Eclectic tradition by providing a relatively similar version of it using new, non-radical architectures, in rather the same way as the Amsterdam School was doing. The result is very attractive in urban terms.

Palacio de la Música Music Hall 1924-28   M 7
Gran Vía 35
Zuazo
One of Zuazo's early works, it nonetheless provides clear indications of where he was going and his role in making modern Madrid look like it does. He opposed his Rational Academicism, albeit with Baroque overtones, to the Eclecticism of his teachers, moving on the path towards out-and-out Modernism.

Palacio de la Prensa Building 1924-28   M 8
Pza. del Callao 4 c/v Gran Vía
Muguruza
This Eclectic metropolitan press building is representative of Muguruza's style. His skillful incorporation of different scales into the design help integrate its volumes into the landscape of the surrounding streets, while the tower provides a landmark to help passers-by locate Pza. de Callao.

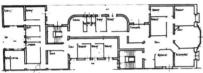

Four Apartment Buildings 1925-27
Miguel Angel 18, 20, 22 and 24
Fernández Balbuena
In this successful residential design that had to provide high-density housing, the inevitable break-up of the façade was incorporated as part of the urban building method which rejected grandiose continuous façades in favour of the kind perhaps best expressed in Zuazo's Casa de las Flores (see M 20) or in other examples of U-shaped layouts around an open courtyard. This highly cultured architect shed any hint of Academicism to propose an attractively varied 19th c. style of composition with brick and cement plaster, thus establishing a new urban vocabulary. Fernández Balbuena also drew up the in-depth study of Madrid that served as the basis for the competition to create further suburbs in 1929 (see M 42). He also designed the house on Pinar 18 in 1920.

Telefónica Head Office 1925-29
Gran Vía 28 c/v Fuencarral c/v Valverde
Cárdenas, I. de
The building housing the Telephone Society is emblematic of the development of the second part of the Gran Vía and is still one of the highest buildings in the city. The design was based on the previous study done by Lewis S. Weeks (New York), an ITT architect. Its concrete-clad steel structure was erected in record time with powerful cranes to move its enormous steel girders. Some say that it was the first skyscraper in Europe. True or not, it was widely held to represent European progress at the time. For all its American roots, it chose Madrilenian Late-Baroque for the decoration of its façades, which somewhat undermines its power as a symbol of the new skyscraper age. It was extended in 1951-55 according to the plans of the original design.

Apartment and Office Building 1926-28
Cedaceros 4
Ferrero, L./Ferrero, F.J.
A unique building between party walls, it represents a Modernism that stands back from the strictures of Rationalism. Francisco Javier Ferrero also designed the Fish Market in Puerta de Toledo (1935), refurbished by R. Aroca and M. Domínguez in 1990 to turn it into a high-fashion designer shopping mall.

ABC Building 1926-31 • 1991-95   M 12
Serrano 61 and Paseo de la Castellana 34
López Sallaberry/González, A./Anasagasti •
conversion: **Bayón**

Originally the office and printing premises for the *ABC* daily newspaper, it was begun by López Sallaberry in Spanish Neo-Plateresque style (1899, façade on the Serrano street side), and continued by Aníbal González in his own personal Historicist style, based on the Sevillian Regionalism of the early 20th c. (façade on the Castellana side). Anasagasti then updated it "American-style" (office building parallel to the Castellana). Later, in 1995, when the newspaper moved to the outskirts of Madrid, Bayón converted the entire complex in a refined Modern style. After bringing order to the labyrinthian set of buildings, he created a shopping mall that is articulated around a central courtyard covered by double-vaulted roofing.

Porto Pi Petrol Station 1927 • 1996   M 13
Alberto Aguilera c/v Vallehermoso
Fernández Shaw

The highly successful reconstruction of this petrol station, recently carried out, carefully followed even the smallest details of the original plans for the Rationalist canopy designed by the highly revered architect, Fernández Shaw, representative of the first Modernist architecture in Spain.

Europa Cinema 1927-29   M 14
Bravo Murillo 160
Gutiérrez Soto

This building is a clear statement of the architect's Rationalism, which he skillfully mixed with Expressionist overtones during his Modernist period prior to the Civil War. It is representative of his designs for cinemas which have added character to the city. In 1997 it was undergoing transformation.

La Unión y El Fénix Building 1928-30   M 15
Alcalá 23 c/v Virgen de los Peligros
López Otero

An interesting example of the tail-end of the Eclecticist movement, it is partially based on the work by the Viennese, Otto Wagner. The building is constructed as a tower in order to avoid overshadowing the next-door Calatravas Church (1670-78), wanting to create some kind of urban identity.

University Campus 1927-
On the NW edge of the city
López Otero
(Director of the Technical Office)

This campus provided an ideal opportunity to expand and modernise the urban structure of Madrid as part of the state-run initiatives of architectural renewal current at the time. Modesto López Otero, Professor of the School of Architecture and Head of the Technical Office team, was placed in charge of the enormous project, planning the whole with a modern rendering of the Eclecticist Classicist style, inspired in the *Beaux Arts* tradition of the best American campuses. He brought to it a broad-ranging vision of how to landscape the city in order to create aesthetically pleasing growth and avoid urban sprawl. It is structured along a generously proportioned central avenue that runs through what used to be the open fields of the Moncloa Palace, leading up to a lozenge-shaped main auditorium, the *Paraninfo*, which despite repeated designs has never been built. It links the city with various independent department buildings that articulate a unity which admits the autonomy of its parts.

López Otero set up a team of high-quality young architects (Miguel de los Santos, Agustín Aguirre, Luis Lacasa, Manuel Sánchez Arcas and Pascual Bravo) to design the different buildings (see M 17, M 18, M 25, M 31, M 32, M 34, M 40). Their work here made them representative of the low-key Modernism current in Madrid at the time. Created at the personal initiative of Alfonso XIII in 1927, under Primo de Rivera's dictatorship, it was continued under the Republic, but then became a front line in the Civil War, when it was completely destroyed. During the first years of Franco's regime, it was rebuilt and then expanded, emphasising its Neo-Historicist features, to be more directly linked to the city. The campus continues to be one of the most attractive neighbourhoods in Madrid, despite the overcrowding of new buildings, put up with little respect to the original order in the plan, and the fact that important buildings like the auditorium have still not been built, leaving a vacuum in the focal point of the plan, which, absurdly enough, is occupied by sports fields that have gradually consolidated themselves on this prime urban land.

Medical School 1928-35 • 1941-45   M 17
Pza. de Ramón y Cajal s/n, Ciudad Universitaria
Santos, M. de los

The axis of the Medical School presides over the biggest and most important sub-campus area of the university campus (see M 16). The building was designed by the architect who worked most closely with the head of overall planning, Modesto López Otero, and enjoyed his ongoing guidance. It was set together with the Departments of Pharmacy (1928-35, by Agustín Aguirre) and Dentistry (1928-36, also by Aguirre) to form a large landscaped square opening onto the main avenue that has become a key part of the university campus. The complex but successful layout of the building over a wide area and its low-key Academicism have provided a composition based on linear pavilions with the systematic use of unique pieces.

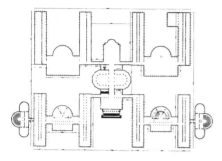

San Carlos University Hospital 1928-36   M 18
Isaac Peral s/n, Ciudad Universitaria
Sánchez Arcas/Torroja Miret [eng.]

A Sánchez Arcas masterpiece, this design shows a skillful layout of the complex, dense mass of different open pavilions and succeeds in using its immensity to configurate the area located in this cornice of the city. The building's architecture is the most radical example of the generally more muted Rationalist movement in Madrid. Total, naked simplicity, without any concessions to figurativism, depends on the clever use of large volumes and the repetition of window and door openings. In this way, it is close to Central European "New Objectivity". It was rebuilt in 1941-46, without Sánchez Arcas, by then in exile. The architect also worked with Lacasa on the Rockefeller Foundation (1927-30), on Serrano 113-117, now the CSIC, Council of Scientific Research.

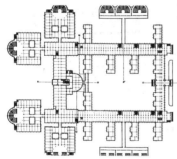

Figaro Cinema 1930-32   M 19
Doctor Cortezo 5
López Delgado

An interesting example of Madrid Rationalism in the thirties, this building is representative of the work of its high-quality, low-output architect, who also made other brilliant buildings, now disappeared, all showing the same graceful, refined and comprehensive design. Now it is in a state of abandon.

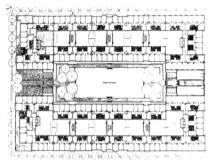

Casa de las Flores Building 1930-32   M 20
Hilarión Eslava c/v Gaztambide c/v Meléndez
Valdés c/v Rodríguez Sampedro
Zuazo. coll: **M. Fleischer**

The complete block of housing known as
the Casa de las Flores (literally Flower
House) is the masterpiece of the great
Basque-born but Madrid-based architect,
Secundino Zuazo Ugalde. It is also probably
the best and most representative design of
its class in the Spanish architectural scene of
the thirties, characterised by a desire for
modernisation without breaking with some
of the more traditional values. Constructed
on an urban block in the expansion grid
planned by Castro in the second half of
the 19th c., the Casa de las Flores respects
the aesthetic and urban meaning and unity
of the 19th c. blocks, with their continuous
walls perforated with window openings.
However, the layout of the block also
proposes a new way of ordering space to
improve and transform it into something
more open: two enormous open blocks,
parallel to each other to make room for a
large garden area, open to two of the side
streets, without in any way breaking up the
continuity of line along them. Moreover,
there is also a generous, almost continuous
inner courtyard, which is only interrupted
by staircases and spaces for clothes lines.
The urban lucidity of the layout, which
has become a widely admired model, still
used even today, is further enhanced by
the successful moderation of the buildings'
brickwork on the load-bearing walls,
with subtle, attractive decoration and a
composition that fits in just as well with the
typical Madrid houses and their balconies
as it would with architecture from the
Amsterdam School that the architect
himself stated to be one of his sources of
inspiration.

Apartment Building 1930-35   M 21
Alcalá 98 c/v Goya 91
García Lomas/Martí

An excellent example of the type of building
taking place in Madrid in the early thirties, it
shows an interesting way of understanding
urban volume in the acute-angled corners.
Its architects clearly followed Mendelsohn's
lesson in a "Rational" translation of Expressionist language for urban buildings.

Other works. The period from 1920 to the mid-thirties left some exemplary buildings, such as the Secessionist Cort palatial house in the Quinta de los Molinos neighbourhood (1925), Ctra. de Aragón 87, by Cort y Botí; the Victoria Eugenia Tuberculosis Clinic (1927-28) on Andrés Mellado 31, by Amos Salvador Carreras; and the apartment buildings on Miguel Angel 16 (1928-29), by Marsá Prat, and on Alcalá 118 (1930), by Arzadún.

Barceló Cinema 1930   M 22
Pza. de Barceló 11
Gutiérrez Soto

The Barceló is probably the most successful cinema building of the many that Gutiérrez Soto designed during a career that spanned nearly forty years, from the twenties to the sixties. Most are located in Madrid, although several can also be found in provincial towns. Built on a corner site, its oblong plan was oriented along the diagonal axis of the corner as appreciated by Neufert, who included it as an example in his well-known book on functional layouts. The external volume codifies the Rationalist Expressionist language to define the urban space that it occupies, a traditional closed city street. For several years now, the building has ceased to be used as a cinema and instead houses the well-known Madrid discotheque, Pachá.

Vizcaya Bank 1930-34   M 23
[now **Banco de Comercio**]
Alcalá 45
Galíndez/Arzadún

These banking offices were built between party walls on the site of an extinct theatre. The building was one of the best works designed by Manuel Galíndez, a Basque architect from Bilbao. Its architecture is full of Academic references, but its use of proportion and its attractive line also have roots in *Art Déco*, managing to put across the image of a solid, metropolitan institution. It forms part of the enormous change that took place on Alcalá street in the first third of the century, from Pza. de Cibeles to the Puerta del Sol circus, which turned it into a central thoroughfare and created a business area around it, replacing the old housing blocks that used to exist there. Conscious that it would play a key role in defining this area, Galíndez made a design that would meet the onerous requirements, placing special emphasis on the external part of the building so that it would define itself and its surrounding area.

Capitol Building 1931-33 M 24
Gran Vía 41 c/v Jacometrezzo 5
Martínez Feduchi/Eced

The winning design of a competition, the Capitol building – also known as the Carrión building – is probably one of the best examples of the architecture that lines the Gran Vía. It stands out for the intense Modernity of its bearing, the clever urban effect of its elaborate volumetrics and the complexity of uses that its design had to be open to: as a large metropolitan building, it was a king of hold-all, containing a hotel, apartments, a cinema and several shops and offices. Its language and the details both on its exterior and in its interior spaces are especially fine, as was the magnificent collection of furnishings and fittings made specially for it, now mostly disappeared. An architecture in the style of Mendelsohn, it fits in harmoniously with the volumes of its unique and difficult terrain. Only the large cinema still conserves the original interior well, a spectacular theatre, carefully restored to its old grandiosity, perhaps the best in the city.

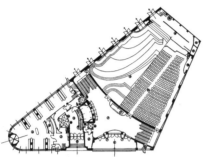

Department of Philosophy 1931-33•1941-42
Ciudad Universitaria M 25
Aguirre

Together with its twin building opposite it, the Philosophy School gives character to the free space around it. The two buildings are laid out in a symmetrical composition in different parts, established in an attractive Modernist language. It has carefully designed interiors with a superb main hall.

Other works. Other interesting works from the thirties designed by Fernández Shaw (see J 2, M 13 and M 26) include the apartment building (1934-35) on Menéndez y Pelayo 15, whose serrated façade solves the problems caused by the irregular-shaped site, and the apartment building (1934) on Marqués de Riscal 11. Of Luis Laciana's works, note the corner building (1935) between Paseo Pintor Rosales and Altamirano.

Coliseum Building 1931-33 M 26
Gran Vía 78
Muguruza/Fernández Shaw

This interesting building for housing and a cinema, the result of excellent cooperation between two unique and very different architects, is rather typical of the Gran Vía. The verticality and the "American" look of the façade are noteworthy, as is the attractive space inside the cinema hall.

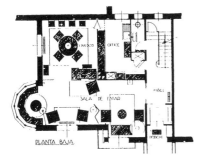

Parque Residencia Estate 1931-33   M 27
Paseo de la Castellana, Joaquín Costa, Vitrubio
Bergamín/Blanco Soler
Precursor of the larger and better known
Colonia de El Viso (see M 41), this small
estate was the product of reflection on the
realities of urban expansion as Madrid spread
inexorably beyond the suburban limits
established under Castro's 19th c. expansion
plan. A new town planning approach was
required from architects: after many earlier
estates, which were conceived as a juxtaposition of sites, each containing a house in
its centre, the architects decided to tackle
the issue rather differently, building houses
for a growing middle class, with money and
education, who could identify with more
Modern architecture and were no longer
bound to the old Historicist principles of
design that had, until then, been the norm
for suburban housing.

Women's Hall of Residence 1932-33   M 28
Miguel Angel 12 c/v Martínez Campos 46
Arniches
This small building successfully plays its dry
volume off against the delicate details of
Rationalism. It thus manages to take its due
place in the order of an important corner in
an attractive traditional sector. The building
has been well restored in recent years by
Junquera and Pérez Pita.

Instituto Escuela   M 29
Kindergarten 1932-35
Serrano 127
Arniches/Domínguez/Torroja Miret [eng.]
A string of open-air classrooms with their
own courtyard, protected by an interesting
concrete canopy (another storey was added
later), formed part of the larger school, the
Instituto Escuela, whose library and assembly
hall were turned into a church (see M 47).

Viaduct 1932-40   M 30
Bailén
Ferrero/Aracil [eng.]/Aldaz [eng.]
The viaduct is an interesting display of urban
engineering, done by architects, with an
outstanding sense of scale for the place. Its
parabolic arches, support elements and *Art
Déco* finishing touches now form an integral
part of the landscape in the historical city
centre.

Thermal Power Plant 1932-35 • 1941-43   M 31
Av. Gregorio del Amo, Ciudad Universitaria
Sánchez Arcas/Torroja Miret [eng.]
The radical Modernism of this small, rather
impressive piece made it stand out from the
rest of the university campus, both in terms
of its use and its very nature, although it has
been somewhat disfigured by an unsuccessful
refurbishment. Sánchez Arcas, who also
designed the University Hospital (see M 18)
and the Rector's Offices (1930), was the
most forward-looking of the members of the
team that worked on the campus, and the
furthest removed from the Eclectical ideas of
the head of the Technical Office in charge
of its construction (see M 16). The plant
incorporates technical machinery into the
landscape in a natural, attractive manner,
using a stark language with few concessions
to a more figurative approach which works
well and became typical for the architect.

Law School 1931-32 • 1941-56   M 32
Ciudad Universitaria
Aguirre
A partial replica of the architect's earlier
Philosophy Department (see M 25), it was
built some 20 years later, after the Civil War,
using a new ground plan and programme.
Although more complex and attractive than
its sibling, the two work together to define
the exterior space of this part of the campus.

New Ministries 1932-36 • 1940-53   M 33
Paseo de la Castellana 67
Zuazo/Torroja Miret [eng.]
Keystone of the prolongation of the Paseo
de la Castellana, aimed at turning it into the
main thoroughfare of the city and opening it
up to further development, this Government
building was started under the Republic –
commissioned by the Minister of Public
Works, Indalecio Prieto – and finished under
Franco's regime. After Zuazo was deported
to the Canary Islands, his project was taken
over by Diz, Gómez Mesa, Rodríguez Cano
and García Lomas. It marked the beginning
of the straight line that still cleaves through
the city from the site of the old racetrack
(transferred to the outer suburbs) up to
Pza. de Castilla. In the Academic style, very
much in line with the Government buildings
of the time, its ground plan is more Modern
in inspiration, with a very open layout.

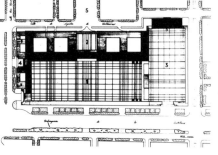

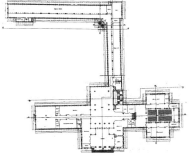

School of Architecture 1932-36 • 1941-43
Av. de Juan de Herrera, Ciudad Universitaria
Bravo, P./García de Castro
Although probably the best-quality building
in all the university campus, from outside,
the small Architecture School looks dry and
even conventional. However, its intriguing
Modernist layout organisation sets it apart,
with independent, open pavilions starting
from a common core that contains attractive
vestibules that are repeated three times
on different storeys. These spaces, and
other ones of interest, are accompanied
by the moderate but exquisite design of
elements, fittings and furnishings, many of
which have been conserved. It was built in
exposed brickwork and reconstructed with
limestone cladding by the same architect,
following damage inflicted during the Civil
War, when it was on the entrenched front-
line of battle.

Student Hall of Residence 1932-36   M 35
[now **Colegio Mayor Cisneros**]
Av. de Séneca s/n, Ciudad Universitaria
Lacasa
This is the only work by Luis Lacasa (see p.
333) in the university campus, in which he
assumed the moderate, sober style of the
overall project, whilst adding the attractive,
refined atmosphere of the Modern American
Student Dormitory.

Apartment Building 1932-42   M 36
Almagro 26 c/v Zurbarán
Gutiérrez Soto
The first of the brilliant bourgeoise housing
designed by Gutiérrez Soto as part of the
Castro expansion plan for Madrid, it is
considered exemplary for the way its layout
nestles into an irregular site and the way it
uses terraces of restrained elegance to
increase the surface area.

Nursing School 1933   M 37
Sinesio Delgado c/v Melchor Fernández Almagro
Bergamín/Blanco-Soler
Another example of the moderate Rationalism of Rafael Bergamín, it shows the peculiar
Madrid-style interpretation of the Modern
architecture of the time. The building is
located close to the El Viso housing estate
(see M 41), in a part of the city that Bergamín
populated with his designs.

Casa del Barco House 1933-34
Joaquín Costa 27 c/v Guadalquivir 3
Bergamín

Despite its unique features, this detached, luxurious house is directly related to the architecture of the Parque Residencia Estate in which it stands (see M 27) and, above all, to that of the El Viso estate (see M 41), all designed by the same architect. Although, strictly speaking, it is not part of the El Viso housing estate, it is close enough to it to constitute a clear unity with it, especially since it displays what the architectural principles applied to El Viso could look like when scaled down to meet the demands of this size of house. The presence of a well-designed poligonal bay giving onto the front street and the general characteristics of the architect's restrained style make it representative of Rationalist architecture and also led to the "boat" nickname, which is still used.

Apartment Building 1933-35
José Abascal 53
Figueroa

An exceptionally attractive apartment building between party walls, it has an excellent composition to its façade, which is beautifully clad in granite rock. Its design is representative of the very personal, independent stance that its architect took vis-à-vis the Modernism of his day.

Department of Physical Sciences,
Chemistry and Mathematics 1934-36
Ciudad Universitaria
Santos, M. de los/Torroja Miret [eng.]

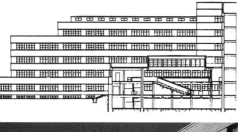

The architect, who was the closest to López Otero, the head of the design team for the university campus, had already designed the large Medical School (see M 17) when he was commissioned the sub-campus for Sciences, facing the Department of Philosophy, across the never-built central main auditorium (see M 16). Along with the University Hospital (see M 18) designed by Sánchez Arcas, this sub-campus for the Science Departments, with its two buildings establishing an L-shaped layout around an open space, offers the most sober, radical interpretation of the Modernist architecture that pervades the entire campus, providing a clear expression of the way that Madrid architects understood the new ideas of the thirties.

41 **El Viso Residential Estate** 1933-36
Serrano (central axis), Guadalquivir, Daniel
Urrabieta, Tormes, Concha Espina, Sil, Nervión
Bergamín. coll.: **L.F. Vivanco**

This residential estate is located on the prolongation of Serrano, to the NE of the city.
Despite its relatively small size, with time its
cultural significance has come to be widely
recognised. It ranks alongside the other big
urban planning projects of its time, such as
the university campus and, above all, the
suburbs of Madrid developed under the
Zuazo plan, which covered the area around
the prolongation of the Castellana (see
M 42), but also with the construction of the
New Ministries (see M 33) and the underground rail links running N-S. The El Viso
estate followed the pilot project of the Parque Residencia Estate (see M 27), in which
the same architects had already much
improved on earlier suburban housing
estates with their simple juxtaposition of
detached houses in the centre of their own
small gardens. But here, they further
developed their new ideas of harmonious
urban planning, proposing a wide-ranging
plan of terraced housing, with a small

courtyard to provide access from the street and a back garden with secondary access via a
footpath. The architecture also changed, shedding all traces of the Eclectic and Historicist
styles fashionable until then, in favour of a new Rationalism, that would be more in keeping
with the aspirations of the increasingly liberal and better educated middle class that was
flourishing in Madrid. This growing middle class came into its own under the Second Republic
and was proud to proclaim its identity with the new Modernist architecture. However, the
Rationalism of El Viso is not a radical interpretation of the new Modernist principles: thus, it
cannot be compared to Le Corbusier's work, but rather to that of Loos, albeit without his
intense play of space. The purist looks, despite some very picturesque variations, were
achieved above all by the rounded or poligonal bays that characterise the corners. For later
Madrid cultural critics, they represented the brilliant beginnings of a new, significant fashion
that became legendary, not so much because of its own intrinsic value as because of the
Historicist regression that hit Madrid following the Civil War.

**Prolongation of the Castellana
and Madrid Expansion Plan** 1930-54
Zuazo/Jansen • Bidagor

Secundino Zuazo and the German architect, Hermann Jansen presented their expansion plan
to the 1929 competition sponsored by the Municipality and organised by Fernández Balbuena.
As runners-up (the first prize was not awarded) they were chosen to put their project into
operation. This entailed the prolongation of the Paseo de la Castellana (by removing the
racetrack that stood in the way) which, by the first third of the century, was already recognised

as a pressing need. Zuazo and Jansen led
the great avenue in one sweeping stroke up
to what is now Pza. de Castilla, where it
joined the old road to France – now Bravo
Murillo street – and then directed it on to
the village of Fuencarral. Because of the
ambiguous outcome of the competition,
Zuazo ended up working both for the City
Council and the Ministry of Public Works.
Later, he drew up another version of the
prolongation that substituted the schematic,
parallel Rationalist housing blocks looking
south in simple order with blocks such as
those of the Casa de las Flores (see M 20),
but he left a primary scheme that, with
time, was followed. At the commission of
the Socialist minister of Azaña's government
under the Second Republic, Indalecio Prieto,

Zuazo also took over the enormous work of the underground rail tunnels running N-S under
the old and the new avenue, and initiated the construction of the New Ministries (see M 33),
which marked the starting point of the new stretch of the Castellana. After the Civil War,
when Zuazo was exiled to the Canary Islands for collaborating with the Republic, Pedro
Bidagor, who had been his assistant, drew up the 1941 General Urban Plan for the city with
his new team. This left the prolongation of the Castellana very much as it had originally been
planned, but turned its housing into conventional closed urban blocks, planned a central focal
point (the AZCA shopping and office area) and set the Real Madrid football stadium opposite
it. The avenue was opened to traffic during the post-war period and gradually became the
directional focus of the city and the backbone for an important residential area.

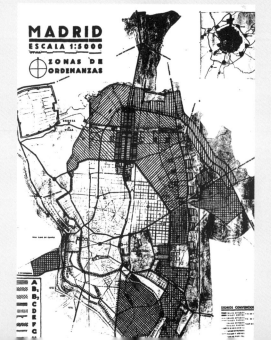

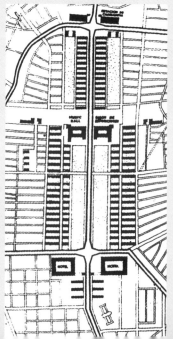

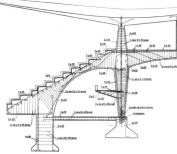

La Zarzuela Racetrack 1935-36
Autovía A-6 de La Coruña km 7
Arniches/Domínguez/Torroja Miret [eng.]

The expansion of the city projected in the thirties prolonged the Castellana (see M 42) and required the removal of the old racetrack which was standing in the way. Today's Zarzuela Racetrack was the winning design of a competition and the result of genuine collaboration between two great Modern architects of the day, Arniches and Domínguez, and the renowned engineer, Eduardo Torroja. Architecture and engineering – especially as understood by these designers – melded together seamlessly, creating one of the most unique and attractive works of Modern architecture in the Madrid of the thirties. It became an emblem of modernity, as expressed in the bold engineering of its repeated white, airy vaulted canopies, made of reinforced concrete sheets jutting out above the tiered seating. It was completed with arches in the base around it and the detailing of an architecture that is to a large extent traditional, which bear witness to the inherent Eclecticism of Madrid taste. Not very well-treated since then, although it has not been as mutilated as some other very important works, the racetrack definitely deserves the kind of restoration that should be given to such an important part of the city's heritage.

Other works. Apart from the New Ministries (see M 33), the rail tunnels, the General Staff Building (see M 54) and the Institute for Agricultural Development (see M 56), there are several works that are linked to the prolongation of the Castellana planned by Zuazo (1929-36) and modified by Bidagor (1941 plan, approved in 1946). The most important is the Real Madrid Stadium (1944-50) by Muñoz Monasterio and Alemany, which ushered football in as a mass spectator sport (reformed and disfigured by Alemany et al. in 1982 and by Lamela in 1992). Also of interest is the low-budget San Cristóbal housing estate (1948) that Zuazo built for the employees of the Madrid bus company, EMT, on Paseo de la Castellana 284-300. The AZCA shopping area, originally planned as a Classical style conglomeration of shops under the 1941 plan, was redesigned along more Modern lines by Antonio Perpiñá (1957-64), then populated with buildings by many different architects (see M 116, M 122, M 131 and M 133).

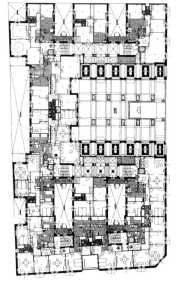

Apartment Building 1936-41
Miguel Angel 2, 4 and 6 c/v Rafael Calvo
Gutiérrez Soto

One of the first and most brilliant pieces of housing designed by Gutiérrez Soto for an especially good area in the new suburbs that sprung up under the 19th c. expansion plan, it manages to place its mark on the street in a way that previous Eclectical housing had not. On a corner site, the architect set the building around a large courtyard opening onto the street, as if he were transferring the great lesson of Zuazo's Casa de las Flores (see M 20) to a smaller work. Without the order inherent to Zuazo's famous house, in part due to the irregularity of the terrain and the dense programme of small and medium-sized apartments that had to be fitted into the building, the architect still showed the skill in handling complex layouts which was always evident in his work. The exterior volume provides a correct shaping for the corner and continues the frontage from the courtyard outwards. Thus, the building is characterised by the use of a restrained composition, supported by a systematic layout of hexagonal cantilevered bodies, similar to those often used by the Chicago School. But the language is somewhat transformed when it reaches the courtyard, by terraces and arches, with magnificent results in terms of urban design.

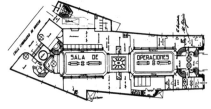

Commercial and Industrial Bank
[now Madrid Community Administration Building] 1936-42 • 1942-45
Alcalá 31
Palacios Ramilo

The last work by Palacios was built with all the pomp and circumstance of the Classicism with which he substituted his earlier Eclecticism. The bank, with its spectacular façade built to look like a triumphal arch, constitutes a unique volume that consolidated the transformation of this part of Alcalá street into an area of banks and government offices during the first third of the century (see M 1). It is characterised by a large trading floor under a vaulted inner courtyard, which joins up the two streets. Despite the architect's much vaunted opposition to Modernism, some exterior details nonetheless reflect the unavoidable ubiquitousness of the Modernist vocabulary in the thirties.

Airforce Ministry 1940-51   M 46
Pza. de la Moncloa s/n
Gutiérrez Soto
Emblematic of the nationalist obsessions in public building following the Civil War, it is built in the style of the Hapsburg heritage in Madrid and El Escorial, and is an expressive example of the architect's Eclectic education and his skill in providing excellent designs in whatever style the customer required.

Espíritu Santo Chapel 1942-43   M 47
Serrano 117
Fisac
The best example of the Historicist style adopted by the architect, Miguel Fisac in his youth, it has interesting interiors and murals by Stolz Viciano. Constructed after the Civil War, it brutally used and destroyed what had previously been the Assembly Hall of the Instituto Escuela (see M 29).

Museum of America 1942-48 • 1984-92   M 48
Av. Reyes Católicos 6
Moya, L./Martínez Feduchi •
Capitel/Martorell/Ortega/Hernández
With greater restraint than in the Technical Colleges of Gijón and Zamora, this building shows Moya's determination to recover the Spanish Classical tradition in counterposition to international Modernism, whilst at the same time expressing the government's interest in a return to a more Academic style in university campuses after the Civil War. Built in palatial style, with vaulted naves with 12 m spans set around a central courtyard, it was made totally in brick. Its incomplete cloister and other missing parts were finally completed when the building was restored and modern facilities installed in recent years, with careful, detailed design of the furniture and fittings, which has made it possible to appreciate the integrity of the whole.

Other works. The period from 1939-49 also produced the Valle de los Caídos (close to San Lorenzo de El Escorial, 46 km from Madrid, which Franco ordered to be built using political prisoners as navvies), by Muguruza and Méndez, an example of ultra-conventional Classical triumphal architecture, and the Seminary of Carabanchel (1942-44) by Luis Moya, amongst the most top-quality architecture. Also note Marsá Prats' apartment building (1945) on Almagro 33 and the large metropolitan-style skyscraper buildings on Pza. de España, the Edificio España (1947-53) and the Torre de Madrid (1954-57), both by the Otamendi brothers, which led to heated debate as to their impact on the traditional city skyline as seen from the Manzanares River looking W. The combination of blocks and tower for the housing complex (1949) on Av. de América 2-14, by Ignacio and Gonzalo de Cárdenas, is also interesting.

Apartment Building 1944
Pza. Gregorio Marañón c/v Paseo Castellana 63
Gutiérrez Soto
Probably the best residential building for the burgeoning middle classes designed by the architect, Gutiérrez Soto in his post-war Historicist style, it featured a delicate, well-ordered urban volume, despite the difficult shape of the site and the curved frontage onto the circus.

Virgen del Pilar Social Housing
Complex [Phase 4] 1945-49
Mataelpino c/v Quintiliano
Cabrero
This attractive low-budget housing complex brought the technique of ordinary brick vaulting enclosure to make split-level, maison-ette-style apartments accessed off a common corridor, and terraces at two levels. It has been very poorly maintained.

Trade Union Building 1948-49
[now **Ministry of Health**]
Paseo del Prado 20
Cabrero/Aburto
The winning design of a competition and the masterpiece of these architects, the Trade Union building is a brilliant example of the transition from Academicism to Modernism that Spain passed through in the fifties, for the second time. It is definitely the best large government building constructed in Madrid under the entire Franco regime. Facing the 18th c. Prado Museum, the crowning glory of Juan Villanueva's career, this building accepted his materials and the imposing nature of his building, using the enormous mass of the design, laid out in cubic form, to achieve the necessary monumentality in an out-and-out abstract style. Thus, a base of 7 storeys is adapted to the irregular shape of the site, on which a central 16-storey cube is erected. Ceramic brick is used to cover the structural skeleton, whilst the lower areas are clad in granite stonework. The building requirements for internal communications were met by making the building open, but without courtyards, and the solidity of the urban space on the Paseo del Prado was achieved whilst respecting the smaller scale and different character of the side streets, despite all the problems entailed in placing a new building in such an important place.

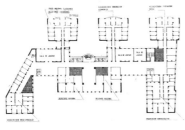

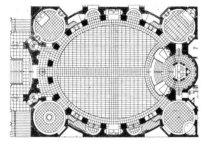

Church of San Agustín 1949
Joaquín Costa 10
Moya

This masterpiece by Luis Moya, the architect of late Classical tradition, is highly representative of his intention to continue working in the Classical language despite the ubiquitousness of Modernism. In this respect, the building forms a group with his Seminary of Carabanchel and his Museum of America (see M 48). Conceived as a kind of urban tumulus, the ground plan is elliptical, integrating the idea of the central church and the nave, and is covered by an interesting brick groin vault. Made completely in brickwork, the façade looks out onto the street in the Baroque style, like an urban standard announcing the importance of the place of worship to all passers-by. It is one of the most unique, interesting examples of late Historicism in the post-war years.

Library of the Institute of Scientific Research 1949-50
Medinaceli 4
Fisac

A pioneer work in the Modern interior design of post-war Madrid, the building is characterised by its use of natural materials (brick, stone) and by the restrained, organic simplicity of its design, which recognises its inspiration in North European architecture.

General Staff Headquarters 1949-53
Vitrubio 1-3 c/v Paseo de la Castellana
Gutiérrez Soto

This building represented a new change in Gutiérrez Soto's architecture, as he moved towards a final acceptance of the Modern architecture that he had abandoned in order to bow to the late Historicism that marked the post-war years under the Franco regime, in which he was a key figure, with his Airforce Ministry (see M 46). Located opposite Zuazo's immense New Ministries (see M 33), the architect established similarities between the two buildings in terms of their materials and figurative style, to fit the official building into the overall unity marking the prolongation of the Paseo de la Castellana (see M 42). However, he also used Modern elements, such as the *brise-soleil*. In 1976, the volume on the corner between Vitruvio and Maestro Ripoll was altered.

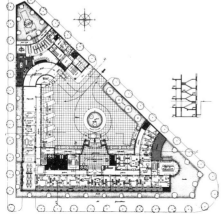

Apartment Building 1949 M 55
Fernando el Católico 47
Sáenz de Oíza
An early but brilliant example of how Sáenz
de Oíza and the architects who graduated
after the Civil War managed to bring back
Modernist architecture. The use of Modern
language in the cantilevered balconies is
made compatible with a volume suitable to
the surrounding urban area.

National Institute for Agricultural M 56
Development and Reform 1950-54
Paseo de la Castellana c/v Joaquín Costa
Tamés
This example of institutional architecture,
like the General Staff HQ (see M 54), found
a figurative balance between tradition and
Modernism. In this sense, it is linked with the
New Ministries (see M 33) in consolidating
the prolongation of the Castellana (see M 42).

United States Embassy 1951-55 M 57
Serrano 75
Architecture Division,
State Department, US/Garrigues
The embassy was built following an interest-
ing American design but with building works
directed by a Spaniard. It was the first big
Modern building (albeit low-key Modern)
constructed in the old part of the Paseo de
la Castellana after the Civil War.

Cabrero House I 1952-53 M 58
Cabeza de Hierro 5, Puerta de Hierro
Cabrero
This is one of the few buildings in which
Cabrero displays signs of affinity with the
Organic style. Although his interpretation of
it is very personal, it is reminiscent of Fisac.
The building fits snugly into the terrain, its
walls, roof and different areas adapted to
the terracing of the earth.

Apartment Building 1953-54 M 59
Juan Bravo c/v Velázquez
Gutiérrez Soto
A brilliant piece of residential architecture
built by Gutiérrez Soto in the inner suburbs
of Madrid in the fifties, its clever layout
covers the requirements for good middle-
class housing and short-term rental apartments. The building's solid volume is fitting
for its urban setting.

Richmond Hotel 1953-54 M 60
Pza. de la República Argentina c/v Dr. Arce 2
Gutiérrez Soto
Built on the edge of the El Viso residential
estate, the Richmond hotel is one of the
best examples of Gutiérrez Soto's work
after his return to Modern architecture.
Unfortunately, reform works on the façade
of the building have disfigured the original
line.

Teachers Technical College 1953-55 M 61
[now **Escuela Universitaria de Estadística**]
Av. Puerta de Hierro s/n (Autovía A-6, km 5.5)
Fisac
Built around the same time as the Daimiel
Institute (1951-53, Ciudad Real) and the
Apostolic School of the Dominican Fathers
in Valladolid (1952, see VA 1) and only a
few years before the Theological School of
the Dominican Fathers in Alcobendas,
(1955, see M 157), this college forms part
of one of the most brilliant architectural
phases in Miguel Fisac's entire career. The
layout is Rationalist, ordered around open
courtyards, thereby revealing the Organic
approach, which is further emphasised in
the two fan-shaped lecture halls and the
attractive, ondulated porticos in concrete
sheets. This use of concrete announces the
arrival of Fisac's next stage, when he would
take up the potential of this material fully.

Santo Tomás de Aquino M 62
Hall of Residence 1953-57
Paseo de las Moreras s/n, Ciudad Universitaria
García de Paredes/La Hoz
This hall of residence was one of the first
buildings to expand the university campus's
residential area towards the slopes where
the "Metropolitana" estate is located, at the
end of the road marking the edge of the
suburbs created under Castro's expansion
plan. The residence bears witness to the
total return to Modern architecture, here in
its International Style manifestation, among
the second generation of architects after
the Civil War. With an attractive serrated-
style layout of the volumes, which configure
an abstract and very attractive image, the
rooms, every two of which share a bathroom
of sophisticated design, are accessed from
the outside. In 1957, the building recieved
the National Architecture Award.

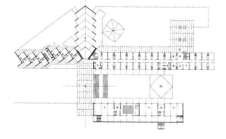

Neighbourhood Absorption Units and Managed Settlements 1954-66

The creation of an "organic", multi-clustered metropolis, with several rather independent towns focussed around the capital, was at the heart of Zuazo's expansion plan (1930-36), continued under Bidagor (1941-46). In the post-war period, some neighbourhoods were built in the Historicist style, with their own urban structure. However, it was not until the mid-fifties that the Greater Madrid Commission took up this new approach to town planning, with the systematic creation of new urban sectors in and outside the city. These were sometimes formed around existing core settlements, other times built from scratch, to absorb the mass influx of rural population. Many operations were run by the state and other official or trade-union bodies. Laguna, the head architect on the Commission, decided to bring in the most prestigious young architects to work on this and thus speeded up the return to Modern architecture in an area where its use made obvious social and economic sense, given the space constraints and building standards. The resulting areas were called Managed Settlements (*Poblados Dirigidos*) when their structure was urban and the buildings made to last, and Neighbourhood Absorption Units (*Unidades Vecinales de Absorción*, or UVAs) when they were put up provisionally (even if some have lived on *ad infinitum*). Several generations of architects contributed to them: from Sáenz de Oíza (who made the most and the best) to Higueras, establishing a sound tradition of good social housing. They include the settlements in Fuencarral (de la Sota, Sáenz de Oíza and Romaní, 1954-56, see photographs and plan); Villaverde (Aburto, 1954-55); Entrevías (see M 73); Caño Roto (see M 75 and M 94); and Almendrales (Carvajal, Corrales, García de Paredes and Molezún, 1963-66); the neighbourhood absorption units in Erillas and El Calero (Cubillo, Romaní, Sáenz de Oíza and Sierra, 1955 and 1958); Usera (Aburto, 1957); and Hortaleza (Higueras, Miró, Cabrera, Espinosa and Weber, 1963); and the estates in Puerta Bonita (Fisac, Romaní, Sánchez, Lozano et al., 1957); El Batán (see M 68); Loyola (see M 83); Juan XXIII (see M 92). As of the mid-sixties, the need for this type of housing decreased as the migratory flow shifted abroad.

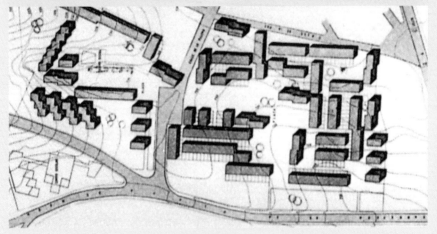

Apartment Building 1954-57   M 64
Pedro de Valdivia 8
Moya
One of the few residential buildings designed
by this late Classicist, Luis Moya, after he
had given up his fight against Modernism
and embraced its basic tenets, it shows
outstanding skill in the ground plan for
middle-class town-housing, laid out around
a circular services courtyard.

Apartment Building 1954-58   M 65
Pza. de Cristo Rey 4
Carvajal
An excellent example of how the post-war
generation of Spanish architects used the
International Style, which they later developed
along more Organicist lines within the
Madrid School. This development is also
represented in the architect's own house in
Somosaguas, Madrid (1965).

Four Apartment Buildings 1955   M 66
Boix y Morer c/v Cea Bermúdez
Zuazo
Apart from working on the city plan, Zuazo
also designed some excellent private-sector
housing in the post-war period. These buildings show his residential architecture after
building the housing on Pza. de Salamanca
c/v Ortega y Gasset (1944-45) and the EMT
housing estate (see p. 239).

Cajal Institute, CSIC 1950-52/55   M 67
Velázquez c/v Joaquín Costa
Fisac
This excellent, original building by Miguel
Fisac is representative of his Modern period
after his initial Historicist stage. Built shortly
after the Instituto de Optica (1949, in the
CSIC, Serrano 113-117), these two buildings both formed part of the important
architectural project for the Scientific Research Council. The Cajal Institute building
should be considered as an exponent of
the International Style, despite the Organicist overtones, which are actually more
representative of Fisac's personal style. Its
volume, clad in a type of hollow brick for
exteriors invented by Fisac, creates an
attractive urban landscape with an open
feel to it. Unfortunately, deterioration and
external changes have undermined its
appearance.

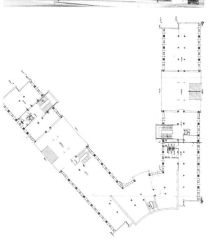

El Batán Housing Estate 1955-61
Between Casa de Campo and Ctra. N-5
Romaní/Sáenz de Oíza/Sierra
This low-income estate (see M 63) was built
to maximise a tight budget. A total return to
Rationalism managed to meet the requirements whilst respecting money and size
constraints. It shows an incipient "Organic"
approach vis-à-vis the site and the town-
planning of the neighbourhood.

Spanish Pavilion
at the Brussels Expo'58 1956-58
Casa de Campo
Corrales/Molezún
Historically considered by critics and essay-
ists as the moment when Franco's regime
unreservedly opened its arms to Modern
architecture, this pavilion is proof of the
government's final acceptance that Historicism was no longer the ideal way to represent
Spain abroad. By winning the national
competition for the pavilion, Corrales and
Molezún consolidated their reputation as
outstanding architects, two of the best of
the post-war generation, who were also
responsible for the very sophisticated,
contemporary Herrera del Pisuerga Secondary School in Palencia (see PA 2). But the Brussels
pavilion also contains an intriguing ambiguity. It stood proudly for the triumph of the authentic
values of Modernism in Spain, as reflected in its International Style – in the play of glass and
steel, in its formal vocabulary, in its use of randomness alongside modularity, and in its vision
of structure – while, at the same time and with equal intensity, it held the seeds of the
Organicist architecture that would shortly take hold over the most avant-garde cultural
circles in Madrid. This is clearly evident in the powerful relationship between form and
structure, the crystallographic layout in a Wright-style hexagonal plan, and in the coherence
of the geometry throughout. Recognising the high quality of the design, after winning the
Gold Medal at the Expo for the best pavilion the whole building was transferred to the
Casa de Campo park in Madrid, under the supervision of its architects. There, it had to be
built in a slightly different way in order to adapt to the features of the terrain. This outstanding
building, part of Europe's architectural heritage, is now in a state of advanced ruin.

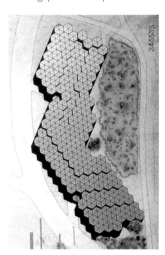

Apartment Building 1956-57
Príncipe de Vergara c/v O'Donnell
Lamela
This building had an immediate impact on
the definition of its surrounding urban landscape. Lamela went on to design several
buildings that established a distinguishable
visual presence in Madrid. In this case, as in
many others, he worked in the style of the
master architect, Gutiérrez Soto.

National School of Catering 1956-58   M 71
Casa de Campo
Cabrero/Ruiz
One of the most representative examples
of the purist Rationalism of the Madrid
School, influenced by the Italian post-war
style, it has been ruined by the incorporation
of an additional volume in the courtyard,
along with other modifications. A sensitive
reform could restore its original beauty.

Apartment Building 1956-59   M 72
Espalter 8
Cano Lasso
This skillfully designed apartment building
stands on a long narrow site between party
walls, next to the Botanical Gardens. The
layout was established with the help of inner
courtyards and cleverly placed spaces on the
façades, anticipating the solution Coderch
used in his Girasol building (see M 98).

Entrevías Settlement 1956-60   M 73
Between Av. de Entrevías and Ronda del Sur
Sáenz de Oíza/Sierra/Alvear
The underlying urbanistic approach tried to
go beyond, or at least further develop the
Modern premises in a clustering layout of
housing. In the Entrevías settlement, the
terraced houses were designed to provide
the minimum living requirements on a minimum budget with the help of Rationalist
instruments. Set together in terraces and
conceived as if they were in fact one single
building, the houses are only 3.60 m wide
and group together the common services
for greatest economic efficiency. They do,
however, include a front and rear courtyard
(at a time of isolated economy, land in
Entrevías was the only cheap component).
Their current deterioration is the inevitable
outcome of time and rock-bottom building
specifications.

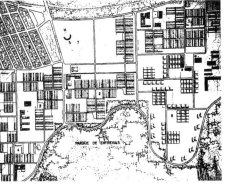

Apartment Building 1957-58
Paseo de la Castellana 121-123
Lamela
In this smart design, the professional skills of Lamela, then in his early career, were used to successfully try out the idea of an open residential building on the prolongation of the Castellana. The style is quite personal, albeit perhaps influenced by an informality that can be traced to Italian sources.

Caño Roto Settlement [Phase 1] 1957-59
Between Vía Carpetana and Laguna
Iñiguez de Onzoño/Vázquez de Castro
Whereas Sáenz de Oíza's Entrevías settlement (see M 73) was the low-budget, low-specs project *par excellence* in the whole Managed Settlements plan (see M 63), where radical Rationalism was used to solve the problems of providing decent housing at minimum cost, Caño Roto used the same set of instruments to meet more demanding specs, with a wider range of possibilities. Thus, conventional blocks were set next to split-level apartment blocks and single houses around different kinds of private courtyards. The diversity of types nonetheless created a whole, which the architects designed on the urban scale of traditional city settlements. The mixed content reflects the Eclecticism of Spanish architecture and already hints at the forthcoming Organicist style.

Apartment and Office Building 1957-66
María de Molina 1-5 c/v Paseo de la Castellana
Gutiérrez Soto
This is probably the most attractive of the large apartment buildings that Gutiérrez Soto designed for the middle classes in key parts of Madrid. Another example is his Carlos III building, on Goya 5 (designed in 1945), which includes apartments, a cinema and shops. In this case, the building, made up of two volumes containing the apartments which flank a narrow tower block with the offices, establishes the image of a break in the Paseo de la Castellana, at the Pza. de Gregorio Marañón, in an especially felicitous manner. The stark parallelepiped starts from the street with a portico. The façades of the lower volumes follow the street alignment and are the most representative of the fully developed Modern style of this great architect.

Office Building 1959
Concha Espina 65
Laorga/López Zanón
A small, isolated building in a residential part of Madrid that was developed at the end of the fifties for the well-off middle classes, it is characterised by continuity with Rationalist architecture in a skillful, radical figurative style that establishes the tone for the entire neighbourhood.

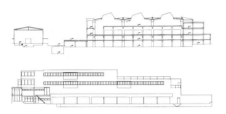

CLESA Dairy Complex 1959-63
Av. Cardenal Herrera Oria c/v Isla de Sicilia, Fuencarral
Sota, A. de la
This unique building in de la Sota's portfolio was built at a time when the success of the monumental Civilian Government Building in Tarragona (see TA 1) encouraged him to try out another style, more technical and modern and less sculptural or compositional. Given the building's requirements, for processing and bottling milk, he conceived the design in strict terms of Rationalist architecture, exploiting the direct, Brutalist signature of the materials (reinforced and prestressed concrete) and the presence of the service facilities, whilst achieving the functional expression of the singularity of its diversified programme.

Santa María School 1959-60
Av. de los Madroños, Parque Conde de Orgaz
Fernández Alba, Antonio
The first example of Fernández Alba's work in Madrid, it has an Aalto-style Rationalism which nonetheless contains the seeds of the Organicism that he would show in his later career, and which would come to characterise Madrid architecture in the sixties, following the triumph of the International Style.

Brazil House 1959-62
Av. de la Victoria s/n, Ciudad Universitaria
D'Escragnolle
An interesting piece of foreign architecture in Madrid, it reflects the prevailing trends in Niemeyer's Brazil. The project consists of various simple, prismatic blocks resting on small stanchions. The bedrooms are closed with a blind façade onto the avenue and open to the garden with large windows.

Fisac, whose style followed a very personal development, reached another peak in his career with the Ministry of Public Works's Institute for Hydrographic Studies. After his initial Historicist stage, he then moved into a more Organic architecture, with works such as the Teachers Technical College in Madrid's university campus (see M 61), the Church of the Dominican Fathers in Alcobendas (see M 157) and the Apostolic School in Valladolid (see VA 1). Constructed on the banks of the Manzanares river, to the SW of the city, the architect designed it using one of his most important inventions: the hollow large-span girders made out of prestressed concrete, explicity inspired in Organicism which led him to nickname them "bones". Tried out in 1959 in the Madrid-based Made Laboratories and used in many other works (not necessarily of similar characteristics, including housing and religious buildings), these girders were of key importance in this Hydraulics Laboratory. With their aid, Fisac managed to cover a 22 m span without ground support, whilst also giving the space overhead lighting. Entirely built out of reinforced concrete, the building is divided into two pavilions, set at an angle to each other. The first is a 7-storey office block and the other a large laboratory hall, 80 x 22 m, where he used the "bones" roof. The building's urban façade towards the river placed its mark on the riverside scenery with its very simple, clearcut Rationalist volume, which could be perceived as just another manufacturing building, but in fact represents one of the most successful and carefully thought-out pieces of radical architecture in Madrid.

Other works. Of the Spanish architectural works that were constructed during the years of autarchic isolation in the fifties, note should be taken of the Eduardo Torroja Institute for Construction and Cement (1955-58), in Ciudad Lineal on the edge of the M-30 ringroad, on the corner with Torroja y Serrano Galvache, by Echegara and Barbero; Cano Lasso's house-studio (1958-89) in La Florida, on Guecho 27, a design that he worked upon and perfected, if not throughout his professional life, definitely throughout the thirty years from his first design until its second extension; and the housing (1959-60) located next to the Viaduct, on Bailén.

Maravillas School Gymnasium 1960-62
Joaquín Costa 21
Sota, A. de la

Alongside Tarragona's Civilian Government
Building (see TA 1), this is the second of the
great masterpieces by de la Sota, and easily
the most famous of his entire career. It
represents a different kind of architecture
from the official building in Tarragona, in
that the very different kind of requirements

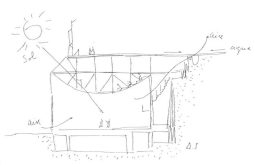

compelled him to abandon the abstract, compositional style that he had so brilliantly wielded
in the other. He constructed the gymnasium as a kind of containing wall for the school,
thereby solving the problem of the steep slope between the school and the street level of
Joaquín Costa. Above all, the design is characterised by the transversal section of the sports
ground, which is covered by enormous curved trusses that allow light to filter in from high
up over the walls, and which actually contain special teaching rooms between them. De la
Sota went out of his way to compatibilise his refined style with an expressly Brutalistic intention,
both in the visible presence of the structure and the service facilities, which are used as a
language of their own, and also in the figurative weight of the most immediate materials, in

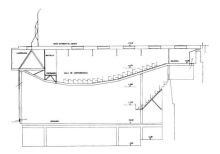

which the most obvious are the exposed isolation materials, used to finish off ceilings and
walls. In this very characteristic section, the building is presented as a true celebration of
space, anticipating the more extreme version of this celebration that would turn Stirling into
a figure of international renown some years later. The outside is brick and steel, where the
architect's own laid-back, compositional style is most obvious. He combines abstraction with
figurative insets alluding to the traditional bay windows of his native Galicia, whilst making
them compatible with an almost puritanical concern for even the smallest constructional
details. Thus he endowed the building with a very attractive appearance on a difficult
street. This gymnasium has always been considered as one of the best, most representative
examples of the full-blown Modern style of Spanish architecture during this period.

Loyola Housing Estate 1960-62   M 83
Carabanchel Alto
Sáenz de Oíza/Romaní/Mangada/Ferrán
Another example of Sáenz de Oíza and his
team's work with low-budget housing, it
shows a change in approach to architecture
and town planning. Here, they have shifted
away from out-and-out Rationalism to a
style that can be related to Team X in its
concept of whole entities.

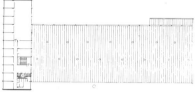

Arriba Newspaper Building 1960-63   M 84
[now **Centre for Cadastral Management
and Tax Cooperation**]
Paseo de la Castellana 272 c/v Mauricio Legendre
Cabrero
Along with de la Sota, Cabrero represents
the way in which Rationalism was identified
with truly Modern architecture and developed
along a continuum that outlived all revisionism. Also the architect of the magnificent
Trade Union Building (see M 51), here
Cabrero exhibits his perennial skill at designing offices along intense yet refinedly simple
lines. Characterised by the relief of its metal
supports and the precision of its cuboid
modular proportions, the Arriba Building
adds quality to the urban landscape on the
Castellana, with its attractive appearance
and its front-on placement. It is now a
Government office and has been restored
with admirable respect and restraint.

School of Telecommunications   M 85
Engineering 1960-71
Av. Complutense s/n, Ciudad Universitaria
Carvajal/García de Paredes, J.M.
A very skillful example of the International
Style in Madrid, at its mature stage, when it
had already become almost establishment
architecture, it nonetheless has early hints of
the architects' later Organicist tendencies in
the design.

Chapel of the   M 86
Santa María del Pilar School 1961-65
Reyes Magos 3
Moya/Domínguez Salazar
The first of Moya's ecclesiastical designs after
he had exhausted his Classicist period with
the elliptical ground plans of San Agustín,
Gijón and Torrelavega (see M 52, O 16 and S 7),
it features a saddle-shaped brickwork roof.
The neighbouring school is also interesting.

Cabrero House II 1961-62 M 87
Av. de Miraflores, Puerta de Hierro
Cabrero

This was Cabrero's own family home, the second he built for himself. On the one hand, it represents the continuity of Rationalism at a time when Madrid architecture was tending towards greater Organicism. On the other, it shows how some traditional principles and conventions can be absorbed into that Rationalism. The language, space and materials are pure International Style, but the house is really a modern version of the old courtyard house, built in a double L-shape enclosing the garden. The design also features a metal-sheeting roof, but raked in such a way that it slopes down to an *impluvium*. This is an excellent example of a quality single-family house in the capital city and probably one of the best examples of Rationalist housing.

Readers' Digest Selections 1961-65 M 88
Torrelaguna 58 c/v Av. de América
Corrales/Molezún/Cavero

Exemplary of the minor works of Corrales and Molezún, and characterised by the ceramic tile bands around it, it is typical of a time when both architects were experimenting with the Modern concepts that were beginning to expand beyond the limits of the International Style.

Artistic Restoration Centre M 89
[now Instituto de C. y Restauración] 1961-70
El Greco 4, Ciudad Universitaria
Higueras/Miró

An important building, along with Sáenz de Oíza's Torres Blancas building (see M 90), it is almost the only true example of full-blown Organicism in Madrid. Representative of Higueras and Miró's endeavours to develop a contemporary vocabulary completely set apart from the Rationalist tradition and the International Style, it is characterised by its monumentality and its difficult but emphatic centrality: it is a circle with a 40 m radius. The building uses reinforced concrete as a means of attaining richness of form and a sense of space, whilst also bringing together the tough, resistent structure with the general shape. Unfinished for many years, it was only completed a quarter of a century after it was designed.

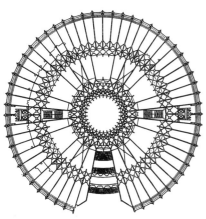

Torres Blancas Building 1961-68
Corazón de María 2 c/v Av. de América 37
Sáenz de Oíza

The masterpiece of Spanish Organicism, it is one of the most important buildings designed by Sáenz de Oíza during his entire career, which saw him move from Radical Rationalism to Organicist architecture. The building was initially conceived as a pair of buildings which were meant to be configured along Corbusian lines, with a tower block of self-sufficient apartments linked to the standard living cells of villa homes, all made entirely out of concrete. However, Sáenz de Oíza was also trying to incorporate the Wrightian ideals implicit in the Price Tower: respecting the identity between form and structure, the biological analogy and the tree-like structure, a coherence between the general shape and the details, and a non-Cartesian geometry. To this synthetic way of incorporating these ideals, that is indicative of Spanish syncretic talents, he also added a sculptural sense that managed to follow the latest Le Corbusier as well as the extreme Organicists, such as Saarinen and Utzon. The result is one of the most ambitious and successful pieces of radical Organic architecture in the world whose sculptural appearance, then, should not be understood as pure, direct form, but rather as a function of all the keys described above. It was also the synthesis of contrary forces – although for Saénz de Oíza Rationalism and Organicism were not opposing tendencies – between which a tension was created, and a debate brought about that produced the most advanced Spanish architecture of the sixties. Today the building stands as a visual landmark at the entrance to the city from the airport of Barajas and the Barcelona road [the neon billboard installed on the top is a shockingly degrading addition].

Other works. During the sixties, at the height of the economic boom and frenetic speculative building activity which ignored order and quality, other points of reference are some of the lesser works of great architects, such as the stark parish church complex of Nuestra Señora de la Luz (1967), on Fernán Núñez and Alfonso XIII, by Fernández del Amo, consisting of a church, offices and ancillary buildings; the dignified Chaminade Hall of Residence (1963), a Modern work by the Classicist, Moya; and the Retiro Tower (1968), on Av. Menéndez Pelayo c/v Anunciación, one of the later works of Gutiérrez Soto.

Parish Church
of Nuestra Señora de Fuencisla 1962-65
Santa Cruz de Mudela, Poblado de Almendrales
García de Paredes, J.M.

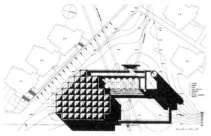

This is an attractive example of a modest
parish church conceived for an interesting
neighbourhood (one of the Managed Settlements, see M 63). Without the usual church
nave and the normal requirement of an
enormous span for the roof, it instead tried
out a space featuring a set of columns: thin
supports like those found in mosques. The
Moorish inspiration had something to do
with the architect's Andalusian heritage and
his fascination with the Córdoba Mosque.
However, it is also related to the impact
that Corrales and Molezún's Pavilion for the
Brussels Exhibition (see M 69) had on him.
These two architects and Javier Carvajal
also worked with García de Paredes on the
Almendrales settlement.

Juan XXIII Housing Estate 1962-66   M 92
Av. General Tabanera, Carabanchel Alto
Ferrán/Mangada/Romany
This intriguing set of low-budget housing
(see M 63) shows how purely Rationalist
principles were superseded, both in terms
of architecture, with Brutalist and Realist
touches, and of urban planning, very much
in line with the thinking behind Team X and
some British town-planning models.

School of Road, Canal and Port   M 93
Engineers 1963-67
Ciudad Universitaria
Laorga/López Zanón
A building showing the continuity of Radical
Rationalism, it is representative of the work
of these architects at the time. Its successful
sculptural touch and use of seen concrete
seem to refer directly to the contents of
the curriculum of the Engineering School.

Caño Roto Settlement [Phase 2] 1963-69   M 94
Between Vía Carpetana and Laguna
Iñiguez de Onzoño/Vázquez de Castro
A continuation of the original, well designed
settlement of Caño Roto (see M 75), it is
one of the most interesting of the Managed
Settlements built in Madrid. This phase was
carried out with a different architecture,
more open to Organicist principles and
concerned with calligraphical aspects.

Banco de Madrid
Carrera de San Jerónimo 13
Bonet Castellana
This building, constructed with a radical glass curtain wall despite the fact that it stands on an important street in the historical part of Madrid, successfully deals with the figurative problems of this kind of bank architecture and is representative of Bonet's receptivity towards Mies's principles.

Glass Pavilion
in the Casa de Campo Park 1964-65 M 96
Casa de Campo
Cabrero/Labiano/Ruiz
This glass pavilion is one of the most radical examples of the continuity of the Rationalist style in the work of Francisco Cabrero, who also designed the Trade Union building (see M 51) and the Arriba Newspaper building (see M 84). Originally planned and designed to be put up very quickly, the building is a large-span container of pure space, built out of a mixed structure of concrete in the lower part and steel in the upper section. Cabrero's exuberant style stretched his work beyond the limitations of the German master, Mies, as is clearly evident from the conception of the internal and external space. The pavilion's elegant Purist volume and its refined, minimalist line is in no way undermined by the sloping roof.

Apartment Buildings in
the Salamanca Neighbourhood 1964-67 M 97
Lagasca, Ortega y Gasset, Claudio Coello
Ruiz de la Prada
Ruiz de la Prada designed several upmarket housing blocks in the best residential areas of Madrid during the seventies: in Aravaca, Salamanca and Chamberí. All were very similar, some of them nearly identical. At the time, they represented the configuration of a new domestic, urban language of elegant synthesis. The aesthetics of the buildings went beyond that of Gutiérrez Soto's own models, which had reigned supreme in the tastes of the upper middle classes until then. The aspect of these suburban areas was improved by the erection of these fine buildings, whose brick banding established an appearance of systematisation that actually hides the differences in the specifications that the different owners required.

Girasol Building 1964-66
José Ortega y Gasset 23 c/v Lagasca
Coderch/Valls
The Catalan architect, Coderch, used an intense design for this block of luxury apartments. In an attempt to go beyond the principles reigning in the suburban area of Salamanca, he avoided the inner courtyards used to bring in light by establishing interesting, deep apartments overlooking the street with their courtyards turned outside. The layout of the standard apartments, set at an angle to the street, is exceptional, giving all apartments the characteristics of a single-family house with well established volumes. However, the corner placement was not so well executed in terms of ground plan or volume. To place the apartments with their courtyards over the street, the lifts had to be individualised and a mezzanine access storey introduced to the general design.

Profidén Laboratories 1964
Ferrocarril c/v Autovía A-1
Corrales/Molezún
A minor work by Corrales and Molezún, it nonetheless has an attractive impact on the surrounding urban landscape. The design uses a composition of horizontal volumes of an Organicist style, but which seem to be rooted in the Mies of the Rosa Luxemburg monument or some of Wright's work.

Nuestra Señora de Luján
Hall of Residence 1964-70
Av. Martín Fierro s/n, Ciudad Universitaria
Baliero/Córdova [head architect: Feduchi]
This building shows how close Argentinian Organicism was in some ways to that of Madrid. The student's bedrooms open onto an inner garden in a shape that suggests a tiered amphitheatre, whilst the street façade is directly closed off.

San Juan Evangelista
Hall of Residence 1965-67
Av. Gregorio del Amo 4, Ciudad Universitaria
Suárez-Inclán/Viloria
Exemplary of the direct architecture related to English Brutalism and the principles of Team X, as well as to what was to become *Arte Povera*, it shows the designers will to avoid any hint of pretentiousness, whether of Rationalist or Organicist hues.

Centro Building 1964-66 M 102
Orense 11
Alas/Casariego
This attractive, 10-storey office block is an example of the Rationalist continuation of the International Style in its unconventional attention to the subject, using concrete and steel to establish a very good-looking building with a simple, clear-cut volume of straight lines, well-proportioned and worthy of its excellent site in the new part of Madrid. Its symmetric plan is laid out around an interesting, octagonally-shaped, glazed inner courtyard with a creatively designed, brightly lit stairway. The building is a good example of the works made by these sound, sensible architects who, 25 years later, continue to make up-to-date buildings, such as their competition-winning design for the Tres Cantos railway station (1986-90), with its interesting portico.

Huarte House 1965-66 M 103
Turégano 1 c/v Isla de Oza, Puerta de Hierro
Corrales/Molezún
This house, which became justly famous in the mid-sixties, marked the final capitulation of the great architects, José Antonio Corrales and Ramón Vázquez Molezún, to the supremacy of Organicism, giving up any trace of their earlier Rationalism. However, the house is only traditional in the way it is laid out around several courtyards, for its shapes, space and language endeavour to establish a Modern alternative, whose remote origins might lie with Wright and Aalto and with a certain way of interpreting vernacular architecture. Characterised by the richness and expressiveness of its large, simple sloping roofs and the use of ceramic materials on all the external surfaces, the house can be considered one of these architects' greatest masterpieces.

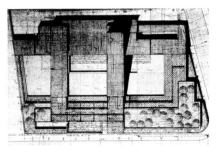

School in Caño Roto 1965-69 M 10
Vía Carpetana and Laguna
Iñiguez de Onzoño/Vázquez de Castro
An example of Organicist architecture with Brutalist overtones, it marks the mature style of the architects that designed the famous first Managed Settlement (see M 75) during the late fifties. The complex can also be related to Fernández Alba's architecture of the same period.

La Unión y El Fénix Building 1965-71
Paseo de la Castellana 37
Gutiérrez Soto
One of Gutiérrez Soto's later works, it is
representative of the changing face of the
Castellana, where it was one of the few
praiseworthy large new projects of the late
sixties. The tower block avoids the already
conventional Miesian tradition, to evoke
New York-style metropolitan profiles.

Saconia, Ciudad de los Poetas 1965-79   M 106
Dehesa de la Villa
Perpiñá/de Miguel/Iglesias • Briones/Marzal [eng.]
A large, private-sector housing estate, it is
adapted to the sloping terrain and separates
the pedestrian alleys from the road, with
access to apartments (average 80 m^2) and
shops solely from the pedestrian precincts.
The blocks are laid out on an Organicist,
non-linear ground plan in a frieze pattern.

Old IBM Building 1966-68   M 107
Paseo de la Castellana 4 c/v Hermosilla 1
Fisac
An interesting office building on an important
site, it shows the full potential of reinforced
concrete in establishing its own language,
even when it was not used here for the
structure but only for protecting the west-
facing façades from the sometimes strong
afternoon sun in Madrid.

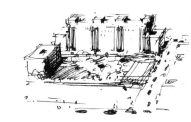

Apartment Building 1966-74   M 108
Basílica 23 c/v General Moscardó 17
Cano Lasso
A fascinating piece of architecture, quite the
opposite of Coderch's Girasol building
(see M 98) it uses the old principles of the
Salamanca suburb, set out in the 19th c., to
establish the layout of the apartments, which
are average sized, and to give a balanced
urban appearance to the entire building.
The layout around an open inner courtyard
makes almost direct reference to Zuazo's
Casa de las Flores (see M 20). In figurative
terms, the bay windows are reminiscent of
Gutiérrez Soto's housing on Calle Miguel
Angel (see M 44), while its restrained design
links it to the kind of architecture practised
by Sánchez Arcas. It was very much praised
in its day by the younger generation, who
saw it as a successful attempt to return a
sense of "urbanity" to housing.

César Carlos Hall of Residence 1967-68　M 109
Ramón Menéndez Pidal 3, Ciudad Universitaria
Sota, A. de la/López Candeira
An interesting work by Alejandro de la Sota, who managed to recover here some of the compositional, abstract and purist brilliance that he had displayed in his masterpiece, the Civilian Government Building in Tarragona (see TA 1). The design bears witness to his continuing Rationalism, which was already becoming rare by the late sixties. The programme was ordered by a curious analytical criterion, dividing the building into the high-rise, monumental volume of the pavilion where the bedrooms are located, and the low-rise block for the central services, in the style of a house, thereby situating the two objects on a horizontal field, almost as if they were two characters united only by language and colour. The high-rise pavilion, with a large central gap, seems to imitate a triumphal arch, as if paying homage to the Emperor Charles V, whose name this hall of residence bears.

Apartment Building 1968　M 110
Señores de Luzón 8
Aroca
The first and one of the few buildings in the old part of the city that tried to create an environmentally valid Modern architecture that would fit in, without being imitative, it uses Aroca's own relaxed version of Brutalism, which had already been successfully tried out in other apartment buildings in Madrid.

Other works. Works of the transition from the sixties to the seventies include the Mutua Madrileña Automovilista (1968) on Almagro 40, by Iñiguez de Onzoño and Vázquez de Castro, with its interesting urban façade, and the Cuzco IV office building (1970-79) on Pza. de Cuzco, by García Benito, projecting a successful metropolitan image onto the Castellana with its 3 bays in which the 2 smaller, lateral ones are shifted off-centre.

Torre de Valencia Building 1968-70　M 111
O'Donnell c/v Menéndez Pelayo
Carvajal
An example of the Organicist style of Javier Carvajal, who took advantage of the exceptional position overlooking the Retiro Park to put up an expressive tower as part of the city skyline. Its volume is more appealing from near than from afar, which made it a very polemical building in its day.

Magariños Sports Centre 1968-70
Serrano 127 c/v Jorge Manrique
Iñíguez de Onzoño, J.L./Vázquez de Castro

M 112

This building has an interesting interior space and fits in well in an area that is characterised by the presence of great architectural works such as Arniches and Domínguez's Instituto Escuela (see M 29), Bergamín's Nursing School (see M 37) and Fisac's CSIC and Espíritu Santo Chapel (see M 47).

Parish Church of
Nuestra Señora de la Araucana 1970-71
Puerto Rico 29
Moya

M 113

A late work by Luis Moya, who had already left behind his Classical stage but was still interested in the spatial potential of mural brickwork, it can be seen as a precursor to certain features that Moneo included later in his Museum of Roman Art (see BA 5).

Juan March Foundation 1971-75
Castelló 77 c/v Padilla
Picardo

M 114

This building tried out a new way of fitting into the 19th c. suburban part of Madrid, with a volume detached from the surrounding buildings although occupying only part of an urban block. The formal continuity and the symmetry achieve the kind of unique character required for a cultural foundation.

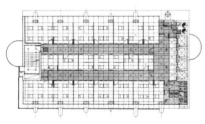

Old Bankunion Building 1970-75
Paseo de la Castellana 46
Corrales/Molezún

M 115

This design won an important competition. It is representative of the new search for truly Modern principles that the architects initiated, having exhausted the possibilities of the Organic style in the Madrid School, whose best buildings never respected any line of continuity. Placed perpendicular to the avenue, standing apart from the other buildings and the street that runs up behind it, the volume reaches upwards, with special care paid to its silhouette, which ends in rounded, semi-cylindrical vaulting. Its compositional calligraphy is supported by use of the service installations to add expression to the whole. Constructed at a time of uncertainty towards the end of Franco's rule, it was much praised in its day as a pointer along the right road towards the future.

Banco de Bilbao 1971-81
[now **BBV, Banco de Bilbao Vizcaya**]
Paseo de la Castellana 79-81
Sáenz de Oíza

Second of the great skyscrapers that Sáenz
de Oíza built in Madrid, after Torres Blancas
(see M 90) it is considered to be one of his
greatest works, if not the greatest. The winner of a restricted-entry competition, the
architect returned to a completely Modern
look after his dalliance with unusual sculptural
effects in Torres Blancas. The building was
to be 30 storeys and 107.8 m high, placed
above one of the train tunnels running under
the Paseo de la Castellana, thus requiring a
rather special structure. This affected the
general conception of the building, whose
engineer was Carlos Fernández Casado. The
resulting union between shape and structure
was highly organic. This meant that the load-
bearing structure was planned at a scale suitable to a tower block and not as a simple
sum of small-scale structures, which was the
habitual way of constructing in these cases.
Two main "trunks" of concrete were laid out
to enclose the vertical installation ducts and
the communications systems. These trunks
also supported large slabs and cantilevers
every 5 storeys, on which metal stanchions
were set to support the intermediate floors.
This arborium style of vertical layout was
enclosed within an enormous self-oxidising
steel curtain wall, which wraps up the entire
building like a skin. The curtain wall is light
and its continuity is shown by the rounded
corners and further emphasised by the cleaning galleries that run around it. The original

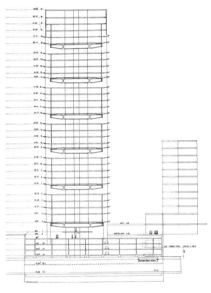

conception boldly attempted to wed the Wright idea of the tower block as a structure
identified with a tree shape, to the Mies schema of the rectangular groundplan and a curtain
wall identical on both façades and symmetrical at the corners. One cannot fail to be aware
of the effort that went into this reconciliation, whose final effect is just short of brilliant. The
building was the object of great admiration in the seventies for its consolidation of Modern
architecture in Madrid. It is still considered to be one of the masterpieces of Spanish 20th c.
architecture, adding nobility to the urban landscape of Madrid and offsetting the disappointing, never-quite-finished feel of the AZCA Centre (see M 42 and p. 239).

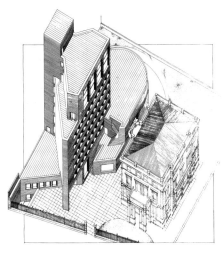

Bankinter Building 1973-77
Paseo de la Castellana 29 c/v Marqués de Riscal
Moneo/Bescós
Probably the most famous building in Spain in the seventies, especially among the small-size designs of young architects, it contributed to the recognition of Moneo's talent in establishing a solution that offered the hopes of continuity following the deep crisis of the end of the sixties. Constructed as the extension to one of the 19th c. palatial build-ings on the Castellana, it was presented as an alternative to total demolition at a time when conservation was not yet foremost on the agenda and several similar buildings were being demolished to make way for anodine blocks of offices and housing. This building also showed a transcendental change in the cultural approach of architecture towards its own obligations. The ingenious solution in the ground plan established the transition between the closed-block layout prevailing in the rear streets and the open building on the Castellana, with a frontal composition based on the silhouette, the use of the same bricks as the old residence and a simple ordering of door and window openings. With the careful application of these elementary but efficient principles, the building proved that architectural resources are not slave to fashion, but can preserve a timeless validity. Brilliant and eclectic, the Bankinter extension also provides the keys to understanding Moneo's architecture: the attention he pays to the placement in the surrounding context, the programme and character of the

design, the use of techniques and elements available to Modern architecture. Here, he combines references to other architects (Cabrero, Sullivan, Aalto, Venturi and Rossi), whilst demonstrating his ability to create a fully functional building.

Caja Postal Calculation Centre
and Securities Deposit 1973-75
Monforte de Lemos c/v Ginzo de Limia
Sota, A. de la/Capella
A minor but interesting work by de la Sota, whose project, of a very specific character and use, divided the plan into two identical twin buildings, cube-shaped Rationalist containers which go a long way to defining the urban landscape around them.

Northern Junction 1973-74
Prolongation of Paseo de la Castellana
**C. Fernández Casado, S.L.,
Manterola/Fernández Troyano [engs.]**
These bridges constitute a Spaghetti junction of motorways crossing over each other at three levels, two with elevated ramps. To avoid visual overcrowding, the architects minimised the supports and lintels: the pillars were reduced to cylindrical columns of 1.2 m diameter; the lintels become an unbroken ribbon that forms an integral part of the roads. The two elevated ramps were made of prestressed concrete in 8 curved spans, 80 m in radius, 11.5 m wide and 1 m deep.

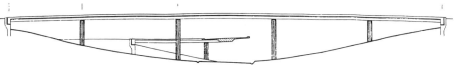

Bank Building 1973-75
Serrano 38
Carvajal
This office building set between party walls, with an attractive vestibule and a façade closed with an elegant curtain wall, shows how good Modern architecture can make a positive contribution to the look and feel of an important street. The interior space has been spoiled by reforms.

Apartment Building 1974-79
Paseo de la Habana 71
Moneo
This singular residential building by Moneo managed to take advantage of its independent site and the big garden by adapting an interpretation of Aalto's open ground plans to the requirements of the placement, whilst closing the building off with façades whose language is strictly Modern.

Windsor Building 1974-78
Raimundo Fernández Villaverde 65
Alas/Casariego
This 28-storey building standing next to Sáenz de Oíza's Banco de Bilbao building makes a positive contribution to defining the visible volume and image of the AZCA Centre. The Windsor shows the high quality of the Rationalist heritage in the office buildings of the architects, Alas and Casariego.

Parque La Arganzuela Residential Complex 1975-80

M 123

Paseo de las Yeserías 59

Junquera/Pérez Pita

One of the first interesting apartment buildings built by the generation that graduated at the end of the sixties, it is representative of the later works of its architects. In this case, the wide, free-standing building is well laid out and correctly dimensioned to enhance its urban environment.

Apartment Building 1975-78

M 124

Arturo Soria c/v Herrera de Tejada

Bayón/Aroca/Bisquert/Martín

A superb cooperative block, planned in such a way that the user could complete the layout to his own taste, it is successful in fitting in with the rest of the housing on Arturo Soria. Indeed, the sophisticated design of the structure on its façade has added to the urban landscape.

Block of Housing and Shops 1977-84

M 125

Pradolongo and other streets, Orcasitas

Mapelli/De Miguel/Romaní/Valdés/Vega/Vellés

One of the first remodelling works done on the outskirts of Madrid, it skillfully combined open town planning with an attempt to recover a town of streets and squares, zoning the area into tower blocks and urban blocks. These blocks were the first to follow the new approach to town planning of the seventies.

Adriática Building 1978-81

M 126

Paseo de la Castellana 39

Carvajal

One of the most successful new buildings in the old part of the Castellana, where the new stands next to the old , this completely independent building establishes a sound relationship with its surroundings. This relationship was sadly undermined by the subsequent construction of another building nextdoor. A glazed, abstract parallelepiped volume houses the office space and is accompanied by another of concrete, which houses the facilities and services, thereby adapting to the irregularities of the terrain. These volumes show the sculptural potential of Carvajal's Organic Rationalism and his ability to use it to form coherent entities. Indeed, this is the kind of building for which he became justly famous.

Barrio de Orcasur
Casas, M. de las/Casas, I. de las

Part of the Orcasur remodelling project, it was one of many reforms to the peripheral areas of Madrid carried out by the democratic regime involving many teams of town planners and architects, including Sáenz de Oíza, Corrales, Aroca and Gómez Carballo. The sector planned by the Casas brothers was intended to look decidedly urban, with long, low-rise blocks of housing defining the space of the streets, with courtyard-style gardens to the back and elegant tower blocks at the end. The final outcome is a complex of strict and purist language, very well-cared for construction and intelligent groundplans in which the tower blocks stand out for the way in which they manage to define a kind of canonic repetition that adds character to the whole.

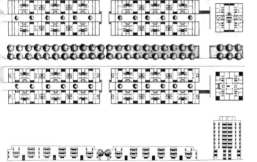

M 128 **Palomeras and Madrid Sur** 1979-
To the south of the capital

Following Franco's death, the neighbourhood associations took advantage of the newly legalised possibility of lobbying to demand thorough changes and responsible planning for the peripheral areas of Madrid. The first areas to be remodelled were the Meseta de Orcasitas (see M 125) and Orcasur (see M 127), followed by the biggest sector of all, Palomeras, which was completed later and expanded to become what is now known as Madrid Sur. The party in government after the first democratic elections applied a social-democratic policy from the central administration, later continued under the socialist government and then devolved to the regional government, where architect Eduardo Mangada carried it through. In the first stage, Palomeras (S of Vallecas, SE of Madrid) had to provide housing for large numbers, working on a dense urban plan that was not convincing but whose architecture was surprisingly successful, with high-quality buildings both in terms of individual typology and overall urban landscape, which was the main concern in this area where disorder had previously prevailed. In the second stage, the architects did not have to provide such dense housing and enjoyed greater flexibility in choice of volumes and placement. Palomeras was a living laboratory of housing and town planning policy. It was much influenced by the new architectural culture focussed around the School of Architecture, and the results were first class. The operation entailed a new edition of the Greater Madrid Managed Settlements (see

1,016 Social Housing Apartments 1979-84

Av. Pablo Neruda and other streets, Palomeras
Casas, M. de las/Casas, I. de las   M 129

These blocks stand in a high-density sector of the Palomeras plan (see M 128), the biggest housing project taken on by the democratic governments to reform the peripheral areas of Madrid. Aimed at providing mass housing for maximum numbers in high-rise buildings, the idea was to establish ordered repetition of enormous, wide blocks which define the landscape around them as an unashamedly urban environment. The area is made especially attractive by the architects' use of space and their ability to spread the houses' area of influence outwards, as well as their excellent sense of volume and their design of each housing unit in an L-shape, distributed through an internal corridor, thus arriving at an excellent Corbusian solution to the living requirements.

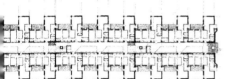

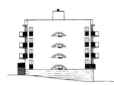

M 63), and indeed, it was often these settlements that were being replaced. Linking with Palomeras, Madrid Sur is at the edge of the sector, bordering with the city centre. Unlike Palomeras, Madrid Sur is on previously unbuilt-up land zoned with a grid of closed or half-closed urban blocks, where the emphasis is on geometrical order, leading to great uniformity. However, the sector has been completed and now stands as an exemplary piece of urban planning. The size of an entire town, it adds a new metropolitan focal point to the southern peripheries.

Apart from the works included separately (see M 129, M 130, M 132, M 137, M 141 and M 154) special reference should be made to the housing on Las Marismas 2 to 55 and the miniature industrial estate on Cerámica street, by Frechilla, López-Peláez and Sánchez (both from 1984-87) and the apartment building with courtyard in SE Palomeras, by Bayón (1986-90). Many good professionals worked in this area, including Prats, Villanueva and Muelas; Bravo, Martínez Ramos and de Miguel; Ruiz Larrea, Rubio Carvajal and Alvarez Sala.

Four Apartment Buildings 1979-82   M 13
Andaluces, Rafael Alberti, Palomeras Sureste
Junquera/Pérez Pita
An interesting contribution to the important
area of Palomeras (see M 128) in its most
densely populated SE part, the layout entails
a system of open, high-rise blocks, where
figurative mechanisms have been successfully used to offset the potentially overbearing
scale of the estate.

Torre Picasso Building 1979-89   M 13
AZCA Centre
Yamasaki/Mir/Coll
A minor work by the architect of the World
Trade Center in New York, its architecture
is competent rather than outstanding. It is
currently the city's highest building (165 m),
and was planned as such in the AZCA Centre
project (see M 42). Its construction was well
directed by Alas, Casariego and Antolín.

Apartment Building 1981-83   M 13
Av. la Albufera c/v Av. Rafael Alberti, Palomeras
Frechilla/López-Peláez/Sánchez
This is another of the apartment buildings in
Palomeras (see M 128) which had to handle
the requirements for high-density, high-rise
housing. A detached building, its composition
follows a rigorous strictness, enhanced by
the brick facing. Its staggered profile makes
attractive viewing from all around.

Sollube Office Building 1982-88   M 13
Pza. Carlos Trías Beltrán 4, AZCA Centre
Iñiguez de Onzoño, J.L./Iñiguez de Onzoño, F.
This work shows the continuing relevance
of Rationalist principles in Madrid. A building
of notable elegance and great architectural
merits, the small size of the Sollube office
building has prevented it from overcoming
the lack of coherence in its surroundings,
the AZCA Centre.

Reform and Completion   M 13
of the Church of Monserrat 1982-89
San Bernardo c/v Quiñones
Capitel/Rivière/Martorell
The complete overhaul of a long unfinished
Baroque church was completed with a new
chancel. The treatment of the chancel, the
head wall and many other modern elements
and details provides an exquisite balance
between the old and the new.

Social Services Centre 1982-89 M 135
Puerta de Toledo c/v Bailén
Navarro Baldeweg
This centre, a complex of three buildings, won the competition for the overall remodelling of the sector of San Francisco el Grande in the old city centre, baptised after the church (1761-84) of the same name. The competition led to the discovery of the then almost unknown architect and painter, Juan Navarro Baldeweg. The sector was designed to close off the Puerta de Toledo circus, which was completed later with the Pedro Salinas Library (see M 151). The large drop in level to the rear streets was resolved using a base on which the three volumes are set. All of these try to establish continuity with the neighbouring buildings, but without being interconnected, the plinth alone being responsible for defining the round space of the circus.

Planetarium 1984-86 M 136
Parque Enrique Tierno Galván
Pérez Arroyo/Mañoso/Morencos
An architecture that aspires to the state-of-the-art style of foreign buildings, at least in its language, it actually boils down to a sound conviction in the continuity of modern progress. The unique content is expressed by an emphasis on high-tech details that could have benefitted from a higher budget.

726 Social Housing Apartments 1984-87 M 137
Av. de la Albufera, Pol. Norte, Palomeras
Casas, M. de las/Casas, I. de las
A complex within the Palomeras plan, this one belongs to a later stage, when density was no longer at a premium. The low-rise tower blocks were erected on a layout similar to that used in Orcasur (see M 127). The order is open, so as not to lose the over-riding urban quality of the whole.

National Auditorium 1984-88 M 138
Príncipe de Vergara 146
García de Paredes, J.M.
This building had to overcome its placement with an architecture that would look imposing from the outside, yet fit into the tradition of the domestic Madrid vernacular. The inside, however, is an interesting interpretation of the Scharoun Philharmonic Hall, which the architect often used as a model.

Reform and Extension of the Atocha Train Station 1984-92
M 13

Glorieta de Carlos V
Moneo

The restricted-entry competition programme entailed conserving the old Southern Station (1888-92) whilst fitting it out with new inter-city and commuter train facilities and the terminal for the high speed train, the AVE, in an area with enormous height differences. The new entrance was taken to the back, where a pointed pavilion with overhead windows provides access to the restrained but beautifully designed underground commuter station, which then leads through to the airy, streamlined architecture of the high-speed train station. The complex was conceived in urbanistic terms as a "basilica" (the old station) with a "belfry" (the clock tower) and a "baptistry" (the access pavilion), in a superb restoration exercise.

República de Brasil State School 1985
M 14

Av. de los Fueros s/n, Barrio de San Fermín
Campo Baeza

This is a good example of the ascetic, compositional nature of Campo's architecture which was much influenced by the Neo-Rationalism prevalent in the US. Although he had previously worked mainly on designing houses, in this school his attributes take on their full expressive power.

Apartments in Palomeras
M 14

[Unit 15] 1986
Pedro Laborde, Palomeras
Cano Lasso

Part of the enormous housing operation for the inhabitants of the south of Madrid (see M 128), here the architect tried to solve the design in urbanistic terms by grouping the blocks of 73 apartments in such a way as to create a town within a city.

Family House in Puerta de Hierro 1986
M 14

Pedralaves 2, Puerta de Hierro
Alonso de Santos

An almost unique display of the singular personality of Alonso de Santos, a student and follower of Alejandro de la Sota and Sáenz de Oíza, this house is a very personal and attractive alternative to the refinement of de la Sota's style that he so admired.

Social Housing on the Edge of the M-30 Ringroad 1986-90
Félix Rodríguez de la Fuente
Sáenz de Oíza

This was Sáenz de Oíza's powerful response to the need to make a free-standing building right on the edge of an urban motorway. The organic approach conceives the outer façade as a fortress-like enclosure and the inner façade as a private courtyard wall.

M 143

Housing Complex 1989-92
Divina Pastora 1-3, Fuencarral
Bayón

These two buildings were designed for the old part of the former village of Fuencarral. Perpendicular to each other, they form a small plaza that, with its simple materials and rhythmic arcades tries to pay homage to local roots without stooping to imitation or self-consciously avoiding abstract language.

M 144

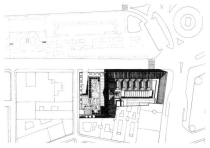

Thyssen-Bornemisza Museum 1989-92
Paseo del Prado 8
Moneo

The work entailed the interior remodelling of the Neoclassical Palace of Villahermosa (built in 1805 on top of a 16th-17th c. estate house), which had already been turned into a bank by Moreno Barbera in 1970-75. Moneo designed a completely new ground plan that was more in keeping with the noble, compact volume of the space. He established an inside courtyard, covered with long skylights, which centralises access and circulation, and also articulates the different rooms leading off it. This courtyard also provides total coherence between the interior and the façade, without mimicking styles or even establishing a clear contrast between old and new, but rather simply adding to what was already there to create a new, harmonious whole.

M 145

Apartment Building 1989-93
Valderribas 86
Abalos/Herreros

On an E-facing site on the edge of the M-30 ringroad, the architects used glazed galleries on the front of the buildings to give the in-habitants a view of the road from the day-time parts of their apartments. The building is clad in a high-tech skin that fits in well with the industrial nature of the neighbourhood.

M 146

Madrid Community Sports Stadium 1989-94

Av. de los Arcentales and M-40 Ringroad
Cruz/Ortiz

The architects won an important, restricted-entry competition for an ambitious project, of which in 1997 only this Stadium had been completed. It was the second of their large-scale works, after the Santa Justa Train Station in Seville (see SE 34). The running track was excavated into the terrain and surrounded by an initial set of tiered seating secured to the ground, followed by an enormous tribune. The spectacular tribune is oblong shaped, built on large curved elements that form thick shell-walls, supporting it. It conveys both the elite-sport image and the functional purpose of the stadium, popularly known as "La Peineta" (ornamental comb). This is the most recent large-scale, top-quality building constructed in Madrid.

UNED Library 1989-94

Senda del Rey, Ciudad Universitaria
Linazasoro

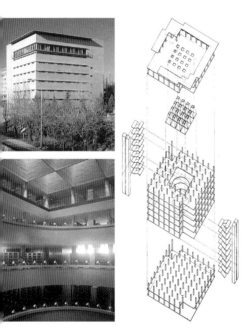

The first, brilliant example of this Basque architect's work in Madrid bears witness to the recuperation of the Rationalist tradition in end-of-century Spain. It is a free-standing building on the lower cornice of the River Manzanares, shaped like a low-rise square tower-block, characterised by its large single space on a base-level access storey. This space is in some way reminiscent of Louis Kahn's library in the Phillips Exeter Academy, but is even more unitary. It is defined by the large round inserts that give it its form, on the edge of which are the reading cubicles, and by the system of skylight windows. All in all, it is a building of cultured architecture which is capable of turning its references and overtones into top-quality operational instruments.

Office Building 1990-91

Alcalá Galiano 4
Alvarez-Sala/Rubio/Ruiz Larrea

In a 19th c. residential area, this marvellous open-plan office building has a façade giving onto an inner courtyard that bears witness to the continuity of Rationalism in the Madrid School of the nineties, developed here in a refined emulation of Mies that is representative of the latest style of its architects.

Display Greenhouses in the Royal Botanical Garden 1990-93
M 150

Pza. de Murillo 2

Fernández Alba, Angel

These constitute an interesting example of how a modern-style space, designed on a section that is shifted along linewise, can successfully emulate the tradition of 19th c. greenhouses in the historical garden created by Juan de Villanueva in 1774.

Pedro Salinas Public Library 1990-94
M 151

Puerta de Toledo

Navarro Baldeweg

The second part of the municipal buildings on the Puerta de Toledo commissioned from Navarro Baldeweg following the competition for the entire San Francisco el Grande area lacked the problems of the drop in levels that affected the first part of the complex (the Social Services Centre, see M 135). The architect made the reading room as a cylindrical space on a plinth, letting the plinth define the shape of the plaza and allowing the room to find its own form of expression. The internal distribution responds to the requirements of a general public library and another specialised library. The complex's quality is based on many merits, including its successful definition of a public space without making use of an inward-looking design.

UNED Department of Economics and Business Studies 1991-94
M 152

Senda del Rey, Ciudad Universitaria

Linazasoro

This highly successful university building in the Rationalist tradition, with refined overtones of Kahn, is almost contiguous with the library for the UNED distance university (see M 148), with which it attains a distant but clear unity of intention.

UNED Department of Psychology 1992-95

Senda del Rey, Ciudad Universitaria

M 153

Linazasoro

The third academic building designed by the architect Linazasoro for the Madrid-based distance university, it also features a comb-layout, like the Economics Department (see M 152), but has different figurative intentions and incorporates allusions to the style of Asplund and Terragni.

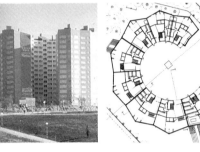

Apartment Building 1992-94 M 154
Puerto del Milagro, Madrid Sur
Martínez Lapeña/Torres Tur
This building was planned under the regional urban management of architect Eduardo Mangada as a figurative and typological counterpoint in the urban landscape to the overly stark, repetitive look of the system of closed blocks placed on a grid layout in the Madrid Sur estate (see M 128), next to Palomeras and Vallecas. Martínez Lapeña and Torres Tur designed the high-rise building following the style of Scharoun in the "Julia" of the Stuttgart complex, although toning down the severe exterior in a way that makes the final product reminiscent of Aalto's apartment buildings. Very successful in satisfying the urbanistic and architectural objectives, the tower-block stands next to a small, low-density complex by the same architects.

Reform of the Teatro Real 1994-97 M 155
Pza. de Oriente 5
Rodríguez de Partearroyo
An efficient reform of the Royal Theatre that seems to have been undergoing reform works ever since it was built in 1818-50, its shape and volume, which Moya improved in his post-war reform, has become a key part of the Madrid landscape. Its spatial and technical fittings are top class.

More on the capital. Note the public residential projects, such as Vázquez Consuegra's on Sierra Elvira c/v M-30 (1987-91), and Cruz and Ortiz's social housing in Carabanchel (1987-91), on Arbol del Cielo c/v Vidauba. Amongst the big projects in the city, the KIO Towers (1990-96) by Philip Johnson and John Burgee, twin tower-blocks that slope inwards towards each other over Pza. de Castilla, have changed the look of northern Madrid. Also by non-Spanish architects are the J. M. Churruca office building (1990-96) on Almansa, university campus, by Kevin Roche (with Fullaondo and González Cruz) and the interior reform of the Banco de Santander offices (1991-93) on Paseo de la Castellana 24-26, by Hans Hollein. Amongst the rehabilitation works, Carlos Puentes' Casa de América (1990-92) on Paseo de Recoletos 2 is interesting, as is the sophisticated technical work for the administration offices of the Ministry of the Interior (1991-93) on Ctra. de Canillas s/n, by Abalos and Herreros.

The outskirts of Madrid. The Madrid region is an old, extensive metropolitan configuration around the capital city. Amongst its magnificent historical towns, Alcalá de Henares, 33 km to the NE, with 159,355 inhabitants, the old Roman *Complutum* and the Muslim *al-Qalaa*, the birthplace of Cervantes, conserves some of its city walls, an interesting old city centre, and a valuable Plateresque façade to the old 16th c. University, which is now being rehabilitated by the new university. There are some peripheral towns belonging to Madrid (Aravaca, to the E, predominantly high-income and middle class residential area; Barajas to the NE, 14 km from the centre, marked by its international airport), that have been located as "outskirts" in this guide. Then there are a mass of what used to be small rural villages that have seen their population multiply exponentially over the last three decades and become satellite cities to the capital: to the N, Alcobendas, San Sebastián de los Reyes (see p. 278), and the new city of Tres Cantos (see page 284). To the NW, along the A-6 motorway, Pozuelo de Alarcón, 10 km from the centre, with 37,889 inhabitants living in small high-quality estates, has become indistinguishable from other Madrid residential suburbs; Majadahonda, 17 km out, is another predominantly residential town, with 23,000 inhabitants, mainly young professionals. It also has an interesting sewage plant (1987-88) by Abalos and Herreros on the road to Villanueva de la Cañada. 18 km NW from the capital, Las Rozas and its outlying satellite, Las Matas, have 14,000 inhabitants in luxury housing estates. 12 km

further down the A-6, in the mountain foothills, is Torrelodones (6,000 inhabitants), with several weekend homes. Rather different in character is the area along the A-5 motorway towards Portugal, whose towns were built up with mass housing in the seventies, such as Alcorcón, 12 km from the centre, with 141,153 inhabitants; Getafe, nearby at 13 km from the centre, is a traditional manufacturing centre, with 143,153 inhabitants. 27 km along the A-3 road towards Valencia, Arganda del Rey is a town of light industry, with 29,224 inhabitants. 20 km along the A-2 motorway towards Barcelona, Torrejón de Ardoz, with over 80,000 inhabitants, is an important industrial centre and a densely populated dormitory town. Finally, there are still some villages that continue to be villages, such as Buitrago (75 km from Madrid, 1,334 inhabitants), Cercedilla (56 km, 1,240 m alt., 3,877 inhabitants), Loeches (30 km, 2,760 inhabitants), Miraflores de la Sierra (50 km, 1,150 m alt., 3,500 inhabitants) and Valdelaguna (47 km, 540 inhabitants).

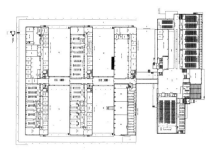

Pharmacy Department
University of Alcalá 1981-85

M 156

Campus nuevo. **Alcalá de Henares**
López-Cotelo/Puente

The Pharmacy Department was the first important project carried out by López Cotelo and Puente, both assistants to Alejandro de la Sota for some time. Since both were interested in further developing the ideas of their teacher, their work shows the continuity of Rationalism from one generation to the next. This is especially clear both in the ground plan (a rigid schema of a chain of open pavilions linked by a passage, which thus form a double series of open courtyards) and in the appearance of the final product. The project is an interesting attempt to make the idealism and abstraction of the designers' composition compatible with a Brutalist style of building.

Alcobendas. The population of the municipality of Alcobendas, estimated to be 25,000 inhabitants in 1970, tripled in the last three decades of the century to around 80,000 in 1997. Only 16 km N from Madrid, it has good communications with the capital along the A-1 motorway to France via the Basque Country and also the M-30 Ringroad, which has really turned it into another suburb of Madrid. High-class residential estates with free-standing homes for high-income families, such as La Moraleja and El Soto de la Moraleja, lie alongside modern industrial estates, business office buildings and shopping malls with a wide range of entertainment facilities. Next to Alcobendas, what used to be the old farming village of San Sebastián de los Reyes now has over 40,000 inhabitants and is even more industrial and densely populated (see M 178).

Church and Theological School   M 157
of the Dominican Fathers 1955-60
Av. de Burgos 204. **Alcobendas**
Fisac
Alongside the Apostolic School in Valladolid (se VA 1), the Church of the Theological School in Alcobendas, on the outskirts of Madrid, is probably the most successful of all of Fisac's prodigious output of ecclesiastical buildings. In it, the great architect eloquently expresses his early Modern manner, which he had already used successfully in previous works and which had become his trademark, following on from his style of unobtrusive Historicism. This monasterial complex for the Dominican monks is one of his most outstanding designs: it shows his genius in using a totally Modern style which he did not develop in the Rationalist key, trying to make a church look like any other large secular building, but in his own original way. In this sense, he drew from the intentions underlying Scandinavian architecture, in which Asplund was the key name. His layout, in a double fan, placed the nave and the choir on either side of the altar. In turn, the cone shapes of the double hyperbola contained a chapel and a courtyard for the Theological School. The space thus created is attractive and mystical in its feel, an effect that is dramatically enhanced by the studied play of light shed from the stained glass windows and the overhead roof windows. Following an age old tradition, from the outside the bulk of the church as such cedes its figurative role to the belfry, which is a highly original modern tower. This attractive emblem caused quite a stir in its day, even outside professional circles. Indeed, at a time when Modern architecture was not given much room in the general press, the general public identified Miguel Fisac as the Spanish contemporary architect *par excellence*.

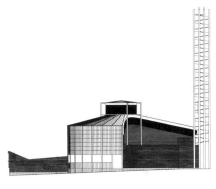

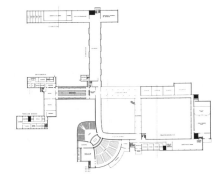

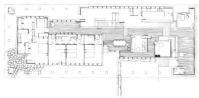

Gómez Acebo House 1966-68 M 158
Urb. Soto de la Moraleja. **Alcobendas**
Moneo
This interesting single-family house is located
in a very up-market residential estate, only a
few minutes from the centre of Madrid (see
p. 278). The house reflects the revision of
the International Style that Rafael Moneo's
generation, including Spanish architects Peña
Ganchegui, Higueras and Miró, brought
about while working in designs of a similar
type, adding elements to the international
vocabulary that could only be termed as
traditionally Spanish. The Gómez Acebo
house is reminiscent of Wright's Prairie
Houses, but it also embraces many of the
values of vernacular architecture. The single
pavilion roof, held up by large pilasters on
each edge, creates a truly rich, free and
eclectic sense of space that is characteristic
of Moneo's mature work.

Red Eléctrica Central Offices 1991-93 M 159
Paseo Conde de los Gaitanes 77, La Moraleja.
Alcobendas
Junquera/Pérez Pita
This work won the first prize in a restricted-
entry competition for expanding the existing
buildings and adding another completely
new one to round off the project. The
winning solution is characterised by the
glass façades and the 25,400 m² of building.

198 Social Housing Apartments 1993-96 M 160
Espino de Cuquillo. **Alcobendas**
Casas, M. de las
These apartments show how social housing
can be of outstanding quality and define the
area in which they stand. The architect laid
out the blocks in the shape of a comb, some
perpendicular to the road and others parallel
to the midline, visually closing the complex
and creating a sense of urban unity.

Town Hall 1973 M 161
Pza. de España 1. **Alcorcón**
Cabrero
In this interesting sample of municipal architecture, Cabrero incorporates the typical
elements of Spanish town halls into Modern
language. The building is easily identifiable
with its function and also adds architectural
distinction to the town as a whole. It was
later extended by the same architect.

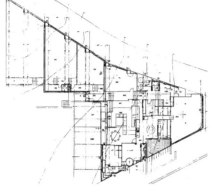

Corrales House 1978   M 162

Fuente del Rey 13, duplicado. **Aravaca**
Corrales

This sophisticated architect's house successfully combines timeless Organic and Natural-
ist principles with the language of Rationalism.
The adaptation of volumes to the irregular
site by laying the house out triangularly and
by terracing the earth to solve the gradient
problem is organic; yet the amplitude and
openness of the ground floor is Rationalist.
This is given over to a professional studio,
which forms an immense, split-level open
space, conceived almost as a landscape in
itself. A system of large sliding doors can be
brought into operation to join or separate
different parts of this space. On the whole,
the building is planned as an object in which
precision, complexity and craftsmanship are
given full rein in the design of the fittings and
other details.

Carretas School Pavilion 1990-92   M 163

Grupo Escolar 1. **Arganda del Rey**
Madridejos/Sancho

An interesting example of Madrid-style Neo-
Rationalism, in many ways it is reminiscent
of de la Sota's purist, compositional works
but very much along the International lines
that Campo Baeza made popular in Spain
during the seventies. It incites expectations
of a promising career for its two architects.

TABSA Aeronautical Workshops 1957-58

Madrid-Barajas Airport. **Barajas**   M 164
Sota, A. de la

This attractive design combines Rationalist
Purism with an exaltation of Functionality,
which is very much in keeping with a high-
tech manufacturing building like this. It is a
clear antecedent to the Maravillas Gymnasium (see M 82). Sadly, recent reforms have
jeopardised the integrity of the design.

Satellite Communications Station 1966-67

Ctra. de Gandullas, km 3. **Buitrago de Lozoya**   M 165
Cano Lasso/Ridruejo

This communications complex shows Cano
Lasso's Organic style at its most spatial,
fullest blown representation, although his
Eclecticism comes across clearly both in the
Functionalist decomposition of the ground
plan and in the purely sculptural intentions
underlying the volume.

Bowery for Excursion Services 1976-79   M 166
Cercedilla (ICONA mountain precinct)
Vellés/López Sardá
A brilliantly sophisticated design to cover an
area for leisure services and swimming on a
protected hillside, it was built with the idea
to set up a wooden framework that would
structure space, closing in service elements,
and could be extended to the rest of the
site, providing shade, without modifiying it.

Municipal Hall 1994-95   M 167
Mayor s/n. **Ciempozuelos**
Puente
The complex programme (exhibition hall,
multi-purpose room, 2 offices, information
area, canteen, 3 teaching rooms and library)
was set in three storeys over a trapezoid-
shaped site, with party walls on three sides.
The strict discipline ever-present in de la
Sota's students here exceeds expectations.

Hangar in Cuatro Vientos 1950   M 168
Cuatro Vientos Airfield. **Cuatro Vientos**
Torroja Miret [eng.]
After the Iberia hangar in Barajas (1945,
similar to the Torrejón hangar, see M 179),
for this military aerodrome Torroja designed
a metal roof of tri-articulated arches, with a
span of 35 m each and variable depth, that
interweave to establish a very rigid but at
the same time highly flexible structure.

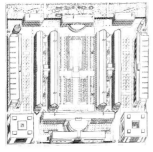

Reform of the old Artillery Barracks   M 169
for the Carlos III University 1988-90
Madrid 126. **Getafe**
Rodríguez de Partearroyo
A broad-ranging conversion of a complex of
military buildings of architectural value, the
architect managed to add further value to
the site by using a contemporary architectural
vocabulary, enriching the complex in both
functional and compositional terms.

Five Bridges over the A-6 Motorway 1964
Between **Las Rozas** and Collado-Villalba   M 170
Fernández Casado [eng.]
In the thirties, this engineer developed the
idea of single-span bridges in reinforced
concrete. In the sixties, he expanded the
idea to these bridges, now made out of
prestressed concrete, with spans of between
30 m and 50 m and with a deck of varying
depth made with gusset plates.

National Nederlanden Building 1990-93
Severo Ochoa 2, Parque Empresarial. **Las Rozas**
Cano Lasso
This office building design won a restricted-
entry competition for the way it solved the
building's image as seen from the motorway.
Cano Lasso decided to work along the lines
of Terragni in the Fascio House, thereby
showing his own special Eclecticism and his
drive for continuous renewal.

Family House in Las Matas 1991-92 M 17
Cabo Finisterre, Urb. del Golf, Las Matas.
Las Rozas
Vicens/Ramos
This house is based on the kind of made-in-
US Neo-Rationalism that the architect often
used, but enriched by his ability to find a
meeting place between formal puritanism
and a certain hedonism in the colours and
textures that is reminiscent of Barragán.

Caja de Madrid Offices
and Calculation Centre 1991-95 M 17
Gabriel García Márquez 1. **Las Rozas**
Junquera/Pérez Pita
The architectural and sculptural features of
this building are similar to those of the offices
that Cano Lasso designed for the National
Nederlanden (see M 171), although larger and
more complex. The exterior is also similar,
although Kahn's influence is also evident.

Montfort School 1962-65 M 17
Av. de la Constitución s/n. **Loeches**
Fernández Alba, Antonio
This is an interesting example of the way in
which Fernández Alba was revising Modern
architecture in the sixties. As a teacher at
the Madrid School, he wanted to place it in
a position relatively close to the mastery of
many of Aalto's works. In this sense, with
the Monfort school he continued down the
road which he had already set out on with
his highly successful El Rollo Abbey, located
in Salamanca (see SA 2), albeit with a different
theme and very diverse nuances. A central
body around a covered courtyard, which is
the key focus of the school, lays out linear
elements that take on their own sculptural
values at the edges of the design, where
they coincide with unique classrooms. The
ceramic material and the clever system of
roofs unify the school complex.

Olympic Ice Skating Rink 1995-96   M 175
Fresa 6, Pol. El Carralero II. **Majadahonda**
Soto/Maroto
The architects had little time and money,
but they made excellence with a design
focussed around a standard section, a single
building technique and a single façade; an
enormous 4,000 m^2 roof to take rain to the
ground; repetition of the transversal section
and a translucent glass wall.

Residence for Workers'   M 176
Children 1957-58
Miraflores de la Sierra
Corrales/Sota, A. de la/Molezún
One of the many merits of this highly original,
attractive building is that it brought together
the talents of de la Sota, Corrales and
Molezún. The base of the building fits snugly
to the slope of the hill with stone terraces,
as does the roof, whose light, almost continuous planes create a pleasing sculptural
effect. A component of almost complete
spatial unity was added to the interesting
volume that this creates, half organic, half
purist. Another component was also added
for technical purposes: a prefabricated
structure, made out of steel, glass, wood
and corrugated iron, to be assembled in this
rather remote site 50 km from Madrid. It
has been recently transformed without
consuting the original architects.

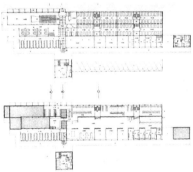

Turégano House 1986-90   M 177
Constantino Rodríguez, 17. **Pozuelo de Alarcón**
Campo Baeza
This brilliant domestic-scale expression of
Campo's Neo-Rationalist Purism has very
interesting light and space effects and a
wonderful play of volumes and composition.
Affected by Minimalist aspirations, but with-
out lacking warmth, the house is one of the
best this architect ever designed.

Infantas Elena y Cristina   M 178
State School 1983-84
Camino de Moscatelar s/n. **San Sebastián de**
los Reyes
Campo Baeza
An interesting example of Campo's Minimalist
Purism, exercised with great feeling for the
sculptural and compositional aspects, which
opened up a new line of architecture in Spain,
influenced by the American Neo-Rationalists.

INTA Hangars 1950   M 17
Base Aérea. **Torrejón de Ardoz**
Torroja Miret [eng.]
In this large rectangular nave, 180 × 47 m, one of the 180 m sides opens completely with sliding doors. Torroja's design won the competition with a polyhedric steel roof (maximum height of 18.3 m and minimum height of 9 m) of exemplary functionality, lightness and economy.

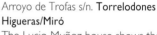

Lucio Muñoz House 1960-63   M 18
Arroyo de Trofas s/n. **Torrelodones**
Higueras/Miró
The Lucio Muñoz house shows the position the architects, Higueras and Miró adopted towards Modern architecture when they declared themselves enemies of Rationalism and searched for some kind of "Romantic" Organicism, based on a modern interpretation of history and tradition. In this sense, the house shows similarities with Peña and Moneo's domestic architecture, and perhaps represents the stance of an entire generation. Its design is based on an ideal of integrating the building into its site and its landscape, with allusions to Wright's more modern works, just as the roofing and volumes refer more to Wright's Prairie houses. An equally idealist use of the structure completes the domestic interpretation of this attractive design.

Tres Cantos. Established by a government decree in 1971 and developed through successive plans along the lines of the French *nouvelles villes* and the American new towns, the city had 27,715 inhabitants in 1996. It lies 20 km N of Madrid's town centre, to which it is connected by the C-607 dual carriageway to Colmenar and the C-1 district railway line, for which Alas and Casariego (coll.: Casariego Córdoba) designed the station (1986-90) and main square.

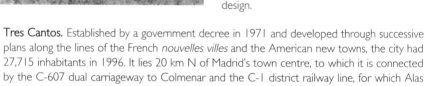

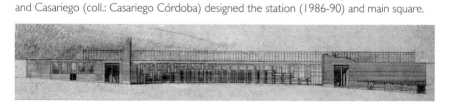

Parish Church of Santa Teresa 1986-91   M 18
Av. de la Vega. **Tres Cantos**
Perea, A./Palao/Franco
This rather interesting example of religious architecture exploits the sculptural freedom and the spatial openness of the Modern tradition whilst starting from a more figurative (and informal) approach that plays with high-tech elements.

Office Building 1990-92
Pza. de las Once Colmenas 1. **Tres Cantos**
Perea

The architecture for the offices links them directly to the church, despite the rather different functionality of the two. Perea's Neo-Organic position is thus reinforced by a voluntary drive to find a biological analogy between the secular and the non-secular that is expressed in high-tech vocabulary.

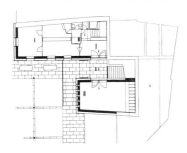

Town Hall and Square 1983-86
Pza. del Valle de la Laguna 1. **Valdelaguna**
López-Cotelo/Puente

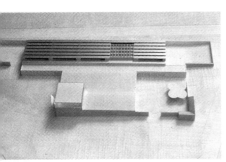

This building was a real test of López-Cotelo and Puente's ability to carry out the restoration of the old elements that needed to be conserved, without sacrificing their own radical Purism in the process, which they developed following the principles of their mentor, de la Sota. Their language, however, is even more flexible here, producing a truly valuable piece of work in which one can recognise some aspects reminiscent of Terragni, in terms of their commitment to the pre-existing context. What stands out in the design is both the way it fits into the environment and the value given to the old parts as representing the way a town hall should look. This work differs in many aspects from the architects' other designs and substantially enriches their repertoire.

Municipal Hall 1992-97
Olivar 8. **Villanueva de la Cañada**
Navarro Baldeweg

This interesting small building had to stand on a site opposite a new and characterless open area, which explains why the architect turned the building in upon itself, organising its own environment. The centre is simply laid out with a system of almost continuous rooms along a routing axis that divides them from the specific purpose-oriented areas. The rooms give onto perimetral courtyards, all held in by a massive container wall, only occasionally broken by large but simple wall openings. A well-studied system of skylights provides the set of rooms with the special lighting that characterises Navarro's designs, and an elegant modern glass pavilion adds the finishing touch to the library. Both are intense expressions of a Minimalist language handled with masterly skill.

MURCIA

Under the new democracy, this region was turned into a single-province Autonomous Community whose population is concentrated on the River Segura, its tributaries and the Mediterranean coast. Inhabited back in remote history, the Iberian culture flourished here over 2,500 years ago, followed by the Carthaginian, the Roman, the Alani (5th c.) and the Byzantine (6th c.). During the 7th c. it was ruled from the Visigothic capital of *Spania* in Toledo before becoming a Muslim stronghold for five centuries, from 743 to 1266, when it was reconquered by Christian Castile, although Morisco influence held strong until the expulsion of the Moriscos in the 17th c. Today it is a centre for service industries, although some heavy industry still flourishes (ship-building in Cartagena, oil refinery in Escombreras, petrochemicals, mining, food processing...) The capital, Murcia, was founded by Abd ar-Rahman in 831. Now a big modern city, approached on the main road from Alicante or Cartagena, it is a unique sight: a city of 338,250 inhabitants dominated by the high tower of its cathedral (Gothic, 14th c., with a splendid Baroque façade by J. Bort, 18th c.) and surrounded by fields and farms. Its rehabilitated historic centre is focussed on two shopping streets, pedestrian precincts mediaeval in name and shape: La Platería (silver-smiths' street) and La Trapería (drapers' street). The Casino, a glazed gallery from the early 20th c., is of special interest. To the south, the city overlooks the Segura, its river front dotted with monumental architecture: the Town Hall, the Episcopal Palace and the Bishop's Lodge. The Old Bridge leads to the Carmen Quarter and the New (or Iron) Bridge to the new residential estate of Don Juan Manuel. Gaspar Blein designed the most emblematic building of Murcian Rationalism, the Coy Department Store (1935) in Madre de Dios 10 c/v Pascual. The Carbonell and Blein reform plans in the fifties divided the historic city with a new road, the Gran Vía Francisco Salzillo, running from the Old Bridge in the south through the city to the north, which became the main thoroughfare in the city. Although some important monuments have been lost, the historic layout and the scale of the city squares have been conserved. New interventions have respected the old urban environment and the religious monumentality of the original centre. Face-lifts and intelligent town planning (around San Esteban) have made Murcia a pleasant, pedestrian-friendly provincial city.

Geography: 11,317 km², set in the low-lying coastal area and mountainous interior, with the Murcian Depression between the two mountain chains. Climate: Mediterranean, warm and dry. Rainfall: approx. 280 mm and 90 days. Sunshine: 2,985 hrs. Temperatures: 36°-18° and 5°-23° C. Population: 1,089,612. GDP: 81% of nat. av.

Adaptation for the Architects' Chamber of Murcia 1978
MU
Jara Carrillo 5
Arana
The conservation of the historical façade and the new monumental space around the stairs are the keys to the new design. Services and lifts are grouped tightly in a band, acting as elevation for the service space and as filter towards the rest of the open-plan area.

Segura River Mills Cultural Centre and Water Museum 1983-88
Pza. de los Molinos s/n
Navarro Baldeweg

In the 18th c., the containing walls along the Segura river, the mills and the old bridge were built as a single complex. Navarro Baldeweg's restoration of the site followed criteria aimed at bringing out the authentic character of the mills, showing the original prism construction, part of Spain's industrial archaeological heritage. His reform is unpretentious, successfully enhancing the true nature of the complex as a whole. His treatment of light, filtered through an airy dome in the conference hall, and his use of local stone and other materials make this rehabilitation project one of great impact, with the personal signature of an architect who shows all due respect to the old building and its environment.

Auditorium 1987-95
Av. Primero de Mayo s/n
García de Paredes/García Pedrosa

Cleanly laid out on a triangle plan, with elevations over the river and the city, the hypotenuse acts as the building's main façade. Classical but in the best contemporary style, its use of space is generous, with highly functional rooms and halls and exquisite aesthetic harmony in the details of design.

State Library 1988-94
Av. Juan Carlos I
Torres-Nadal

The design uses the functional requirements of a library to re-shape a stark building along the lines of Robert Venturi's architectural theory. After his interesting experience on a smaller scale, in the Murcia Savings Bank (1978-83, with Carbonell Messeguer) on Gran Vía Francisco Salzillo 23, Torres-Nadal obtained surprising results, such as the strong, highly coloured porticos on the south and east façades. The north elevation is determined by the communication and service elements behind it. By grouping them together in a complex manner, he liberated three platforms (36 x 83 m) that can be used with no constraints other than furnishing, renouncing the concept of compartmentalisation but emphasising the library's singularity and complexity with a clever use of skylights.

Extension of the Town Hall and Layout of the Town Hall Square 1991-97
Cardenal Belluga 2
Moneo
The simplicity and functionality of the building interior, with stronger light than expected, is offset by the complexity of the main façade, whose stone portico is a scaled replica of the monumental Baroque façade on the cathedral. An English-style courtyard is set within the new town hall square.

Three Family Houses amongst Lemon Groves 1984-86
Finca La Gavirana. **Cabezo de Torres**
Torres-Nadal
Austere volumes, subtle innovations in the distribution, small complexities and twists, perfect pointing in the brickwork, and free layout of windows, drawn in by a horizontal band of concrete, are some of the efficacious Minimalist resources used in these houses.

Seven Family Houses 1990-92
Paz 17. **La Alberca**
Martínez Gadea/Pérez Pinar
The houses stand on a gulley with a canal running through it, making a perfect garden. The contrasts between volumes and lines, verticality and horizontality, opaqueness and transparency, stone and high-tech, create a canny equilibrium between the whole, its individual parts and its surroundings.

More on Murcia. The crafts centre was designed by Molina Serrano (1992), in the Jardín de la Pólvora park, as a kind of box – a white, high-tech cube – placed upside down and separated from the ground by a slit to show craft exhibits in interesting spatial layouts. The reform of the Fontes palace, by Batlle, Roig Durán and López Miguel (1985-92), on Pza. de Fontes 1, is a fine demonstration of how to relate an historical building to new architectural realities. Recent social housing can be seen in Alcantarilla (7 km away from Murcia), with a complex of 85 housing units (1989) on Calle del Carmen, where vandalism has not managed to deface the architectural value of the two blocks where Alvarez, Carbonell, Martínez Gadea and Moreno created an unusual play of windows, doors, portico and different materials.

CARTAGENA. The excellent natural harbour turned the city into the naval base for the Spanish Mediterranean, and has been its focal point ever since it was founded by Asdrubal. The Romans named it *Carthago Nova*. When Charles III opened it up to trade with the Americas in 1765, he created the most important shipyard in the peninsula. The city flourished again in the 19th c. with the mining industry set up by La Unión, which was reflected in its Modernist architecture, currently being rehabilitated, around Mayor street. In 1932, during the Second Republic, Ros Costa built the German schools (now San Isidoro and Santa Florentina schools) in pure Rationalist style, on Paseo Alfonso XIII 6. Industrial estates, such as that of Cabezo Beaza, show how Cartagena has industrialised in recent years. Origin: Iberian *Mastia*, Carthaginian *Qart Hadasht*, 228 BC. Population: 173,061.

Centro de Empresas e Innovación

[CEIC Business Centre] 1991-92
Pol. Industrial Cabezo Beaza
Martínez Gadea/Retes
Consisting of modules and an iterative composition where one axis of the facilities starts from a building clearly differentiated from the other offices, the centre has simple, forceful, state-of-the-art, symbolic volumes conveying the idea of business efficiency.

UNED Distance University 1995
MU 9

Comandante Ripoll s/n
Brugarolas/Corbi/Chacón/Sola
A box, elementary in its cubical geometry, houses a series of unique spaces, perfectly brought together as a whole whilst also able to stand alone. On the outside there is an exciting tension between the open spaces, the solid structural blocks and the glazed areas. Inside, the box hangs over a slightly raked ground floor, uninterrupted by stanchions or supports and clearly related to the surroundings outdoors. Tiered terraces form the anteroom to the saloon, reflecting the empty central space that opens up vertically into two courtyards, separated by a foyer on the third floor. The play of scales, materials, spatial relations, the transparency in the upper part of the teaching rooms all denote a creative maturity that is at odds with the architects' relative youth.

LA MANGA DEL MAR MENOR. 83 km from Murcia, the Mar Menor is a natural saltwater lagoon, 185 km², separated from the Mediterranean by a spit of dunes and beaches known as La Manga (literally "the sleeve"), between 80 and 700 m wide and 24 km long, hardly broken by any communication between the two bodies of water. Its exceptional natural characteristics have been exploited by mass tourism since the sixties with excessively dense, commercial development. Bonet Castellana's 1961-64 plan has scarcely left any traces. But there are a few examples of good architecture: Bonet Castellana's Hexagonal tower (1966) and the Soling apartments by Corrales and Molezún (1979). Car access is only via Cabo de Palos, and severe traffic problems have led to proposals to open the spit from the other end, opposed by environmental groups.

Galúa Hotel 1965-67. Extension 1971-72
MU 10

La Manga del Mar Menor
Corrales/Molezún
Conceived for an exceptional site, on the headland, like a boat pointing prow-first to the sea, the hotel has an interesting plan, well composed volumes and nautical terraces which, slightly below the rooms, draw the gaze towards the sea. Later reform on the window aprons undermines this directionality.

NAVARRE

Ever since the Middle Ages, the stretch of the Pilgrim's Way that passes through Navarre has been trod by millions of travellers on their way to the burial place of Saint James the Greater in Santiago de Compostela (Galicia). All European pilgrims had to make their way through Navarre, since the different routes meet in Puente de la Reina, and then, after passing through Estella, cross the River Ebro at Logroño (La Rioja). Like the voyagers, history has seen villages, hostels, hospitals and churches spring up along the pilgrimage route, served by traders offering everything the travellers might need. This influx of people from all over Europe led the region to improve its infrastructure, increase its service quality, and enjoy the rich intercultural exchange and substantial commercial benefits that still persist to this very day. Foreigners have not always been welcome, though. In the past, Charlemagne was unable to conquer this land, nor could the Arabs put down roots here. Navarre had its own kingdom for six hundred years, resisting pressures from its powerful neighbours: Castile and Aragón. Its frontiers only collapsed in 1512 (still later than the stubborn independent Muslim Kingdom of Granada) in the face of Ferdinand I and Isabella I's drive to unify Spain and establish a modern nation. Even then, Navarre refused to give up its special empowerment charters, the *fueros*.

The capital, Pamplona, began as a Roman camp in 75 BC, named *Pompaelo* after the military commander, Pompey. Its geographical location made it an important defensive enclave, protecting the peninsula against invasion from N Europe. Although changes were made by military engineers to provide more civil housing inside the city walls, this military orientation in the urban structure was maintained until 1915, when the old walls were partially demolished to allow its suburbs to spread outwards and give rise to the development of modern Pamplona. Real architectural modernity arrived much later, however, after the private University of Navarre set up its own School of Architecture in 1964. The professors there also actively exercised their profession, and their pupils graduated to play a key role in changing the face of the urban environment. The teachings of Javier Carvajal over the last twenty years brought the ideas of Rationalism and clarity as a guiding principle in construction to generations of Navarran architects. In the first third of the 20th c., only Víctor Eusa achieved national recognition, stamping his work with his own strong personality and giving free rein to his poetic expressiveness, which stood out in Pamplona's Misericordia house (1927) and Tafalla's old people's home (1933). Since then, Sáenz de Oíza and Moneo have become undisputed masters of Spanish 20th c. architecture. Navarran Sáenz de Oíza actually only has one building in the region, but Moneo, who started work in Tudela in 1965, has continuously accepted local commissions. Both have worked with the Navarran construction company of Félix Huarte – Sáenz de Oíza in his Torres Blancas building in Madrid (see M 90) and Moneo in his renovation of the bullring in Pamplona – and both can attest to the way that Huarte's strong character, his love of building and his professionalism have marked the development of Navarran construction, imprinting it with high quality standards.

Geography: 10,421 km², very varied, between the steep valleys of the Pyrenees (peaks up to 2,400 m) and the flat Ebro river plains. Climate in Pamplona: Mediterranean. Rainfall: approx. 680 mm and 144 days. Sunshine: 2,240 hrs. Population: 523,563. GDP: 114% of nat. av.

San Miguel School 1926-28
Olite 1
Eusa

The large site gave Eusa the opportunity to show off his compositional talents on three façades with three corners, working in an Expressionist style that had achieved full maturity. On the corner between Olite and Arrieta, he placed a tower that unbalances the building's proportions.

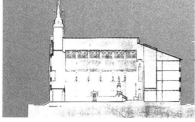

La Milagrosa Church and Abbey 1928
Av. de Zaragoza 23
Eusa

Bringing together the church and the abbey in a single building helped to enhance its impact on the surrounding landscape. Víctor Eusa designed the building at the height of his Expressionist period, using reinforced concrete for both the structure and the decorative elements, in combination with brick. The language thus achieved is very close to that used in the Central European architecture of the time. Inside the church is a nave, which is a prime example of his skill with the use of light and his ability to create an atmosphere of spirituality very close to that of Gothic cathedrals without, however, falling into the neo-Gothicism so common at the turn of the century. Some experts have noted references to Gaudí in the way Eusa designed and decorated this building, as well as in several other works. However, Eusa's architecture is a compilation of very diverse influences, all contained within a geometrical rigour that Gaudí would never have contemplated.

Apartment Building 1930
Fernández Arenas 4
Eusa

This modest residential building gave Eusa an opportunity to engage in another exercise of streetcorner enhancement. As the corner rises up, the composition becomes more complicated, with concrete cornices and aprons that form a kind of sculptural crown for the entire building.

Other works. In Pamplona, the prolific Víctor Eusa also designed the Casa de la Misericordia or Mercy House (1927), on Vuelta del Castillo 1, and the Eslava Casino (1931), on the Plaza del Castillo, where he used curved lines which, although exceptional for him, he treated with surprising naturalness. In Tafalla (10,249 inhabitants), 38 km away from Pamplona, he was responsible for the design of the Old People's Home (1933).

Huarte Towers 1963-64
Vuelta del Castillo 3-5
Redón/Guibert
The partnership between Fernando Redón's studio and the builder, Félix Huarte, resulted in this residential complex, an example of strict compositional discipline, modulation and good use of resources. The Huarte towers marked a watershed in house building in Pamplona and were much imitated.

Plaza de los Fueros 1970-75
Moneo/Cuadra Salcedo
When asked to do something with this no-man's land where different traffic flows cross, the architects came up with the solution of leaving it empty. Not only did they not fill it, but they emptied it, digging out a pedestrian plaza that adds to the contrast with the surrounding buildings, including Eusa's La Milagrosa Abbey (see N 2).

Cordobilla Erreleku Restaurant 1978-80
San Cosme y San Damián 1, Cordobilla
Iñiguez/Ustarroz
This design was a watershed in the Basque and Navarran architecture of the end of the seventies, showing a clear tendency to return to more classical styles. Iñiguez and Ustarroz have referred to their work as "an analogical restoration project on a pre-existing building."

Navarre Museum 1986-90
Cuesta de Santo Domingo s/n
Garcés/Sòria
In 1952, the abortive attempt to turn the Misericordia Hospital into a museum brought about the virtual disappearance of the old Renaissance factory in vain. Later, Garcés and Sòria took all the due steps to turn it into a working museum, filling the exhibition spaces with meaningful content.

Health Centre 1989-93
Luis Morondo 5, Azpilagaña
Miguel, E. de/Leache
This building is closed off from the outside, opening onto two inner courtyards. The choice of brick as the only material for the outer walls, taking advantage of its building potential, adds unmeasurable value to this architectural gem, exemplary in the way it blends in with its surroundings.

Special Education Resources Centre 1991-92

Pedro I 27, Fuente del Hierro
Alonso del Val/Hernández
The greatest success in this low-budget building is the way its succession of teaching rooms, interspersed with courtyards, joins up the urban centre with the fringes of the town. Its architecture contains references to its functionality as a teaching centre.

Department of Social Sciences 1994-96

Campus Universitario
Vicens/Ramos
In a privileged location, on the slope joining central Pamplona with the campus, this building stands apart from its surroundings, imposing a certain distance from its neighbours. The solidity of its exterior contrasts with the subtlety expressed inside, where there is an almost mystic atmosphere with convent overtones. With the exception of the large central vestibule, the building communicates with the outside via openings that let light in without establishing any visual link with the landscape. The overhead lighting, the exclusive use of concrete, both for the interior and the exterior, the latticework used to cover window openings, and the profusion of interior courtyards all contribute to create an atmosphere of contemplation, as if the building were looking in on itself.

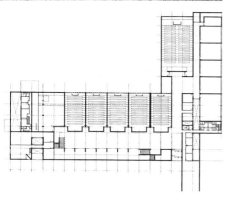

Other works. The Navarre University campus also features a notable Sports Centre (1991-92) designed by Alonso del Val and Hernández. A second university, the Universidad Pública (1989-92), with its rigidly structured campus in Sadar, was designed by Sáenz de Oíza. Mangado has become one of the exponents of Navarran quality architecture of the end of the 20th c. Together with Apezteguía he has designed two interesting works: the Iturrama Health Centre (1990) in Pamplona and the Marco Real Wineries (1991) in Olite (3,049 inhabitants), 43 km away from Pamplona, a town well known for its 16th c. palace (the favourite residence of the Navarran royal family of the time). The Pza. de Carlos III (1987), designed by Mangado, is also in Olite, as is the Casa de Cultura Municipal Hall (1994), that he made in cooperation with Alzugaray.

Vocational Training Centre 1972-74

Av. de Villava. **Burlada**
Cano Lasso/Campo Baeza
This centre is an example of the fruits of the cooperation between these two architects, of different generations, who worked jointly throughout Spain during these years. Here, they used some of the elements that marked their composition and construction style in a similar building they designed in Vitoria.

Autovía A-15 near **Castejón**
Carlos Fernández Casado, S.L.,
Fernández Troyano/Manterola [engs.]

Under the guidance of the master builder, Carlos Fernández Casado, the engineers, Manterola and Fernández Troyano – all of them professional bridge builders of international renown for their technical know-how – designed a slender cable-stayed bridge characterised by the unfussy beauty of its form, which at once serves man and establishes an in-depth dialogue with nature. Since the riverway was 100 m wide at the point where the dual carriageway had to cross the River Ebro, the engineers chose to span the river with a single, moderately-sized deck. However, given that at that point the riverway was asymmetrical – the right margin of the river being heavily rugged, while the left was smooth and subject to river floods in a large area – the engineers decided to let this uneven topography dictate the design. The result was an asymmetrical bridge with a 137 m span consisting of a main deck (crossing the riverway) hanging from a single tower and auxiliary decks in the flooding areas. The bridge was suspended from three sets of tied beams: the front one linking with the bridge axis and the two back sets, anchored at the borders of the carriageway, forming a 120° angle. Thus, the geometry of the bridge responds to the interacting polygonal forces. Further, the double inclination of the tower, which is broken at the height of the road surface, owes its nature to the composition of the axil forces acting on both elements. The tower was conditioned at its base by the width of the dual carriageway's dividing section, and at its cusp by the suspension cable anchorages which form the 120° angle mentioned above. Consequently, the cusp is wider than the base, which explains why the pile widens from the base to the cusp on its transversal axis, but narrows on its longitudinal axis. All in all, this work of engineering stands as a lesson for those wanting to design bridges perfectly adapted to their surroundings.

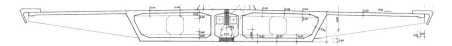

Bridge over the River Aragón 1967-69
Caparroso
Fernández Casado/Fernández Troyano/
Manterola [engs.]
This continuous prestressed concrete bridge
over the River Aragón is 197 m long. Of its
two sections, the first is 104 m long, cover-
ing the main 50-m span crossing the river.
The larger span consists of a cantilevered
box girder.

Health Centre 1992-94
Erreniega 26. Cizur Mayor
Apezteguía/Martín
The building is articulated around a courtyard, giving access to the exterior, with the
waiting rooms and corridors looking out onto it. The difference in height between the
area where the surgeries are held and the
other rooms create a balance of volumes
that enriches the initial simplicity of the plan.

Plaza de los Fueros 1990-93
Estella
Mangado
The architect's main aim was to return this
urban space, the most significant in the city,
to its original state as an open space. He
grouped together the different elements
and left the façades surrounding the central
area open to view, adding texture to the
ground space by the creative use of paving.

Apartment Building 1978-80
Ctra. de Larraga s/n. Mendigorría
Garay/Linazasoro
One of the last joint designs by Garay and
Linazasoro, it shows their deepening interest
in vernacular architecture whilst still respecting the supremacy of geometry and the
protagonism of the materials used, which
were to become a hallmark of Linazasoro's
later work.

Piher Factory 1965-69
Ctra. de Corella s/n. Tudela
Martorell/Bohigas/Mackay
This factory is one of the three that the MBM
group of architects designed for the Piher
company, although this one is now called
the NACESA factory. The other two are in
Catalonia (see B 104). The expressive nature
of the facilities and the subtlety of the container are characteristics shared by all three.

Ulzama Golf Club 1965-67

Guerendiain. **Valle de Ulzama**
Redón/Guibert
The references to Wright are undeniable in this club house design, where the unitary tiled roof over the building houses a fragmented interior, with linked spaces that develop an Organicism that, in Fernando Redón's later one-man designs, was to become even more pronounced.

Alloz Aqueduct 1939

On the River Salado, between **Yerri** and **Arizala**
Torroja Miret [eng.]
The aqueduct is formed by a repetition of the structural sections, each 40 m long and supported by pillars set 20 m apart. With this layout, Torroja managed to reduce the number of joints. But, above all, what the great engineer aimed at and successfully achieved was to avoid the appearance of cracks and their consequent leaks, whilst maintaining an aesthetic harmony with maximum economy. The aqueduct was also a pioneer in prestressing with cables.

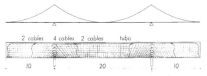

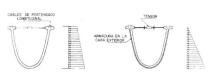

Golf Club 1993-95

San Andrés s/n. **Zuasti**
Mangado
The elements making up the complex are all relatively small, establishing relations between each other and with the environment to create intermediate spaces that form part of the basic idea. The design makes clear reference to the outbuildings scattered around the old rural estates.

Other works. In Tudela (26,163 inhabitants), 84 km from Pamplona, with a Cistercian-style cathedral from the transition from the Romanesque to the Gothic, is the Misericordia house (1968-82), by Moneo, whose construction was much delayed, with the consequent stylistic time lag. In Estella (13,569 inhabitants), 41 km away, Leache, working in cooperation with de Miguel, built the industrial building for Gráficas Lizarra (1994) on Ctra. de Tafalla 1.

BASQUE COUNTRY

Set between the Cantabrian and the Pyrenees mountain ranges, the Basque Country consists of the provinces of Alava (capital, Vitoria), Guipúzcoa (capital, San Sebastián) and Vizcaya, or Biscay (capital, Bilbao). Its mountains are relatively low, with woody valleys and grazing land. Its hunter-gatherer tribes were taken over by the Romans in the 1st c. BC. Later the Islamic culture stopped on the S edge of the Cantabrian mountains in the 8th c. Converted to Christianity in the 8th-10th c., it became part of Castile in the 11th c, with its own empowerment charters or *fueros*. In the Middle Ages, cities began to spring up (Diego López de Haro, lord of Biscay, founded Bilbao in 1300) and, later, entrepreneurs established the first iron-and-steel works and developed a sea trade for exporting Castilian wool. This industrialist culture triggered the intense industrialisation of the mid-19th c. (iron and steel, ship-building, chemicals, etc.), building on the general prosperity under Isabella's rule, until the first third of the 20th c., when Vizcaya was producing three quarters of Spain's steel and half its iron. Basque architecture of the beginning of the 20th c. reflects this flourishing economy, with architects studying in Madrid and Barcelona. Vallejo and Aizpurúa's contribution to the second CIAM was out-standing, and they were much involved, shortly afterwards, in setting up the Northern Group of GATEPAC. After the Civil War, with many promising professionals dead or exiled, architecture here and throughout Spain lost contact with the European move-ments. In the fifties and sixties, business in the Basque Country boomed and housing had to be built on a grand scale for all the immigrant labour flowing into the industrial city of Bilbao and the Nervión valley. Juan D. Fullaondo was a key figure, renowned for his critical work and dissemination of the ideas blossoming in Basque artistic circles in the seventies, through the *Nueva Forma* journal and under Huarte's sponsorship (see p. 290), establishing links with the sculpture of Oteiza, Chillida and Basterretxea. He was also involved as an artist in works with Olabarría and Líbano. In the seventies, architects such as the Iñiguez de Onzoño brothers, Basáñez and Aguinaga in Vizcaya; Erbina in Alava, and Marquet and Zulaica in Guipúzcoa maintained their commitment to modern archi-tecture, establishing ideas that would survive as alternatives to post-Modernism in the eighties. Luis Peña was a case apart, with his personal interpretation of the place, managing to re-angle the constants of the Basque architectural tradition to consolidate one of the main lines of critical revision to the Modern movement. The younger architects, Linazasoro and Garay followed the guidelines established by Rossi and Grassi in Italy and founded a strictly disciplined architectural style. This theoretical embryo was at the heart of the San Sebastián Architecture School, set up in 1977. At the end of the 20th c., the panorama varied from one province to the next. In Guipúzcoa, theoretical work revolved around the San Sebastián School. In Vizcaya, most of the large-scale designs for renovating Bilbao have gone to foreign architects. In Vitoria, municipal urban policy has encouraged young architects to try a road towards restrained expressiveness and strict constructional techniques, identified with contemporary Navarran architecture.

Geography: 7,261 km², hilly (Basque Hills with peaks up to 1,500 m), with narrow river plains at the estuaries, short, fast-flowing rivers and the treacherous Cantabrian Sea. Climate: ocean climate on the coast, continental inland. Population: 2,109,009. GDP: 117% of nat. av.

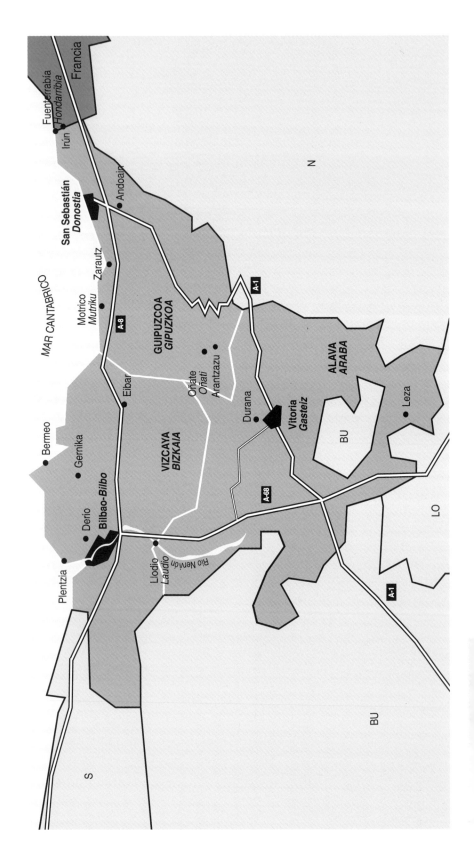

MAR CANTABRICO

Francia

Fuenterrabía
Hondarribia

Irún

Andoain

San Sebastián
Donostia

Zarautz

Motrico
Mutriku

A-8

Eibar

GUIPUZCOA
GIPUZKOA

Oñate
Oñati

Arantzazu

A-1

Bermeo

Gernika

VIZCAYA
BIZKAIA

Durana

Vitoria
Gasteiz

ALAVA
ARABA

Leza

Derio

Bilbao-Bilbo

BU

Plentzia

Llodio
Laudio

Río Nervión

A-68

A-1

LO

N

S

BU

VITORIA. The city known as Vitoria in Spanish and Gasteiz in Basque has been well developed, with high quality architecture in its individual buildings and people-friendly spatial relations resulting from the municipal control over urban planning and growth in recent years. The city was originally founded in 1181 by Sancho of Navarre on the old Visigothic town of *Gasteiz*,

as a defensive enclave on the top of a hill. Since then, its development has always been kept in control, and even the urban sprawl that was rampant throughout Spain from the fifties to the mid-seventies did not spoil the harmony of the city's layout. Although over the last four decades of the 20th c. there has been more building activity in Vitoria than during its entire history, the old city centre has been kept intact. Its mediaeval street pattern, with its characteristic heart or almond shape has been conserved, and an acceptable new town has grown up on an orderly layout with plenty of green spaces. In the province of Alava (Araba in Basque), 4 km N of Vitoria is Durana; 49 km NW along the A-6 motorway is Llodio, an industrial town, the second biggest in the province (20,551 inhabitants); and 60 km S, at the foot of the Sierra de Cantabria, is Leza (170 inhabitants). Altitude: 524 m. Rainfall: 770 mm and 180 days. Sunshine: 1,940 hrs. Temperatures: 27°-9° and 1°-14° C. Population: 209,704.

Church of Los Angeles 1958-60　　　VI 1
Bastiturri 4
Carvajal/García de Paredes
The power of the geometry in this religious building is the result of a highly stylised architectural idea: a pointed arrow, shaped to represent the heavenward thrust of communion through asceticism. This elevated idea is expressed in simple materials: yellow brick, slate and an interior structure formed by unadorned metal stanchions. The light, always a key part of religious architecture, is indirect and reflected, so that the roof, from inside, seems to be taking off from the walls, as if it were suspended in thin air.

Church of La Coronación 1958-60　　　VI 2
Eulogio Serdán 9
Fisac
Miguel Fisac designed this church as he was developing from Classicism towards Organicism. In it, he developed the idea of movement, which arises from the relationship between two walls, one curved, white and smooth, without any focal points, the other rugged, straight and pitted with scaled vertical openings. The convergence and conjunction of these two opposites creates a dynamic yet intensely spiritual effect.

Kas Soft Drinks Factory 1962 VI 3
Av. de los Olmos 2, Pol. Industrial de Gamarra
Fargas/Tous
In this industrial complex, the bottling plant, designed by Fargas and Tous, stands out with its structure of clamped reinforced concrete paraboloids. The cladding on the façade, which was later applied to the office block, is made of a series of modulated panels with metal profiles, which are closed with insulated plates. The plant's roof is made of the same laminated structure of reinforced concrete with horizontal gutters and vertical drainpipes of cement fibre running through the centre pillar.

Vocational Training Centre 1972 VI 4
José Achótegui 1
Cano Lasso/Campo Baeza
The building unfolds around a set of routes that set out from the vestibule, which soars up high, then run out along the edges of the centre around two inner courtyards. These courtyards serve to provide light to the in-side of the building, and the plants growing in the open spaces provide some visual relationship that could otherwise be missing between the two functional cores: the lecture rooms and the administration offices. They add a sense of a close link between the artificial and the natural, the inside and the outside, to the simple composition of brick walls. The routes and functions are structured by a very human-sized spatial hierarchy. The overall impression is moving and at the same time the design displays a beautiful formal clarity and precision.

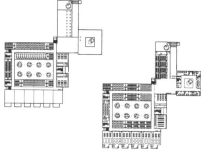

Plaza de los Fueros 1979 VI 5
Pza. de los Fueros
Peña Ganchegui. coll.: Chillida [sculptor]
This plaza provided a second opportunity for the architect and sculptor to work together, albeit with less impressive results than in the Plaza del Tenis (see SS 4). The creation of a split level in such a small space, the crowd-ing of elements and a design that could be a security risk undermine the project.

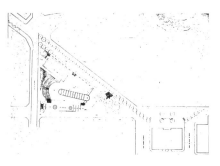

Municipal Hall 1979   VI 6
Paseo de la Florida 9
Fernández Alba, Antonio/Erbina
The first time that Fernández Alba worked
with the local architect, José Erbina, resulted
in a design that opens onto the Florida Park
and is closed off from the neighbouring
buildings. On his own, Erbina designed an
interesting housing complex on the Paseo
de Cervantes.

San Martín Health Centre 1988-90   VI 7
Pintor Teodoro Dublang 23
Uriarte
A prism-shaped building, established within
the comprehensive symmetry that allowed
the centre to fulfill its objectives, its two
storeys, plus a basement and an attic, can
be seen from inside through some vertical
shafts that let the daylight in from the roof
down to the basement.

Lakua Civic Centre 1991-97   VI 8
Senda de los Echánove s/n
Ercilla/Campo
This building, originally designed as a sports
centre, was later expanded to become a
civic centre using the original language. The
use of brick in the original and the extension
accentuates the restrained nature of the
work, where the sections show how it has
been adapted for new uses.

Treasury Department Building 1992   VI 9
Samaniego 14
Catón/Ercilla/Campo
Since this building had to stand in a residential
area, the architects respected the height of
the neighbouring housing blocks by staggering the different volumes upwards from
them in such a way as to achieve both
monumentality and a sense of scale. The
final geometrical feel is very satisfactory.

Azol-Gas Building 1992-93   VI 10
Landalucía 9, Pol. Industrial de Júndiz
Mozas
The building was constructed in two stages.
The first established a clear split between
the assembly hall and the office area, using
different materials and distinct languages.
The second added onto the office area
with more abstract volumes, as the formal
containers of the functional programme.

Dr. Gómez House 1960 VI 11
Ctra. de Vergara 10-12. **Durana**
Sáenz de Oíza
Oíza used this exercise to go beyond the Modern movement and immerse himself in the Organicism then spreading throughout Europe. The result is a house that revolves around the hearthplace, with walls spreading out spiderweb-style and three columns holding up the treble-pitch roof.

Sanatorium 1934 VI 12
Ctra. Vitoria-Logroño, km 59. **Leza**
Zabalo
An interesting example of a single hospital block, a model that arose parallel to a new kind of medicine during the interwar period, with more private spaces made available, as more individualised care was given, its S façade is covered by a mesh of individual balconies, whilst the N one is more closed.

Special Education Centre 1984-86 VI 13
Lateorro. **Llodio**
Ercilla/Uriarte/Martín
The simplicity of the layout and the austere use of resources is what makes this building special. The architects managed to take advantage of a difficult, N-facing orientation by using successive interior courtyards, protected from the elements, and a clear layout of uses and routing.

SAN SEBASTIAN. The physical geography of the city could not have been better. Two hills, the Igeldo and the Ugrull, frame the almost perfect semicircle of the Concha bay. Throughout its history, the city has consistently adapted to this natural environment, enhancing it in its urban planning, which has taken into account the topography and views with a moderation worthy of special mention. The architecture has also followed similar lines of discreet charm. The 19th c. air to San Sebastián is real enough, for the city was almost entirely rebuilt after the Duke of Wellington's troops, having expelled Napoleon's troops in 1813, set fire to the garrison in the closing stages of the Peninsular War. The city became a favoured sea resort amongst the aristocracy of the early 20th c. The seafront and the part built under Antonio Cortázar's 1860 expansion plan are good examples of Basque Romanticism. In 1977, Luis Peña founded the San Sebastián School of Architecture (first part of the Barcelona School and later as an independent body), which has created a special theoretical drive. The initial ideological con-

nections between much of its staff and the Italian Tendenza and the Revisionism of the Modern movement has been maintained and has established a clearcut style that has informed architecture throughout Guipúzcoa. Rainfall: 1,500 mm and 210 days. Sunshine: 1,770 hrs. Temperatures: 24°-9° and 6°-17° C. Population: 176,019.

Sailing Club 1929
Igentea 9
Aizpurúa/Labayen

Located at the end of the Paseo de la
Concha, San Sebastián's seaside promenade,
and opposite the old Gran Casino (now the
town hall offices) built by Aladrén and
Morales in 1882, the Sailing Club is
considered to be one of the most important
works of the Modern movement in Spain. It
was the only building included in Henry Russell Hitchcock and Philip Johnson's book *The
International Style: Architecture since 1922*, which included the most outstanding examples
of this style in both Europe and America. José Manuel Aizpurúa received the commission
when he was only 25, and the building bears, as Sanz Esquide shows in his writings, resem-
blances to Le Corbusier in Villa Savoye, despite the fact that he finished it when work had
scarcely even begun on Le Corbusier's famous house. It was really a commission to extend
the existing club house, which stood in a small building on the ramp down to the quay,
whose roof was a metre higher than the level of the Paseo de la Concha and had been turned
into an easily accessible terrace. The clubroom was located in a construction on top of this,
with wooden panelling. Aizpurúa and Labayen reformed their design several times whilst
works were still in progress, although they remained true to the spirit of the initial plan. They
took advantage of the existing building on the ramp, which was made of brickwork, with
small gaps between the bricks to provide defense against storms, and simply extended it

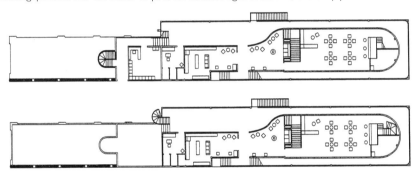

lengthwise to make room for the new changing rooms. They used the old walls to hold up the
main storey, which was built of concrete, to house the members' rooms, and a second storey,
where they placed the restaurant. This terminated at one end in a semicircular projection
and a line of sliding windows that accentuate the ship-like horizontality of the composition.
The open layout, the metalwork on the façade and the clear references to naval architecture
are also unmistakable features of the more heroic stage of the Modern movement.

Equitativa Building 1933
Pza. de Euskadi 1
Arzadún
In this building, the architect of Villa Kikumbera (see BI 20) used *Art Déco* techniques to compose a cornered façade, where the play of shadows creates interesting alignments and the parts jutting out provide an expressiveness that is very characteristic of Arzadún's work.

Urumea Building 1969-73
Paseo de Ramón María Lilí, 3-4
Moneo/Marquet/Unzurrunzaga/Zulaica
This complex of 111 homes occupies half an urban block on the edge of the Urumea river. It was designed by Moneo working with a local architectural studio (Marquet, Unzurrunzaga and Zulaica) from San Sebastián. The front façade appears to be made up of curved folds that wrap around the corners. The horizontality achieved by using sliding windows contrasts strongly with the verticality of the corner volumes, which frame the river façade, whilst successfully integrating the entire building into its urban environment.

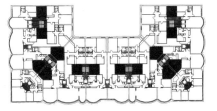

Plaza del Tenis 1975-76
Paseo del Peine del Viento s/n
Peña Ganchegui/Chillida [sculptor]

The Plaza del Tenis was the second project in San Sebastián in which Luis Peña was involved. After his success with the Plaza de la Trinidad in 1963, which gave meaning to an area that had originally appeared as some kind of afterthought between the Monte Urgull and the old part of town, the City Council commissioned him to do something similar on the site at the end of the Paseo del Tenis, so that it could provide a backdrop for Chillida's group sculpture, the *Peine del Viento* (wind comb). Peña took on the project, thinking that his plaza would serve as a foreword to introduce the sculptures, without melding into them. He interpreted the power of the place as the beginning and end of the town, an area where town met with nature, respecting it and using it to give shape to the design. The very constraints imposed by the site, which arrogantly resisted any attempt at interference, became suggestions for creativity.

Miraconcha Apartment Building 1981-86
Paseo de la Fe 20-30   SS 5
Peña Ganchegui
Apart from the housing design, this work
with 30 apartments and garages is also an
example of how to order space in a steeply
sloping site with stringent traffic requirements. Peña solved the problems with a
platform that was set upon a plinth to
articulate the entire complex.

Santa Teresa Carmelite Convent 1991   SS 6
Camino Andereño Elvira 3
Linazasoro/Sesé
Linazasoro, with the collaboration of Luis
Sesé, built up his design for the Carmelite
convent on the old abbey and church
constructed by Semosiain in 1666. Rejecting
Historicist elements, he preferred a more
technical flavour. This marked a seachange
in his work.

Other works. The Modern movement spawned many of Mocoroa's designs, such as his
1934 project of housing and a petrol station on the corner of Av. de la Zurriola, 32-34, in
which he tried out some façade compositions based on the play of cornices. The workers
canteen in the Laborde Hermanos factory in Andoain (15 km S), designed in 1939 by the
engineers, M. and E. Laborde and the draftsperson, L. Tolosa, follows the same principles.

Thus, he laid out a series of stepped
platforms, along the lines of the Greek
temple *crepidoma*, which he covered using
granite paving from Porriño. Aware that the
place where the sculptures were to stand
would gain almost transcendental importance,
he designed this part of the plaza as a *temenos*, the sacred precinct to Greek temples,
without adding anything that was not already
present in the place. Thus, he built a thick,
low wall, which gave a sea view as impressive
as the one the fishermen had enjoyed in the
thirties, when they congregated on the
pipeline that ran around the Monte Igueldo.
This old engineering feat, now no longer
used, was given the noble mission of taking
the water to the subsoil under the plaza
and bringing it up, on stormy days, through
the seven orifices in the lowest platform.
The complex, with Chillida's sculpture
placed amidst the rocks, has become a
landmark not just in the town, but also in
international architecture.

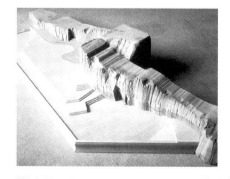

Kursaal Conference Hall and Auditorium 1990-

Paseo de la Zurriola, Urumea estuary and the sea

Moneo

Rafael Moneo won the competition held in 1990 by the San Sebastián City Council to use a site, known as Site K, empty ever since the old Kursaal Casino was demolished in 1972, located on the Gros suburbs to the NE of the town, near the Urumea estuary and the new Zurriola beach. Rafael Moneo's proposal played with the metaphor of two beached boulders, as if they were a geographical accident, albeit connected to the built-up area of San Sebastián. The result are two compact volumes that provide an internal continuity whilst permitting freedom of organisation and overcoming the risk of fragmentation that the programme entailed without making any changes to the Urumea estuary. One of the two cube-shaped glass volumes houses the auditorium in its prismatic body of 60 x 48 x 27 m. The other holds the conference hall in its slightly sloping prism of 42 x 35 x 24 m. The exhibition rooms, meeting rooms, restaurants and other services are contained in the platform that is set at the level of the Paseo de la Zurriola. The calendered glass in which the two cubes are enclosed is, according to the architect, just the right material to enhance the abstract nature of the buildings, set apart from their surroundings. In Rafael Moneo's career, the Kursaal was the first building in which he chose glass as the sole material for covering the façades, giving it the same poetic feel that he had previously reserved for brick and stone. He especially commissioned expert companies to make an original prototype of ondulated, calendered glass that would give his design the character he wanted for it.

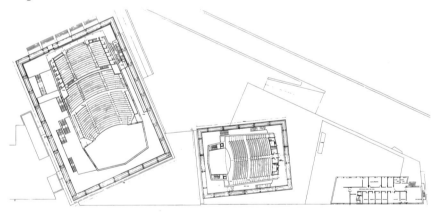

Other works. Oriol designed the EUTG university complex (1961) on Mundaiz 50, where the play of roofs and the fragmentation of the programme into small clusters of buildings are of special interest. The University campus (1989-97) on Av. de Tolosa cannot be considered an architectural whole, since it was developed by many architects in competition with each other (Garay and Barea; Iriarte, Brena and Múgica; Montero) working to common standards, so that its differences are really its defining feature. In the province of Guipúzcoa, 64 km along the A-8 motorway to the W is the industrial town of Eibar (32,108 inhabitants), whilst 46 km along the coastal road is Motrico or Mutriku (4,466 inhabitants). To the E, 23 km along the A-8 towards France, is Fuenterrabía or Hondarribia, a beach tourist resort (13,974 inhabitants), and 20 km away, on the French border, is Irún (53,861 inhabitants).

Mendiola House 1978 SS 8
Barrio Saravilla. **Andoain**
Garay
The design must be analysed in terms of the
revisionist Modernism of the end of the
seventies. The return to Classical architecture,
the rejection of out-and-out Functionalism,
the importance of type and the routing to
achieve best views turn the house into
something almost monumental.

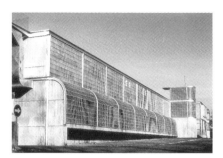

Unión Farmacéutica Guipuzcoana SS 9
(Pharmaceutical Factory) 1971-76
Av. de Bilbao 18. **Eibar**
Peña Ganchegui
The first of Peña's two commissions for this
company involved extending and remodelling the existing pavilion, in which he tried
out glass block walls, which he later used
more widely in the Igara warehouse in Irún
in 1974-77 [shown in photograph].

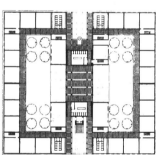

Ikastola Basque School 1974-78 SS 10
Ctra. N-I, Barrio Jaisubía. **Fuenterrabia**
Garay/Linazasoro
The Hondarribia *Ikastola* (Basque school)
was built during the transition from Franco's
dictatorship to democracy, when it marked
a watershed in the theoretical debate then
being held in Spain. The architects wanted
to turn it into a piece of propaganda for the
movement known as Tendenza, and they
succeeded in making a paradigm of a certain
way of understanding architecture. It was
solidly rooted in the surroundings, with a
geometry that did not make any concessions
to the landscape, using a language more
suited to inner cities. This was further
enhanced with the use of white rough coating to accentuate the volumes and disclose
the architects' ambitions to achieve purist
lines. In the nineties, Garay built an extension
on his own, which was a separate work.

Painter's House 1989-90 SS 11
Usótegui 7, Jaizkibel. **Irún**
Aguinaga/Azqueta
This single-family house stands on a gently
sloping, fan-shaped site, which is articulated
around a courtyard with chimney. The adaptation to the terrain on three different levels
develops a play of volumes, allowing the
interior spaces to alternate with the outer
ones, which mutually protect each other.

Aizetzu Housing Complex 1964-65 SS 12

Av. J. M. Alcíbar 19. **Mutriku**

Peña Ganchegui

The way this cluster of houses has been laid out is paradigmatic in Basque landscaping. The Aizetzu housing complex stands on a pronounced slope, set on three staggered platforms, which compensate for the differences in height and provide the economic benefit of avoiding contention walls. It comes into contact with the ground on supports that form a covered access porch. The macle of the three volumes through the two stairboxes endow it with a sculptural value. Finally the choice of the cladding materials (slate for the roof, brick for the façades and metalwork for the window and door frames) give the whole complex an unusually monumental finish, despite the small scale, which fits into the context without in any way jarring.

Imanolena House 1964 SS 13

Paseo de San Nicolás. **Mutriku**

Peña Ganchegui

This is perhaps the most outstanding single-family house designed by Peña. In its day, many interpreted it as a critical revision of vernacular architecture, when it is really a compendium of the Classical tradition and the international influences that the architect assimilated and placed in the local context.

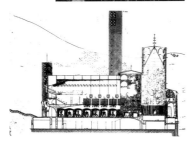

Arantzazu Basilica 1949 SS 14

Arantzazu. **Oñati**

Laorga/Sáenz de Oíza

In expanding the old basilica, various diverse circumstances came together that made the final outcome much more than the sum of its architectural values. It was Sáenz de Oíza's first work, won in a competition, working with Laorga and the Basque sculptor, Oteiza. Sáenz de Oíza himself referred to it as a training exercise, with several mistakes. However, it was way ahead of its time, anticipating the changes that would come about in religious architecture a decade later. His layout did not adhere to classical patterns, but maintained the Latin cross plan. The language employed, including Oteiza's frieze of the apostles for the façade and Chillida's entrance gates, triggered off a heated debate that delayed the termination of the works by twelve years.

Vista Alegre Tower 1958
Parque de Vista Alegre. **Zarautz**
Peña Ganchegui/Encio
In his first work, Peña accepted the challenge
of building three 3-storey maisonettes in
what was meant to be a residential area.
The idea of baring the structure on the
façade helped to maintain a compositional
order in which the interior sections were
reflected.

BILBAO. The new distribution of interests in modern-day Europe has made cities like Bilbao (with approx. 1 million inhabitants in its greater area) widen their focus beyond their immediate region. This has given rise to the phenomenon known as the Atlantic Arch, which stretches from Lisbon to Glasgow, linking towns and cities that have maintained close trading links in the past. Bilbao (in competition with Bordeaux) aims at becoming the keystone of this arch. Having lost much of its traditional dynamism as a result of the crisis experienced in its traditional heavy industries, Bilbao is now following a successful policy to bring new life to the city by other means in order to open it to the outside world. Although not an official capital, the city is acknowledged as N Spain's leading metropolis. Even so, it still needs to update its somewhat dilapidated image with a commercial operation that can make it competitive and bring in the foreign investment required to reestablish its leadership. The city of Bilbao is thus developing its network of services and infrastructures, planning and carrying out projects in obsolete industrial areas, which will give the city a complete facelift in the next few years. The end of the 20th c. is a time of changes as important as those that were triggered off in 1876, when the general plans for expansion over the Abando area were approved and the city officially crossed the wide estuary of the River Nervión. Before that, the old mediaeval cluster of the city founded by Diego López de Haro in 1300 and laid out along three parallel streets was extended to seven streets in the 15th c., which are still recognisable in the old quarter. Until then, Bilbao had been clustered around its old city centre, on the right bank of the Nervión, with industrial and port facilities along the river. Shifting the old port downriver to the new one, which is being constructed in a municipality of the seawards side of the estuary, has freed up lands close to the city centre, previously occupied by shipyards and machinery, so that both sides of the river can now be replanned. The layout of Bilbao had always been actively focussed away from the river, but now the general plans are intent on reorientating its focal area in such a way that the river will join the two banks and act as a fulcrum between them. Thus, the estuary will become a sheet of water that will reflect the urban life taking place in the large, beautifully equipped buildings on its banks. The architecture of Bilbao has always been open to different styles and tendencies, its main characteristic being precisely its permeability to outside influences. Its last stage is no exception, with imported architecture (designed by Foster and Gehry, among others) that fits in superbly with the city. Alluding to Colin Rowe's book, Fullaondo calls Bilbao a "great collage". Bilbao is that but it is also its industry, warehouses, roads, bridges, nodal stations and a splendid cumulation of architectures. In the year 2000, the city will hold its 7th centenary. Rainfall: 1,210 mm and 200 days. Sunshine: 1,760 hrs. Temperatures: 27°-14° and 4°-16° C. Population: 372,054.

Post Office Building 1927
BI 1

Alameda de Urquijo 15

Zuazo

The Post Office building located on Alameda de Urquijo was a watershed in Secundino Zuazo's work, indicating the moment when he moved on from his first, highly traditionalist stage. Until 1927, his work had been characterised by its Eclecticism and loyalty to the old order of things. It was not that Zuazo was ignorant of the new winds of change, but that he was too honest to borrow a language that he did not yet master. However, in the Bilbao Post Office, designed immediately after a trip abroad, he felt ready to declare his support of the principles underlying the Modern movement. Although the design still features Historicist elements (such as the Baroque entrance) the emphatic quality of the stark volume, the simplicity with which the façades are composed and the choice of materials used in its construction identify it as the clearcut precursor of what would be his masterpiece, the Casa de las Flores, in Madrid (see M 20).

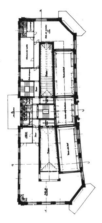

Other works. The first attempt to build Minimalist housing blocks was made by Bastida, who followed the Central European examples when, in 1923, he designed the Torre Urizar suburb (Rekalde, to the S) with 5-storey blocks. In 1931, Amann improved on the original idea with his social housing in Solokoetxe (Pza. Zumarraga, in the old town), where he applied Rationalist criteria, proposing a U-shaped block and avoiding any waste of space.

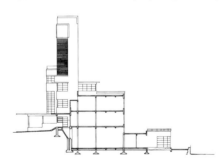

Luis Briñas School 1932-33
BI 2

Pza. Lauaxeta c/v Iturriaga

Ispízua

After having built another much more conventional commission for a school in Bilbao, Ispízua applied a new, more Rationalist vision to this one, which some attribute to the influence of an unknown assistant and others to the competition for a school in the San Francisco neighbourhood that he judged, where he had the chance to see the plans presented by the most prestigious members of GATEPAC. This time, his design was firmly placed in the Modernist movement, with a rich composition that turned the difficulties of the sharply sloping site and the complex functional brief into clear advantages. The visual power of the building (now cramped in between neighbouring blocks) merely reveal its authentically Expressionist language.

Casa Elejabeita Building 1933 BI 3
Av. Lehendakari Aguirre next to Pza. San Pedro
Basterra
Basterra's works are characterised by an absence of expressive resources that insert them in the Rationalist framework of the thirties. This building, whose layout separates the living quarters from the service areas in a unique composition of volumetric balance, is proof of this.

Apartment Building 1933 BI 4
Ripa 6
Bilbao
The location of the apartments between party walls obliged Bilbao to give up some of the prevailing Rationalist principles. However, the play of volumes on the façade are the saving grace that turn the design into one of the leading examples of Rationalist architecture in the city.

Equitativa Building 1934 BI 5
Colón de Larreategui c/v Alameda de Mazarredo
Galíndez
After having designed several different types of housing in Madrid and Bilbao, Galíndez was commissioned to make this building in the Abando suburb. The combination of a brief requiring housing units in the upper storeys and offices on the ground and first floor, and the corner location, between a narrow street and a broad avenue with a view of the Albia Gardens, gave Galíndez a chance to make a more monumental building than would have been necessary for housing alone. However, what makes the building unique is the double-angle solution (as Galíndez called it) that enabled him to adapt the cant of the design to the two streets of different widths and avoid the more common solution of a central tower. The use of a single cladding material (stone veneer) and the blind volume containing the clock like a clock tower distinguish it from other works where he used a mass of materials and compositional details that sometimes crowded the façades.

Other works. In 1945, another initiative of great importance for social housing was taken when the Saint Ignatius Loyola Group worked on the area of Deusto (which gave its name to a prominent private university). Imaz, Aguirre and Blanc designed houses that developed the ideas of Minimalist housing prevalent prior to the Civil War (see p. 297), maintaining their spatial and urbanistic values, whilst adding to the range of types.

La Aurora Building 1934-35 BI 6
Pza. de Federico Moyúa 4
Galíndez

This insurance company commissioned Galíndez to design a building of housing and offices on a site between two axial roads , which allowed him to produce a balanced play of curves between three façades. Its restrained Formalism is typical of his work during the thirties.

Apartment Building 1936 BI 7
Dr. Areilza 10
Ispízua

With this building, Ispízua continued to grow closer to the Rationalism he had begun to develop in the Briñas school complex, which he went on alternating with a more Classical style during the forties. Here, he applied the curved cant and framed it with the side volumes.

Aviación y Comercio Building 1944 BI 8
Pza. Venezuela 1
Ispízua/Arzadún

This apartment and office building conserves some of the Rationalist touches found in Arzadún's early works, although Ispízua added his own characteristically Eclectic monumentalism. A key building in the urban landscape, it is close to the Naviera Aznar building (see BI 11), another area landmark.

Apartment Building 1947-49 BI 9
Gran Vía 69-71
Ispízua

Here, Ispízua developed the Rationalism already present in earlier works, but now adding special ornamental touches, such as the balustrade around the curved chamfer which announce his progressive shift away from Rationalism towards a more Eclectic approach.

Office Building 1947 BI 10
Arbietio c/v Diputación
Fontán

Rafael Fontán's skill in dealing with corners is especially manifest in this building, into which he incorporated a more Eclectic language than in earlier works, to make it more monumental, although the site's location makes it almost impossible to get a full view of it.

Naviera Aznar Building 1948   BI 11
Ibáñez de Bilbao c/v Ripa
Galíndez
This building could be considered to be Manuel Galíndez's most transparent and also most complex work. The commission to erect the central offices of this shipping company on the riverbank inspired him to imagine a prow pointing seawards and to follow up on the metaphor by making a curved façade on the E side. He completed the initial idea with a composition of façades in which different languages are given free rein to adapt to the requirements of each elevation and its visual potential, just as he had in the Equitativa building (see BI 5). Later, in 1950, he built the Banco Hispano Americano building on Gran Vía 4, where he also played with three façades, although he incorporated a much more Classical language.

Apartment Building 1954-57   BI 12
Gran Vía 56
Aguinaga/Imaz/Aguirre
This is an excellent example of how the architects achieved restraint and elegance in design, whilst remaining open to the best influences of their time. Here, the lively feel of the façades is added to by the clever layout of window openings, which also facilitates the cleaning of the windows.

Department of Economics 1962   BI 13
Av. Lehendakari Aguirre 83, Parque de Sarriko
Basterrechea
The criteria the architect followed in this building was to respect the topography of the site and its grove of trees. The result was a building whose central volume is related to a set of staggered seminar rooms. The style cannot be considered Organicist, since the architect vehemently rejected any distinction between Functionalism and Organicism. However, it does show a distance from his earlier works, which were much more compact, and it also brings in the use of wood combined with glass on the façades, which was very innovative in its day. As in Basterrechea's other designs, what is most impressive is the building's simplicity and absence of decorative elements.

Apartment Building 1962-67   BI 14
Gran Vía 59, Estraunza
Iñiguez de Onzoño, J.L./Iñiguez de Onzoño, F.
This upmarket apartment building is firmly located in an outstanding site of the city's expansion suburb, where the restrained subtlety of its composition of straight lines and the materials employed on the façade (granite, wood and translucent glass) are especially significant.

Municipal Housing 1964-69   B 15
Larrako Torre c/v Islas Canarias
Basañez/Argárate/Larrea
At the beginning of their career, Basañez and two young architects won a municipal competition with their brave proposal to create a different social housing complex of split-level apartments on two storeys with a Brutalist language that Basañez never used again in his later works.

Girls School 1966-69   B 16
Pol. Txurdinaga
Fullaondo/Líbano
This is the second and most successful of Fullaondo and Líbano's joint projects, where each contributed the best of his own style, making a building in which Líbano's know-how in construction techniques allowed Fullaondo's talents in formal design to find full expression. The building is articulated in two open-plan volumes contained within a curtain wall, where the classes are located on either side of a central corridor. By way of contrast, the element that acts as a hinge is opaque, almost blind, and houses the services. The result added new possibilities to the range of styles in school architecture, very much in keeping with the theoretical and teaching work that Fullaondo was doing as editor of the *Nueva Forma* journal.

Abando-Ibarra. In its reconversion plan, Bilbao wanted to reuse the land left empty with the dismantling of the old heavy industries. The original idea was to use Abando-Ibarra (the banks of the estuary opposite the Deusto University) for an American-style business centre, with a complex of green spaces joining up the suburb with the estuary. In 1992, César Pelli won the architectural competition. But three years later, the market had changed: in the mid-nineties, housing was more economically efficient than the services industry, which meant changing the basic specifications. Pelli's powerful initial proposal was subjected to various reconsiderations and by mid-1997, it was still not clear what would happen with the area, where other notable buildings had already been built, such as the Guggenheim Museum (see BI 18), the Euskalduna Conference Hall (see BI 19) and Calatrava's footbridge, locally referred to as the Zubizuri, or "white bridge".

Underground Stations 1988-96

Bilbao

Foster et al.

Sir Norman Foster & Partners won the competition held in 1988 by the Basque Government's Department of Transport for the stations of the underground network. Foster's design condensed the basic essence of travelling underground, adding poetic touches to the idea. Not all the stations are the same. Eleven have been designed, of which nine are in horizontally bored tunnels, like caves, and two are built in false tunnels, using the Austrian cut and cover system. The image of an egg or the maternal womb was used

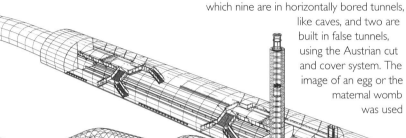

in the first kind (the horizontally bored tunnels). As Foster put it: "A tunnel... is such an organic response to natural forces and is such a beautiful shape, that it is a shame to hide it instead of working with it." Thus, Foster preferred to leave the cavernous form open to the eye, with all its elementary power. The platforms, bridges, and other elements are added in such a way as to avoid any distortion of the purity in this fecund egg-shape. It is meant to be an organic conduit in which the structure and the coating are the same thing. Travelling underground is associated to the protection of darkness. The route towards the surface is made as if it were a journey towards the light. In the cave-like stations, the exterior element continues with the tunnel cross-section. It is treated with the same coating as in the part that projects outwards, with

the same curved shape. The change of material, from concrete inside to glass outside, reinforces this leap towards transparency. In the Sarriko station, in a false tunnel, the level is much deeper, making it possible to have a spectacular concourse reached by long escalators. With the change of scale in this station, the platforms and bridges are not metal, as in the others, but have a larger section and are made of concrete. However, the total volume continues to play a key role, with the materials as extra elements. The large canopy at Sarriko also adopts a much larger scale, allowing natural light to reach down into the station. The suspended platforms are of a minimal width and are held up on walls by prefabricated concrete supports. In the summer of 1997, the second underground line was being developed along the left side of the estuary.

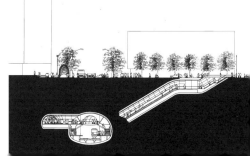

 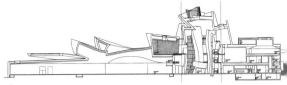

BI 18 **Guggenheim Museum** 1991-97

Av. Abando Ibarra 2

Gehry

The Basque authorities wanted to build a contemporary art museum to provide a focal point that could add new life to an old industrial area in terminal decline. Since they did not want to start from scratch, they went into partnership with the New York Guggenheim Foundation to take advantage of its international reputation. This museum brought part of its collection to Bilbao, to which the local authorities may add works purchased in Spain. The partnership, which made the event more newsworthy than a new local museum would be, gave the Foundation the right to choose the architect for the building in a restricted-entry competition which was won by Frank O. Gehry. Once the location was established, Gehry was delighted to learn that it was the most chaotic site imaginable: overlooking the estuary, with a large bridge crossing it to the city centre, in the area where the old port buildings stood and with a view of old farmhouses scattered over the nearby mountainside. Out of this chaos, Gehry extracted the energy and movement he wanted for his building: a movement of shapes that is vibrantly alive. Gehry's personal way of doing things marked a distance between the volumes of this museum and those built according to the rules of architecture as an autonomous discipline, so that it became part of the world of art it was meant to house. The Bilbao museum was not conceived as a whole, whose values are permanence and stability, but rather as an organism, an artistic body, a set of fragments and images for cultural consumers. The way the building moves is reminiscent of fish swimming. The titanium cladding, with its velvety finish, also recalls the soft scaliness of fish. However, all this dynamism in the estuary area becomes even more pronounced on the city side. The cladding of the administrative facilities is quite different, using sandstone with windows that are very similar to those in the conventional housing buildings nearby. According to Gehry, this is the best way to make the building fit into its environment, whilst managing to enhance its own power. Inside, the central atrium soars up 50 m, a kind of central pivot for the museum. The three exhibition floors housing the permanent collection stem out from it, connected by curved passage ways and panoramic lifts. The temporary exhibitions are displayed in a large open-plan hall, 130 x 25 m. Even before its inauguration, the Californian architect's building had become a symbol for the new vigour of the city.

Euskalduna Conference Hall and Auditorium 1994-

Av. Abando Ibarra
Soriano/Palacios

The 1992 competition-winning design took many by surprise, not so much because of the emphatic power of the idea as for the fact that the jury should come out in favour of such an unconventional looking building for this kind of purpose. The game is clear: to turn the image of a ship into a building, the ribs into porticoes for the structure, and the water pressure into gravity. The site was, until recently, a shipyard. The formal image of the auditorium represents the remains of a phantom boat run aground in the estuary. A certain dichotomy with the Guggenheim also comes into play here. Two buildings in one: the closer it is to the city, the more it looks like a building; the closer it is to the estuary, the more it looks like a boat.

Villa Kikumbera 1930
BI 20

Ctra. de Mundaka, by the port. **Bermeo**
Arzadún

Built on a cliff, and joined up to the road by a bridge that leads to its upper storey, the villa's four storeys stem from a stairway shaped like a tower. Its unashamedly Rationalist style does not prevent it from maintaining certain constants from verna-cular architecture.

Multi-Purpose Hall 1987-89
BI 21

Colegio de la Sagrada Familia. **Derio**
Cenicacelaya/Saloña

The structure, on concrete pillars, is left open to the eye on the inside of the hall, although outside it is enclosed in a brick contention wall. Large expanses of window between the pillars turn the building into a kind of crystal box. The two-pitch roof is very narrow.

Footbridge 1990-91
BI 22

Plentzia
Manterola/Fernández Troyano [engs.]

This metal arch structure has a lower deck with a span of 117.6 m. The two arches holding up the footbridge (braced together by steel box girders) are semi-circles with an 18-m rise, set on inward-sloping planes. The beauty of this footbridge lies in the economy and efficiency of its engineering.

LA RIOJA

In 1982, the small province of Logroño was turned into an Autonomous Community called La Rioja, after the municipal area of this same name that it shares with Alava, and that runs along the S bank of the NW stretch of the River Ebro. La Rioja is an abundant producer of vegetable products and the famous Rioja wines. Although always an area of overlapping influences from its more powerful neighbours N and S, it has maintained its own distinctive character. First part of the kingdom of Navarre and then of Castile, it was the birthplace of the Spanish language over 1,000 years ago. Logroño, the capital, traditionally the bridgehead of the Road to Santiago over the Ebro, contains half of the province's population. Haro (8,939 inhabitants), 48 km NW, is the wine capital. Alfaro (9,432 inhabitants), 70 km E, lives off its food industry. La Unión, 14 km S, is part of Clavijo. Anguiano is SW, 45 km along the C-113 road.

Geography: 5,034 km², mainly mountainous, with altitudes of up to 2,262 m. and a flat corridor along the Ebro valley. Climate: continental. In Logroño, rainfall: approx. 450 mm and 135 days. Sunshine: approx. 2,360 hrs. Temperatures: 32°-11° and 2°-16° C. Population: 267,943. GDP: 124% of nat. av.

LOGROÑO. Celtic settlement of *Vareia* (1st c. BC), it was reconquered from the Arabs for the kingdom of Navarre in 755 and united with Castile in 1076. Its 20th c. architecture has revolved around Fermín Alamo and Agapito del Valle, masters of the Eclecticism prevailing in the early 20th c. who then moved towards a watered-down Rationalism. The religious buildings by Gerardo Cuadra are also noteworthy. Altitude: 384 m. Population: 122,254.

Apartment Building 1928-29   L R 1
Doce Ligero de Artillería 31-33
Alamo
Alamo's prolific output developed in parallel with international movements, from which he borrowed references that he combined with his own Eclecticism, as in this building. The emphatic character of the brackets on which the bay windows are set is its most characteristic feature.

Apartment Building 1939   L R 2
Vara del Rey 7
Valle, A. del
The architect was tied up in the Rationalist and Expressionist movements during his early years, of which this building, the first of his big commissions, is a clear example. After the Civil War, he was overwhelmed by the dominant principles of the official architecture under the new regime.

Tax Office Building 1956   L R 3
Víctor Pradera c/v Av. de Portugal
Romero Aguirre, M. /Romero Aguirre, J.
The merit of the design lies in its challenge to the prevailing norms of official buildings. Rationalism shines through, despite a clear tendency towards monumentalism. The language is not drowned by ornamentation and the site allowed the architects to put their ideas across clearly.

Other works. The marketplace (1928) on Sagasta street is a design by Alamo. Of special importance amongst Gerardo Cuadra's many works is his Priests' Residence (1968) on Ctra. de Zaragoza, which has an expressive interplay of volumes; from amongst Cano Lasso and Campomanes', the Centre for Technical Colleges (1973), on Ctra. de Soria; and from amongst León and García's, the Law School (1990-94) on Cigüeña street. In Alfaro, the Gonzalo de Berceo Technical College (1953-34), by Corrales, has been much altered.

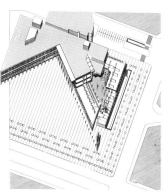

Town Hall 1973-81   L R 4
Av. de la Paz 11
Moneo
As Franco's regime drew to a close, Rafael Moneo conceived this building as a point of reference for what official designs could hope to achieve under the new democratic constitution. His guiding idea was to create the feeling of a coherent town centre. In the entire block previously occupied by the Alfonso XII barracks, Moneo designed a building of great urban elegance. Its lines are clearcut and the dimensions suitable for its civic mission, whilst also endowing its surroundings with meaning. Apart from housing the town hall offices, it also has several access spaces and surrounding areas in the porticos and archways, as well as a large triangular plaza that orders the throughflows and the layout of the whole. The use of a light colonnade in front of the windows to define the façade and the introduction of light into the inner spaces are amongst the design's most outstanding innovations.

El Carmen Housing Complex 1978   L R 5
Belchite
Dols/Inza/Sols
The architectural quality of this complex lies in its attempt to lay out the urban block without interior courtyards, but whilst still ensuring sunlight for all the apartments. Its double-T plan manages to make use of the leisure areas of the site, located opposite a small wood.

Apartment Building Complex 1981   L R 6
Rua Vieja c/v San Gregorio
Moneo (team coordinador) et al.
Using a basic plan, the team of 13 architects coordinated by Rafael Moneo recovered an historic part of the town. The building complex consists of 116 apartments which have been built on the old site but have been adapted to the new needs by the construction of interior courtyards.

Espartero Health Centre 1990-94   L R 7
Pza. de la Alhóndiga c/v General Espartero
León/García
Making maximum use of the site, this free-standing, rectangular, 4-storey building has been organised around an interior courtyard. The limestone façades reflect the functions of the building behind standard window openings whose pattern is only interrupted for specially important areas.

Aqueduct over the River Najerilla 1981-88
Anguiano   L R 8
Fernández Casado [eng.]
The engineer built this aqueduct over the Najerilla for a hydroelectric station. Its 60-m span is supported by two rings with a constant width of 0.55 m and a variable depth. The arch is elegantly narrow, its structure strictly distributed using simple, minimalist elements.

Reconstruction of the Bretón de los   L R 9
Herreros Theatre 1980
Monseñor Rodríguez 36. **Haro**
Frechilla/López Peláez/Sánchez
The theatre was designed in the Italian Style by Martín Saracibar in 1814. The architects showed respect towards the few historical elements that remained from the original design whilst bringing in new elements to satisfy the requirements of the programme.

Church of Santiago 1965-67   L R
La Unión de los Tres Ejércitos. Clavijo
Cuadra
Although small, the church is of enormous architectural value, especially due to the spatial differentiation achieved through the use of light and the clear distinction between volumes; the materials employed and the way it is scaled down to fit in with its rural surroundings.

VALENCIA

Located on the E coast of the Iberian Peninsula, this Autonomous Community occupies a long strip of land between the Mediterranean and the Castilian Meseta and consists of the provinces of Castellón de la Plana, Valencia (whose capital gave the community its name) and Alicante. Settled from very early on (Paleolithic caves), its ancient civilisation was soon in contact with Phoenicians and Greeks, turning the area into an urban focal point for Iberian culture (7th c. BC), with opulent sculpture as evidenced in the Dama de Elche. After a period under Roman rule, with the rest of *Hispania*, it achieved greatest splendour from the 8th c. as part of the Hispano-Muslim kingdom of *Al Andalus*. Five centuries of Islamic rule left practices such as the cultivation of rice, citrus and other fruits, and a system of water distribution (originally Roman) through a network of channels in the rich, fertile *Huerta* (literally "farmland") of Valencia that is still the source of the region's wealth. James I the Conqueror reconquered it in the 13th c. when he constituted the Kingdom of Valencia, under the Crown of Aragón, with its own court and charters until these were suppressed in Philip V's drive to form a new centralised state in the 18th c. More Baroque than most other parts of Spain in its art, popular culture and architecture (the 17th c. Basilica of the Virgin and the 18th c. Palace of the Marquis of Dos Aguas, in Valencia), this industrious region combines a dense network of small and medium-sized enterprises oriented towards the export of fruit, rice, furniture, shoes, toys and textiles with large factories of big multinational companies, like Ford (car manufacturing) and IBM (electronic components). Trade, transport and tourism on the Azahar Coast and the beaches of Alicante complete its economy, where the services sector predominates.

There were several outstanding architects between the wars, including Rieta (the Tecles building, Valencia, 1936) and Artal Ros (apartment building on Gran Vía Germanías, Valencia, 1936, designed with Testor and Romaní). During the postwar autarchy drive, the Committee for Devastated Regions gave priority to the reconstruction of the areas on the previous war fronts, such as Nules and Segorbe (Castellón) and the maritime villages of Valencia. Housing policy continued throughout the fifties with much social housing, especially following the River Turia floods (1949 and 1957), with the state also building territorial infrastructures, such as the South Plan in the metropolitan area of Valencia, and linking up with the increasingly popular and broad-ranging urban planning projects in Alicante and Valencia, which reflected the expansive economy of the sixties. The fervoured drive to develop land during these years and the resulting property speculation brought about a deep transformation in the cities and their peripheral areas, changing the urban and rural landscape and, especially, the appearance of the coastal areas, with the onslaught of mass tourism. Benidorm is still the epitome of this kind of development. Under the later democracy, the policy of reequiping and rehabilitating historical buildings became more notable (see V 9, V 15 and the recovery of the Reales Atarazanas (1989-93) in Valencia, by Portaceli). There are now two Schools of Architecture (Valencia, 1968 and Alicante, 1996) which are turning out excellent professionals.

Geography: 23,305 km², with a mountainous interior (peaks of up to 1,500 m), a long litoral plain and short, steep rivers with rapid, irregular flows. Climate: very benign and Mediterranean (see data in each town). Population: 3,923,841. GDP: 101% of nat. av.

ALICANTE. The city runs from the port and beaches to the foot of Monte Benacantil, crowned by the Santa Barbara Castle, originally a Carthaginian fortress. Its core, the Muslim structure (*Vila Vella*), was taken over and expanded by the Christians after the Reconquest (*Vila Nova*), with further additions in the 16th-18th c. resulting from the importance of its port and defensive structure, including the fortifications on the neighbouring isle of Tabarca. In the 19th c., the walls were demolished and a train link established with Madrid (the first link between the capital and the seaside), triggering further growth oriented to leisure services, such as its sea parade, the Paseo de la Explanada. The city was rezoned at the end of the 19th c., and subsequent changes altered it further in the 20th c., including the 1955 plan which gave it its present appearance. Since the seventies, Alicante has become much favoured by tourists for its benign weather, even in winter. The immediate post-war period saw the Albert Ballesteros' building (1934) on Av. Federico Soto c/v Colón. More recently, outstanding buildings include the Bernabeu Institute (1993-97), by Alonso and García-Solera Vera, a clinic in Vistahermosa. Origin: Hellenic settlement of *Akra Leuke* (the

White City) and Roman *Lucentum*. Rainfall: approx. 300 mm and 80 days. Sunshine: 2,930 hrs. Temperatures: 31°-17° and 6°-22° C. Population: 275,110.

La Adriática Building 1935   A 1
Rambla Méndez Núñez c/v Coronel Chapulí
López Gonsálvez
The extension of the small, earlier building uses an Expressionist vocabulary clearly evident in its horizontality and rounded corner. The extension is borne by the dividing load-bearing wall, but the new metal structure makes it possible for the façade to be free of structural elements.

CESA, Centro de Estudios Superiores   A 2
de Alicante 1965
Av. de Denia s/n, Vistahermosa
García Solera
The layout of this building in pavilions brings in the exterior space through porticos that become points of inter-relation and passage. The work has a Miesian flavour, its strict geometry and modern functionalism set in a beautiful pinewood.

Family House with Greenhouse 1986   A 3
Urb. Lomahermosa
García-Solera Vera
The interesting plan gravitates around the twofold purpose of the greenhouse, which is both an articulation fulcrum and the workplace of the owner, a biologist. Domestic comfort is achieved by a clever layout, the treatment of light and refined fittings.

High Performance Centre   A 4
for Rhythmic Gymnastics 1989-93
Foguerer José Ramón Gilabert Davó 12
Miralles/Pinòs/Miás
The design of this gymnastics training centre
wanted to underline its uniqueness, starting
with the idea of dynamism and seeking the
sculptural exuberance of its gymnasts. Walls,
structure, spectacular metal trusses, sloping
pillars and ramps all evoke a creative and
vibrant topography.

Trade Fair Grounds 1990-92   A 5
Ctra. N-340 Alicante-Elche, km 731
Magro/Martín/Del Rey Aynat
Re-using a hypermarket, whose identity
dissolved before the expressive power of
the longitudinal body annexed to it (now
the vestibule and front façade), its glazed
architecture reaches up to the metal roof,
merging vernacular expression with the late
Modern style associated with Le Corbusier.

Regional Government Building 1992-96   A 6
Tucumán 8
García-Solera Vera/Payá
The basic prism is sawn in half by an inner
street, turned into the vital nerve of the
design which, along with the use of the courtyard and another side street to separate the
building from the neighbouring buildings,
provides excellent light conditions and a
convincing articulation of space.

Business School 1994-96   A 7
Campus Universitario, San Vicente de Raspeig
García-Solera Vera
The half-buried, open-air courtyard of this
austere university building, with an access-
way in the shape of a corridor to bridge the
gap, makes it unique. The plan has an ideal
distribution and well-lit interiors which were
both meticulously finished and impeccably
executed in terms of materials.

The province. 55 km N of Alicante is Alcoy (64,579 inhabitants, altitude 545 m), attractively
located between rivers and gulleys crossed by Arab bridges. Its 19th c. bourgeoisie created
the modern industrial city *par excellence*, and further urban renewal is now being planned.
The social housing and rehabilitation of Barbacana (90 apartments, 1986-92) was designed
by Alonso de Armiño and Vidal, while the La Fábrica health centre (1988-91), on Alcolecha 4,
was designed by Colomer and Alcácer. Cocentaina (10,567 inhabitants) is 5 km from Alcoy.
Aspe (15,923 inhabitants) is 24 km W of Alicante, and the villages of El Realengo and San
Isidro de Albatera, 40 and 50 km SE. Calpe (10,962 inhabitants) is a tourist resort with an
attractive beach, where the Peñón de Ifach (332 m) juts out into the sea.

Peñas Blancas Kindergarten 1978-82   A 8
Barítono Almodóvar s/n. **Aspe**
Campo Baeza
The rectangular plan of this introverted, white, restrained, geometrical building is perforated by two courtyards onto which the schoolrooms look. From the outside, the verticality of the chimneys stands out, along with the large access volume and some niches that are set shallow in the silent walls.

La Manzanera, Xanadú Apartments   A 9
and La Muralla Roja 1969
Partida Manzanera. **Calpe**
Bofill
These three buildings, designed for a certain social class of tourists, are characterised by their expressive appearance, recreating the spontaneity of several popular buildings, and their unconventional typologies. La Manzanera is of special interest.

Jover Factory 1973-75   A 10
Ctra. N-340, km 136. **Cocentaina**
Vidal Vidal
This factory exemplifies high-class industrial architecture of considerable typological discipline and size. Its strictly modulated plan contrasts with the complexity of its section, which cuts through the casing of a staggered metal roof, with long eaves and natural lighting.

El Realengo Settlement 1957   A 11
Fernández del Amo
Located near San Isidro de Albatera and designed along similar lines, the central core is laid out on a grid pattern (church, town hall, schools, social centre, administration building, clinic, shops), with 115 homes for tenant farmers and 20 for workers laid out on streets around the edge, which can also have farming lands attached to them.

A 12   **San Isidro de Albatera**
Settlement 1953
Fernández del Amo
This design extracts the very essence of vernacular architecture in its building logic, functionality, simplicity and harmony with the surroundings. In an ethical drive against trivialising this valuable legacy, the architect synthesized, reinterpreted and updated it through abstraction. Originally planned on

CASTELLON DE LA PLANA. The city of Castellón de la Plana stands in the fertile area of La Plana, on the site decreed by James I after the Christian Reconquest of the original village in the 13th c. Economic activity focusses on exporting oranges, furniture, consumer goods and tiles. Its trading port, El Grao, is 5 km away. Benicassim (6,151 inhabitants), 13 km NE, is a tourist and residential town, with many villas that sprung up at the beginning of the 20th c. Inland, in the Maestrazgo district, 106 km from the capital, is Morella (2,717 inhabitants), at an altitude of 960 m, a small gem with its castle and 14th c. church, walled mediaeval old-town of steeply winding streets and well-preserved vernacular architecture. Rainfall: approx. 400 mm and 85 days. Sunshine: approx. 2,850 hrs. Temperatures: 31°-16° and 5°-21° C. Population: 138,489.

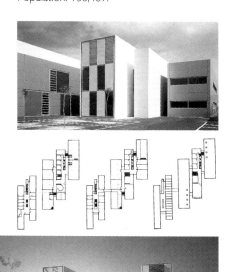

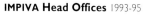

IMPIVA Head Offices 1993-95   CS 1
Av. del Mar s/n
Ferrater
The design shows total autonomy from its rather chaotic, suburban surroundings through its staggered layout of prismatic volumes that display their headwalls instead of a façade and present a wise combination of the emphatic with the ambiguous in an abstract, contemporary discourse. The result is an outstanding sculptural quality. The building, skillfully executed, has been set aside by the Valencian regional government for seeding and incubating companies, and meets their heterogeneous needs by decomposing its parts, split apart or united accordingly, to establish offices, laboratories, warehouses, meeting rooms and two vestibules that distribute the circulation flows into two groups of containers, linked by a transparent, upper walkway.

Santa Agueda Apartments 1966-67   CS 2
Las Villas de Benicassim. **Benicassim**
Martorell/Bohigas/Mackay
The complex shows a new way of under-standing collective life on a tourist coast. It is inspired by the vernacular, grouping together the apartments to give them good views of the sea or mountains, emphasising the highly expressive volumetric dynamism and the craftwork elements.

an orthagonal pattern, the settlement's scale and flexibility in its borders allow it to fit into a flat landscape of palm trees, where the 150 homes with agricultural facilities for tenant farmers and another 34 for workers as well as public buildings were built. The architecture is full of a poetical charm, conceived to help the new community take root. It has been much altered in the face of the authorities' disregard.

Boarding School 1995   CS 3
Paseo de la Alameda s/n. **Morella**
Miralles/Pinòs

The school design shows a deep relationship between architecture and place, which
was essential to the project definition. Like a
land art experiment, the building acts visually
on the physical environment, integrating
into it with its own identity, eloquently
contemporary in its complex geometry and
its fragmentation, which recreate an artificial
topography that matches the slope of the
mountain, suggesting the idea of a plinth
with sharp edges for the walls and for the
old castle that crowns the splendid landscape. The school and lodging programme
was shared out over the two downward
parts, adapted to the terrain in a different
way based on the multipurpose hall and the
common access via a ramp. The schoolrooms are prolonged outside with terraces
open to the panoramic views. Light fills all
the parts, which have adopted the same
layout as local housing in search of the best
orientation. The roofing acts like a genuine
façade, illustrating the innovative spatial
articulation of the complex.

VALENCIA. On the alluvial plains next to a bend in the River Turia, 3 km before its estuary, the
Roman fort of *Valentia* was founded in 138 BC. Under Muslim rule from the 8th-13th c., it
reached its peak of splendour in the 15th c., after it was reconquered, as reflected in the
great Gothic buildings then added to the cathedral (12th-18th c.) and the Gothic octagonal
Miguelete Belfry, the city's symbol (14th c.); the Serranos and Quart Towers (old archways
into the original walled city), the Lonja (old silk market), and the Generalitat Palace (the old
parliament building) standing at the beginning of the historical street of Caballeros. The 1356
walls stood until 1865, when they were demolished and where the ringroad now runs (Xáti-
va and Guillem de Castro streets), at the edge of the old city, the *Ciutat Vella*. Between
1887 and 1911, the first expansion (on a geometrical layout) and the inner reform took
place, creating the Gran Vía, with Modernist architecture near it, such as the Estación
del Norte (1906-17) by Ribes, and in the interesting street of La Paz. Planned after 1893,
the emblematic axis was the Paseo al Mar (now Av. Blasco Ibáñez), which includes the
University campus and buildings such as the Júcar Water Authority Building (1962-65) by
Colomina. With the economic boom experienced in the sixties, the city outskirts grew

and the capital absorbed the surrounding
villages. The riverbed was diverted to avoid
periodic flooding, and the old dry bed
awaits further treatment to fully integrate it
into city life. At the end of the 20th c.,
Valencia is now a metropolitan area with a
radius of some 15-20 km and an ever-
expanding suburban population. Rainfall:
approx. 390 mm and 85 days. Sunshine:
2,450 hrs. Temperatures: 31°-17° and 7°-
22° C. Population: 777,409.

Finca Roja Building 1929-33 V I
Jesús c/v Marvá c/v Maluquer
Viedma Vidal
A work on the way to Modernism, the Finca
Roja's volumetrics provide it with a strong
identity, turning it into a unique image, with
a figuration close to the Dutch Wendingen
Group, but also incorporating solutions
from the Viennese "Hof" in the collectivist
orientation of its programme. It contains
500 apartments for workers around a landscaped courtyard, with the planned shops
reached through alleys. The hierarchy of the
cants is revealed through the towers, which
are set up as deposits, and whose sculptural
silhouette emerges from a skin, rhythmically
folded to hold bay windows, sharing a set of
expressive resources that, along with the
construction, define the very quality of the
building. The structure is made of concrete.

Apartment Building 1933-34 V 2
Donoso Cortés 1 c/v Pza. del Barón de Cortés
Pecourt Betés
Valencia's first approximation to the Modernist postulates, adopted by an architect who
had been related to the GATEPAC as a
student, is reflected in its austere façades,
the composition of the windows and doors,
the treatment of the corner and the severe
balcony railings.

Rialto Cinema 1935 V 3
Pza. del Ayuntamiento 17 and Moratín 10
Borso di Carminati
Located on a highly irregular site, the
complex requirements of the cinema and
apartment building were laid out in a clever
section and distribution by storeys. Its main
façade with *Art Déco* overtones is bravely
designed, using iron and glass, materials that
insinuate an interesting curtain wall at the
back.

Torre de Valencia Building 1956 V 4
Gran Vía Marqués del Turia 77
Gutiérrez Soto
The architect, who is often falsely believed
to have circumscribed all of his work to
Madrid, designed this Valencian milestone,
interpreting the possibilities of high-rise buildings. It features apartments with terraces,
window boxes and other interesting changes
in the layout that orders the day areas.

Agentes Comerciales Cooperative 1958-61
Santa María Micaela 12   V 5
Artal Ríos
Three blocks of strictly modulated housing,
mostly split-level apartments, stand around a
common area with pool and walkways. The
composition is based on the expression of
the structure and a rigorous study of common
services and routing, which emphasise the
social orientation of the avant-garde movements, updated with the Team X revision.

Guadalaviar School 1958-60   V 6
Av. Aragón c/v Av. Blasco Ibáñez
Martínez García-Ordoñez
A refined example of architecture scattered
over gardens, its inside-outside dialogue is
established in an especially pleasing, almost
lyrical manner. It contains dignified references
to the renewal experiments of international
culture of its time.

Law School 1959-60   V 7
Av. Blasco Ibáñez 30
Moreno Barberá
This open building with green spaces plays a
key role in the new way of understanding
the city. The assimilation of Le Corbusier is
evident in the strong sun protection system
that uses *brise-soleils* and concrete latticework to create a high-profile image. It is a
functionally efficient and precise work.

IVAM Julio González Centre 1987-89   V 8
Guillém de Castro 118
Giménez/Salvadores
The museum's appearance and set-up
shows great sobriety in the lineal layout of
its rooms parallel to the façade. Its glazed
bay window announces the vestibule, which
has an exuberant stairway. The well-scaled,
user-friendly, metropolitan building stands
next to the river.

Adaptation of the Benicarló Palace   V 9
for the Valencian Parliament 1988-95
Pza. de San Lorenzo 4
Salvadores/Portaceli
The adaptation opened the building to an
updated, sequential reading of its historical
parts, with Gothic and 19th c. remains. The
original central chamber, which stands
proud of the building and can be seen from
outside, was expanded outwards.

Bridges and Underground Station 1991-95
Calatrava   V 10

Together with the underground station below it and the Nueve de Octubre bridge (144-m span, 1986-89), the Alameda bridge was constructed on the dried-out bed of the River Turia and shows how Calatrava sought for icons whose formal monument-ality could make a statement about the place where they are located. Less integrated into the urban landscape than the Nueve de Octubre bridge, the Alameda bridge displays a prominent sloping arch with stays, embedded in a curved deck. Below, the roofing of the underground station, sub-terranean, white and airy, stems from the girder sustaining the bridge structure, with a central zone of concrete spokes and ribbed outer areas where the concourses fit in the stairwells.

Four Underground Stations 1994-96   V 11
Underground Line 4
Meri/García Sogo/Armiño/Vidal/Huet [eng.]

Good architecture, with its ideas of order, sobriety and excellence, using well-selected materials and fittings has turned these public works into something rather special. The three subterranean stations are the same size (100 x 15 x 7.5 m), distinguished by their colours, all with granite flooring and wall cladding up to 2.1 m high. The rocky mass of the outside walls contrasts with the light-filled platforms, and the compositional freedom in their volumetric simplicity and attractive appearance hint at a de la Sota touch.

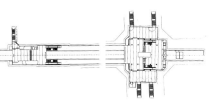

San Pío V Museum of Fine Arts 1996-97 V 12
Av. San Pío V, 9
Portaceli/Gómez-Ferrer

The refurbishment and extension was ordered around the old octagonal church (now the vestibule), like a socket joint between two main axes. The landscaping, overall restraint and the spaciousness of the new exhibition halls stand out in this cultured historical restoration. [Final phase still unfinished]

Other works. In the Technology Park in Paterna, 4 km W of Valencia, Ros built the CESGA building (1991-93) for water treatment and meeting rooms. Xativa (23,755 inhabitants, 10 m), first an Iberian settlement, then a Roman town and then the Muslim *Hateba,* is 59 km S, with its castle. Formerly the site of the first paper manufacturing plant in Europe, nowadays it is home to the Inelcom Factory (1995), designed by Gradolí, Herrero and Sanz.

Technical College 1967-69   V 13
Ctra. Valencia-Madrid s/n. **Cheste**
Moreno Barberá
The assimilation of a Le Corbusier-style culture is at the heart of this small location of 5,000 students, built in one year on old dry-farming lands, then totally relandscaped. Moreno Barberá achieved an over-riding sculptural feel by exploiting the expressive potential of concrete and the powerful image of the sun-protection systems, which were designed according to their solar orientation. The ambitious educational programme clusters the building's different uses together, avoiding the sense of mass-ification and avoiding any alteration of the topography. Staggered downwards, the excellence of the building, its modulation, functionality and overall planning are truly outstanding.

Gavina School 1979-81   V 14
Partida de la Martina. **Picanya**
Portaceli/Gregorio
Set amidst beautiful orange groves, the design begins with an elementary square-based shape around a 2-storey core, as a multipurpose key to the whole. The appear-ance of the prismatic volume, perforated by courtyards is restrained and incorporates Modern references.

Roman Theatre Rehabilitation 1985-93   V 15
Castillo s/n. **Sagunto**
Grassi/Portaceli
This ambitious intervention, which aroused much controversy, raised the imposing outer walls to block the view from outside of the ruins that people had always thought should be open, although in fact Roman theatres, unlike Greek ones, were always closed in. The final work is true to the original, having respected the inseparable union between the tiers and the stage in a single volume. The architects distinguish between the new parts and the old ones. Their use of brick-work, stone and concrete refers back to ancient building techniques. The classical profile of the tiers is recreated, and the reconstructed theatre can be visited from the corridor running through it. It has thus recuperated its civic nature as a space that is a monument to civilisation, as it was in its times of splendour (2nd c.).

CASTING SHADOWS
Notes on the Work of Spanish Architects Outside Spain

This guide would be incomplete if it failed to cover the work done by Spanish architects beyond Spain. When we speak of Spanish architecture, we think of buildings that are anchored down to the ground, an intrinsic part of the nation's landscape. But the architects of the buildings are not so firmly tied down to their country, and if we were to omit exploring the vast territory of their achievements outside Spain, it would be like drawing a portrait of Spanish architecture without its shadows. These discontinuous shadows loom large and cross far distant lands. Sometimes clearer than others, they run over exotic topographies, adopting themselves to their folds, rippling over their rugged surfaces, but conserving a certain something that (at least to us) suggests a way of looking (a special light perhaps) which will always be attached to its roots.

The discontinuity of the shadows arises from the diversity of the buildings we shall visit, product of different times and different causes. We have divided them into three groups. The first consists of the works of the Spaniards who went into exile at the end of the Spanish Civil War (1936-1939). Especially in America, these architects worked within the invisible folds of Modernism, and their designs brim over with a belief in the power of style to shape reality.

The second group includes the works of architects designing institutional buildings to represent Spain abroad in diplomatic missions and international exhibitions. In this area, there is always an interesting tension between what we are and what we would like to be, leaving space for intense, vibrant architectural feats of imagination. And then the third group is the one which has forged the prestige that Spanish architecture has come to enjoy over recent years, its reputation slowly but surely spreading over new lands. Its architects display a heady drive to internationalism, based on a strong awareness of how to make shadows solid.

1. The Architects in Exile
The modern, radical voice of Spanish architecture was silenced in April 1939, after a civil war during which it had expressed the social commitments of Modernist thought in journals and trenches alike. Architects who had upheld these ideas had to renounce them or leave the country, impoverishing yet further an avant-garde[1] that had already lost some of its leading exponents (Aizpurua, of the Falangist Party, shot in San Sebastián and Torres-Clavé, who fought on the Republican side, see SS 1 and B 16, respectively).

1. In July 1942, Franco's Government officially removed many architects' professional accreditation. The full list of "cleansed professionals", as they were officially called at the time, can be found in Oriol Bohigas, *Arquitectura Española de la Segunda República*, Tusquets, Barcelona, 1970.

Spanish Pavilion,
1937 Paris Exhibition,
by Sert and Lacasa
[rebuilt in 1992
in Barcelona
by Espinet, Ubach and
Hernández de León]

Before that time, enlightenment and reason had their swan-song in the **Spanish Pavilion** (representing the legally elected government of the Republic) at the **1937 Paris International Exhibition**. Designed by Josep Lluis Sert and Luis Lacasa during the Civil War, it struck a fine balance between Modern Abstractionism and a passion for the earth, floating upwards on piles and strapped down by stairs and ramps. Photographs show a courtyard occupying the lower part of the building and containing some important works of art, dramatic cries from a country racked by war (including Miró's *El pagès català i la revolució*, Picasso's *Guernica* and Calder's *Fountain of Mercury*, which the architect, Bonet Castellana helped install). Never had Modernism been so heartfelt. The drama was expressed in its very flesh and bones; its anguish was palpable in its material face; it screamed its desperation at an onslaught of unbearable reality. In the pavilion, however, it managed to retain some of its Mediterranean lightness and this equilibrium was perhaps best caught by the firm gaze of Julio González's harvester, *La Segadora*. Like her, with its eyes on the horizon, the Spanish avant-garde watched its world closing in around it for decades to come.

Several years later, in 1948, at the suggestion of Pierre Vago, Bernardo Giner de los Ríos, who had been a minister under the Republic, called the Spanish architects who were living in exile to an International Meeting of Architects in Lausanne. In very general terms, the work of these exiled Spaniards was exemplified in the designs of Félix Candela in Mexico; Antoni Bonet Castellana in Argentina, and Josep Lluis Sert in the United States. Even from a distance, their buildings retain a distinctive flavour. Other exiles include:

Argentina: Antoni Bonet Castellana. *Chile:* Fernando Echevarría, Germán Rodríguez Arias, Pedro Zavala. *Colombia:* Santiago Esteban de la Mora, Alfredo Rodríguez Orgaz, Germán Tejero. *Cuba:* Martín Domínguez (in the United States since 1960). *Dominican Republic:* Domingo Fábregas. *France:* Domingo Escorsa, Gabriel Pradal. *Mexico:* Tomás Auñón, Francisco Azorín, José Luis Mariano Benlliure, Tomás Bilbao, Emilio Blanch, Ovidio Botella, Félix Candela, José Caridad, Oscar Coll, Francisco Detrell, Ignacio Faure, Roberto Fernández Balbuena, Fernando Gay, Bernardo Giner de los Ríos, Cayetano de la Jara, J. Larrosa, Juan de Madariaga, Esteban Marco, Jesús Martí, Jaime Ramonell, Juan Rivaud, Eduardo Robles, Mariano Rodríguez Orgaz, Arturo Sáenz de la Calzada, Enrique Segarra. *Norway:* Jordi Tell. *United States:* Josep Lluis Sert, Martín Domínguez (since 1960). *USSR:* Luis Lacasa, Manuel Sánchez Arcas. *Venezuela:* Deu Amat, Rafael Bergamín, Juan Capdevila, Francisco Iñiguez, H. de Manchovas, Joaquín Ortiz, Amós Salvador, Fernando Salvador, José Lino Vaamonde, Javier Yámoz. [2]

2. Arturo Saenz de la Calzada, "La arquitectura en el exilio" (by several authors) in *El exilio español de 1939*, Taurus, Madrid, 1978; Arturo Souto Albarce, "Arquitectura" (by several authors) in *El exilio español en México*, 1939-1982, Fondo de Cultura Económica y Salvat Editores, México City, 1982.

Sert House, Cambridge, MA, 1958

Josep Lluis Sert was easily the most widely known Spanish architect working in international circles. In June 1939 he arrived in New York, after being banned from exercising his profession at the end of the Civil War. After his involvement in the *Athens Charter*, he was commissioned to write a book, *Can Our Cities Survive?* The task brought him into contact with an earlier generation of European refugees in the States: Neutra, Breuer, Mies van der Rohe and Gropius, whom he replaced as Director of the Architecture Department and Dean of the School of Design at the University of Harvard, where he had already become a frequent lecturer. Throughout his life, Sert maintained a broad-ranging vision of his vocation, leading him to deal with urbanistic issues, taking into account climate and the delimitation of open spaces as well as rationalist criteria, and to do in-depth studies of housing. Yet he never fell into the trap of considering his subject from a purely theoretical viewpoint, so that his lectures were a workshop where students could study the links between ideas and reality.

Sert's house with courtyard in Cambridge, Massachusetts, built in 1958, is a living example of how the architect put his ideas into practice, which can be summed up as a vocational search for unity: his house sprung from a desire to make something that could be repeated, that could form a town. The house is inhabited by works of art, an interest that he had maintained ever since the 1937 Pavilion, and which would blossom in South America. But what shines through most strongly is the way Rationalism was set within the regional context, as if modern values could be revived when grafted onto the open spaces and climate identified with the Mediterranean civilisation. What is so attractive about this architecture, which is also true of the **Aimé and Marguerite Maeght Foundation** (Saint Paul-de-Vence, France 1958), Joan Miro's studio in Palma de Mallorca (1955, see PM 1) and the design for **Braque's House** (Saint Paul-de-Vence, France, 1960), is the way Modernism exchanges attributes with the Mediterranean, breaking down the frontiers between the two, bringing out abstract ideas in a way that is tangible and material, intimately linked to light and nature. Perhaps Sert (like Le Corbusier at the end of his life) suddenly realised that nature is a "straight line that unites Man and the Cosmos, as uncurvable as the horizon of the sea" and that, without the aid of materiality to give life, without the graft of things in ideas, the power of style (the Modern style) would be little more than a fantasy.

Some other works by Sert in the United States and Latin America:
Presidential Palace, Havana, Cuba (1955-58); Central Campus, Boston University, United States
[Tower Block Housing the Law and Pedagogy Departments, the Boston Union Building and the
General Boston University Library] (1960-67); Central Campus, Guelph University, Ontario, Canada
[Students Residence, Central Library and Arts and Humanities Department] (1964-66); Central
Campus, Cambridge University, United States [Centre for World Religion Studies, Holyoke Centre,
Administrative Building and Health Centre, Married Students Quarters, F.B. Peabody Terrace (1962-
64), Undergraduate Science Department], Martin Luther King Elementary School (1958-70); Estate
of 1,000 houses on Roosevelt Island, New York, United States (1962-64); Design for the Saint
Botolph Chapel, in the Boston Civic Centre, United States (1966); Riverview Housing Estate,
Yonkers, New York, United States (1972-76).

Planning and Urbanism:
Cidade dos Motores, Brazil (1945); Ciudad Nueva de Chimbote, Peru (1948); General Plan for
Medellín, Colombia (1949); General Plan for Bogotá, Colombia (1953); Pilot Plan for Havana, Cuba
(1958); Design for Remodelling the South Station, Boston, United States (1966); Remodelling the
urban centre of Worcester, Massachusetts, United States (1967).

The second exiled Spanish architect whose work received international renown
at this time was Antoni Bonet Castellana. Immediately after finishing the Spanish
Pavilion at the Paris 1937 Exhibition, he worked with Le Corbusier on the **Jaoul
House**, impressing the great French architect with the way he managed to combine
the creative freedom of Surrealism with the rigours of Rationalist architecture.

This freedom also triggered a
mysterious alchemical reaction
between Rationalism and
nature, which characterised
all of his later work. It
seemed that he was trying to
create a time, rather than a
space, in nature, in an effort to
conceive a fascinating architecture in which Modernism
opened up to life, love and
suffering. This is especially clear
in his work in Argentina and
Urguay, where his designs for
the **Punta Ballena Estate** (1945-
48), in Maldonado, achieve real
beauty.

Some other works by Bonet
Castellana in America:
Building on Calle Paraguay, Buenos
Aires, Argentina (1938-39).
Hotel, restaurant and night club, La
Solana del Mar, Punta Ballena, Mal-
donado, Uruguay (1946-48).
Berlingieri House in Punta Ballena,
Maldonado, Uruguay (1947).
Housing block and shopping arcade,
Galería Rivadavia, Buenos Aires,
Argentina (1956-59).

La Rinconada, Punta Ballena (Uruguay), by Bonet, 1948

Experimental hyperbolic paraboloid umbrella, Colonia Vallejo, Mexico City, by Félix Candela, 1953

Last, but by no means least, in this list of outstanding architects in exile is Félix Candela, who emigrated to Mexico in 1939, becoming naturalised there in 1941. Together with his family, he set up the building company, Cubiertas Alas, S.A., in which he spent twenty years designing and constructing laminate structures. Amongst his many works in Mexico City, the most characteristic is perhaps the **Iglesia de la Virgen de la Medalla Milagrosa** church (1953), but besides works like this he was also involved in structural design and construction (his two great passions) in projects such as the **Los Manantiales Restaurant** (Xochimilco, Mexico, 1957, together with the architect, Alvarez Ordóñez) and the Sports Centre for the XIX Olympic Games (1968, together with the architects, Castañeda and Peyri). Candela was both architect and engineer by training, and could see architecture in terms of structural logic. More a builder than a designer (as he himself used to insist), he declared himself a seeker of form, understood as "the qualities that make each thing what it is". He thought of Formalism[3] as a kind of scientific research into the configuration of space. We can now imagine his work as two figures: form and gravity, the two in constant battle, wrestling with each other until they eventually meld together into one.

Some of Candela's works in America:
Capilla de Nuestra Señora de la Soledad chapel in Coyoacán, Mexico City [with E. de la Mora] (1956-58).
Lederie Pharmaceutical Laboratories in Calzada de Tlalpan, Mexico City (1957).
Texas Instruments Factory in Dallas, US (1957).
La Jacaranda Night Club in Acapulco, Mexico (1957).
Bacardi Factory, Mexico-Queretaro Highway, Tultitlán (1958-60; offices: Mies van der Rohe).
Iglesia de San José Obrero church in Monterrey, Mexico (1959).
Capilla de San Vicente Paul chapel in Coyoacán, Mexico City (1959-60).

Vírgen de la Medalla Milagrosa Church, Mexico City, by Félix Candela, 1953

3. Felix Candela, "En Defensa del Formalismo", paper given in *La Casa del Arquitecto*, Mexico, April 1956.

2. Spain Away from Spain

The distance between Sert's 1937 Pavilion and Salvador Dalí's mise en scène in the New York World Fair in 1939[4] is the distance separating the collective dream from the personal subconscious. In the latter, nothing remains of the drama of war, which was not allowed to compete with the drama of Dalí's flamboyant gestures. Perhaps the only thing these two artists had in common was their true respect for Gaudí.

With the **Spanish Pavilion** in the 9th Milan Triennial in 1950, Coderch and Valls obtained international recognition. As in other cases, their avant-garde ideas were emptied of ideological content and were reduced to a personal interiorisation of constructive language. Within this group of emblematic designs, works such as the **Pantheon of the Spaniards** in Rome, and the **Spanish Stand** at the 11th Milan Triennial, both by M. García de Paredes and Javier Carvajal (1957), should also be mentioned.

A special case is that of the **Spanish Pavilion** built for the **1958 Brussels Universal Exposition** (see M 69), for which José Antonio Corrales and Ramón Vázquez Molezún won the competition with a design that struck a fine balance between nature and abstraction. Despite its structural purity, its clarity, it is in no way removed from the land on which it is set. There are no abstract axes. Rather it meets the paradoxical condition of being stuck to the ground, conceived from the ground up, whilst at the same time being able to stand anywhere (and was indeed later reinstalled in Madrid). The Pavilion is a model of growth that reminds many of the Córdoba Mosque, a structure which, once the rules are established, provides a space that can be expanded in any direction. The pavilion manipulates the constructional geometry of Modernism through approximations that, given the times, could not be very personal. Thus, the process of construction sheds its own light over the space, which is seamless. What is most moving about this pavilion is its attempt at wholeness: the umbrella is at once the roofing and the drainage, the structure, the lighting and the space, without any of these being a separate part of it. Everything is everything. But at the same time, since it is resting on the earth, leaving its footprint in this one place, what is always the same here appears as something very different. There is identity and difference at once: like the fingers of our hand, like human faces. There is nothing more beautiful that this simultaneous presence of what Kant called *Mitgefühl*, human sympathy with inanimate objects. The architects give life to their buildings so that they can behave like natural formations. Nature is called forth again in these structures, at the same time new yet different.

Spanish Pavilion, Brussels Expo'58, by Corrales and Molezún, later reinstalled in Madrid

4. Salvador Dalí, *Dream of Venus* Pavilion at the 1939 New York World Fair. According to Maite Muñoz, this was "...a possible Spanish Pavilion at an impossible date."

After many decades of international isolation, first, and then openness as a result of the political change and also in the wake of tourism, in the eighties Spain joined the European Community as a full-fledged democracy and became fashionable, finding an international identity more in keeping with its history, language, culture and economy. This also provided an unparalleled opportunity for several excellent Spanish architects to show off their prowess in representational buildings.

The Spanish Ministry of Foreign Affairs has been especially active in this respect, commissioning several top-quality professionals to design the Spanish diplomatic mission buildings abroad: Bohigas/Martorell/Mackay, Julio Cano Lasso, Pablo Carvajal, Manuel de las Casas, Cruz/Ortíz, Angel and Antonio Fernández Alba, Rafael de la Hoz, Junquera/Pérez Pita, López Cotelo/Puente, Juan López Jaén, López-Peláez/Frechilla Herrero/Sánchez, Gerardo Mingo, Rafael Moneo, Francisco Rodríguez de Partearroyo, Luis Peña Ganchegui, Francisco J. Sáenz de Oíza, Alejandro de la Sota, Ignacio Vicens... Their designs can be referenced in the catalogue to the exhibition, *Arquitectura de Representación, España de Oriente a Occidente*, Spanish Ministry of Foreign Affairs, Madrid, 1995.

3. Contemporaries

Whether through international competitions or direct commissions, many Spanish architects have put up their buildings beyond Spanish frontiers. A pioneer in this stage was the beautiful **House in Pantelleria**, Italy (1972-75) by Clotet and Tusquets.

Amongst the current works of interest, we can include Alberto Campo Baeza's plans for the house for the fashion designer, Tom Ford, in Santa Fe; the Marugame Hirai Museum (1993), in Japan, and the designs for the Swatch-Mercedes exhibition and sales rooms (1993) by Alfredo Arribas; the Art Museum in Kumamoto (1990-92) and Les Follies in Osaka (1989-90), Japan, by Martínez Lapeña and Torres Tur; the housing Boris Podrecca commissioned to Josep Llinás in Conegliano, Italy (1996); José Luis Mateo's housing in the Netherlands (1993); Cruz and Ortíz's design for the Basel Train Station area (1996) and Bohigas' housing estate for the Berlin IBA.

House in Pantelleria, by Clotet and Tusquets, 1975

Of all the buildings and designs of the last few years, Ricardo Bofill and Santiago Calatrava's stand out in quantity, and Rafael Moneo and Juan Navarro Baldeweg's for their intensity.

Ricardo Bofill must be given due recognition for following in the worthy footsteps of Josep Lluis Sert and Antoni Bonet Castellana, and managing to have established what may be a new record for the number of Catalan designs that have been built outside Spain.

Some of Bofill's works outside Spain:
Les Arcades du Lac and Le Viaduc, Saint-Quentin-en-Yvelines, France (1978-81).
Le Palais d'Abraxas, Marne la Vallée, France (1978-83).
Antigone, Montpellier, France (1979-83).
Social housing consisting of 270 units, 78 rue du Château, Paris, France (1985).
Shepherd School of Music, Rice University, Houston, Texas, United States (1992).
R.R. Donnelly Center, Chicago, United States (1992).
Officies, public facilities and shops, Place du Marché Saint-Honoré, Paris, France (1993).

Santiago Calatrava, architect and engineer, is in some ways close to Félix Candela. What most surprises in his designs is his ability to swap around the attributes that engineering, architecture and sculpture are traditionally given. By shuffling together his scales, building methods, three-dimensional prowess and origins, he obtains amazing effects, all the more beautiful for being shorn of stylistic frills. Indeed, his early work, especially, achieves enormous intensity by rejecting any need to impose the kind of personal style, the distinctive stamp that some customers demand.

Some works by Calatrava outside Spain:
Portal to train station concourse, Lucerne, Switzerland (1984-89).
Heritage Plaza and Gallery, Toronto, Canada (1987).
Train station, Zurich, Switzerland (1983-90).
Train station in Satolas Airport, Lyon, France (1989-93).

There are architects who place their faith in the validity of an expression handed down to them, but there are others who mistrust a preconceived formal outcome and think that the way the work develops and the way that objects reveal themselves is what gives personality to their design. These architects believe that the character of the building – the form that ideas take – should not be predetermined; that it is there, mysteriously waiting to be shaped.

Le Palais d'Abraxas, by Bofill, 1978-83

Stadelhofen Station, Zurich, Calatrava, 1982-90

Perhaps Navarro Baldeweg and Moneo are the Spanish architects most bound up with this way of working, albeit approaching their works from very different angles (at least when seen from close to). Juan Navarro Baldeweg's architecture takes form from the presence of things. There is nothing literary or representative of something else in his designs. His lines are like tightropes joining up the abstract and the material. He fits his work into the space between these two extremes, where the simultaneity of opposites creates something vibrant and tense. Things and ideas adopt the same profile and somehow appear in all their powerful purity. It is here, in the metamorphosis of what already exists in potentiality, where his creativity gives life.

Some works and designs by Navarro Baldeweg abroad:
Design for Conference Centre in Salzburg, Austria (1992-, competition).
Design for the Salvador Allende Museum and Cultural Centre in Santiago de Chile (1993-).
Woolworth Music Center in Princeton University, United States (1994-).
Design for the Hertzian Library in Rome, Italy (1996-).

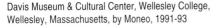

Davis Museum & Cultural Center, Wellesley College, Wellesley, Massachusetts, by Moneo, 1991-93

Hertzian Library, Rome, by Navarro Baldeweg, 1996-

Finally, we must refer to the work of José Rafael Moneo, who provides coincidental symmetry to the century by becoming the Dean at the Harvard Graduate School of Design in 1987, a post that Sert had occupied in 1953. Moneo is the Spanish architect with greatest international recognition both for his buildings and for his commitment to teaching and theory. In 1996, he won the prestigious Pritzker Prize for Architecture. Apart from the **Potsdamer Platz Hotel and Office Block** in Berlin (1993, still under construction as of autumn 1997) and the design for the Spanish Ambassador's Residence in Washington (1995), his activity has been mainly directed towards public buildings, such as the design for the Venice Film Festival headquarters (Lido, 1991, first prize in competition) and various museum buildings: the **Davis Museum and Cultural Center, Wellesley College** (1991-93, Wellesley, Massachusetts), the **Houston Museum** (1992, still under construction as of autumn 1997) and the **Stockholm Museums of Modern Art and Architecture** (1991-97, competition).

In all these projects, as elsewhere in his work, there is a common way of seeing things, rather than a common style of doing them. Each building takes its form from a key concept, always abstract (and never predetermined), which is hidden with the observation or reflection of this concept through the structure, the construction, the light and the space. And the true achievement lies in bringing together all these different ways of seeing, at least different in principle, until they refocus together and restore the act of expressing ideas in shapes and forms. When seen from a close distance, the shape of the building can be made out (naturally, one of these ways of seeing is the very process of building). In Moneo's

1. Stockholm Museums of Art and Architecture, by Moneo, 1991-97 2. Passenger Terminal, Yokohama, by Zaera and Moussavi, 1995-2001 3. Meditation Pavilion, Unazuki, by Miralles, 1991-93
4. Follie No. 7, Osaka, by Martínez Lapeña and Torres Tur, 1989-90

understanding of architecture itself, in his vocation to achieve unity, his buildings always contain a lesson, a critique of their own contemporaneity, as if their conscious materiality were ordered around the belief that buildings should always look both ways at once: their necessary tactile materiality faces nature, touched by human hand, but the way in which it is ordered refers to culture, to ideas. That is how abstraction and concretion coincide. Moneo's latest important commission outside Spain is to discover the form that the Los Angeles Cathedral (1996-) is to take in California.

Apart from Enric Miralles, who although known internationally, has in fact only erected two small buildings outside Spain – his intense **Meditation Pavilion** in Unazuki (1991-93) and the new **access to Takaoka Station**, both in Japan – we will have to wait for the next millennium to see the finished outcome of the attractive designs with which young Spanish professionals have won international competitions: the **Borghetto Flaminio Complex** in Rome, by García de Paredes and Pedrosa, and the **Passenger Terminal in the Yokohama Port** in Japan, by Zaera and Moussavi. The passenger terminal, although highly experimental, returns to the search for unity, the vocation to combine the extremely abstract with the extremely material, that we consider to be the distinguishing mark of the best Spanish architecture of all times.

Luis Moreno Mansilla and Emilio Tuñón Alvarez
Madrid, 1997

BIOGRAPHICAL DATA AND ADDRESSES

A ABALOS VAZQUEZ, Iñaki [1956, grad. 1978]
ABALOS/HERREROS
Víctor Hugo 1   28004 Madrid
Tel. 523 44 04   Fax 523 45 53
ABARCA, Miriam [1959, grad. 1987]
See Cano Pintos/Cosín/Fariña
ABURTO RENOVALES, Rafael de [1913, grad. 1943]
AGUILA RADA, Antonio del, eng. [1893, grad. 1916, † 1962]
AGUINAGA Y AZQUETA, Eugenio M. de [1910, grad. 1934]
AGUINAGA CHURRUCA, Eugenio M. de [1943, grad. 1969]
Orense 49   28020 Madrid
Tel. 597 48 85   Fax 597 38 65
AGUIRRE LOPEZ-CARBONELL, Agustín [1896, grad. 1920, † 1985]
AIZPURUA AZQUETA, José M. [1902, grad. 1927, † 1936]
ALAMO FERRER, Fermín [1887, grad. 1911, † 1937]
ALAS RODRIGUEZ, Genaro [1926, grad. 1953]
ALAS CASARIEGO ARQUITECTOS
San Hermenegildo 12   28015 Madrid
Tel. 593 90 15   Fax 593 04 35
ALBERT BALLESTEROS, Luis [1902, grad. 1928, † 1968]
ALBERTO NOGUEROL + PILAR DIEZ
Pza. María Pita 11   A Coruña
Tel./Fax 20 48 26
ALBIÑANA CORRALE, Francisco [1887, grad. 1911, † 1936]
ALCACER GARCIA, Vicente [1947, grad. 1973]
See Cano/Colomer
ALCANTARA MONTALVO, Fernando [1895, † 1964]
ALDAZ MUGUIRO, Luis, eng. [1907, grad. 1930]
ALEMANY SOLER, Luis [1897, grad. 1922, † 1970]
ALOMAR, Gabriel [1910, grad. 1934]
ALONSO VERA, Dolores [1951, grad. 1976]
Paseo Ramiro 3   03002 Alicante
Tel. 514 03 66   Fax 521 96 78
ALONSO DE ARMIÑO PEREZ, Luis Carlos [1948, grad. 1974]
Botánico Cavanilles 16   46010 Valencia
Tel. 369 06 18   Fax 369 06 18
ALONSO DEL VAL, Miguel A. [1956, grad. 1979]
ALONSO, HERNANDEZ & ASOCIADOS
Ciudadela 9   31001 Pamplona
Tel. 21 17 50   Fax 21 17 91
ALVAREZ CASTELAO, Ignacio [1910, grad. 1936, † 1984]
ALVAREZ-SALA WALTHER, Enrique [1952, grad. 1977]
See 3AC Estudio de Arquitectura
ALVAREZ SANDOVAL, Antonio [1947, grad. 1977]
See Martínez Gadea, Vicente
ALVEAR CRIADO, Jaime [1925, grad. 1952]
General Oraa 9   28006 Madrid   Tel. 563 74 90
ALZUGARAY LOS ARCOS, Alfonso [1955, grad. 1979]
See Mangado Belloqui, Francisco
AMADO CERCOS, Roser [1944, grad. 1968]
See Roser Amadó/Lluis Domènech, Arquitectes

AMANN Y AMANN, Calixto E. [1882, grad. 1907, † 1942]
AMP ARQUITECTOS
San José 2   38002 Santa Cruz de Tenerife
Tel. 24 51 49   Fax 24 40 33
ANASAGASTI Y ALGAN, Teodoro [1880, grad. 1906, † 1938]
ANTOLIN GARCIA, Fernando [1955, grad. 1982]
See Alas Casariego Arquitectos
APEZTEGUIA ELSO, María Teresa [1956, grad. 1979]
Sancho el Mayor 2   31002 Pamplona
Tel. 21 19 98   Fax 21 19 98
ARACIL BELLOD, José Joaquín [1930, grad. 1957]
Burgo de Osma 57   28033 Madrid   Tel./Fax 302 90 27
ARANA AMURRIO, José Luis [1942, grad. 1966]
ARANA/AROCA, ESTUDIO
Guzmán el Bueno 123   28003 Madrid
Tel. 553 02 20   Fax 553 02 20
ARANGUREN/GALLEGOS ARQUITECTOS
La Masó 2   28034 Madrid
Tel. 734 19 01   Fax 734 19 01
ARANGUREN LOPEZ, María José [1958, grad. 1983]
See Aranguren/Gallegos Arquitectos
ARANTXA BASTERRA/CARLES LLINAS
Paseo de San Juan 57   08009 Barcelona   Tel. 232 21 81
AREVALO CARRASCO, Rafael [1898, grad. 1922, † 1952]
ARGARATE URIA, Esteban [1926, grad. 1957]
ARNICHES MOLTO, Carlos [1897, grad. 1922, † 1955]
AROCA HERNANDEZ-ROS, María [1942, grad. 1964]
See Arana/Aroca, Estudio
AROCA HERNANDEZ-ROS, Ricardo [1940, grad. 1965]
Rafael Calvo 9   28010 Madrid
Tel. 448 25 05   Fax 448 25 06
ARQUITECTURA PERDIGO/RODRIGUEZ
Pza. Manuel Girona 15-24   08034 Barcelona
Tel. 203 57 44   Fax 203 52 58
ARRIBAS, Alfredo [1954, grad. 1977]
Balmes 345   08006 Barcelona
Tel. 417 33 37   Fax 417 35 91
ARRIOLA I MADORELL, Andreu [1956, grad. 1981]
Mallorca 293   08037 Barcelona   Tel./Fax 457 03 57
ARTAL ROS, Lorenzo [1895, grad. 1922]
ARTAL RIOS, Santiago [1931, grad. 1957]
ARTENGO RUFINO, Felipe [1954, grad. 1978]
See AMP Arquitectos
ARTENGO RUFINO, Francisco [1942, grad. 1968]
ARTENGO RUFINO/JDOMINGUEZ ANADON, ARQUITECTOS
Carlos Hamilton 12   38001 Santa Cruz de Tenerife
Tel. 28 07 50   Fax 24 70 63
ARTIGUES CODO, Ramón [1936, grad. 1967]
ARTIGUES & SANABRIA ARQUITECTOS
Aribau 230-240   08006 Barcelona
Tel. 414 42 00   Fax 414 41 90

ARZADUN E IBARRARAN, Fernando [1893, grad. 1919, † 1951]
ASENSIO PEÑA, José Miguel [1949, grad. 1971]
ASENSIO PEÑA/BENITEZ CASTRO
Pza. Cardenal Toledo 15   14001 Córdoba
Tel. 47 86 39   Fax 47 86 39
AYALA HERNANDEZ, Gerardo [1940, grad. 1968]
Bretón de los Herreros 66   28003 Madrid
Tel. 441 75 58   Fax 399 17 63
AYMERICH AMADIOS, Manuel [1919, grad. 1946, † 1982]
AZQUETA SANTIAGO, Alfonso [1959, grad. 1988]
See Aguinaga Churruca, Eugenio M. de

B BACH NUÑEZ, Jaume [1943, grad. 1970]
BACH-MORA, ARQUITECTES
Herzegovina 24   08006 Barcelona
Tel. 200 70 66   Fax 200 73 96
BADIA RODRIGUEZ, Jordi [1961, grad. 1989]
Aribau 119   08036 Barcelona   Tel. 454 96 07
BALIERO, Horacio
Buenos Aires, Argentina
BAR BOO, Xosé [1922, grad. 1957, † 1994]
BARBA CORSINI, Francisco Juan [1916, grad. 1945]
Pza. Eguilaz 10   08017 Barcelona
Tel. 204 42 06   Fax 417 85 06
BARRIONUEVO FERRER, Antonio [1947, grad. 1973]
Muñoz Olivé 2   41001 Seville
Tel. 422 23 41   Fax 421 05 09
BARRIONUEVO FERRER, Francisco [1943, grad. 1970]
Av. de la Constitución 34   41001 Seville
Tel. 421 48 78   Fax 421 91 42
BASAÑEZ BILLELABEITIA, Rufino de [1929, grad. 1956, † 1991]
BASSO BIRULÉS, Francesc [1921, grad. 1947]
BASTERRA BERASATEGUI, Diego [1883, † 1959]
BASTERRA ZARANDONA, Arantxa [1959, grad. 1986]
See Arantxa Basterra/Carles Llinas
BASTERRECHEA AGUIRRE, Jesús Rafael [1908, grad. 1934]
BASTIDA BILBAO, Ricardo de [1879, grad. 1902, † 1953]
BATLLE DURANY, Enric [1956, grad. 1980]
BATLLE Y ROIG, ARQUITECTOS
Provenza 355   08037 Barcelona
Tel. 457 98 84   Fax 457 12 07
BAU ARQUITECTOS
Pza. del Cordón 2   28005 Madrid
Tel. 542 15 69   Fax 542 87 08
BAYON ALVAREZ, Mariano [1942, grad. 1967]
Santa Engracia 19   28010 Madrid
Tel. 593 89 84   Fax 593 89 90
BELLMUNT I CHIVA, Jordi [1954, grad. 1979]
See Brú i Bistuer, Eduard
BELLOSILLO AMUNATEGUI, Francisco Javier [1948, grad. 1973]
Av. General Perón 22   28020 Madrid
Tel. 533 30 79   Fax 533 30 79
BELTRAN NAVARRO, José [1902, grad. 1930, † 1974]
BENITEZ CASTRO, Jorge [1949, grad. 1972]
See Asensio Peña/Benítez Castro
BENTO COMPANY, Carlos [1950, grad. 1973]
See Ferrater Lambarri, Carlos
BERGAMIN GUTIERREZ, Rafael [1891, grad. 1918, † 1970]
BESCOS DOMINGUEZ, Ramón [1936, grad. 1961, † 1993]
BIDAGOR LASARTE, Pedro [grad. 1931, † 1996]
BILBAO HOSPITALET, Tomás [1890, grad. 1918, † 1954]
BISQUERT SANCHEZ, Emilia [1937, grad. 1965, † 1984]
BLANCO-SOLER PEREZ, Luis [1894, grad. 1918, † 1988]
BLEIN ZARAGOZA, Gaspar [1902, grad. 1924, † 1975]
BLEIN ZARAGOZA, José [1904, grad. 1927, † 1975]
BLOND GONZALEZ, Alejandro [1915, grad. 1944]
See Estudio Cano Lasso

BOFILL LEVI, Ricardo [1939, grad. 1979]
Av. Industria 14   08960 Sant Just Desvern, Barcelona
Tel. 499 99 00   Fax 499 99 50
BOHIGAS GUARDIOLA, Oriol [1925, grad. 1951]
See MBM Arquitectes
BONA PUIG, Eusebi [1890, grad. 1915, † 1972]
BONELL I COSTA, Esteve [1942, grad. 1970]
Córcega 288   08008 Barcelona
Tel. 237 32 12   Fax 237 73 04
BONET BERTRAN, Pep [1941, grad. 1965]
Pujades 63   08005 Barcelona
Tel. 485 54 94
BONET CASTELLANA, Antoni [1913, grad. 1936, † 1989]
BORDES CABALLERO, Félix Juan [1939, grad. 1964]
León y Castillo 277   35005 Las Palmas de Gran Canaria
Tel. 23 36 77   Fax 23 40 92
BOROBIO OJEDA, José [1907, grad. 1931, † 1984]
BOROBIO OJEDA, Regino [1895, grad. 1920, † 1976]
BORSO DI CARMINATI, Cayetano [1900, grad. 1925, † 1972]
BOSCH GENOVER, Jordi [1949, grad. 1973]
BOSCH-TARRUS-VIVES, ARQUITECTES
Pelayo 48   08001 Barcelona
Tel. 301 63 74   Fax 301 61 50
BRAVO DURA, Carmen [grad. 1976]
BRAVO/MARTINEZ RAMOS, ARQUITECTOS
Arturo Soria 214   28033 Madrid
Tel. 359 74 06   Fax 350 68 84
BRAVO SANFELIU, Pascual [1893, grad. 1918, † 1984]
BRIONES, Ignacio, eng.
BRINGAS CAMINO, Manuel [1907, grad. 1941, † 1969]
BRONER, Erwin [1898, † 1971]
BRU I BISTUER, Eduard [1950, grad. 1975]
Herzegovina 27   08006 Barcelona
Tel. 414 10 33   Fax 414 13 45
BRUGAROLAS MARTINEZ, Carlos [1966, grad. 1989]
BRUGAROLAS/SOLA
Av. Río Segura 1   30002 Murcia
Tel. 21 54 56   Fax 21 54 56
BRULLET I TENAS, Manuel [1941, grad. 1966]
Av. Coll del Portell 52-54   08024 Barcelona
Tel. 210 53 01   Fax 284 88 18
BURGEE, John
See Philip Johnson Architects
BURILLO LAFARGA, Luis [1949, grad. 1976]
BURILLO/LORENZO
Travesía de Islas Cabo Verde 6   28035 Madrid
Tel. 373 72 82   Fax 373 72 82
BUSQUETS SINDREU, Xavier [1917, grad. 1947, † 1990]
BUSTO DELGADO, Manuel del [1874, grad. 1898, † 1948]
BUSTO GONZALEZ, Juan Manuel del [1905, grad. 1929, † 1967]
CABRERA, Antonio [1952, grad. 1977]   **C**
See González Cordón, Antonio
CABRERA DOMINGUEZ, Agustín [1954, grad. 1980]
CABRERA & FEBLES, ARQUITECTOS
Rafael Arocha Guillama 61   38008 Santa Cruz de
Tenerife   Tel. 20 58 06   Fax 20 58 06
CABRERO TORRES-QUEVEDO, Francisco [1912, grad. 1942]
CADARSO DEL PUEYO, Angel [1918, grad. 1946]
CALATRAVA VALLS, Santiago [grad. 1969, grad. eng. 1979]
Hoschagasse 5   8008 Zürich   Switzerland
Tel. 422 75 00   Fax 422 56 00
CALATAYUD CORRAL, Manuel [1920, grad. 1951, † 1992]
CAMPO BAEZA, Alberto [1946, grad. 1971]
Almirante 9   28004 Madrid
Tel./Fax 521 70 61

CAMPO DIAZ, Miguel Angel [1949, grad. 1974]
See Ercilla/Campo
CAMPOMANES, R.
See Estudio Cano Lasso
CAMPOS DE MICHELENA, Pascuala [1939, grad. 1967]
See Portela Fernández-Jardón, César
CANALIS HERNANDEZ, Oscar [1957, grad. 1982]
Morey 4   07001 Palma de Mallorca
Tel. 72 44 05   Fax 72 44 05
CANDELA OUTERIÑO, Félix [1910, grad. 1935, † 1997]
6341 Wynbrook Way   Raleigh, NC 27612   US
Tel. (919) 848 33 03   Fax (919) 676 24 98
CANO/COLOMER
Av. Marqués de Sotelo 1   46002 Valencia
Tel. 351 76 59   Fax 394 18 33
CANO DOMINGUEZ, Alfonso [1963, grad. 1988]
See Cano Pintos/Cosín/Fariña
CANO LASSO, Julio [1920, grad. 1949, † 1996]
See Estudio Cano Lasso
CANO PINTOS, Alfonso [1960, grad. 1986]
CANO PINTOS/COSIN/FARIÑA
Argensola 19   28004 Madrid
Tel. 308 06 82   Fax 308 06 82
CANO PINTOS, Diego [1954, grad. 1978]
See Estudio Cano Lasso
CANO PINTOS, Gonzalo [1956, grad. 1985]
See Estudio Cano Lasso
CANOVAS, ELENA [1963, grad. 1992]
See San Martín/Ortíz
CANTALLOPS VALERI, Lluis [1942, grad. 1968]
Dalmases 41-43   08017 Barcelona
Tel. 212 18 12   Fax 212 18 12
CAÑAS DEL RIO, Ramón [1901, grad. 1929, † 1971]
CAPELLA CALLIS, Juan [1935, grad. 1962]
See Sota, Alejandro de la
CAPITEL, Antón [1947, grad. 1971]
CAPITEL/ARBEROLA/MILLAN/MARTORELL
García de Paredes 38   28010 Madrid
Tel./Fax 593 07 68
CARBAJAL NAVARRO, José Antonio [1942, grad. 1968]
Salado 3   41010 Seville
Tel. 427 80 57
CARBONELL MESSEGUER, Enrique [1950, grad. 1976]
See Martínez Gadea, Vicente
CARDENAS PASTOR, Ignacio de [1898, grad. 1924, † 1979]
CARDENAS PASTOR, Manuel de [1877, † 1954]
CARIDAD MATEO, José [1900, grad. 1931]
CARLOS FERNANDEZ CASADO
Grijalba 9   28006 Madrid
Tel. 561 58 49   Fax 563 01 01
e-mail: ccasado@lander.es
CARMEL GRADOLI - ARTURO SANZ
Convento de Santa Clara 6   46002 Valencia
Tel. 394 20 78   Fax 351 21 64
CARRASCAL CALLE, Fernando [1948, grad. 1977]
CARRASCAL/FERNANDEZ
Paseo de Colón 19   41001 Seville
Tel. 422 57 59   Fax 456 09 34
CARRASCO LOPEZ, Rodolfo [1954, grad. 1982]
Donoso Cortés 17 A   06002 Badajoz
Tel. 22 46 82   Fax 22 47 48
CARRASCO MUÑOZ, Jesús [1900, grad. 1930]
CARVAJAL FERRER, Francisco Javier [1926, grad. 1953]
Goya 7   28001 Madrid
Tel. 575 64 07   Fax 576 05 24
CASARES AVILA, Alfonso [1942, grad. 1967]

CASARES AVILA Y RUIZ YEBENES
Jorge Juan 7   28001 Madrid
Tel. 577 06 63   Fax 576 97 35
CASARIEGO CORDOBA, Juan [1958, grad. 1983]
See Alas Casariego Arquitectos
CASARIEGO CORDOBA, María [1956, grad. 1981]
See Vellés Arquitectos
CASARIEGO HERNANDEZ-VAQUERO, Pedro [1927, grad. 1953]
See Alas Casariego Arquitectos
CASARIEGO TERREROS, Pedro [1890, grad. 1916, † 1958]
CASAS GOMEZ, Ignacio de las [1947, grad. 1971]
See Casas Gómez, Manuel de las
CASAS GOMEZ, Manuel de las [1940, grad. 1964]
Arturo Soria 214   28033 Madrid
Tel. 359 84 95   Fax 359 84 95
CASAS LLOMPART, Francisco [1905, grad. 1929, † 1977]
CASTILLO MORENO, Miguel [1906, grad. 1933, † 1988]
CATA CATA, Enric
CATON SANTAREN, José Luis [1948, grad. 1971]
Pza. de la Provincia 5   01001 Vitoria
Tel. 18 18 18   Fax 18 17 54
CENDOYA BUSQUETS, Modesto [grad. 1885, †]
CENICACELAYA, Javier [1951, grad. 1975]
CENICACELAYA & IÑIGO SALOÑA ARQUITECTOS
General Concha 8   48008 Bilbao
Tel. 444 74 32   Fax 444 74 31
CENTELLAS SOLER, Miguel [1956, grad. 1980]
Virgen del Mar 6   04738 Vícar (Almería)
Tel. 34 21 95
CHACON, José Manuel [1963, grad. 1990]
See Brugarolas/Sola
CHUECA EDO, Rafael, eng. [1942, grad. 1965]
See José Antonio Torroja Oficina Técnica
CHURRUCA DOTRES, Ricard [1900, grad. 1926, † 1963]
CIRICI I ALOMAR, Cristián [1941, grad. 1965]
Pujades 63   08005 Barcelona   Tel. 485 47 52
CLOTET BALLUS, Lluis [1941, grad. 1965]
CLOTET I PARICIO, ASSOC.
Pujades 63   08005 Barcelona
Tel. 485 36 25   Fax 309 05 67
CODERCH DE SENTMENAT, José A. [1913, grad. 1940, † 1984]
COLL PUJOL, Rafael [1943, grad. 1970]
Teodora Lamadrid 43   08022 Barcelona
Tel. 434 05 00
COLOMER SENDRA, Vicente [1948, grad. 1974]
See Cano/Colomer
CORBI, Camilo [1965, grad. 1990]
See Brugarolas/Sola
CORDOVA, Carmen
Buenos Aires, Argentina
CORELLA ARROQUIA, Jorge [1960, grad. 1986]
See Cano Pintos/Cosín/Fariña
CORONA BOSCH, Antonio [1954, grad. 1983]
See N. Tres Arquitectos
CORRALES GUTIERREZ, José A. [1921, grad. 1949]
Bretón de los Herreros 57   28003 Madrid
Tel. 442 37 43   Fax 399 06 23
CORREA RUIZ, Federico [1924, grad. 1953]
CORREA-MILA, S.C. - ARQUITECTOS
Pza. San Jaime 2   08002 Barcelona
Tel. 317 80 62   Fax 412 22 17
CORT BOTI, César [1893, grad. 1916, † 1978]
COSIN ZURRIARAIN, Eduardo [1957, grad. 1989]
See Cano Pintos/Cosín/Fariña
CRAFFORD, Clive
See Peña Ganchegui, Luis

CRUZ/ORTIZ
Santas Patronas 36   41001 Seville
Tel. 422 16 74   Fax 456 16 89
CRUZ VILLALON, Antonio [1948, grad. 1971]
See Cruz/Ortiz
CUADRA E IRIZAR, Fernando de la [1904, grad. 1928]
CUADRA RODRIGUEZ, Gerardo [1926, grad. 1953]
República Argentina 9   26002 Logroño
Tel. 24 61 78   Fax
DAROCA BRUÑO, Francisco [1950, grad. 1978]
See Estudio El Brillante
D DELGADO BRACKENBURY, José, eng. [1873, †]
DIAZ GOMEZ, Carles M. [1946, grad. 1969]
See Tusquets • Díaz & Assoc.
DIAZ-LLANOS, Javier [1935, grad. 1960]
DIAZ-LLANOS/SAAVEDRA ARQUITECTOS
Valentín Sanz 4   38003 Santa Cruz de Tenerife
Tel. 24 69 42   Fax 24 18 95
DIAZ LOPEZ, José [1960, grad. 1986]
See Estudio El Brillante
DIAZ RECASENS, Gonzalo [1947, grad. 1972]
Ciudad de Ronda 8   41004 Seville
Tel./Fax 442 16 96
DIEGO LLACA, Andrés [1955, grad. 1982]
Hermanos Pidal 24   35005 Oviedo
Tel. 25 48 93   Fax 21 92 58
DIEZ VAZQUEZ, Pilar, artist [1945, grad. 1975]
See Noguerol+Díez
DOLS MORELL, Heliodoro [1933, grad. 1960]
Menéndez y Pidal 5   50009 Zaragoza
Tel./Fax 976 35 71 48
DOMENECH GUIRBAU, Lluis [1940, grad. 1964]
See Amadó/Domènech Arquitectes
DOMENECH ROURA, Pedro [1881, † 1962]
DOMINGO SANTOS, Juan [1961, grad. 1986]
Recogidas 3   18005 Granada
Tel. 25 55 50
DOMINGUEZ ANADON, José Angel [1944, grad. 1968]
See Artengo Rufino/Domínguez Anadón, Arquitectos
DOMINGUEZ ESTEBAN, Martín [1897, grad. 1922,
† 1970]
DONATO FOLCH, Emili [1934, grad. 1960]
Pedró de la Creu 48   08034 Barcelona
Tel. 203 44 39   Fax 280 10 13
DURAN NIETO, Victoria [grad. 1981]
See Torres Martínez, Francisco
DURAN REYNALS, Raimon [1897, grad. 1926, † 1996]
E ECED ECED, Vicente [1923, grad. 1955, † 1994]
ECHAIDE ITARTE, Rafael [1902, grad. 1927, † 1978]
ENCIO CORTAZAR, Juan Manuel [1928, grad. 1955]
See Peña Ganchegui, Luis
ERBINA ARREGUI, José [1930, grad. 1961]
See Fernández Alba, Antonio
ERCILLA ABAITUA, Roberto [1950, grad. 1976]
ERCILLA/CAMPO
Pza. de España 13   01001 Vitoria
Tel. 23 10 60   Fax 14 75 25
ESCRAGNOLLE FILHO, Luis Alfonso d'
ESPIAU MUÑOZ, José [1894, grad. 1907, † 1938]
ESTUDIO CANO LASSO
Guecho 27, La Florida 28023 Madrid
Tel. /Fax 307 70 73
ESTUDIO EL BRILLANTE
Av. del Brillante 43   14012 Córdoba
Tel. 27 29 02
EUSA RAZQUIN, Víctor [1894, grad. 1920, † 1990]

FARGAS I FALP, Josep María [1926, grad. 1952]   **F**
FARGAS ASS.
Muntaner 477   08021 Barcelona
Tel. 417 90 07   Fax 417 68 05
FARIÑA MARTINEZ, Francisco [1961, grad. 1987]
See Cano Pintos/Cosín/Fariña
FEBLES BENITEZ, María Nieves [1957, grad. 1981]
See Cabrera & Febles Arquitectos
FEDUCHI, Javier [1929, grad. 1959]
Valenzuela 7   28014 Madrid
Tel. 532 99 21   Fax 531 55 08
FEDUCHI CANOSA, Pedro [1959, grad. 1985]
See Capitel/Arberola/Millán/Martorell
FERNANDEZ ALBA, Angel [1943, grad. 1970]
Hilarión Eslava 49 28015 Madrid
Tel. 544 26 29   Fax 544 25 90
FERNANDEZ ALBA, Antonio [1927, grad. 1957]
Hilarión Eslava 49 28015 Madrid
Tel./Fax 543 32 35
FERNANDEZ-ALBALAT LOIS, Andrés [1924, grad. 1956]
Príncipe 4   15001 A Coruña
Tel./Fax 20 86 44
FERNANDEZ BALBUENA, Gustavo [1888, grad. 1913, † 1931]
FERNANDEZ CASADO, Carlos. eng. [1905, grad. 1924, † 1988]
See Carlos Fernández Casado
FERNANDEZ DE CASTRO, Manuel [1945, grad. 1972]
See Díaz Recaséns, Gonzalo
FERNANDEZ DEL AMO, José Luis [1914, grad. 1942, † 1995]
FERNANDEZ MARTINEZ, Luis [1948, grad. 1976]
FERNANDEZ MARTINEZ/PASTOR RODRIGUEZ
Arapiles 15   04001 Almería
Tel. 23 58 99   Fax 26 62 17
FERNANDEZ ORDOÑEZ, José Antonio, eng. [1933, grad. 1959]
See IDEAM
FERNANDEZ DE LA PUENTE IRIGOYEN, José M. [1947, grad. 1977]
See Carrascal/Fernández
FERNANDEZ-SHAW ITURRALDE, Casto [1896, grad. 1919,
† 1978]
FERNANDEZ TROYANO, Leonardo, eng. [1938, grad. 1963]
See Carlos Fernández Casado
FERNANDO NANCLARES/NIEVES RUIZ ARQUITECTES
Principado 8   33007 Oviedo
Tel. 521 16 71   Fax 522 95 24
FERRAN ALFARO, Carlos [1934, grad. 1960]
Av. de Portugal 57 28011 Madrid
Tel. 479 83 14   Fax 470 21 25
FERRATER LAMBARRI, Carlos [1944, grad. 1971]
Bertrán 67   08023 Barcelona
Tel. 212 04 66   Fax 212 04 66
FERRERO Y LLUSIA, Francisco J. [1891, grad. 1917, † 1936]
FERRERO Y LLUSIA, Luis [1893, grad. 1917, † 1992]
FIGUEROA ALONSO MARTINEZ, Eduardo [1899, grad. 1923,
† 1984]
FISAC SERNA, Miguel [1913, grad. 1942]
Cerro del Aire s/n   28050 Madrid
Tel. 302 48 81   Fax 302 48 81
FLORENSA FERRER, Adolfo [1889, grad. 1914, † 1969]
FLOREZ URDAPILLETA, Antonio [1877, grad. 1904, † 1941]
FOLGUERA GRASSI, Francesc [1891, grad. 1917, † 1960]
FONTAN SAENZ, Rafael [1898, grad. 1925, † 1986]
FOREIGN OFFICE ARCHITECTS
58 Belgrave Road   London SWIV 2BP
Tel. (0171) 976 59 88   Fax (0171) 630 97 54
e-mail: foa@easynegrad.co.uk
FOSTER, Norman [1935, grad. 1960]
See Norman Foster & Partners

FRAILE OCHARAN, María [1960, grad. 1983]
FRAILE/REVILLO ARQUITECTOS
Gran Vía 1   28013 Madrid   Tel./Fax 522 56 66
FRANCO LA HOZ, Luis [1952, grad. 1976]
FRANCO/PEMAN
Pza. de Santa Cruz 13-15   50003 Zaragoza
Tel. 976 39 57 71   Fax 976 20 10 93
FRANCO LOPEZ, Julián [1955, grad. 1979]
FRANCO/PALAO ASOCIADOS
Saturnino Calleja 16   28002 Madrid
Tel. 519 55 61   Fax 519 43 27
FRECHILLA CAMOIRAS, Javier [1949, grad. 1972]
FRECHILLA & LOPEZ PELAEZ ARQUITECTOS
Gabriel Lobo 6   28002 Madrid
Tel. 562 59 27   Fax 562 10 03
FULLAONDO Y ERRAZU, Juan D. [1936, grad. 1961, † 1994]
FUSES COMALADA, Josep [1954, grad. 1977]
FUSES-VIADER/ARQUITECTES
Bonaventura Carreras Peralta 5   17004 Girona
Tel. 21 74 58   Fax 21 74 58

G GALARRAGA ALDAONDO, Iñaki [1944, grad. 1969]
See Peña Ganchegui, Luis
GALI CAMPRUBI, Elisabeth [1950, grad. 1982]
Rambla dels Caputxins 74   08002 Barcelona
Tel. 412 68 78   Fax 412 64 57
GALINDEZ ZABALA, Manuel I. [1892, grad. 1918, † 1980]
GALLEGO JORRETO, Manuel [1936, grad. 1963]
Piñeiro Pose 2   15006 A Coruña
Tel. 28 20 80   Fax 28 30 75
GALLEGOS BORGES, Gabriel [1956, grad. 1980]
See J.C. Sanz y Gallegos
GALMÉS NADAL, Andrés [1880, grad. 1920, † 1970]
GALNARES SAGASTIZABAL, José [1904, grad. 1932, † 1977]
GARAY ORMAZABAL, Miguel [1936, grad. 1970]
Villa Bide-ertz, Aldapeta 74   20009 San Sebastián
Tel. 46 10 53   Fax 46 10 53
GARCÉS BRUSES, Jordi [1945, grad. 1970]
Boquería 10   08002 Barcelona
Tel. 317 31 88   Fax 317 31 88
GARCIA BARBA, Federico [1953, grad. 1977]
San Fernando 6   38001 Santa Cruz de Tenerife
Tel. 28 40 25   Fax 29 38 53
GARCIA-BARBON, Lorenzo [1906, grad. 1944]
GARCIA DE PAREDES FALLA, Angela [1958, grad. 1982]
See García Pedrosa/García de Paredes
GARCIA DE PAREDES BARREDA, José M. [1924, grad. 1950, † 1990]
GARCIA GARCIA Francisco Javier [1947, grad. 1973]
GARCIA GARCIA/LEON PABLO ARQUITECTOS
Bretón de los Herreros 33   26001 Logroño
Tel. 20 82 58   Fax 20 82 60
GARCIA LOMAS, Miguel [1912, † 1976]
GARCIA MARQUEZ, Purificación [1959, grad. 1986]
See García/Rubiño/Rubiño Arquitectos
GARCIA MERCADAL, Fernando [1896, grad. 1921, † 1985]
GARCIA/RUBIÑO/RUBIÑO ARQUITECTOS
Imagen 4   41003 Seville
Tel. 421 81 69   Fax 421 81 69
GARCIA PEDROSA, Ignacio [1957, grad. 1983]
GARCIA PEDROSA/GARCIA DE PAREDES
Bretón de los Herreros 55   28003 Madrid
Tel. 441 72 15   Fax 442 60 96
GARCIA SOGO, Lourdes [1959, grad. 1989]
See Meri Cucart, Carlos
GARCIA-SOLERA, Juan A. [1929, grad. 1953]
Av. Ramón y Cajal 3   03001 Alicante
Tel. 521 86 44   Fax 521 86 44

GARCIA-SOLERA VERA, Javier [1958, grad. 1984]
San Ildefonso 4   03001 Alicante
Tel. 5219678   Fax 5219678
GARCIA VAZQUEZ, Carlos [1961, grad. 1987]
See González Cordón, Antonio
GARRIGUES DIAZ-CAÑABATE, Mariano [1902, grad. 1928, † 1994]
GEEST, Uwe [1941, grad. 1966]
See Donato Folch, Emili
GEHRY, Frank O. [1929]
1520 B Cloverfield Blvd.   Santa Monica, CA 90404   US
Tel. (310) 828 60 88   Fax (310) 828 20 98
GIL GONZALEZ, Francisco [1905, grad. 1962]
GIL GUITART, Josep María [1950, grad. 1978]
See Bonell i Costa, Esteve
GILI MOROS, Joaquim [1916, grad. 1947, † 1984]
GIMÉNEZ JULIAN, Emilio [grad. 1963]
See Salvadores Navarro, Carlos
GIMÉNEZ LACAL, José F. [1876, †]
GIRALDEZ DAVILA, Guillermo [1925, grad. 1951]
Ronda General Mitre 139   08022 Barcelona
Tel. 417 85 06   Fax 417 85 06
GODAY I CASALS, Josep [1882, grad. 1905, † 1936]
GOMEZ ESTERN, Luis [1909, grad. 1934, † 1979]
GOMEZ-FERRER BAYO, Alvaro [1939, grad. 1965]
See Portaceli Roig, Manuel
GOMEZ-GONZALEZ G. DE LAS BUELGAS, Juan [1922, grad. 1947]
See Estudio Cano Lasso
GONZALEZ ALVAREZ-OSSORIO, Aníbal [1876, grad. 1902, † 1929]
GONZALEZ CORDON, Antonio [1950, grad. 1975]
San Vicente 60   41002 Seville
Tel. 438 20 02   Fax 438 18 47
GONZALEZ EDO, José Joaquín [1894, grad. 1919]
GONZALEZ GALLEGOS, José [1958, grad. 1983]
See Aranguren Gallegos Arquitectos
GONZALEZ GARCIA, María Luisa [1953, grad. 1978]
Triana 67   33002 Las Palmas de Gran Canaria
Tel./Fax 36 34 62   e-mail: mgg@servercda.ul gc.es
GONZALEZ MORIYON, Juan [1952, grad. 1978]
See Fernando Nanclares/Nieves Ruiz Arquitectos
GONZALEZ PEREZ, Primitivo [1951, grad. 1978]
Teresa Gil 18   47002 Valladolid
Tel. 21 18 84   Fax 27 37 82
GONZALEZ VILLAR, Rafael [1887, grad. 1910, † 1941]
GRADOLI I MARTINEZ, Carmel [1961, grad. 1986]
See Carmel Gradoli - Arturo Sanz
GRASSI, Giorgio [1935, grad. 1960]
Via Leopardi 19   20123 Milan   Italy
Tel. 498 19 14   Fax 498 19 14
GREGORIO, Joaquin [1945, grad. 1971]
See Portaceli Roig, Manuel
GRUPO MONARK
Temporary association: Juha Jääskeläinen, Juha Kaakko,
Petri Rouhiainen, Matti Sanaksenaho, Jari Tirkkonen
GRUPO PER
See different entries for Clotet, Tusquets, Bonet, Cirici
GUIBERNAU ZABALA, Joan [1963, grad. 1991]
See Ferrater Lambarri, Carlos
GUIMON EGUIGUREN, Pedro [grad. 1902, †]
GUINEA Y ORTIZ DE URBINA, Pedro, eng. [1923, grad. 1950]
GUTIERREZ HERREROS, Virgilio [1958, grad. 1982]
See Sosa Díaz-Saavedra, José A.
GUTIERREZ SOTO, Luis [1900, grad. 1923, † 1977]
HENRIQUEZ HERNANDEZ, Rubéns [1925, grad. 1950]   **H**
Suárez Guerra 40   38002 Santa Cruz de Tenerife
Tel. 24 19 96   Fax 24 19 97

HERNANDEZ MINGUILLON, Rufino J. [1958, grad. 1982]
See Alonso, Hernández & Asociados
HERNANDEZ SANDE, Enrique [1957, grad. 1981]
HERNANDEZ SANDE, Manuel [1954, grad. 1981]
HERNANDEZ SANDE Y PEREA ARQUITECTOS
Instituto 16   33201 Gijón
Tel. 535 01 86   Fax 535 01 86
HERRERA CARDENETE, Emilio [1951, grad. 1976]
See Soler Márquez, Rafael
HERRERO AYLLON, Alejandro [1911, grad. 1940, † 1977]
HERRERO GARCIA, Luis Francisco [1957, grad. 1986]
See Carmel Gradolí - Arturo Sanz
HERREROS GUERRA, Juan [1958, grad. 1985]
See Abalos/Herreros
HIGUERAS DIAZ, Fernando [1930, grad. 1959]
Av. de América 14   28028 Madrid
Tel. 355 16 71   Fax 725 63 63
HUBMAN, Erich [grad. 1988]
HUBMAN/VASS
Viktorgasse 22/2   1040 Vienna   Austria
Tel. 504 58 28   Fax 503 43 09

I

IDEAM
Hermosilla 59   28001 Madrid
Tel. 435 83 80   Fax 576 31 62
IGLESIAS MARTI, Luis [1926, grad. 1956]
IGLESIAS PICAZO, Pedro [1958, grad. 19826]
See Tuñón Alvarez, Emilio
ILLESCAS MIROSA, Sixto [1903, grad. 1928, † 1986]
IMAZ ARRIETA, Hilario [grad. 1923, † 1968]
INZA CAMPOS, Francisco de [1929, grad. 1959, † 1978]
IÑIGUEZ DE ONZOÑO Y ANGULO, Félix [1927, grad. 1951]
See Iñiguez de Onzoño, José L.
IÑIGUEZ DE ONZOÑO Y ANGULO, José L. [1927, grad. 1957]
Serrano 112   28006 Madrid
Tel./Fax 564 51 18
IÑIGUEZ DE VILLANUEVA, Manuel [1948, grad. 1972]
ISOZAKI, Arata [1931, grad. 1954]
9-6-7 Akasaka, Minato-ku   Tokyo 107   Japan
Tel. 05 15 26   Fax 75 52 65
ISPIZUA SUSUNAGA, Pedro [1895, grad. 1920, † 1976]

J

J.C. SANZ Y GALLEGOS
Curtidores 1A   47006 Valladolid
Tel./Fax 34 06 95
JÄÄSKELÄINEN, Juha
See Grupo Monark
JARAMILLO ESTEBAN, Angel [1939, grad. 1965]
See Torres Martínez, Francisco
JEAN-PAUL VIGUIER S.A. D'ARCHITECTURE
16 rue du Champ de l'Alouette   75013 Paris   France
Tel. (01) 44 08 62 00   Fax (01) 44 08 62 02
http ://www.planet.fr/viguier
JIMENEZ TORRECILLAS, Antonio [1962, grad. 1988]
See Domingo Santos, Juan
JODRY, Jean François
See Jean-Paul Viguier s.a. d'architecture
JOHNSON, Philip
See Philip Johnson Architects
JOSE ANTONIO TORROJA OFICINA TECNICA
Príncipe de Vergara 103   28006 Madrid
Tel. 564 24 12   Fax 561 43 41
JOYA CASTRO, Rafael de la [1921, grad. 1950]
Av. Osa Mayor 32   28023 Aravaca (Madrid)
Tel. 307 10 40   Fax 307 10 42
JUAN-ARACIL SEGURA, José, eng. [1905, grad. 1930, † 1982]
JUAREZ RODRIGUEZ, Agustín [1939, grad. 1964]
See Bordes Caballero, Félix

JUJOL, Josep María [1879, grad. 1906, † 1949]
JULIA I CAPDEVILA, Josep María [1954, grad. 1965]
Mallorca 184   08036 Barcelona   Tel. 453 33 61
JUNCOSA IGLESIAS, Enrique [1902, grad. 1928, † 1975]
JUNQUERA GARCIA DEL DIESTRO, Jerónimo [1943, grad. 1969]
JUNQUERA/PÉREZ PITA ARQUITECTOS
Saturnino Calleja16   28002 Madrid
Tel. 413 63 93   Fax 415 50 51

K

KAAKKO, Juha
See Grupo Monark
KEVIN ROCHE, JOHN DINKELOO & ASS.
20 Davis Street   Hamden, CT 06517-0127   US
Tel. (203) 777 72 51   Fax (203) 776 22 99

L

LABAYEN TOLEDO, Joaquín [1900, grad. 1927, † 1996]
LACASA NAVARRO, Luis [1899, grad. 1921, † 1966]
LACIANA GARCIA, Angel 1905, grad. 1928, † 1985]
LA HOZ ARDERIUS, Rafael de [1924, grad. 1950]
Paseo de la Castellana 82   28046 Madrid
Tel. 563 65 44   Fax 561 78 03
LAMELA MARTINEZ, Antonio [1926, grad. 1954]
O'Donnell 34   28009 Madrid
Tel. 574 36 00   Fax 574 44 79
LANGLE RUBIO, Guillermo [1895, grad. 1921, † 1981]
LAORGA GUTIERREZ, Luis [1919, grad. 1954, † 1990]
LARREA BASTERRA, Julián María de [1925, grad. 1957]
Gran Vía 15   48001 Bilbao
Tel. 415 84 00   Fax 415 84 00
LASAOSA, María José [1954, grad. 1977]
See Torres Martínez, Francisco
LASTRA MERIANO, Deogracias de la [grad. 1918, †]
LEACHE RESANO, Jesús [1962, grad. 1987]
Gorriti 34   31003 Pamplona
Tel./Fax 24 83 53
LEON PABLO, José Miguel [1947, grad. 1974]
See García García/León Pablo Arquitectos
LEONHARDT, Fritz, eng. [1909, grad. 1931]
LEONHARDT, ANDRAE UND PARTNER
Lenzhalde 16   70192 Stuttgart   Germany
Tel. 711 2 50 60   Fax 711 250 62 00
LEON Y DIAZ CAPILLA, José Luis de [grad. 1925]
LERDO DE TEJADA, José María [1952, grad. 1978]
See González Cordón, Antonio
LIBANO PÉREZ-ULIBARRI, Alvaro [1921, grad. 1952]
Rodríguez Arias 9   48008 Bilbao
Tel. 443 43 50   Fax 444 82 48
LINAZASORO RODRIGUEZ, José Ignacio [1947, grad. 1972]
Lagasca 126   28006 Madrid
Tel. 561 63 97   Fax 561 63 97
LLINAS CARMONA, Carles [1957, grad. 1987]
See Arantxa Basterra/Carles Llinás
LLINAS CARMONA, Josep A. [1945, grad. 1969]
Av. República Argentina 62   08023 Barcelona
Tel. 212 37 14   Fax 417 65 69
LLORET HOMS, Joaquim [1890, grad. 1915, † 1988]
LOPEZ ALVAREZ, Jorge [1954, grad. 1978]
Donoso Cortes 17   06002 Badajoz
Tel. 22 46 82   Fax 22 47 48
LOPEZ COTELO, Víctor [1947, grad. 1969]
Pasaje Doña Carlota 8   28002 Madrid
Tel. 519 53 30   Fax 519 53 33
LOPEZ DELGADO, Felipe [1902, grad. 1928, † 1981]
LOPEZ GONSALVEZ, Miguel [1907, grad. 1931, † 1976]
LOPEZ IÑIGO, Pedro [1926, grad. 1951, † 1997]
LOPEZ OTERO, Modesto [1885, grad. 1910, † 1962]
LOPEZ-PELAEZ MORALES, José Manuel [1945, grad. 1970]
See Frechilla & Lopez Peláez Arquitectos

LOPEZ SARDA, María Luisa [1948, grad. 1973]
See Vellés Arquitectos
LOPEZ ZANON, José [1925, grad. 1954]
Pirineos 45   28020 Madrid
LORENZO GARCIA, Ricardo [1927, grad. 1953, † 1989]
LORENZO SAIZ-CALLEJA, Jaime [1949, grad. 1976]
See Burillo/Lorenzo
LUPIAÑEZ GELY, Gabriel [1900, grad. 1927, † 1942]

M M. DEL REY AYNAT/I. MAGRO DE ORBE, ARQUITECTOS
Maestro Clave 3   46002 Valencia
Tel./Fax 351 97 80
M. IÑIGUEZ/A. USTARROZ ARQUITECTOS
Zapatería 54   31001 Pamplona
Tel./Fax 22 15 20
MACKAY, David [1933, grad. 1956]
See MBM Arquitectes
MADRIDEJOS, Sol [1958, grad. 1983]
See BAU Arquitectos
MAGRO DE ORBE, Iñigo [1950, grad. 1975]
See M. del Rey Aynat/I. Magro de Orbe, Arquitectos
MANGADA SAMAIN, Eduardo [1932, grad. 1959]
See Ferrán Alfaro, Carlos
MANGADO BELLOQUI, Francisco J. [1957, grad. 1981]
Vuelta del Castillo 5   31007 Pamplona
Tel. 27 62 02   Fax 17 65 05
MANRIQUE, César, artist [1919, grad. 1950, † 1992]
MANSILLA+TUÑON ARQUITECTOS
Ríos Rosas 11   28003 Madrid
Tel. /Fax 399 30 67
e-mail: circo@arch-mag.com
MANTEROLA ARMISÉN, Javier, eng. [1936, grad. 1962]
See Carlos Fernández Casado
MAP ARCHITECTS
Paseo de Gracia 108   08008 Barcelona
Tel. 218 63 58   Fax 218 52 92
e-mail: map.ars@coac.es
MAPELLI CAFFARENA, Luis [1943, grad. 1970]
See Vellés Arquitectos
MARI MARTIN, Jesús [grad. 1927]
MARIN DE LA VIÑA, Mariano [grad. 1923]
MARIN DE TERAN, Luis [1936, grad. 1962]
Hombre de Piedra 22   41002 Seville
Tel. 437 50 08   Fax 490 44 59
MAROTO, Javier [1958, grad. 1981]
See Soto/Maroto
MARQUET ARTOLA, Javier [1935, grad. 1964]
See Moneo Vallés, Rafael
MARRERO REGALADO, José E. [1897, grad. 1926, † 1956]
MARSA PRAT, Antonio [grad. 1925, † 1983]
MARTIN ESCANCIANO, Miguel
See Estudio Cano Lasso
MARTIN FERNANDEZ DE LA TORRE, Miguel [1894, grad. 1920,
† 1980]
MARTIN GIL, Francisco, eng. [1896, grad. 1912, † 1933]
MARTIN MARTIN, Eduardo [1955, grad. 1980]
MARTIN MARTIN, Luis Javier [1957, grad. 1983]
MARTIN/MARTIN/RUIZ
Mesones 37   18001 Granada
Tel./Fax 26 54 69
MARTIN MENIS, Fernando [1952, grad. 1978]
See AMP Arquitectos
MARTIN SANCHEZ, Sigifredo [1948, grad. 1975]
Gorriti 39   31003 Pamplona
Tel. 23 47 33   Fax 23 47 46
MARTIN VELASCO, Miguel [1950, grad. 1975]
See M. del Rey/I. Magro, Arquitectos

MARTINEZ ARTOLA, Pedro L., eng. [1899, grad. 1926, † 1966]
MARTINEZ CALZON, Julio, eng. [1938, grad. 1962]
MC - 2 Estudio de Ingeniería
Víctor de la Serna 21   28016 Madrid
Tel. 413 38 02   Fax 519 74 72
MARTINEZ DELGADO, José A. [1950, grad. 1981]
See Soler Márquez, Rafael
MARTINEZ DURBAN, Jesús [1946, grad. 1971, † 1989]
MARTINEZ-FEDUCHI BENLLIURE, Javier [1929, grad. 1959]
See Feduchi, Javier
MARTINEZ-FEDUCHI RUIZ, Luis [1901, grad. 1927, † 1975]
MARTINEZ GADEA, Vicente [1948, grad. 1975]
La Paz 17   30150 La Alberca (Murcia)
Tel./Fax 84 28 05
MARTINEZ GARCIA, Eustaquio [1955, grad. 1981]
See N. Tres Arquitectos
MARTINEZ GARCIA-ORDOÑEZ, Fernando [1922, grad. 1953]
Colón 82   46004 Valencia
Tel./Fax 352 04 62
MARTINEZ GUTIÉRREZ, J.
MARTINEZ LAPEÑA, José A. [1941, grad. 1968]
MARTINEZ LAPEÑA & TORRES TUR, ARQUITECTOS
Roca y Batlle 14   08023 Barcelona
Tel. 212 14 16   Fax 418 65 44
MARTINEZ RAMOS, Jaime [1942, grad. 1969]
See Bravo/Martínez Ramos, Arquitectos
MARTINEZ SANTA-MARIA, Luis [1960, grad. 1985]
La Unión 1   28013 Madrid
Tel. 559 20 73
MARTINEZ PARICIO, Pelayo [1898, † 1985]
MARTORELL AROCA, Consuelo [1955, grad. 1983]
See Capitel/Arberola/Millán/Martorell
MARTORELL, BOHIGAS, MACKAY
See MBM Arquitectes
MARTORELL CODINA, Josep María [1925, grad. 1951]
See MBM Arquitectes
MARZAL, Ignacio, eng.
MAS GUINDAL, Antonio [1950, grad. 1973]
See Estudio Cano Lasso
MATEO MARTINEZ, Josep Lluis [1949, grad. 1974]
See Map Architects
MBM ARQUITECTES
Plaça Reial 18   08002 Barcelona
Tel. 317 00 61   Fax 317 72 66
e-mail: mbmarq@bcn.servicom.es
MEDINA BENJUMEA, Felipe [1910, grad. 1934]
MEDINA BENJUMEA, Rodrigo [1909, grad. 1934, † 1979]
MEIER Richard
See Richard Meier & Partners Architects
MENDEZ GONZALEZ, Diego [1906, grad. 1932]
MENENDEZ FERNANDEZ, Jesús [1957, grad. 1984]
See Fernando Nanclares/Nieves Ruiz
MERI CUCART, Carlos Joaquín [1957, grad. 1982]
Duque de Calabria 17   46005 Valencia
Tel. 333 27 11   Fax 333 27 11
MIAS GIFRE, Josep [1966]
See Miralles Moya, Enric
MIES VAN DER ROHE, Ludwig [1886, † 1969]
MIGUEL ARBONES, Eduardo de [1959, grad. 1983]
General Sanmartín 7 46004 Valencia
Tel./Fax 394 13 63
MIGUEL GONZALEZ, Carlos de [1904, grad. 1934, † 1986]
MIGUEL RODRIGUEZ, José Luis de [1944, grad. 1969]
See Vellés Arquitectos
MILÁ SAGNIER, Alfonso [1924, grad. 1952]
See Correa-Milà, S.C. - Arquitectos

MILLANES MATO, Francisco, eng. [1951, grad. 1973]
See IDEAM
MINGO PINACHO, Gerardo [1952, grad. 1974]
MIQUEL SUAREZ-INCLAN, Luis [1929, grad. 1957]
Infantas 21   28004 Madrid
Tel. 521 70 34
MIR VALLS, Jorge [1929, grad. † 1957, 1993]
MIRALLES MOYA, Enric [1955, grad. 1978]
Pasaje de la Paz, 10 bis   08002 Barcelona
Tel. 412 53 42   Fax 412 37 18
MIRO VALVERDE, Antonio [1930, grad. 1959]
See Higueras Díaz, Fernando
MITJANS MIRO, Francesc [1909, grad. 1940]
MOLINA SERRANO, Juan Antonio [1944, grad. 1969]
Pza. Santa Catalina 6   30004 Murcia
Tel. 21 46 90   Fax 22 08 11
MOLINER SALINAS, Jordi [1957, grad. 1982]
See Map Architects
MOLINI ULIBARRI, Luis, eng. [1845, grad. 1871, † 1933]
MONEO VALLÉS, José Rafael [1937, grad. 1961]
Cinca 5   28002 Madrid
Tel. 564 22 57   Fax 563 52 17
e-mail: cinca5@genio.infor.es
MONRAVA LOPEZ, José María [grad. 1929]
MORA BERENGUER, Francisco de [1898]
MORA GRAMUNT, Gabriel [1941, grad. 1966]
See Bach-Mora, Arquitectes
MORAGAS I GALLISSÀ, Antoni [1913, † 1985]
MORENO BARBERA, Fernando [1913, grad. 1940]
Serrano 169   28002 Madrid
Tel. 853 05 95   Fax 853 97 03
MORENO GARCIA-MANSILLA, Luis [1959, grad. 1983]
See Mansilla+Tuñón Arquitectos
MORENO PASCUAL, Miguel [1947, grad. 1977]
See Martínez Gadea, Vicente
MORENO PERALTA, Salvador [1947, grad. 1972]
Av. Andalucía 27   29006 Málaga
Tel. 234 03 70   Fax 231 99 32
MOSHER, Robert [c. 1900, †]
MOUSSAVI, Fassid [1965]
See Foreign Office Architects, Ltd.
MOYA BLANCO, Luis [1904, grad. 1927, † 1990]
MOZAS LÉRIDA, Javier [1956, grad. 1982]
General Alava 15   01005 Vitoria
Tel. 13 36 09   Fax 13 49 01
MUGURUZA OTAÑO, Pedro [1893, grad. 1916, † 1952]
MUÑOZ MOLINA, Ricardo [1957, grad. 1986]
See Estudio El Brillante
MUÑOZ MONASTERIO, Manuel [1904, grad. 1928,
† 1969]

N N. TRES ARQUITECTOS, S. L.
San Juan Bautista 4   38002 Santa Cruz de Tenerife
Tel. 24 18 06   Fax 24 73 25
NADAL I OLLER, Lluís [1929, grad. 1957]
Rosellón 188   08008 Barcelona
Tel. 453 60 40
NANCLARES FERNANDEZ, Fernando [1947, grad. 1971]
See Fernando Nanclares/Nieves Ruiz Arquitectes
NEBOT TORRENTS, Francesc [1883, grad. 1909, † 1965]
NAVARRO BALDEWEG, Juan [1939, grad. 1965]
Oria 13   28002 Madrid
Tel. 562 68 01   Fax 562 16 51
NIETO Y NIETO, Enrique [1883, grad. 1909, † 1954]
NOEL, Martín S. [1888, † 1963]
NOGUEROL DEL RIO, Alberto [1943, grad. 1974]
See Alberto Noguerol + Pilar Díez

NORMAN FOSTER & PARTNERS
Riverside Three, 22 Hester Road
London SW11 4AN   Great Britain
Tel. (0171) 738 04 55   Fax (0171) 738 11 07
ONTAÑON CABRERA, Guillermo, eng. [1941, grad. 1965]   **O**
INTECSA   Orense 70   28020 Madrid
Tel. 583 29 86   Fax 583 22 11
OPPEL, Richard Ernst [1888, grad. 1918, † 1910]
ORIOL E YBARRA, Miguel de [1933, grad. 1959]
Campomanes 3   28013 Madrid
Tel. 542 75 98   Fax 541 36 97
ORTEGA VIDAL, Javier [1952, grad. 1976]
See Rodríguez de Partearroyo, Francisco, see Capitel
ORTIZ ALBA, Manuel [1961, grad. 1993]
See San Martín/Ortiz
ORTIZ-ECHAGÜE RUBIO, César [1927, grad. 1952]
Diego de León 14   28006 Madrid
Tel. 563 41 42
ORTIZ GARCIA, Antonio [1947, grad. 1974]
See Cruz/Ortiz
OTAMENDI MACHIMBARRENA, Joaquín [1874, grad. 1910, †
1960]
OTAMENDI MACHIMBARRENA, Julián [1899, grad. 1916, † 1966]
OTERO GONZALEZ, Rafael [1952, grad. 1979]
Veedor 10   11003 Cádiz   Tel. 22 32 42
Fax 22 12 89   e-mail: rotero@arconegrad.es   **P**
PALACIOS DIAZ, Dolores [1960, grad. 1987]
See Soriano & Asociados, Arquitectos
PALACIOS RAMILO, Antonio [1874, grad. 1900, † 1945]
PALAO NUÑEZ, José M. [1956, grad. 1982]
See Franco/Palao Asociados
PARICIO ANSUATEGUI, Ignacio [1944, grad. 1969]
See Clotet, Paricio & Assoc., S. L.
PASTOR RODRIGUEZ, Luis [1948, grad. 1975]
See Fernández Martínez/Pastor Rodríguez
PAYA BENEDITO, Alfredo [1961, grad. 1988]
San Ildefonso 4   03001 Alicante
Tel./Fax 521 96 78
PECOURT BETÉS, Enrique [1903, grad. 1930, † 1982]
PEMAN GAVIN, Mariano [1952, grad. 1977]
See Franco/Pemán
PENELA FERNANDEZ, Alfonso [1952, grad. 1980]
Pza. Constitución 3   36202 Vigo (Pontevedra)
Tel. 22 53 71   Fax 43 79 00
PEÑA GANCHEGUI, Luis [1926, grad. 1959]
Av. Alcalde Elósegui 209   20015 San Sebastián
Tel. 27 51 07   Fax 27 51 11
PERDIGO NARDIZ, Ricardo [1942, grad. 1966]
See Arquitectura Perdigo/Rodríguez
PEREA CAVEDA, Enrique [1946, grad. 1971]
See Hernández Sande y Perea Arquitectos
PEREA ORTEGA, Andrés [1940]
Pintor Ribera 22   28016 Madrid
Tel. 413 69 84   Fax 519 36 02
PEREZ AMARAL, Arsenio [1958, grad. 1982]
See N. Tres Arquitectos
PEREZ ARROYO, Salvador [1945, grad. 1973]
Pza. de la Constitución 9   28200 San Lorenzo de
El Escorial (Madrid)   Tel. 896 13 45   Fax 896 14 70
PEREZ CARASA, José María [1889, grad. 1913, † 1962]
PEREZ ESCOLANO, Víctor [1945, grad. 1971]
Abad Gordillo 6   41002 Seville
Tel. 456 00 80   Fax 490 60 13
PEREZ JOVE, Pau [1947, grad. 1972]
Ctra. de Salou 68   43205 Reus (Tarragona)
Tel. 77 23 28

PEREZ LATORRE, José Manuel [1947, grad. 1979]
Paseo María Agustín 39   50004 Zaragoza
Tel. 976 23 67 78   Fax 976 23 99 64
PEREZ PIÑERO, Emilio [1935, grad. 1962, † 1972]
PEREZ PITA, Estanislao [1943, grad. 1969]
See Junquera/Pérez Pita Arquitectos
PEREZ ROLLANO, Antonio Diego [1947, grad. 1976]
Paseo Almería 45   04001 Almería
Tel. 26 47 48   Fax 27 03 13
PERPIÑA SEBRIA, Antonio [1918, grad. 1948, † 1995]
PHILIP JOHNSON ARCHITECTS
375 Park Avenue   New York, NY 10022-4834   US
Tel. (212) 319 58 80   Fax (212) 319 58 81
PICARDO CASTELLON, José Luis [1919, grad. 1950]
Carbonero y Sol 14   28003 Madrid
Tel. 561 69 54
PINEDA ALVAREZ, Albert de [1953, grad. 1980]
Travessera de Dalt 93   08024 Barcelona
Tel. 265 19 66   Fax 231 27 00
PINOS DESPLAT, Carme [1954, grad. 1980]
Av. Diagonal 490   08006 Barcelona
Tel. 416 03 72   Fax 415 37 19
PIÑON PALLARES, Helio [1942, grad. 1966]
See Viaplana/Piñón Arquitectos
PIQUERAS COTOLI, Manuel [1888, † 1963]
PORTACELI ROIG, Manuel [1942, grad. 1971]
Gran Vía Marqués del Turia 44   46005 Valencia
Tel. 395 64 55   Fax 395 55 68
PORTELA FERNANDEZ-JARDON, César [1937, grad. 1967]
García Camba 8   36001 Pontevedra
Tel. 85 89 16   Fax 86 02 43
POSADA RODRIGUEZ, Fabriciano [1954, grad. 1982]
See Vellés Arquitectos
POZO SERRANO, Aurelio del [1942, grad. 1970]
Tomás de Ybarra 32   41001 Seville
Tel./Fax 456 17 65
POZO SORO, Félix [1952, grad. 1975]
POZO SORO/TORRES GALAN
Tetuán 19   41001 Seville
Tel./Fax 422 53 52
PRIETO FERNANDEZ, Julián [1953, grad. 1979]
Donoso Cortes 17   06002 Badajoz
Tel. 22 46 82   Fax 22 47 48
PRIETO-MORENO PARDO, Francisco [1907 grad. 1931, † 1985]
PUENTE FERNANDEZ, Carlos [1944, grad. 1973]
Fernández de la Hoz 62   28010 Madrid
Tel./Fax 442 77 16
PUIG ANDREU, Ramón María [1940, grad. 1964]
See Domènech Girbau, Lluis
PUIG I GAIRALT, Antoni [1888, grad. 1918, † 1935]
PUIG TORNE, José [1929, grad. 1957]
Av. Sarriá 52-54   08029 Barcelona
Tel. 322 74 12   Fax 439 91 49
PUJOL NIUBO, Antoni [1942, grad. 1966]
See Arquitectura Pérdigo/Rodríguez
PUJOL I SEVIL, Antoni [1902, grad. 1927]
Q   QUADRA SALCEDO Y GAYARRE, Estanislao de la
See Moneo Vallés, Rafael
R   RAHOLA AGUADE, Victor [1945, grad. 1973]
Gran Vía 700   08010 Barcelona
Tel. 265 10 17   Fax 265 38 29
RAMOS ABENGOZAR, José A. [1958, grad. 1982]
See Vicéns/Ramos, Arquitectos
RAVENTOS FERRARONS, Ramón [1892, grad. 1917, † 1976]
REBOLLO DICENTA, José [1914, grad. 1942]
REBOLLO PUIG, Angel [1951, grad. 1976]

REBOLLO PUIG, Gabriel [1947, grad. 1972]
Carbonell y Morán 3   14001 Córdoba
Tel./Fax 47 37 28
RECASENS MENDEZ QUEIPO DE LLANO, Luis [1916, † 1989]
REDON HUICI, Fernando [1929, grad. 1957]
Paseo Lurbeltzeta 19   31190 Cizur Menor (Navarre)
Tel./Fax 18 91 58
RELAÑO LAPUEBLA, José [1907, grad. 1934, † 1989]
RETES, Fernando de [1949, grad. 1975]
Trapería 19   30001 Murcia
Tel. 22 16 77   Fax 21 14 57
REVENTOS I ROVIRA, Manuel, eng. [1956, grad. 1982]
Calders 8   08003 Barcelona
Tel./Fax 268 32 05
REVILLO PINILLA, Javier [1959, grad. 1983]
See M. Fraile /J. Revillo, Arquitectos
REY AYNAT, Miguel del [1948, grad. 1974]
See M. del Rey Aynat/I. Magro de Orbe, Arquitectos
REY PEDREIRA, Santiago [1902, grad. 1928, † 1959]
RIBAS CASAS, José María [1899, † 1978]
RIBAS I PIERA, Manuel [1925, grad. 1950]
Rambla de Cataluña 11   08007 Barcelona
Tel. 301 76 75   Fax 318 67 95
RICHARD MEIER & PARTNERS ARCHITECTS
475 Tenth Avenue   New York, N.Y. 10018   US
Tel. (212) 967 60 60   Fax (212) 967 32 07
RICO SANTAMARIA, Marcos [1908, grad. 1934, † 1995]
RIDRUEJO BRIEVA, Juan A. [1935, grad. 1959]
See Estudio Cano Lasso
RIUS BALAGUER, Teodoro [grad. 1913]
RIUS I CAMPS, Francesc [1941, grad. 1967]
Av. Coll del Portell 52   08024 Barcelona
Tel./Fax 210 36 51
RIVIERE GOMEZ, Antonio [1950, grad. 1977]
See Capitel/Arberola/Millán/Martorell
ROBLES JIMENEZ, Francisco
ROCHE, Kevin
See Kevin Roche, John Dinkeloo & Ass.
RODRIGO DALMAU, Jaume [1932, grad. 1959, † 1965]
RODRIGUEZ ARIAS, Germán [1902, grad. 1926, † 1987]
RODRIGUEZ FRADE, Juan Pablo [1957, grad. 1983]
Añastro 5   28037 Madrid
Tel./Fax 766 80 72
RODRIGUEZ COLL, Tomás [1943, grad. 1966]
See Arquitectura Pérdigo/Rodríguez
RODRIGUEZ DE PARTEARROYO, Francisco [1948, grad. 1970]
Génova 14   28004 Madrid
Tel. 319 60 70   Fax 308 46 96
e-mail: arquimat@ctv.es
RODRIGUEZ-NORIEGA, José Luis [1946, grad. 1972]
See Tuñón Alvarez, Emilio
RODRIGUEZ-PASTRANA MALAGON, José M. [1954, grad. 1977]
See AMP Arquitectos
ROIG DURAN, Joan [1954, grad. 1981]
See Batlle y Roig, Arquitectos
ROMANI, José
See Vellés Arquitectos
ROMANI VERDAGUER, Angel [1893, grad. 1920, † 1973]
ROMANY ARANDA, José Luis [1921, grad. 1950]
Av. de Portugal 53   28011 Madrid   Tel. 464 09 86
ROMERO AGUIRRE, José [1924, grad. 1954, † 1987]
ROMERO AGUIRRE, Manuel [1920, grad. 1947, † 1986]
ROS Y COSTA, Lorenzo [1890, grad. 1913, † 1989]
ROSER AMADO/LLUIS DOMENECH, ARQUITECTES
Aribau 152   08036 Barcelona
Tel. 218 23 08   Fax 218 64 16

ROSSI, Aldo [1935, † 1997]
ROUHIAINEN, Petri
See Grupo Monark
RUBIÑO CHACON, Ignacio [1957, grad. 1986]
See García/Rubiño/Rubiño Arquitectos
RUBIÑO CHACON, Luis [1959, grad. 1986]
See García/Rubiño/Rubiño Arquitectos
RUBIO CARVAJAL, Carlos [1950, grad. 1977]
See 3AC Estudio de Arquitectura
RUBIO I TUDURI, Nicolás María [1891, grad. 1916, † 1981]
RUISANCHEZ CAPELASTEGUI, Manuel [1957, grad. 1982]
RUISANCHEZ-VENDRELL, ARQUITECTES S.C.P.
Aribau 282-284   08006 Barcelona
Tel. 414 16 14   Fax 414 43 33
RUIZ CABRERO, Gabriel [1946, grad. 1971]
Felipe Campos 12   28002 Madrid
Tel. 561 68 81   Fax 563 75 08
RUIZ DE LA PRADA SANCHEZ, Juan Manuel [1929, grad. 1958]
José Abascal 50   28003 Madrid
Tel./Fax 399 50 69
RUIZ FUENTES, Raúl [1956, grad. 1983]
See Martín/Martín/Ruiz
RUIZ FERNANDEZ, Nieves [1947, grad. 1970]
See Fernando Nanclares/Nieves Ruiz, Arquitectos
RUIZ LARREA, César [1950, grad. 1976]
See 3AC Estudio de Arquitectura
RUIZ RUIZ, Jaime [1914, grad. 1943]
RUIZ YÉBENES, Reinaldo [1943, grad. 1968]
See Casares Avila y Ruiz Yebenes
S   SAAVEDRA MARTINEZ, Vicente [1937, grad. 1960]
See Díaz-Llanos/Saavedra Arquitectos
SAENZ DE OIZA, Francisco Javier [1918, grad. 1946]
General Arrando 11   28010 Madrid
Tel. /Fax 448 79 90
SAIZ HERES, Vidal [1901, grad. 1928, † 1967]
SALOÑA, Iñigo [1958, grad. 1981]
See Cenicacelaya & Iñigo Saloña Arquitectos
SALVADOR CARRERAS, Amós [1877, grad. 1902, † 1936]
SALVADORES NAVARRO, Carlos [1948, grad. 1975]
María Ros 50   46100 Burjassot (Valencia)
Tel. 390 36 99   Fax 390 36 98
SAN MARTIN GAVAS, Antonio [1958, grad. 1983]
SAN MARTIN/ORTIZ
Av. del Tibidabo 10   08022 Barcelona
Tel. 418 86 26   Fax 418 04 42
e-mail: ASMO@coac.es
SANABRIA BOIX, Ramón [1950, grad. 1973]
See Artigues & Sanabria, Arquitectos
SANAHUJA ROCHERA, Jaime [1957, grad. 1983]
See Ferrater Lambarri, Carlos
SANAKSENAHO, Matti
See Grupo Monark
SANCHEZ ARCAS, Manuel [1897, grad. 1920, † 1970]
SANCHEZ-CUENCA MARTINEZ, Felipe [1931, grad. 1960]
D'Alt Murada 2   07001 Palma de Mallorca
Tel./Fax 72 35 64   e-mail: szcuenca@arquired.es
SANCHEZ ESTEVE, Antonio [1897, grad. 1921, † 1977]
SANCHEZ LOPEZ, Eduardo [1948, grad. 1973]
See Frechilla & López Peláez Arquitectos
SANCHEZ PUCH, Daniel [1913, grad. 1940, †]
SANCHEZ DEL RIO, Ignacio, eng. [1898, grad. 1922, † 1980]
SANCHO OSINAGA, Juan Carlos [1957, grad. 1982]
See BAU Arquitectos
SANMARTI VERDAGUER, Jaime [1941, grad. 1964]
See Domènech Girbau, Lluis
SANTOS NICOLAS, Miguel de los [1896, grad. 1919, † 1991]

SANZ BLANCO, Juan Carlos [1953, grad. 1980]
See J.C. Sanz y Gallegos
SANZ MARTINEZ, Arturo [1963, grad. 1988]
See Carmel Gradolí - Arturo Sanz
SCHWARTZ PEREZ, Carlos [1942, grad. 1968]
See Artengo Rufino - Domínguez Anadón, Arquitectos
SEGUI PÉREZ, José [1946, grad. 1971]
Olmo 5, Cerrado de Calderón   29018 Málaga
Tel. 229 18 38   Fax 229 71 58
e-mail: jsegui@microcad.es
SERT LOPEZ, Josep Lluis [1902, grad. 1929, † 1983]
SESE MADRAZO, Luis [grad. 1985]
See Linazasoro Rodríguez, José Ignacio
SEIGNEUR, François
See Jean-Paul Viguier s.a. d'architecture
SIERRA DELGADO, José Ramón [1945, grad. 1972]
SIERRA DELGADO, Ricardo [1950, grad. 1975]
SIERRA/SIERRA
Monsalves 13   41001 Seville   Tel./Fax 422 76 74
SIERRA NAVA, Manuel [1923]
See Romany, see Sáenz de Oíza, see Vázquez de Castro
SIZA VIEIRA, Alvaro [1933]
Rua da Alegria 399-A   4000 Oporto   Portugal
Tel. 57 08 50   Fax 51 03 518
SOLA SANCHEZ, Francisco [1964, grad. 1989]
See Brugarolas/Sola
SOLA-MORALES DE ROSELLO, Manuel de [1910, grad. 1932]
SOLA-MORALES RUBIO, Ignasi de [1942, grad. 1966]
L'Avenir 1   08006 Barcelona
Tel. 414 37 14   Fax 414 62 29
SOLA MORALES RUBIO, Manuel de [1939, grad. 1963]
Santa Magdalena Sofía 5   08017 Barcelona
Tel 203 47 98   Fax 280 07 35
SOLA SUSPERREGUI, Bernardo de
Caspe 35   08010 Barcelona
Tel. 301 67 61   Fax 302 08 78
SOLER MARQUEZ, Rafael [1956, grad. 1980]
San Antón 73   18005 Granada
Tel. 26 76 02   Fax 26 77 73
SOLS LUCIA, Santiago [1945, grad. 1970]
Castellví 27   08190 Sant Cugat del Vallés (Barcelona)
Tel./Fax 589 42 50
SOMOLINOS CUESTA, Francisco [1908, grad. 1934]
SOMOZA ESCUDERO, Francisco [1962, grad. 1985]
See Vellés Arquitectos
SORIA BADIA, Enric [1937, grad. 1934]
Boquería 10   08002 Barcelona   Tel./Fax 317 31 88
SORIANO PELAEZ, Federico [1961, grad. 1986]
SORIANO & ASOCIADOS ARQUITECTOS
Lirios 13   28016 Madrid
Tel.7Fax 413 45 27   e-mail: fsorian@ibm.net
SOSA DIAZ-SAAVEDRA, José A. [1957, grad. 1980]
Sor Ana s/n   Monte Lentiscal 35310 Las Palmas de
Gran Canaria   Tel. 43 05 30   Fax 43 03 27
SOSTRES MALUQUER, Josep María [1915, grad. 1946, † 1984]
SOTA MARTINEZ, Alejandro de la [1913, grad.1941, † 1996]
SOTERAS MAURI, Josep [1907, † 1989]
SOTO, Alvaro [1958, grad. 1981]
SOTO/MAROTO
Barquillo 44   28004 Madrid
Tel. 308 55 43   Fax 308 33 94
e-mail: javier.maroto@mad.servicom.es
SUAREZ VALIDO, Fermín [1907, † 1969]
SUBIAS FAGES, Xavier [1926, grad. 1951]
Ronda del General Mitre 139   08022 Barcelona
Tel./Fax 417 85 06

SUBIRANA I SUBIRANA, Joan Bautista [1904, grad. 1930, † 1978]

SUNYER I VIVES, Antoni [1954, grad. 1979]
Jesús y María 31   08022 Barcelona
Tel./Fax 212 24 44

T TALAVERA Y HEREDIA, Juan [1880, grad. 1909, † 1960]

TAMÉS ALARCON, José [1905, grad. 1932]

TARRAGO I SALA, Gemma [1955, grad. 1979]
See Brú i Bistuer, Eduard

TARRUS GALTER, Joan [1945, grad. 1971]
See Bosch-Tarrús-Vives, Arquitectes

TENREIRO BROCHON, Antonio
See Fernández-Albalat Lois, Andrés

TENREIRO RODRIGUEZ, Antonio [1893, grad. 1919, † 1969]

TERESA, Enrique de [1940, grad. 1983]
See González Pérez, Primitivo

TESTOR GOMEZ, José Luis [1896, grad. 1922, † 1968]

TIRKKONEN, Jari
See Grupo Monark

TOBIAS PINTRE, Basilio [1954, grad. 1977]
Paseo de Ruiseñores 23   50006 Zaragoza
Tel. 976 38 73 10   Fax 976 38 73 97

TORBADO FRANCO, Juan [1900, grad. 1929]

TORO BUIZA, Alfonso [1909, grad. 1934, † 1979]

TORRES CLAVE, José María [1906, grad. 1929, † 1939]

TORRES GALAN, Alberto [1949, grad. 1975]
See Pozo Soro/Torres Galán

TORRES LOPEZ, Ramón de [1953, grad. 1979]
Pza. Doctor Gómez Campana 1   04002 Almería
Tel. 26 37 23

TORRES MARTINEZ, Francisco [1948, grad. 1972]
Ensenada 3   41003 Seville
Tel. 421 12 68   Fax 421 94 11

TORRES NADAL, José María [1947, grad. 1973]
Calderón de la Barca 5   30001 Murcia
Tel. 21 46 85   Fax 21 56 65

TORRES TUR, Elías [1944, grad. 1968]
See Martínez Lapeña & Torres Tur, Arquitectos

TORROJA CAVANILLAS, José Antonio, eng. [1933, grad. 1956]
See José Antonio Torroja Oficina Técnica

TORROJA MIRET, Eduardo, eng. [1899, grad. 1923, † 1961]

TOSCANO, A. M., eng.

TOUS I CARBO, Enric [1925, grad. 1953]
See Fargas Ass.

TRAVER Y TOMAS, Vicente [1889, grad. 1912, † 1970]

TRILLO DE LEYVA, Juan Luis [grad. 1971]
Lorenzo de Sepúlveda 8   41012 Seville
Tel. 461 36 09

TRILLO DE LEYVA, Manuel [grad. 1966]
Sor Gregoria Santa Teresa 10   41012 Seville
Tel. 461 42 97

TUÑON ALVAREZ, Emilio [1958, grad. 1981]
See Mansilla+Tuñón Arquitectos

TUSQUETS GUILLEN, Oscar [1941, grad. 1965]

TUSQUETS • DIAZ & ASSOC.
Cavallers 50   08034 Barcelona
Tel. 280 55 99   Fax 280 40 71

U UNZURRUNZAGA GOICOECHEA, Javier [1937, grad. 1964]
See Moneo Vallés, Rafael

URIARTE ALDAITURRIAGA, Luis María [1950, grad. 1980]
Goikoplaza 20   01400 Llodio (Alava)
Tel./Fax 672 54 47

URCOLA LAZCANOTEGUI, Francisco de [grad. 1899, †]

USTARROZ CALATAYUD, Alberto [grad. 1980]
See M. Iñiguez/A. Ustarroz Arquitectos

Jørn UTZON
Boessemagergade 77   31050 Hellebaex   Denmark
Tel. (45) 4970 97 05

VALDES RUIZ DE ASSIN, Alfonso [1944, grad. 1973]   **V**
See Vellés Arquitectos

VALLE, Agapito del [1895, grad. 1922, † 1969]

VALLEJO REAL DE ASUA, Luis [grad. 1926]

VALLEJO ALVAREZ, Antonio [1903, grad. 1927]

VALLS VERGES, Manuel [1912, grad. 1942]

VALVERDE ABRIL, Rafael [1960, grad. 1986]
See Estudio El Brillante

VAQUERO PALACIOS, Joaquín [1903, grad. 1928]

VASS, Andreas [grad. 1988]
See Hubman/Vass

VAZQUEZ DE CASTRO, Antonio [1929, grad. 1955]
Calle del Estudio 7   28023 Aravaca (Madrid)
Tel. 357 22 81   Fax 357 22 81

VAZQUEZ CONSUEGRA, Guillermo [1945, grad. 1972]
Laraña 6   41003 Seville
Tel. 421 35 90   Fax 421 96 73

VAZQUEZ MOLEZUN, Ramón [1922, grad. 1948, † 1994]

VEGA Y FERNANDEZ REGATILLO, Javier [1942, grad. 1970]
See Vellés Arquitectos

VELLES MONTOYA, Javier [1943, grad. 1971]

VELLES ARQUITECTOS
Génova 19   28004 Madrid   Tel. 310 10 21

VENDRELL SALA, Xavier [1955, grad. 1983]
See Ruisánchez-Vendrell, Arquitectes S.C.P.

VIADER MARTI, Joan M. [1953, grad. 1977]
See Fuses-Viader/Arquitectes

VIAPLANA VEA, Albert [1933, grad. 1966]

VIAPLANA/PIÑON ARQUITECTOS
Aribau 18   08006 Barcelona   Tel. 200 61 75

VICENS Y HUALDE, Ignacio [1950, grad. 1976]

VICENS • RAMOS, ARQUITECTOS
Barquillo 29   28004 Madrid
Tel. 521 00 04   Fax 521 65 50

VIDAL VIDAL, Vicente Manuel [1939, grad. 1973]
Balmes 11   03803 Alcoy (Alicante)   Tel./Fax 552 26 82

VIEDMA VIDAL, Enrique [1889, grad. 1915, †]

VIGUIER, Jean-Paul [1946, grad. 1970]
See Jean-Paul Viguier s.a. d'architecture

VILLAR LUENGO, José María de, eng. [1945, grad. 1969]
See José Antonio Torroja Oficina Técnica

VILORIA GARCIA, Antonio [1928, grad. 1958]
Alameda 6   28014 Madrid   Tel./Fax 420 07 16

VILLANUEVA SANDINO, Fernando [1943, grad. 1968, † 1992]

VIÑUELA RUEDA, Luis, eng. [1949, grad. 1974]
Corazón de María 62   28002 Madrid
Tel. 416 80 18

VIVANCO BERGAMIN, Luis Felipe [1907, grad. 1932, † 1975]

VIVES SANFELIU, Santiago [1948, grad. 1973]
See Bosch-Tarrús-Vives, Arquitectes

YARZA GARCIA, José [1907, grad. 1933, † 1995]   **Y**

YARNOZ LARROSA, José [1884, grad. 1910, † 1966]

YORDI DE CARRICARTE, Luciano J., eng. [1917, grad. 1946, † 1978]

ZABALO BALLARIN, Pedro [1891, grad. 1918, † 1961]   **Z**

ZAERA-POLO, Alejandro [1963]
See Foreign Office Architects Ltd.

ZUAZO UGALDE, Secundino [1887, grad. 1921, † 1970]

ZULAICA ARSUAGA, Luis María [1940, grad. 1964]
See Moneo Vallés, Rafael

3AC ESTUDIO DE ARQUITECTURA
Lagasca 21   28001 Madrid
Tel. 435 26 78   Fax 575 09 30

Apartment Building on Menéndez y Pelayo, 232
Apartment Building on Miguel Angel (1928), 231
Apartment Building on Miguel Angel (1936), 240:
    M 44, 261
Apartment Building on Muntaner (1930), 144: B 10
Apartment Building on Muntaner (1964), 156: B 42,
    158
Apartment Building on Nicaragua, 155: B 39
Apartment Building on Paseo de la Castellana, 250:
    M 74
Apartment Building on Paseo de la Habana, 266:
    M 121
Apartment Building on Paseo Pintor Rosales, 232
Apartment Building on Pedro de Valdivia, 247: M 64
Apartment Building on Príncipe de Vergara, 249:
    M 70
Apartment Building on Prior, 123: SA 1
Apartment Building on Puerto del Milagro, 276: M 154
Apartment Building on Pza. de Cristo Rey, 247: M 65
Apartment Building on Pza. de Salamanca, 247
Apartment Building on Pza. de San Miguel, 95
Apartment Building on Pza. del Instituto, 95: O 13
Apartment Building on Pza. Gregorio Marañón, 242:
    M 49
Apartment Building on Pza. Tirant lo Blanc, 173, 174:
    B 92
Apartment Building on Ripa, 311: BI 4
Apartment Building on Señores de Luzón, 262: M 110
Apartment Building on Tavern, 150: B 23
Apartment Building on the Old Bus Depot in Sarriá,
    36, 157: B 46
Apartment Building on Valderribas, 273: M 146
Apartment Building on Vara del Rey, 318: LR 2
Apartment Building on Via Augusta, 143: B 9
Apartment Building on Viriato , 225: M 5
Apartment Buildings in the Salamanca Neighbour-
    hood, 258: M 97
Apartment Buildings on Boix y Morer, 247: M 66
Apartment Buildings on Núñez de Balboa, 130: ZA 1
Apartments in Cerdanyola, 181: B 111, 186
Apartments in Guadalmina Baja, 61
Apartments in Nerja, 61
Apartments in Palomeras (Unit 15), 272: M 141
Apartments in Sant Feliú de Guixols, 191
Apostolic School of the Dominican Fathers, 128:
    VA 1, 245, 252, 278
Aqueduct over the River Najerilla, 32, 320: LR 8
Aragón Public Library, 89: Z 7
Aramo Building, 91
Arantzazu Basilica, 308: SS 14
Archery Pavilion, Vall d'Hebron, 171: B 86
Architects' Chamber of Catalonia, 153: B 31
Architects' Chamber of the Canary Islands, 114: TF 5
Architects' Chamber of Western Andalusia, 72: SE 19
Architects' Chambers of Catalonia, Delegation of
    Tarragona, 197
Arco de les Fosses Bridge, 192: GI 10
Argentina Pavilion, 1929 Exhibition, Seville, 65
Arquitecte Jujol State School, 164: B 70
Arriba Newspaper Building (Centre for Cadastral
    Management), 254: M 84, 258
Artistic Restoration Centre, 255: M 89
Arturo Estévez House, 220: PO 8
Astilleros Españoles Gantry Cranes, 49

Astoria Building, 145: B 13
Atalaya Building, 158
Atlantic Centre of Modern Art, 110: GC 11
Auditorium and Music Centre, Barcelona, 168: B 80
Auditorium, Conference and Exhibition Centre,
    Pontevedra, 218: PO 4
Auditorium, Murcia, 287: MU 3
Auditorium, Santiago de Compostela, 214
AVE Train station, Córdoba, 55
Avenida de Blasco Ibáñez, 326
Aviación y Comercio Building, 312: BI 8
AZCA Centre, 238, 239, 264, 266, 270
Azol-Gas Building, 301: VI 10
Bach de Roda-Felipe II Bridge, 166: B 74
Ballvé House, 192: GI 9
Banca Catalana Building, 156: B 43
Banco de Bilbao Building, 38, 264: M 116, 266
Banco de España, Girona, 190: GI 1
Banco de España, Jaén, 61: J 1
Banco de España, Santander, 117
Banco de Madrid, 258: M 95
Banco Hispano Americano, 313
Banco Pastor Head Offices, 210
Bank Building on Serrano, 266: M 120
Bankinter Building, 38, 223, 265: M 117,
Bar and Lecture Room, Law School, Barcelona, 151
Barceló Cinema, 231: M 22
Barcelona General Metropolitan Plan (1976), 139
Baró de Viver Housing Development, 167
Barraquer Clinic, 147: B 17
Barriada de la Plata, 52: CA 13
Barrios de Luna Bridge, 122: LE 3
Belén Garden Houses, 59
Belesar Dam Offices and Sluice Gate Outhouse, 216
Bernabeu Institute, 322
Besós Park, 185: B 129
Blanquerna School (Menéndez Pelayo Institute), 140
Bloc House Workers' Housing, 145: B 12
Block of Housing and Shops, 267: M 125, 268
Boarding School, 326: CS 3
Bodegas San Patricio Cellars, 55
Boenders House, 38, 104: IB 5
Bofarull House, 28, 198: TA 6
Borghetto Flaminio Complex, Rome, 341
Bowery for Excursion Services, 281: M 166
Brazil House, 251: M 80
Bridge over the River Aragón, 295: N 13
Bridge over the River Guadiana, 205
Bridge over the River Sella, 94: O 11
Bridges and Underground Station, 329: V 10
Bridges over the A-6 Motorway, 281: M 170
Broner House, 102: IB 1
Building on Av. Federico Soto, 322
Building on Av. L'Hospital Militar, 151
Building on Pza. de Compostela, 220
Building on Zamora, 120
Bus Station and Housing, Seville, 64, 69: SE 11
Bus Station, Almería, 47: AL 2
Bus Station, Granada, 59: GR 6
Bus Station, Huelva, 60: HU 1
Bus Station, Málaga, 61
Business School, Alicante, 323: A 7
Business School, Burgos, 121: BU 1, 122
Cabeza del Moro Housing Complex, 137: TO 9

Dalí Museum-Theatre and Geodesic Dome, 191
Dam across the River Eume, 34, 212: C 9
Dam in Belesar, 212, 216
David Chipperfield Summer House, 212
Davis Museum and Cultural Centre, Wellesley, 340
Department of Agriculture, Palencia, 122: PA 1
Department of Arts and Crafts, Sant Sadurní d'Anoia,
    188: B 138
Department of Biology, Oviedo, 94: O 8
Department of Computer and Mathematics, Las
    Palmas, 110
Department of Dentistry, Madrid, 229
Department of Economic Sciences and Library, Vigo,
    221: PO 10
Department of Economics, Bilbao, 313: BI 13
Department of Pharmacy, Madrid, 229
Department of Philology, Santiago de Compostela,
    214: C 15
Department of Philosophy, Madrid, 232: M 25, 234,
    236
Department of Physical Sciences, Chemistry and
    Mathematics, Madrid, 236: M 40
Department of Science, Seville, 38, 70: SE 16
Department of Social Sciences, Pamplona, 293:
    N 10
Diagonal-Carles III Underpass, 158: B 49
Diestre Factory, 88: Z 5
Display Greenhouses in the Royal Botanical Garden,
    275: M 150
Diversion of the River Guadalquivir, 32, 65, 76
Diversion of the River Turia, 326
Domínguez House, 219: PO 6
Domus Museum (Casa del Hombre), 211: C 8
Dr. Gómez House, 302: VI 11
Drago State School, 50
Duclós House, 64, 68: SE 9
Ebro Water Authority Building, 88: Z 3
Edificio España Building, 241
Eduard Fontseré State School (La Teixonera), 161:
    B 60
Eduardo Torroja Institute for Construction and
    Cement, 252
El Alamillo Bridge and Viaduct, 82: SE 44
El Almacén Cultural Centre, 112
El Batán Housing Estate, 246, 248: M 68
El Calero Neighbourhood Absorption Unit , 246
El Carmen Housing Complex, 319: LR 5
El Guincho Natural Pool, 113
El Guix de la Meda House, 193: GI 11
El Noticiero Universal Building, 156: B 40
El Paraguas Urban Canopy, Oviedo, 97
El Porvenir Housing Block, 71: SE 18
El Ralengo Settlement, 323, 324: A 11
El Rollo Abbey, 36, 124: SA 2, 127, 282
El Sardinero District, 117
El Termómetro Building, 92, 93: O 4
El Viso Residential Estate, 30, 107, 233, 235, 236,
    237: M 41, 245
Electrical Power Plant, Aboño, 97
Electrical Power Plant, Grandas de Salime, 34, 97:
    O 17
Electrical Power Plant, Miranda, 97
Electrical Power Plant, Proaza, 97
Electrical Power Plant, Tanes, 97

Enlargement and Renovation of the Maqueda Castle,
    136: TO 5
Entrevías Managed Settlement, 246, 249: M 73, 250
Equitativa Building, Bilbao, 311: BI 5, 313
Equitativa Building, San Sebastián, 304: SS 2
Erillas Neighbourhood Absorption Unit, 246
Escarrer House, 100: PM 5
Escorial Housing Estate, 151
Eslava Casino, 291
Espartero Health Centre, 320: LR 7
Espíritu Santo Chapel, 241: M 47, 263
Esquivel Settlement, 32, 63, 84: SE 55
Europa Cinema, 227: M 14
Euskalduna Conference Hall and Auditorium, 314,
    317: BI 19
EUTG University Complex, 306
Exhibition Casino, 65, 67: SE 5
Experimental Hyperbolic Paraboloid Umbrella, 336
Extension of the Town Hall, Ceuta, 201
Extension of the Town Hall and Layout of the
    Square, 288: MU 5
Extension to the Advanced Technical School of
    Architecture, Barcelona, 161: B 59
Extension to the Godo y Trías Factory, 182: B 115
Extension to the Law Courts, Zaragoza, 90: Z 10
Extension to the Picasso Museum, 162: B 64
F.C. Barcelona Stadium, 150: B 24
Fábregas Building, 147
Family House in Canyamars, 181: B 110
Family House in Esplugas de Llobregat, 182: B 114
Family House in Finca El Machacón, 137: TO 10
Family House in Las Rozas, 282: M 172
Family House in Puerta de Hierro, 272: M 142
Family House with Greenhouse, 322: A 3
Family Houses in Cabezo de Torres, 288: MU 6
Family Houses in La Alberca, 288: MU 7
Federico Mayo Group of Fishermen Houses, 60:
    HU 2
Fénix Español Building, 140
Fénix Hotel, 99: PM 2
Fierro House, 61
Fifteenth Century Pavilion, Expo'92, 77
Figaro Cinema, 229: M 19
Finca Roja Building, 327: V 1
Fine Arts Circle, 224: M 1
Fine Arts Section, Museum of Cáceres, 206: CC 3
Finland Pavilion, Expo'92 , 40, 77, 82: SE 46
Fitness Centre, 172
Follie No. 7, Osaka, 341
Fortuny Apartments and Swimming Pool, 186: B 131
Fossar de la Pedrera, 164: B 69
Four Apartment Buildings in Palomeras, 270: M 130
Four Apartment Buildings on Miguel Angel, 226: M 9
France Pavilion, Expo'92, 77, 82: SE 45
Francés House, 104
Frare Negre Residential Complex, 148: B 20
Frégoli I Building, 159: B 52
Fuencarral Managed Settlement, 246
Fullá Housing Block, 157: B 45
Galician Biological Centre, 217: PO 1
Galician Centre of Contemporary Art, 42, 215: C 16
Gallego House in O Carballo, 213: C 13
Gallego Summer House, 212
Galúa Hotel, 289: MU 10

UNED Library, Madrid, 274: M 148, 275
Unión Farmacéutica Guipuzcoana Factory, 307: SS 9
United States Embassy, Madrid, 244: M 57
Universidad Autónoma Train Station, Bellaterra, 166:
    B 72
Universidad Pública, Sadar, 293
University Campus, Madrid, 28, 228: M 16, 229, 234,
    235, 236, 237, 241, 245, 252
University Campus, San Sebastián, 306
University Campus, Tafira, 110: GC 12
University Campus, Valencia, 326
University Campus, Zaragoza, 88, 90
University Hostel in Sierra Nevada, 59
University Library, Las Palmas, 110
University Research Institutes, Santiago de
    Compostela, 216: C 19
Urban Block of Housing in Las Palmeras, 56: CO 5
Urban Planning of Las Palmas de Gran Canaria, 107:
    GC 4
Urban Solid Waste Incineration Plant, 197: TA 3
Uriach House, 183: B 118
Urumea Building, 304: SS 3
Usera Neighbourhood Absorption Unit, 246
Utzon House, 102: PM 10
Valle de los Caídos, 241
Vega House, 109: GC 7
Vegaviana Settlement, 34, 133, 206, 207: CC 5
Veracruz Religious Shrine, 32, 217: OR 2
Via Júlia, 164: B 68
Viaduct, Madrid, 233: M 30
Victoria Eugenia Tuberculosis Clinic, 231
Vilamarta Theatre, 55
Vilassar de Mar Schools, 188
Villa Kikumbera, 304, 317: Bl 20
Villa Molina, 209: C 1
Villa Pepita, 60
Villalba de Calatrava Settlement, 34, 133: CR 2, 207
Villaverde Managed Settlement, 246
Virgen de la Medalla Milagrosa Church, Mexico, 336
Virgen del Pilar Social Housing Complex (Phase 4),
    242: M 50
Vista Alegre Tower, 309: SS 15
Vizcaya Bank (Banco de Comercio), 231: M 23
Vocational Training Centre, Burlada, 293: N 11
Vocational Training Centre, Vitoria, 300: VI 4
Walden Building (Phase 1), 187: B 136
Wholesalers Market, Algeciras, 51: CA 9
Wind Energy Park, 48, 54: CA 21
Windsor Building, 266: M 122
Women's Hall of Residence, 233: M 28
World Trade Center, 77
Zamora Museum, 130: ZA 3
Zubizuri Footbridge, 314

ALPHABETICAL LIST OF PLACE NAMES

Cendoya, 57, see Catà et al.
Cenicacelaya/Saloña, 317: BI 21
Centellas, 47
Chacón, See Brugarolas et al.
Chipperfield, 212
Chueca [eng.], See Torroja Cavanillas [eng.] et al.
Churruca, 147: B 18
Cirici, See Solà-Morales, I. de/Ramos/Cirici, see Bonet
    Bertrán/Cirici
Cirici/Bonet Bertrán, 104
Clotet, SeeTusquets/Clotet 168
Clotet/Paricio, 59, 181: B 109, 190: GI 1
Clotet/Tusquets, 157: B 45, 181: B 111, 183: B 119,
    186: B 131, 338
Coderch, 18, 19, 24, 36, 101: PM 8, 103, 174, 249,
    138, 157: B 46, 158: B 48, 161: B 59,188, 191, 261
Coderch/Valls, 34, 118: S 5, 149: B 22, 260: M 104,
    152: B 29, 154: B 35, 157: B 44, 180: B 108,
    183: B 118, 189: B 140, 190, 192: GI 9, 194: GI 15,
    337, 338
Coll, See Yamasaki et al.
Colomer/Alcácer, 323
Colomina, 324
Committee for Devastated Regions 30, 55, 56,
    231
Conde, 25
Corbi, See Brugarolas et al.
Córdova, See Baliero et al.
Corea/Gallardo/Manino, 146
Corella, See Abarca et al.
Corona, See Martínez et al.
Corrales, 54: CA 19, 210, 317, 136: TO 4, 223, see
    Carvajal et al., 268, 280: M 162
Corrales/Sota. A. de la/Molezún, 283: M 176
Corrales/Molezún, 34, 42, 100: PM 3, 122: PA 2,
    210: C 4, 248: M 69, 259: M 99, 260: M 103,
    263: M 115, 289, 289: MU 10, 337
Corrales/Molezún/Cavero, 255: M 88
Correa, 40, see Buxadé et al.
Correa/Milà, 100, 182: B 114, 182: B 115, 191: GI 6
Correa/Milá/Sanz Magallón, 158
Cort y Botí, 231
Cosín, See Abarca et al.
Cruz/Ortiz, 40, 42, 46, 50: CA 4, 52: CA 10, 60,
    60: H 1, 64, 71: SE 17, 73, 74, 74: SE 27, 74,
    78: SE 34, 83: SE 51, 201, 274: M 147, 276
Cuadra, Gerardo, 316, 317, 320: LR 10
Cuadra e Irízar, 52: CA 13
Cuadra e Iríza/Torroja Cavanillas [eng.], 53: CA 14
Cubillo/Romany/Sáenz de Oíza/Sierra, 246
Cuenca, 55
Daroca/Díez/Muñoz/Valver, 56: CO 5
Delgado Brackenbury [eng.], 65
D´Escragnolle, 251: M 80
Díaz, See Tusquets & Díaz Asoc.
Díaz-Llanos/Saavedra, 105, 113, 114: TF 5,
    115: TF 12, 116: TF 13
Díaz Recaséns, 77: SE 30, 85: SE 58
Diego Llaca, 97: O 18
Díez, See Daroca et al.
Díez Vázquez, See Noguerol/Díez
Diz, 234
Dols, See Inza/Dols
Dols/Inza/Sols, 319: LR 5

Domènech i Guirbau, See Amadó/Domènech, 170,
    188, see Amadó et. al.
Domènech/Puig/Sanmartí, 195: LL 1
Domènech Roura, See Catà et al.
Domingo Santos/Jiménez Torrecillas, 59
Domínguez, M., See Aroca/Domínguez
Domínguez Anadón, See Artengo et al.
Domínguez Esteban, See Arniches/Domínguez, see
    Arniches/Domínguez/Torroja [eng.], 333
Domínguez Salazar, See Moya/Domínguez Salazar
Donato/Geest, 161: B 60
Durán Nieto, See Torres Martínez 73: SE 23
Durán Reynals, 147: B 16
Durán Reynals/Martínez Paricio, 141: B 5
Eced, See Martínez Feduchi/Eced
Echaide, See Ortiz Echagüe/Echaide
Echegaray/Barbero, 252
Encio, See Peña Ganchegui/Encio
Erbina, See Fernández Alba, Antonio/Erbina
Ercilla, See Catón et al.
Ercilla/Campo, 301: VI 8
Ercilla/Uriarte/Martín, E., 302: VI 13
Espiau Muñoz, 64, see Espiau/Urcola
Espiau/Urcola, 66: SE 3
Espinosa, See Higueras et al.
Estellés, See Tenreiro/Estellés
Eusa, 87, 291: N 1, 291: N 2, 291: N 3, 291, 292
Fargas/Tous, 156: B 43, 300: VI 3
Fariña, See Abarca et al.
Fathy, 99
Febles, See Cabrera Domínguez/Febles
Feduchi, 49: CA 3, see Baliero et al.
Fernández Alba, Angel, 101: PM 9, 122: PA 1,
    274: M 149, 338
Fernández Alba, Antonio, 36, 124: SA 2, 124:
    SA 3, 127, 223, 251: M 79, 259, 282: M 174,
    338
Fernández Alba, Antonio/Erbina, 301: VI 6
Fernández-Albalat, 208
Fernández-Albalat/Tenreiro Brochón, 209: C 3
Fernández Balbuena, 222, 226: M 9, 238
Fernández Casado/Fernández Troyano/Manterola
    [engs.], 294: N 12
Fernández Casado [eng.], 32, 264, 281: M 170, 320: LR 8
Fernández de Castro, See Díaz Recasens
Fernández de la Puente, See Carrascal/Fernández de
    la Puente
Fernández del Amo, 34, 63, 132: AB 1, 133: CR 2,
    207: CC 5, 256, 324: A 11, 324: A 12
Fernández Martínez/Pastor Rodríguez, 47
Fernández Ordóñez, See Martínez Calzón/Fernández
    Ordóñez
Fernández-Shaw, See Aguila/Fernández-Shaw, 205,
    222, 227: M 13, 232, see Muguruza/Fernández-
    Shaw
Fernández Troyano [eng.], See Manterola/Fernández
    Troyano [engs.], see Carlos Fernández Casado,
    S.L. et al., see Manterola et. al., see Fernández
    Casado et al.
Fernández Troyano/Manterola [engs.], Carlos
    Fernández Casado, S.L., 159: B 51
Ferrán, See Sáenz de Oíza et al.
Ferrán/Mangada/Romaní, 257: M 92
Ferrater, 162: B 62, 173, 193: GI 11, 193: GI 12

Higueras, 112, 1241
Higueras/Manrique, 111: LZ 1
Higueras/Mirò, 255: M 89, 279, 284: M 18
Higueras/Mirò/Cabrera/Espinosa/Weber, 246
Hollein, 276
Hubmann/Vass, 58: GR 4
Iberduero, Technical Department, Director: Martínez
    Artola [eng.], 126: SA 6
Iberduero, Technical Department, Guinea/Galíndez
    [engs.], 126: SA 7
Iglesias Martí, See Perpiñá et al.
Iglesias Picazo, See Tuñóñ et al.
Imaz, See Aguinaga/Imaz/Aguirre
Imaz/Aguirre/Blanc, 311
Instituto Nacional de Colonización, 63
Inza/Dols, 127: SG 2, see Dols et al.
Iñiguez/Ustarroz, 292: N 6
Iñiguez de Onzoño, Félix, See Iñiguez de Onzoño,
    José L.
Iñiguez de Onzoño, José L., 270: M 133, 314: BI 14
Iñiguez de Onzoño, J. L./Vázquez de Castro, 250:
    M 75, 257: M 93, 259: M 101, 262, 263: M 112
Iriarte/Brena/Múgica, 306
Isozaki, 41, 169: B 81, 170, 184: B 123
Isozaki/Portela, 211: C 8
Ispízua, 310: BI 2, 312: BI 7: BI 9
Izpízua/Arzadún, 312: BI 8
Jackson & Ass., See Sert/Jackson & Ass.
Jansen, See Zuazo/Jansen
Jaramillo, SeeTorres López et al.
Jiménez Torrecillas, See Domingo Santos/Jiménez
    Torrecillas
Jodry, See Viguier et al.
Johnson/Burgee, 39, 41, 276
Juan-Aracil, See Ferrero et al.
Juárez, See Bordes/Juárez
Jujol, 28, 140, 186: B 134, 187: B 135, 197: TA 4,
    198: TA 6: TA 7, 200: TA 13
Juliá i Capdevila, See Sola Susperregui/Julià i
    Capdevila
Juncosa, 99, see Sert et al.
Junquera/Pérez Pita, 59: GR 7, 61, 233, 267: M 123,
    270: M 130, 279: M 159, 282: M 173, 338
La Hoz, See García de Paredes/Hoz 46, 56: CO 3,
    56: CO 4, 338
Labayen, See Aizpurúa/Labayen
Laborde, M. [eng.]/Laborde, E. [eng.], 305
Lacasa, 23, 228, see Sánchez Arcas/Lacasa, 235: M 35
Lacasa/Sert, 30, 333
Laciana, 232
Laforet, see Martín Fernández de la Torre/Laforet
Lamela, 133: CR 1, 239, 249: M 70, 250: M 74
Langle Rubio, 46, 47: AL 1: AL 2
Laorga, 217
Laorga/López Zanón, 213: C 11, 251: M 77,
    257: M 94
Laorga/Sáenz de Oíza et al., 308: SS 14
Larrea, See Basáñez et al.
Lasaosa, See Torres López et al.
Lastra, 117, 117: S 1
Leache, See Miguel, E. de/Leache
Leache/Miguel E. de, 296
León/García, 319, 320: LR 7
León, J. L. de, 86

Leonhardt/Viñuela, 81: SE 43
Lerdo de Tejada, See Cabrera et al.
Líbano, See Fullaondo/Líbano
Linazasoro, See Garay/Linzasoro, 129: VA 3,
    274: M 148, 275: M 151, 276: M 153
Linazasoro/Sesé, 305: SS 6
Llinás, Carles, See Basterra et al.
Llinás, Josep, 141, 151, 167: B 77, 168, 176: B 99,
    185: B 127, 191: GI 5, 196, 197: TA 4, 200,
    200: TA 12, 338
Lloret Homs, 147: B 17
López, See Sota, A. de la/López
López Alvarez, See Carrasco López et al., 205: BA 7
López Cotelo/Puente, 89: Z 7, 124: SA 4, 277:
    M 156, 285: M 184, 338
López Delgado, 229: M 19
López Gonsálvez, 322: A 1
López Iñigo, See Giráldez et al.
López Otero, 28, 227: M 15, 228: M 16, 229, 236
López-Peláez, See Frechilla et al.
López Sallaberry, See Anasagasti/López Sallaberry,
    227: M 12
López Sardá, See Vellés/López Sardá
López Zanón, See Laorga/López Zanón
Lorenzo, See Burillo/Lorenzo
Lorenzo/Calatayud, 119
Luna, See Brullet/Luna
Lupiáñez, See Arévalo/Lupiáñez
MacKay, See MBM Arquitectos, see Martorell et al.
Madridejos/Sancho, 280: M 163
Magro/Martín/Rey Aynat, 323: A 5
Makovecz, 41, 77
Mangada, See Sáenz de Oíza et al., see Ferrán et al.,
    268, 275
Mangado/Apezteguía, 293
Mangado, See Mangado/Alzugaray, 295: N 14,
    296: N 19
Mangado/Alzugaray, 293
Manino, See Corea et al.
Manrique, 111, see Higueras/Manrique, 112
Manterola/Fernández Troyano [engs.], 38, 94: O 11,
    122: LE 3, see Carlos Fernández Casado et al.,
    317: BI 2
Manterola/Fernández Troyano [engs.], Carlos
    Fernández Casado, S.L., 266: M 119
Manterola, See Fernández Casado et al., see
    Fernández Troyano et al.
Mapelli/Miguel de/Romaní/Valdés/Vega/Vellés,
    267: M 125
Margarit, See Buxadé et al.
Marín de Terán/Pozo, A. del, 73: SE 24, 78: SE 31
Marín de Terán/Pozo, A. del/Haro, 72
Marín de la Viña, 91
Mariscal, 211
Maroto, See Soto/Maroto
Marquet, See Moneo et al.
Marrero, 105, 113, 113: TF 1: TF 2: TF 3, 114: TF 4,
    118: S 2
Marsá Prat, 231, 241
Martí, See García-Lomas/Martí
Martín, E., See Ercilla et al.
Martín, E./Martín, L. I./Ruiz, 59: GR 8
Martín Escanciano, See Cano Lasso et al.
Martín Fernández de la Torre, 30, 105, 106,

106: GC 1, 106: GC 2, 107: GC 4, 108,
   108: GC 6, 109: GC 8, 109: GC 9, 118
Martín Fernández de la Torre/Laforet, 108: GC 5
Martín Fernández de la Torre/Oppel, 106: GC 3,
   109: GC 7
Martín Gil/Villalba/Salazar/Torroja Miret [engs.],
   131: ZA 6
Martín Gómez, See Bayón et al.
Martín Menis, See AMP Arquitectos, S. L.
Martín Sánchez, See Apezteguía/Martín
Martín Velasco, See Magro et al.
Martínez Artola [eng.], See Iberdrola
Martínez Calzón/Fernández Ordóñez, 78: SE 32
Martínez del Valle/Yárnoz, 117
Martínez Durbán, 47
Martínez Feduchi, See Moya/Martínez Feduchi, 222
Martínez Feduchi/Eced, 232: M 24
Martínez Gadea, 288: MU 6
Martínez Gadea, See Alvarez/Carbonell et al.
Martínez Gadea/Retes, 289: MU 8
Martínez García, A., See Trillo, M./Trillo, J.L.
Martínez García-Ordoñez, 328: V 5
Martínez Gutiérrez, 68: SE 6
Martínez Lapeña/Torres Tur, 38, 40, 100: PM 5,
   103: IB 3, 103: IB 4, 104: IB 5, 173, 174: B 92,
   194: GI 17, 199: TA 8, 275: M 152, 338, 341
Martínez Paricio, See Durán Reynals/Martínez Paricio
Martínez/Pérez Amaral/Corona, 115: TF 9
Martínez Ramos, See Bravo Durá/Martínez Ramos
Martínez Santa-María, 110
Martorell, See MBM Arquitectes, see Bohigas/
   Martorell, see Alemany et al., see Capitel/
   Hernández/Martorell, see Capitel/Rivera/Martorell
Martorell, Consuelo, See Capitel et al.
Martorell/Bohigas/Mackay/Puigdòmenech, 172: B 89
Marzal [eng.], See Perpiñá et al.
Más, See Cano Lasso et al.
Mateo, 166: B 73, 194: GI 18, 338
Mateo/Moliner, 179: B 106
Mateos, See Soler et al.
MBM Arquitectes, 36, 77, 100: PM 5, 153: B 32,
   155: B 37, 159: B 53, 160: B 55, 162, 162: B 63,
   181: B 110, 189: B 142, 295: N 16, 325: CS 2, 338
Medina Benjumea, F. et al., 70: SE 15
Medina Benjumea, R., 46, 64, 69: SE 11
Medina Benjumea, R./Gómez Estern/Toro Buiza, 69:
   SE 13
Meier & Partners, 41, 168: B 79
Méndez, See Muguruza/Méndez
Menis, See AMP Arquitectos, S. L.
Meri/Gacía Sogo, 329: V 11
Mestres i Fosses, 140
Miás, See Miralles/Pinòs/Mías
Mies van der Rohe, 28, 29, 33, 35, 37, 125, 131, 142: B
   6, 154, 260, 334, 335
Miguel, Carlos de, See Perpiñá et al.
Miguel, Eduardo de/Leache, 293: N 9, see Leache/
   Miguel, E. de
Miguel, José L. de, See Mapelli et al.
Milà, See Correa et al., see Buxadé et al.
Mingo, 134: GU 1, 338
Miquel, See Aracil et al.
Miquel/Viloria, 259: M 100
Mir, See Yamasaki et al.

Miralles, 40, 163, 341
Miralles/Pinós, 25, 86: HU 1, 171: B 86, 173,
   179: B 105, 182: B 117, 189: B 141, 326: CS 3
Miralles/Pinòs/Miás, 323: A 4
Miró, See Higueras et al., see Higueras/Miró
Mitjans Miró, 148, see García-Barbón et al., see
   Alemany et al., 153: B 33
Mocoroa, 305
Molina Serrano, 288
Molezún, See Vázquez Molezún
Moliner, See Mateo/Moliner
Moliní [eng.], 65
Mondrilla, 65
Moneo, 25, 40, 42, 43, 46, 61: J 1, 74: SE 25,
   79: SE 36, 88: Z 5, 100: PM 6, 124, 125, 136,
   168: B 80, 197, 202, 203, 203: BA 4, 204: BA 5,
   319: LR 4, 223, 263, 266: M 121, 272: M 139,
   273: M 145, 279: M 158, 284, 288: MU 7, 296,
   306: SS 7, 338, 339, 340, 341
Moneo (team coordinator), 320: LR 6
Moneo/Bescós, 38, 265: M 117
Moneo/Quadra Salcedo, 292: N 5
Moneo/Marquet/Unzurrunzaga/Zulaica, 304: SS 3
Moneo/Solà-Morales, M. de, 42, 167: B 76
Monravá/Pujol Sevil, 197: TA 2
Montero, 302
Mora, See Bach/Mora
Moragas, 148: B 21, 151, 152, 178: B 103
Moreno, See Alvarez/Carbonell et al.
Moreno Barberá, See Cano Lasso/Moreno Barberá,
   273, 328: V 6, 330: V 13
Moreno Mansilla/Tuñón Alvarez, 130: ZA 3
Moreno Peralta, 61, 201
Mosher/Relaño, 62: MA 1
Moya, L., 32, 91, 96: O 16, 119: S 7, 124, 223,
   243: M 48, 243: M 52, 247: M 64, 256,
   263: M 113, 276
Moya, L./Moya, R./Ramírez, P., 130: ZA 2
Moya, L./Domínguez Salazar, 254: M 86
Moya, L./Martínez Feduchi, 241: M 48
Moya, R., See Moya, L. et al.
Mozas, 301: VI 10
Muelas, 269
Múgica, See Iriarte et al.
Muguruza, 225: M 8
Muguruza/Méndez, 241
Muguruza/Fernández-Shaw, 232: M 26
Muñoz, See Daroca et al.
Muñoz Monasterio/Alemany, 239
Nadal, 161: B 58
Nanclares/Ruiz Fernández, 94: O 9
Nanclares/Ruiz/González Moriyón, 91, 95: O 15
Navarro Baldeweg, 25, 26, 40, 42, 43, 104,
   110: GC 12, 119: S 6, 125: SA 5, 202, 203,
   205: BA 6, 271: M 135, 275: M 150, 285: M 185,
   287: MU 2, 338, 339, 340
Nemec/Stengel, 77
Nebot, 140: B 3
Nieto, 201
Noel, 65
Noguerol/Díez, 84: SE 53, 210, 212, 214: C 15,
   215: C 18, 219: PO 7
Ochoa [eng.], See Sert et al.
Oppel, See Martín Fernández de la Torre/Oppel, 118

Torres Martínez, See Barrionuevo/Torres Martínez, 59: GR 6, 68: SE 8, see Torres Martínez/Durán Nieto, 73: SE 23, 77
Torres Nadal, 287: MU 4, 288: MU 5
Torres Tur, 25, see Martínez Lapeña/Torres Tur
Torroja Cavanillas [eng.], See Cuadra e Irízar/Torroja Cavanillas [eng.]
Torroja Cavanillas/Chueca/Villar [engs.], 183: B 121
Torroja Miret [eng.], 32, 36, see Sánchez Arcas/ Torroja Miret [eng.], see Zuazo/Torroja Miret [eng.], see Santos, M. de los/Torroja Miret [eng.], see Arniches/Domínguez/Torroja Miret [eng.], 280: M 164, see Martín Gil et al., 284: M 180, 296: N 18
Toscano [eng.], 49: CA 2
Tous, See Fargas/Tous
Traver, 67: SE 5
Trillo, J. L., See Trillo, M. et al.
Trillo, M./Trillo, J L./Martínez, 72: SE 20, 73: SE 22
Tuñón Alvarez, See Moreno Mansilla/Tuñón Alvarez
Tuñón/Rodríguez-Noriega/Iglesias, 135: TO 1
Tusquets, See Clotet/Tusquets
Tusquets/Bassó, 168
Tusquets/Clotet, 161: B 57, 193: GI 13
Tusquets & Díaz Asoc., 110: GC 13, 163: B 66
Unzurrunzaga, See Moneo et al.
Urcola, See Espiau/Urcola
Uriarte, 301: VI 7, see Ercilla et al.
US State Department, Architectural Section, See Garrigues
Ustarroz, See Iñiguez/Ustarroz
Utzon, 102: PM 10
Valdés, See Mapelli et al.
Valle, A. del, 318, 318: LR 2
Valls, See Coderch/Valls
Valverde, See Daroca et al.
Vaquero Palacios, 34, 42, 91, 94: O 7, 97: O 17, 214: C 14
Vaquero Palacios/Casariego Terreros, 92: O 3
Vass, See Hubman/Vass
Vázquez Consuegra, 40, 46, 50: CA 5, 51: CA 7, 64, 75: SE 28, 75, 77, 79: SE 35, 81: SE 42, 85: SE 56, 85: SE 57, 202, 203: BA 3, 221, 276
Vázquez de Castro, 77, see Iñiguez de Onzoño/ Vázquez de Castro
Vázquez Molezún, 36, 48, See Corrales/Molezún, see Carvajal et al., 218: PO 4, 223, see Corrales et al., see Carvajal et al.
Vega, See Mapelli et al.
Vellés, 53: CA 15, 201, see Mapelli et al.
Vellés/Casariego/Somoza/Posada, 130
Vellés/López Sardá, 281: M 167
Vendrell, See Ruisánchez/Vendrell
Viader, See Fuses/Viader
Viaplana/Piñón, 40, 163: B 65, 166: B 75, 173, 174: B 93, 175: B 98, 176: B 100, 185: B 129, 186: B 133
Vicéns/Ramos, 137: TO 10, 282: M 172, 293: N 10, 338
Vidal, 324: A 10, see Alonso de Armiño/Vidal
Viedma Vidal, 327: V 1
Viguier/Jodry/Seigneur, 82: SE 45
Villalba [eng.], See Martín Gil et al.

Villanueva, 269
Villanueva, 64, see Barrionuevo Ferrer/Villanueva
Villar [eng.], See Torroja Cavanillas [eng.] et al.
Viloria, See Aracil et al., see Miquel/Viloria
Viñuela, See Leonhardt/Viñuela
Viñuela/Reventós, 192: GI 10
Vivanco, 237
Vives, See Bosch/Tarrús/Vives
Weber, See Higueras et al.
Weeks, 226
Yamasaki/Mir/Coll, 38, 270: M 131
Yárnoz, See Martínez del Valle/Yárnoz
Yárnoz, Javier 333
Yarza, 89: Z 6
Yordi de Carricarte [eng.], 212: C 9, 216
Zabalo, 302: VI 12
Zaera/Moussavi, 341
Zóbel [painter], See Rueda et al.
Zuazo, 28, 30, 88: Z 2, 225: M 7, 226, 230: M 20, 237, 238, 239, 240, 243, 246, 247: M 66, 261, 306: BI 1
Zuazo/Jansen, 222, 238
Zuazo/Torroja Miret [eng.], 234: M 43
Zulaica, See Moneo et al.

Dam across the River Eume, 34, 212: C 9
Dam in Belesar, 212, 216
Diversion of the River Guadalquivir, 32, 65, 76
Diversion of the River Turia, 326
Electrical Power Plant, Aboño, 97
Electrical Power Plant, Grandas de Salime, 34, 97: O 17
Electrical Power Plant, Miranda, 97
Electrical Power Plant, Proaza, 97
Electrical Power Plant, Tanes, 97
Majadahonda Sewage Plant, 277
Salto del Jándula Dam, 60, 61: J 2

Bridges and Viaducts
Alfonso XIII Bridge, 28, 65
Arco de les Fosses Bridge, 192: GI 10
Bach de Roda-Felipe II Bridge, 166: B 74
Barrios de Luna Bridge, 122: LE 3
Bridge over the River Aragón, 295: N 13
Bridge over the River Guadiana, 205
Bridge over the River Sella, 94: O 11
Bridges and Underground Station, 329: V 10
Bridges over the A-6 Motorway, 281: M 170
Centenary Bridge, 78: SE 32
Diagonal-Carles III Underpass, 158: B 49
El Alamillo Bridge and Viaduct, 82: SE 44
La Cartuja Bridge, 81: SE 43
Martín Gil Railway Viaduct over the River Esla, 32, 131: ZA 6
Northern Junction, 266: M 119
Nueve de Octubre Bridge, 329
Plentzia Footbridge, 317: BI 22
Sancho III El Mayor Bridge, 38, 294: N 12
Suspended Footbridge, 159: B 51
Twin Bridges over the River Llobregat, 183: B 121
Viaduct, Madrid, 233: M 30
Zubizuri Footbridge, 314

Road Infrastructures
Alhambra Accessways and Parking Area, 57, 58: GR 4
Bowery for Excursion Services, 281: M 166
El Paraguas Urban Canopy, Oviedo, 97
Housing and Petrol Station on Av. de la Zurriola, 305
Los Enlaces Service Station, 89: Z 6
Pergolas on Av. de Icària, 173
Petrol Station, Las Palmas, 109: GC 10
Petrol Station, Tenerife, 115: TF 8
Porto Pi Petrol Station, 61, 227: M 13
Service Station, Huelva, 60
Underground Rail Tunnels, Madrid, 238

PUBLIC BUILDINGS AND OFFICES
Public Administration Buildings
Adaptation of 18th c. House for the Andalusian Architectural Institute, 75
Adaptation of the Benicaó Palace for the Valencian Parliament, 328: V 9
Adaptation of the San Pelayo Convent for Government Use, 93
Administration Building for the Regional Government, Oviedo, 94: O 10
Airforce Ministry, 241: M 46, 243
Arriba Newspaper Building (Centre for Cadastral Management), 254: M 84, 258
Cabildo Insular Building, Las Palmas, 30, 108: GC 5

Cabildo Insular Building, Tenerife, 113: TF 2
Civilian Government Building, Tarragona, 34, 196: TA 1, 251, 253, 262
Commercial and Industrial Bank (Madrid Community Building), 240: M 45
Correction Centre, 184: B 124
Ebro Water Authority Building, 88: Z 3
Enlargement and Renovation of the Maqueda Castle, 136: TO 5
Extension of the Town Hall and Layout of the Square, 288: MU 5
Extension of the Town Hall, Ceuta, 201
Extension to the Law Courts, Zaragoza, 90: Z 10
General Staff Headquarters, 239, 243: M 54, 244
Headquarters for the Provincial Government, Seville, 83: SE 51
Institute for Agricultural Development, 239, 244: M 56
Júcar Water Authority Building, 326
Law Courts, Badalona, 179: B 106
Law Courts, Girona, 190: GI 3
Law Courts, Mahón, 104: ME 1
Meteorological Centre, Barcelona, 175: B 95
Ministry of the Interior Administration Offices, 276
New Ministries, 234: M 33, 237, 238, 239, 243, 244
Police Station in Cortijo de Cuarto, 83: SE 49
Recovery of the Reales Atarazanas, 321
Reform of the Fontes Palace for government use, 288
Refurbishment of the Banco de España for the Regional Government, 94: O 9
Regional Department of Agriculture and Fisheries, Seville, 67: SE 4
Regional Department of Agriculture, Toledo, 135: TO 2
Regional Government Building, Gran Canaria, 110: GC 14
Regional Government Building, Guadalajara, 134: GU 1
Regional Government Building, Valencia, 323: A 6
Regional Government Buildings, Mérida, 205: BA 6
Rehabilitation of the San Telmo Palace (Phase I) for the Regional Government of Andalusia, 75
Remodelling of the Aljafería Palace for the Regional Parliament, 90
Sant Jordi Building (Catalonian Ministry of Justice), 143: B 8
Tax Office Building, Logroño, 319: LR 3
Torretriana Building, 80: SE 39
Town Hall and Square, Valdelaguna, 285: M 183
Town Hall, Alcorcón, 279: M 161
Town Hall, Cangas de Morrazo, 219: PO 7
Town Hall, Collserola, 172
Town Hall, Library and Constitution Square, Camas, 84: SE 53
Town Hall, Logroño, 319: LR 4
Town Hall, Pontecesures, 219
Town Hall, Porriño, 219
Trade Union Building (Ministry of Health), 32, 242: M 51, 254, 258
Transformation of Fuensaldaña Castle for the Parliament of Castile and León, 129
Treasury Department Building, Vitoria, 301: VI 9
United States Embassy, Madrid, 244: M 57
Banks
Banca Catalana Building, 156: B 43

GLOSSARY

Abstract art Non-figurative or non-representational art in which the shapes and colours in themselves move the spectator. It derives from cubism and was first introduced by Kandinsky c. 1910.

Abutment The solid masonry placed to counteract the lateral thrust of an arch or vault.

Academicism A movement that showed respect for the spirit, methods and techniques of the widely accepted architectural tradition, especially in the early 20th c., and that was symbolised by the tenets of the Schools of Fine Arts. See Beaux Arts.

Almohade art Art of the Muslim Berber dynasty that established its rule in Western Islam and Spain during the 12th-13th c. and reached its zenith under Yacub Yusuf (1163-1184) in Seville.

Amsterdam School Amsterdam-based architects (Michel de Klerk, van der Mej) and works marked by their Expressionist manner, c. 1910-20.

Art Déco An expression derived from the Paris Exhibition of Decorative Arts in 1925, it refers to the Jazz Age style made fashionable concurrently with the Modern movement in the twenties and thirties. Characterised by a lack of functional intent and the use of streamlined motifs, the style found its most noteworthy expression in the skyscrapers of New York, such as the Chrysler building and the Rockefeller Center.

Art Nouveau A movement away from the imitation of the past, its origins lie in the designs of William Morris and the mediaeval theories of John Ruskin. Its principal centres from 1892 on were Brussels (Horta, Hankar, van de Velde), Paris (Guimard) and Italy (Sommaruga). Its main architectural exponent was the Spanish architect, Antoni Gaudí (1852-1926), who used undulated forms and floral motifs. See Modernism.

Arte Povera An Italian movement (Kounellis and others, 1967) that elevates banality to the category of art through the use of humble materials, effects and techniques.

Avant-garde Term applied to the group of artists thought at any given time to be most advanced in their techniques or subject matters. An artistic movement away from traditional or established tastes and languages.

Axonometric projection A geometrical drawing that shows a building in three dimensions. The plan appears at an angle and the verticals are projected to scale in order to arrive at a representation whose dimensions on a horizontal plane and verticals are to scale, but whose diagonals and curves on a vertical plane are distorted.

Barcelona School See Realism.

Baroque architecture This style originated in Rome c. 1630, after the Renaissance, and spread throughout Europe until the advent of Neo-Classicism, c. 1750. It was characterised by the use of expansive curvaceous forms, exuberant decoration, a sense of mass, sweeping vistas and spatially complex, large-scale compositions.

Barrel vault The simplest type of vault, also known as a tunnel or wagon vault, consists of a continuous arched structure of semicircular or pointed sections, unbroken in its length by cross vaults.

Base The lower part of a building (or a section of it) on which the whole work seems to rest. The body formed by the plinth and pedestal of a column.

Bastion A five-sided defensive fortress that juts out from the angle formed by two walls. See bulwark.

Bauhaus A school of architecture, arts and crafts founded by Walter Gropius (1919) in Weimar to design functional architecture in which art (painters included Klee, Kandinsky and others) and technology are intergrated within the framework of high-tech industry. In 1925-26 the school moved to Dessau. The growth of National Socialism led to the dismissal of the director, Mies van der Rohe, in 1932, and to the closing down of the school by the Nazis in 1933, giving rise to the dispersal of its staff, nearly all of whom emigrated to the United States.

Bay A vertical division of the exterior or interior of a building marked by fenestration, units of vaulting or buttresses. Space between two supporting walls.

Bay window The angular or curved projection of a house front filled with fenestration. When curved it is also called a bow window, while when on an upper floor only it is called an oriel window.

BBPR An architects studio founded by Banfi, Belgoioso, Rogers and Peressutti in Milan (1932).

Beaux Arts style From the French École des Beaux Arts (School of Fine Arts), a classical, ornamental style that was favoured by the Schools of Fine Arts in the 19th c. Garnier's Opera House in Paris is its most representative work. See Academicism.

Belvedere See Gazebo.

Blind A screen formed by slats, 2-3 cm wide, used to deflect or redirect light or to restrict vision from without. Also known as window shutter or shade.

Brace A secondary length of timber, be it straight or curved, used to strengthen a structure.

Bracket A small supporting piece of stone or other material to carry a projecting weight.

Brise-soleil A French term meaning "sun-break" or check, it is often used to designate the arrangement of horizontal or vertical fins used in hot and sunny climates to shade the window openings.

Brutalism A term coined in the fifties to designate the style of Le Corbusier at the moment of Marseille and Chandigarh, and later by the Smithsons and Stirling in England, Vigano in Italy, Rudolph in the US, and Tange in Japan. Rather than conceal materials and structures, it handles them with over-emphasis, often using concrete exposed at its roughest.

Bulwark A solid wall-like structure for defense.

Canopy A hood suspended or projected over a door or window, usually to protect from the rain.

Carmen A detached villa with garden typical of Granada whose architecture is influenced by Mudejar and Moorish Andalusian tradition.

Castrum A circular or oval layout of elliptical-shaped houses, with stone bases and straw roofs, located on hilltops or strategic places and surrounded by stone ramparts. In Spain they were first built by the Iberians, Celts and Celtiberians, later by the Romans.

Centering The wooden framework used in arch and vault construction; it is removed when the voussoirs have been placed and the mortar has set.

Chicago School A disputed term understood as referring to a group of architects (Jenney, Burnham, Sullivan, Wright) working in Chicago between 1880 and 1910 and their design of utilitarian multi-storey buildings characterised by their verticality, external expression of the skeleton frame and repetitious use of identical fenestration for storeys of similar plan.

Churrigueresque style The lavish, over-decorated style used to describe Late Baroque architecture in Spain and Latin America in the late 17th c. and early 18th c.

CIAM The *Congrès International d'Architecture Moderne*, founded in 1928 in La Sarraz (Switzerland), became the key instrument for the dissemination of Modernist ideas on architecture and town planning. Dominated by Le Corbusier in the thirties, it underlined functionalism and rational planning. The last meeting of CIAM took place in 1959.

Cladding An external covering or skin applied to a structure for protective or aesthetic purposes.

COAC *Colegio Oficial de Arquitectos de Cataluña*, the Architects' Chamber of Catalonia.

COAM *Colegio Oficial de Arquitectos de Madrid*, the Architects' Chamber of Madrid.

Colonisation [town] See INC.

Committee for Devastated Regions A committee created by Franco in 1938 to reconstruct the towns damaged during the Civil War (192 towns lost 60%

of their buildings). The committee worked actively for two decades, until 1957, mainly in rural areas (towns in the N of Spain, near Oviedo, Bilbao and Aragón; in the S of Spain, near Córdoba and Jaén; and in central Spain, near Madrid), but also in cities, such as Teruel, Oviedo and Toledo.

Concrete A type of building material formed by sand, cement, stone, water and, at times, additives, that is used wet when it can be easily worked and moulded and that becomes a rock-hard, durable, weather-resistant material when it sets and dries.

Constructivism An aesthetic movement derived from cubism and headed by Malevich, Tatlin, Gabo, Lissitsky, Melnikov and others in Russia in 1913-20, whose most important achievements were in design and architecture. Its spirit of utilitarian simplicity, iconoclasm and respect for the logic of materials have lived on in Russia and in the West, where it was disseminated through the Bauhaus.

Cornice The ornamental moulding or projecting structure along the top of a wall, arch or exterior of a building to prevent rainwater from filtering into the wall.

Cortijo In Andalusia, a complex formed by houses, storage and farm buildings. This rural unit centres around a large interior courtyard formed by the main house, the stables and the workers' houses.

Crepidoma The stepped base of a Greek temple.

Cross A figure or mark formed by two intersecting lines.

Cross vault A vault formed by the intersection of two or more simple vaults. See groin vault.

Crossing The space at the intersection of a nave, chancel and transept of a church.

CSCAE *Consejo Superior de Colegios de Arquitectos de España*, Spanish Council of Architects' Chambers.

Cubism The first abstract art style of the century, an attempt to represent fully and exhaustively on a flat surface all aspects of what the artist saw in three dimensions by eliminating perspective, it reached its zenith in 1907-14. Led by Picasso, Braque, Gris and Léger, it gave rise to the most important aesthetic revolution since the Renaissance.

Curtain wall A non-load-bearing wall which can be applied in front of a framed structure to keep out the weather. A continuous wall of steel and glass that hangs infront of the main frame, thus separating structure from cladding.

Dado The solid block that forms the body of a pedestal between the plinth and the cornice.

Dam A barrier, be it a bank of earth or a masonry wall (stone or concrete), built across a watercourse to confine and restrain the flow of water.

Deconstructivism This term was borrowed from deconstructive philosophy in the late eighties to loosely group the contemporary architects using fragmented forms and new lines with an almost generalised disdain for function in order to present a disordered group of abstract shapes. Some of the varied architects included in this group are Gehry, Eisenman, Hadid, Libeskind et al.

De Stijl A Dutch art and architecture movement founded in 1917 by Theo van Doesburg (the group disbanded after his death in 1931) and dominated by the painter, Mondrian. Influenced by Lissitsky (Constructivism) and Wright, the group's most prominent members included Oud, Rietveld and van't Hoff and exerted great influence on Modern 20th c. architecture.

Dolmen A prehistoric, Megalithic monument from the Neolithic and Bronze age consisting of three or more large blocks of stone forming a table.

Dubbing out The rough rendering of a wall with a layer of mortar to even the surface, hiding building imperfections before plastering.

Eclecticism The term applied to works of art and architecture combining elements and techniques from two or more historical styles, especially during the 19th c. and the first quarter of the 20th c.

Eixample Catalan term for the expansion of a city.

ENI The *Ente Nazionale Idrocarburi*, an Italian holding founded in 1953.

Enlightenment A Central European movement that attempted to advance human knowledge through the light of reason in the 18th c.

EU European Union.

Expansion The extension or spread of a city, the urban space allotted for its future development. In the 19th c., the industrial and demographic revolution brought about the demolition of many European city walls, which were substituted by ringroads and boulevards beyond which the *ensanche* (*eixample* in Catalan) or new city was planned on the basis of previously established grid layouts. In Spain, the key expansion plans were drawn up by Castro for Madrid and by Cerdà for Barcelona (both from 1860).

Expressionism The aesthetic movement developed in northern Europe towards 1910-25 as a reaction towards Impressionism was characterised by a distortion of reality in order to express the artists' emotions and inner visions. Main exponents in the world of art included Munch, Klee, Ensor; in cinema, Wiene, Lang, Murnau; in architecture, Michel de Klerk, van der Meij, Poelzig and Mendelsohn; and in music, R. Strauss and Schönberg.

Facing The surface applied to the exterior of a building to finish it off. It can have a protective and decorative function.

Fenestration The arrangement, proportioning and design of windows and doors in a building.

Figurative art Representational art which portrays, in however altered or distorted a form, the things perceived in the visible world.

Fourierism Fourier's plan for the reorganisation of society into cooperative communities of small producer and consumer groups living in common. By extension, the term is also applied to collective housing units. Also called Phalansterianism.

Foyer The space in a public building, such as lobby, entrance hallway or vestibule, that connects the access with the different circulation flows. It is especially representative in theatres.

Frottage The technique used to reproduce a given texture or relief design by laying a piece of paper over it and rubbing with charcoal or crayon. The Surrealists, especially Max Ernst, used it with all types of objects as a way of questioning matter in the development of images.

Functionalism The theory popular in the twenties which held that a building should first and foremost fulfil its function well and that artistic and aesthetic considerations should be of secondary importance. Functionalism has a long history in aesthetic theory, although it is best known in architecture through Sullivan's slogan, "Form follows Function", and the writings of Otto Wagner and Adolf Loos.

Futurism An Italian artistic and literary movement whose first manifesto was published by Marinetti and which exerted considerable influence over the world of art.

Gablet An ornamental motif in the form of a small gable used in the portals of Gothic buildings, it is formed by two lines that meet at an angle at the cusp and is decorated with bosses.

Gallery A long room, often on an upper floor, or a platform or mezzanine supported on columns or brackets overlooking the main interior space of a building. In religious architecture, an upper storey over an aisle opening on to the nave.

Gantry crane A bridge crane in which the beam or bridge is carried at each end by a trestle that runs on parallel tracks to carry large pieces.

GATCPAC *Grupo de Artistas y Técnicos Catalanes para el Progreso de las Artes Constructivas* (Group of Catalan Artists and Technicians for the Progress of the Building Arts) is the Catalan section of the Spanish GATEPAC group.

GATEPAC *Grupo de Artistas y Técnicos Españoles para el Progreso de las Artes Constructivas* (Group of Spanish Artists and Technicians for the Progress of the Building Arts) was founded in 1930 in Zaragoza to design an architecture that met the Rationalist postulates of the Bauhaus and Le Corbusier. It expressed its aims and views in the *AC* magazine before the Civil War cut short its activities.

Gazebo A small look-out tower or balcony on the roof of a house that offers good views.

Gothic architecture An architectural style founded in France, it evolved from the Romanesque from the 12th c. until the advent of the Renaissance in the 15th c. (16th c. in England) and was typified by pointed arches, rib vaults, flying buttresses, tracery on windows, a minimising of walls and a tendency to vertical features such as steeples.

Gravity dam A concrete dam, usually of triangular profile, which resists the pressure of the water from the mere weight of the wall.

Gresite The brand name of a small piece of glazed grès used for decorative panelling and cladding.

Groin vault Also known as cross vault, it is formed by the intersection at right angles of two barrel vaults of identical shape.

Group R A group of young architects in Barcelona (Moragas, Sostres, Gili, Bassó, Bohigas, Martorell, Pratmarsó, Ribas, Coderch, Valls, Monguió, Vayreda, Balcells, Giráldez) who tried to break the silence in which architects had fallen since the Civil War by reactivating professional debate in the fifties through courses and exhibitions.

Hacienda Farm estate. In Andalusia, olive *haciendas* are rural complexes that include housing and olive pressing facilities, warehouses and stables gathered around the main house following a Hispano-Roman *villae* structure, plus chapels, towers (added in the Visigothic era), gardens and orchards (added in the Islamic era).

High Tech An approach to architecture based on the visual expression of engineering, construction and other space technologies and characterised by exposed steel structures and services (pipes, ducts) and smooth impervious glass skins, it may be the most outstanding stylistic constribution of English architects of the seventies (Foster, Rogers) to 20th c. architecture.

Historicism A style that followed the Neo-Classical in the 19th c., it respected, adopted and used the norms and styles of the past, either singly or jointly. A wide gamut of Historicist buildings can be seen in Vienna's Ringstrasse (1859).

Hof The large social housing complexes built in the twenties by the social democratic municipality of Vienna, whose ideological message and architectural expression (large community areas and services) became a symbol of the new collective identity of the city's inhabitants.

Hórreo Originally a Roman structure, in the rural architecture of Asturias and Galicia it is a small granary perched on stone or wooden piles to keep grain dry.

Horseshoe arch An arch in which the centre of the circle is above the springing line, so that the curves start to come together at the level of the imposts.

Hypostyle A hall or other large space over which the roof is supported by rows of columns like a forest.

IBA The *Internationale Bauausstellung* (International Building Fair) founded in Berlin in 1987 under Josef Paul Kleihues, who acted as planification manager.

Impluvium The rectangular basin or water cistern in the centre of a Roman and Ethruscan house used to receive the rain-water from the surrounding roofs.

Impost A member in the wall, usually formed by a projecting bracket-like moulding, on which the end of an arch appears to rest.

INC *Instituto Nacional de Colonización* (Land Settlement Institute), the state body created by Franco in 1939 to irrigate dry lands, furnish poor farmers with lands and farming tools, and build rural housing and even small rural towns.

INI The *Instituto Nacional de Industria* (National Industry Institute), an industrial holding founded in 1941 under Franco's regime to industrialise Spain at a time of autarchy and international isolation.

Intercolumniation The space between columns measured in diameters.

International style A term coined to designate the new architectural style of the 20th c. by Henry Russell Hitchcock and Philip Johnson in their book, *The International Style: Architecture since 1922*, which included the most noteworthy examples of Modern architecture of the time.

Intradós The inner curve or underside of an arch, also called soffit.

INV *Instituto Nacional de la Vivienda* (National Housing Institute).

Irrigation ditch Canal built to water land artificially.

Isabellino style The highly ornamental Gothic style with Mudejar influence developed in Spain under the reign of the Castilian crown (Ferdinand and Isabella) in the late 15th c. and early 16th c.

Isotropy The quality or state of an element that exhibits equal tendencies to growth in all directions, lacks predetermined axes or exhibits properties with the same values when measured along axes in all directions.

Jamb The vertical side supports of a doorway, arch, window or fireplace.

Keystone The central stone of an arch or rib vault.

Lantern A small turret, circular or polygonal in plan, placed at the top of a roof or dome to let in air and light.

Late Modern A term used to refer to architectural works based on Modern principles or vocabularies built at a time when these were no longer current or ignoring the later developments of Organicism and the architecture of the sixties.

Lattice A framework or structure of wood or metal made by crossing laths or other thin strips to form a network that enables people to see through them without being seen.

Lintel A horizontal beam of wood, stone or other material bridging an opening and supporting the wall above.

Loggia A gallery or room, open on one or more sides, sometimes pillared. It can also be a separate structure.

Louvre Also slat, one of a series of overlapping slips of glass or boards to admit air and exclude rain.

Madrid School A rich, suggestive, yet imprecise term to refer to the architectural culture created around the teachings of key Madrid architects from the generation of the forties (Cabrero, Sota, Fisac, Sáenz de Oíza, Corrales, Molezún and others) to that of the sixties (Moneo and others).

Malpaís In Spanish-speaking countries, territories of slag-like lava.

Managed settlements The new approach to town planning adopted in the mid-fifties by the Greater Madrid Commission resulted in the construction of new urban areas in and outside Madrid to absorb the mass influx of population to the city. Designed by prestigious young architects, they speeded the return of Modern architecture in an area where it made obvious social and economic sense given the space constraints and building standards. When their structure was urban and the buildings made to last they were called Managed Settlements (*Poblados Dirigidos*). When they were put up provisionally they were called Neighbourhood Absorption Units (*Unidades Vecinales de Absorción*).

Mannerism The acceptance of a manner rather than its meaning. In art and architecture, the term designates the style developed in Italy from the early 15th c. (Michelangelo) to the end of the 16th c. The term also applies to Spanish (Herrera) and French architecture of the 16th c., although its use in the northern countries is controversial.

Masía In Catalonia, a rural farmhouse generally made of stone.

MBM Martorell, Bohigas and Mackay's studio.

Megaron A large square or oblong room with a hearth traditional in Greece since Mycenaean times and thought to be the ancestor of the Doric temple.

Minimal art A term coined to denote the art which abandons all pretensions at either expressiveness or illusion, reducing works to simple geometrical forms and chromatic relations. The style originated (Judd, Flavin, Richard Serra, Frank Stella) in the US in the sixties as a reaction against Figurative art and, more specifically, Pop art. In architecture, the term applies to a style derived from the Bauhaus and Mies van der Rohe's paradigm, "Less is More".

Modern movement The term refers to the style of architecture that "lacks style" (absence of shapes from the past) adopted by the avant-garde circles of the twenties. It is best known for its asymmetrical compositions; stark, smooth cube-shaped buildings; use of horizontal fenestration; open floor plan, and white renderings.

Modernism The name given to the succession of avant-garde styles in art and architecture that have dominated Western culture through most of the 20th c.

Modernisme See Art Nouveau. The term given to a regional style which flourished in Catalonia from 1880-1920, similar to Art Nouveau, which had its best exponent in Antoni Gaudí (1852-1926).

Morisco Descendants of the Spanish Muslims that stayed in Christian territories (see Mudejar). As a style it is also known as Moresque, a style of intricate surface decoration derived from Islamic art and made popular in rural or popular architecture.

Mozarabic The architecture of the Christians that lived in the Iberian peninsula under Muslim rule, particularly during the 10th c. It is characterised by its combination of Visigothic shapes and techniques with Spanish Muslim features, such as the Cordoban horseshoe arch and the rolled modillion.

Mudejar The architecture of the Spanish Muslims living in Christian areas, particularly from the 12th to the 15th c. It is characterised by its combination of Islamic structures and materials (use of brick, wood and glazed tiles in cube-shaped spaces) with Christian dispositions and concepts (Roman and

Gothic elements, decorations incorporating shapes from nature, etc.).

Nasrid Art and architecture of the Muslim dynasty founded by Yusuf ben Nasar, who governed the Kingdom of Granada from the 13th c. to the 15th c., during which time the Alhambra was built.

Naveta Megalithic monument found in the Balearic Islands shaped like an upturned boat or pyramid trunk.

Neighbourhood Absorption Units New urban sectors put up provisionally (although often they have lived on indefinitely) in and around Madrid by the Greater Madrid Commission in the mid-fifties. See Managed Settlements.

Neo-Classicism The style based on Ancient Greek and Roman architecture that developed in Europe during the 18th c. (in Spain, from 1730 on, with its apogee under Charles III), with an emphasis on the linear and symmetrical, formal and spatial qualities of architecture and a rejection of incorrect motifs.

Neo-Rationalism A reaction against the Modern Movement, it was also known as the "Tendenza", led by Aldo Rossi, which rejected Functionalism in favour of an autonomous architecture concerned with formal essences and not with technology. Its seminal texts included books by Gregotti (1966), Rossi (1966) and Grassi (1967). Architects in the movement included Rob Krier in Austria; Reinhart and Reichlin in Switzerland; Ungers and Kleihues in Germany.

Novecentism [Noucentisme in Catalan] In Spain, the cultural trend led by Eugenio d'Ors from 1901 on against the Romantic tradition and Modernism, preferring Classical aesthetics and elaborate creative processes over the natural spontaneity favoured in the 19th c. In Italy, the movement led by Botempelli around the *'900* magazine (1926-29), in which different writers (Moravia and others) searched for a new era in which to consolidate all the "isms" found in Europe between the First and the Second World War.

Oculus A circular opening or window on a wall.

Organicism Wright and Aalto led a conception of architecture based on nature's shape and function. "Nature is the mother of architecture... *Organic* architecture means *natural* architecture. It means *belonging to*, instead of *presiding over*. [In it] the nature of the thing suggests its shape... it is built from the inside out... it will be natural as regards its purpose...", wrote Wright.

Orthogonal That which lies or intersects at right angles. See axonometric projection.

OSED The *Obra Sindical de Educación y Descanso* (Union's Education and Entertainment Organisation) was the trade union body operating under Franco's regime in charge of coordinating vocational training, entertainment and holiday trips for the working classes.

OSHA The *Obra Sindical del Hogar y Arquitectura* (Union's Housing and Architecture Organisation) was the trade union body founded in 1941 to build social housing.

Panelling The lining of walls with wood, stone or metal panels.

Pantheon In ancient Greece, a temple dedicated to all the gods. A building serving as a burial place or containing memorials to the dead.

Party wall The wall between two adjoining houses.

Phalansterianism See Fourierism.

Pilaster A rectangular column that projects only slightly from a wall for support or decoration.

Pilotis A French term for pillars or stilts that carry a building, raising it to first floor level and leaving the ground floor open.

Plastering The lining of a dubbed wall with a layer of plaster, gypsum, stucco or cement to obtain a smooth and uniform surface.

Plateresque Ornate style with intricate details that developed in the 16th c. from Moorish and Gothic architecture.

Plinth The projecting base of a building, wall or column pedestal. In the latter case, it is slightly larger than the dado and is chamfered at the top.

Pointing Exposed mortar finishing to masonry and brick.

Pompier A pejorative French term to designate the tritely or insipidly academic, marked by pretentious and stereotypical themes and lacking in originality.

Pop Art Art which makes use of the imagery of consumerism and mass culture (comics, packaging) with a balanced mixture of irony and celebration. It began in the fifties in the US and blossomed in the sixties, when Warhol, Jasper Johns, Oldenburg, Rauschenberg, Lichtenstein and others presented their works at the Venice Biennale of 1964.

Popular architecture See vernacular architecture.

Porch The small, covered entrance to a building. A grander and more ostentatious type of porch is a portal. A roofed entrance supported by a classical colonnade is a portico.

Post-Modernism A term coined in the forties and given currency by Charles Jencks in the seventies for the reaction to Modernism and other contemporary movements, such as High Tech, which encouraged Eclecticism and favoured "elements which are hybrid rather than pure" and "messy vitality over obvious unity". After Venturi's seminal book (1966), *Complexity and Contradiction in Architecture*, Post-Modernist works were designed by Graves, Hollein, Johnson, Moore, Stern and others.

Prairie School An architectural movement in mid-west America *c.* 1900-1916, inspired by Sullivan but led by Wright, characterised by horizontality, open plans and an emphasis on natural materials.

Prestressed concrete Concrete that contains steel cables fed through ducts which are stretched and pulled before the concrete is cast into position.

Purism An art movement founded in 1915 which deprived works of unnecessary elements, returning to simple, extremely generalised basic forms.

Rambla Dry riverbed. In Spanish Mediterranean cities, a wide, tree-lined boulevard layed out on a former watercourse.

Rationalism An Italian movement led by Gruppo 7, founded in 1926 by Terragni (its most prominent figure), Figini, Pollini and others, and expanded in 1928 by Libera et al. to form the MIAR (*Movimiento Italiano per l'Architettura Razionale*, or the Italian Movement for Rational Architecture). Its "modern" programme derived partly from Sant'Elia's Futurist projects. The movement foundered in its alliance with Fascism, which led to its decline and the rise of Eclecticism.

Realism Term attributed to Bohigas, who defended the architectural works of the Barcelona School in the sixties. The "realist" attitude adapts Rationalism of the twenties and thirties to Spain's circumstances (obsolete industries), respecting client's demands while searching for a rational and modern use of traditional materials.

Regionalism A Spanish architectural trend that tried to establish a style rooted in the vernacular tradition of an area, reflecting the idiosyncracy of the region in the selection of stylistic elements from the past. In the early 20th century, Leonardo Rucabado (from Cantabria to the Basque Country) and Aníbal González (in SW and central Seville) were its main representatives.

Reinforced concrete Concrete reinforced with metal (iron or steel), in the form of wires, bars or cables that enhance the naturally great compression resistance of the concrete to produce a building material of enormous strength.

Renaissance An era that began in Italy *c.* 1420 and continued to the mid-16th c., with the advent of the Baroque. It was based on the restoration of Ancient Roman standards and motifs, with special attention to stability and poise.

Revival The reappearance of, or renewed interest in, architectural styles of the past.

Rise [of an arch or vault] The vertical distance between the underside at the crown or the apex of the intrados and the level of the springing line.

Rococo architecture Rather than a style in itself, it is the last phase of the Baroque, characterised by a lightness in colour and rocaille decoration (shell-like motifs, S-shaped curves, etc.) initiated in France.

Romanesque A style developed by the Cistercian monks in Christian Europe between the 10th and the 13th c., until the advent of Gothic architecture, it was characterised by clear schemes of planning and elevation, rounded arches and barrel vaults.

Rooflight See skylight.

Rounded arch In the shape of a semicircle, the arch centre is in the middle point of the springing line.

Rubble masonry Rough, unhewn building stones or flints used for rubble walling.

Rubble walling A style of coarse walling consisting of rough stones of irregular size, not necessarily flat bedded, bonded with thick mortar.

Scratchwork coating A decorative technique where the first layer of the plastered surface of a wall is scratched according to a former design to obtain a contrast between two different tonalities.

Secessionism [also Sezessionism] A group of painters (Klimt) and architects (Olbrich, Hoffmann) seceded from the conservative academy in Vienna to establish the Wiener Sezession in 1987. When they were joined by Otto Wagner, the Secessionist style became very influential.

Segmental arch An arch in the shape of a segment of a circle centred below the springing line.

Siedlung Originally, a group of single-family houses with gardens in low density residential areas that interested Dutch and German architects of the Modern movement in the twenties. These architects experimented with domestic spaces and typologies, increasing their density and grouping them in rows and blocks, turning them into powerful advertising instruments of the new architecture.

Skeleton construction A building method that uses a framework and an outer covering which takes no load, often revealing the skeleton.

Skylight A window of glass or other translucent material set into a roof or ceiling to provide top lighting. It may be open or fixed.

Slat See louvre.

SOM The architects studio founded by Skidmore, Owings & Merrill, one of the largest in the US.

Span The horizontal distance between the supports of a roof, arch or bridge.

Split-level apartment A flat that consists of two floors joined by an interior stairway.

Strut A bar designed to resist pressure in the direction of its length.

Surrealism An aesthetic movement in literature and the visual arts, its first manifiesto was published by André Breton in 1924, in which it is described as "pure automatism". It combined reason with lack of reason and used dreams and chance effects to create a new reality.

Symbolism This influential aesthetic movment in European literature and art, from 1885-1910, rejected objectivity in favour of subjectivity and tried to suggest ideas by means of ambiguous yet powerful symbols.

Talayot A Megalithic monument from the Bronce Age in the Balearic Islands in the shape of a tower, inside which there is a chamber with a false vault.

Taula A Megalithic monument in the Balearic Islands consisting of a large vertical stone slab and another horizontal slab in the shape of a T.

Team X The group (Candilis, Bakema, van Eyck, the Smithsons) responsible for preparing the tenth CIAM in Otterlo (1959), it established contact with others in search of innovative architectural and urban solutions, like Erskine, van den Broek, DeCarlo and Coderch, and used Dutch magazine *Forum* and English magazine *Architectural Digest* to criticise the Modern movement from 1941 to the late sixties.

Tectonics The science or art of construction, both in relation to its use and its artistic design.

Temenos A temple enclosure or court.

Tendenza See Neo-Rationalism [Italian].

Terrace A horizontal or gently sloping ridge or offset made in a hillside to take full advantage of the earth for cultivation, landscaping or domestic use.

Tie beam The main horizontal, transverse timber carrying the feet of the principals at wall-plate level.

Town planning The idea or concept of viewing the layout of a town or city as a whole entity.

Troglodyte [dwellings] The most primitive and rudimentary habitat for human beings: caves, pits and other natural holes in the rocks. In extremely poor Mediterranean regions, some inhabitants lead troglodytic lives in artificially made caves and pits offering protection from the heat and the humidity, as in the caves of Apulia and Calabria in Italy, and those of Almería and Granada in Spain.

Truss A framework of timbers placed laterally across a building to carry the longitudinal roof timbers that support the common rafters. See centering.

UCD *Unión de Centro Democrático*, the centre party in government after the first democratic elections following Franco's death, responsible for initiating the transition to democracy under Adolfo Suárez's presidency from 1979-81.

UIA *Union International d'Architectes* (International Union of Architects).

Underpin To replace or strengthen the foundation of a wall or building.

Urban renewal The replanning of existing areas to improve traffic flows and ammenities in towns.

Vault An arched integral roof or ceiling. See barrel vault, cross vault and groin vault.

Vault dam A concrete dam built in the shape of an arch, with the convex part of the vault heading up-water. Most of the pressure of the water falls on the abutments, which transmit it to the sides of the dam as a result of the arch effect. Vault dams can only be built in narrow valleys.

Vernacular architecture A term recently coined for architecture (by analogy with linguistics, referring to native or local tongues) to designate architecture built out of local or regional materials (brick, wood, stone, as opposed to the impersonal materials such as cement, glass and steel used by the Modern movement), usually of unknown authorship, following traditional methods and techniques that make little or no reference to the chief styles or theories of architecture. Also known as popular architecture.

Voussoir A brick or wedge-shaped stone forming one of the units of an arch or vault.

VPO *Viviendas de protección oficial*, subsidised, low-cost or council housing, one of the categories of social housing currently being promoted by the Spanish government.

Window opening An opening in a wall for lighting and ventilation, which also permits those inside to view the surroundings. Other types include door openings (to access and exit a building) and inter-columniations.

BIBLIOGRAPHY

The acronyms used in this bibliography stand for the following Architects' Chambers:
COAAoc: Western Andalusia.   COAAor: Eastern Andalusia.   COAAr: Aragón.   COAAs: Asturias.
COAB: Balearic Islands.   COAC: Catalonia.   COACa: Canary Islands.   COAG: Galicia.   COAM: Madrid.
COAMu: Murcia.   COACV: Valencia.   COAVN: Basque Country and Navarre.

Ajuntament de Barcelona: *Urbanisme a Barcelona. Plans cap al 92*, Ayuntamiento de Barcelona, 1987.

Alonso Gómez, M. et al.: *José Espiau y Muñoz, arquitecto, 1884-1938*, Seville, 1984.

Alonso Pereira, José R.: *Historia general de la arquitectura en Asturias*, COAAs, Oviedo, 1996.

— *Asturias. 50 años de arquitectura*, COAAs, Oviedo, 1990.

Aranda, J.: *Los arquitectos de Gijón alrededor del racionalismo: los años treinta*, COAAs, Oviedo, 1981.

Architektur Zentrum Wien (ed.): *Neues Bauen heute Europäische Architektur der neunziger Jahre*, Birkhäuser, Basel, 1995.

Armesto, A.; Padró, J.: *Atlantic Houses. Galicia and Northern Portugal*, Gili, Barcelona, 1996.

Arqués Soler, M.: *Miguel Fisac*, Pronaos, Madrid, 1996.

Arredondo, F.: *La obra de Eduardo Torroja*, Instituto de España, Madrid, 1977.

Artengo, F. et al.: *Artengo. Menis. Pastrana. Obras y proyectos en Canarias*, (exhibition catalogue), Architektur-Galerie, Stuttgart, Gobierno Autónomo Canario, Santa Cruz de Tenerife, 1993.

Ayala, G.: *Gerardo Ayala*, Munilla-Lería, Madrid, 1994.

Baldellou, Miguel A.: *Arquitectura moderna de Galicia*, Madrid, Electa, 1995.

— *Lugar, memoria y proyecto. Galicia 1974-1994*, Electa, Madrid, 1995.

Baldellou, M. A.; Capitel, A.: *Summa Artis. Historia general del arte. XL. Arquitectura española del siglo XX*, Espasa Calpe, Madrid, 1995.

Bastlund, K.: *José Luis Sert. Architecture, City Planning, Urban Design*, Les Editions d'Architecture, Zurich, 1967.

Bayón, M.: *Mariano Bayón*, Architektur - Galerie am Weissenhof, Stuttgart, 1992.

Benevolo, L.: *Storia della architettura moderna*, 1960 (English edition, Cambridge, MA, 1971).

Blaser, Werner (ed.); Frampton, K.; Nicolin, P.: *Santiago Calatrava*, Gili, Barcelona, 1989.

Bohigas, Oriol: *Barcelona, entre el Pla Cerdà i el barraquisme*, Edicions 62, Barcelona, 1963.

— *Contra una arquitectura adjetivada*, Seix Barral, Barcelona, 1969.

— *Reconstrucción de Barcelona*, MOPU, Madrid, 1986.

— *Garcés y Sòria*, Gili, Barcelona, 1988.

Bohigas, O.; Buchanan, P.; Magnago Lampugnani, V.: *Barcelona, arquitectura y ciudad, 1980-92*, Gili, Barcelona, 1990.

Borràs, María L.: *Sert, Arquitectura Mediterrània*, Ediciones Polígrafa, Barcelona, 1972.

Bosch, J.; Rubió, M.; Domínguez, C.; Solà-Morales, I. de: *Nicolau María Rubió i Tudurí, 1891-1981, jardinero y urbanista*, Doce Calles, Aranjuez, 1993.

Botia, L. (ed.): *Fernando Higueras*, Xarait, Madrid, 1987.

Bru, E.; Mateo, J.L.: *Arquitectura española contemporánea*, Gili, Barcelona, 1987.

Buchanan, Peter (introduction): *Vázquez Consuegra*, Gili, Barcelona. 1992.

Buchanan, P. (introduction); Bonell, E.: *Bonell, Rius, Gil*, Tanais Ediciones, Seville, 1998.

Buchanan, P.; Quetglas, J.: *Lapeña /Torres*, Gili, Barcelona, 1990.

Buil, C. et al.: *Regino y José Borobio Ojeda, 1924-1958* (exhibition catalogue), Zaragoza, 1991.

Cabrero, Félix: *Casto Fernández Shaw*, Madrid, 1980.

Calafell, B.; Piñera, G. (comps.): *Abrir Vigo o mar. Proxecto de recuperación urbana da Beiramar central*, COAG-Consorcio da Zona Franca de Vigo, Vigo, 1995.

Campo Baeza, Alberto: *La idea construida*, COAM, Madrid, 1996.

— *Campo Baeza*, Munilla-Lería, Madrid, 1996.

Campos, C.; Vidal, J.M.: *Arquitectura del Mediterráneo. Comunidad Valenciana*, COACV, Valencia, 1990.

Capitel, Antón: *La arquitectura de Luis Moya Blanco*, COAM, Madrid, 1982.

— *Arquitectura española, años 50 - años 80*, Dirección General de Arquitectura y Edificación, MOPU, Madrid, 1986.

— *Artículos y ensayos breves 1976-1991*, COAM, Madrid, 1993.

— see Baldellou.

Capitel, A.; Mateo, J.L.; Pérez Escolano, V.; Fullaondo, J.D. et al.: *Architecture espagnole: trente oeuvres.*

Années 50 - années 80, Europalia catalogue, MOPU, Madrid, 1985.

Capitel, A.; Solà-Morales, I. de: *Contemporary Spanish Architecture. An Eclectic Panorama*, Rizzoli, New York, 1986.

Capitel, A.; Wang, W.; Ezquiaga, J.M.; Kleihues, J.P.; Pechinski, M.; Feduchi, P.; Solà-Morales, I. de; Ruiz Cabrero, G.: *Tradición y cambio en la arquitectura de seis ciudades europeas*, Consorcio para la Organiación de Madrid, Capital Europea de la Cultura 1992, Madrid, 1993.

Carazo, E.; Otxotorena, J.M.: *Arquitecturas en Valladolid. Tradición y Modernidad (1900-1950)*, Valladolid, 1989.

Carreras Moysi, B.; Duró i Pifarrer, J.; Candela, F.; Cabrero, F. de A.; Corrales Gutiérrez, J. A.; Peña Ganchegui, L. (selection committee): *Muestra de Arquitectura Española 1991-1993*, MOPTMA, CSCAE, Universidad I. Menéndez Pelayo, Madrid, 1994.

Casariego, P.; Iñiguez de Onzoño, J.L.; Llinás, J.; Nanclares, F.; León, I.; Vázquez Consuegra, G.; De la Dehesa, M.; León, I.; Maruri, J. (selection committee): *Il Bienal de Arquitectura Española 1991-1992*, MOPTMA, CSCAE, Universidad I. Menéndez Pelayo, Madrid, 1993.

Casas, M. de las, et al.: *Arquitectura de Regiones Devastadas*, MOPU, Madrid, 1989.

Castro Borrego, F.: *La arquitectura en los siglos XIX y XX. Canarias*, Anaya, Madrid, 1980.

Castro López-Villarino, F. (exhibition commissar): *Antonio Palacios*, COAG, A Coruña, 1991.

Cerrillo, Rubio, M.I.; García Pozuelo, D.; Sáez Hernández, C.: *La obra del arquitecto Agapito del Valle (1895-1969)*, Logroño, 1986.

Chueca Goitia, F.: *Invariantes castizos de la arquitectura española. El Manifiesto de La Alhambra*, Seminarios y Ediciones, Madrid, 1971.

Climent, Javier (introduction): *Francisco Cabrero, arquitecto*, Xarait, Madrid, 1979.

Coderch, José A.: "No son genios lo que necesitamos ahora", in *Arquitectura*, num. 38, Madrid, 1962 (first published in *Domus*, num. 384, Milan, 1961).

— *J.A. Coderch, 1945-1976*, Xarait, Madrid, 1978.

— *Conversaciones con Enric Sòria*, Colegio de Aparejadores de Murcia, Murcia, 1997.

Cohn, D. (introduction), Gallego Jorreto, M.: *Manuel Gallego*, Tanais Ediciones, Seville, 1998.

Corredor, J.: *Antoni de Moragas Gallisà*, Gili, Barcelona, 1989.

Cortés, J.A.: *Escritos sobre Arquitectura Contemporánea 1978-1988*, COAM, Madrid, 1991.

— *El racionalismo madrileño. Casco antiguo y ensanche. 1925-45*, COAM, Madrid, 1992.

Costa, X.; Landrove, S.: *Arquitectura del Movimiento Moderno. Registro DOCOMOMO Ibérico*, Fundación Mies van der Rohe - DOCOMOMO, Barcelona, 1996.

Cruells, B.: *Ricardo Bofill. Taller de arquitectura*, Gili, Barcelona, 1992.

Curtis, William J.R.: *Modern Architecture Since 1900*, Phaidon, 3rd edition, London, 1996.

Domènech Girbau, L.: *Arquitectura española contemporánea*, Blume, Barcelona, 1974.

— *Arquitectura de siempre. Los años cuarenta en España*, Tusquets, Barcelona, 1978.

Domínguez Ortiz, A.; Bonet Correa, A.; Pérez Villalta, G.; Mosquera Adell, E.; Pérez Cano, M.T.; Martín, M.; Rodríguez Baberán, F.J.; Pérez Escolano, V.: *1492-1992. Transformaciones de cinco siglos de arquitectura en Andalucía*, COAAoc, Seville, 1992.

Drew, Philip: *Real Space. The Architecture of Martorell, Bohigas, Mackay, Puigdomènech*, Ernst Wasmuth, Tübingen/Berlin, 1993.

Faes, Rosa María: *Manuel del Busto, arquitecto*, COAAs, Oviedo, 1997.

Fernández Alba, A.: "25 años de arquitectura española 1939-64", in *Arquitectura*, num. 64, April 1964.

— *La crisis de la arquitectura española. 1939-1972*, Edicusa, Madrid, 1972.

Fernández del Amo, José L., *Palabra y obra*, COAM, Madrid, 1995.

Fernández Casado, Carlos: *La arquitectura del ingeniero*, Alfaguara, Madrid, 1975.

Fernández-Galiano, L. (introduction): *Francisco Mangado*, Gili, Barcelona, 1994.

— *La quimera moderna: Los poblados dirigidos de Madrid*, Blume, Madrid, 1988.

Fernández Troyano, L.: *Tierra sobre el agua. Visión histórica universal*, Colegio de Ingenieros de Caminos, Canales y Puertos, Madrid, 1988.

Ferrater, C. (direction); Cruz, A.; Ercilla, R.; Garcés, J.; Herreros, J.; Mingo, G.; León, I.; Fernández-Galiano, L.; Ibáñez, J. (jury): *Cuarta Bienal de Arquitectura Española 1995-1996*, Ministerio de Fomento, CSCAE, Universidad I. Menéndez Pelayo, Universidad de Alcalá, Madrid, 1997.

Fleming, J.; Honour, H.; Pevsner, N.: *The Penguin Dictionary of Architecture*, 4th edition, Penguin Books, London, 1991.

Flores, Carlos: *Arquitectura Española Contemporánea*, Aguilar (first edition, 1961), Madrid, 1989.

— *Sobre arquitecturas y arquitectos*, COAM, Madrid, 1994.

Fochs, Carles (ed.): *J.A. Coderch de Sentmenat: 1913-1984*, Gili, Barcelona, 1995.

Forestier, Jean Claude N.: *Jardines andaluces*, Arquitectura, T. IV, 1922.

Frampton, Kenneth: *Modern Architecture: A Critical History*, 3rd edition, Thames and Hudson, London, 1992.

Frampton, K. (introduction): *Luoghi d'architettura europea*, Carte Segete, Rome, 1989.

Frampton, K. (introduction); Campo Baeza, A.; Poisay, C.: *Young Spanish Architecture*, COAM, Universidad Politécnica de Madrid, 1985.

Frampton, K.; Capitel, A.; Pérez Escolano, V.; Solà-Morales, I. de: *Building in a New Spain*, The Art Institute of Chicago - Gili, Chicago - Barcelona, 1992.

Frechilla, J.; Carreras Moysi, B.; Duró Pifarré, J.; Lluch, E.; Bonell, E.; Campo Baeza, A.; Gallego, J.M.; Mangado, F.J. (selection committee and jury): *III Bienal de Arquitectura española. 3rd Biennial*

Spanish Architecture, MOPTMA - CSCAE - Universidad I. Menéndez Pelayo, Madrid, 1991.

Freixa, Jaume: *Josep Lluis Sert*, Gili, Barcelona, 1995.

Fullaondo, Juan D.: *Juan Daniel Fullaondo*, Munilla-Lería, Madrid, 1996.

— *Fernando García Mercadal, arquitecto*, COAM, Madrid, 1984.

— *La bicicleta aproximativa: conversaciones en torno a Francisco Javier Sáenz de Oíza*, Kain, Madrid, 1991.

— *Las arquitecturas de Bilbao. A la búsqueda del tiempo perdido (sobre todo ecléctico)*, COAVN, Bilbao, 1993.

Fullaondo, J.D.; Muñoz, M.T.: *Historia de la arquitectura española contemporánea,* vol. 1, Kain Editorial, Madrid, 1993.

— *Historia de la arquitectura española contemporánea,* vol. 2, Munilla-Lería, Madrid, 1995.

— *Historia de la arquitectura española contemporánea,* vol. 3, Molly Editorial, Madrid, 1995.

González Capitel, Antonio: see Capitel, Antón.

Grandas, M.C.: *L'Exposició Internacional de Barcelona de 1929*, Barcelona, 1988.

Granell, Enrique: *Bankinter, 1973-76, de R. Moneo y R. Bescós*, COAAor, Almería, 1994.

Güell, Xavier: *Mediterranean Houses. Costa Brava 2*, Gili, Barcelona, 1994.

Gutiérrez Burón, J.: *Antonio Palacios Ramilo en Madrid*, Madrid, 1987.

Hernández Pezzi, C.: *José María García de Paredes*, COAAor, Málaga, 1992.

Herrera, J.M.: *Joaquín Rieta Sister. Arquitecto valenciano,* Valencia, 1983.

Hervás Avilés, José M.: *Cincuenta años de arquitectura en Murcia*, COAMu, Murcia, 1982.

Insausti, P.; Llopis, T.; Pérez Escolano, V.: *Arquitectura valenciana. La década de los ochenta,* IVAM, Valencia, 1992.

Jencks, Charles: *Modern Movements in Architecture,* New York, 1973.

Lahuerta, J.J.: "Razionalismo e architettura in Spagna negli anni trenta", in various authors, *L'Europa dei razionalisti*, Electa, Milan, 1989.

Levene, R.; Márquez Cecilia, F.; Ruiz Barbarín, A.: *Arquitectura española contemporánea 1975-1990*, 2 volumes, El Croquis Editorial, Madrid, 1989.

Llano Cabado, P. de: *Alejandro de la Sota. O nacemento dunha arquitectura,* Diputación de Pontevedra, Pontevedra, 1995.

Llinás, Josep A.; Sarrá, Jordi (photographs): *Josep María Jujol,* Taschen, Cologne, 1992.

López-Peláez, J.M.; Corrales, J.A.; Vázquez Molezún, R.: *Corrales y Molezún. Obra Completa*, Tanais Ediciones, Seville, 1998.

López Sardá, María L. (exhibition commissar): *Arquitecturas de Representación. España de Oriente a Occidente*, Ministerio Asuntos Exteriores, MOPTMA, Fundación Cultural del COAM, Madrid, 1995.

Mannino, E.; Paricio, I.: *J.Ll. Sert: construcción y arquitectura*, Gili, Barcelona, 1983.

Manrique, César: *Lanzarote. Arquitectura inédita*, Cabildo Insular de Lanzarote, Arrecife, 1988.

Manterola Armisen, J.: "Personalidad y obra de Carlos Fernandez Casado", in *Revista de Obras Públicas*, Madrid, 1988, 135: 1013-1026.

Marchán, Simón: *Linazasoro*, Gili, Barcelona, 1989.

Martorell, J.M.; Bohigas, O.; Mackay, D.; Puigdomènech, A.: *La Villa Olímpica: Barcelona 92: The Olympic Village*, Gili, Barcelona, 1991.

Mas Serra, Elías: *50 años de arquitectura en Euskadi*, Gobierno Vasco, Consejería de Obras Públicas, Vitoria, 1990.

Maure Rubio, Lilia: *Zuazo*, COAM, Madrid, 1987.

Mitjans, Francesc: *Francesc Mitjans, arquitecte,* Barcelona, 1996.

Moneo, Rafael: "La llamada Escuela de Barcelona", in *Arquitectura*, num. 121, Madrid, 1969.

— *Sobre el concepto de tipo en arquitectura*, ETSAM, Madrid, 1991.

— *Contra la Indiferencia como Norma. Anyway*, Ediciones ARQ, Universidad Católica de Chile, Escuela de Arquitectura, Santiago de Chile, 1995.

Moneo, R. (introduction), Cruz, A.; Ortiz, A.: *Cruz/Ortiz*, Princeton Architectural Press, New York, 1996.

Montaner, J.M.: *La modernidad superada. Arquitectura, arte y pensamiento del siglo XX*, Gili, Barcelona, 1997.

— *Después del movimiento moderno. Arquitectura de la segunda mitad del siglo XX*, Gili, Barcelona, 1993.

— *Museos para el nuevo siglo*, Gili, Barcelona, 1995.

— "España", in Benevolo, op. cit.

Monteys, Xavier (coord.): *La arquitectura de los años cincuenta en Barcelona* (exhibition catalogue), Dirección General para la Vivienda y la Arquitectura del MOPU - Escuela T.S. de Arquitectura del Vallés, Madrid - Barcelona, 1987.

Mosquera Adell, E.; Pérez Cano, M.T.; Moreno Pérez, J.R.: *De la Tradición al Futuro*, Congreso de Arquitectura Contemporánea en Andalucía, COAAoc, Seville, 1992.

Mosquera, E.; Pérez Cano, M.T.: *La vanguardia imposible*, Junta de Andalucía, Consejería de Obras Públicas, Seville, 1990.

Moya Blanco, Luis: *La arquitectura cortés y otros escritos. T.2. Bóvedas tabicadas*, COAM, Madrid.

Nanclares, F.: *Ignacio Alvarez Castelao, arquitecto*, COAAs, Oviedo, 1983.

Narbona, C.; Duró i Pifarrer, J.;Lluch, E.; Gil, M.D.; Vázquez Molezún, R.; Mateo, J.L.; Botey, J.M.; Molinero, J. (selection committee): *I Muestra de 10 años de Arquitectura Española 1980-1990*, MOPTMA, CSCAE, Universidad I. Menéndez Pelayo, Madrid, 1991.

Navarro Baldeweg, Juan: *Navarro Baldeweg*, Tanais Ediciones, Seville, 1998.

Navarro Segura, María Isabel: *Racionalismo en Canarias*, Act, Santa Cruz de Tenerife, 1989.

— *Marrero Regalado (1897-1956). La arquitectura como escenografía*, COACa, Santa Cruz de Tenerife, 1992.

Neufert, E.: *Bauentwurfslehre*, Berlin, 1936, 33rd edition, 1992.

Palerm Salazar, Juan M. et al.: *Arquitectura y urbanis-mo en Canarias, 1968-1988*, Escuela T.S. de Arquitectura, Las Palmas de Gran Canaria, 1989.

Peña, R.; Sangalli, M.: *Luis Peña Ganchegui. Arquitec-turas 1958-1994*, Universidad del País Vasco, San Sebastián, 1994.

Peña Ganchegui, L.; Solà-Morales, I. de; Fernández-Galiano, L.; Kleihues, J.P.; Coquhoum, A.; Grassi, G.; Waisman, M.; Buchanan, P.R.; Benet, J. (inter-national jury): *I Bienal de Arquitectura Española. 1991*, MOPTMA, CSCAE, Universidad I. Menéndez Pelayo, Madrid, 1991.

Pérez Arroyo, S.: *Salvador Pérez Arroyo*, Fundación COAM, Madrid, 1992.

Pérez Escolano, Víctor: *Aníbal González, Arquitecto. 1876-1929*, Diputación de Sevilla, Seville, 1973.

— "Una década prodigiosa", in *1978-1988. Andalu-cía: diez años de cultura*, Junta de Andalucía, Con-sejería de Cultura, Seville, 1988.

Pérez Escolano, V.; Pérez Cano, M.T.; Mosquera Adell, E.; Moreno Pérez, J.R: *50 años de arquitectu-ra en Andalucía. 1936-1986* (exhibition catalogue), Junta de Andalucía, Consejería de Obras Públicas y Transportes, Seville, 1986.

Pérez Escolano, V.; Solà-Morales, I. de: *España: Arqui-tecturas de hoy*, MOPT, Madrid, 1992.

Pérez Escolano, V.; Sierra Delgado, J.R.; Torres, F.: *Arquitectura pública en Andalucía*, Junta de Anda-lucía, Consejería de Obras Públicas, Seville, 1994.

Pérez Lastra, José R.: *Vaquero Palacios, arquitecto*, COAAs, Oviedo, 1992.

Pérez Parrilla, Sergio T.: *La arquitectura racionalista en Canarias. 1927-1939*, Cabildo Insular de Gran Canaria, Las Palmas de Gran Canaria, 1977.

— *La arquitectura de Las Palmas en el primer tercio del siglo XX*, Cabildo Insular de Gran Canaria, Las Palmas de Gran Canaria, 1981.

— *Apuntes sobre arquitectura contemporánea. Historia del arte en Canarias*, Edirca, Las Palmas de Gran Canaria, 1982.

Pérez Rojas, F.J.: *Cartagena (1874-1936). Transforma-ción urbana y arquitectónica*, Murcia, 1986.

— *Art Déco en España*, Cátedra, Madrid, 1990.

Pérez i Sánchez, M. (ed.): *Vint-i-cinc anys d'arquitectura barcelonina. 1914-1938*, COAC, Barcelona, 1981.

Piñón, H.: *Arquitecturas de las neovanguardias*, Gili, Barcelona, 1984.

Piñón, H.; Català-Roca, F.: *Arquitectura moderna en Barcelona (1951-1976)*, Edicions UPC, ETSAB, Barcelona, 1996.

Pizza, Antonio: *Dispensario antituberculoso, 1933-37*, COAAor, Almería, 1993.

— (ed. and exhibition commissar): *J. Ll. Sert y el Mediterráneo*, CAC - Ministerio de Fomento, Barcelona - Madrid, undated.

Poisay, C.; Hassine, R.B. (eds.): *Architecture en Espagne. 1974-1984*, (exhibition catalogue), Paris, 1985.

Pozo Municio, José M.: *Regino Borobio Ojeda (1895-1976)*, COAAr, Zaragoza, 1990.

Quetglas, Josep: "Al margen de una imposible Escue-la de Barcelona", in *Jano Arquitectura*, num. 48, Barcelona, 1977.

— *Der Gläserne Schrecken. Imágenes del Pabellón de Alemania*, Montreal, 1991.

Quetglas, J.; Alonso, F.; López-Peláez, J.M. et al.: *Conversaciones en torno a Alejandro de la Sota*, Departamento Proyectos ETSAM, Madrid, 1996.

Rábanos Faci, Carmen: *Vanguardia frente a tradición en la arquitectura aragonesa (1925-39). El racio-nalismo*, Guara, Zaragoza, 1984.

Rispa, R.; Aguaza, M.J. (eds.), Dal Co, F. (foreword); Pellón, J.; Pérez Escolano, V.; Polano, S.: *Expo'92 Seville. Architecture and Design*, Expo'92 S.A.-Electa - Abbeville, Seville - Milan - New York, 1992.

Rodríguez, C.; Torres, J.: *Grup R*, Gili, Barcelona, 1994.

Rodríguez Cheda, José B.: *Alejandro de la Sota*, COAG, 1994.

Roig, J.; Alvarez, F.; Pich-Aguilera, F.: *La Ricarda*, Bar-celona, 1996.

Rossi, Aldo: *L'architettura della città*, Padua, 1966 (English edition, Cambridge, MA, 1982).

Rovira, J.M.: *Urbanización en Punta Martinet, Ibiza, 1966-1971*, COAAor, Almería, 1996.

Rubió i Tudurí, N.M.: *Jardines modernos*, Barcelona, 1929.

— *Del Paraíso al jardín latino*, Barcelona, 1981.

Ruiz Cabrero, Gabriel: *El Moderno en España. Arquitectura 1945-2000*, Tanais Ediciones, Seville, 1998.

Rykwert, J. (introduction); Güell, X. (ed.): *Spanish Contemporary Architecture. The Eighties*, Gili, Barcelona, 1990.

Sáenz de Oíza, F.J.; Capitel, A.; Sáenz Guerra, J.: *Javier Sáenz de Oiza, arquitecto*, Pronaos - Ministerio de Fomento, Madrid, 1996.

Sambricio, Carlos: *Cuando se quiso resucitar la arqui-tectura*, Colegio de Aparejadores/Librería Yerba/ Consejería de Cultura, Murcia, 1983.

Sanz Esquide et al.: *Archivo de arquitectura en el País Vasco, años 30*, Delegación en Bizkaia del COAVN - Gobierno Vasco, Vitoria, 1990.

Schneider, Friederike (assistance: Axel Haase, Ria Stein): *Grundrißatlas Wohnungsbau. Floor Plan Atlas Housing*, Birkhäuser, Basel, 2nd edition, 1997.

Sebastián, S.; Alonso, A.: *Arquitectura mallorquina moderna y contemporánea*, Palma de Mallorca, 1981.

Seguí, M.: *Arquitectura contemporánea en Baleares, 1900-1947*, Universitat-COAB, Palma de Mallorca, 1990.

Sert, Josep Lluís: *Can Our Cities Survive?*, Cambridge, 1942.

— *Ibiza, fuerte y luminosa*, Ediciones Polígrafa, Barce-lona, 1967.

Sert, J.L.; Thyrwhitt, J.; E.M. Rogers, E.M.: *The Heart of the City*, London, 1952.

Sobrino Simal, Julián: *Arquitectura Industrial en España (1830-1990)*, Cátedra, Madrid, 1996.

Solà-Morales, Ignasi de: *Diferencias. Topografía de la arquitectura contemporánea*, Gili, Barcelona, 1996.

— *Bach/Mora Arquitectos*, Gili, Barcelona, 1996.

— "L'arquitectura a Catalunya. 1939-1970", in E. Jardí, *L'art català contemporani*, Aymá, Barcelona, 1972.

— "Arquitectura española: balbuceos y silencios", in Bozal/Lloréns (eds.), *España. Vanguardia artística y realidad social, 1936-1976*, Gili, Barcelona, 1976.

— "L'Exposició Internacional de Barcelona (1914-29) com instrument de política urbana", .n *Recerques*, 6 (1976), pp. 137-148.

— *Eclecticismo y vanguardia. El caso de la arquitectura moderna en Catalunya*, Gili, Barcelona, 1980.

— "La arquitectura de Josep M. Jujol", in various authors, *Josep María Jujol, arquitecte (1879-1942)*, Barcelona, 1989.

— see Capitel.

Solà-Morales, I. de; Cirici; C.; Ramos, F.: *Mies van der Rohe. Barcelona Pavilion*, Gili, Barcelona, 1993.

Solana Suárez, E.: *El patrimonio de la arquitectura moderna en la ciudad de Las Palmas G. C. 1922-1960*, Conferencia Internacional de Conservación de Centros Históricos, 1994.

Soler Márquez, R.: "50 años de arquitectura en Granada, 1940-1990. Apuntes para un relato incompleto", in various authors, *Granada ante el 92. Un proyecto cultural*, Universidad de Granada, Granada, 1992.

Sòria Badia, Enric: *Coderch*, Blume, 1979.

Sostres, Josep M.: *El funcionalismo y la nueva plástica*, Madrid, 1950.

— *Opiniones sobre arquitectura*, COAMu, Murcia, 1983.

Sota, A. de la (introduction), Llinás, J.: *Josep Llinás*. Whitney Library of Design, New York, 1997.

Steiner, D.: *José Luis Mateo*, Gili, Barcelona, 1992.

Tabuenca, F. (ed): *Víctor Eusa, arquitecto*, Pamplona, 1989.

Terán, Fernando de: *Planeamiento urbano en la España contemporánea (1900-1980)*, Alianza Editorial, Madrid, 1982.

Trillo de Leyva, Manuel: *La Exposición Iberoamericana. La transformación urbana de Sevilla*, Ayuntamiento de Sevilla, Seville, 1980.

Uría, L. (introduction): *Antonio Fernández Alba. Arquitec-tura 1957-1980*, Xarait, Madrid, 1980.

Urrutia, Angel: *Arquitectura española. Siglo XX*, Cátedra, Madrid, 1997.

Var. authors: *Manifiesto de La Alhambra*, 1953.

Var. authors: *Alas Casariego arquitectos, 1955-1995*, MOPTMA, Madrid, 1995.

Var. authors: *Xosé Bar Bóo, arquitecto*, COAG, 1996.

Var. authors: *Antonio Bonet Castellana 1913-1989*, COAC - Ministerio de Fomento, Barcelona - Madrid, 1996.

Var. authors: *Félix Candela*, MOPTMA, Madrid, 1994.

Var. authors: *Julio Cano Lasso*, CSCAE, Madrid, 1992.

Var. authors: *Cano Lasso, 1949-1995*, MOPTMA, Madrid, 1995.

Var. authors: *José Luis Fernández del Amo*, Museo Centro Nacional de Arte Reina Sofía, Madrid, 1995.

Var. authors: *Fisac*, Ministerio de Fomento - CSCAE, Madrid, 1997.

Var. authors: *Rafael González Villar e a sua época*, COAG, Vigo, 1975.

Var. authors: *La obra de Luis Gutiérrez Soto*, 2nd edition, COAM, Madrid, 1988.

Var. authors: *La Arquitectura racionalista de Miguel Martín Fernández de la Torre, 1927-39* (exhibition catalogue), Ayuntamiento de Arucas, 1977.

Var. authors: *Miguel Martín. Arquitecturas para la gran ciudad* (exhibition catalogue), Centro Atlántico de Arte Moderno, Las Palmas de Gran Canaria, 1995.

Var. authors: *Cinco proyectos de vivienda social en la obra de Javier Sáenz de Oíza*, Pronaos, Madrid, 1996.

Var. authors: *Josep Lluis Sert, arquitectura y diseño urbano*, Ministerio de Cultura, Madrid, 1978

Var. authors: *Informes de la Construcción*, num. 137, monograph on Eduardo Torroja, Instituto Eduardo Torroja, Madrid.

Var. authors: *Barcelona Olímpica*, A&V: Monografías de Arquitectura y Vivienda, num. 37, Madrid, 1992.

Var. authors: *Arquitectura y espacio rural en Ibiza*, CAOB - La Gaya Ciencia, Palma de Mallorca - Barcelona, 1985.

Var. authors: *El Cabildo Insular y la ciudad racionalista*, Cabildo Insular de Gran Canaria, Las Palmas de Gran Canaria, 1987.

Var. authors: *Sevilla 1992*, A&V: Monografías de Arqui-tectura y Vivienda, num. 20, Madrid, 1989.

Var. authors: *Sevilla Expo*, A&V: Monografías de Arqui-tecura y Vivienda, num. 34-35, Madrid, 1992.

Var. authors: *Especial Expo92. Análisis crítico de Arqui-tectura y Diseño*, Diseño Interior, num. 15, Madrid, 1992.

Var. authors: *Arquitectura para después de una guerra, 1939-1949* (exhibition catalogue), COACB, Barcelona, 1977.

Var. authors: *Casas Españolas*, A&V: Monografías de Arquitectura y Vivienda, num. 60, Madrid.

Var. authors: *Diez años de planeamiento urbanístico en España, 1979-1989*, MOPU, Madrid, 1989.

Var. authors: *El gran arte en la arquitectura*, Salvat, Barcelona, 1988.

Var. authors: *El Noucentisme. Un projecte de moder-nitat*, Generalitat de Catalunya, Barcelona, 1994.

Var. authors: *Els darrers cent anys. Arquitectura i ciutat*, Generalitat de Catalunya, Barcelona, 1988.

Var. authors: *Arquitectura a Catalunya. L'era democrática 1977-1996*, Generalitat de Catalunya, Departament de Cultura, Barcelona, 1996.

Var. authors: *Galicia Jacobea*, A&V: Monografías de Arquitectura y Vivienda, num. 41, Madrid.

Var. authors: monograph on contemporary architecture in Madrid and Barcelona, in *L'Architecture d'Aujourd'hui*, num. 149, Paris, 1970.

Var. authors: monograph on Spain, in *Architectural Review*, num. 1071, London, 1986.

Var. authors: monograph on Spanish architecture of the 70s, in *Controspazio*, year IV, num. 4, July-August 1979, Rome.

Var. authors: monograph on Spain, in *Deutsche Bau-zeitung*, num. 6, 1992.

Var. authors: monograph on Spain, in *Werk, Bauen und Wohnen*, num. 9, 1984.

Var. authors: monograph on Spanish architecture of the 60s, in *Zodiac*, num. 15, Milan, 1965.

Var. authors: monograph on J.M. Sostres, in *2C. Construcción de la ciudad*, num. 4, Barcelona, 1975.

Venturi, Robert: *Complexity and Contradiction in Architecture*, New York, 1966.

Viaplana, A.; Piñón, H.: *Albert Viaplana, Helio Piñón*, Barcelona, 1996.

Villar Movellán, A.: *Arquitectura del Regionalismo en Sevilla, 1900-1935*, Diputación de Sevilla, Seville, 1979.

Zabalbeascoa, A.: *The New Spanish Architecture*, Rizzoli, New York, 1993.

Zaera, Alejandro: *Abalos & Herreros*, Gili, Barcelona, 1993.

Zevi, Bruno: *Arquitectura de Sert en la Fundació Miró*, Ediciones Polígrafa, Barcelona, 1977.

Spanish Journals and Magazines

The journals that are currently being published on a regular basis are **highlighted** in bold italics.

2 C, Construcción de la Ciudad, Barcelona.

3ZU, Barcelona.

A.C., published from 1931 to 1935 by GATEPAC.

Aldaba, Zaragoza, since 1983.

Anales de Arquitectura, Valladolid.

Anuario de la Asociación de Arquitectos de Cataluña (yearbook), from 1899 to 1930.

Aparejadores, Seville.

ARDI, Barcelona.

Arquitectos, Madrid., from 1975 to 1981 and from 1984 on.

Arquitectura, published uninterruptedly since 1918 by the Sociedad Central de Arquitectos, Madrid, it is currently the COAM's journal.

Arquitectura, Seville.

Arquitectura Andalucía Oriental, Granada.

Arquitectura Española, from 1923 to 1928.

Arquitectura i Urbanisme, Barcelona, 1931 and others.

Arquitectura Viva, Madrid, since 1988.

Arquitectura y Construcción, from 1897 to 1923.

Arquitecturas Bis, Barcelona, from 1974 to 1985.

Arte y Cemento, Madrid.

Arte y Parte, Madrid.

a+t, Vitoria, since 1992.

A & V. Monografías de Arquitectura y Vivienda, Madrid, since 1985.

Babelia, El País (daily) cultural supplement.

Basa, COACa, Santa Cruz de Tenerife, since 1982.

BAU, 1989 and others.

Boden, Madrid.

Boletín de la Dirección General de Arquitectura, (bulletin) Madrid.

Boletín de la Sociedad Central de Arquitectos (bulletin), Madrid, 1876-1877 (see *Revista* below).

Carrer de la Ciutat, Barcelona.

CAU, Construcción, Arquitectura, Urbanismo, Barcelona.

Cercha, Madrid, since 1990.

Circo, Madrid.

Ciudad y Territorio, Madrid.

Común, Bilbao, 1979 and others.

Composición arquitectónica, Bilbao, 1988 and others.

Cortijos y Rascacielos, Madrid, from 1929 to 1953.

Cota Cero, COAAs, Oviedo, from 1985 to 1988.

Cuadernos de Arquitectura y Urbanismo, from 1944 to 1981 [*Quaderns* since 1981], Barcelona.

Cuadernos de Construcción, Seville.

Cuadernos del Departamento de Teoría de la Arquitectura, Seville.

Cuadernos, Dirección General de Arquitectura y Edificación, Madrid.

Cuadernos de Proyectos, Seville.

D'A, COAB, Palma de Mallorca, 1989 and others.

d.d.A. Detalles de Arquitectura.

De Diseño, Madrid.

DiseñoInterior, Madrid.

Documentos de Arquitectura, Almería, since 1987.

El Croquis, Madrid, since 1982.

El Inmueble.

Experimenta, Madrid.

Figura, Seville.

Gaceta de Arte, from 1932 to 1936.

Geometría, Málaga, since 1986.

Hogar y Arquitectura, Madrid, from 1956 to 1977

Informes de la Construcción, Instituto Eduardo Torroja, Madrid, since 1948.

Jano-Arquitectura, Barcelona.

La Ciudad Lineal, from 1896 to 1932.

La Construcción Moderna, from 1903 to 1936.

La construcción y las artes decorativas, in the 20s.

La Escuela de Madrid, Madrid, 1984 and others.

La Gaceta de Obras Públicas, Madrid, 19th c. to 1929.

Lápiz. Revista mensual de arte, Madrid.

MOPU, MOPU, Madrid.

MOPTMA, MOPTMA, Madrid.

Neutra, Seville.

Nueva Forma, Madrid, from 1966 to 1975.

Nuevas Formas, Madrid, from 1934 to 1936.

Obradoiro. Revista de Arquitectura, Santiago de Compostela, since 1978.

Obras, from 1931 to 1985.

Oeste, 1983 and others.

ON Diseño, Barcelona.

Periferia, Seville, 1984 and others.

Q, C.S.C.A.E., Madrid, from 1981 to 1984.

Quaderns d'arquitectura i urbanisme, COAC, Barcelona

Reconstrucción, Madrid, 1940 and others.

Restauración & Rehabilitación, Madrid.

Resúmenes Arquitectura, since 1875.

Revista Nacional de Arquitectura, Madrid, from 1939 to 1959.

Revista de Obras Públicas, Colegio de Ingenieros de Caminos, Canales y Puertos de Madrid, since 1843.

Revista Técnica, Barcelona.

Tecnología y Arquitectura, Vitoria, since 1988.

Tectónica, Madrid, since 1996.

Temas de Arquitectura y Urbanismo, Madrid, 1959 and others.

UR. Urbanismo Revista, Barcelona.

Urbanismo, COAM, Madrid.

WAM, Barcelona, 1997.

The drawings, ground plans and photographs of the works featured in this guide have been made available to the *Register of Spanish Architecture* by the architects, engineers, or their firms, who were requested to furnish materials for which they hold the official copyright. The other illustrations and photographs used – identified as *a, b, c*... from left to right and from top to bottom in each page – have been furnished by the individuals and companies that follow. The acronyms of the Architects' Chambers used are explained in page 393.

Abalos&Herreros 273e, 129d. Aguinaga 307e. Alas Casariego 260a,b, 266e, 284e; Alas Casariego-R. Royal 270b. Alonso del Val 293a. Alumnos ETSA de San Sebastián 303b,c. Alvarez Sala 274f. Amadó/Domènech 195b; Amadó/Domènech-L. Casals 169d; Amadó/Domènech-H. Suzuki 167d. AMP 115a,c. Apezteguía 295b. Arana 286b. Aranguren/González 206b. Aroca 262d. Arriola & Fiol-L. Casals 175c. Artengo/Domínguez Anadón/Schwartz 114f. Artigues/Sanabria-F. Freixa 186b. Arxiu Coderch 101d, 118e. Ayala 83a,d, 206a.
Bach/Mora 87a, 164e, 166a,b, 185c, 187e,f,g, 197b. M.A. Baldellou 117b, 121b, 130a, 201a, 318b. Barrionuevo, A. 74e. Barrionuevo, F. 71c,d. Barrionuevo/Torres 52b. Batlle/Roig 175b. Bayón 227b, 267b; Bayón-J. Azurmendi 118d, 269e, 273b; Bayón-H. Suzuki 77b. Bellosillo 128a. Bofill 154a,b, 155d, 185a, 187d; Bofill-S. Vergano 187c, 324b; Bofill-D. von Shaewen 339a. Bohigas-cb foto 178e; Bohigas/Martorell-cb foto 159e. Bonell 159c ,165b, 179c,f; Bonell-L. Casals 165c,d, 176d; Bonell-cb foto 165a, 179d,e; Bonell-.F. Freixa 190d. Bonell/Gil/Rius 174a. Bosch/Tarrús-F. Catalá Roca 182c. Bru 171e,f, 184b. Brugarolas 289b,c. Brullet 173a; Brullet-F. Freixa 173b, 183c. Burillo/Lorenzo 90c,d. 136c. CAAM 106b, 106c, 108d, 109c; CAAM-Sosa 110a; CAAM-T. Edo Hierro 107c,d, 108b. Cabrera/Febles 116c. Cabrero 242b,c,d,e,f, 254b,c, 255a,b, 258b,c,d; Cabrero-Férriz fotógrafo industrial 244d, 249b, 279f. Campo Baeza 54e, 272c, 283d,e, 324a, Candela 336a,b. Cantallops-Maspons+Ubiña 156c. A. Capitel 96a,b,c, 101a, 119c,d, 130b,c, 144a,e, 230c, 240a, 241d, 242a, 243b, 248a, 254a, 270e, 281a, 308d,e; Capitel/Hernandez/Martorell 241c. Carbajal Navarro 84a; Carbajal-M. Laguillo 51a. Carlos Fernández Casado, S.L. 122a,b, 158c, 159a,b, 266a,b, 281e, 294b, 295a, 317e, 320c; Carlos Fernandez Casado, S.L.-FCP 294a,c,d; Carlos Fernández Casado, S.L.-L. Montoto 94e. Carrascal/Fernández de la Puente 83c. Carrasco López 203a. Carvajal 151c, 247b, 262 e, 266c, 267d,e,f. CA,s.a 17b,c,d, 76a, 82b,d,e,f. Casas 129c, 135c, 137c,e, 218c, 268b,c, 269b; Casas-J. Azurmendi 135d, 137d; Casas-L. Casals 137a,b, 268a, 269a; Casas-C. Delgado 80f; Casas-J. González 271d; Casas-E. Sánchez 131a, 279e. Catón/Ercilla/Campo 301d. Cenicacelaya/Saloña 317d. Clotet/Paricio 181a,c; Clotet/Paricio-L. Casals 190a; Clotet/Tusquets 157b, 183b, 186a, 338; Clotet/Tusquets-E. Berenguer 157c. COAAs 92a,b,e,f, 93b,d, 97a,b; COAAs-M. Morilla 92c, 95a, 97c,d. COAB 102d, 103c; COAB/*D'A* 99b. COAC 142b,c,d, 143e, 145d, 146b, 149b, 150c,d, 151e, 152b,d, 153b,c, 156b, 158b, 170d, 180c, 184c,e, 188d, 191a, 192a, 193d,e, 199d, 333, 334, 335; COAC Tarragona 197a. COACa Tenerife 113b,c,d, 114a, 118 b. Colegio O. de Arquitectos de Castilla y León - Segovia 127e. COAM 99c, 224b, 226b, 228c, 229b,d, 231b, 232b, 233b, 234f, 235b, 236c,d, 237c,d, 238b,c, 240c,e, 243e, 246c, 249e, 250e, 259b, 261b; COAM/*Arquitectura* 227d. COAV Alicante 322a. *Composición Arquitectónica* 214a,b. Corrales, 54b, 100a, 122d,e, 123c,d, 136b, 210a,b,c, 248b,c,d, 255c, 259c, 260c,d, 263d,e, 280a,b, 283b,c, 289b, 337. Correa/Milà 182a, 191d; Correa/Milà-D. von Schoewen 182b. Cruz/Ortiz, S.L. 50b, 71a,b, 74,f, 78f, 274 a; Cruz/ Ortiz, S.L.-D. Malagamba 27 b, 50a, 52a, 78e, 60a, 83e. Cuadra 320f.
Daroca 56d. Díaz Llanos/Saavedra 114b,c,d, 116b; Díaz Llanos/Saavedra-E. Pintos 115e, 116a. Díaz Recaséns 85c. Diego Llaca 97e. DoCoMoMo Ibérico 62a, 68e, 87c, 88b, 89a, 97f,g, 103b, 127a,b, 144b,c, 145c, 150f, 184d, 237b,e, 317c, 328b. Domènech, Ll. 195a. Donato 161d.
Ercilla 302c; Ercilla/Campo 301c. Estudio Cano Lasso 47c, 111e, 217a, 249c, 261d,e, 272d, 280d, 293d, 300e.
Fargas/Tous 156e, 300a,c. FCC 81c,d. Feduchi 49c. Fernández Alba, Angel 122c, 275a; Fernández Alba, Angel-M. Pyykkö 101e. Fernández Alba, Antonio 124a,b,c,d, 251e, 282e,f, 301a. Fernández-Albalat 209 d. R. Fernández del Amo 132a, 133d, 207 b; R. Fernández del Amo-Kindel 63a,b, 132b, 133 b,c, 207 c, 324d, 325e,f; R. Fernández del Amo-Paisajes Españoles 63c,d, 207a, 324e. Ferrater 162a, 193a,b, 325a,c; Ferrater-L. Casals 192b; Ferrater-cb foto 192c, 325b. Fisac 128c, 243c, 245b,c, 247e, 252a,b,c, 278a,b,c,d; Fisac-M. García Moya 247d; Fisac-Kindel 128b,d; Fisac-A.S. Koch 299c; Fisac-A. Schommer 299d. Foreign Office Architects, Ltd. 341b. Foster 171a,b, 315b,d; Foster-R. Davies 315a,c; Foster-John E. Linden 171c. Fraile/Revillo 131b. Frechilla/López-Peláez/Sánchez 83b, 127a, 136a, 269c,d,f, 320d,f; Frechilla/López-Peláez-J. Azurmendi 270c. Fris Imatge 175a. Fullaondo 314c,d,e. Fundación A. de la Sota 23, 70c,d, 84d, 85d,e, 90b, 121c,d, 123a,b, 217d,e, 218a,b, 219a,b, 251b,c,d, 253a,b,c,d, 262a,b,c, 265d, 280d. Fundación César Manrique 112a,b,c,d. Fundación Rodríguez Acosta 57b; Fundación Rodríguez Acosta-J.J. Blassi 57a,c. Fuses/Viader-D. Malagamba 190b,c.
Gali 164d, 170b, 210e. Gallego 211c, 216b. Gallego-P. Gallego 210d,f, 211a,b, 213e, 216a,c; Gallego-X. Lobato 216e; Gallego-H. Suzuki 216d. Garay 295d, 307a,c,d. Garcés/Sòria, 116e, 161e, 162c,d, 188a, 194b, 292d; Garcés/Sòria-L. Casals 183e. Garcia Barba 115d. García de Paredes 58b,c,d, 62c,d, 245d,e, 257b, 271e; García de Paredes-L. Casals 58e; García de Paredes-Pando Fotógrafos 55a; García de Paredes-A. Schommer 62b, 257a. García de Paredes/García Pedrosa 287c. García Solera 322c. García-Solera Vera 322d, 323c,d. García/Rubiño/Rubiño-D. Malagamba 54c, 84c. Frank O. Gehry & Associates 316a,b,c,d,e,f. González Cordón 52c,d, 53d, 60c, 67b, 72d, 77c, 80e. González, Mª Luisa-L. Casals 110e.
Henríquez 114e. Herederos de Martín Fernández de la Torre 107a,b, 108c, 109d. Herederos de R. Vazquez Molezún 218d. Higueras 111b,c,d, 255d,e, 284b,c. HSP Arquitectos, S.L.-D. Malagamba 94d. Hubman / Vass 58f.
Iberdrola 126d. Instituto Eduardo Torroja 131c,d,e, 239c, 281c, 284a, 296c,d,e. Iñiguez de Onzoño 250b,c,d, 257e,f, 260e, 263a, 270d, 314a. Iñiguez/Ustarroz 292c. Isozaki 169b,c.
C. Jordá 211b, 326d, 327b,c,d,e,f. Junquera/Pérez Pita 59c, 267a, 270a, 279c,d, 282c,d. Junta de Andalucía, Consejería de Obras Públicas, Dirección General de Arquitectura y Vivienda 55b,c, 69e; Junta de Andalucía, Consejería de Obras

Públicas, Dirección General de Arquitectura y Vivienda-J. Andrade 47b, 53e, 54a, 56e, 58a, 60b; Junta de Andalucía, Consejería de Obras Públicas, Instituto Cartográfico de Andalucía 48c, 61d.
P. Lizancos 213a,b. L. Llorente 127c,d. La Hoz 56b,c. Lamela-M. Garcia Moya 133a, 249a, 250a. León/García 320b.
Linazasoro 129b, 274c,d,e, 275d,e, 305b. Llinás 176b, 196a,b, 197e; Llinás-cb foto 185b, 191b; Llinás-L. Jansana 151f, 176a, 197c,d, 200b; Llinás-H. Suzuki 141d, 167c. López Alvarez 205d. López Cotelo 124e, 277b,c, 285b,c; López Cotelo/Puente 89b,c,d.
Madridejos/Sancho-H. Suzuki 280c. Magro-Pepa Balaguer 323b. Mangado 295c, 296f. María Vázquez 218e. Marín de Terán 78a; Marín de Terán-L.Casals 73e. Martín/Martín/Ruiz 59d. Martínez Gadea 288c, 289a. Martínez Lapeña/Torres Tur 100b, 103d, 104a, 174b, 194c, 199a,b,c, 276a,b,c, 341d; Martínez Lapeña/Torres-L. Casals 104b; Martínez Lapeña/Torres-L. Jansana 103a. Martínez/Pérez Amaral/Corona 115b. Martorell/Bohigas 172 b. Mateo 166c, 194d,e; Mateo-H. Suzuki 179b. MBM Arquitectes 100c, 159d, 162b, 173 c, 326c; MBM-F. Catalá Roca 155a, 160c, 189c, 181b; MBM-cb foto 155b. Meier 168a; Meier-Scott Frances 168b. Meri 329d; Meri/García Sogo 329e. Miguel, E. de 292e. Mingo-Numay 134d. Ministerio de Defensa, Centro de Publicaciones 65b.
Ministerio de Fomento, Dirección General de la Vivienda, la Arquitectura y el Urbanismo, Servicio de Estudio y Fomento de la Arquitectura 17a, 67c, 68d, 70a, 88c, 106d, 108a, 109a,b, 141b,c, 147a, 148d, 150b, 170c, 178b,c, 181e, 187b, 188c, 191c, 198b, 200a,d, 205e, 224d, 225e, 227a,c, 233e, 254d, 257c, 261c, 291a,b,c,d,e, 292b, 295e, 299b, 300b,d, 302a,b, 304a, 328a, 339b; Ministerio de Fomento, Dirección General de la Vivienda, la Arquitectura y el Urbanismo, Servicio de Estudio y Fomento de la Arquitectura-F. Catalá Roca 101c, 149a, 151a, 157a, 178d, 180a, 183a, 189a, 192d, 194a; Ministerio de Fomento-Ricardo 56a; Ministerio de Fomento, Dirección General de la Vivienda, la Arquitectura y el Urbanismo, Servicio de Estudio y Fomento de la Arquitectura-Arxiu González-Torán 140d, 143f, 144f, 148e, 150e, 153a,d, 155c, 156a, 157d,e, 160a; Ministerio de Fomento, Dirección General de la Vivienda, la Arquitectura y el Urbanismo, Servicio de Estudio y Fomento de la Arquitectura/Tanais 256a; Ministerio de Fomento, Dirección General de la Vivienda, la Arquitectura y el Urbanismo, Servicio de Estudio y Fomento de la Arquitectura/J. Utzon 102b; Ministerio de Fomento, Dirección General de la Vivienda, la Arquitectura y el Urbanismo, Servicio de Estudio y Fomento de la Arquitectura/J. Utzon-F. Bo Andersen 102a. Ministerio de Fomento, Centro Nacional de Información Geográfica/Tanais 99a, 102c, 106a, 111a, 113a, 209a, 220c, 299a, 302d, 309b.
Miquel Suarez-Inclán 259e. Miralles 341c; Miralles-F. Freixa 179a. Miralles/Pinòs 182e, 326c. Miralles/Pinòs-D. Malagamba 86b, 171d, 182d, 189 b, 323a, 326a,b. Moneo 64, 74a,c,d, 88d,e,f, 100d, 167b, 168c,e, 203c, 204b,c,d, 265a,c, 266d, 272a,b, 273d, 279b, 288a, 304b,c, 306b, 319b; Moneo-Ake:E son Lindman 79e, 319b, 341a; Moneo/ D. Biggi 61a, 204, 265b, 279a; Moneo-L. Casals 25, 74b, 167a, 168d, 204e, 306a; Moneo-J. Latova 273c; Moneo-D. Malagamba 79d, 100e; Moneo-S. Rosenthal 340a. Moreno Barberá 328c; Moreno Barberá-Estudios Pando 330b; Moreno Barberá-Paisajes Españoles 330a. Moreno Mansilla/Tuñón-L. Asin 130d. Mozas- a+t / C. San Millán 301e. Museo de Arte Abstracto Español 134a,c; Museo de Arte Abstracto Español-P. Cerezo, R. Luna, F. Mendoza 134b.
Nanclares/Ruiz 94c, 95d. Navarro Baldeweg 110c, 119b, 125a, 205c, 271a,b, 275b, 287a; Navarro Baldeweg-J. Azurmendi 285d,e; Navarro Baldeweg-J. Bretón 110b; Navarro Baldeweg-L. Casals 287b; Navarro Baldeweg-N. Casla 340b; Navarro Baldeweg-J.Mª G. Chutichaga 119a; Navarro Baldeweg-D. Malagamba 26, 104c, 125b,c,d, 205a,b; Navarro Baldeweg-H. Suzuki 275c. Noguerol/Díez 84b, 214d, 219d, 215e; Noguerol/Díez-J. Rodríguez 219c.
Oriol 206c,d. Otero 51e; Otero-M. Laguillo 51d.
Paisajes Españoles 135a, 268d. Penela 221a. Peña Ganchegui 300f, 304d, 305a,c,d, 307b, 308a,b,c, 309a. Perea-J. Azurmendi 211d, 284f, 285a. Pérez Arroyo 221c. V. Pérez Escolano 47a. Pérez Jové 199e. Pérez Latorre 89e,f,g. R. Pico Valimaña 51f. Portaceli 328e, 329f, 330c,d,e. Portela 220a,b, 221c. Prieto Fernandez 202a,b. Puente 281b.
Rahola 198a. Redón 292a, 296a,b. Revista de ObrasPúblicas/Tanais-A. Garrido 126a,b,c. Rius Camps 158d. J. Rodríguez 215 a,c,d. Rodríguez de Partearroyo 121a, 281d. Rodríguez Frade 59a. Ruisánchez/Vendrell 174e; Ruisanchez/Vendrell-cb foto 169f; Ruisanchez/Vendrell-M. Roselló 169e, 174d. G. Ruiz Cabrero 24, 72a,b, 238a. Ruiz de la Prada 258f. Ruiz Larrea 47d.
Sáenz de Oíza 80c,d, 101b, 244a, 249d, 256b, 264a,b,c,d. Salvadores 328d. San Martín 87b. Sevillana de Electricidad 54d. Sierra J.R./Sierra R. 73b,c, 78c,d; Sierra, J.R./Sierra, R.-L.Casals 80a,b. Siza 215 b. Sola Susperregui 164c; Sola Susperregui-cb foto 164b. Solà-Morales, I. de 176e. Solà-Morales, M. de 156d, 164a. Soriano/Palacios 317a,b. Sosa/Gutiérrez 116d. Soto/Maroto 283a. Sunyer-H. Suzuki 172 a.
Tanais: front cover flap or p.403, inside front cover or p.404-405, 46, 61b,c, 66b,c, 76b, 86a, 91, 98, 105, 117a, 120, 132a, 138, 160b, 177, 178a, 201a, 202a, 208, 222, 239d, 277a, 286a, 290, 297, 298, 318a, 321, inside back cover or p.406-407; Tanais-a+t ediciones 310b,c, 311d, 313b,e; Tanais-L. Alonso Lamberti 220d; Tanais-M. Benítez 282a; Tanais-R. Cuevas 72c, 73a, 78b, 82a; Tanais-A. Elías 66a, 67a, 69b,c, 139, 140a,b,c, 141a, 142a, 143a,b,d, 146a,c,d, 147d, 148a,b, 151d, 152c, 154d, 181d, 186d,e, 224a, 226c,d,e, 227e, 228a, 230a,b,d, 231c,d, 232d, 235a, 236a,c, 239a,b,e, 240d, 244e, 245a, 247a, 254e, 259a, 263b, 264e; Tanais-N. González 109e; Tanais-Ikatz 313c, 318c, 319a,d, 320a; Tanais-P. Jiménez 62e,f, 65a, 66c, 68b, 225c, 229c, 232a,c, 233a,f, 234d, 235d,e, 236e, 240b, 241b, 243a,d, 244b, 250f, 258a,e, 261a, 263c, 272e, 276d; Tanais-G. Landrove 18, 88a, 90d, 95c, 143c, 144d, 145a,b,e,f, 147b,c, 148c, 149c, 150a, 151b, 152a, 153e, 154c, 158a, 160d, 161b,c, 166d, 169a, 170a, 180b, 184a, 185e, 187a, 188b, 198c,d, 200c,e; Tanais-P. Lizancos 209b,c, 212a,b,c, 213c,d, 214c, 217b,c; Tanais-M.A. Martí 329a,b,c; Tanais-Paisajes Españoles 203d; Tanais-A. Prieto 48d, 49a,b, 52e, 53a, 69a,d, 70b; Tanais-R. Rispa 65c, 68a, 77a, 81e, 136d,e, 228b,d, 229a, 234a,b,c,e, 235c, 237a, 246a,b, 251a, 257d, 259d, 273a; Tanais-C. San Millán 310a,d, 311a,b,c, 312a,b,c,d,e, 313a,d, 314b; Tanais-I. Unzurrunzaga 303a,d; Tanais-V. Martín Chico 92d, 93a,c,e, 94a,b, 95b, 118a,c, 224c,e, 225a,b,d, 226a, 229e, 230e, 231a, 233c,d, 241a, 244c, 247c, 251f. Tobías 90a. Torres 48a,b, 59b, 68c, 73d. Torres Nadal 287d,e, 288b. Torroja Cavanillas 183d. E. Tuñón 135b. Tusquets 161a; Tusquets, Díaz & Assoc. 110d, 163e,f, 193c.
Uriarte 301b
Vázquez Consuegra 50d, 75b, 79b,c, 81a, 221d; Vázquez Consuegra-L. Casals 75a, 85a; Vázquez Consuegra-D. Malagamba 50c,e, 51b,c, 79a, 81b, 203b, 221b; Vázquez Consuegra-M. Moreno 85b; Vázquez Consuegra-H. Suzuki 75c. Vellés 53c, 201 b; Vellés-A. Müller 267c; Vellés-H. Suzuki 53b. Viaplana/Piñón 163a,b,c,d, 166e, 175d,e, 185d, 186c; Viaplana/Piñón-L. Casals 174c, 176c; Viaplana/Piñón-cb foto 175f. Vicens/Ramos 137f, 282b, 293c; Vicens/Ramos-D. Malagamba 293b. Vidal Vidal 324c. Viedma Vidal 327a. Viguier-Graphix 82c. Viñuela 192e.

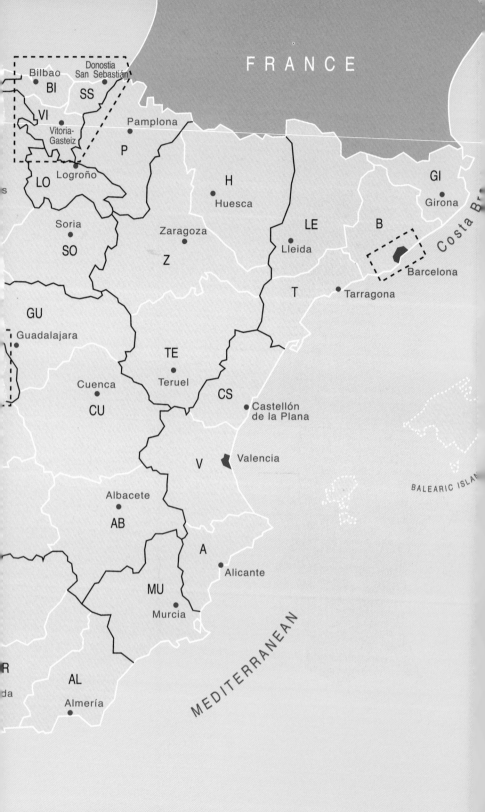

I ANDALUSIA	AL	Almería	CA	Cádiz
	CO	Córdoba	GR	Granada
	HU	Huelva	J	Jaén
	MA	Málaga	SE	Seville
II ARAGÓN	H	Huesca	TE	Teruel
	Z	Zaragoza		
III ASTURIAS	O	Oviedo		
IV BALEARIC ISLANDS	PM	Majorca		
	IB	Ibiza		
	ME	Minorca		
V CANARY ISLANDS	GC	Gran Canaria		
	LZ	Lanzarote		
	TF	Tenerife		
VI CANTABRIA	S	Santander		
VII CASTILE AND LEÓN	BU	Burgos	LE	León
	PA	Palencia	SA	Salamanca
	SG	Segovia	SO	Soria
	VA	Valladolid	ZA	Zamora
VIII CASTILE-LA MANCHA	AB	Albacete	CR	Ciudad Real
	CU	Cuenca	GU	Guadalajara
	TO	Toledo		
IX CATALONIA	B	Barcelona		
	GI	Girona		
	LL	Lleida		
	TA	Tarragona		
X CEUTA and MELILLA	CE	Ceuta		
	ML	Melilla		
XI EXTREMADURA	BA	Badajóz		
	CC	Cáceres		
XII GALICIA	C	A Coruña		
	LU	Lugo		
	OR	Ourense		
	PO	Pontevedra		
XIII MADRID	M	Madrid		
XIV MURCIA	MU	Murcia		
XV NAVARRE	N	Pamplona		
XVI BASQUE COUNTRY	VI	Alava		
	SS	Guipúzcoa		
	BI	Vizcaya		
XVII LA RIOJA	LR	Logroño		
XVIII COMUNIDAD VALENCIANA	A	Alicante		
	CS	Castellón de la Plana		
	V	Valencia		

Peter Buchanan
Architecture critic and historian, London
Antón Capitel
Architect (PhD), Professor at the Madrid School of Architecture
Javier Cenicacelaya
Architect (PhD), Professor at the San Sebastián School of Architecture
Aurora Fernández
Editor of the architectural journal *a + t*, Vitoria
Eduardo Fernández-Abascal
Architect, Torrelavega (Santander)
José Mª Fernández-Isla
Architect, architecture critic and writer, Madrid
Federico García Barba
Architect, Santa Cruz de Tenerife, former director of the journal *Basa*
Carlos García Vázquez
Architect, Lecturer at the Seville School of Architecture
Carmen Jordá
Architect (PhD), Associate Professor at the Valencia School of Architecture
Susana Landrove
Architect, Mies van der Rohe Foundation, Barcelona
Plácido Lizancos
Architect, Lecturer at the A Coruña School of Architecture
Pedro de Llano
Architect (PhD), Professor at the A Coruña School of Architecture
Javier Mozas
Architect, director of the architectural journal *a + t*, Vitoria
Juan Francisco Noguera
Architect (PhD), Associate Professor at the Valencia School of Architecture
Luis Moreno Mansilla
Architect, Lecturer at the Madrid School of Architecture
Víctor Pérez Escolano
Architect (PhD), Professor at the Seville School of Architecture
Ramón Pico Valimaña
Architect, Lecturer at the Seville School of Architecture
Massimo Preziosi
Architect, researcher of contemporary Spanish architecture, Barcelona
Gabriel Ruiz Cabrero
Architect (PhD), Professor at the Madrid School of Architecture
Ignasi de Solà-Morales
Architect (PhD), Professor at the Barcelona School of Architecture
Emilio Tuñón Alvarez
Architect, Lecturer at the Madrid School of Architecture